Fashion Institute of Design and Merchandising Edition

America's History

Volume Two

Fashion Institute of Design and Merchandising Edition

America's History

Volume Two

Sixth Edition

James A. Henretta
University of Maryland

David Brody
University of California, Davis

Lynn Dumenil
Occidental College

Bedford / St. Martin's
Boston • New York

For Bedford/St.Martin's

Executive Editor for History: Mary Dougherty
Director of Development for History: Jane Knetzger
Senior Developmental Editor: William J. Lombardo
Senior Production Editor: Bridget Leahy
Senior Production Supervisor: Joe Ford
Executive Marketing Manager: Jenna Bookin Barry
Editorial Assistants: Holly Dye and Amy Leathe
Production Assistants: Amy Derjue and Lidia MacDonald-Carr
Copyeditors: Barbara Bell and Lisa Wehrle
Text Design: Catherine Hawkes, Cat and Mouse Design
Indexer: EdIndex
Photo Research: Pembroke Herbert and Sandi Rygiel/Picture Research Consultants & Archives
Cover Design: Donna Lee Dennison
Cover Art: Expansive view of newly built houses jammed side-by-side, divided by a never-ending street clogged
   with moving vans unloading families' possessions on moving day. © J R Eyerman. Getty Images / Time & Life
   Pictures.
Cartography: Mapping Specialists Limited
Composition: TechBooks
Printing and Binding: R.R. Donnelley & Sons Company

President: Joan E. Feinberg
Editorial Director: Denise B. Wydra
Director of Marketing: Karen Melton Soeltz
Director of Editing, Design, and Production: Marcia Cohen
Managing Editor: Elizabeth M. Schaaf

Manufactured in the United States of America.

5 4 3 2
f e d c

For information, write: Bedford/St. Martin's, 75 Arlington Street, Boston, MA 02116
(617-399-4000)

ISBN-10: 0–312–57052–X ISBN-13: 978–0–312–57052–1

Acknowledgments

*Acknowledgments and copyrights can be found at the back of the book on pages C-1–C-2, which constitute an
extension of the copyright page.*

PART FIVE

The Modern State and Society, 1914–1945   *670*

24   Redefining Liberalism: The New Deal, 1933–1939   *737*

25   The World at War, 1939–1945   *767*

PART SIX

The Age of Cold War Liberalism, 1945–1980   *798*

26   Cold War America, 1945–1960   *801*

27   The Age of Affluence, 1945–1960   *831*

28   The Liberal Consensus: Flaming Out, 1960–1968   *861*

29   The 1970s: Toward a Conservative America   *895*

PART SEVEN

Entering a New Era: Conservatism, Globalization, Terrorism, 1980–2006   *924*

30   The Reagan Revolution and the End of the Cold War, 1980–2001   *927*

31   A Dynamic Economy, A Divided People, 1980–2000   *957*

DOCUMENTS   *D–1*
APPENDIX   *A–1*
GLOSSARY   *G–1*
CREDITS   *C–1*
INDEX   *I–1*

The New Deal's Impact on Society 749
    The Rise of Labor 749
    Women and Blacks in the New Deal 750
    Migrants and Minorities in the West 755
    A New Deal for the Environment 759
    The New Deal and the Arts 760
    The Legacies of the New Deal 762

Summary 764
    Connections: Economy 764

Timeline 765

For Further Exploration 765

■ COMPARING AMERICAN VOICES
Ordinary People Respond to the New Deal 740

■ VOICES FROM ABROAD
Odette Keun: A Foreigner Looks at the Tennessee Valley Authority 758

■ READING AMERICAN PICTURES
Interpreting the Public Art of the New Deal 761

Note: This custom edition of *America's History, Volume Two*, Sixth Edition, omits Chapters 15 through 23 and Chapter 32.

Brief Contents *v*
Maps *x*
Figures and Tables *xi*
Special Features *xii*

25 **The World at War, 1939–1945** *767*

PART FIVE

The Modern State and Society, 1914–1945 *670*

24 **Redefining Liberalism: The New Deal, 1933–1939** *737*

The New Deal Takes Over, 1933–1935 738
    Roosevelt's Leadership 738
    The Hundred Days 739
    The New Deal under Attack 744

The Second New Deal, 1935–1938 746
    Legislative Accomplishments 746
    The 1936 Election 747
    Stalemate 748

The Road to War 768
    The Rise of Fascism 768
    Isolationists versus Interventionists 769
    Retreat from Isolationism 770
    The Attack on Pearl Harbor 771

Organizing for Victory 774
    Financing the War 774
    Mobilizing the American Fighting Force 775
    Workers and the War Effort 777
    Politics in Wartime 781

Life on the Home Front 782
    "For the Duration" 782
    Migration and Social Conflict 783
    Civil Rights during Wartime 784

Fighting and Winning the War 787
    Wartime Aims and Tensions 787
    The War in Europe 788
    The War in the Pacific 791
    Planning the Postwar World 791

Summary *796*
> Connections: Government *796*

Timeline *797*

For Further Exploration *797*

> ■ READING AMERICAN PICTURES
> U.S. Political Propaganda on the Homefront during World War II *776*

> ■ COMPARING AMERICAN VOICES
> Women in the Wartime Workplace *778*

> ■ VOICES FROM ABROAD
> Monica Itoi Sone: Japanese Relocation *786*

PART SIX

The Age of Cold War Liberalism, 1945–1980 *798*

26 **Cold War America, 1945–1960** *801*

The Cold War *802*
> Descent into Cold War, 1945–1946 *802*
> George Kennan and the Containment Strategy *803*
> Containment in Asia *810*

The Truman Era *813*
> Reconversion *813*
> The Fair Deal *815*
> The Great Fear *815*

Modern Republicanism *818*
> They Liked Ike *818*
> The Hidden-Hand Presidency *819*
> Eisenhower and the Cold War *819*
> Containment in the Post-Colonial World *822*
> Eisenhower's Farewell Address *827*

Summary *828*
> Connections: Diplomacy and Politics *828*

Timeline *829*

For Further Exploration *829*

> ■ VOICES FROM ABROAD
> Jean Monnet: Truman's Generous Proposal *807*

> ■ COMPARING AMERICAN VOICES
> Hunting Communists and Liberals *820*

> ■ READING AMERICAN PICTURES
> Why a Cold War Space Race? *823*

27 **The Age of Affluence, 1945–1960** *831*

Economic Powerhouse *832*
> Engines of Economic Growth *832*
> The Corporate Order *834*
> Labor-Mangement Accord *835*

The Affluent Society *837*
> The Suburban Explosion *837*
> The Search for Security *841*
> Consumer Culture *842*
> The Baby Boom *844*
> Contradictions in Women's Lives *846*
> Youth Culture *847*
> Cultural Dissenters *847*

The Other America *849*
> Immigrants and Migrants *849*
> The Urban Crisis *850*
> The Emerging Civil Rights Struggle *852*

Summary *858*
> Connections: Economy *858*

Timeline *859*

For Further Exploration *859*

> ■ VOICES FROM ABROAD
> Hanoch Bartov: Everyone Has a Car *840*

> ■ READING AMERICAN PICTURES
> The Cold War and the Civil Rights Movement *854*

> ■ COMPARING AMERICAN VOICES
> Challenging White Supremacy *856*

28 **The Liberal Consensus: Flaming Out, 1960–1968** *861*

John F. Kennedy and the Politics of Expectation *862*
> The New Politics *862*
> The Kennedy Administration *863*
> The Civil Rights Movement Stirs *864*
> Kennedy, Cold Warrior *868*
> The Kennedy Assassination *870*

Lyndon B. Johnson and the Great Society 871
   The Momentum for Civil Rights 871
   Enacting the Liberal Agenda 872

Into the Quagmire, 1963–1968 877
   Escalation 877
   Public Opinion on Vietnam 879
   Student Activism 879

Coming Apart 884
   The Counterculture 884
   Beyond Civil Rights 885

1968: A Year of Shocks 888
   The Politics of Vietnam 888
   Backlash 891

Summary 892
   Connections: Diplomacy and Politics 892

Timeline 893

For Further Exploration 893

  ■ **COMPARING AMERICAN VOICES**
    The Toll of War *880*

  ■ **VOICES FROM ABROAD**
    Che Guevara: Vietnam and the World Freedom
    Struggle *883*

  ■ **READING AMERICAN PICTURES**
    War and Its Aftermath: Images of the Vietnam Conflict, 1968
    and 1982 *890*

29 **The 1970s: Toward
a Conservative
America** 895

The Nixon Years 896
   Nixon's Domestic Agenda 896
   Détente 896
   Nixon's War 898
   The 1972 Election 901
   Watergate 901

Battling for Civil Rights: The Second Stage 902
   The Revival of Feminism 903
   Enforcing Civil Rights 906

Lean Years 911
   Energy Crisis 911
   Environmentalism 912
   Economic Woes 913

Politics in the Wake of Watergate 917
   *Jimmy Carter: The Outsider as
    President* 917
   Carter and the World 920

Summary 922
   Connections: Society 922

Timeline 923

For Further Exploration 923

  ■ **COMPARING AMERICAN VOICES**
    Debating the Equal Rights Amendment *908*

  ■ **READING AMERICAN PICTURES**
    A Near Meltdown at Three Mile Island, 1979 *914*

  ■ **VOICES FROM ABROAD**
    Fei Xiaotong: America's Crisis of Faith *919*

PART SEVEN

**Entering a New Era: Conservatism,
Globalization, Terrorism, 1980–2006** *924*

30 **The Reagan Revolution
and the End of the Cold
War, 1980–2001** *927*

The Rise of Conservatism 928
   Reagan and the Emergence of the New Right 928
   The Election of 1980 929

The Reagan Presidency, 1981–1989 933
   Reaganomics 933
   Reagan's Second Term 936

Defeating Communism and Creating a New World
  Order 938
   The End of the Cold War 939
   The Presidency of George H. W. Bush 943
   *Reagan, Bush, and the Middle East,
    1980–1991* 944

The Clinton Presidency, 1993–2001 946
   Clinton's Early Record 946
   The Republican Resurgence 948
   Clinton's Impeachment 950
   Foreign Policy at the End of the Twentieth Century 951

Summary 954
   Connections: Government and Politics 954

Timeline 955

For Further Exploration 955

  ■ **COMPARING AMERICAN VOICES**
    Christianity and Public Life *930*

■ READING AMERICAN PICTURES

Image Warfare: Fighting to Define the Reagan
Presidency *934*

■ VOICES FROM ABROAD

Zhu Shida: China and the United States: A Unique
Relationship *940*

31 **A Dynamic Economy,
A Divided People,
1980–2000** *957*

America in the Global Economy and Society *958*
The Economic Challenge *958*
The Turn to Prosperity *961*
Globalization *963*

The New Technology *970*
The Computer Revolution *970*
*Technology and the Control of Popular
Culture* *973*

Culture Wars *975*
An Increasingly Pluralistic Society *976*
*Conflicting Values: Women's and
Gay Rights* *983*

Summary *986*
Connections: Society and Technology *986*

Timeline *987*

For Further Exploration *987*

■ COMPARING AMERICAN VOICES

Cheap Labor: Immigration and
Globalization *978*

■ VOICES FROM ABROAD

Janet Daley: A U.S. Epidemic *981*

■ READING AMERICAN PICTURES

The Abortion Debate Hits the Streets *985*

Appendix *A-1*
Glossary *G-1*
Credits *C-1*
Index *I-1*

MAPS

24 Redefining Liberalism: The New Deal, 1933–1939

Popular Protest in the Great Depression, 1933–1939   *751*

The Dust Bowl and Federal Building Projects in the West, 1930–1941   *756*

The Tennessee Valley Authority, 1933–1952   *760*

25 The World at War, 1939–1945

World War II in the North Atlantic, 1939–1943   *772*

Japanese Relocation Camps   *785*

World War II in Europe, 1941–1943   *788*

World War II in Europe, 1944–1945   *789*

World War II in the Pacific, 1941–1942   *792*

World War II in the Pacific, 1943–1945   *793*

26 Cold War America, 1945–1960

Cold War in Europe, 1955   *806*

The Korean War, 1950–1953   *811*

Presidential Election of 1948   *815*

American Global Defense Treaties in the Cold War Era   *824*

The Military-Industrial Complex   *826*

27 The Age of Affluence, 1945–1960

Shifting Population Patterns, 1950–1980   *838*

Connecting the Nation: The Interstate Highway System, 1930 and 1970   *839*

28 The Liberal Consensus: Flaming Out, 1960–1968

Decolonization and the Third World, 1943–1990   *865*

The Civil Rights Struggle, 1954–1965   *866*

The United States and Cuba, 1961–1962   *869*

Black Voter Registration in the South, 1964 and 1975   *873*

Presidential Election of 1964   *873*

The Vietnam War, 1968   *877*

Presidential Election of 1968   *892*

29 The 1970s: Toward a Conservative America

States Ratifying the Equal Rights Amendment, 1972–1977   *906*

From Rust Belt to Sun Belt, 1940–2000   *916*

30 The Reagan Revolution and the End of the Cold War: 1980–2001

Presidential Election of 1980   *932*

U.S. Involvement in Latin America and the Caribbean, 1954–2000   *937*

The Collapse of the Soviet Union and the Creation of Independent States, 1989–1991   *942*

Presidential Election of 1992   *947*

31 A Dynamic Economy, A Divided People, 1980–2000

Growth of the European Community, 1951–2005   *965*

Hispanic and Asian Populations, 2000   *977*

FIGURES AND TABLES

Figures

Government Military and Civilian Spending as a
  Percentage of GDP, 1920–1980   *774*

National Defense Spending, 1940–1965   *813*

Gross Domestic Product, 1930–1972   *833*

Labor Union Strength, 1900–1997   *836*

The American Birthrate, 1860–1980   *845*

Legal Immigration to the United States by Region,
  1931–1984   *849*

Americans in Poverty, 1959–2000   *876*

U.S. Troops in Vietnam, 1960–1973   *878*

U.S. Energy Consumption, 1900–2000   *911*

The Inflation Rate, 1960–2000   *915*

The Annual Federal Budget Deficit (or Surplus),
  1940–2005   *935*

Productivity, Family Income, and Wages, 1970–2004   *958*

The Increase in Two-Worker Families   *960*

Boom and Bust in the Stock Market   *964*

American Immigration, 1920–2000   *976*

Tables

American Banks and Bank Failures, 1920–1940   *739*

Major New Deal Legislation   *747*

Major Great Society Legislation   *874*

SPECIAL FEATURES

■ Comparing American Voices

Ordinary People Respond to the
  New Deal   740

Women in the Wartime Workplace   778

Hunting Communists and Liberals   820

Challenging White Supremacy   856

The Toll of War   880

Debating the Equal Rights Amendment   908

Christianity and Public Life   930

Cheap Labor: Immigration and Globalization   978

■ Reading American Pictures

Interpreting the Public Art of the New Deal   761

U.S. Political Propaganda on the Homefront during World
  War II   776

Why a Cold War Space Race?   823

The Cold War and the Civil Rights Movement   854

War and Its Aftermath: Images of the Vietnam Conflict,
  1968 and 1982   890

A Near Meltdown at Three Mile Island, 1979   914

Image Warfare: Fighting to Define the Reagan
  Presidency   934

The Abortion Debate Hits the Streets   985

■ Voices From Abroad

Odette Keun: A Foreigner Looks at the Tennessee Valley
  Authority   758

Monica Itoi Sone: Japanese Relocation   786

Jean Monnet: Truman's Generous Proposal   807

Hanoch Bartov: Everyone Has a Car   840

Che Guevara: Vietnam and the World Freedom
  Struggle   883

Fei Xiaotong: America's Crisis of Faith   919

Zhu Shida: China and the United States: A Unique
  Relationship   940

Janet Daley: A U.S. Epidemic   981

Fashion Institute of Design and Merchandising Edition

America's History

Volume Two

PART FIVE | The Modern State and Society

1914–1945

	GOVERNMENT	DIPLOMACY	ECONOMY	SOCIETY	CULTURE
	The Rise of the State	**From Isolation to World Leadership**	**Prosperity, Depression, and War**	**Nativism, Migration, and Social Change**	**The Emergence of a Mass National Culture**
1914	▶ Wartime agencies expand power of federal government ▶ High taxes on the wealthy and on corporations	▶ United States enters World War I (1917) ▶ Wilson's Fourteen Points (1918)	▶ Shift from debtor to creditor nation ▶ Agricultural prosperity	▶ Southern blacks migrate to factory work in North ▶ Attacks against German Americans ▶ "Red Scare" (1919–1920)	▶ Wartime promotion of national unity ▶ Americanization campaign ▶ Silent screen; Hollywood becomes movie capital of the world
1920	▶ Republican ascendancy ▶ Prohibition (1920–1933) ▶ Business-government partnership ▶ Nineteenth Amendment gives women the vote	▶ Treaty of Versailles rejected by U.S. Senate (1920) ▶ Washington Conference sets naval limits (1921) ▶ Dawes Plan (1924)	▶ Economic recession (1920–1921) ▶ Booming prosperity (1922–1929) ▶ Automobile age begins ▶ Rise of welfare capitalism	▶ Rise of nativism and revival of KKK ▶ National Origins Act (1924) ▶ Mexican American immigration grows ▶ Harlem Renaissance	▶ Advertising promotes consumer culture ▶ New media — radio, movies — create national popular culture ▶ Image of "Roaring Twenties"
1930	▶ Franklin Roosevelt becomes president (1933) ▶ The New Deal: vast government intervention in economy ▶ Social welfare liberalism	▶ Good Neighbor Policy toward Latin America (1933) ▶ Isolationism grows ▶ U.S. neutrality proclaimed (1939)	▶ Great Depression (1929–1941) ▶ TVA aids development ▶ Rise of CIO and organized labor	▶ Farming families migrate from dust bowl states to California ▶ Indian New Deal ▶ Reverse migration to Asia and Mexico	▶ Documentary impulse in arts ▶ Works Project Administration assists artists
1940	▶ Government mobilizes industry for war output ▶ Massive war budgets and debt ▶ Universal income tax system	▶ United States enters World War II (1941) ▶ Allies defeat fascist powers ▶ Atomic bombing of Japan (1945) ▶ United Nations created (1945)	▶ War spending ends depression ▶ Business executives join government ▶ Labor unions prosper ▶ Married women enter workforce	▶ Internment of Japanese Americans ▶ Segregation in armed forces ▶ Rural whites and blacks migrate to war jobs in cities	▶ Movie industry expands and aids war effort ▶ Rationing limits consumer culture

In the 1930s journalist Mark Sullivan described World War I as a "fundamental alteration, from which we would never go back." Sullivan was correct in viewing the war as a pivotal point in world history, but many of the important factors that were transforming America were in place before the war. By 1914 industrialization, massive immigration, and the growth of cities had set the foundations for distinctly *modern* American society: diverse, prosperous, and urban. This new society was also more organized, more bureaucratic, and more complex. And by 1945, after having mobilized its resources to fight two world wars and the Great Depression, it was more wealthy and powerful, with a much larger national government. The edifice of the new society was largely complete.

GOVERNMENT An essential feature of modern American society was a strong national state. This state came late and haltingly to the United States compared with those of the industrialized countries of western Europe. American participation in World War I called forth an unprecedented mobilization of the domestic economy, but policymakers quickly dismantled the centralized wartime bureaucracies in 1919. During the 1920s the Harding and Coolidge administrations embraced a philosophy of business-government partnership, believing that corporate capitalism would provide for the welfare of the American people. It took the Great Depression, with its countless business failures and unprecedented levels of unemployment, to overthrow that long-cherished idea. Franklin D. Roosevelt's New Deal dramatically expanded federal responsibility for the economy and the welfare of ordinary citizens. An even greater expansion of the national state resulted from the massive mobilization following America's entry into World War II. Unlike the experience after World War I, the new state apparatus remained in place when the war ended.

DIPLOMACY A second defining feature of modern America was its slow but steady movement toward a position of world political leadership, which it continues to hold today. World War I provided the first major impetus: Before 1914 the world had been dominated by European nations, but from that point on the United States grew increasingly influential in international economic and political affairs. In 1918 American troops provided the margin of victory for the Allies, and President Wilson helped to shape the treaties that ended the war. Although the United States refused to join the League of Nations, its dominant economic position meant that it played an active role in world affairs in the 1920s and 1930s. America's global presence accelerated in 1941, when the nation threw all its energies into a second world war waged against fascist nations in Europe and Asia. Of all the major powers, only the United States emerged physically unscathed from that devastating global conflagration. The country was also the only one to possess a dangerous new weapon—the atomic bomb. Within wartime decisions and strategies lay the roots of the Cold War that followed.

ECONOMY The dominant world position of modern America was the result of a robust domestic economy. Between 1914 and 1945 the nation boasted the world's most productive economic system. Even the Great Depression, which hit the United States harder than any other industrialized nation, did not permanently undermine America's global economic standing. American businesses successfully competed in world markets, and American financial institutions played the leading role in international economic affairs. Large-scale corporate organizations replaced smaller family-run businesses. The automobile industry symbolized the ascendancy of mass-production techniques. Many workers shared in the general prosperity but also bore the brunt of economic downturns. These uncertainties fueled the dramatic growth of the labor movement in the 1930s.

SOCIETY The character of modern American society was shaped by the great wave of European immigration between 1880 and 1914 and the movement of native-born Americans from farms to cities. The growth of metropolitan areas gave the nation an increasingly urban tone, and geographical mobility broke down regional differences. Many old-stock white Americans viewed these processes with alarm; in 1924 they secured legislation limiting immigration to countries in the Western Hemisphere. Migration across the border from Mexico continued to shape the West and Southwest. And the internal movement of people continued: African Americans moved north and west to take factory jobs, dust bowl farmers migrated to the Far West, and Applachian whites took jobs in World War II defense plants around the country.

CULTURE Finally, modern America saw the emergence of a mass national culture. By the 1920s advertising and the new entertainment media—movies, radio, and magazines—disseminated the new values of consumerism, and the Hollywood movie industry exported this vision of the American experience worldwide. Not even the Great Depression could divert Americans from their desire for leisure, self-fulfillment, and consumer goods. The emphasis on consumption and a quest for a rising standard of living would define the American experience for the rest of the twentieth century.

RFA11

RADIO

RURAL ELECTRIFICATION ADMINISTRATION

24 Redefining Liberalism: The New Deal

1933–1939

"**W**HAT IS GOING TO BECOME OF US?" asked an Arizona man. "You can't sleep, you know. You wake up at 2 A.M. and you lie and think." Many Americans went sleepless in 1933, as the nation entered the fourth year of the worst economic contraction in its history. Times were hard — very hard — and there was no end in sight.

In his inaugural address in March 1933, President Franklin Delano Roosevelt tried to dispel the gloom and despondency that gripped the nation. "The only thing we have to fear is fear itself," Roosevelt declared. His demeanor grim and purposeful, Roosevelt issued a ringing call "for action, and action now," and promised strong presidential leadership. He would ask Congress for "broad Executive power to wage a war against the emergency, as great as the power that would be given to me if we were in fact invaded by a foreign foe." With these words, Roosevelt launched a program of federal activism — which he called the *New Deal* — that would change the nature of American government.

The New Deal represented a new form of liberalism, the ideology of individual rights that had long shaped the character of American society and politics. To protect those rights, "classical" nineteenth-century liberals had sought to keep governments small and relatively powerless. Their successors, the "regulatory" liberals of the Progressive era, had

The New Deal Takes Over, 1933–1935
Roosevelt's Leadership
The Hundred Days
The New Deal under Attack

The Second New Deal, 1935–1938
Legislative Accomplishments
The 1936 Election
Stalemate

The New Deal's Impact on Society
The Rise of Labor
Women and Blacks in the New Deal
Migrants and Minorities in the West
A New Deal for the Environment
The New Deal and the Arts
The Legacies of the New Deal

Summary
Connections: Economy

◄ **New Deal Art**

The Rural Electrification Administration used this poster, designed by Lester Beall in 1937, to celebrate the power of radio and to encourage farmers to form cooperatives to bring electric power to their localities. The radio gave rural folk immediate access to news of farm prices and world events, soap operas, and advertising — making them part of modern American life.
The Wolfsonian-Florida International University, Miami Beach, Florida, The Mitchell Wolfson, Jr. Collection.

safeguarded the liberty of individuals by bolstering the authority of the state and federal governments to oversee and, if necessary, to control large business corporations. The New Deal activists went much further — their **"social welfare" liberalism** expanded individual rights. Beginning in the 1930s and continuing until the 1970s, they increased the amount and scope of national legislation; created an increasingly centralized federal administrative system; and instituted new programs, such as Social Security, that gave the national government responsibility for the welfare of every American citizen. Their efforts did not go unchallenged. Critics of the New Deal charged that its program of "big government" and "social welfare" directly repudiated traditional **classical liberal** principles and, beginning with the "Reagan Revolution" of the 1980s, would seek to undo many of its programs.

The New Deal Takes Over, 1933–1935

The Great Depression destroyed Herbert Hoover's political reputation and boosted that of Franklin Delano Roosevelt. Although some Americans, especially wealthy conservatives, hated the new Democratic president, he was immensely popular; millions called him by his initials — FDR — which became his nickname. Ironically, the ideological differences between Hoover and Roosevelt were not vast. Both were committed to maintaining the nation's basic social and institutional structures. Both believed in the morality of a balanced budget and extolled the values of hard work, cooperation, and sacrifice. But Roosevelt's personal charm, his political savvy, and his willingness to experiment made all the difference. Above all, his New Deal programs put people to work, instilling hope for the nation's future.

Roosevelt's Leadership

Roosevelt immediately established a close rapport with the American people. More than 450,000 letters poured into the White House in the week after his inauguration, and they continued to come at a rate of 5,000 a week throughout the 1930s. Whereas one person had handled public correspondence under Hoover, a staff of fifty was required by the new administration. Roosevelt's masterful use of the new medium of radio, especially the "fireside chats" during his first two terms, bolstered his relationship with the people. Many citizens thanked him personally for their successes, saying "He gave me a job" or "He saved my home" (see Comparing American Voices, "Ordinary People Respond to the New Deal," pp. 740–741).

FDR

Franklin Delano Roosevelt was a successful politician partly because he loved to mix with a crowd. Despite Roosevelt's upper-class background, he had a knack for relating easily to those from all occupations. Although a well-dressed crowd turned out to greet him in Elm Grove, West Virginia, as he campaigned for the presidency in 1932, Roosevelt took care to be photographed shaking hands with coal miner Zeno Santanella. Courtesy of the Franklin D. Roosevelt Library.

Roosevelt's charisma allowed him to continue the expansion of presidential powers begun in the administrations of Theodore Roosevelt and Woodrow Wilson. He dramatically enlarged the role of the executive branch in setting the budget and initiating legislation. For policy formulation, he relied heavily on his "Brain Trust" of professors from Columbia and Harvard universities: Raymond Moley, Rexford Tugwell, Adolph A. Berle, and Felix Frankfurter. He turned as well to his talented cabinet, which included Secretary of the Interior Harold L. Ickes, Frances Perkins at Labor, Henry A. Wallace at Agriculture, and Henry Morgenthau, Jr., the secretary of the Treasury. Financier Bernard Baruch was also influential. This array of intellectual and administrative talent attracted hundreds of highly qualified recruits to Washington. Young professors and newly trained lawyers streamed out of Ivy League law schools into the expanding federal bureaucracy, where they had a direct hand in shaping legislation. Inspired by the idealism of the New Deal, many of them would devote their lives to public service and the principles of social welfare liberalism.

The Hundred Days

Roosevelt promised "action now," and he kept his promise. The first months of his administration produced a whirlwind of activity in Congress, which was controlled by Democrats elected with Roosevelt in 1932. In a legendary legislative session, known as the "Hundred Days," Congress enacted fifteen major bills. This legislation focused primarily on four major problems — banking failures, agricultural overproduction, the business slump, and soaring unemployment.

The Emergency Banking Act. The president and Congress first addressed the banking crisis. Since the stock market crash, bank failures had cut into the savings of nearly nine million families; to prevent more failures, dozens of states had closed their banks. On March 5, the day following his inauguration, FDR declared a national "bank holiday" — a euphemism for closing all the banks — and called Congress into special session. Four days later Congress passed the Emergency Banking Act — the debate in the House took only thirty-eight minutes — which permitted banks to reopen if a Treasury Department inspection showed they had sufficient cash reserves.

The act worked because Roosevelt convinced the public that it would. In his first Sunday night fireside chat, to a radio audience estimated at 60 million, the president reassured citizens that federal scrutiny would ensure the safety of their deposits. When the banking system reopened on March 13, deposits exceeded withdrawals, restoring stability to one of the nation's prime financial institutions. "Capitalism was saved in eight days," quipped Roosevelt's advisor Raymond Moley. A second banking law of 1933, the Glass-Steagall Act, further restored public confidence; it created the Federal Deposit Insurance Corporation (FDIC), which insured deposits up to $2,500. Four thousand banks had collapsed in the months prior to Roosevelt's inauguration, but only sixty-one closed their doors in all of 1934 (Table 24.1).

The avalanche of legislation now began. Congress created the Home Owners Loan Corporation to refinance home mortgages threatened by foreclosure. It then established the Civilian Conservation Corps (CCC), which mobilized 250,000 young men to do reforestation and conservation work. Two controversial measures also won quick approval. One set up the Tennessee Valley Authority (TVA), a government-owned corporation that would produce cheap hydroelectric power and encourage economic development in the flood-prone river valley (see Map 24.3 on p. 760); critics assailed it as creeping socialism. The second act legalized the sale of beer, offending moral reformers; but full repeal of Prohibition, by constitutional amendment, was already in the works and came eight months later, in December 1933.

The Agricultural Adjustment Act. Because farmers formed more than a quarter of the workforce, Roosevelt considered effective agricultural legislation

TABLE 24.1	American Banks and Bank Failures, 1920–1940		
Year	**Total Number of Banks**	**Total Assets ($ billion)**	**Bank Failures**
1920	30,909	53.1	168
1929	25,568	72.3	659
1931	22,242	70.1	2,294
1933	14,771	51.4	4,004
1934	15,913	55.9	61
1940	15,076	79.7	48

SOURCE: *Historical Statistics of the United States: Colonial Times to 1970* (Washington, D.C.: U.S. Government Printing Office, 1975), 1019, 1038–1039.

Ordinary People Respond to the New Deal

Franklin Roosevelt's fireside chats and his relief programs prompted thousands of ordinary Americans to write directly to the president and his wife Eleanor. Taken together, they offer a vivid portrait of depression-era America and of popular support for, and opposition to, the New Deal.

MRS. M.H.A.

Mrs. M.H.A. worked in the County Court House in Eureka, California.

June 14, 1934
Dear Mrs. Roosevelt:

I know you are overburdened with requests for help and if my plea cannot be recognized, I'll understand it is because you have so many others, all of them worthy....

My husband and I are a young couple of very simple, almost poor families. We married eight years ago on the proverbial shoe-string but with a wealth of love.... We managed to build our home and furnish it comfortably.... Then came the depression. My work has continued and my salary alone has just been sufficient to make our monthly payments on the house and keep our bills paid.... But with the exception of two and one-half months work with the U.S. Coast and Geodetic Survey under the C.W.A. [Civil Works Administration], my husband has not had work since August, 1932.

My salary could continue to keep us going, but I am to have a baby.... I can get a leave of absence from my job for a year. But can't you, won't you do something so my husband can have a job, at least during that year?...

As I said before, if it were only ourselves, or if there were something we could do about it, we would never ask for help. We have always stood on our own feet and been proud and happy. But you are a mother and you'll understand this crisis.

Very sincerely yours,
Mrs. M. H. A.

UNSIGNED LETTER

This unsigned letter came from a factory worker in Paris, Texas.

November 23, 1936
Dear President,

[N]ow that we have had a land Slide [in the election of 1936] and done just what was best for our country ... I do believe you Will Strain a point to help the ones who helped you mostly & that is the Working Class of People I am not smart or I would be in a different line of work & better up in ever way yet I will know you are the one & only President that ever helped a Working Class of People....

I am a White Man American age, 47 married wife 2 children in high School am a Finishing room foreman I mean a Working foreman & am in a furniture Factory here in Paris Texas where thaire is 175 to 200 Working & when the NRA [National Recovery Administration] came in I was Proud to See my fellow workmen Rec 30 Per hour in Place of 8 cents to 20 cents Per hour....

I can't see for my life President why a man must toil & work his life out in Such factories 10 long hours ever day except Sunday for a small sum of 15 cents to 35 cents per hour & pay the high cost of honest & deason living expences....

please see if something can be done to help this one Class of Working People the factories are a man killer not venelated or kept up just a bunch of Republickins Grafters 90/100 of them Please help us some way I Pray to God for relief. I am a Christian ... and a truthful man & have not told you wrong & am for you to the end.

[not signed]

R.A.

R.A. was 69 years old and an architect and builder in Lincoln, Nebraska.

May 19/34
Dear Mrs Roosevelt:

In the Presidents inaugural address delivered from the capitol steps the afternoon of his inauguration he made mention of The Forgotten Man, and I with thousands of others am wondering if the folk who was borned here in America some 60 or 70 years a go are this Forgotten Man, the President had in mind, if we are this Forgotten Man then we are still Forgotten.

We who have tried to be diligent in our support of this most wonderful nation of ours boath social and other wise, we in our younger days tried to do our duty without complaining....

And now a great calamity has come upon us and seemingly no cause of our own it has swept away what little savings we had accumulated and we are left in a condition that is imposible for us to correct, for two very prominent reasons if no more.

First we have grown to what is termed Old Age, this befalls every man.

Second, . . . we are confronted on every hand with the young generation, taking our places, this of corse is what we have looked forward to in training our children. But with the extra ordinary crises which left us helpless and placed us in the position that our fathers did not have to contend with. . . .

We have been honorable citizens all along our journey, calamity and old age has forced its self upon us please do not send us to the Poor Farm but instead allow us the small pension of $40.00 per month. . . .

Mrs. Roosevelt I am asking a personal favor of you as it seems to be the only means through which I may be able to reach the President, some evening very soon, as you and Mr. Roosevelt are having dinner together privately will you ask him to read this. And we American citizens will ever remember your kindness.

Yours very truly.

R. A.

M.A.

M.A. was a woman who held a low-level salaried position in a corporation.

Jan. 18, 1937

[Dear Mrs. Roosevelt:]

I . . . was simply astounded to think that anyone could be nitwit enough to wish to be included in the so called social security act if they could possibly avoid it. Call it by any name you wish it, in my opinion, (and that of many people I know) is nothing but downright stealing. . . .

I am not an "economic royalist," just an ordinary white collar worker at $1600 per [year—about $21,700 in 2007]. Please show this to the president and ask him to remember the wishes of the forgotten man, that is, the one who dared to vote against him. We expect to be tramped on but we do wish the stepping would be a little less hard.

Security at the price of freedom is never desired by intelligent people.

M. A.

M.A.H.

M.A.H. was a widow who ran a small farm in Columbus, Indiana.

December 14, 1937

Mrs. Roosevelt:

I suppose from your point of view the work relief, old age pensions, slum clearance and all the rest seems like a perfect remedy for all the ills of this country, but I would like for you to see the results, as the other half see them.

We have always had a shiftless, never-do-well class of people whose one and only aim in life is to live without work. I have been rubbing elbows with this class for nearly sixty years and have tried to help some of the most promising and have seen others try to help them, but it can't be done. We cannot help those who will not try to help themselves and if they do try a square deal is all they need, . . . let each paddle their own canoe, or sink. . . .

I live alone on a farm and have not raised any crops for the last two years as there was no help to be had. I am feeding the stock and have been cutting the wood to keep my home fires burning. There are several reliefers around here now who have been kicked off relief but they refuse to work unless they can get relief hours and wages, but they are so worthless no one can afford to hire them. . . . They are just a fair sample of the class of people on whom so much of our hard earned tax money is being squandered and on whom so much sympathy is being wasted. . . .

You people who have plenty of this worlds goods and whose money comes easy have no idea of the heart-breaking toil and self-denial which is the lot of the working people who are trying to make an honest living, and then to have to shoulder all these unjust burdens seems like the last straw. . . . No one should have the right to vote theirself a living at the expense of the tax payers.

M. A. H.

SOURCES (IN ORDER): Robert S. McElvaine, *Down and Out in the Great Depression* (Chapel Hill: University of North Carolina Press, 1983), 54–55; Michael P. Johnson, ed., *Reading the American Past*, 3rd ed., 2 vols. (Boston: Bedford/St. Martin's, 2005), 2: 166–167; Robert D. Marcus and David Burner, eds., *America Firsthand*, 7th ed. (Boston: Bedford/St. Martin's, 2007), 184, 182–184.

ANALYZING THE EVIDENCE

➤ How do you explain the personal, almost intimate, tone of these letters to the Roosevelts?

➤ How have specific New Deal programs helped or hurt the authors of these letters?

➤ What are the basic values of the authors? Do they differ between those who support and oppose the New Deal?

"the key to recovery." The federal government had long assisted farmers: through cheap prices for land, the extension services of the Department of Agriculture, and the Federal Farm Loan Act of 1916. But the Agricultural Adjustment Act (AAA), a measure jointly developed by administration officials and major farm organizations, represented a new level of government involvement in the farm economy. To solve the problem of overproduction, which resulted in low prices for farm crops, the AAA set up an allotment system for seven major commodities (wheat, cotton, corn, hogs, rice, tobacco, and dairy products). The act provided cash subsidies to farmers who cut their production of these crops; to pay these subsidies, the act imposed a tax on the processors of these commodities, which they in turn passed on to consumers. New Deal policymakers hoped that farm prices would rise as production (and supply) fell, spurring consumer purchases by farmers and assisting a general economic recovery.

By dumping cash in farmers' hands (a special-interest policy that continues to this day), the AAA stabilized the farm economy. But the act's benefits were not evenly distributed. Subsidies went primarily to the owners of large- and medium-sized farms, who often cut production by reducing the amount of land they rented to tenants and sharecroppers. In the South, where many sharecroppers were black and the landowners and government administrators were white, such practices forced 200,000 black families off the land. Some black farmers tried to protect themselves by joining the Southern Tenant Farmers Union (STFU), a biracial organization founded in 1934. "The same chain that holds you hold my people, too," an elderly black farmer reminded his white colleagues. But landowners had such economic power and such support from local politicians and sheriffs that the STFU could do little. Dispossessed of access to land and denied government aid, hundreds of thousands of black sharecroppers and white smallholders moved to the cities.

The National Recovery Act. The New Deal's initial response to depressed levels of business activity was the National Industrial Recovery Act. The act drew on the regulatory approaches of Bernard Baruch's War Industries Board during World War I and Herbert Hoover's trade associations of the 1920s. It also reflected "corporatist" theories of a government-planned economy popular in Europe and implemented in Italy by Benito Mussolini. The government agency charged with implementing the act, the National Recovery Administration (NRA), established a system of self-government in more than six hundred industries. Each industry — ranging from large businesses such as coal, cotton, and steel to small ones such as dog food and costume jewelry — regulated itself by hammering out a government-approved code of prices and production quotas, similar to those for farm products. These agreements had the force of law and covered workers as well as employers. The codes outlawed child labor and set minimum wages and maximum hours for adult workers. One of the most far-reaching provisions, Section 7(a), guaranteed workers the right to organize and bargain collectively "through representatives of their own choosing." This right to union representation was an important spur to the growth of the labor movement in the 1930s.

In many instances the trade associations set by Hoover in the 1920s, which were controlled by large companies, dominated the code-drafting process. As a result, the NRA solidified the power of large businesses at the expense of smaller enterprises, labor unions, and consumer interests. To sell the program to skeptical consumers and businesspeople, the NRA launched an extensive public relations campaign, complete with plugs in Hollywood films and "Blue Eagle" stickers with the NRA slogan, "We Do Our Part."

Unemployment Legislation. The early New Deal also addressed the critical problem of unemployment and impoverished working families. By 1933, local governments and private charities had exhausted their resources and looked to Washington for assistance. Roosevelt responded reluctantly because he feared a budget deficit. Nonetheless, he asked Congress to fund relief for millions of unemployed Americans. In May, Congress established the Federal Emergency Relief Administration (FERA). Directed by Harry Hopkins, a hard-driving social worker from New York, the FERA provided federal funds to the states for relief programs. In his first two hours in office, Hopkins distributed $5 million. Over the program's two-year existence, FERA spent $1 billion.

Roosevelt and his advisors had strong reservations against the "dole," the popular name for these government welfare payments. As Hopkins worried, "I don't think anybody can go year after year, month after month, accepting relief without affecting his character. . . . It is probably going to undermine the independence of hundreds of thousands of families." To maintain a commitment to individual initiative, the New Deal tried to put people to work. Early in 1933, Congress appropriated $3.3 billion

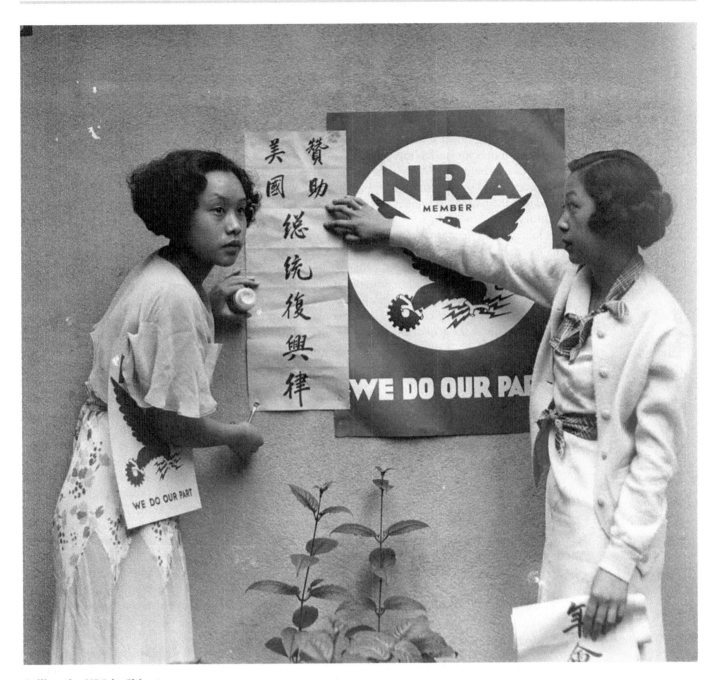

Selling the NRA in Chinatown

To mobilize support for its program, the National Recovery Administration (NRA) distributed millions of posters to businesses and families, urging them to display the "Blue Eagle" in shops, factories, and homes. Here Constance King and Mae Chinn of the Chinese Y.M.C.A. affix a poster (and a Chinese translation) to a shop in San Francisco that is complying with the NRA codes. Copyright Bettmann / Corbis.

for the Public Works Administration (PWA), a construction program directed by Secretary of the Interior Harold L. Ickes. However, Ickes's cautious approach to approving public works projects limited the agency's effectiveness in providing jobs or spurring recovery. So in November 1933 Roosevelt established the Civil Works Administration (CWA), named Harry Hopkins as its head, and gave it $400 million in PWA funds. Within thirty days, Hopkins had put 2.6 million men and women to work; at its peak in January 1934, the CWA funded the employment of 4 million Americans in public works' projects: repairing bridges, building highways, constructing public buildings, and setting up community projects. The CWA, a stopgap measure to get the country through the winter of 1933–1934, lapsed the next spring after spending all its funds.

When an exhausted Congress recessed in June 1933, it had accomplished much: banking reform, recovery programs for agriculture and industry, unemployment relief, and a host of other measures. Few presidents had so dominated a legislative session and won the passage of so many measures (the only future president to do so would be Lyndon Baines Johnson in 1965; see Chapter 28). A mass of "alphabet" agencies (the CCC, CWA, FERA, AAA, NRA), as the New Deal programs came to be known, began to flow from Washington. But if the avalanche of new laws and programs halted the downward psychological spiral of the Hoover years, they had yet to break the grip of the depression.

Financial Reform. As Roosevelt waited anxiously for the economy to revive, he turned his attention to the reform of Wall Street, where insider trading, fraud, and reckless speculation had triggered the financial panic of 1929. In 1934, Congress established the Securities and Exchange Commission (SEC) to regulate the stock market. The commission had broad powers to regulate companies that issued stock and bonds to the public, set rules for margin (credit) transactions, and prevent stock sales by those with inside information on corporate plans. The Banking Act of 1935 authorized the president to appoint a new Board of Governors of the Federal Reserve System, placing control of interest rates and other money-market policies at the federal level rather than with regional banks.

The New Deal under Attack

As Congress and the president consolidated the New Deal, their work came under attack from many quarters. Roosevelt saw himself as the savior of the American system of democratic capitalism, declaring simply: "To preserve we had to reform." Many bankers and business executives disagreed. To them, FDR became "That Man," a traitor to his class. In 1934, Republican business leaders joined with conservative Democrats in a "Liberty League" that lobbied against the "reckless spending" and "socialist" reforms of the New Deal. Reflecting their outlook, Herbert Hoover condemned the NRA as a "state-controlled or state-directed social or economic system"; and that, the former president declared, is "tyranny, not liberalism."

The Supreme Court likewise repudiated many New Deal measures. In May 1935, the Court unanimously ruled that the National Industrial Recovery Act represented an unconstitutional delegation of Congress's legislative power to a code-writing agency in the executive branch of the government. The case, *Schechter v. United States,* arose when a firm in Brooklyn, New York, sold diseased chickens to local storekeepers in violation of NRA codes. In addition to the delegation issue, the Court declared that the NRA unconstitutionally extended federal authority to *intrastate* (as opposed to *interstate*) commerce. Roosevelt publicly protested that the Court's narrow interpretation would return the Constitution "to the horse-and-buggy definition of interstate commerce," but he could only watch helplessly as the Court also struck down a raft of New Deal legislation in 1935: the Agricultural Adjustment Act, a Railroad Retirement Act, and the Frazier-Lemke debt relief act.

Challenges from the Left. If business executives and the Supreme Court thought the New Deal had gone too far, other Americans believed it had not gone far enough. Francis Townsend, a Long Beach, California, doctor, spoke for the nation's elderly, most of whom had no pension plans and feared poverty in their old age. In 1933 Townsend proposed the Old Age Revolving Pension Plan, which would give $200 a month (about $3,000 today) to citizens over the age of sixty. To receive payments the elderly would have to retire from their jobs, thus opening their positions to younger workers, and agree to spend the money within a month. Townsend Clubs soon sprang up across the country, particularly in the Far West. These clubs mobilized mass support for old-age pensions and helped win passage of the far less ambitious Social Security Act of 1935 (see p. 746).

Father Charles Coughlin also challenged Roosevelt's leadership and attracted a large following, especially in the Midwest. A priest in a Catholic parish in Detroit, Coughlin had turned to the radio in the mid-1920s to enlarge his pastorate. By 1933, about forty million Americans listened regularly to the Radio Priest's broadcasts. Coughlin initially supported the New Deal but turned against it when Roosevelt refused to nationalize the banking system and expand the money supply. To promote these programs, which resembled the proposals of the Populist Party of the 1890s (see Chapter 19), Coughlin organized the National Union for Social Justice and continued to attack the administration's policies.

The most direct political threat to Roosevelt came from Senator Huey Long. As the Democratic governor of Louisiana, the flamboyant Long had achieved stunning popularity by lowering utility bills, increasing taxes on corporations, and building new highways, bridges, hospitals, and schools. Long's accomplishments came at a price: To push through these measures, he had seized almost dictatorial control of the state government. In 1934, Long broke with the New Deal and, like Townsend and Coughlin, established a national movement. His "Share Our Wealth Society," which boasted over four million followers, argued that the depression did not stem from overproduction but from underconsumption. The unequal distribution of wealth prevented ordinary families from buying goods and stimulating economic activity. To put money in the hands of millions of consumers, the Society advocated a tax of 100 percent of all income over $1 million and all inheritances over $5 million. Long hoped that this program would carry him into the White House.

Although somewhat simplistic, the economic proposals offered by Townsend, Coughlin, and Long were no more radical than the NIRA or the AAA. Like the New Deal measures, they were plausible responses to the depression; in fact, some of them were subsequently endorsed by social welfare liberals. It was the constitutional views of Coughlin and Long that separated them from most politically engaged Americans: Neither man had much respect for representative government. "I'm the Constitution around here," Long declared during his governorship, while Coughlin suggested that dictatorial rule might be necessary to preserve democracy. Voters seemed not to mind. As their policies won increasing popularity, Roosevelt and his advisors feared that Long might join forces with Coughlin and Townsend to form a third party that would appeal to many Democratic voters. This prospect encouraged Republicans, who hoped that a split among between New Dealers and other reformers might return their party, and its ideology of small government and free enterprise, to political power in the 1936 election.

The Kingfish

Huey Long, the Louisiana governor and senator, called himself "the Kingfish" because, he said, "I'm a small fish here in Washington. But I'm the Kingfish to the folks down in Louisiana." An exceptionally charismatic man and a brilliant campaigner, he attracted a significant following with his "Share Our Wealth" plan, which aimed to redistribute the nation's wealth. Democrats worried that he might run for president in 1936 on a third-party ticket, threatening Franklin Roosevelt's reelection. But in September 1935 Long was killed (apparently by his bodyguard) during an assassination attempt by a young doctor over a Louisiana political dispute. Long is seen here shaking hands with a Louisiana supporter. Louisiana State Museum.

> ➤ What were the major differences between the approaches of Herbert Hoover and Franklin D. Roosevelt to the crisis of the depression?

> ➤ What were the main programs of the New Deal's "Hundred Days"? Why did FDR and the Democrats believe that these programs would work?

> ➤ Define the criticism of the New Deal from the political right and left. Who were the New Deal's major critics, and what were their alternative programs?

The Second New Deal, 1935–1938

As attacks on the New Deal from the conservative right and the liberal left mounted, Roosevelt and his advisors abandoned the middle ground and moved to the left. Historians have labeled this new course the Second New Deal. Acknowledging his inability to win the support of big business, Roosevelt openly criticized the "money classes," proudly stating: "We have earned the hatred of entrenched greed." And he moved decisively to counter the rising popularity of Townsend, Coughlin, and Long by stealing parts of their programs and, he hoped, much of their thunder. The administration's Revenue Act of 1935 proposed a substantial tax increase on corporate profits and higher income and estate taxes on wealthy citizens. Conservatives called the legislation an attempt to "soak the rich," and Congress moderated its rates, so that it boosted revenue only by $250 million a year. But FDR was happy. He had met Huey Long's Share Our Wealth plan with a plan of his own.

Legislative Accomplishments

The Revenue Act symbolized the administration's new outlook. Unlike the First New Deal, which focused on economic recovery, the Second New Deal emphasized social justice: the use of national legislation to enhance the power of working people and the security and welfare of the old, the disabled, and the unemployed.

The Wagner Act. The first beneficiary of Roosevelt's move to the left was the labor movement. The rising number of strikes in 1934 — about 1,800 job actions involving a total of 1.5 million workers — reflected the dramatic growth of rank-and-file militancy. When the Supreme Court voided the NIRA in 1935, thereby invalidating Section 7(a), labor unions demanded new legislation that would protect workers' rights to organize and bargain collectively. Named for its sponsor, Senator Robert F. Wagner of New York, the Wagner Act (1935) upheld the right of industrial workers to join unions; because of the opposition of southern Democrats, who represented the interest of planters and landlords, it did not apply to farm workers. The act outlawed many practices used by employers to squelch unions, such as firing workers for organizing activities. It also established the National Labor Relations Board (NLRB), a federal agency with the authority to protect workers from employer coercion, supervise elections for union representation, and guarantee the process of collective bargaining.

The Social Security Act. A second initiative, the Social Security Act of 1935, had an even greater impact. Other industrialized societies, such as Germany and Britain, had created national old-age pension systems around 1900, but American Progressives had failed to muster political support for a similar program in the United States. But now millions of citizens had joined the Townsend and Long movements; their demands gave political muscle to pension advocates within the administration, such as Grace Abbott, head of the Children's Bureau, and Secretary of Labor Frances Perkins. They won the president's support for a Social Security Act that provided old-age pensions for most privately employed workers and established a joint federal-state system of compensation for unemployed workers. Because of southern Democratic opposition in Congress, farm workers and domestic servants were excluded from both programs.

Roosevelt had his own concerns. Knowing that compulsory pension and unemployment legislation would be controversial, he refused to include a provision for national health insurance because that would make it more difficult to get the measure through Congress. A firm believer in personal responsibility, the president also insisted that workers bear part of the cost of the new pension and unemployment plans. Consequently, the act was not funded out of general tax revenues but by mandatory contributions paid by workers and their employers. Decades later, this funding mechanism protected the Social Security system from the attempt of "New Right" conservatives to abolish it; having contributed to the pension fund, millions of workers demanded that they receive its benefits (see Chapter 30).

The Social Security Act was a milestone in the creation of an American welfare state. Never before had the federal government assumed such responsibility for the well-being of a substantial majority of the citizenry. In addition to pension and unemployment coverage, the act mandated aid to various categories of Americans: the blind, deaf, and disabled as well as dependent children. These categorical assistance programs to the so-called "deserving poor" grew dramatically after the 1930s. Aid to Dependent Children covered only 700,000 youngsters in 1939; by 1994, its successor, Aid to Families with Dependent Children (AFDC), enrolled 14.1 million Americans, 60 percent of whom were African American or Hispanic. A minor program during the New Deal, AFDC had become one of the central facets of the American welfare system and one of the most controversial (see Chapter 30).

The Works Progress Administration. Roosevelt was never enthusiastic about public relief programs. But with the election of 1936 on the horizon and 10 million Americans still out of work, FDR won funding for the Works Progress Administration (WPA). Under the energetic direction of Harry Hopkins, the WPA became the main federal relief agency. Whereas the Federal Emergency Relief Administration of 1933–1934 had supplied grants to state relief programs, the WPA put workers directly onto the federal payroll. Between 1935 and 1943 the WPA spent $10.5 billion and employed 8.5 million Americans. The agency's workers constructed or repaired 651,087 miles of roads; 124,087 bridges; 125,110 public buildings; 8,192 parks; and 853 airports. Though the WPA was an extravagant operation by the standards of the 1930s, it reached only about one-third of the nation's unemployed. Wages were low — on average $55 a month ($800 today) — so as not to compete with private-sector jobs. But most WPA workers were thankful for any job that allowed them to eke out a living.

The 1936 Election

As the 1936 election approached, new voters joined the Democratic Party. Many had personally benefited from New Deal programs or knew those who had (Table 24.2). Roosevelt could count on a potent coalition of organized labor, midwestern farmers, white ethnic groups, northern blacks, and middle-class families concerned about unemployment and old-age dependence.

In addition, he commanded the support of Jews, intellectuals, and progressive Republicans. The Democrats also held on, though with some difficulty, to their traditional constituency of white southerners.

The Republicans realized that the New Deal was too popular to oppose directly. So they chose as their candidate the progressive governor of Kansas, Alfred M. Landon. Landon accepted the legitimacy of most New Deal programs but stridently criticized their inefficiency and expense.

TABLE 24.2	Major New Deal Legislation

Agriculture

1933	Agricultural Adjustment Act (AAA)
1935	Resettlement Administration (RA) Rural Electrification Administration
1937	Farm Security Administration (FSA)
1938	Agricultural Adjustment Act of 1938

Finance and Industry

1933	Emergency Banking Act Glass-Steagall Act (created the FDIC) National Industrial Recovery Act (NIRA)
1934	Securities and Exchange Commission (SEC)
1935	Banking Act of 1935 Revenue Act (wealth tax)

Conservation and the Environment

1933	Tennessee Valley Authority (TVA) Civilian Conservation Corps (CCC) Soil Conservation and Domestic Allotment Act

Labor and Social Welfare

1933	Section 7(a) of NIRA
1935	National Labor Relations Act (Wagner Act) National Labor Relations Board (NLRB) Social Security Act
1937	National Housing Act
1938	Fair Labor Standards Act (FLSA)

Relief and Reconstruction

1933	Federal Emergency Relief Administration (FERA) Civil Works Administration (CWA) Public Works Administration (PWA)
1935	Works Progress Administration (WPA) National Youth Administration (NYA)

The Republican candidate also pointed to authoritarian regimes in Italy and Germany, directed by Benito Mussolini and Adolf Hitler respectively, and hinted that FDR harbored similar dictatorial ambitions.

These charges fell on deaf ears. Roosevelt's victory in 1936 was one of the biggest landslides in American history. The assassination of Huey Long in September 1935 had deflated the threat of a serious third-party challenge; the candidate of the combined Long-Townsend-Coughlin camp, Congressman William Lemke of North Dakota, garnered fewer than 900,000 votes (1.9 percent) for the Union Party ticket. Roosevelt received 60.8 percent of the popular vote and carried every state except Maine and Vermont. The New Deal was at high tide.

Stalemate

"I see one-third of a nation ill-housed, ill-clad, ill-nourished," the president declared in his second inaugural address in January 1937. But any hopes that FDR had for expanding the liberal welfare state were quickly dashed. Within a year, staunch opposition to New Deal initiatives arose in Congress and the South, and a sharp recession undermined confidence in Roosevelt's economic leadership.

The Fight over the Supreme Court. Roosevelt's first setback came when he stunned Congress and the nation by asking for fundamental changes in the Supreme Court. In 1935 the Court had struck down a series of New Deal measures and a minimum wage law in New York State by the narrow margin of 5 to 4. With the Wagner Act, the TVA, and Social Security coming up on appeal, the future of the New Deal lay in the hands of a few elderly, conservative-minded judges. To diminish their influence, the president proposed to add a new justice for every member over the age of seventy. Roosevelt's opponents protested that he was trying to "pack" the Court; concerned by this blatant attempt to alter a traditional institution, Congress rejected the proposal after a bitter months-long debate.

If Roosevelt lost the battle, he won the war. Swayed by FDR's overwhelming election victory in 1936, the Court upheld a California minimum wage law and the Wagner and Social Security Acts. Moreover, a series of resignations allowed Roosevelt to reshape the Supreme Court; his new appointees, who included Hugo Black, Felix Frankfurter, and William O. Douglas, viewed the Constitution as a "living document" that had to be interpreted in the light of present conditions and generally supported New Deal measures.

Nonetheless, the court-packing fiasco revealed Roosevelt's vulnerability and energized congressional conservatives. Throughout Roosevelt's second term a conservative coalition composed mainly of southern Democrats and rural Republicans blocked or impeded social legislation. The president did win passage of the National Housing Act of 1937, which mandated the construction of low-cost public housing, and the Fair Labor Standards Act of 1938, which made permanent the minimum wage, maximum hours, and anti-child labor provisions in the NRA codes. But Congress rejected or modified other administration initiatives, including a far-reaching plan for reorganizing the executive branch of the federal government.

The Roosevelt Recession. The "Roosevelt recession" of 1937–1938 dealt the most devastating blow to the president. From 1933 to 1937 the gross domestic product had grown at a yearly rate of about 10 percent; by 1937 industrial output and real income had finally returned to 1929 levels. Unemployment had declined from 25 percent to 14 percent. "The emergency has passed," remarked Senator James F. Byrnes of South Carolina.

Acting on this assumption, Roosevelt slashed the federal budget, which had been running a modest deficit. Congress cut the WPA's funding in half, causing layoffs of about 1.5 million workers; the Federal Reserve, fearing inflation, raised interest rates. The results halted the economic recovery. The stock market dropped sharply, and unemployment soared to 19 percent. Quickly reversing course, Roosevelt spent his way out of the recession by boosting funding for the WPA and resuming public works projects. Although improvised, this spending program accorded with the theories advanced by John Maynard Keynes, a British economist who proposed that governments use **deficit spending** (funds obtained by borrowing rather than through taxation) to stimulate the economy when private spending proved insufficient. Untested and sharply criticized by Republicans and conservative Democrats in the 1930s, **Keynesian economics** gradually won wider acceptance as defense spending during World War II ended the Great Depression. Beginning in the 1940s, Democratic administrations endorsed Keynesian principles and after 1980, Republican administrations engaged in massive deficit spending, both to stimulate the economy and offset the effects of tax cuts (see Chapters 26 and 30).

To restore the vitality of the New Deal, Roosevelt decided to "purge" the Democratic Party of some of his most conservative opponents. During the primary elections in 1938, the president campaigned against members of his own party who had been hostile to New Deal initiatives. His purge failed abysmally and opened the door for a Republican resurgence. Profiting from the "Roosevelt recession" and court-packing fiasco, Republicans picked up eight seats in the Senate, eighty-one in the House, and thirteen state governorships.

The New Deal had run out of steam. Roosevelt's political mistakes were partly responsible for this outcome, but so too were his successes. By 1939, the challenge posed by the Great Depression to American capitalist and democratic institutions had been met. The economy was back on course and so too was normal party politics; Americans had rejected the simplistic solutions proposed by demagogic politicians and the allure of fascist and communist alternatives to the American tradition of liberal individualism. A reformer rather than a revolutionary, Roosevelt had done his part to save capitalism and democracy. He lacked a new domestic agenda and the political power to enact it. Had it not been for the outbreak of a major war in Europe, FDR probably would have served out his second term and retired from the scene. In any event, by 1939 the New Deal was over.

➤ How did the Second New Deal differ from the first? What were FDR's reasons for changing course?

➤ Why did the New Deal reach a stalemate?

➤ Describe Keynesian economics. How important was it to the New Deal?

The New Deal's Impact on Society

Whatever the limits of the New Deal, it had a tremendous impact on the nation. Its ideology of social welfare liberalism fundamentally altered Americans' relationship to their government, providing assistance to a wide range of groups: the unemployed, the elderly, white ethnic workers, women, and racial minorities. To serve these diverse constituencies, New Dealers created a sizeable federal bureaucracy; the number of civilian federal employees increased by 80 percent between 1929 and 1940 and reached a total of one million. The expenditures—and deficits—of the federal government grew at an even faster rate. In 1930 the Hoover administration spent $3.1 billion and had a surplus of almost $1 billion; in 1939 New Dealers expended $9.4 billion and ran a deficit of nearly $3 billion. But the real step toward major government spending came with World War II (and later military buildups), when federal outlays routinely totaled $95 billion and deficits grew to $50 billion. In peace or in war, power increasingly centered in the nation's capital, not in the states.

The Rise of Labor

Exploiting their dominant position in national politics, Democrats used legislation and tax dollars to cement the allegiance of blocs of voters to their party. One of their prize targets were the millions of workers with ties to the labor movement. Demoralized and shrinking organizations at the end of the 1920s, labor unions rose to influence as they took advantage of increased worker militancy and New Deal legislation. Thanks to Section 7(a) of the National Industrial Recovery Act and the Wagner Act, unions found it easier to organize workers, to win recognition from management, and to bargain for higher wages, seniority systems, and grievance procedures. By the end of the decade, the number of unionized workers had tripled to almost nine million, or 23 percent of the nonfarm workforce.

The Congress of Industrial Workers (CIO) served as the cutting edge of the union movement. It did so by promoting "industrial unionism"—that is, it organized all the workers in an industry, both skilled and unskilled, into one union. John L. Lewis, leader of the United Mine Workers (UMW), was the foremost exponent of industrial unionism. By 1935, Lewis had rejected the philosophy of the American Federation of Labor (AFL), which favored organizing workers on a craft-by-craft basis, and helped to create the CIO.

The CIO scored its first major victory in the automobile industry. On December 31, 1936, General Motors workers in Flint, Michigan, staged a sit-down strike, vowing to stay at their machines until management agreed to collective bargaining. The workers lived in the factories and machine shops for forty-four days before General Motors recognized their union, the United Automobile Workers (UAW). Shortly thereafter the CIO won another major victory at the U.S. Steel Corporation. Despite a history of bitter opposition to unionization, as demonstrated in the 1919 steel strike (see Chapter 22),

"Big Steel" executives capitulated without a fight in March 1937 and recognized the Steel Workers Organizing Committee (SWOC). Another group of companies, "Little Steel," refused to negotiate, sparking a protest at the Republic Steel Corporation in Chicago that took the lives of ten strikers; only in 1941 did workers in Little Steel win union recognition.

The 1930s constituted one of the most active periods of labor solidarity in American history (Map 24.1). The sit-down tactic spread rapidly and reached a high point in March 1937, when a total of 167,210 workers staged 170 sit-down strikes. Labor unions called nearly 5,000 strikes that year and won favorable terms in 80 percent of them. Large numbers of middle-class Americans opposed the sit-down tactics, which they considered a violation of private property. In 1939, the Supreme Court accepted this argument and upheld a law that banned the sit-down tactic.

Organize

The Steel Workers Organizing Committee was one of the most vital labor organizations contributing to the rise of the CIO during the late 1930s. Note that artist Ben Shahn chose a man who might be of either European or African ancestry to represent the steel workers, part of a conscious effort to build a labor movement across racial and ethnic lines. This iconography also reinforced the notion that the typical worker was male, despite the large number of women who joined the CIO. Library of Congress.

The CIO welcomed new groups to the labor movement. Unlike the AFL, which had long excluded or segregated African American workers, the CIO actively organized blacks in the steel and meatpacking industries. In California, its organizers set out to win equal pay for Mexican American women who worked in the canning industry. Corporate giants such as Del Monte, McNeill, and Libby paid women around $2.50 a day, while their male counterparts received $3.50 to $4.50. These differentials shrank following the formation in 1939 of the United Cannery, Agricultural, Packing, and Allied Workers, an unusually democratic union in which women played leading roles. Altogether, some 800,000 women workers joined CIO unions.

Labor's new vitality spilled over into political action. The AFL generally had stood aloof from partisan politics, but the CIO quickly allied itself with the Democratic Party, hoping to persuade the Party to nominate candidates sympathetic to labor. The CIO gave $770,000 (about $12 million today) to Democratic campaigns in 1936, and its Political Action Committee became a major Democratic contributor during the 1940s.

Despite its successes during the 1930s, the labor movement did not develop into a dominant force in American life. Roosevelt never made the growth of the labor movement a high priority, and many workers remained suspicious of unionization, especially as New Deal programs provided unemployment assistance and pension benefits. And while the Wagner Act helped unions to achieve better working conditions for their members, it did not redistribute power in American industry. Managers retained authority over most corporate affairs. In fact, business executives found that unions could be used as a buffer against rank-and-file militancy; likewise, National Labor Relation Board officials, concerned about rising consumer prices, pressed unions to moderate their demands for higher wages and benefits. The road to union power, even with New Deal protection, continued to be a rocky and uncertain one.

Women and Blacks in the New Deal

Although the New Deal did not directly challenge gender inequities and racial injustice, its programs generally enhanced the welfare of women and African Americans.

Women in Government. Women won the vote in 1920, but only with the New Deal did they enter the higher ranks of government in significant numbers.

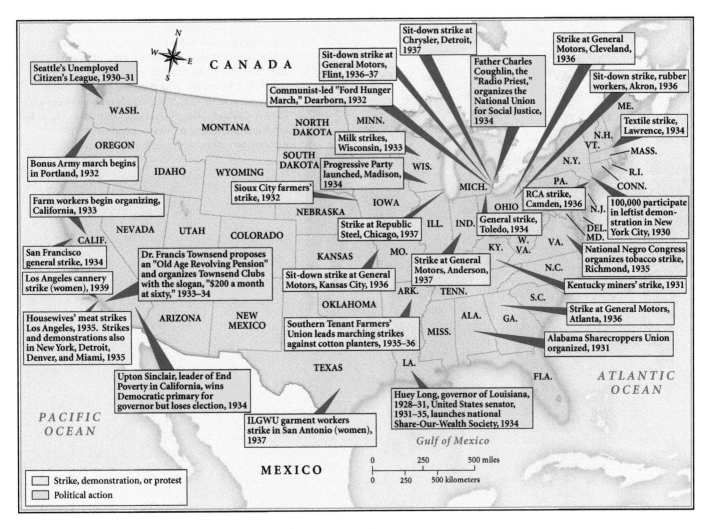

MAP 24.1   Popular Protest in the Great Depression, 1933–1939

The depression forced Americans to look closely at their society, and many of them did not like what they saw. Some citizens expressed their discontent through popular movements, and this map suggests the geography of discontent. The industrial Midwest witnessed union movements, strikes, and Radio Priest Charles Coughlin's demands for social reform. Simultaneously, farmers' movements — tenants in the South, smallholders in the agricultural Midwest — engaged in strikes and dumping campaigns, and rallied behind the ideas of progressives in Wisconsin and Huey Long in the South. Protests took diverse forms in California, which was home to strikes by farmworkers, women, and — in San Francisco — all wage workers. The West was also the seedbed of two important reform proposals: Upton Sinclair's "End Poverty in California" movement and Francis Townsend's "Old Age Revolving Pension" clubs.

Frances Perkins, the first woman named to a cabinet post, served as secretary of labor throughout Roosevelt's presidency. Molly Dewson, a social reformer turned politician, headed the Women's Division of the Democratic National Committee, where she pushed an issue-oriented program that supported New Deal reforms. Roosevelt's women appointees also included the first female director of the mint, the head of a major WPA division, and a judge on a circuit court of appeals. Many of those women were close friends as well as professional colleagues and cooperated in an informal network to advance feminist and reform causes.

Eleanor Roosevelt exemplified the growing prominence of women in public life. In the 1920s she had worked closely with other reformers to expand positions for women in political parties, labor unions, and education. During her years in the

White House, Mrs. Roosevelt emerged as an independent and influential public figure. She held press conferences for women journalists, wrote a popular syndicated news column called "My Day," and traveled extensively throughout the country. By descending deep into coal mines to view working conditions and meeting with African American antilynching advocates, she became the conscience of the New Deal, pushing her pragmatically minded husband to do more for the disadvantaged. "I sometimes acted as a spur," Mrs. Roosevelt later reflected, "even though the spurring was not always wanted or welcome." And she knew the limits of her power with the president: "I was one of those who served his purposes."

Without the vocal support of Eleanor Roosevelt, Frances Perkins, and other prominent women, New Deal policymakers might have completely overlooked the needs of women. Despite their efforts, a fourth of the NRA codes set a lower minimum wage for women than for men performing the same jobs; only 7 percent of the workers in the Civil Works Administration were female; and the Civilian Conservation Corps excluded women entirely. Women fared better under the Works Progress Administration; at its peak, 405,000 women were on the job rolls. Still, most policymakers and most Americans viewed the depression primarily as a crisis for male breadwinners and gave priority to their needs. When asked in a 1936 Gallup poll whether wives should work when their husbands had jobs, 82 percent of those interviewed said no. Reflecting such sentiments, many state legislatures enacted laws that prohibited married women from working. Not until the 1970s would women's quest for equal rights begin to be addressed.

Blacks Join the New Deal Coalition. Especially in the South, African Americans remained in the lowest paying jobs and faced harsh social and political discrimination. In a celebrated 1931 case in

Scottsboro, Alabama, nine young black men were accused of rape by two white women who had been riding a freight train. The women's stories contained many inconsistencies, but in interracial matters a southern white woman was usually taken at her word. Within two weeks, a white jury convicted all nine defendants of rape; eight received the death sentence. After the U.S. Supreme Court overturned the sentences on grounds that the defendants had been denied adequate legal counsel, five of the men were again convicted and sentenced to long prison terms. The Scottsboro case received wide coverage in black communities across the country, as did the rise in the number of lynchings; white mobs lynched twenty blacks in 1930 and twenty-four in 1934.

This violence, and the dispossession of sharecroppers by the AAA, prompted a renewal of the "Great Migration" of African Americans to the cities of the North and Midwest. One destination was Harlem, where housing was already at a premium because of the black influx during the 1920s. Because residential segregation kept African Americans from moving to many sections of New York, they had to pay high rents to live in crowded and deteriorating buildings. Jobs were scarce. White-owned stores in Harlem would not employ blacks; elsewhere in New York City hard-pressed whites took over the menial jobs traditionally held by blacks — as waiters, domestic servants, elevator operators, and garbage collectors. Unemployment in Harlem rose to 50 percent, twice the national rate. These conditions triggered a major race riot in March 1935 as blacks went on a rampage. Before order was restored, four rioters were killed and millions of dollars in property was destroyed.

For the majority of white Americans, the events in Scottsboro and Harlem reinforced their beliefs that blacks were a "dangerous class." Consequently, there was little support for federal intervention to secure the civil rights of African Americans. In fact, many New Deal programs reflected prevailing racist attitudes. CCC camps segregated blacks and whites, and many NRA codes did not protect black

Scottsboro Defendants

The 1931 trial in Scottsboro, Alabama, of nine black youths accused of raping two white women became a symbol of the injustices African Americans faced in the South's legal system. Denied access to an attorney, the defendants were found guilty, and eight were sentenced to death. When the U.S. Supreme Court overturned their convictions in 1932, the International Labor Defense organization hired the noted criminal attorney, Samuel Leibowitz, who eventually won the acquittal of four defendants and jail sentences for the rest. This photograph, taken in a Decatur jail, shows Leibowitz conferring with Haywood Patterson, in front of the other eight defendants. Brown Brothers.

Mary McLeod Bethune

This 1943 painting by Betsy Graves Reyneau captures the strength and dignity of one of the twentieth century's most important African Americans. Behind Bethune is a picture of the first building at the Daytona Literary and Industrial School for Training of Negro Girls, which later became Bethune-Cookman College. National Portrait Gallery, Smithsonian Institution / Art Resource, NY.

workers from discrimination. Most tellingly, Franklin Roosevelt repeatedly refused to support legislation to make lynching a federal crime, arguing it would antagonize southern Democrats whose support he needed to pass New Deal measures.

Nevertheless, blacks received significant benefits from New Deal relief programs directed toward poor Americans. Reflecting their poverty, African Americans made up about 18 percent of the WPA's recipients, although they constituted only 10 percent of the population. The Resettlement Administration, established in 1935 to help small farmers and tenants buy land, fought for the rights of black tenant farmers until angry southerners in Congress drastically cut its appropriations. Such help from New Deal agencies, and a belief that the White House—or at least Eleanor Roosevelt—cared about their plight, caused blacks to change their political allegiance. Since the Civil War, African Americans had staunchly supported the party of Abraham Lincoln, the Great Emancipator; even in the dark depression year of 1932, black voters in

northern cities overwhelmingly supported Republican candidates. But in 1936 black Americans outside the South (where few blacks were allowed to vote) gave Roosevelt 71 percent of their votes. In Harlem, where state and federal relief dollars increased dramatically in the wake of the 1935 riot, African American support for the president was an extraordinary 81 percent. Black voters have remained strongly Democratic ever since.

Mary McLeod Bethune: Black New Dealer. African Americans supported the New Deal in part because the Roosevelt administration appointed many blacks to federal office. Among the most important of these was Mary McLeod Bethune. Born in 1875 in South Carolina, Bethune was the child of former slaves who founded a school that eventually became the prestigious Bethune-Cookman College. Becoming an educator herself, Bethune served during the 1920s as president of the National Association of Colored Women (NACW)—a leading black women's organization. In 1935 she organized the National Council of Negro Women (NCNW), a coalition of the major associations of black women.

Bethune joined the New Deal in 1935, serving first as a member of the advisory committee of the National Youth Administration and then as director of the NYA's Division of Negro Affairs. In that position she emerged as the leader of the Federal Council of Negro Affairs, a group of black administrators who met on Sunday nights at her home in Washington. Along with NAACP general secretary Walter White, she had access to the White House and pushed continually, though often without success, for New Deal programs that would directly assist African Americans.

The Indian Reorganization Act. The New Deal had a greater direct impact on Native Americans. Indian peoples had long made up one of the nation's most disadvantaged and powerless minorities. Their average annual income in 1934 was only $48, and their unemployment rate was three times the national average. The plight of Native Americans won the attention of Secretary of the Interior Harold Ickes and Commissioner of the Bureau of Indian Affairs John Collier. They pushed for an Indian Section of the Civilian Conservation Corps and earmarked FERA and CWA work relief projects for Indian reservations.

More ambitious was the Indian Reorganization Act of 1934, sometimes called the "Indian New Deal." That law reversed the Dawes Act of 1887 by promoting Indian self-government through formal constitutions and democratically elected tribal

A Bitter Harvest

In the early 1930s California was rocked by strikes, and one of the largest was the cotton pickers' strike of 1933. Demanding higher wages and better working conditions, the predominantly Mexican American workforce set up camps for the duration of the strike. While the men stood on the picket line, their wives and daughters took care of the cooking, cleaning, and child care. Bancroft Library, University of California, Berkeley.

councils. A majority of Indian peoples—some 174—accepted the reorganization policy, but 78 refused to participate, primarily because they preferred traditional consensus-seeking methods of making decisions. New Deal administrators

accepted their decision. Influenced by academic anthropologists, who celebrated the unique character of native cultures, government officials no long attempted to assimilate Native Americans into mainstream society. Instead, they embraced a policy of **cultural pluralism** and pledged to preserve Indian languages, arts, and traditions.

Migrants and Minorities in the West

Over the course of the late nineteenth and twentieth centuries, the American West—and especially California—grew dramatically in population and wealth (see Chapter 16). During the 1920s and 1930s, agriculture in California became a big business—large scale, intensive, and diversified. Corporate-owned farms produced specialty crops—lettuce, tomatoes, peaches, grapes, and cotton—whose staggered harvests required lots of transient labor during picking seasons. Thousands of workers, initially migrants from Mexico and Asia and later from the midwestern states, trooped from farm to farm harvesting those crops for shipment to eastern markets. Some of these migrants also settled in the rapidly growing cities along the West Coast, especially the sprawling metropolis of Los Angeles. Until the Great Depression, many foreign migrants viewed California as the promised land.

Mexicans and Asians. The economic downturn brought dramatic changes to the lives of thousands of Mexican Americans. The 1930 census reported 617,000 Mexican Americans; by 1940 the number had dropped to 377,000. A formal deportation

A New Deal for Indians

John Collier, the New Deal's commissioner for Indian affairs, was a former social worker who had become interested in Native American tribal cultures in the 1920s. A longtime opponent of the assimilationist policies of the Dawes Act of 1887, Collier led successful efforts to provide Native American peoples with communally controlled lands and self-government. Here, Collier speaks with Chief Richard of the Blackfoot Nation, one of the Indian leaders attending the Four Nation celebration at historic Old Fort Niagara, New York, in 1934. Corbis-Bettmann.

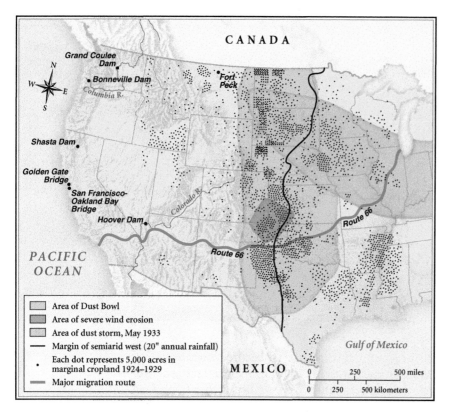

MAP 24.2 The Dust Bowl and Federal Building Projects in the West, 1930–1941

A U.S. Weather Bureau scientist called the drought of the 1930s "the worst in the climatological history of the country." Conditions were especially severe in the southern plains, where farming on marginal land threatened the environment even before the drought struck. As farm families migrated west on U.S. Route 66, the federal government began a series of massive building projects that provided flood control, irrigation, electric power, and transportation facilities to residents of the states of the Far West.

policy for illegal immigrants instituted by the Hoover administration was partly responsible for the decline in numbers, but even more Mexicans left voluntarily in the first years of the depression. Working as migrant laborers, they knew that local officials would ship them back to Mexico rather than support them on relief during the winter.

Under the New Deal, the situation of Mexican Americans improved. Those migrants living in Los Angeles, El Paso, and other cities qualified for relief more easily, and there was more relief to go around. New Deal initiatives supporting labor unions indirectly encouraged the acculturation of Mexican immigrants; joining the CIO was an important stage in becoming Americans for many Mexicans. Other immigrants heeded the call of the Democratic Party to join the New Deal coalition. Los Angeles activist Beatrice Griffith noted, "Franklin D. Roosevelt's name was the spark that started thousands of Spanish-speaking persons to the polls."

The farm union organizer César Chavez grew up in such a family. In 1934, when Chavez was ten, his father lost his farm near Yuma, Arizona, and the family became part of the migrant workforce in California. They experienced continual discrimination, even in restaurants where signs proclaimed "White Trade Only." César's father joined several bitter strikes in the Imperial Valley, part of a wave of job actions across the state. All of the strikes failed, including one in the San Joaquin Valley that

mobilized 18,000 cotton pickers. But these strikes set the course for the young Chavez, who founded the United Farm Workers, a successful union of Mexican American workers, in 1962 (see pp. 886–887).

Men and women of Asian descent — mostly from China, Japan, and the Philippines — formed a tiny minority of the American population but were a significant presence in some western cities and towns. Immigrants from Japan and China had long faced discrimination; for example, a California law of 1913 prohibited immigrants from owning land. Japanese farmers, who specialized in fruit and vegetable crops, circumvented this restriction by putting land titles in the names of their American-born children. As farm prices declined during the depression and racial discrimination undermined the prospects of rising generation for nonfarm jobs, about 20 percent of the migrants returned to Japan.

Chinese Americans were even less prosperous than their Japanese counterparts were. Only 3 percent of Chinese Americans worked in professional and technical occupations, and discrimination kept them out of most industrial jobs. In San Francisco, most Chinese worked in small ethnic businesses — restaurants, laundries, and firms that imported textiles and ceramics. In the hard times of the depression, they turned for assistance both to traditional Chinese social organizations such as *huiguan* (district associations) and to local authorities; in 1931, about one-sixth of San Francisco's Chinese population

Drought Refugees

Like the Joad family in John Steinbeck's powerful novel *The Grapes of Wrath* (1939), many thousands of poor people hit hard by the drought, dust, and debt of farm life in the Great Plains loaded their possessions into pickup trucks and hoped for brighter futures in the West. This photograph, shot in 1937 by Dorothea Lange, shows a family of Missouri drought refugees taking a break on Highway 99 near Tracy, California. Library of Congress.

was receiving public welfare aid. Few benefited from the New Deal. Until the repeal of the Chinese Exclusion Act in 1943, Chinese immigrants were classified as "aliens ineligible for citizenship" and therefore excluded from most federal programs.

Because Filipino immigrants came from a U.S. territory, they were not affected by the ban on Asian immigration passed in 1924 (see Chapter 23). During the 1920s their numbers swelled to about 50,000, many of whom worked as laborers on large corporate-owned farms. As the depression cut wages, Filipino immigration slowed to a trickle and was virtually cut off by the Tydings-McDuffie Act of 1934. The act granted independence to the Philippines (which since 1898 had been an American dependency), classified all Filipinos in the United States as aliens, and restricted immigration to fifty persons per year.

Dust Bowl Migration to California. Even as California lost its dazzle for Mexicans and Asians, it became the destination of tens of thousands of displaced farmers from the "dust bowl" of the Great Plains. Between 1930 and 1941, a severe drought afflicted farmers in the semiarid states of Oklahoma,

Texas, New Mexico, Colorado, Arkansas, and Kansas. But the dust bowl was primarily a human creation. Farmers had pushed the agricultural frontier beyond its natural limits, stripping the land of its native vegetation and destroying the delicate ecology of the plains (Map 24.2). When the rains dried up and the winds came, nothing remained to hold the soil. Huge clouds of thick dust rolled over the land, turning the day into night.

This ecological disaster prompted a mass exodus. Their crops ruined and their debts unpaid, at least 350,000 "Okies" (so-called whether or not they were from Oklahoma) loaded their meager belongings into beat-up Fords and headed to California. Many were drawn by handbills distributed by commercial farmers that promised good jobs and high wages; instead, they found low wages and terrible living conditions. Before the depression, white native-born workers made up 20 percent of the migratory farm labor force of 175,000; by the late 1930s, Okies accounted for 85 percent of the workers. John Steinbeck's novel *The Grapes of Wrath* (1939) immortalized them and their journey, and New Deal photographer Dorothea Lange's haunting images of migrant camps in California gave a

Odette Keun

A Foreigner Looks at the Tennessee Valley Authority

In 1936 French writer Odette Keun visited the United States and was so impressed by the Tennessee Valley Authority (TVA) that she wrote a book about it. Keun was struck not only by the vast size of the TVA but also by its imaginative scope. By promoting such projects, she argued, democratic governments could ward off popular support for fascist solutions to the Great Depression.

The vital question before democracy is, therefore, not how to bring back an economic freedom which is irretrievably lost, but how to prevent the intellectual freedom, which is still our heritage, from being submerged. It is already threatened. It will be threatened more and more strongly in the years ahead—and the menace, of course, is dictatorship. But to fight dictatorship it is necessary first to understand in what circumstances it arises, and then to think out the counterattack which democracy can launch against its approaching force.

Dictatorship springs from two very clear causes. One is the total incapacity of parliamentary government: total, as in Germany in 1933 and in Spain in 1935. To such a breakdown neither the democratic nations of Europe nor America have yet been reduced, although everywhere there are very ominous creaks and cracks, and the authority and prestige of parliamentary institutions have greatly and perilously diminished. The other cause, infinitely closer to us and more dynamic, is the failure of the economic machine to function properly, and by functioning properly I mean ensuring a livelihood for the entire population. No system can survive if it cannot procure food and wages for the people who live under it. Man has to get subsistence from his rulers, for the most immediate and the most imperious law of our nature is that the belly must be filled. It is perfectly futile to orate on fine, high, and abstract principles to human beings who are permanently hungry, permanently harassed, permanently uncertain, who hear their wives begging for the rent and their children crying out for nourishment....

One of the main tenets of liberalism—I reiterate this like a gramophone, but I must get it to sink in—is that all necessary overhauling and adjustment ought to be done in a manner which will minimize the shock to the greatest number, and soften as much as possible the unavoidable human suffering which these changes entail. This opposition to extremes, this practice of a graduated change, we can call "the middle of the road in time and space." But it is not nearly enough to conceive it and to bestow upon it a name. We must reach it. It is unutterably foolish to look at the middle of the road, to talk of the middle of the road, to hope for the middle of the road—and never get there.

Now I have tried to show that the middle of the road is already being laid down in America. The Tennessee Valley Authority is laying it down. Handicapped and restricted though it is in all sorts of ways, it is the noblest, the most intelligent, and the best attempt made in this country or in any other democratic country to economize, marshal, and integrate the actual assets of a region, plan its development and future, ameliorate its standards of living, establish it in a more enduring security, and render available to the people the benefits of the wealth of their district, and the results of science, discovery, invention, and disinterested forethought. In its inspiration and its goal there is goodness, for goodness is that which makes for unity of purpose with love, compassion, and respect for every life and every pattern of living. The economic machine, bad though it is, has not been smashed in the Tennessee Watershed; it is being very gradually, very carefully, very equitably reviewed and amended, and the citizens are being taught and directed, but not bullied, not coerced, not regimented, not frightened, within the constitutional frame the nation itself elected to build. It is not while the Tennessee Valley Authority has the valley in its keeping that despair or disintegration can prepare the ground for a dictatorship and the loss of freedom. The immortal contribution of the TVA to liberalism, not only in America but all over the world, is the blueprint it has drawn, and that it is now transforming into a living reality, of the road which liberals believe is the only road mankind should travel.

SOURCE: Odette Keun, "A Foreigner Looks at the TVA," in *This Was America*, ed. Oscar Handlin (Cambridge, MA: Harvard University Press, 1949), 547–549.

ANALYZING THE EVIDENCE

➤ According to Keun, why has dictatorship come to Germany and Spain? Why might the TVA prevent such an outcome in the United States?

➤ What does the term *liberalism* mean to Keun, and why does she consider the TVA an example of that ideology?

personal face to some of the worst suffering of the depression.

A New Deal for the Environment

Concern for the land was one of the dominant motifs of the New Deal, and the shaping of the public landscape was among its most visible legacies. Franklin Roosevelt and Interior Secretary Harold Ickes were avid conservationists and used public concern over the drought and devastation in the dust bowl to spread "the gospel of conservation." Their national resources policy stressed scientific management of the land and the often aggressive use of public authority to preserve or improve the natural environment.

The Tennessee Valley Authority. The most extensive New Deal environmental undertaking was the Tennessee Valley Authority (TVA). Since World War I, experts had recommended the building of dams to control severe flooding and erosion in the Tennessee

The Human Face of the Great Depression

Migrant Mother by Dorothea Lange is one of the most famous documentary photographs of the 1930s. Lange spent only ten minutes in the pea-picker's camp in California where she captured this image and did not even get the name of the woman whose despair and resignation she so powerfully recorded. She was later identified as Florence Thompson, a full-blooded Cherokee from Oklahoma. Library of Congress.

River Basin, a seven-state area with some of the country's heaviest rainfall (Map 24.3). But when progressive reformers in the 1920s proposed a series of flood-control dams that would also generate cheap electricity, private utility companies blocked the project. As governor of New York, FDR had waged a similar unsuccessful battle to develop public power in the Niagara region. So in 1933 he encouraged Congress to fund the Tennessee project. The TVA was the ultimate watershed demonstration area, integrating flood control, reforestation, electricity generation, and agricultural and industrial development, including the production of chemical fertilizers. The dams and their hydroelectric plants provided cheap electric power for homes and industrial plants and ample recreational opportunities for the valley's residents. The project won praise around the world (see Voices from Abroad, "Odette Keun: A Foreigner Looks at the Tennessee Valley Authority," p. 758).

The TVA also contributed to the efforts of the Roosevelt administration to keep farmers on the land by enhancing the quality of rural life. The Rural Electrification Administration (REA), established in 1935, was central to that goal. Fewer than one-tenth of the nation's 6.8 million farms had electricity, and private utilities balked at the expense of running lines to individual farms. The REA addressed this problem by promoting the creation of nonprofit farm cooperatives. For a $5 down payment, local farmers could join the coop and apply for low-interest federal loans covering the cost of installing power lines. By 1940, 40 percent of the nation's farms had electricity; a decade later, 90 percent did.

Electricity brought relief from the drudgery and isolation of farm life. Electric milking machines and water pumps saved hours of manual labor. Electric irons, vacuum cleaners, and washing machines eased women's burdens, and radios enlivened the lives of the entire family. Electric lights extended the time children could read, women could sew, and families could eat their evening meals. One farm woman remembered, "I just turned on the light and kept looking at Paw. It was the first time I'd ever really seen him after dark." Along with the automobile, electricity probably did more than any other technological innovation to break down the barriers between urban and rural life in twentieth-century America.

Still, the dust bowl disaster focused the attention of urban dwellers and government planners on rural issues of land management and ecological balance. Agents from the Soil Conservation Service in the Department of Agriculture taught farmers to prevent soil erosion by tilling hillsides among the contours of the land. Government

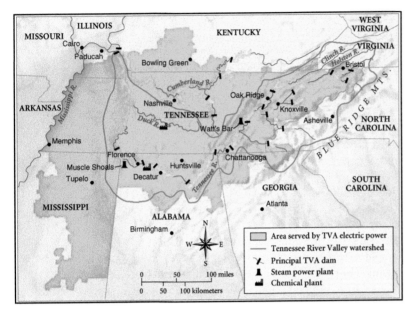

MAP 24.3 The Tennessee Valley Authority, 1933–1952

The Tennessee Valley Authority was one of the New Deal's most far-reaching environmental projects. Between 1933 and 1952, the TVA built twenty dams and improved five others, taming the flood-prone Tennessee River and its main tributaries. The cheap hydroelectric power generated by the dams brought electricity to hundreds of thousands of area residents, and artificial lakes provided extensive recreational facilities. Widely praised at the time, the TVA came under attack in the 1970s for its practice of strip mining and the pollution caused by its power plants and chemical factories.

agronomists also tried to remove marginal farms from cultivation. One of their most widely publicized programs was the Shelterbelts, the planting of 220 million trees running north along the ninety-ninth meridian from Abilene, Texas, to the Canadian border. Planted as a windbreak, the trees also prevented soil erosion.

New Deal projects that enhanced people's enjoyment of the natural environment can be seen today throughout the country. CCC and WPA workers built the famous Blue Ridge Parkway, which connects the Shenandoah National Park in Virginia with the Great Smoky Mountain National Park in North Carolina. In the West, government workers built the San Francisco Zoo, Berkeley's Tilden Park, and the canals of San Antonio. The CCC helped to complete the East Coast's Appalachian Trail and the West Coast's Pacific Crest Trail through the Sierra Nevada. In state parks across the country, cabins, shelters, picnic areas, lodges, and observation towers stand as monuments to the New Deal ethos of recreation coexisting with nature.

The New Deal and the Arts

Many American artists redefined their relationship to society in response to the Great Depression, and many became politically engaged. Never had there been a decade, critic Malcolm Cowley noted in 1939, "when literary events followed so closely on the flying coat-tails of social events." Because the New Deal funded many arts projects, the link between politics and the arts was both close and controversial.

Federal Arts Projects. As the economic downturn dried up traditional sources of private patronage, creative artists, like other Americans, turned to Washington. A WPA project known as "Federal One" put unemployed artists, actors, and writers to work, but its spirit and purpose extended far beyond relief. New Deal administrators encouraged artists to create projects of interest to the entire community, not just the cultured elite. "Art for the millions" became a popular New Deal slogan and encouraged the painting of murals in hundreds of public buildings (see Reading American Pictures, "Interpreting the Public Art of the New Deal," p. 761).

The Federal Art Project (FAP) gave work to many young artists who would become the twentieth century's leading painters, muralists, and sculptors. Jackson Pollock, Alice Neel, Willem de Kooning, and Louise Nevelson all received support. The Federal Music Project employed fifteen thousand musicians, and government-sponsored orchestras toured the country, presenting free concerts of both classical and popular music. Like many New Deal programs, the Music Project emphasized American themes. The composer Aaron Copland wrote his ballets *Billy the Kid* (1938) and *Rodeo* (1942) for the WPA, basing the compositions on western folk motifs. The federal government also employed the musicologist Charles Seeger and his wife, the composer Ruth Crawford Seeger, to catalog hundreds of American folk songs.

The Federal Writers' Project (FWP) gave work to five thousand writers and produced more than a thousand publications. It collected the oral histories

Interpreting the Public Art of the New Deal

"The Promise of the New Deal," Ben Shahn (1938). Roosevelt Arts Project.

Murals are perhaps the most pervasive artistic legacy of the New Deal. They decorate federal buildings throughout the nation today. The goals of the agencies that commissioned murals were to give employment to artists, bring art to the masses, and celebrate the American people and their nation. All murals were "realistic" in style and many embodied the decade's emphasis on regionalism by depicting the history of a locality and its people at work and play. This image comes from a large, three panel mural by well-known artist Ben Shahn that adorns a public school in Roosevelt, New Jersey.

Originally called the Jersey Homesteads, the town was created by the Farm Security Administration as a planned community for poor immigrant Jewish garment workers from New York City. The first two panels of the mural depict Jewish immigrants and their work. The third panel, pictured here, features in the left corner a teacher instructing workers about the history of unions. Seated at the right are New Deal planners and labor leaders. The figures behind them are the prospective residents of the new community. For the full mural, go to **www.scc.rutgers.edu/njh/ homesteads/mural.htm.**

ANALYZING THE EVIDENCE

➤ What does this third panel of Shahn's mural tell us about the character and the goals of the New Deal?

➤ Note the blueprint of the street plan and the houses depicted on the mural (top center). Then turn to the cartoon in Chapter 27 (p. 837) which depicts Levittown, a famous housing development built by a private corporation in the late 1940s. What does a comparison of those two images suggest?

➤ How does this mural fit with the discussion of the documentary impulse discussed in this chapter?

of many Americans, including two thousand narratives by former slaves, and published a set of popular state guidebooks. Young FWP employees who later achieved fame included Saul Bellow, Ralph Ellison, Tillie Olsen, and John Cheever. The black folklorist and novelist Zora Neale Hurston finished three novels while in the Florida FWP, among them *Their Eyes Were Watching God* (1937). And Richard Wright won the 1938 *Story* magazine prize for the best tale by a WPA writer. Wright used his spare time to complete *Native Son* (1940), a novel that took a bitter look at racism.

Of all the New Deal arts programs, the Federal Theatre Project (FTP) was the most ambitious. Under the gifted direction of Hallie Flanagan, the FTP reached an audience of 25 to 30 million people in the four years of its existence. Talented directors, actors, and playwrights, including Orson Welles, John Huston, and Arthur Miller, offered their services. Because many FTP productions took a critical look at American social problems, it was attacked in Congress as sympathetic to communism and its funding was cut off in 1939.

The Documentary Impulse. The WPA arts projects reflected a broad artistic trend called the "documentary impulse." Documentary artists focused on actual events that were relevant to people's lives and presented them in ways that aroused the interest and emotions of the audience. It influenced practically every aspect of American culture — literature, photography, art, music, film, dance, theater, and radio. It is evident in John Steinbeck's *Grapes of Wrath* and in John Dos Passos's *USA* trilogy, which used actual newspaper clippings and headlines in its fictional story. *The March of Time* newsreels, which movie audiences saw before feature films, presented images of world events for a pre-television age. New photojournalism magazines, including *Life* and *Look,* carried this documentary approach into millions of living rooms.

The federal government played a leading role in compiling the documentary record of the 1930s. It sent journalist Lorena Hickok, writer Martha Gellhorn, and many other investigators into the field to report on the conditions of people on relief. And the Historical Section of the Farm Security Administration compiled a remarkable series of photographs of the American scene. Under the direction of Roy Stryker, a talented group of photographers — Dorothea Lange, Walker Evans, Ben Shahn, and Margaret Bourke-White — produced haunting images of sharecroppers, dust bowl migrants, and urban homeless, permanently shaping the image of the Great Depression.

Building the American Future

Margaret Bourke-White's photograph of the Fort Peck Dam in Montana, with the two human figures in the foreground establishing its huge scale, graced the inaugural cover of *Life* magazine in 1936. Fort Peck was one of a series of dams built by the Works Projects Administration to control floods on the Missouri River. *Life*'s first issue also contained a photo essay about the town nearest to the Fort Peck Dam, which was named, appropriately, New Deal, Montana. Margaret Bourke-White, *Life Magazine,* copyright 1936 Time Warner, Inc.

The Legacies of the New Deal

The New Deal did much more than simply reinforce and extend the "regulatory" liberalism of the Progressive era. By creating a powerful national bureaucracy and laying the foundation of a social welfare state, it redefined the meaning of American liberalism. For the first time the federal government became an ongoing part of everyday life. During the 1930s, millions of people began to pay taxes directly to the Social Security Administration and the Internal Revenue Service, and more than a third of the population received direct government assistance from new federal programs, including old-age pensions, unemployment compensation, farm loans, relief work, and mortgage guarantees. Furthermore, the government stood ready to intervene in the economy when private enterprise failed to produce economic stability. New legislation regulated the stock market, reformed the Federal Reserve System, and subjected business corporations to federal regulation.

Like all major social transformations, the New Deal was criticized by those who thought it did too much and those who protested that it did too little. "Classical" liberals, who gave high priority to small government and individual freedom, pointed out that the New Deal state intruded deeply into the personal and financial lives of the citizenry. The Social Security Act, for example, imposed compulsory taxes on workers and forced families to comply with ever more complicated bureaucratic regulations. As one historian has written, the act instigated a "mercantilist regulation of family life not seen since the eighteenth century." Conversely, advocates of social welfare liberalism complained that the New Deal's safety net had many holes, especially in comparison with the far more extensive welfare systems provided by the governments of western Europe. These critics pointed out that there was no provision for a national health-care system; that domestic workers and farm laborers were excluded from most welfare programs; and that, in the many New Deal programs administered by state governments, benefits were often low.

Despite recurring debate about the increased presence of the state in American life, the New Deal set a pattern of government involvement in the life of the society that would persist for the rest of the twentieth century. There was a significant expansion of social welfare programs in the 1960s during the "Great Society" initiative of President Lyndon Johnson, and most of those programs remained intact in the wake of the "Reagan Revolution" of the 1980s (see Chapters 28 and 30).

The New Deal Coalition. Whatever the fate of the depression-era social welfare liberalism, there is no question that it was brilliant politics. The Democratic Party courted and won the allegiance of citizens who benefited from New Deal programs. Organized labor aligned itself with the administration that had made it a legitimate force in modern industrial life. Blacks voted Democratic as economic aid began to flow into their communities. The Women's Division of the Democratic National Committee elicited grassroots political support from 80,000 women who praised what the New Deal had done for their communities. The unem-

ployed also looked kindly on the Roosevelt administration. According to one of the earliest Gallup polls, 84 percent of those on relief voted the Democratic ticket in 1936.

Roosevelt's magnetic personality and the New Deal's farm relief and social security programs also brought millions of middle-class voters into the Democratic fold. Many were first- or second-generation immigrants from southern and central Europe — Italians, Poles, Slovaks, and Jews — who had now found a secure place in American life. The New Deal completed the transformation of the Democratic Party that had begun in the 1920s. Its coalition of ethnic groups, city dwellers, organized labor, blacks, and a broad cross-section of the middle class formed the nucleus of the northern Democratic Party for decades to come, and provided support for additional liberal reforms.

From its inception, the New Deal coalition also contained a potentially fatal contradiction involving the issue of race. Roosevelt and the Democratic Party depended heavily on white voters in the South, who strongly preferred to keep African Americans poor and powerless. Such policies faced increasing opposition not only from northern liberals but also from the increasing number of northern black Democrats. As the struggle over civil rights for African Americans entered the national agenda beginning in the late 1940s, it would gradually destroy the Roosevelt coalition. Even in the late 1930s, southern Democrats refused to support the expansion of federal power, fearing it would undermine white rule in the South. Thanks in part to this southern Democratic opposition, the New Deal, as we have seen, ground to a halt. The darkening international scene was also important. As Europe moved toward war and Japan flexed its muscles in the Far East, Roosevelt became increasingly preoccupied with international relations and pushed domestic reform further and further into the background.

➤ What impact did the New Deal have on organized labor, women, and racial and ethnic minorities?

➤ Under the New Deal, the government's involvement in the environment and in the arts was unprecedented. What were the major components of this new departure?

➤ What were the most significant long-term results of the New Deal? What were its limitations?

SUMMARY

We have seen the ways in which Franklin Delano Roosevelt's First New Deal concentrated on stimulating economic recovery, providing jobs and relief to the unemployed, and reforming banks and other financial institutions. His goal was to restore Americans' confidence in their society and institutions. The Second New Deal was different. Influenced by the persistence of the depression and the popularity of Huey Long's Share Our Wealth Society, FDR promoted social welfare legislation that would provide economic security for American citizens.

We also explored the impact of the New Deal on various groups of citizens, especially blacks, women, and unionized workers. Our survey focused on the depression-era experiences of migrants in the West, particularly the Mexicans, Asians, and Okies who worked in the farms and factories of California. Because New Deal legislation and programs assisted such groups, they gravitated to the Democratic Party. Its coalition of white southerners, ethnic urban workers, farmers, and a cross-section of the middle classes gave the party overwhelming majorities in Congress and provided FDR with a landslide presidential victory in 1936.

Finally, we examined the accomplishments and legacies of the New Deal. In the short run, it pulled the nation out of the crisis of 1933, provided relief, and preserved capitalist economic institutions and a democratic political system. Over the longer run, it expanded the size and power of the federal government and, through the Social Security system, farm subsidy programs, and public works projects, extended its presence into the lives of nearly every American. Great dams and electricity projects sponsored by the Tennessee Valley Authority in the Southeast, the Works Project Administration in the West, and the Rural Electrification Administration made permanent contributions to the quality of national life.

Connections: Economy

As we noted in the essay that opened Part Five (p. 671), between 1914 and 1945 the United States "boasted the world's most productive economic system." But the performance of the American economy varied widely over the decades. In Chapter 22 we saw how spending for military mobilization during World War I invigorated the industrial sector and food shortages in Europe ushered in a boom time for American farmers. But after the war, the farm economy fell into a two-decades-long crisis. As Chapter 23 explained, during the 1920s food surpluses cut farm prices and farm income, and Presidents Coolidge and Hoover vetoed farm relief legislation. Chapter 24 described the farm policies of the New Deal, which both subsidized farm owners and forced many tenant and sharecropping families off the land. As we will see in Chapter 25, new shortages of goods during World War II restored the prosperity of the farm sector, which was now increasingly dominated by the operators of large-scale farms.

The evolution of the industrial economy followed a roughly similar pattern. As we saw in Chapter 23, there was a sharp postwar economic recession in the early 1920s but then a quick recovery, thanks to the demand for new consumer goods: automobiles and many kinds of electrical goods. However, the wages paid to workers were not sufficient to sustain the boom, which collapsed in 1929. As this chapter explained, the various economic policies of the New Deal preserved the capitalist system and demonstrated the crucial importance of government intervention in smoothing out the business cycle and maintaining prosperity. Chapter 25 will show how massive government spending ended the Great Depression and, in the process, confirmed the economic theories of John Maynard Keynes.

CHAPTER REVIEW QUESTIONS

➤ Some historians have seen the New Deal as an evolution of Progressivism, but others have argued that it represented a revolution in social values and government institutions. What do you think?

➤ In what ways did Roosevelt's personality, values, and political style affect the policies and programs of the New Deal?

➤ What changes took place during the depression era with respect to the lives of women, workers, and racial and ethnic minorities? What role did the New Deal play?

TIMELINE

1931–1937	Scottsboro case: trials and appeals
1933	FDR's inaugural address and first fireside chats
	Emergency Banking Act begins the Hundred Days
	Civilian Conservation Corps (CCC) created
	Agricultural Adjustment Act (AAA)
	National Industrial Recovery Act (NIRA)
	Tennessee Valley Authority (TVA) established
	Townsend Clubs promote Old Age Revolving Pension Plan
	Twenty-first Amendment repeals Prohibition
1934	Securities and Exchange Commission (SEC) created
	Southern Tenant Farmers Union (STFU) founded
	Indian Reorganization Act
	Senator Huey Long promotes Share Our Wealth Society
	Father Charles Coughlin founds National Union for Social Justice
1935	Harlem race riot
	Supreme Court voids NRA in *Schechter v. United States*
	National Labor Relations (Wagner) Act
	Social Security Act creates old-age pension system
	Works Progress Administration (WPA) created
	Huey Long assassinated
	Rural Electrification Administration (REA) established
	Supreme Court voids Agricultural Adjustment Act
	Congress of Industrial Organizations (CIO) formed
1936	General Motors sit-down strike
	Landslide reelection of FDR marks peak of New Deal power
1937	FDR's Supreme Court plan fails
1937–1938	"Roosevelt recession" raises unemployment
1938	Fair Labor Standards Act (FLSA)
1939	Federal Theatre Project terminated

FOR FURTHER EXPLORATION

Robert S. McElvaine, *The Great Depression* (1984), provides a general treatment of the New Deal. Blanche Wiesen Cook's *Eleanor Roosevelt* (vol. 1, 1992; vol. 2, 1999) and Katie Loucheim, ed., *The Making of the New Deal: The Insiders Speak* (1983), portray important New Dealers. For popular reaction to Roosevelt's fireside chats, see Lawrence W. Levine and Cornelia R. Levine, *The People and the President* (2002). Robert S. McElvaine's *Down and Out in the Great Depression* (1983) contains letters written by ordinary people, while Studs Terkel's *Hard Times: An Oral History of the Great Depression* (1970) offers their memories. For audio versions of Terkel's interviews, go to the Chicago Historical Society at **www.studsterkel.org/index.html**. James Agee and Walker Evans's *Let Us Now Praise Famous Men* (1941) is a compelling portrait of southern poverty. For a memoir of a depression-era childhood, see Russell Baker's *Growing Up* (1982). John Steinbeck, *The Grapes of Wrath* (1939); Josephine Herbst, *Pity Is Not Enough* (1933); and Richard Wright, *Native Son*, (1940) are classic novels. See also Harvey Swados, *The American Writer and the Great Depression* (1966).

For two extensive collection of 1930s materials, see the "New Deal Network" at **newdeal.feri.org** and "America in the 1930s" at **xroads.virginia.edu/~1930s/home_1.html**, which includes clips of radio programs. See also the University of Utrecht's "American Culture in the 1930s" at **www.let.uu.nl/ams/xroads/ 1930proj.htm** and the wonderful collection of government-commissioned art at **www.archives.gov/exhibits/new_deal_ for_the_arts/index.html**. The Library of Congress has a multimedia presentation, "Voices from the Dust Bowl," at **memory .loc.gov/ammem/afctshtml/tshome.html** and a superb collection of photographs covering the years 1935–1945 at **lcweb2. loc.gov/ammem/fsowhome.html**. For music, listen to **www.authentichistory.com/1930s.html**. The political cartoons of the day are available in the "FDR Cartoon Archive" at **www.nisk.k12. ny.us/fdr**.

For the impact of the depression and the New Deal on African Americans, go to **memory.loc.gov/ammem/aaohtml/ exhibit/aopart8.html**. For the "'The Scottsboro Boys' Trials: 1931–1937," log on to **www.law.umkc.edu/faculty/projects/ FTrials/scottsboro/scottsb.htm**. For audio reminiscences about racial segregation during this and later decades, listen to "Remembering Jim Crow" at **americanradioworks.publicradio .org/features/remembering**.

TEST YOUR KNOWLEDGE

To assess your command of the material in this chapter, see the Online Study Guide at **bedfordstmartins.com/henretta**.

For Web sites, images, and documents related to topics and places in this chapter, visit **bedfordstmartins.com/makehistory**.

25 The World at War

1939–1945

THE SECOND WORLD WAR WAS "the largest single event in human history, fought across six of the world's seven continents and all of its oceans. It killed fifty million human beings, left hundreds of millions of others wounded in mind or body and materially devastated much of the heartland of civilization" both in Europe and East Asia. So concluded the noted military historian John Keegan, in a grim judgment that still rings true. The war was so vast and so destructive because it was waged both with technologically advanced weapons and with massive armies. The military conflict began in 1939 with a *blitzkrieg* ("lightning war") attack by wonderfully engineered German tanks across the plains of Poland. It ended in 1945 when American planes dropped two atomic bombs, the product of even more breathtaking scientific breakthroughs, on the Japanese cities of Hiroshima and Nagasaki. In between these demonstrations of technological prowess and devastating power, huge armies confronted and destroyed one another on the steppes of Russia, the river valleys of China, and the sandy deserts of North Africa.

Well might soldiers and civilians "jive in the streets" around Times Square in New York City on August 1945, celebrating V-J (Victory over Japan) Day. World War II was finally over. Many American lives had been lost or forever damaged, but the country emerged from the war intact

The Road to War
The Rise of Fascism
Isolationists versus Interventionists
Retreat from Isolationism
The Attack on Pearl Harbor

Organizing for Victory
Financing the War
Mobilizing the American Fighting Force
Workers and the War Effort
Politics in Wartime

Life on the Home Front
"For the Duration"
Migration and Social Conflict
Civil Rights during Wartime

Fighting and Winning the War
Wartime Aims and Tensions
The War in Europe
The War in the Pacific
Planning the Postwar World

Summary
Connections: Government

◄ **One City (and Island) at a Time**

By late 1944, the victory of the United States and its allies was nearly certain, but Japanese and German troops continued to fight with great courage and determination. Many European cities and every Pacific island had to be taken foot by foot. Here, American troops from the 325th Regiment of the 82nd Airborne Division advance slowly through the rubble-filled street of a German city in early 1945. Collection of Jeff Ethell.

and prosperous. As one man told journalist Studs Terkel, "Those who lost nobody at the front had a pretty good time." In fact, many Americans viewed the brutal conflict as the "good war," a successful defense of democratic values from the threat posed by German and Japanese fascism. When evidence of the grim reality of the Jewish Holocaust came to light, U.S. participation in the war seemed even more just.

Although it was not fully apparent at the time, World War II changed the nation's government in fundamental ways. The power of the federal government, which had been increasing since the Progressive era and World War I, grew exponentially during the conflict. Equally important, the government remained powerful after the war ended. Federal laws, rules, and practices put in place during the war—universal taxation of incomes, nationwide antidiscrimination employment standards, a huge military establishment, and multibillion dollar budgets, to name but a few—became part of American life. So too did the active participation of the United States in international politics and diplomacy, a participation all the more important because of the unresolved issues of the wartime alliance with the Soviet Union. A powerful American state, the product of a long "hot" war, would remain in place to fight an even longer, more expensive, and more dangerous Cold War.

The Road to War

The Great Depression disrupted economic life and political life around the world, everywhere endangering traditional institutions. An antidemocratic movement known as fascism, which had developed in Italy during the 1920s, spread to Japan, Germany, and Spain. By the mid-1930s, these states had forsaken their democratic institutions and instituted authoritarian, militaristic governments led by powerful dictators: Adolf Hitler in Nazi Germany, Benito Mussolini in Italy, Francisco Franco in Spain, and, after 1940, Hideki Tojo in Japan. As early as 1936, President Roosevelt warned Americans that other peoples had "sold their heritage of freedom for the illusion of a living" and called on them to work for "the survival of democracy" both at home and abroad. Hampered at first by the pervasive isolationist sentiment in the country, by 1939 FDR was leading the nation toward war against the Fascist powers.

The Rise of Fascism

World War II had its roots in the settlement of World War I (see Chapter 22). Germany deeply resented the harsh terms imposed on it by the Treaty of Versailles, and Japan and Italy revived their dreams of overseas empires that had been thwarted by the treaty makers. The League of Nations, the collective security system established at Versailles, proved unable to maintain the existing international order.

The first challenge came from Japan. In 1930, that small island nation was controlled by a militaristic regime with an expansionist agenda. To become a major industrial power, Japan needed raw materials and overseas markets for its goods. To get them, Japan embarked on a program of military expansion. In 1931, its troops occupied Manchuria, the northernmost province of China, and in 1937 it launched a full-scale invasion of China. In both instances the League of Nations condemned Japan's action but took no action to stop the military invasion.

Hitler

In 1933, Adolph Hitler seized power in Germany, intent on restoring its status as a major power. His ambitions grew steadily: overturning the Versailles treaty, asserting German control of central Europe, dominating Europe and the world. Here, dressed as usual in a military uniform, he salutes army troops and brown-suited members of his National-Socialist German Workers Party (NSDAP or Nazi) at the party's annual meeting in Nuremberg in 1938. Note the swastika — the symbol of his Nazi Party — prominently displayed on the *führer's* sleeve. Time Life Pictures / Getty Images.

Japan's defiance of the League encouraged a fascist dictator half a world away: Italy's Benito Mussolini who had come to power in 1922 and introduced a fascist political system. Fascism in Italy and, later, in Germany rested on an ideology of a powerful state that directed economic and social affairs. It disparaged parliamentary government, independent labor movements, and individual rights and celebrated authoritarian rule; Mussolini called for "a dictatorship of the state over many classes cooperating."

The Italian dictator had long been unhappy with the Versailles treaty, which had not awarded Italy any of the former German or Turkish colonies in Africa or the Middle East. So in 1935 he invaded Ethiopia, one of the few independent countries left in Africa. The Ethiopian emperor, Haile Selassie, appealed to the League of Nations, which condemned the invasion but imposed only limited sanctions. By 1936 the Italians had subjugated Ethiopia and were now an imperial nation.

Hitler and National Socialism. But it was Germany, not Italy, that presented the gravest threat to the world order in the 1930s. There, huge World War I reparation payments, economic depression, fear of communism, labor unrest, and rising unemployment fueled the rise of Adolf Hitler and his National Socialist (Nazi) Party. In 1933 Hitler became chancellor of Germany, and the legislature, the *Reichstag*, granted him dictatorial powers to deal with the crisis. He soon took the title of *führer* (leader) and outlawed other political parties.

Hitler's goal was nothing short of European domination and world power, as he made clear in his book *Mein Kampf* (*My Struggle*). Hitler's plan was to overturn the territorial settlements of the Versailles treaty, unite Germans living throughout central and eastern Europe in a great German fatherland, and annex large areas of eastern Europe. The "inferior races" who lived in these lands — Jews, Gypsies, and Slavs — would be removed or subordinated to the German "master race." A virulent anti-Semite, Hitler had long blamed Jews for Germany's problems. Once in power, he began a sustained and brutal persecution of Jews, which expanded to a campaign of extermination when the war began.

Hitler's strategy for restoring Germany's lost territories and military power was to provoke a series of minor crises — daring Britain and France to go to war to stop him. In 1935, Hitler announced that he planned to rearm the nation in violation of the Versailles treaty. No one stopped him. In 1936 Germany sent troops into the Rhineland, a region that had been declared a demilitarized zone under the treaty; once again, France and Britain took no

action. Later that year, Hitler and Mussolini joined forces in the Rome-Berlin Axis, a political and military alliance. Also in 1936, Germany signed an Anti-Comintern Pact with Japan. Its announced purpose was to oppose the Comintern, a Soviet-backed worldwide organization that spread communist ideology, but the pact was really a military alliance between Japan and the Axis Powers.

Isolationists versus Interventionists

While these events were taking place in Europe, the Roosevelt administration focused its energies on restoring the American economy and, diplomatically, on consolidating American influence in the Western Hemisphere. Secretary of State Cordell Hull implemented a Good Neighbor Policy, under which the United States voluntarily renounced the use of military force and armed intervention in Latin America. As part of this effort, in 1934 Congress repealed the Platt Amendment, a relic of the Spanish-American War, which asserted the U.S. right to intervene in Cuba's affairs (see Chapter 21). However, the United States kept (and still maintains) a major naval base at Cuba's Guantanamo Bay, and its diplomats continued to intervene in various Latin American countries on behalf of American business interests there.

Congress and the American public accepted such economic intervention, but they were increasingly resistant to diplomatic initiatives that might result in political entanglements. In part, the growing support for political isolationism reflected disillusionment with American participation in World War I. In 1934 Gerald P. Nye, a progressive Republican senator from North Dakota, began a congressional investigation into the profits of munitions makers during World War I and then widened the investigation to determine their influence (and that of the banks that lent millions to the Allies) on America's decision to declare war. Nye's committee concluded that war profiteers, whom it called "merchants of death," had maneuvered the nation into World War I for financial gain.

Although the Nye committee failed to prove this charge, its factual findings gave momentum to the isolationist movement and resulted in the passage of a series of legislative acts. All were explicitly designed to prevent a recurrence of the events that helped to pull the nation into World War I. Thus, the Neutrality Act of 1935 imposed an embargo on arms trading with countries at war and declared that American citizens traveled on the ships of belligerent nations at their own risk. In 1936 Congress expanded the act to ban loans to belligerents, and in

1937 it adopted a "cash-and-carry" provision: If a country at war wanted to purchase nonmilitary goods from the United States, it had to pay for them in cash and pick them up in its own ships.

The Popular Front. Other Americans, especially writers, intellectuals, and progressive social activists, responded to the rise of fascism in Europe by advocating interventionist policies. Some of them joined the American Communist Party, which had taken the lead in organizing opposition to fascism and which was also gaining supporters as the depression revealed deep flaws in the capitalist system. Between 1935 and 1938, Communist party membership peaked at about 100,000, from a wide range of social groups: African American farmers in Alabama, white electrical workers in New York, union organizers, even a few New Deal administrators. Many intellectuals did not join the party, but considered themselves "fellow travelers." They sympathized with the party's objectives, wrote for the *Daily Worker*, and supported organizations sponsored by the party.

The courting of intellectuals, union members, and liberal organizations reflected a shift in the strategy of the Communist Party. Fearful of German and Japanese aggression, the Soviet Union instructed its followers in western Europe and the United States to join in a Popular Front with other opponents of fascism. The Popular Front strategy became even more urgent with the outbreak of the Spanish Civil War in 1936. Armed forces led by Generalissimo Francisco Franco, strongly supported by the Fascist regimes in Germany and Italy, led a rebellion against Spain's democratically elected Republican government. Backed only by the Soviet Union and Mexico, the Republicans, or Loyalists, relied heavily on military volunteers from other countries, including the 3,200-strong American Abraham Lincoln Brigade. The governments of the United States, Great Britain, and France, despite their Loyalist sympathies, remained neutral — a policy that ensured a Fascist victory. American intellectuals strongly supported the Spanish Loyalists but grew increasingly uneasy with the Popular Front because of the rigidity of their Communist associates and the cynical brutality and political repression of Soviet leader Joseph Stalin.

The Failure of Appeasement. Further encouraged by the passivity of the Allied Powers during the Spanish Civil War, Hitler expanded his aggression in 1938. He sent troops to annex German-speaking Austria, while simultaneously scheming to seize a part of Czechoslovakia. Because Czechoslovakia had an alliance with France, war seemed imminent. But at the Munich Conference in September 1938, Britain and France again capitulated, agreeing to let Germany annex the Sudetenland — the German-speaking border areas of Czechoslovakia — in return for Hitler's pledge to seek no more territory. The agreement, declared British Prime Minister Neville Chamberlain, guaranteed "peace for our time."

Within six months, however, Hitler's forces had overrun the rest of Czechoslovakia and were threatening to march into Poland. Britain and France, realizing that their policy of appeasement had been disastrous, now prepared to take a stand. Then in August 1939 Hitler and Stalin shocked the world by signing a Nonaggression Pact. The pact had advantages for both sides. It protected Russia from a German invasion but only at the cost of destroying the Popular Front and severely weakening support for the Communist Party in western Europe and the United States. For Germany, the results of the pact were all positive. It assured Hitler that he would not have to wage a two-front war. Now protected in the east, on September 1, 1939, Hitler launched a *blitzkrieg* ("lightning war") against Poland; two days later Britain and France declared war on Germany. World War II had begun.

Retreat from Isolationism

Because the United States had become a major world power, its response would affect the course of the European conflict. Two days after the European war started, the United States officially declared its neutrality. Roosevelt made no secret of his sympathies and pointedly rephrased Woodrow Wilson's declaration of 1914 (see p. 675): "This nation will remain a neutral nation, but I cannot ask that every American remain neutral in thought as well." The overwhelming majority of Americans — some 84 percent, according to a poll in 1939 — supported Britain and France rather than Nazi Germany, but most Americans did not want to be drawn into another war.

At first the need for American intervention seemed remote. After the German conquest of Poland in September 1939, a false calm settled over Europe. But then on April 9, 1940, Nazi tanks overran Denmark. Norway fell to the Nazi *blitzkrieg* next, and the Netherlands, Belgium, and Luxembourg followed. Finally, on June 22, 1940, France fell. Britain stood alone against Hitler's plans for domination of Europe.

Support for Intervention Grows. What *Time* magazine would later call America's "thousand-step road to war" had already begun. After a bitter battle in Congress in 1939, Roosevelt won a change in the neutrality laws to allow the Allies to buy arms on a cash-and-carry basis. Interventionists, led by the journalist William Allen White and his Committee to Defend America by Aiding the Allies, became increasing vocal. In response, isolationists, including the aviator Charles Lindbergh and Senator Gerald Nye, formed the America First Committee to keep the nation out of the war; they attracted strong support in the Midwest and from conservative newspapers.

Despite the efforts of the America Firsters, in 1940 the United States moved closer to involvement in the war. In May Roosevelt created the National Defense Advisory Commission and laid the basis for a bipartisan defense effort by bringing two prominent Republicans, Henry Stimson and Frank Knox, into his cabinet as secretaries of war and the navy, respectively. During the summer, the president traded fifty World War I destroyers to Great Britain in exchange for the right to build military bases on British possessions in the Atlantic, thus circumventing the nation's neutrality law by executive order. In October, a bipartisan vote in Congress approved a large increase in defense spending and instituted the first peacetime draft registration and conscription in American history.

While the war expanded from Europe to its colonial possessions in North Africa and the oil-rich Middle East, the United States was preparing for the 1940 presidential election. The conflict had convinced Roosevelt that he should seek an unprecedented third term. Overcoming strong opposition from conservative Democrats, Roosevelt chose the liberal secretary of agriculture, Henry A. Wallace, as his running mate. The Republicans nominated Wendell Willkie of Indiana, a former Democrat who supported many New Deal policies. The two parties' platforms differed only slightly. Both parties pledged aid to the Allies, and both candidates pledged not to send "one American boy into the shambles of another war," as Willkie put it. Willkie's spirited campaign resulted in a closer election than those of 1932 or 1936; nonetheless, Roosevelt and the Democrats won 55 percent of the popular vote and a lopsided total in the Electoral College.

Lend-Lease and the Atlantic Charter. With the election behind him, Roosevelt concentrated on persuading the American people to increase aid to Britain, whose survival he viewed as the key to American security. In an address to Congress in January 1941, he outlined "four essential freedoms" (freedom of speech and of religion, freedom from want and fear) that he believed it was necessary to protect. Two months later, with Britain no longer able to pay cash for arms, Roosevelt convinced Congress to pass the Lend-Lease Act. The legislation

authorized the president to "lease, lend, or otherwise dispose of" arms and other equipment to any country whose defense was considered vital to the security of the United States. When Hitler abandoned his Nonaggression Pact with Stalin and invaded the Soviet Union in June 1941, the United States promptly extended lend-lease to the Soviets, who became part of the Allied coalition. The implementation of lend-lease marked the unofficial entrance of the United States into the European war.

Roosevelt underlined his support for the Allied cause by meeting in August 1941 with Winston Churchill, who had become Britain's prime minister. Their joint press release, which became known as the Atlantic Charter, provided the ideological foundation of the Western cause. Like Wilson's Fourteen Points and Roosevelt's Four Freedoms, the charter called for economic collaboration and guarantees of political stability after the war to ensure that "all men in all the lands may live out their lives in freedom from fear and want." The charter also supported free trade, national self-determination, and the principle of collective security.

As in World War I, when Americans started supplying the Allies, Germany attacked U.S. and Allied ships. By September 1941 Nazi submarines and American vessels were fighting an undeclared naval war in the Atlantic, unknown to the American public (Map 25.1). Without a dramatic enemy attack, however, and with the public reluctant to enter the conflict, Roosevelt hesitated to ask Congress for a declaration of war.

The Attack on Pearl Harbor

The final provocation came not from Germany but from Japan. Throughout the 1930s, Japanese military advances in China had upset the balance of political and economic power in the Pacific, where the United States had long enjoyed the benefits of the open-door policy (see Chapter 21). After Japan's invasion of China in 1937, Roosevelt denounced "the present reign of terror and international lawlessness," suggesting that aggressors be "quarantined" by peace-loving nations. Despite such rhetoric, the United States refused to intervene when Japanese troops sacked the city of Nanking, massacred 300,000 Chinese residents and raped thousands of women, and sank an American gunboat in the Yangtze River.

As Japan pacified coastal areas of China, its imperial ambitions expanded. In 1940 Japan signed a formal military alliance with Germany and Italy, and its troops occupied the northern section of the French colony of Indochina (present-day Vietnam). Its goal was to create and dominate a Greater East

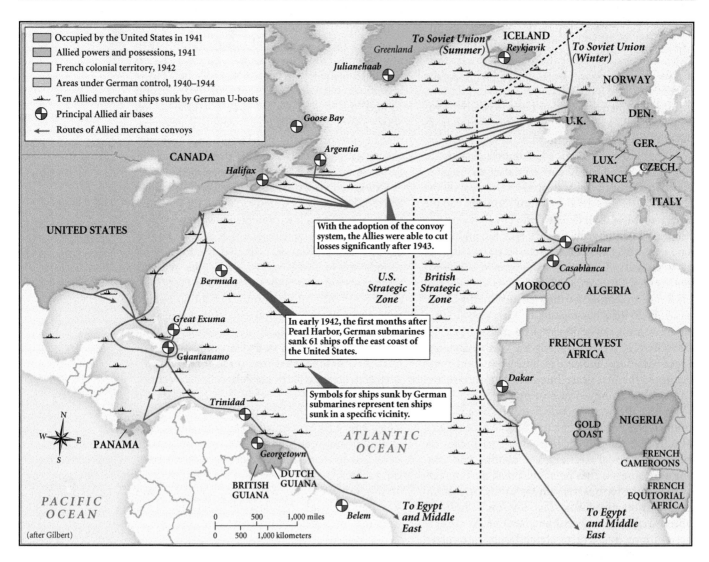

Map 25.1 World War II in the North Atlantic, 1939–1943

After the start of the war in Europe in September 1939, Germany escalated its submarine attacks on Allied and American merchant shipping in the Atlantic. Continued German advances spurred Congress to pass the Lend-Lease Act in March 1941 and President Roosevelt and Prime Minister Churchill to issue the Atlantic Charter in August. A pivotal factor in the Allied victory in Europe would be countering the German submarine threat in the Atlantic. With the establishment of the convoy system — the protection of merchant vessels with destroyers armed with sonar and depth charges — the Atlantic shipping lanes became safer, allowing the transport of troops and materials to Great Britain and North Africa.

Asia Co-Prosperity Sphere stretching from Indonesia to Korea. The United States responded to the invasion of Indochina by restricting trade with Japan, especially aviation-grade gasoline and scrap metal. Roosevelt hoped these economic sanctions would deter Japanese aggression. But in July 1941 Japanese troops occupied the rest of Indochina. Roosevelt now froze Japanese assets in the United States and instituted an embargo on all trade with Japan, including vital oil shipments that accounted for almost 80 percent of Japanese consumption.

In September 1941 the government of Prime Minister Hideki Tojo began secret preparations for war against the United States. By November American military intelligence knew that Japan was planning an attack but did not know where it would come. Early on Sunday morning, December 7, 1941, Japanese bombers attacked Pearl Harbor in Hawaii, killing more than 2,400 Americans. They destroyed or heavily damaged eight battleships, three cruisers, three destroyers, and almost two hundred airplanes.

Pearl Harbor, December 7, 1941

Sailors at the Naval Air Station stare in disbelief as a huge explosion rocks the battleship USS *Arizona*, anchored at Pearl Harbor. The Japanese bombed both the American fleet and the nearby military airfields to prevent a counterattack against the aircraft carriers that had launched the strike. U.S. Naval Historical Foundation.

Although the assault was devastating, it united the American people (as the September 11, 2001, terrorist attacks would do some sixty years later). The next day Roosevelt went before Congress. Calling December 7 "a date which will live in infamy," he asked for a declaration of war against Japan. The Senate voted unanimously for war, and the House concurred by a vote of 388 to 1. The lone dissenter was Jeannette Rankin of Montana, who had also opposed American entry into World War I. Three days later Germany and Italy declared war on the United States, and the United States in turn declared war on those nations.

➤ Compare the impact of the depression on the politics and political institutions of the United States, Italy, and Germany. What are the similarities and differences?

➤ As the world edged toward war in the late 1930s, many Americans were committed to political isolationism. What were the sources of this isolationism, and how was it manifest?

➤ Why did the United States join the fight in World War II? What are the key events leading to America's involvement?

Organizing for Victory

The task of fighting a global war greatly accelerated the influence of the federal government on all aspects of American life. Coordinating the changeover from civilian to war production, raising an army, and assembling the necessary workforce required a vast increase in the scope and size of government agencies. Mobilization on such a scale also demanded close cooperation between business executives in major corporations and political leaders in Washington, solidifying a partnership that had been growing since World War I. But the most dramatic expansion of power occurred at the presidential level when Congress passed the War Powers Act of December 18, 1941, giving President Roosevelt unprecedented authority over all aspects of the conduct of the war. This act marks the beginning of what historians call the Imperial Presidency — the far-reaching use (and abuse) of executive authority during decades of American world dominance, from 1945 to the present.

Financing the War

Defense mobilization definitively ended the Great Depression. In 1940, the gross national product stood at $99.7 billion; in 1945 it reached $211 billion. After-tax profits of American businesses nearly doubled, and farm output grew by a third. Federal spending of $186 billion on war production powered this advance; by late 1943, two-thirds of the economy was directly involved in the war effort (Figure 25.1). The government paid for these military expenditures by raising taxes and borrowing money. The Revenue Act of 1942 dramatically expanded the number of people paying income taxes from 3.9 million to 42.6 million; the annual revenue rose to $35.1 billion, facilitated by a payroll deduction system instituted in 1943. Most citizens willingly paid their income taxes as an expression of patriotism. Thanks to this revolutionary — and apparently permanent —

change in government financing, taxes on personal incomes and business profits paid for half the cost of the war, compared with 30 percent of the cost of World War I. The government borrowed the rest, both from wealthy Americans and ordinary citizens, who invested some of their wartime wages in long-term Treasury bonds. The **national debt** grew steadily, topping out at $258.6 billion in 1945.

The war also brought a significant expansion in the federal bureaucracy. The number of civilians employed by the government increased almost fourfold, to 3.8 million — a far more dramatic growth than during the New Deal. Leadership of federal agencies also changed as the Roosevelt administration turned from New Deal reformers to business executives. These executives became known as "dollar-a-year men" because they accepted only a token government salary and remained on the payroll of their corporations. Donald Nelson, a former executive at the Sears, Roebuck Company headed the powerful War Production Board (WPB). The Board awarded defense contracts, evaluated military and civilian requests for scarce resources, and oversaw the conversion of industry to military production. To encourage businesses to convert to war production, the board granted generous tax write-offs for plant construction and approved contracts with "cost-plus" provisions that guaranteed a profit and promised that businesses could keep the new factories after the war.

Henry J. Kaiser: "Miracle Man." In the interest of maximum production, the WPB preferred to deal with major corporations rather than with small businesses. America's fifty-six largest corporations received three-fourths of the war contracts; the top ten received a third. The best-known contractor was Henry J. Kaiser. Already highly successful from building roads in California and the Hoover and Grand Coulee dams, Kaiser turned to industrial production. At his Richmond, California, shipyard, he revolutionized ship construction by applying

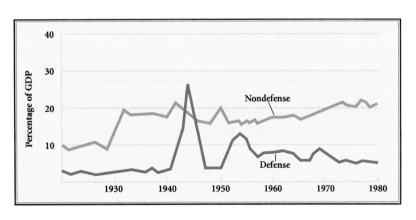

Figure 25.1 Government Military and Civilian Spending as a Percentage of GDP, 1920–1980.

Government military spending was about 3 percent of the gross domestic product (GDP) in the 1920s and 1930s, but it ballooned to more than 25 percent during World War II, to 13 percent during the Korean War, and to nearly 10 percent during the Vietnam War. Federal government spending for civilian purposes doubled during the New Deal and has remained at about 17 to 20 percent of GDP ever since.

The Miracle Man

Henry Kaiser knew how to run a business with no-nonsense efficiency. He built towns to house his workers, provided them with superior medical care, and organized them to build ships in record time. Here Kaiser uses an 81-piece, 14-foot-long model to show ship owners and Navy brass how his workers built a 10,400-ton Liberty freighter in the amazing time of 4 days, 15 hours, and 26 minutes. Corbis-Bettmann.

Henry Ford's techniques of mass production. Previously, most shipbuilding had been done by skilled workers who had served lengthy apprenticeships. To meet wartime production schedules, Kaiser broke the work process down into small, specialized tasks that newly trained workers could do quickly. Soon each of his work crews was building a "Liberty Ship," a huge vessel to carry cargo and troops to the war zone, every five days. The press dubbed him the "Miracle Man."

The Kaiser shipyards were also known for their corporate welfare programs, which boosted workers' productivity almost as much as his efficient assembly system. Kaiser offered his workers day care for their children, financial counseling, subsidized housing, and low-cost health care. The Kaiser Permanente Medical Care Program, founded in 1942, provided subsidized, prepaid health care for the shipyard workers and their families (and lives on today, as one of the nation's largest and most successful health maintenance organizations).

Central to all of Kaiser's business miracles was a close relationship with the federal agencies. The government financed the great dams he built during the depression and, through the Reconstruction Finance Corporation, lent him $300 million to build shipyards and manufacturing plants during the war. One historian has aptly called Kaiser a "government entrepreneur," the model for a new breed of business executive that prospered because of government contracts (and continue to do so, today). As Secretary of War Henry Stimson put it, in capitalist countries at war "you had better let business make money out of the process or business won't work."

Working together, American business and government turned out a prodigious supply of military hardware: 86,000 tanks; 296,000 airplanes; 15 million rifles and machine guns; 64,000 landing craft; and 6,500 cargo ships and naval vessels. The system of allotting contracts, along with the suspension of the antitrust prosecutions during the war, hastened the trend toward large corporate structures. In 1940, the largest one hundred companies produced 30 percent of the industrial output; by 1945, their share had soared to 70 percent. These same corporations formed the core of the nation's military-industrial complex of the Cold War era (see Chapters 26 and 27).

Mobilizing the American Fighting Force

Going to war meant mobilizing human resources, both on the battlefield and the home front (see Reading American Pictures, "U.S. Political Propaganda on the Home Front During World War II," p. 776). During World War II, the armed forces of the United States numbered more than 15 million men and women. The draft boards registered about 31 million men between the ages of eighteen and forty-four, but more than half the men failed to meet the physical standards, many because of defective teeth. The military tried to screen out homosexuals but had little success. Once in the services, homosexuals found opportunities to participate in a gay culture more extensive than that in civilian life.

Racial discrimination was part of military life, directed mainly against the approximately 700,000 blacks in uniform. The National Association for the Advancement of Colored People (NAACP) and other civil rights groups chided the government with reminders such as "A Jim Crow army cannot fight for a free world," but the military continued to segregate African Americans and to assign them the most menial duties. In contrast, Native Americans and Mexican Americans were never officially segregated and usually welcomed into combat units.

U. S. Political Propaganda on the Homefront during World War II

This is the Enemy

WINNER R. HOE & CO., INC. AWARD – NATIONAL WAR POSTER COMPETITION
HELD UNDER AUSPICES OF ARTISTS FOR VICTORY, INC.–COUNCIL FOR DEMOCRACY–MUSEUM OF MODERN ART

IS YOUR TRIP NECESSARY?

NEEDLESS TRAVEL
interferes with the War Effort
OFFICE OF DEFENSE TRANSPORTATION

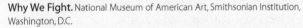

Why We Fight. National Museum of American Art, Smithsonian Institution, Washington, D.C.

Please Stay Home. Picture Research Consultants & Archives.

In times of war, governments use visual imagery to motivate the public and frame the meaning of the war both at home and abroad. During World War II, as we point out in the text, the United States government made every effort to convince the American people to understand and support the war. But what can visual imagery tell us about the nature of World War II? These two pictures—produced in the U.S. during the war—provide some answers. The first is a 1942 lithograph by two artists, Karl Koehler and Victor Ancona, de-picting a Nazi officer. The second is a poster of bus travelers produced by the Office of Defense Transportation.

ANALYZING THE EVIDENCE

➤ How might these images affect a viewer? What visual cues or elements do the image-makers employ to create an impact? List some of these items and compare them across the two images. Is one image more convincing than the other? Why?

➤ What kind of message does each image convey? Are these messages consistent with each other? Can you combine the messages into a larger statement explaining the U.S. perspective on fighting the war?

Approximately 350,000 American women enlisted in the armed services. About 140,000 served as army WACS (Women's Army Corps) and 100,000 as naval WAVES (Women Accepted for Volunteer Emergency Service). One-third of the nation's registered nurses, almost 75,000 overall, volunteered for military duty. In addition, about 1,000 WASPs (Women's Airforce Service Pilots) ferried planes and supplies in noncombat areas. The armed forces limited the types of duty assigned to women, as it did with blacks. Women officers could not command men, and WACS and WAVES were barred from combat duty, although female as well as male nurses served close to the front lines, risking capture or death. Most of the jobs women did in the military—clerical work, communications, and health care—reflected stereotypes of women's roles in civilian life.

Workers and the War Effort

As millions of working age citizens joined the military, the nation faced a critical labor shortage. The backlog of depression-era unemployment quickly disappeared, as defense industries alone provided jobs for about seven million new workers. Substantial numbers of women and blacks joined the industrial workforce; unions, benefiting from the demand for their members, negotiated higher wages and improved conditions for America's workers.

Rosie the Riveter. Government and corporate recruiters drew on patriotism as they urged women to take jobs in defense industries. "Longing won't bring him back sooner . . . GET A WAR JOB!" one poster beckoned, while the artist Norman Rockwell's famous "Rosie the Riveter" beckoned to women from the cover of the *Saturday Evening Post*. The government directed its publicity at housewives, but many working women gladly abandoned low-paying "women's" jobs as domestic servants or file clerks for higher-paying work in the defense industry. Suddenly the nation's factories were full of women working as airplane riveters, ship welders, and drill-press operators. Women made up 36 percent of the labor force in 1945, compared with 24 percent at the beginning of the war. Women war workers often faced sexual harassment on the job and usually received lower wages than men did. In shipyards women with the most seniority and responsibility earned $6.95 a day, whereas the top men made as much as $22.

When the men came home from war and the nation's plants returned to peacetime operations, Rosie the Riveter was out of a job. But many married women refused to put on aprons and stay home, and women's participation in the labor force rebounded steadily for the rest of the 1940s. The wartime expansion of the female workforce, especially among married women, began a trend that would continue for the rest of the twentieth century and change the character of family life (see Comparing American Voices, "Women in the Wartime Workplace," pp. 778–779).

Organized Labor. Workers used wartime mobilization to extend the gains in unionization and

A Real "Rosie" at Work

Elegant posters by artists J. Howard Miller (1942) and Norman Rockwell (1943) celebrated the work of the six million women who worked in the defense industry during World War II, as did the song that gave them a generic name: Rosie the Riveter. As this photograph suggests, the work itself had more grease and grime than elegance. This young woman operates a high-powered lathe, a boring machine that makes engine parts to precise specifications. Library of Congress.

Women in the Wartime Workplace

During World War II, millions of men served in the armed forces and millions of women worked in war-related industries. A generation later, some of these women workers recounted their wartime experiences to historians in oral interviews.

EVELYN GOTZION
Becoming a Union Activist

Evelyn Gotzion went to work at Rayovac, a battery company in Madison, Wisconsin, in 1935; she retired in 1978. While at Rayovac, Gotzion and her working husband raised three children.

I had all kinds of jobs. [During the war] we had one line, a big line, where you'd work ten hours and you'd stand in one spot or sit in one spot. It got terrible, all day long. So I suggested to my foreman, the general foreman, that we take turns of learning everybody's job and switching every half hour. Well, they [the management] didn't like it, but we were on the side, every once in a while, learning each other's job and learning how to do it, so eventually most all of us got so we could do all the jobs, [of] which there were probably fifteen or twenty on the line. We could do every job so we could go up and down the line and rotate. And then they found out that that was really a pretty good thing to do because it made the people happier. . . .

I one day I was the steward, and they wouldn't listen to me. They cut our rates, so I shut off the line, and the boss came up and he said, "What are you doing?" I said, "Well, I have asked everybody that I know why we have gotten a cut in pay and why we're doing exactly the same amount of work as we did. . . . So, anyhow, we wrote up a big grievance and they all signed it and then I called the president of the union and then we had a meeting. . . . At that point the president decided that I should be added to the bargaining committee so that I would go in and argue our case, because I could do it better than any of the rest of them because I knew what it was. . . . We finally got it straightened out, and we got our back pay, too. From then on I was on the bargaining committee all the years that I worked at Rayovac.

SOURCE: Michael E. Stevens and Ellen D. Goldlust, eds., *Women Remember the War, 1941–1945* (Madison: State Historical Society of Wisconsin Press, 1993), 26–29.

FANNY CHRISTINA (TINA) HILL
War Work: Social and Racial Mobility

After migrating to California from Texas and working as a domestic servant, Tina Hill, an African American, got a wartime job at North American Aircraft. After time off for a pregnancy in 1945, Hill worked there until 1980.

Most of the men was gone, and . . . most of the women was in my bracket, five or six years younger or older. I was twenty-four. There was a black girl that hired in with me. I went to work the next day, sixty cents an hour. . . . I could see where they made a difference in placing you in certain jobs. They had fifteen or twenty departments, but all the Negroes went to Department 17 because there was nothing but shooting and bucking rivets. You stood on one side of the panel and your partner stood on this side and he would shoot the rivets with a gun and you'd buck them with the bar. That was about the size of it. I just didn't like it . . . went over to the union and they told me what to do. I went back inside and they sent me to another department where you did bench work and I liked that much better. . . .

Some weeks I brought home twenty-six dollars . . . then it gradually went up to thirty dollars [about $400 in 2007]. . . . Whatever you make you're supposed to save some. I was also getting that fifty dollars a month from my husband and that was just saved right away. I was planning on buying a home and a car. . . . My husband came back [from the war, and] . . . looked for a job in the cleaning and pressing place, which was just plentiful. . . . That's why he didn't bother to go out to North American. But what we both weren't thinking about was that they [North American] have better benefits because they did have an insurance plan and a union to back you up. Later he did come to work there, in 1951 or 1952. . . .

When North American called me back [after she left to have a baby] was I a happy soul! . . . It made me live better. It really did. We always say that Lincoln took the bale off of the Negroes. I think there is a statue up there in Washington, D.C., where he's lifting something off the Negro. Well, my sister always said—that's why you can't interview her because she's so radical—"Hitler was the one that got us out of the white folks' kitchen."

SOURCE: Excerpted from Sherna B. Gluck, *Rosie the Riveter Revisited* (Boston: G. K. Hall & Co., 1987), 37–42.

PEGGY TERRY
War: Wider Horizons and Personal Tragedies

Peggy Terry was born in Oklahoma, grew up in Paducah, Kentucky, and worked in defense plants in Kentucky and Michigan before settling in Chicago.

The first work I had after the Depression was at a shell-loading plant in Viola, Kentucky. It is between Paducah and Mayfield. They were large shells: anti-aircraft, incendiaries, and tracers. . . . We made the fabulous sum of thirty-two dollars a week [about $445 in 2007]. To us it was just an absolute miracle. Before that, we made nothing.

You won't believe how incredibly ignorant I was. I knew vaguely that a war had started, but I had no idea what it meant. . . . I was eighteen. My husband was nineteen. We were living day to day. When you are involved in stayin' alive, you don't think about big things like a war. It didn't occur to us that we were making these shells to kill people. It never entered my head. . . . We were just a bunch of hillbilly women laughin' and talkin'. . . .

I worked in building number 11. I pulled a lot of gadgets on a machine. The shell slid under and powder went into it. Another lever you pulled tamped it down. Then it moved on a conveyer belt to another building where the detonator was dropped in. You did this over and over.

Tetryl was one of the ingredients and it turned us orange. Just as orange as an orange. Our hair was streaked orange. Our hands, our face, our neck just turned orange, even our eyeballs. We never questioned. None of us ever asked, What is this? Is this harmful? . . . The only thing we worried about was other women thinking we had dyed our hair. Back then it was a disgrace if you dyed your hair. . . .

I think of how little we knew of human rights, union rights. We knew Daddy had been a hell-raiser in the mine workers' union, but at that point it hadn't rubbed off on any of us women. Coca-Cola and Dr. Pepper were allowed in every building, but not a drop of water. You could only get a drink of water if you went to the cafeteria, which was about two city blocks away. Of course you couldn't leave your machine long enough to go get a drink. . . .

The war just widened my world. Especially after I came up to Michigan. . . . We made ninety dollars a week [about $1,000 in 2007]. We did some kind of testing for airplane radios. Ohh, I met all those wonderful Polacks. They were the first people I'd ever known that were any different from me. A whole new world just opened up. I learned to drink beer like crazy with 'em. They were all very union-conscious. I learned a lot of things that I didn't even know existed. . . .

My husband was a paratrooper in the war, in the 101st Airborne Division. He made twenty-six drops in France, North Africa, and Germany. . . . Until the war he never drank. He never even smoked. When he came back he was an absolute drunkard. And he used to have the most awful nightmares. He'd get up in the middle of the night and start screaming. I'd just sit for hours and hold him while he just shook. We'd go to the movies, and if they'd have films with a lot of shooting in it, he'd just start to shake and have to get up and leave. He started slapping me around and slapped the kids around. He became a brute.

SOURCE: Studs Terkel, *"The Good War": An Oral History of World War II* (New York: Pantheon, 1984), 102–111.

ANALYZING THE EVIDENCE

➤ What common themes appear in the working lives of these three women? For example, how do labor unions affect their conditions of employment?

➤ How did the war change the lives of these women?

➤ These interviews occurred long after the events they describe. How might that long interval have affected the women's accounts of those years?

working conditions made in the New Deal. By 1945 almost 15 million workers belonged to a union, up from 9 million in 1939. These gains stemmed in part from organized labor's embrace of patriotism. In December 1941, representatives of the major unions made a "no-strike" pledge—nonbinding in character—for the duration of the war. In January 1942 Roosevelt set up the National War Labor Board (NWLB), composed of representatives of labor, management, and the public. The NWLB established wages, hours, and working conditions and had the authority to order government seizure of plants that did not comply. Forty plants were seized during the war.

During its tenure the NWLB handled 17,650 disputes affecting 12 million workers. It resolved the controversial issue of mandatory union membership through a compromise. New hires did not have to join a union, but those who already belonged had to maintain their union membership over the life of a contract. Agitation for wage increases caused a more serious disagreement. Because managers wanted to keep production running smoothly and profitably, they were willing to pay higher wages. However, pay raises conflicted with the government's efforts to combat inflation, which drove up prices dramatically in the early war years. Incomes rose as much as 70 percent during the war because workers earned pay for overtime work, which was not covered by wage ceilings and greatly increased output.

Despite higher incomes, many union members felt cheated as they watched corporate profits soar in relation to wages. Dissatisfaction peaked in 1943 when a nationwide railroad strike was narrowly averted. Then, John L. Lewis led more than half a million United Mine Workers out on strike, demanding an increase in wages over that recommended by the NWLB. Lewis's tactics won concessions, but they also alienated many Americans and made him one of the most disliked public figures of the 1940s. Congress responded by passing (over Roosevelt's veto) the Smith-Connally Labor Act of 1943, which required a thirty-day cooling-off period before a strike and prohibited strikes in defense industries. The legacy of this public and congressional hostility would hamper the union movement in the postwar years.

African American and Mexican American Workers.

During the war, a new mood of militancy swept through the African American community. "A wind is rising throughout the world of free men everywhere," Eleanor Roosevelt wrote during the war, "and they will not be kept in bondage." Black leaders pointed out parallels between anti-Semitism

Fighting for Freedom at Home and Abroad, 1941
This protester from the Negro Labor Relations League pointedly drew the parallel between blacks serving in the armed forces and winning access to jobs at the Bowman Dairy Company, a Chicago bottler, dried milk producer, and distributor that employed three thousand workers. Library of Congress.

in Germany and racial discrimination in America and pledged themselves to a "Double V" campaign: victory over Nazism abroad and victory over racism and inequality at home.

Even before Pearl Harbor, black labor activism was on the rise. In 1940 only 240 of the nation's 100,000 aircraft workers were black, and most of them were janitors. African American leaders demanded that the government require defense contractors to hire more blacks. When the government took no action, A. Philip Randolph, head of the Brotherhood of Sleeping Car Porters, the largest black union, announced plans for a "March on Washington" in the summer of 1941. Roosevelt was not a strong supporter of civil rights, but he feared the embarrassment of a massive public protest and he worried about a disruption of the nation's war preparations.

In June 1941, in exchange for Randolph's cancellation of the march, Roosevelt issued Executive Order 8802. It prohibited "discrimination in the employment of workers in defense industries or government because of race, creed, color, or national origin," and established the Fair Employment Practices Commission (FEPC). This federal commitment to minority employment rights was both unprecedented and limited: For example, it did not affect segregation in the armed forces, and the FEPC could not require compliance with its orders. Still, the committee resolved about a third of the more than eight thousand complaints it received.

Encouraged by the ideological climate of the war years, the League of United Latin American Citizens (LULAC) — the Latino counterpart to the NAACP — challenged long-standing patterns of discrimination and exclusion. In Texas, where it was still common to see signs reading, "No Dogs or Mexicans Allowed," the organization protested limited job opportunities and the segregation of schools and public facilities. The NAACP itself grew ninefold to 450,000 members by 1945, and in Chicago James Farmer helped to found the Congress of Racial Equality (CORE), a group known nationwide for protesting through direct action, such as rallies and sit-ins. These wartime developments — both federal intervention in the form of the FEPC and resurgent African American militancy — laid the groundwork for the civil rights revolution of the 1960s.

Politics in Wartime

The federal government expanded dramatically during the war years, but there was little attempt to use the state to promote progressive social reform on the home front, as in World War I. Many people, including business leaders, believed that an enlarged federal presence was justified only insofar as it assisted war aims. Moreover, in the 1942 elections Republicans had picked up ten seats in the Senate and forty-seven seats in the House, bolstering conservatives in Congress and cutting back prospects for new social initiatives. As war mobilization brought full employment, Roosevelt ended several popular New Deal programs, such as the Civilian Conservation Corps and the National Youth Administration.

As the war dragged on, Roosevelt began to lay the ideological foundations for new federal social welfare measures. In his State of the Union address in 1944, he called for a second bill of rights, which would guarantee that Americans had jobs, adequate food and clothing, decent homes, medical care, and education. There was some public support for such welfare measures, but Congress was less enthusiastic and extended benefits only to military veterans or GIs (short for "government issue"). The Servicemen's Readjustment Act (1944), popularly known as the "GI Bill of Rights," provided education, job training, medical care, pensions, and mortgage loans for men and women who had served in the armed forces. An extraordinarily influential program, particularly in expanding access to higher education, it distributed almost $4 billion in benefits to nine million veterans between 1944 and 1949; in the 1950s, it was extended to veterans of the Korean War.

The Election of 1944. Roosevelt's call for social legislation was part of a plan to reinvigorate the New Deal political coalition. In the election of 1944, Roosevelt once again headed the Democratic ticket. Party leaders, aware of FDR's health problems and anxious to find a middle-of-the-road successor, dropped Vice President Henry Wallace from the ticket. They feared that Wallace's outspoken support for labor, civil rights, and domestic reform would alienate southern Democrats. In his place they chose Senator Harry S. Truman of Missouri. A direct-speaking, no-nonsense politician, Truman won his seat because of the sponsorship of Thomas Pendergast, the Democratic boss in Kansas City. Truman rose to prominence for heading a Senate investigation of government efficiency in awarding wartime defense contracts.

The Republicans nominated Governor Thomas E. Dewey of New York. Only forty-two years old, Dewey had won fame fighting organized crime as a U.S. attorney. Like drug smuggling today, the bootlegging of liquor during Prohibition generated huge profits and highly organized criminal "families" that subsequently turned to prostitution and the "protection" racket. Dewey took on the mobs in New York and, despite his use of controversial "third-degree" interrogation tactics, won the admiration of many Americans. Because Dewey accepted the general principles of welfare state liberalism domestically and internationalism in foreign affairs, he attracted some of Roosevelt's supporters. But a majority of voters preferred political continuity. Roosevelt received 53.5 percent of the nationwide vote and 60 percent in cities of more than 100,000 people, where ethnic minorities and labor unions strongly supported Democratic candidates. The continuing strength of the New Deal coalition after the economic emergency of the Great Depression had passed indicated that the long era of Republican political dominance (1896–1932) had come to an end.

> ➤ In what ways did World War II contribute to the growth of the federal government? How did it foster what historians now call the "military-industrial complex"?

> ➤ What impact did war mobilization have on women, racial minorities, and organized labor? What legislation or government rules affected their lives as workers, and what effect did it have on their political allegiance?

Life on the Home Front

The United States did not suffer the physical devastation that ravaged much of Europe and East Asia, but the war deeply affected the lives of millions of civilians, in ways good and bad. Americans welcomed the return of prosperity but shuddered every time they saw a Western Union boy on his bicycle, fearing he carried a telegram from the War Department reporting the death of someone's son, husband, or father. Many citizens also grumbled about the annoying government regulations that were a constant fact of life, but accepted that things would be different "for the duration."

"For the Duration"

Just like the soldiers in uniform, people on the home front had jobs to do. They worked on civilian defense committees, recycled old newspapers and scrap material, and served on local rationing and draft boards. About twenty million home "Victory gardens" produced 40 percent of the nation's vegetables. Various federal agencies encouraged these efforts, especially the Office of War Information (OWI), which disseminated news and promoted patriotism. The OWI urged advertising agencies to link their clients' products to the war effort, arguing that patriotic ads would not only sell goods but also "invigorate, instruct and inspire" the citizenry.

Popular Culture. Popular culture, especially the movies, reinforced the connections between the home front and the war effort. Hollywood producers, directors, and actors offered their talent to the War Department. Director Frank Capra created a series of "Why We Fight" documentaries to explain war aims to conscripted soldiers. Movie stars such as John Wayne, Anthony Quinn, and Spencer Tracy portrayed the heroism of American fighting men in many films, including *Wake Island* (1942), *Guadalcanal Diary* (1943), and *Thirty Seconds over Tokyo* (1945). Other movies, such as *Watch on the Rhine* (1943), warned of the danger of fascism at home and abroad, while the Academy Award–winning *Casablanca* (1943) demonstrated the heroism and patriotism of an ordinary American in German-occupied North Africa.

Average weekly movie attendance soared to over 100 million. Demand was so high that many theaters operated around the clock to accommodate defense workers on the swing and night shifts. Many movies had patriotic themes. In the box-office hit *Since You Went Away* (1943), Claudette Colbert starred as a wife who took a defense job after her husband left for war, while Oscar-winning Greer Garson played a courageous British housewife in *Mrs. Miniver* (1942). In this pre-television era, newsreels accompanying the feature films kept the public up-to-date on the war, as did on-the-spot radio broadcasts by Edward R. Murrow and other well-known commentators.

Wartime Prosperity and Rationing. Perhaps the major source of Americans' high morale was wartime prosperity. Federal defense spending had ended the depression, unemployment had disappeared, and per capita income doubled in real terms from $595 in 1939 to $1,237 in 1945. Despite geographical dislocations and shortages of many items, about 70 percent of Americans admitted midway through the war that they had personally experienced "no real sacrifices." A Red Cross worker put it bluntly: "The war was fun for America. I'm not talking about the poor souls who lost sons and daughters. But for the rest of us, the war was a hell of a good time."

For many Americans the major inconveniences of the war were the limitations placed on their consumption. In contrast to the largely voluntaristic approach used during World War I, federal agencies such as the Office of Price Administration subjected almost everything Americans ate, wore, or used during World War II to rationing or regulation. The first major scarcity was rubber. The Japanese conquest of Malaya and the Netherlands Indies cut off 97 percent of America's imports of natural rubber, an essential raw material. An entire new industry, synthetic rubber, was born and by late 1944 was producing 762,000 tons a year. To conserve rubber for the war effort, the government rationed tires, and so many of the nation's thirty million car owners put their cars up on blocks for the duration. As more people walked, they wore out their shoes. In 1944 shoes were rationed to two pairs per person a year, half the prewar average.

The government also rationed fuel oil, so schools and restaurants shorted their hours, and homeowners lowered their thermostats to 65 degrees. To cut domestic gasoline consumption, the government rationed supplies and imposed a nationwide speed limit of 35 miles per hour, which cut highway deaths dramatically. By 1943, the government was regulating the amount of meat, butter, sugar, and other foods Americans could buy. Most people cooperated with the complicated system of rationing points and coupons, but almost a fourth occasionally bought items on the black market, especially meat, gasoline, cigarettes, and nylon stockings. Manufacturers of automobiles, refrigerators, and radios, who had been forced to switch to military production, told consumers to save their money now and buy products once the war ended.

Migration and Social Conflict

The war and government policies determined where many people lived. When men entered the armed services, their families often followed them to training bases or points of debarkation. The lure

of high-paying defense jobs encouraged others— Native Americans on reservations, white southerners in the hills of Appalachia, farmers on marginal lands—to move. About fifteen million Americans changed residences during the war years, half of them moving to another state.

As a major center of defense production for the Pacific war, California was affected more than any other state by wartime migration. The state welcomed nearly three million new residents and grew by 53 percent during the war. "The Second Gold Rush Hits the West," headlined the *San Francisco Chronicle* in 1943. A tenth of all federal dollars flowed into California, and the state's factories turned out one-sixth of all war materials. People went where the defense jobs were—to Los Angeles, San Diego, and the San Francisco Bay area. Some towns grew practically overnight: Within two years of the opening of

A Family Effort

After migrating from the Midwest to Portland, Oregon, fifteen members of the family of John R. Brauckmiller (sixth from left) found jobs at Henry Kaiser's Swan Island shipyard. From 1943 to 1945, the shipyard turned out 152 T-2 Tankers, mostly for use by the U.S. Navy to carry fuel oil. A local newspaper pronounced the Brauckmillers as "the shipbuildingest family in America," and because of the importance of shipbuilding to the war effort, *Life* magazine featured the family in its issue of August 16, 1943. Ralph Vincent, *The Journal*, Portland, OR.

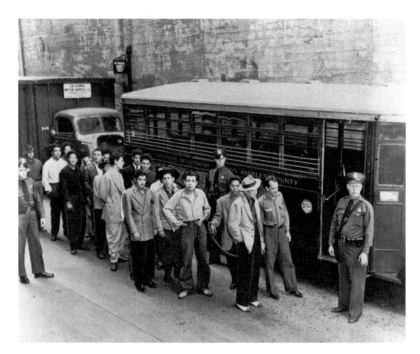

Zoot Suit Youth in Los Angeles

During a four-day riot in June 1943, servicemen in Los Angeles attacked young Latino men wearing distinctive "zoot suits," which were widely viewed as emblems of gang membership and a delinquent youth culture. The police response was to arrest scores of zoot-suiters. Here, a group of handcuffed young Latino men is about to board a Los Angeles County Sheriff's bus to make a court appearance. Note the wide-legged pants that taper at the ankle, a hallmark of the zoot suit. Library of Congress.

the huge Kaiser Corporation shipyard in Richmond, California, the town's population had quadrupled.

The growth of war industries prompted the migration of more than a million African Americans from the rural South to California, Illinois, Michigan, Ohio, and Pennsylvania — a continuation of the "Great Migration" earlier in the century (see Chapter 22). As migrant blacks and whites competed for jobs and housing, racial conflicts broke out in forty-seven cities during 1943. The worst violence took place in the Detroit area. In June 1943, a major race riot erupted, with Polish Americans and southern white migrants on one side and African Americans on the other. It left thirty-four people dead and hundreds injured.

Racial conflict struck the West as well. In Los Angeles, male Hispanic teenagers organized *pachuco* (youth) gangs. Many dressed in "zoot suits" — broad-brimmed felt hats, pegged trousers, and clunky shoes; they wore their long hair slicked down and carried pocket knives on gold chains. The young women who partied with them favored long coats, huarache sandals, and pompadour hairdos. Some blacks and working-class white teenagers in Los Angeles and eastern cities took up the zoot suit style to indicate both their group identity and their rejection of white, middle-class values. To many adults, the zoot suit symbolized wartime juvenile delinquency. When rumors circulated in July 1943 that a *pachuco* gang had beaten a white sailor, it set off a four-day riot. White servicemen roamed through Mexican American neighborhoods and attacked zoot-suiters,

taking special pleasure in slashing their pegged pants. Some attacks occurred in full view of white police officers, who did nothing to stop the violence.

Civil Rights during Wartime

These outbreaks of social violence were sharp but limited. Unlike World War I, which evoked intense prejudice and widespread harassment of German Americans, the mood on the home front was generally calm in the 1940s. Federal officials interned about five thousand potentially dangerous German and Italian aliens during the war. But leftists and Communists, prime targets of government repression at the end of World War I, experienced few problems, in part because the Soviet Union and the United States were allies in the fight against right-wing fascist nations.

Japanese Internment. The internment of Japanese aliens and Japanese American citizens was a glaring exception to this record of tolerance. Immediately after the attack on Pearl Harbor, the West Coast remained calm. Then, as residents began to fear attacks, spies, and sabotage, California's long history of racial antagonism toward Asian immigrants came into play (see Chapters 16, 21, and 24). Local politicians and newspapers whipped up sentiment against Japanese Americans, who numbered only about 112,000, had no political power, and clustered together in ethnic communities in the three West Coast states.

Early in 1942 Roosevelt responded to West Coast fears by issuing Executive Order 9066. The order, and

Behind Barbed Wire

As part of the forced relocation of 112,000 Japanese Americans, Los Angeles photographer Toyo Miyatake and his family were sent to Manzanar, a camp in the California desert east of the Sierra Nevada. Miyatake secretly began shooting photographs of the camp with a handmade camera. Eventually, Miyatake received permission from the authorities to document life in the camp — its births, weddings, deaths, and high school graduations. To communicate the injustice of internment, he also took staged photographs, such as this image of three young boys behind barbed wire with a watchtower in the distance. For Miyatake, it gave new meaning to the phrase "prisoners of war." Toyo Miyatake.

a subsequent act of Congress, gave the War Department the authority to evacuate Japanese Americans from the West Coast and intern them in relocation camps for the rest of the war. Despite the lack of any evidence of disloyalty or sedition activity among the evacuees, few public leaders opposed the plan. "A Jap's a Jap," snapped General John DeWitt, the officer charged with defense of the West Coast. "It makes no difference whether he is an American citizen or not."

The relocation plan shocked Japanese Americans, more than two-thirds of whom were native-born American citizens. (They comprised the Nisei generation, the children of the immigrant Issei generation.) Army officials gave families only a few days to dispose of their property. Businesses that took a lifetime to build were liquidated overnight, and speculators snapped up Japanese real estate for a fraction of its value (see Voices from Abroad, "Monica Itoi Sone: Japanese Relocation," p. 786). The War Relocation Authority moved the internees to hastily built camps in desolate areas in California, Arizona, Utah, Colorado, Wyoming, Idaho, and Arkansas (Map 25.2). Ironically, the Japanese Americans who made up one-third of the population of Hawaii, and presumably posed a greater threat because of their numbers and proximity to Japan,

Map 25.2 Japanese Relocation Camps

In 1942, the government ordered 112,000 Japanese Americans living on the West Coast into internment camps in the nation's interior because of their supposed threat to public safety. Some of the camps were as far away as Arkansas. The federal government rescinded the mass evacuation order in December 1944, but when the war ended in August 1945, 44,000 people still remained in the camps.

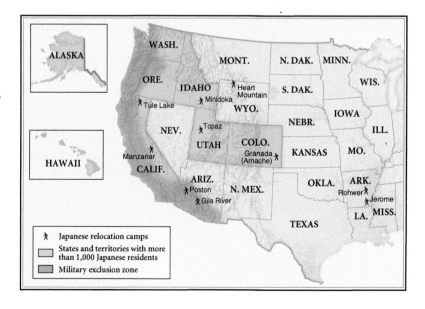

Monica Itoi Sone

Japanese Relocation

As Monica Itoi Sone discovered, her legal status as an American citizen did not keep her from being treated like an unwelcome foreigner. Her autobiography, Nisei Daughter *(1953), tells the story of the relocation and internment of Japanese Americans during World War II. In 1942 Sone was a young woman who had been born and raised in Seattle; she saw herself as an "American." In this selection, Sone ponders the question of national identity as she describes the Itoi family's forced evacuation by the U.S. Army. Her family spent the entire war in an internment camp in Idaho, but in 1943 Sone was allowed to attend college in Indiana.*

We felt fortunate to be assigned to a room at the end of the barracks because we had just one neighbor to worry about. The partition wall separating the rooms was only seven feet high with an opening of four feet at the top, so at night, Mrs. Funai next door could tell when Sumi was still sitting up in bed in the dark, putting her hair up. "Mah, Sumi-chan," Mrs. Funai would say through the plank wall, "are you curling your hair tonight again? Do you put it up every night?" Sumi would put her hands on her hips and glare defiantly at the wall.

The block monitor, an impressive Nisei who looked like a star tackle with his crouching walk, came around the first night to tell us that we must all be inside our room by nine o'clock every night. At ten o'clock, he rapped at the door again, yelling, "Lights out!" and Mother rushed to turn the light off not a second later.

Throughout the barracks, there were a medley of creaking cots, whimpering infants and explosive night coughs. Our attention was riveted on the intense little wood stove which glowed so violently I feared it would melt right down to the floor. We soon learned that this condition lasted for only a short time, after which it suddenly turned into a deep freeze. Henry and Father took turns at the stove to produce the harrowing blast which all but singed our army blankets, but did not penetrate through them. As it grew quieter in the barracks, I could hear the light patter of rain. Soon I felt the "splat! splat!" of raindrops digging holes into my face. The dampness on my pillow spread like a mortal bleeding, and I finally had to get out and haul my cot toward the center of the room. In a short while Henry was up. "I've got multiple leaks, too. Have to complain to the landlord first thing in the morning."

All through the night I heard people getting up, dragging cots around. I stared at our little window, unable to sleep. I was glad Mother had put up a makeshift curtain on the window for I noticed a powerful beam of light sweeping across it every few seconds. The lights came from high towers placed around the camp where guards with Tommy guns kept a twenty-four hour vigil. I remembered the wire fence encircling us, and a knot of anger tightened in my breast. What was I doing behind a fence like a criminal? If there were accusations to be made, why hadn't I been given a fair trial? Maybe I wasn't considered an American anymore. My citizenship wasn't real, after all. Then what was I? I was certainly not a citizen of Japan as my parents were. On second thought, even Father and Mother were more alien residents of the United States than Japanese nationals for they had little tie with their mother country. In their twenty-five years in America, they had worked and paid their taxes to their adopted government as any other citizen.

Of one thing I was sure. The wire fence was real. I no longer had the right to walk out of it. It was because I had Japanese ancestors. It was also because some people had little faith in the ideas and ideals of democracy. They said that after all these were but words and could not possibly insure loyalty. New laws and camps were surer devices. I finally buried my face in my pillow to wipe out burning thoughts and snatch what sleep I could.

SOURCE: Monica Itoi Sone, *Nisei Daughter* (Boston: Little, Brown & Co., 1953), 176–178.

ANALYZING THE EVIDENCE

➤ What was the difference between Sone's legal status and that of her parents? Why were they treated the same, given their different legal statuses?

➤ Based on the information in the text, what answer would the Supreme Court have given to Sone's claim that she deserved a "fair trial" before being imprisoned "like a criminal"?

were not interned. They provided much of the un-skilled labor in the island territory and the Hawaiian economy could not function without them.

Cracks soon appeared in the relocation policy. A labor shortage in farming led the government to furlough seasonal agricultural workers from the camps as early as 1942. About 4,300 college students were allowed to resume their education outside the West Coast military zone. Another route out of the camps was enlistment in the armed services. The 442nd Regimental Combat Team, a segregated unit composed almost entirely of Nisei volunteers, served with distinction in Europe.

Gordon Hirabayashi: Constitutional Rights. Nisei Gordon Hirabayashi was among the few Japanese Americans who actively resisted incarceration. A student at the University of Washington, Hirabayashi was a religious pacifist who had registered with his draft board as a conscientious objector. He challenged internment by refusing to register for evacuation; instead, he turned himself in to the FBI. "I wanted to uphold the principles of the Constitution," Hirabayashi later stated, "and the curfew and evacuation orders which singled out a group on the basis of ethnicity violated them." Tried and convicted in 1942, he appealed his case to Supreme Court in *Hirabayashi v. United States* (1943). In that case, and also in *Korematsu v. United States* (1944), the Court allowed the removal of Japanese Americans from the West Coast on the basis of "military necessity," but avoided ruling on the constitutionality of the internment program. But in *Ex Parte Endo* (1944), the Court held that American citizens of undoubted loyalty could not be confined by government authorities.

The Court's refusal to rule directly on the relocation program underscored the fragility of civil liberties in wartime. Although Congress in 1988 issued a public apology and $20,000 in cash to each of the 80,000 surviving Japanese American internees, it once again gave the government sweeping powers of arrest and detention in the PATRIOT Act of 2001 (see Chapter 32).

➤ What impact did World War II have on everyday life for the majority of Americans?

➤ What distinguished the internal migration of Americans during World War II from that of the World War I era? Who moved and why?

➤ How do you explain the decision to intern Americans of Japanese birth or ancestry?

Fighting and Winning the War

World War II was, literally, a war for control of the world. Had the Axis Powers triumphed, Germany would have dominated, either directly or indirectly, all of Europe and much of Africa; Japan would have controlled most of East Asia. To prevent this outcome, which would have crippled democracy worldwide, destroyed the British and French empires, and restricted American power to the Western Hemisphere, the Roosevelt administration took the United States to war. The United States extended aid to the Allied Powers in the late 1930s, resorted to economic warfare against Germany and Japan in 1940 and 1941, and then fully committed its industrial might and armed forces from 1942 to 1945. Its intervention, and that of the Soviet Union, decided the outcome of conflict and shaped the character of the postwar world.

Wartime Aims and Tensions

Great Britain, the United States, and the Soviet Union were the key actors in the Allied coalition. China, France, and other nations played lesser roles. The "Big Three," consisting of President Franklin Roosevelt, Prime Minister Winston Churchill of Great Britain, and Premier Joseph Stalin of the Soviet Union, set military strategy and diplomatic policy. The Atlantic Charter, which Churchill and Roosevelt had drafted in August 1941, set out the Anglo-American vision of the postwar international order. It called for free trade, national self-determination, and collective security. Stalin had not participated in that agreement and disagreed fundamentally with some of its precepts, such as a capitalist-run international trading system. Moreover, he hoped to protect the USSR from invasion from the West by setting up a band of Soviet-controlled buffer states along his border with Germany and western Europe.

The first major conflict among the Allies concerned military strategy and timing. While they agreed that defeating Germany (rather than Japan) was the top military priority, they argued over how best to do it. In 1941 the German army had invaded the Soviet Union and advanced to the outskirts of Leningrad and Moscow before being halted by hard-pressed Russian forces in early 1942. To relieve pressure on the Soviet army, Stalin wanted the British and Americans to attack Germany in western Europe, opening this "second front" with a major invasion through France. Roosevelt informally assured Stalin that the Allies would open a second front in 1942, but the British opposed an early invasion and American war production was not yet sufficient to support it. For the next eighteen months, Stalin's pleas went unanswered, and the Soviet Union bore the brunt of the fighting. Then, at a conference of the "Big Three" in Tehran, Iran, in November 1943, Churchill and Roosevelt agreed to open a second front in France within six months in return for Stalin's promise to join the fight against Japan. Both sides adhered to this agreement, but the long delay in creating a second front angered Stalin, who became increasingly suspicious about American and British intentions.

The War in Europe

Following the attack on Pearl Harbor, the Allies suffered one defeat after another. German armies pushed deep into Soviet territory in the south; advancing through the wheat fields of the Ukraine and the rich oil fields of the Caucasus, they moved toward the major city of Stalingrad. Simultaneously the Germans began an offensive in North Africa aimed at seizing the Suez Canal. In the Atlantic, German submarines relentlessly and successfully damaged American convoys carrying oil and other vital supplies to Britain and the Soviet Union.

The Allied Advance. Then, in the winter of 1942–1943, the tide began to turn in favor of the Allies. In the epic Battle of Stalingrad, Soviet forces decisively halted the German advance, killing or capturing 330,000 German soldiers, and began to push westward (Map 25.3). By early 1944, Stalin's troops had driven the German army out of the

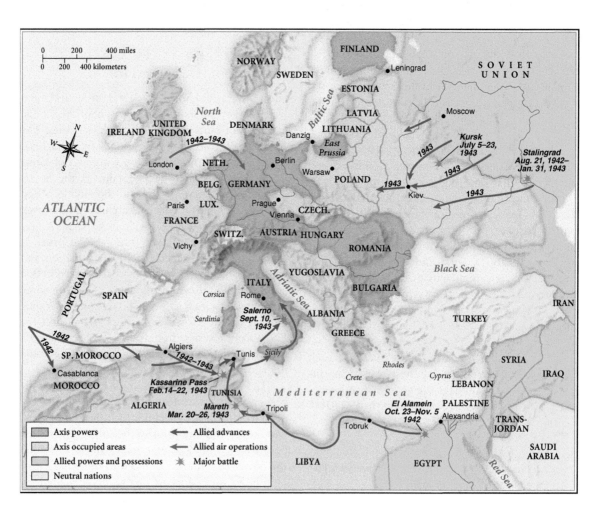

Map 25.3 World War II in Europe, 1941–1943

Hitler's Germany reached its greatest extent in 1942 when Nazi forces had occupied Norway, France, North Africa, central Europe, and much of western Russia. The tide of battle turned in late 1942 when the German advance stalled at Leningrad and Stalingrad. By early 1943, the Soviet army had launched a massive counterattack at Stalingrad, and Allied forces had driven the Germans from North Africa and launched an invasion of Sicily and the Italian mainland.

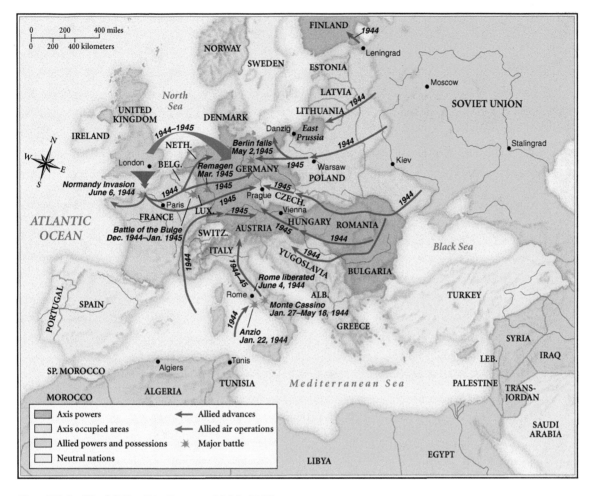

Map 25.4 World War II in Europe, 1944–1945

By the end of 1943, the Russian army had nearly pushed the Germans out of the Soviet Union, and by June 1944, when the British and Americans finally invaded France, the Russians had liberated eastern Poland and most of southeastern Europe. By the end of 1944, British and American forces were ready to invade Germany from the west, and the Russians were poised to do the same from the east. Germany surrendered on May 8, 1945.

Soviet Union. Meanwhile, the Allies launched a major offensive in North Africa, Churchill's substitute for a second front in France. Between November 1942 and May 1943, Allied troops under the leadership of General Dwight D. Eisenhower and General George S. Patton defeated Germany's *Afrika Korps,* led by General Erwin Rommel.

From Africa, the Allied command followed Churchill's strategy of attacking the Axis through its "soft underbelly": Sicily and the Italian peninsula. Faced with an Allied invasion, the Italian king ousted Benito Mussolini's Fascist regime in July 1943. German troops took control of Italy and bitterly resisted the Allied invasion. American and British troops took Rome only in June 1944 and were still fighting German forces in northern Italy when the European war ended in May 1945

(Map 25.4). Churchill's southern strategy proved a time-consuming and costly failure.

The long-promised invasion of France came on "D-Day," June 6, 1944. That morning, after an agonizing delay caused by bad weather, the largest armada ever assembled moved across the English Channel under the command of General Dwight D. Eisenhower. When American, British, and Canadian soldiers hit the beaches of Normandy, they suffered terrible causalities but secured a beachhead. Over the next few days, more than 1.5 million soldiers and thousands of tons of military supplies and equipment flowed into France. In August Allied troops liberated Paris; by September they had driven the Germans out of most of France and Belgium. Meanwhile, long-range Allied bombers had attacked German cities as well as military and

Hitting the Beach at Normandy

These American soldiers were among the 156,000 Allied troops who stormed the beaches of Normandy, France, on D-Day, June 6, 1944; on that day alone, more than 10,000 were killed or wounded. Within a month, one million Allied troops came ashore. Filmmaker Steven Spielberg recreated the carnage and confusion of the landing in the opening scene of *Saving Private Ryan* (1998). Library of Congress.

industrial targets. The air campaign killed some 305,000 civilians and soldiers and wounded another 780,000.

The Germans were not yet ready to give up, however. In December 1944 they mounted a final offensive in Belgium, the so-called Battle of the Bulge, before being pushed back across the Rhine River into Germany. As American and British troops drove toward Berlin from the west, Soviet troops advanced from the east through Poland. On April 30, as Russian troops massed outside Berlin, Hitler committed suicide; on May 8, Germany formally surrendered.

The Holocaust. As Allied troops advanced into Poland and Germany in the spring of 1945, they came face to face with Adolf Hitler's "final solution of the Jewish question": the extermination camps where six million Jews had been put to death, along with another six million Poles, Slavs, Gypsies, homosexuals, and other "undesirables." Photographs of the Nazi death camps at Buchenwald, Dachau, and Auschwitz showed bodies stacked like cordwood

and survivors so emaciated they were barely alive. Quickly published in *Life* and other mass-circulation magazines, the photographs horrified the American public.

The Nazi persecution of German Jews in the 1930s was widely known in the United States. But when Jews began to flee from Germany, the United States refused to relax its strict immigration laws to take them in. American officials, along with those of most other nations, continued this exclusionist policy during World War II, as the Nazi regime extended its control over millions of east European Jews. Among the various factors that combined to inhibit American action, the most important was widespread anti-Semitism: in the State Department, Christian churches, and the public at large. The legacy of the immigration restriction legislation of the 1920s and the isolationist attitudes of the 1930s also discouraged policymakers from assuming responsibility for the fate of the refugees. As later American administrations would learn (as "ethnic cleansing" killed millions in India in the 1940s and Bosnia

The Living Dead

When Allied troops advanced into Germany in the spring of 1945, they came face to face with what had long been rumored — concentration camps, Adolf Hitler's "final solution of the Jewish question." In this picture from Wobbelin concentration camp — liberated by the 82nd Airborne Division of the 9th U.S. Army — emaciated inmates are being taken to a hospital. In the days before the camp was liberated, one thousand of the five thousand prisoners had been allowed to starve to death. U.S. Holocaust Memorial Museum.

and Rwanda in the 1990s), such political considerations often conflict with humanitarian values. Taking a narrow view of the national interest, the State Department allowed only 21,000 Jewish refugees to enter the United States during the war. But the War Refugee Board, established by President Roosevelt in 1944, following a plea by Secretary of the Treasury Henry Morganthau, helped to move 200,000 European Jews to safe havens in various countries.

The War in the Pacific

Winning the war against Japan was as arduous as the campaign against Germany in Europe. After crippling the American battle fleet at Pearl Harbor, the Japanese quickly expanded their military presence in the South Pacific, with seaborne invasions of Hong Kong, Wake Island, and Guam. Japanese forces then advanced into Southeast Asia, conquering

the Solomon Islands, Burma, and Malaya and threatening Australia and India. By May 1942, they had forced the surrender of American forces in the Philippine Islands and, in the Bataan "death march," callously allowed the deaths of 10,000 prisoners of war.

At that dire moment, American naval forces scored two crucial victories. In the Battle of the Coral Sea near southern New Guinea in May 1942, they halted the Japanese offensive against Australia. In June, at the Battle of Midway Island, the American navy inflicted serious damage on the Japanese fleet. In both battles dive bombers and fighters launched from American aircraft carriers provided the margin of victory.

The American military command, led by General Douglas MacArthur and Admiral Chester W. Nimitz, then took the offensive in the Pacific (Map 25.5). For the next eighteen months, American forces advanced slowly toward Japan, taking one island after another in the face of bitter Japanese resistance. In October 1944, MacArthur and Nimitz began the reconquest of the Philippines by winning the Battle of Leyte Gulf, a massive naval encounter in which the Japanese lost practically their entire fleet (Map 25.6).

By early 1945, victory over Japan was in sight. Japanese military forces had suffered devastating losses, and American bombing of the Japanese homeland had killed about 330,000 civilians and crippled its economy. But the closer U.S. forces got to the Japanese home islands, the more fiercely the Japanese fought. On the small island of Iwo Jima, 21,000 Japanese soldiers fought to the death, killing 6,000 American marines and wounding 14,000 more. On Okinawa, the American toll reached 7,600 dead and 32,000 wounded. Desperate to halt the American advance and short of ammunition, Japanese pilots flew *kamikaze* (suicidal) missions, crashing their bomb-laden planes into American ships. Based on the fighting on Okinawa and Iwo Jima, American military commanders grimly predicted millions of casualties in the upcoming invasion of Japan.

Planning the Postwar World

As Allied forces moved toward victory in the Pacific and Europe, Roosevelt, Churchill, and Stalin met in February 1945 at Yalta, a resort on the Black Sea. Roosevelt focused on maintaining Allied unity, which he saw as the key to postwar peace and stability. But two sets of issues, the fate of the British and French colonial empires and of central and eastern Europe, threatened to divide

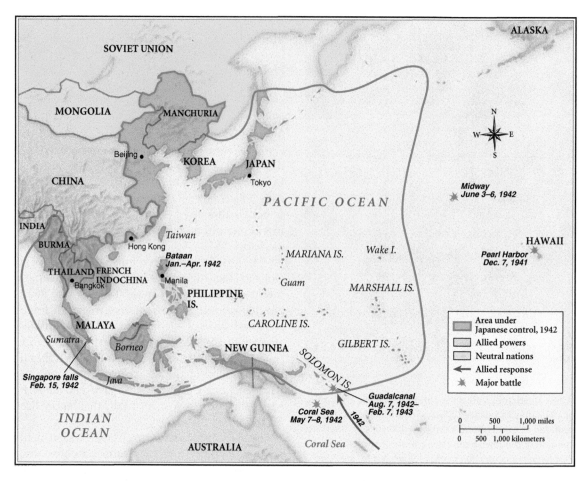

Map 25.5   World War II in the Pacific, 1941–1942

After the attacks on Pearl Harbor in December 1941, the Japanese rapidly extended their domination in the Pacific. The Japanese flag soon flew as far east as the Marshall and Gilbert islands and as far south as the Solomon Islands and parts of New Guinea. Japan also controlled the Philippines, much of Southeast Asia, and parts of China, including Hong Kong. By mid-1942, American naval victories at the Coral Sea and Midway stopped further Japanese expansion.

the Big Three. An independence movement in British India, led by Mahatma Gandhi, had already gathered strength and caused friction between Roosevelt and Churchill. A more serious source of conflict was Stalin's insistence that Russian national security demanded the installation of pro-Soviet governments in central and eastern Europe. Roosevelt pressed for an agreement that guaranteed self-determination and democratic elections in Poland and neighboring countries but, given the presence there of Soviet troops, had to accept a pledge from Stalin to hold "free and unfettered elections" at a future time. The three leaders agreed to divide Germany into four administrative zones, each controlled by one of the four powers (the United States, Great Britain, France, and the Soviet Union) and also to partition the capital city, Berlin, which lay in the middle of the Soviet zone, among the four powers.

Creating the United Nations. To continue and expand their alliance, the Big Three agreed to establish an international body to replace the discredited League of Nations. They decided that the new United Nations organization would have a Security Council composed of the five major Allied powers—the United States, Britain, France, China, and the Soviet Union—and six other nations elected on a rotating basis. They also agreed that the five permanent members of the Security Council should have veto power over decisions of the

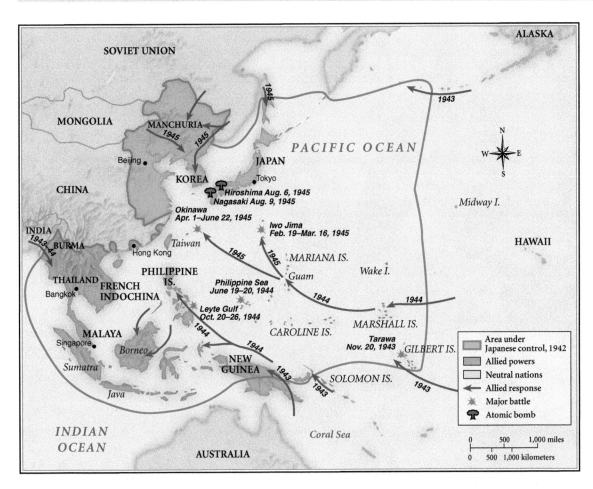

Map 25.6   World War II in the Pacific, 1943–1945

Allied forces retook the islands in the central Pacific in 1943 and 1944 and ousted the Japanese from the Philippines early in 1945. The capture of Iwo Jima and Okinawa put American bombers in position to attack Japan itself. As the Soviet army invaded Japanese-occupied Manchuria in August 1945, the United States dropped atomic bombs on Hiroshima and Nagasaki. The Japanese offered to surrender on August 10.

General Assembly, in which all nations would be represented. Roosevelt, Churchill, and Stalin announced that the United Nations would convene in San Francisco on April 25, 1945.

Roosevelt returned to the United States in February, visibly exhausted by his 14,000-mile trip. The sixty-three-year-old president was a sick man, suffering from heart failure and high blood pressure. On April 12, 1945, during a short visit to his vacation home in Warm Springs, Georgia, Roosevelt suffered a cerebral hemorrhage and died.

The Atom Bomb. When Harry S Truman assumed the presidency, he learned for the first time about the top-secret Manhattan Project,

charged with developing a new weapon—an atomic bomb. European physicists, many of them Jewish, had achieved the theoretical breakthroughs that foreshadowed the atomic age during the first decades of the twentieth century. By the 1930s scientists knew that the tiny nuclei of atoms could be split into yet smaller particles, a process called fission. They also knew that the fission of highly processed uranium would produce a chain reaction and unleash tremendous amounts of energy. Working at the University of Chicago in December 1942, Enrico Fermi and Leo Szilard, refugees from Fascist Italy and Nazi Germany, produced the first controlled chain reaction. With the aid of Albert Einstein, the greatest theorist of modern physics and a refugee

The Big Three at Yalta

With victory in Europe at hand, Roosevelt journeyed in 1945 to Yalta, on the Black Sea, and met for the final time with Churchill and Stalin. The leaders discussed the important and controversial issues of the treatment of Germany, the status of Poland, the creation of the United Nations, and Russian entry into the war against Japan. The Yalta agreements mirrored a new balance of power and set the stage for the Cold War. Franklin D. Roosevelt Library.

scholar at Princeton, they persuaded Franklin Roosevelt to develop an atomic weapon, warning that German scientists were also working on such nuclear reactions.

The Manhattan Project cost $2 billion, employed 120,000 people, and involved the construction of thirty-seven installations in nineteen states—all of this activity hidden from Congress, the American people, and even Vice President Truman. Directed by General Leslie Graves and scientist Robert Oppenheimer, the nation's top physicists assembled the first bomb in Los Alamos, New Mexico, and successfully tested it on July 16, 1945. Overwhelmed by its frightening power, Oppenheimer recalled the words from the *Bhagavad Gita,* the Hindu bible: "I am become Death, Destroyer of Worlds."

Three weeks later, President Truman ordered the dropping of atomic bombs on two Japanese cities, Hiroshima on August 6 and Nagasaki on August 9. Truman was not a reflective man, and he did not question the morality of using such a revolutionary weapon. Administration officials were convinced that Japan's military leaders would never surrender unless their country was utterly devastated, and they knew that an American invasion would cost hundreds of thousands of lives. Truman may also have hoped that use of the bomb would intimidate Stalin and ease his objections to American plans for the postwar world. Whatever the long-range intention or result, atomic bombs achieved the immediate goal. The deaths of 100,000 people at Hiroshima and 60,000 at Nagasaki prompted the Japanese government to offer to surrender on August 10 and to sign a formal agreement on September 2, 1945.

Hiroshima

This aerial view of Hiroshima after the dropping of an atomic bomb on August 6, 1945, shows the terrible devastation of the city. A U.S. Army report prepared in 1946 describes the bomb exploding "with a blinding flash in the sky, and a great rush of air and a loud rumble of noise extended for many miles around the city; the first blast was soon followed by the sounds of falling buildings and of growing fires, and a great cloud of dust and smoke began to cast a pall of darkness over the city." Except for fifty concrete-reinforced buildings designed to withstand earthquakes, every structure within one mile of the center of the bomb blast was reduced to rubble. The physical destruction was second to the human cost: With a population estimated at between 300,000 and 400,000 people, Hiroshima lost 100,000 in the initial explosion, and many thousands more died slowly of radiation poisoning. U.S. Air Force.

Fascism had been defeated, thanks to a strange alliance between the capitalist nations of the West and the communist government of the Soviet Union. The coming of peace would strain, and then destroy, the victorious coalition.

> ➤ Describe the course of the war in Europe and the Pacific. What factors led to the Allied victory in World War II?

> ➤ Explain why the United States used atomic weapons in Japan. Why was the Americans' use of these weapons controversial?

SUMMARY

As we have seen, the rise of fascism and expansionism in Germany, Italy, and Japan led to the outbreak of World War II. Initially, the American public preferred a policy of noninvolvement. But by 1940 President Roosevelt had begun mobilizing public opinion for intervention and converting the economy to war production. The Japanese attack on Pearl Harbor on December 7, 1941, brought the nation into World War II, a global conflict that involved massive military campaigns in both Europe and the Pacific.

As with World War I, mobilization led to a dramatic expansion of the size and power of the federal government. It also increased geographical and social mobility as new defense plants in California and elsewhere created job opportunities for women, rural whites, southern blacks, and Mexican Americans. Government intervention in the economy assisted the labor movement to consolidate its gains during the 1930s. In addition, the ideological climate of fighting Nazism aided the cause of civil rights for African Americans. At the same time, religious and racial animosity blocked the admission of Jewish refugees and prompted the forced internment of 112,000 Japanese Americans, a devastating denial of civil liberties.

As our account makes clear, the prospects of an American and Allied victory were bleak during much of 1942. By 1943 the Allies had taken the offensive, thanks to advances by the Soviet army in Europe and the American navy in the Pacific; by the end of 1944 victory was all but certain. Among the major powers, only the United States emerged physically unharmed from the war, and it alone possessed the atomic bomb, the most lethal weapon of mass destruction ever created. But the most vexing result of World War II was the onset of the Cold War between the United States and the Soviet Union. This conflict would dominate American foreign policy for the next four decades.

Connections: Government

The "Rise of the State" has been a central theme of Part Five. As we stated in the essay that opened Part Five (p. 671), "American participation in World War I called forth an unprecedented mobilization of the domestic economy" by government institutions, a process we described in Chapter 22. Chapter 23 then explained how that wartime collaboration continued in the 1920s. Herbert Hoover and other government officials promoted polices of the "associated state" and "welfare capitalism," which encouraged large corporate businesses to assume broad economic and social responsibilities. When the Great Depression revealed the flaws in these policies and ideologies, Franklin Roosevelt's New Deal instituted a variety of new government programs to spur economic recovery and social welfare. As Chapter 24 made clear, the National Recovery Association, the Agricultural Adjustment Act, the Works Project Administration, and similar measures represented unprecedented levels of government supervision of American economic life. Likewise, the ideology of social welfare liberalism and its partial realization in the Social Security Act of 1935 gave the federal government major responsibility for the welfare of a substantial majority of American citizens. As we saw in Chapter 25, these links between the state and its citizenry grew even closer and more pervasive during World War II, with the creation of universal income taxation and the enactment of the GI Bill of Rights. Moreover, as we noted in the Part Opener, "Unlike the experience after World War I, the new state apparatus remained in place when the war ended." In Part Six, which covers the period from 1945 to 1980, we will explain how the federal government grew in size and power as it both armed the nation to fight a Cold War abroad and worked to end poverty and expand prosperity at home.

CHAPTER REVIEW QUESTIONS

> ➤ According to the oral historian Studs Terkel, World War II was a "good war." Do you agree with this assessment?

> ➤ Overall, what sort of impact — positive or negative — did World War II have on women and minority groups in the United States?

> ➤ Why was there tension among the Allies during the war, and what long-term impact did it have?

TIMELINE

1933	Adolf Hitler becomes chancellor of Germany
1935	Italy invades Ethiopia
1935–1937	U.S. Neutrality Acts
1936	Germany reoccupies Rhineland demilitarized zone Rome-Berlin Axis established Japan and Germany sign Anti-Comintern Pact
1937	Japan invades China
1938	Munich agreement between Germany, Britain, and France
1939	Nazi-Soviet Nonaggression Pact Germany invades Poland Britain and France declare war on Germany
1940	American conscription reinstated Germany, Italy, and Japan sign Tri-Partite Pact
1941	Roosevelt promulgates Four Freedoms Germany invades Soviet Union Lend-Lease Act passed Fair Employment Practices Commission created Atlantic Charter promulgated Japanese attack Pearl Harbor
1942	Allies suffer severe defeats in Europe and Asia Executive Order 9066 leads to Japanese internment camps Battles of Coral Sea and Midway halt Japanese advance Women recruited for war industries
1942–1945	Rationing of scarce goods
1943	Race riots in Detroit and Los Angeles Fascism falls in Italy
1944	D-Day: Allied landing in France GI Bill of Rights enacted Supreme Court avoids issue of the constitutionality of Japanese American internment
1945	Yalta Conference Battles of Iwo Jima and Okinawa Germany surrenders Harry S Truman becomes president after Roosevelt's death United Nations convenes Atomic bombs dropped on Hiroshima and Nagasaki Japan surrenders

FOR FURTHER EXPLORATION

The standard military history of World War II is Henry Steele Commager, *The Story of World War II*, as expanded and revised by Donald L. Miller (1945; revisions 2001). Fifty-three personal stories of war appear in *War Stories: Remembering World War II* (2002), edited by Elizabeth Mullener. An engaging overview of war on the home front is John Morton Blum, *V Was for Victory* (1976). See also "Cents and Sacrifice" at **www.nauticom.net/ www/harts/homefront.html**, a comprehensive site with many links to other valuable resources. The National Archives Administration at **www.archives.gov/exhibit_hall/index.html** has two World War II sites: "A People at War" and "Powers of Persuasion: Poster Art from World War II." An anthology that focuses on popular culture and the wartime experience is Lewis A. Erenberg and Susan E. Hirsch, eds., *The War in American Culture* (1996). Powerful novels inspired by the war include John Hersey, *A Bell for Adano* (1944); James Jones, *From Here to Eternity* (1951); and Norman Mailer, *The Naked and the Dead* (1948).

The Library of Congress exhibit "Women Come to the Front: Journalists, Photographers, and Broadcasters During World War II" at **lcweb.loc.gov/exhibits/wcf/wcf0001.html** and "Rosie Pictures: Select Images Relating to American Women Workers During World War II" at **www.loc.gov/rr/ print/list/126_rosi.html** record the contributions of women during World War II. Sherna B. Gluck, *Rosie the Riveter Revisited* (1988), offers compelling accounts by women war workers.

Many sites cover the Japanese internment, including the interesting one at the University of Washington on Seattle's Japanese American community: **www.lib.washington.edu/exhibits/ harmony/default.htm**. For interviews with detainees and thousands of images, go to **www.densho.org/densho.asp**. The Library of Congress site "Suffering Under a Great Injustice" at **memory.loc.gov/ammem/aamhtml** presents a haunting exhibition of Ansel Adams's photographs of the Manzanar camp.

For "'Man on the Street Interviews' Following the Attack on Pearl Harbor," go to **lcweb2.loc.gov/ammem/afcphhtml/ afcphhome.html**. See also the "Rutgers Oral History Archive of World War II" at **oralhistory.rutgers.edu**.

The decision to drop the bomb remains controversial. An excellent site is Lehigh University Professor Edward J. Gallagher's "*The Enola Gay* Controversy: How Do We Remember a War That We Won?" at **www.lehigh.edu/~ineng/ enola**. See also the masterful biography of the bomb's principal architect: Kai Bird and Martin J. Sherwin, *American Prometheus: The Triumph and Tragedy of J. Robert Oppenheimer* (2005).

TEST YOUR KNOWLEDGE

To assess your command of the material in this chapter, see the Online Study Guide at **bedfordstmartins.com/henretta**.

For Web sites, images, and documents related to topics and places in this chapter, visit **bedfordstmartins.com/makehistory**.

PART SIX | The Age of Cold War Liberalism

1945–1980

DIPLOMACY	POLITICS	ECONOMY	SOCIETY	CULTURE
The Cold War	**Decline of the Liberal Consensus**	**Ups and Downs of U.S. Economic Dominance**	**Social Movements and Demographic Diversity**	**Consumer Culture and Its Critics**
1945 ▶ Truman Doctrine (1947) ▶ Marshall Plan (1948) ▶ Berlin blockade ▶ NATO founded (1949)	▶ Truman's Fair Deal liberalism ▶ Taft-Hartley Act (1947) ▶ Truman reelected (1948)	▶ Reconversion ▶ Strike wave (1946) ▶ Bretton Woods system established: World Bank, IMF	▶ Migration to cities accelerates ▶ Armed forces desegregated (1948)	▶ End of wartime rationing ▶ Rise of television ▶ First Levittown (1947)
1950 ▶ Permanent mobilization: NSC-68 (1950) ▶ Korean War (1950–1953) ▶ U.S replaces France in Vietnam	▶ McCarthyism ▶ Eisenhower's modern Republicanism ▶ Warren Court activism	▶ Rise of military-industrial complex ▶ Industrial economy booms ▶ Labor-management accord	▶ *Brown v. Board of Education* (1954) ▶ Montgomery bus boycott (1955) ▶ Urban crisis emerges	▶ Growth of suburbia ▶ Sun Belt emerges ▶ Religious revival ▶ Baby boom ▶ Youth culture develops
1960 ▶ Cuban missile crisis (1962) ▶ Vietnam War escalates (1965) ▶ Tet offensive (1968); peace talks begin	▶ Kennedy's New Frontier ▶ Kennedy assassinated ▶ Great Society, War on Poverty ▶ Nixon's election (1968) ushers in conservative era	▶ Kennedy-Johnson tax cut, military expenditures fuel economic growth	▶ March on Washington (1963) ▶ Civil rights legislation (1964, 1965) ▶ Student activism ▶ Black Power	▶ Shopping malls spread ▶ Baby boomers swell college enrollment ▶ Hippie counterculture
1970 ▶ Nixon visits China (1972); SALT initiates détente (1972) ▶ Paris Peace accords (1973) end Vietnam War ▶ Carter brokers Camp David accords between Egypt and Israel (1978) ▶ Iranian revolution; hostage crisis	▶ Watergate scandal; Nixon resigns (1974) ▶ Weak presidencies of Ford and Carter	▶ Arab oil embargo (1973–1974); inflation surges, while income stagnates ▶ Onset of deindustrialization	▶ Revival of feminism ▶ *Roe v. Wade* (1973) ▶ New Right urges conservative agenda	▶ Consumer and environmental protection movements ▶ Deepening social divide over ERA and gay rights

"What Rome was to the ancient world," proclaimed the influential journalist Walter Lippmann in 1945, "America is to be for the world of tomorrow." Lippmann's remark captures America's sense of triumphant confidence at the end of World War II. What he underestimated were the challenges, both global and domestic, confronting the United States. In this Part Six, covering the years 1945–1980, we track how the United States fared in its quest to become the Rome of the twentieth century.

DIPLOMACY Hardly had Lippmann penned his triumphant words in 1945 than the Soviet Union challenged America's plans for postwar Europe. The Truman administration responded by crafting the policies and alliances that came to define the Cold War. That struggle spawned two "hot" wars in Korea and Vietnam and fueled a terrifying nuclear arms race. By the early 1970s, as the bi-polar assumptions of the Cold War broke down, the Nixon administration got on better terms with both the Soviet Union and China. The high hopes for détente, however, fell short, and during Carter's tenure Soviet-U.S. relations lapsed into a state of anxious stalemate. The hostage crisis in Iran revealed that, beyond the Cold War, other big challenges, especially from the aggrieved Muslim world, faced the United States.

POLITICS Lippmann's confidence in America's future in part stemmed from his sense of a nation united on the big domestic questions. Except for a brief postwar reaction, which brought forth the Taft-Hartley Act (1947), the liberal consensus prevailed. And while not much headway was made by Truman's Fair Deal, neither did Republicans under Eisenhower attempt any dismantling of the New Deal. Johnson's ambitious Great Society, however, did provoke a conservative response and, beginning with the debacle of the Democratic convention of 1968, the country moved to the right. The interaction of the domestic and global — the links between liberalism and the Cold War — was especially clear at this juncture because it was Vietnam that, more than anything, undermined the Great Society and the liberal consensus. By the end of the 1970s, with a big assist from the Carter administration, the Democrats had lost the grip they had won under FDR as the nation's dominant party.

ECONOMY In no realm did America's supremacy seem so secure in the postwar years as in economics. While the war-torn countries of Europe and Asia were picking through the rubble, the American economy boomed, fed both by the military-industrial complex and by a high-spending consumer culture. Real income grew, and collective bargaining became well entrenched. In the 1950s, no country was competitive with America's economy. By the 1970s, however, American industry had been overtaken, and a sad process of dismantling, of deindustrialization, began. At the same time, the inflationary spiral that had begun during the Vietnam War speeded up under the impact of the oil embargo of 1973. A decade of "stagflation" set in, and with it a suspicion that America's vaunted economic powerhouse had seen its best days.

SOCIETY The victory over Nazism in World War II spurred demands for America to make good on its promise of equality for all. In great waves of protests beginning in the 1950s, African Americans — and then women, Latinos, and other minorities — challenged the status quo. Starting with the Supreme Court's landmark *Brown v. Board of Education* (1954) decision, the country began to outlaw the practices of segregation, discrimination, and disfranchisement that had held minorities down. In the 1970s, however, reaction set in, fueled in part by the growing militancy of blacks and others, in part by the discovery of a resentful "silent majority" by conservative politicians. Achieving equality, it turned out, was easier said than done.

CULTURE America's economic power in the postwar years accelerated the development of a consumer society that cherished the tract house, the car, and television set. As millions of Americans moved into suburban subdivisions, the birth-rate speeded up, spawning a baby boom generation whose social influence would be felt for the next seventy-five years. Under the surface calm of the 1950s, a mood of cultural rebellion took hold. In the 1960s, it would burst forth in the hippie counterculture and the antiwar movement. Although both subsided in the early 1970s, they left a lasting impact on the country's politics, in particular, as fuel that fed the resurgence of American conservatism.

Walter Lippmann died in 1974. He had lived long enough to see his high hopes of 1945 blasted by the Cold War, by economic troubles, and by the collapse of the liberal consensus.

26 Cold War America

1945–1960

O N MAY 1, 1950, THE RESIDENTS OF Mosinee, Wisconsin, staged a mock Communist takeover of their small papermill town. Secret police interrogated citizens. The mayor was carted off to jail. The local paper reappeared as a mini-*Pravda*. And restaurants served only potato soup and black bread. Dreamed up by the American Legion, Mosinee's "Day Under Communism" was a sensational media event that conveyed a chilling message: America's way of life was under siege by the Communist menace.

The Mosinee episode captured a towering irony of the postwar period. Americans in 1945 had indeed been anxious over what would follow victory. But their anxiety was not directed at the Soviet Union. Weren't we all part of the Grand Alliance? No, what worried Americans was closer to home. Defense plants were shutting down, war workers being laid off, and twelve million job-seeking veterans on the way home. Might the country slide back into the Great Depression? In short order, those fears dissipated. Home building picked up. Cars flowed from the assembly lines. Consumers began to spend like crazy the savings they had piled up during the war. The economy was in fact entering the strongest boom in American history. But instead of being able to settle back and enjoy their prosperity, the good people of Mosinee worried about a Soviet coup in their town. They had exchanged one fear — of economic hard times — for another: the Communist menace.

The Cold War
Descent into Cold War, 1945–1946
*George Kennan and the Containment
    Strategy*
Containment in Asia

The Truman Era
Reconversion
The Fair Deal
The Great Fear   .

Modern Republicanism
They Liked Ike
The Hidden-Hand Presidency
Eisenhower and the Cold War
*Containment in the Post-Colonial
    World*
Eisenhower's Farewell Address

Summary
Connections: Diplomacy and Politics

◄ **The Perils of the Cold War**

In this detail of a 1948 Pulitzer Prize–winning cartoon, Rube Goldberg depicts the perilous nature of America's postwar peace — one that was based largely on the threat of nuclear annihilation. University of California at Berkeley, Bancroft Library.

The conflict that emerged between the Soviet Union and the United States, while not leading to any direct engagement on the battlefield, inaugurated a long twilight era of international tension — a Cold War — when either side, armed with nuclear weapons, might have tipped the entire world into oblivion.

The impact of the Soviet-American confrontation on domestic affairs was far-reaching. The Cold War fostered a climate of fear and suspicion of "subversives" in government, education, and the media. It boosted military expenditures, fueling a growing arms race between the two superpowers, creating a "military-industrial complex" in the United States, and undergirding an amazing era of economic expansion (see Chapter 27). That prosperity helped to expand federal power, perpetuating the New Deal state in the postwar era. But the Cold War also now held liberal politics hostage because the ability of the New Deal coalition to advance its agenda at home depended on its prowess as a Cold Warrior abroad. In all these ways, the line between the international and the domestic blurred. That was an enduring legacy of the Cold War.

The Cold War

The Cold War began in 1946. It ended forty-five years later with the collapse of the Soviet Union. In that intervening period, a vast amount was written by historians about why the Cold War had happened. By no means did all blame the Soviets. Eventually, indeed, those holding the opposite view — the "revisionist" historians, so-called — often held the upper hand. But in truth, the debate was ultimately inconclusive because the scholarly conditions that prevailed really precluded definitive history. The Soviet archives, for one thing, were completely closed. More important, perhaps, historians were trying to capture an event that was still happening. Only now that it is over can historians look back and gain the perspective needed for understanding why the Cold War occurred.

Descent into Cold War, 1945–1946

World War II itself set the basic conditions for Cold War rivalry. With Germany and Japan defeated and America's British and French allies exhausted, only the two superpowers remained standing in 1945. Even had nothing else divided them, the United States and the USSR would have jostled against each other as they moved to fill the vacuum. But, of course, the two countries *were* divided — by ideology, by history, by geography and strategic interest, even by relative power (with the advantage, both militarily and economically, heavily on the American side). FDR understood that bridging the divide and maintaining the U.S.-Soviet alliance were essential conditions for postwar stability. But he also believed that permanent peace depended on adherence to the Wilsonian principles of collective security, self-determination, and free trade (see Chapter 22). The challenge was to find a way of reconciling Wilsonian principles with U.S.-Soviet power realities.

Yalta. That was what Roosevelt, Churchill, and Stalin had undertaken at the Yalta Conference of February 1945. They agreed there to go forward with the United Nations, committing themselves to a new international forum for resolving future conflicts and fostering world peace. The realist side of that noble arrangement, demanded by the U.S. and the USSR, was that permanent seats with veto rights be reserved for them (and their three major allies) on the Security Council. The paramount problem at Yalta, however, was eastern Europe. Roosevelt and Churchill agreed that Poland and its neighbors would fall under the Soviet "sphere of influence" — thus meeting Stalin's demand for secure western borders. But Yalta also called for "free and unfettered" elections — thus upholding the essential principle of democratic self-determination. Implicit in Yalta's details was an expectation — the nub of the deal — that freely elected governments would consent to Soviet domination.

That actually had happened in Finland and, after Yalta, briefly in Czechoslovakia. It could not happen in Poland. For that, Stalin had himself to blame. With war impending in 1939, he made his infamous secret pact with Hitler for the partition of Poland. When the Nazis invaded, the Soviet Union seized its apportioned share (and reclaimed much of it as sovereign territory when the Nazis retreated in 1944). Then Stalin ordered the execution of the entire Polish officer corps in Russian hands in the Katyn forest, a deed that, when exposed by the Nazis in 1943, caused a rift with the Polish government-in-exile in London. Equally unforgivable was Stalin's betrayal of the Poles of Warsaw late in the war. When they rose against the Germans, the Red Army halted on the outskirts so that any potential anti-Communist opposition could be finished off by the Nazis. Evidently blind to the resentment of his victims, Stalin — American observers reported — was taken aback by the fear and loathing that greeted his approaching armies. So there would be no free elections, a conclusion Stalin had already arrived at before Yalta. He got the puppet regime he required, but never the consent of the Poles, or the Hungarians, Romanians, and other subject peoples of eastern Europe. Stalin's unwillingness — his *inability,* if he was to fulfill his ambitions — to hold free elections was the precipitating event of the Cold War.

Truman Takes Command. Historians doubt that, had he lived, even the resourceful Roosevelt could have preserved the Grand Alliance. With Harry Truman, no such possibility existed. Truman was inexperienced in foreign affairs. As vice president, he had been kept in the dark about Roosevelt's negotiations (or even about the atomic bomb). His blunt instinct was to stand up to Stalin. At a meeting held shortly after he took office, the new president berated the Soviet foreign minister, V. M. Molotov, over the Soviets' failure to honor their Yalta agreements. He abruptly halted lend-lease shipments that the Soviets desperately needed and denied their request for $6 billion in credits. Truman used what he called "tough methods" that July at the Potsdam Conference, which had been called to take up postwar planning. After learning of the successful test of America's atomic bomb, Truman "told the Russians just where they got off and generally bossed the whole meeting," recalled Winston Churchill.

Stalin was not taken by surprise. He had been kept informed by his spy network about the Manhattan Project virtually from its inception in 1942 — far earlier than Truman himself knew about it. Nor was Stalin intimidated. His spies assured him that the small American arsenal posed no immediate threat to the Soviet Union. And his own scientists were on a crash course to producing a Soviet bomb, their efforts much eased by plutonium bomb blueprints stolen from the Manhattan Project. It was a time, as Stalin said, for strong nerves. But the atomic issue did enflame tensions, requiring extra displays of toughness by the Soviets, deepening their suspicions of the West, and, on the American side, encouraging a certain swagger. It was unwise, warned Secretary of War Stimson, for the United States to try to negotiate with "this weapon rather ostentatiously on our hip."

In early 1946, the United States made an effort to head off the impending nuclear race, proposing in the Baruch Plan (after its sponsor, the financier Bernard Baruch) that all weapons-related development and production be placed under the control of a special U.N. atomic agency and that a strict system of inspections and punishments (not sub-ject to Security Council veto) be instituted to prevent violations by individual nations. Once international controls were fully in place, the United States would dispose of its stockpile of atomic bombs. Hot on the trail of their own bomb, the Soviets, although they went through the motions of negotiation, regarded the Baruch Plan as an American trick to dominate them. Its failure foreshadowed a frenzied nuclear arms race between the two superpowers.

By then, Truman's instinctive toughness was being seconded by his more seasoned advisors, a distingished group known collectively as the Establishment for their elite pedigrees and high-placed public service. Close students of diplomacy, some of them, like Averell Harriman and George F. Kennan, experts on Soviet affairs, concluded that Stalin's actions in eastern Europe were not an aberration, but truly reflective of Stalin's despotic regime. A cogent summary of their views came, ironically, from a former Russian foreign minister, Maxim Litvinoff, who had negotiated America's recognition of the Soviet Union with FDR in 1933. Lamenting the end of wartime cooperation, Litvinoff told a CBS Moscow correspondent that the USSR had returned "to the outmoded concept of security in terms of territory — the more you've got, the safer you are." This was because "the ideological concept prevailing here [is] that conflict between Communist and capitalist worlds is inevitable." The Soviet Union was at that time, in early 1946, expanding its reach, maintaining troops in northern Iran, pressing Turkey for access to the Mediterranean, sponsoring a guerrilla war in Greece. If the current Soviet demands were satisfied, the CBS man asked, what then? "It would lead to the West's being faced, after a more or less short time, with the next set of demands," replied Litvinoff.

George Kennan and the Containment Strategy

Just how the West should respond was crystallized in February 1946 by George F. Kennan in an eight-thousand-word cable, dubbed the "Long Telegram," from his post at the U.S. embassy in Moscow. Kennan argued that the Soviet Union was an "Oriental despotism" and Communism just "the fig-leaf" justifying its crimes. For Soviet leaders, hostility to the West provided the essential excuse "for the dictatorship without which they do not know how to rule." The West had no way of altering this perverse internal dynamic. Its only recourse, Kennan wrote in a famous *Foreign Affairs* article a year later, was to meet the Soviets "with unalterable

George F. Kennan

As a diplomat, foreign policy theorist, and historian, George F. Kennan (1904–2005) enjoyed a long and distinguished career spanning more than seventy years. This portrait by Guy Rowe dates from 1955. National Portrait Gallery, Smithsonian Institution/Art Resource, N.Y.

counter-force at every point where they show signs of encroaching upon the interests of a peaceful and stable world." Kennan called for "long-term, patient but firm and vigilant *containment* of Russian expansive tendencies." Containment, the key word, defined America's evolving strategic stance against the Soviet Union, and Kennan, its author, became one of the most influential advisors in the Truman administration.

On its face, containment seemed a counsel of despair, dooming the United States to a draining, inconclusive struggle without end. In fact, Kennan was more optimistic than that. The Soviet system, he argued with notable foresight, was inherently unstable, and eventually — not in Stalin's time, but eventually — it would collapse. Moreover, the Soviets were not reckless. "If . . . situations can be created in which [conflict] is not to [their] advantage," they would pull back. So it was up to the West to create those situations, avoiding an arms race, picking its fights carefully, exercising patience.

Kennan's attentive readers included Stalin, who had quickly obtained a copy of the classified Long Telegram. To keep things even, Stalin ordered his ambassador in Washington to prepare his own Long Telegram, and got back an eerie mirror image of Kennan's analysis, with the United States cast as imperialist aggressor, driven by the crisis of monopoly capitalism, and spending "colossally" on arms and overseas bases. Like Kennan, the Soviet ambassador was confident of the adversary's instability, only in his case, from a rather shorter-term perspective. America's problem was its British alliance, which was "plagued with great internal contradictions" and bound to explode, probably over differences in the Middle East.

The Truman Doctrine. The alliance, in fact, was in some difficulty, not out of conflicting interests, however, but because of British exhaustion. In February 1947 London informed Truman that it could no longer afford to support the anti-Communists in Greece, where a bitter guerrilla war was going on. If the Communists won in Greece, Truman worried, that would embolden the Communist parties in France and Italy and, of more immediate concern, threaten Soviet domination of the eastern Mediterranean. In response the president announced what

Postwar Devastation

Berlin, Germany, was reduced to rubble during World War II. Allied bombing, followed by brutal fighting in April 1945 when Soviet troops entered Berlin, devastated the once impressive capital city. Here, in a telling statement about the collapse of Hitler's Third Reich, German refugees walk in front of what was once Goebbels's Propaganda Ministry. U.S. policymakers feared that the economic disorder following this type of destruction would make many areas of postwar Europe vulnerable to Communist influence. National Archives.

came to be known as the Truman Doctrine. In a speech to the Republican-controlled Congress on March 12, he asserted an American responsibility "to support free peoples who are resisting attempted subjugation by armed minorities or by outside pressures." To that end, Truman requested large-scale assistance for Greece and Turkey. "If we falter in our leadership, we may endanger the peace of the world," Truman declared, and "we shall surely endanger the welfare of our own nation." Despite the open-endedness of this military commitment, Congress quickly approved Truman's request for $300 million in aid to Greece and $100 million for Turkey.

The Marshall Plan. In the meantime, Europe was sliding into economic chaos. Devastated by the war, it was hit by the worst winter in memory in 1947. People were starving, and European credit was near-ing zero. At Secretary of State George C. Marshall's behest, Kennan's small team of advisers came up with a remarkable proposal: a massive infusion of American capital to help get the European economy back on its feet. Speaking at the Harvard commencement in June 1947, Marshall urged the nations of Europe to work out a comprehensive recovery program and then ask the United States for aid, which would be forthcoming.

Truman's pledge of financial aid to European economies met with significant opposition in Congress. Republicans castigated the Marshall Plan as a huge "international W.P.A." But in the midst of the congressional stalemate, on February 25, 1948, came a Communist coup in Czechoslovakia. A stark reminder of Soviet ruthlessness, the coup rallied congressional support for the Marshall Plan. In March 1948 Congress voted overwhelmingly to approve funds for the program. Like most other foreign-policy initiatives of the 1940s and 1950s, the Marshall Plan won bipartisan support.

Over the next four years, the United States contributed nearly $13 billion to a highly successful recovery effort. Western European economies revived, industrial production increased 64 percent, and the appeal of the local Communist parties waned. The Marshall Plan was actually a good deal for the United States, providing stronger markets for American goods and fostering the economic multilateralism and interdependence it wanted to encourage in Europe (see Voices from Abroad, "Jean Monnet: Truman's Generous Proposal," p. 807). And, most notably, the Marshall Plan was a strategic masterstroke. The Soviets had been invited to participate. At first they did, then Stalin, sensing a trap, ordered his delegation home and, on

further reflection, ordered the satellite delegations home as well. It was a clumsy performance, placing the onus for dividing Europe on the Soviets and depriving their threadbare partners of assistance they sorely needed.

The Berlin Crisis. The flashpoint for a hot war, if it existed anywhere, was Germany. This was because the stakes were so high for both sides and the German situation initially so fluid. At Yalta, Germany's future had been left undecided, except that it would be made to pay heavy reparations and be permanently demilitarized. For the time being, a defeated Germany would be divided into four zones of occupation controlled by the Soviet Union, the United States, Britain, and France. A similar arrangement later applied to Berlin (Map 26.1). As it happened, Anglo-American

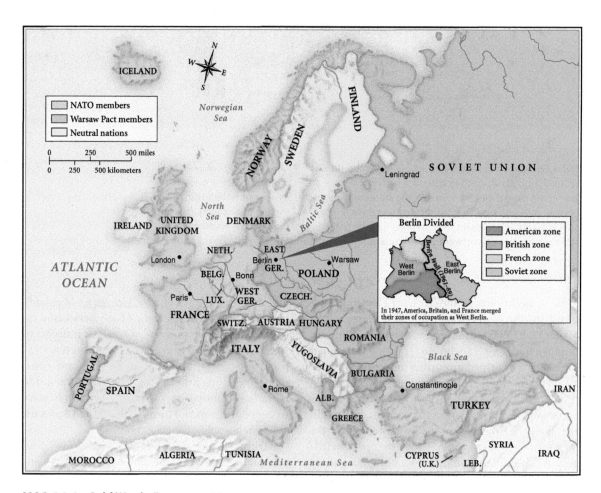

MAP 26.1 Cold War in Europe, 1955

This map vividly shows the Cold War division of Europe as it was in 1955. In green are the NATO countries, allied to the United States; in purple, the Warsaw Pact countries, allied to the USSR. At that point, in 1955, West Germany had just been admitted to NATO, completing Europe's stabilization into two rival camps. But Berlin, Germany's traditional capital, remained divided, and one can see, from its location deep in East Germany, why it was always a flashpoint in Cold War controversies.

Jean Monnet

Truman's Generous Proposal

J ean Monnet was an eminent French statesman and a tireless promoter of postwar European union. As head of a French postwar planning commission, he helped oversee the dispersal of Marshall Plan funds, the importance of which he describes in his memoirs.

So we had at last concerted our efforts to halt France's economic decline; but now, once more, everything seemed to be at risk. Two years earlier [1947], we thought that we had plumbed the depths of material poverty. Now we were threatened with the loss of even basic essentials. . . . Our dollar resources were melting away at an alarming rate, because we were having to buy American wheat to replace the crops we had lost during the winter. . . . A further American loan was soon exhausted.

Nor was this grim situation confined to France. Britain too had come to the end of her resources. In February 1947 she had abruptly cancelled her aid to Greece and Turkey, whose burdens she had seemed able to assume in 1945. Overnight, this abrupt abdication gave the United States direct responsibility for part of Europe. Truman did not hesitate for a moment: with the decisiveness that was to mark his actions as President, he at once asked for credits and arms for both Turkey and Greece. . . . [Soon after], he announced the Truman Doctrine of March 12, 1947. Its significance was general: it meant that the United States would prevent

Europe from becoming a depressed area at the mercy of Communist advance. On the very same day, the Four-Power Conference began in Moscow. There, for a whole month, George Marshall, Ernest Bevin, and Georges Bidault argued with Vyacheslav Molotov about all the problems of the peace, and above all about Germany.

When Marshall returned to Washington, he knew that for a long time there would be no further genuine dialogue with Stalin's Russia. The "Cold War," as it was soon to be known, had begun. . . . Information from a number of sources convinced Marshall and his Under-Secretary Dean Acheson that once again, as in 1941, the United States had a great historic duty. And once again there took place what I had witnessed in Washington a few years earlier: a small group of men brought to rapid maturity an idea which, when the Executive gave the word, turned into vigorous action. This time, it was done by five or six people, in total secrecy and at lightning speed. Marshall, Acheson, [William] Clayton, Averell Harriman, and George Kennan worked out a proposal of unprecedented scope and generosity. It took us all by surprise when we read the speech that George Marshall made at Harvard on June 5, 1947. Chance had led him to choose the University's Commencement Day to launch something new in international relations: helping others to help themselves.

SOURCE: Jean Monnet, *Memoirs*, trans. Richard Mayne (New York: Doubleday, 1978), 264–266.

ANALYZING THE EVIDENCE

➤ Why, according to Monnet, did Europe need massive economic assistance, and fast?

➤ Monnet was writing as an embattled Frenchman about the Marshall Plan. If you compare his account with the textbook's account, what is missing from Monnet's account?

➤ Can you explain, on the basis of Monnet's account of the Marshall Plan, why the North Atlantic Treaty Organization, which was established the following year, proved so durable?

forces, encountering much less German resistance than did the Soviets, could have occupied virtually all of Germany, including Berlin. Churchill pleaded for this, but Roosevelt said no. Even so, Eisenhower's troops ended up a hundred miles inside the Soviet zone at war's end, only to be withdrawn — again over Churchill's protests — at Truman's order. These goodwill gestures proved of no account as tensions mounted and the two sides jockeyed for advantage in Germany. When no agreement for a unified state was forthcoming in 1947, the western allies consolidated their zones and prepared to establish an independent federal German republic, supported by an infusion of Marshall Plan money.

Some of that money was slated for West Berlin, in hopes of making it a capitalist showplace deep inside the Soviet zone. On its face, of course, the Allied presence in Berlin was anomolous, an accident of interim wartime arrangements, and indefensible against the Soviets. That, at any rate, was the way Stalin saw it. In June 1948 he halted all Allied traffic to West Berlin. Instead of giving way, as he had expected, Truman and the British were galvanized into action. They improvised an airlift. For nearly a year American and British pilots, who had been dropping bombs on Berlin only four years earlier, flew in 2.5 million tons of food and fuel — nearly a ton for each resident. The Berlin crisis was the closest the two sides came to actual war, and probably the closest America came — since it had no other military option at the time — to using the atomic bomb against the USSR. But

Stalin backed down. On May 12, 1949, he lifted the blockade. West Berlin became a symbol of resistance to Communism.

The crisis in Berlin persuaded western European nations that they needed a collective security pact with the United States. In April 1949, for the first time since the end of the American Revolution, the United States entered into a peacetime military alliance, the North Atlantic Treaty Organization (NATO). Under the NATO pact, twelve nations — the United States, Canada, Britain, France, Italy, Belgium, the Netherlands, Luxembourg, Denmark, Norway, Portugal, and Iceland — agreed that "an armed attack against one or more of them in Europe or North America shall be considered an attack against them all." In May 1949 those nations also agreed to the creation of the Federal Republic of Germany (West Germany), which joined NATO in 1955. In response, the Soviet Union set up the German Democratic Republic (East Germany) in 1949; an economic association, the Council for Mutual Economic Assistance (COMECON), in 1949; and a military alliance for eastern Europe, the Warsaw Pact, in 1955. In these parallel steps, the two superpowers were institutionalizing the Cold War and thereby translating tense uncertainty into permanent stalemate.

Nuclear Stalemate. The final stage in that process came in September 1949, when American military intelligence detected a rise in radioactivity in the atmosphere — proof that the Soviet Union

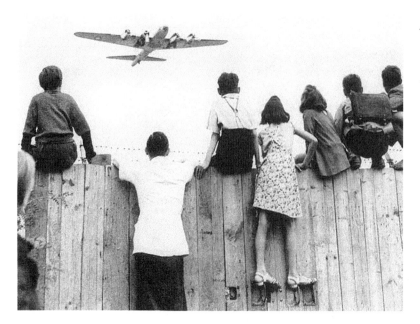

The Berlin Airlift

For 321 days American planes like this one flew missions to bring food and other supplies to Berlin after the Soviet Union had blocked all surface routes into the former German capital. The blockade was finally lifted on May 12, 1949, after the Soviets conceded that it had been a failure. AP Images.

Testing the Bomb

After World War II, the development of nuclear weapons went on apace, requiring frequent testing of the more advanced weapons. This photograph shows members of the 11th Airborne division viewing the mushroom cloud from one such A-bomb test at the Atomic Energy Commission's proving grounds at Yucca flats in Nevada, November 1, 1951. Finally acknowledging the dangers to the atmosphere (and the people in the vicinity or downwind), the United States and the Soviet Union signed a treaty in 1963 banning above-ground testing. J. R. Eyerman/Time Life Pictures/Getty Images.

had detonated an atomic bomb. With America's brief tenure as sole nuclear power over, there was a pressing need for a major reassessment of the nation's strategic planning. Truman turned to the National Security Council (NSC), an advisory body established by the National Security Act of 1947 that also created the Department of Defense and the Central Intellegence Agency (CIA). In April 1950 the NSC delivered its report, known as "NSC-68." Bristling with alarmist rhetoric, the document urged a crash program to maintain America's nuclear edge, including stepped-up production of atomic bombs and the development of a hydrogen bomb, a thermonuclear device a thousand times more destructive than the atomic bombs that had destroyed Hiroshima and Nagasaki. What American intelligence did not know was that Soviet scientists, unlike their American counterparts, had been working on

both tracks all along and were making headway toward a hydrogen bomb. The United States got there first, exploding its first hydrogen bomb in November 1952; the Soviet Union followed in 1953.

Although he accepted the NSC-68 recommendation, Truman had grave misgivings about the furies he was unleashing. This was apparent in his decision to lodge control over nuclear weapons in a civilian agency, not with the military. Truman did not want nuclear weapons incorporated into military planning and treated as a functional part of the nation's arsenal (as they had been at Hiroshima and Nagasaki). Evidence suggests that Stalin, in fact, had similar misgivings. And with the advent of the hydrogen bomb, the utility of nuclear devices as actual weapons shrank to zero. No political objective could possibly be worth the destructiveness of a thermonuclear exchange. One effect was to reinforce the grudging stalemate that had taken hold in Europe. A "balance of terror" now prevailed.

The other, paradoxically, was to magnify the importance of conventional forces. The United States, having essentially demobilized its wartime army, had relied on the atomic bomb as the equalizer against the vast Soviet army. Now, if it wanted a credible deterrent, the only option was a stronger conventional military. To that end, NSC-68 called for increased taxes to finance "a bold and massive program of rebuilding the West's defensive potential to surpass that of the Soviet world." Truman was reluctant to commit to a major defense buildup, fearing that it would overburden the budget. Two months after NSC-68 was completed, events in Asia took that decision out of his hands.

Containment in Asia

Containment aimed primarily at preventing Soviet expansion in Europe. But as tensions built up in Asia, Cold War doctrines began to influence the American position there as well. At first America's attention centered on Japan. After dismantling Japan's military, American occupation forces under General Douglas MacArthur drafted a democratic constitution and oversaw the rebuilding of the economy, paving the way for the restoration of Japanese sovereignty in 1951. Considering the scorched-earth war just ended, this was a remarkable achievement, thanks partly to the imperious MacArthur, but mainly to the Japanese, who put their militaristic past behind them and embraced peace. Trouble on the mainland then drew America's attention, and the Cold War mentality kicked in.

The "Fall" of China. A civil war had been raging in China since the 1930s, as Communist forces led by Mao Zedong (Mao Tse-tung) contended for power with Nationalist forces under Jiang Jieshi (Chiang Kai-shek). Although dissatisfied with the corrupt Jiang regime, American officials did not see Mao as a good alternative, and they resigned themselves to supporting the Nationalists. Between 1945 and 1949 the United States provided more than $2 billion to Jiang's forces, but in August 1949 the Truman administration gave up on the Nationalists and cut off aid. By then their fate was sealed. The People's Republic of China was formally established under Mao on October 1, 1949, and the remnants of Jiang's forces fled to Taiwan.

Initially, the American response was muted. Both Stalin and Truman expected Mao to take an independent line, as the Communist Tito had recently done in Yugoslavia. Mao, however, aligned himself with the Soviet Union, partly out of exaggerated fears that the United States would rearm the Nationalists and send them back to the mainland. As attitudes hardened, many Americans viewed Mao's success as a defeat for the United States. A pro-Nationalist "China lobby" accused Truman's State Department of being responsible for the "loss" of China. Sensitive to these charges, the Truman administration refused to recognize "Red China," and also blocked China's admission to the United Nations, treating the world's most populous country as an international pariah. But the United States pointedly refused to guarantee Taiwan's independence, and in fact accepted the outcome on the mainland. It had not, however, taken account of a country few Americans had ever heard of, Korea, which had been a part of the Japanese Empire since 1910 and whose future now had to be decided.

The Korean War. In Korea, as in Germany, Cold War confrontation grew out of interim arrangements made at the end of the war. The United States and the Soviet Union, both with troops in Korea, had agreed to occupy the nation jointly, dividing their sectors at the thirty-eighth parallel, pending Korea's unification. As tensions rose in Europe, the thirty-eighth parallel hardened into a permanent demarcation line. The Soviets supported a Communist government, led by Kim Il Sung, in North Korea; the United States backed a long-time Korean nationalist, Syngman Rhee, in South Korea. Both were spoiling for a fight, but neither could launch an all-out offensive without the backing of his sponsor. Washington repeatedly said no, and so did Moscow — until Stalin, reading a speech by Secretary of State Dean Acheson declaring South Korea outside America's "defense perimeter," concluded that the United States would not intervene.

On June 25, 1950, the North Koreans launched a surprise attack across the thirty-eighth parallel (Map 26.2). Truman immediately asked the U.N. Security Council to authorize a "police action" against the invaders. Because the Soviet Union was temporarily boycotting the Security Council to protest China's exclusion from the United Nations, it could not veto Truman's request. With the Security Council's approval of a "peacekeeping force," Truman ordered U.S. troops to Korea.

Though fourteen other non-Communist nations sent troops, the rapidly assembled U.N. army in Korea was overwhelmingly American, with General

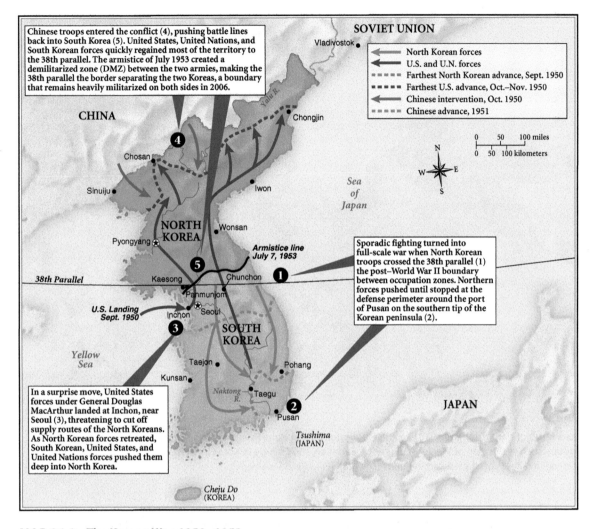

Chinese troops entered the conflict (4), pushing battle lines back into South Korea (5). United States, United Nations, and South Korean forces quickly regained most of the territory to the 38th parallel. The armistice of July 1953 created a demilitarized zone (DMZ) between the two armies, making the 38th parallel the border separating the two Koreas, a boundary that remains heavily militarized on both sides in 2006.

North Korean forces
U.S. and U.N. forces
Farthest North Korean advance, Sept. 1950
Farthest U.S. advance, Oct.–Nov. 1950
Chinese intervention, Oct. 1950
Chinese advance, 1951

Sporadic fighting turned into full-scale war when North Korean troops crossed the 38th parallel (1) the post–World War II boundary between occupation zones. Northern forces pushed until stopped at the defense perimeter around the port of Pusan on the southern tip of the Korean peninsula (2).

In a surprise move, United States forces under General Douglas MacArthur landed at Inchon, near Seoul (3), threatening to cut off supply routes of the North Koreans. As North Korean forces retreated, South Korean, United States, and United Nations forces pushed them deep into North Korea.

MAP 26.2   The Korean War, 1950–1953

The Korean War, which the United Nations officially deemed a "police action," lasted three years and cost the lives of over 36,000 U.S. troops. South and North Korean deaths were estimated at over 900,000. Although hostilities ceased in 1953, the U.S. military and the North Korean army faced each other across the demilitarized zone for the next fifty years.

Douglas MacArthur placed in charge. At first, the North Koreans held an overwhelming advantage, occupying the entire peninsula except for the southeast area around Pusan. But on September 15, 1950, MacArthur launched a surprise amphibious attack at Inchon, far behind the North Korean lines, while U.N. forces staged a breakout from Pusan. Within two weeks the U.N. forces controlled Seoul, the South Korean capital, and almost all the territory up to the thirty-eighth parallel. Although the Chinese government in Beijing warned repeatedly against further incursions, MacArthur's troops crossed the thirty-eighth parallel on October 9, reaching the Chinese border at the Yalu River by the end of the month. Just after Thanksgiving a massive Chinese counterattack of almost 300,000 "volunteers" forced MacArthur's

forces into headlong retreat back down the Korean peninsula. On January 4, 1951, Communist troops reoccupied Seoul.

Two months later American forces and their allies counterattacked, regained Seoul, and pushed back to the thirty-eighth parallel. Then stalemate set in. With public support in the United States for a prolonged war waning, Truman and his advisors decided to work for a negotiated peace.

MacArthur disagreed. Arrogant and brilliant, the general fervently believed that America's future lay in Asia, not Europe. In an inflammatory letter to the House minority leader, Republican Joseph J. Martin of Massachusetts, he denounced the Korean stalemate, declaring "There is no substitute for victory." The strategy backfired. On

The Korean War

As a result of Harry Truman's 1948 executive order, for the first time in the nation's history, all troops, such as the men of the Second Infantry Battalion, shown here in Korea in 1950, served in racially integrated combat units (see p. 853). National Archives.

April 11 Truman relieved MacArthur of his command, accusing him of insubordination. Truman's decision was highly unpopular, but he had the last word. After failing to win the Republican presidential nomination in 1952, MacArthur faded from public view.

The war dragged on for more than two years after MacArthur's dismissal. An armistice was not signed until July 1953, leaving Korea divided at the original demarcation line at the thirty-eighth parallel. North Korea remained firmly allied with the Soviet Union; South Korea signed a mutual defense treaty with the United States in 1954.

The Impact of the Korean War. The Korean War had lasting consequences. Truman's decision to commit troops to Korea without congressional approval set a precedent for future undeclared wars. His refusal to unleash atomic bombs, even when American forces were reeling under a massive Chinese attack, set limiting ground rules for Cold War conflict. The war also expanded American involvement in Asia, transforming containment

into a truly global policy. Finally, it ended Truman's resistance to a major military buildup. Overall defense expenditures grew from $13 billion in 1950, roughly one-third of the federal budget, to $50 billion in 1953, nearly two-thirds of the budget. Although military expenditures dropped briefly after the Korean War, defense spending remained at over $35 billion annually throughout the 1950s. American foreign policy had become more global, more militarized, and more expensive (Figure 26.1). Even in times of peace, the United States now functioned in a state of permanent mobilization.

> Why was the United States unable to avoid entering a Cold War with the Soviet Union?

> How are the ideas of George F. Kennan reflected in Truman's Cold War policies?

> What was the long-term significance of the Korean War?

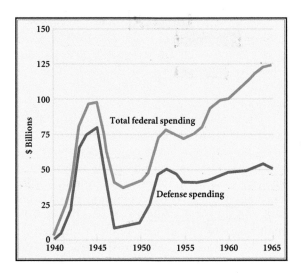

FIGURE 26.1 National Defense Spending, 1940–1965

In 1950 the defense budget was $13 billion, less than a third of total federal outlays. In 1961 defense spending reached $47 billion, fully half of the federal budget and almost 10 percent of the gross domestic product.

The Truman Era

Harry Truman never intended to be a caretaker president. On September 16, 1945, just fourteen days after Japan surrendered and six months after FDR's death, Truman staked his claim to domestic leadership with a plan that called for a dramatic expansion of the New Deal. He intended to fulfill the expansive Economic Bill of Rights that Roosevelt had famously proclaimed in his State of the Union Address in 1944. Truman phrased his proposals in just that way, as rights expected by all Americans — to a "useful and remunerative" job, good housing, "adequate medical care," "protection from the economic fears of old age," and a "good education." Truman had no way of foreseeing on V-J day the confounding forces lying in wait. In the end, his high hopes were crushed, and Truman went down in history not, as he hoped, as FDR's worthy successor, but as a Cold Warrior.

Reconversion

No sooner had Truman finished laying out his ambitious domestic program than he was waylaid by cascading problems over converting the wartime economy to peacetime. Left in the dark about the atomic bomb, government planners had assumed that reconversion would be phased in while Japan

was being subdued. So when the war suddenly ended, no reconversion plan was in place. The hasty dismantling of the vast wartime machine frustrated liberal planners, who had hoped to give small business a headstart in the peacetime market while the big manufacturers were still in war production. What worried Truman, however, was runaway inflation. He wanted to keep the wartime Office of Price Administration (OPA) in place while domestic production caught up with pent-up demand. His efforts at price control were overwhelmed by consumers impatient to spend money and businesses eager to take it from them, with the result that consumer prices soared by 33 percent in the immediate postwar years.

Postwar Strikes and the Taft-Hartley Act. Organized labor was far stronger than it had ever been. Union membership had swelled to over fourteen million by 1945, including two-thirds of all workers in mining, manufacturing, construction, and transportation. Determined to make up for their wartime sacrifices, workers mounted crippling strikes in the automobile, steel, and coal industries. General strikes effectively brought normal life to a halt in half a dozen cities in 1946.

Truman responded erratically. In some cases, he gave way, as, for example, when he lifted price controls on steel in early 1946 so that the industry could grant the wage demands of the strikers. In other instances, Truman tried to show union leaders who was boss. Faced by a devastating railway strike, he threatened to place the nation's railroad system under federal control and asked Congress for the power to draft striking workers into the army — moves that infuriated union leaders but got the strikers back to work. In November 1946, when coal miners called a strike as winter approached, Truman secured a sweeping court order against the union. When its imperious leader John L. Lewis, having been slapped with a huge fine, tried to negotiate, Truman turned him away. He was not going to have "that son of a bitch" in the White House.

If Truman outraged organized labor, an important partner in the Democratic coalition, his display of toughness did little to placate the Republicans, who, having gained control of both houses of Congress in 1946, moved quickly to curb labor's power. In alliance with conservative southern Democrats, they passed the Taft-Hartley Act (1947), a sweeping overhaul of the 1935 National Labor Relations Act. Some of the new provisions aimed at perceived abuses — the **secondary boycott**, crippling national strikes, unionization of supervisory employees. Ultimately of greater significance, however, were skillfully crafted changes in procedures and language that over time eroded the law's stated purpose of protecting the right of workers to organize and engage in collective bargaining. Unions especially disliked Section 14b, which allowed states to pass "right-to-work" laws prohibiting the **union shop**. Truman issued a ringing veto of the Taft-Hartley bill in June 1947, but Congress easily overrode the veto.

The 1948 Election. By 1947, most observers wouldn't have bet a nickel on Truman's future. His popularity ratings had plummeted, and "To err is Truman" had entered the political language. Democrats would have dumped him for 1948 had they found a better candidate. As it was, the party fell into disarray. The left wing split off and formed the Progressive Party, nominating as its candidate Henry A. Wallace, an avid New Dealer whom Truman had fired as secretary of commerce in 1946 because of his vocal opposition to the Cold War. The right-wing challenge came from the South. When northern liberals such as Mayor Hubert H. Humphrey of Minneapolis pushed through a strong civil rights platform at the Democratic convention, the southern delegations bolted and,

calling themselves Dixiecrats, nominated Governor J. Strom Thurmond of South Carolina for president. The Republicans meanwhile renominated Thomas E. Dewey, the politically moderate governor of New York who had run a strong campaign against FDR in 1944.

Truman surprised everyone. He launched a strenuous cross-country speaking tour in which he hammered away at the Republicans for opposing legislation for housing, medical insurance, civil rights, and, in general, for running a "do-nothing" Congress. By combining these issues with attacks on the Soviet menace abroad, Truman began to salvage his troubled campaign. At his rallies enthusiastic listeners shouted, "Give 'em hell, Harry!"

Truman won a remarkable victory, receiving 49.6 percent of the vote to Dewey's 45.1 percent (Map 26.3). The Democrats also regained control of both houses of Congress. Strom Thurmond carried only four southern states, while Henry Wallace failed to win any electoral votes. Truman retained the support of organized labor, Jewish and Catholic voters in the big cities, and black voters in the North. Most important, he appealed effectively to people like himself from the farms, towns, and small cities in the nation's heartland.

Truman Triumphant

In one of the most famous photographs in American political history, Harry S Truman gloats over a headline in the *Chicago Daily Tribune*. Pollsters had predicted an easy victory for Thomas E. Dewey. Their primitive techniques, however, missed the dramatic surge in support for Truman during the last days of the campaign. © Bettmann/Corbis.

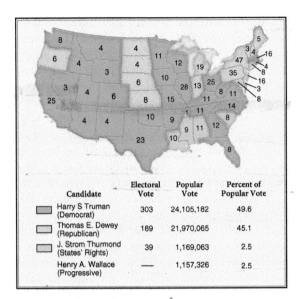

Candidate	Electoral Vote	Popular Vote	Percent of Popular Vote
Harry S Truman (Democrat)	303	24,105,182	49.6
Thomas E. Dewey (Republican)	189	21,970,065	45.1
J. Strom Thurmond (States' Rights)	39	1,169,063	2.5
Henry A. Wallace (Progressive)	—	1,157,326	2.5

MAP 26.3 Presidential Election of 1948

Truman's electoral strategy in 1948 was to concentrate his campaign in areas where the Democrats had their greatest strength. In an election with a low turnout, Truman held onto enough support from Roosevelt's New Deal coalition of blacks, union members, and farmers to defeat Dewey by more than two million votes.

The Fair Deal

In his 1949 State of the Union address, Truman rechristened his program the Fair Deal. It incorporated the goals he had set out initially — national health insurance, aid to education, a housing program, expansion of Social Security, a higher minimum wage, and a new agricultural program — but also struck out in some new directions. In its attention to civil rights (see Chapter 27), the Fair Deal reflected the growing importance of African Americans to the Democratic Party's coalition of urban voters. And the desire to raise the living standards of an ever-greater number of citizens reflected a new liberal vision of the role of the state.

Truman was inspired by the renown English economist, John Maynard Keynes, who had argued that government was capable by means of its fiscal powers of preventing economic depressions. In bad times, deficit spending would "prime the pump," re-igniting consumer spending and private investment and restoring prosperity. The Employment Act of 1946, which asserted the government's responsibility and established a Council of Economic Advisers to assist the president, embodied this Keynesian policy. Truman wanted the Employment Act reinforced by raising its goal to "full" employment and by expanding welfare programs that would undergird consumer purchasing power.

Among the opportunities that came and went, most notable, in light of the nation's current health-care crisis, was the proposal for national health insurance. This was a popular idea, with strong backing from organized labor, but it was denounced as "socialized medicine" by the American Medical Association; the insurance industry (which had spotted a new profit center); and big corporations, which (to their everlasting regret) preferred providing health coverage directly to employees. Lobbying groups were equally effective at defeating Truman's agricultural reforms, which aimed at helping small farmers, and federal aid to education. In the end, the only significant breakthrough, other than improvements in the minimum wage and Social Security, was the National Housing Act of 1949, which authorized the construction of 810,000 low-income units.

Despite Democratic majorities, Congress remained a huge stumbling block. The same conservative coalition that had blocked Roosevelt's initiatives in his second term and dismantled or cut New Deal programs during wartime continued the fight against the Fair Deal. On top of this came the Cold War. The outbreak of fighting in Korea in 1950 was especially damaging, diverting national attention and federal funds from domestic affairs. Another potent diversion was the nation's growing paranoia over internal subversion, the most dramatic manifestation of the Cold War's effect on American life.

The Great Fear (ESPIONAGE)

Was there any significant Soviet penetration of the American government? Historians had mostly debunked the idea and so, in earlier editions, did this textbook. But we were wrong. Records opened up since 1991 — intelligence files in Moscow and, among U.S. sources, most importantly the Venona intercepts of Soviet cables — name among American suppliers of information FDR's assistant secretary of the Treasury Department (Harry Dexter White); FDR's administrative aide (Laughlin Currie); a mid-level, strategically placed group in the State Department (including Alger Hiss, who was with FDR at Yalta); and several hundred more, some identified only by code name, working in a range of government departments and agencies.

What are we to make of this? Many of these enlistees in the Soviet cause were bright young New Dealers in the mid-1930s, when Moscow's Popular Front suggested—to the uninformed, at any rate—that the lines between liberal, progressive, and Communist were blurred and permeable (see Chapter 25). At that time, in the mid-1930s, the United States was not at war, nor ever expected to be. And when war did come, the Soviet Union was an American ally. The flow of stolen documents speeded up and kept Soviet intelligence privy to all aspects of the American war effort. What most interested Stalin was U.S. intentions about a second front and—an obsessive fear of his—a separate deal with Hitler. And, of course, the atomic bomb. Even here, people turned a blind eye to Soviet espionage. Many Los Alamos scientists, indeed, thought it a mistake not to tell the Soviets about the bomb. J. Robert Oppenheimer, the director of the Manhattan Project, was inclined to agree. He just didn't like "the idea of having the [secrets] moved out the back door."

Once the Cold War set in, of course, Oppenheimer's indulgent view of Soviet espionage became utterly inadmissible, and the government moved with great fanfare to crack down. In March 1947 President Truman issued an executive order launching a comprehensive loyalty program for federal employees. Of the activities deemed to be "disloyal," the operative one was membership in any of a list of "subversive" organizations compiled by the attorney general. On that basis, federal loyalty boards mounted witch hunts that wrecked the careers of about ten thousand public servants, not one of whom was ever tried and convicted of espionage.

As for the actual suppliers of information to the Soviets, they seem mostly to have left off spying once the Cold War began. For one thing, the professional apparatus of Soviet agents running them was dismantled or disrupted by stepped-up American counterintelligence work. After the war, moreover, most of these well-connected amateur spies moved on to other careers. The State Department official Alger Hiss, for example, was serving as head of the prestigious Carnegie Endowment for International Peace when he was accused in 1948 by a Communist-turned-informant, Whittaker Chambers, of having passed classified documents to him in the 1930s. Skepticism by historians about internal subversion—that it was insignificant—seems justified if we start in 1947, just when the hue-and-cry about internal subversion was blowing up into a second Red Scare (for the first, see Chapter 22).

HUAC. For this, the Truman administration bore some responsibility. It had legitimized making "disloyalty" the proxy for subversive activity. Others, however, were far more ruthless and adept at this technique, beginning with the House Un-American Activities Committee (HUAC), which Congressman Martin Dies of Texas and other conservatives had launched back in 1938. After the war, HUAC helped spark the Great Fear by holding widely publicized hearings on alleged Communist infiltration in the movie industry. A group of writers and directors, soon dubbed the Hollywood Ten, went to jail for contempt of Congress when they cited the First Amendment while refusing to testify about their past associations. Hundreds of other actors, directors, and writers whose names had been mentioned in the HUAC investigation were unable to get work, victims of an unacknowledged but very real blacklist honored by industry executives.

Following Washington's lead, many state and local governments, universities, political organizations, churches, and businesses undertook their own antisubversion campaigns, which often included the requirement that employees take loyalty oaths. In the labor movement, where Communists had been active as organizers in the 1930s, charges of Communist domination led to the expulsion of a number of industrial unions by the CIO in 1949. Civil rights organizations such as the NAACP and the National Urban League also expelled Communists or "fellow travelers"—words used to describe people viewed as Communist sympathizers although not members of the Communist Party. Thus the Great Fear spread from the federal government to the farthest reaches of American associational, cultural, and economic life.

Here, too, however, revelations from the Soviet archives have complicated the picture. Historians have mostly regard the American Communist Party as a "normal" organization, acting in America's home-grown radical tradition and playing by the rules of the game. Soviet archives clearly show otherwise. The American party was taking money and instructions from Moscow. It was in no way independent, so that, when Communists joined other organizations, not only red-baiters found their participation problematic. Consider the expulsion of the Communist-led industrial unions mentioned above. In 1948 the CIO had gone all-out for Truman's reelection, which was the only hope it had of reversing the hated Taft-Hartley Act. The Communist line was to support Wallace's Progressive Party, and that's what the Communist-led unions did, thereby

The Army-McCarthy Hearings

These 1954 hearings contributed to the downfall of Senator Joseph McCarthy by exposing his reckless accusations and bullying tactics to the huge television audience that tuned in each day. Some of the most heated exchanges took place between McCarthy (center) and Joseph Welch (seated, left), the lawyer representing the army. When the gentlemanly Welch finally asked, "Have you no decency left, sir?" he fatally punctured McCarthy's armor. The audience broke into applause because someone had finally had the courage to stand up to the senator from Wisconsin. © Bettmann/Corbis.

demonstrating that they were Communists first, trade unionists second — a cardinal sin for the labor movement. The expulsions left in their wake the wrecked lives of many innocent, high-minded trade unionists, and that was true wherever anti-Communism took hold, whether in universities, school boards, or civil rights organizations.

McCarthyism. The finale of the Great Fear opened with the meteoric rise of Senator Joseph McCarthy of Wisconsin. In February 1950 McCarthy delivered a bombshell during a speech in Wheeling, West Virginia: "I have in my hand 57 cases of individuals who would appear to be either card-carrying members or certainly loyal to the Communist Party, but who nevertheless are still helping to shape our foreign policy [in the State Department]." McCarthy later reduced his numbers, and he never released any names or proof, but he had gained the attention he sought. For the next four years, he was

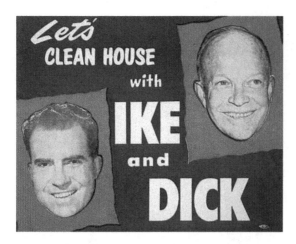

The 1952 Presidential Campaign

The Republican campaign capitalized on scandals involving bribery and influence-peddling that engulfed the Truman administration's second term and on Dwight Eisenhower's popularity. Everyone knew him as "Ike." They didn't particularly know his running mate Richard M. Nixon as "Dick." That was just thrown in for good measure. Collection of Janice L. and David J. Frent.

the central figure in a virulent smear campaign. Critics who disagreed with him exposed themselves to charges of being "soft" on Communism. Truman called McCarthy's charges "slander, lies, character assassination," but could do nothing to curb them. The Republicans, for their part, refrained from publicly challenging their most outspoken senator and, on the whole, were content to reap the political benefits (see Comparing American Voices, "Hunting Communists and Liberals," pp. 820–821).

In early 1954 McCarthy overreached himself by launching an investigation into possible subversion in the U.S. Army. When lengthy hearings—the first of its kind broadcast on the new medium of television—brought McCarthy's smear tactics into the nation's living rooms, support for him declined. In December 1954 the Senate voted 67 to 22 to censure McCarthy for unbecoming conduct. He died from an alcohol-related illness three years later at the age of forty-eight, his name forever attached to a period of political repression of which he was only the most flagrant manifestation.

➤ Why did Harry Truman seem a failure during his first term in the White House?

➤ How does the Fair Deal differ from the New Deal?

➤ Why have historians revised their views about the significance of espionage in American government? Does this make any difference about how we evaluate McCarthyism?

Modern Republicanism

As election day 1952 approached, America seemed ready for change. The question was, How much? With the Republican victory, the country got its answer: Very little. The new president, Dwight D. Eisenhower, set the tone for what his supporters called "modern Republicanism"—an updated GOP approach that aimed at moderating, not dismantling, the New Deal state. Eisenhower and his supporters were—despite themselves—successors of FDR, not Herbert Hoover. Foreign policy revealed a similar continuity. Like their predecessors, Republicans saw the world in Cold War polarities. They embraced the defense buildup begun during the Korean War and pushed containment to the far reaches of the world.

They Liked Ike

The Republicans' problem was that, after twenty years of Democratic rule, they were the minority party. Only one in three registered voters was Republican. The party faithful gave their hearts to Robert A. Taft of Ohio, the Republican leader in the Senate since 1939, but their heads told them that only a moderate, less-well-defined candidate was likely to attract the independent vote. General Eisenhower filled the bill. He was an immensely popular figure, widely admired as the architect of D-Day and victory in Europe. Eisenhower was a man without a political past. Believing that democracy required that the military stand aside, he had never voted. Democrats and Republicans courted him, but it turned out that Eisenhower was a Republican, a believer in balanced budgets and individual responsibility. For regional balance, Eisenhower asked Senator Richard M. Nixon of California to be his running mate. Nixon was youthful, tirelessly partisan, and strongly anti-Communist. He had won his spurs by leading HUAC's investigation of Alger Hiss's espionage past.

The Democrats never seriously considered renominating Harry Truman, who by 1952 was a thoroughly discredited leader, primarily because of the unpopularity of the Korean War, but also because of a series of scandals that Republicans dubbed "the mess in Washington." With a certain relief, the Democrats turned to Governor Adlai E. Stevenson of Illinois, who enjoyed the support of respected liberals, such as Eleanor Roosevelt, and of organized labor. To appease conservative southern voters, the Democrats nominated Senator John A. Sparkman of Alabama for vice president.

Throughout the campaign Stevenson advocated New Deal-Fair Deal policies with an almost literary eloquence. But Eisenhower's artfully unpretentious speeches and "I Like Ike" slogan were more effective with voters. Eager to win the support of the broadest electorate possible, Eisenhower played down specific questions of policy. Instead, he attacked the Democrats with the "K_1C_2" formula — "Korea, Communism, and Corruption."

That November Eisenhower won 55 percent of the popular vote, carrying all the northern and western states and four southern states. His triumph did not translate, however, into a new Republican majority. Republicans regained control of Congress on his coattails, but lost it 1954 and did not recover when Eisenhower easily won reelection over Adlai Stevenson in 1956. For most of his tenure, Eisenhower had to work with a Democratic Congress.

The Hidden-Hand Presidency

Although supremely confident as an international leader, Eisenhower started out a novice in domestic affairs. He did his best to set a quieter national mood after the rancorous Truman years. Disliking confrontation, he was reluctant to speak out against Joe McCarthy, and he was not a leader on civil rights. Yet Eisenhower was no stooge as president. Political scientists have characterized his leadership style as the "hidden-hand presidency." They point out that Eisenhower maneuvered deftly behind the scenes while maintaining a public demeanor of being above the fray. If he sometimes seemed inarticulate and bumbling, that was often a studied effect to mask his real intentions. He in fact ran a tight ship and was always in command.

After 1954, when the Democrats took control over Congress, the Eisenhower administration accepted legislation promoting social welfare. Federal outlays for veterans' benefits, housing, and Social Security were increased, and the minimum wage was raised from 75 cents an hour to $1. The creation of the new Department of Health, Educa-

tion, and Welfare (HEW) in 1953 consolidated government administration of social welfare programs, confirming federal commitments in that area. Welfare expenditures went steadily upward during Eisenhower's tenure, consuming an ever larger share of the federal budget. Like Truman, Eisenhower accepted the government's responsibility for economic performance and, despite his faith in a balanced budget, engaged in deficit spending whenever employment dipped. He intervened even more vigorously when it came to holding in check the inflation sparked by the Korean War.

More striking was the expanded scope of federal activity. In a move that drastically altered America's landscape and driving habits, the National Interstate and Defense Highways Act of 1956 authorized $26 billion over a ten-year period for the construction of a nationally integrated highway system (see Map 27.2, p. 839). To link the Great Lakes with the Atlantic Ocean, the United States and Canada cosponsored in 1959 the construction of the St. Lawrence Seaway. These enormous public works programs surpassed anything undertaken during the New Deal. And when the Soviet Union launched the first satellite, *Sputnik,* in 1957, the startled country went into high gear to catch up in this new Cold War space competition (see Reading American Pictures, "Why a Cold War Space Race?," p. 823). Eisenhower authorized the National Aeronautics and Space Administration (NASA) the following year, and, alarmed that the United States was falling behind in science and technology, he persuaded Congress to appropriate additional money for college scholarships and university research.

Only in the area of natural resources did the Eisenhower administration actually reduce federal activity — turning over offshore oil to the states and private developers, and authorizing privately financed hydroelectric dams on the Snake River. In most other ways — New Deal welfare programs, Keynesian intervention in the economy, new departures in public works, scientific research, higher education — the Eisenhower Republicans had become part of a broad **liberal consensus** in American politics. That was the view of a true conservative, Senator Barry Goldwater of Arizona, who remarked sourly that Ike had run a "Dime Store New Deal."

Eisenhower and the Cold War

Every incoming administration likes to proclaim itself a grand departure from its predecessor.

Hunting Communists and Liberals

The onset of the Cold War created an opportunity for some conservatives to seize on anti-Communism as a weapon to attack the Truman administration. In Senator McCarthy's case, the charge was that the Truman administration was harboring Soviet spies within the government. There was also a broader, more amorphous attack on people not accused of spying but of having Communist sympathies and thus being "security risks" and unsuitable for government positions. For this targeted group, the basis of suspicion was generally membership in organizations that supported policies that overlapped with or seemed similar to policies supported by the Communist Party.

McCARTHYISM
Senator Joseph McCarthy, Speech Delivered in Wheeling, West Virginia, February 9, 1950

Senator McCarthy was actually late getting on board the anti-Communist rocket ship. This was the speech that launched him into orbit. No one ever saw the piece of paper he waved about with the names of fifty-seven spies in the State Department. Over time, the number fluctuated, and never materialized into a single indictable spy. Still, McCarthy had an extraordinary talent for whipping up anti-Communist hysteria. His downfall came in 1954, when the U.S. Senate formally censured McCarthy for his conduct; three years later, he died of alcoholism at the age of 48.

Today we are engaged in a final, all-out battle between communistic atheism and Christianity. The modern champions of communism have selected this as the time. And, ladies and gentlemen, the chips are down — they are truly down. . . .

The reason why we find ourselves in a position of impotency is not because our only powerful potential enemy has sent men to invade our shores, but rather because of the traitorous actions of those who have been treated so well by this Nation. It has not been the less fortunate or members of minority groups who have been selling this Nation out, but rather those who have had all the benefits that the wealthiest nation on earth has had to offer — the finest homes, the finest college education, and the finest jobs in Government we can give. . . .

I have in my hand 57 cases of individuals who would appear to be either card carrying members or certainly loyal to the Communist Party, but who nevertheless are still helping to shape our foreign policy. . . .

THE ORDEAL OF FRANK P. GRAHAM
Fulton Lewis Jr.'s Radio Address, January 13, 1949

The groundwork for McCarthy's anti-Communist crusade was laid by the House Un-American Activities Committee (HUAC), which had been formed in 1938 by conservative southern Democrats seeking to investigate alleged Communist influence around the country. One of its early targets had been Dr. Frank P. Graham, the distinguished president of the University of North Carolina. A committed southern liberal, Graham was a leading figure in the Southern Conference on Human Welfare, the most prominent southern organization supporting the New Deal, free speech, organized labor, and greater rights for southern blacks — causes that some in the South saw as pathways for Communist subversion. After the war, HUAC stepped up its activities and kept a close eye on Dr. Graham.

Among Dr. Graham's duties, one was to serve as the head of the Oak Ridge Institute of Nuclear Studies, a consortium of fourteen southern universities designed to undertake joint research with the federal government's atomic energy facility at Oak Ridge, Tennessee. To enable him to carry on his duties, the Atomic Energy Commission (AEC) granted Dr. Graham a security clearance, overriding the negative recommendation of the AEC's Security Advisory Board. That was the occasion for the following statement by Fulton Lewis Jr., a conservative radio commentator with a nationwide following.

. . . About Dr. Frank P. Graham, president of the University of North Carolina, and the action of the Atomic Energy Commission giving him complete clearance for all atomic secrets despite the fact that the security officer of the commission flatly rejected him . . .

President Truman was asked to comment on the matter today at his press and radio conference, and his reply was that he has complete confidence in Dr. Graham.

. . . The defenders of Dr. Graham today offered the apology that during the time he joined the various subversive and Communist front organizations [like the Southern Conference for Human Welfare] — organizations so listed by the Attorney General of the United States — this country was a co-belligerent with Soviet Russia, and numerous people joined such groups and causes. That argument is going to sound very thin to most American citizens, because the overwhelming majority of us would have no part of any Communist or Communist front connections at any time. . . .

Frank Porter Graham's Telegram to Fulton Lewis Jr., January 13, 1949

One can imagine Graham's shock at hearing himself pilloried on national radio. (He had not even been aware of the AEC's investigation of him.) Following is his response to Lewis.

. . . In view of your questions and implications I hope you will use my statement to provide for my answers. . . . I have always been opposed to Communism and all totalitarian dictatorships. I opposed both Nazi and Communist aggression against Czechoslovakia and the earlier Russian aggression against Finland and later Communist aggression against other countries. . . .

During the period of my active participation, the overwhelming number of members of the Southern Conference were to my knowledge anti-Communists. There were several isolationist stands of the Conference with which I disagreed. The stands which I supported as the main business of the Conference were such as the following: Federal aid to the states for schools; abolition of freight rate discrimination against Southern commerce, agriculture, and industry; anti-poll tax bill; anti-lynching bill; equal right of qualified Negroes to vote in both primaries and general elections; the unhampered lawful right of labor to organize and bargain collectively in our region; . . . minimum wages and social security in the Southern and American tradition. . . .

I have been called a Communist by some sincere people. I have been called a spokesman of American capitalism by Communists and repeatedly called a tool of imperialism by the radio from Moscow. I shall simply continue to oppose Ku Kluxism, imperialism, fascism, and Communism whether in America . . . or behind the "iron curtain."

HOUSE UN-AMERICAN ACTIVITIES COMMITTEE Report on Frank Graham, February 4, 1949

Because of the controversy, HUAC released this report on Dr. Graham.

A check of the files, records and publications of the Committee on Un-American Activities has revealed the following information:

Letterheads dated September 22, 1939, January 17, 1940, and May 26, 1940, as well as the "Daily Worker" of March 18, 1939, . . . reveal that Frank P. Graham was a member of the American Committee for Democracy and Intellectual Freedom. . . . In Report 2277, dated June 25, 1942, the Special Committee on Un-American Activities found that "the line of the American Committee for Democracy and Intellectual Freedom has fluctuated in complete harmony with the line of the Communist Party." The organization was again cited by the Special Committee . . . as a Communist front "which defended Communist teachers." . . .

A letterhead of February 7, 1946, a letterhead of June 4, 1947 . . . and an announcement of the Third Meeting, April 19–21, 1942, at Nashville, Tennessee, reveal that Frank P. Graham was honorary President of the Southern Conference for Human Welfare. . . .

In a report on the Southern Conference for Human Welfare, dated June 16, 1947, the Committee on Un-American Activities found "the most conclusive proof of Communist domination of the Southern Conference for Human Welfare is to be found in the organization's strict and unvarying conformance to the line of the Communist Party in the field of foreign policy. It is also a clear indication of the fact that the real purpose of the organization was not 'human welfare' in the South, but rather to serve as a convenient vehicle in support of the current Communist Party line." . . .

SOURCES: *Congressional Record*, U.S. Senate, 81st Cong., 2d Sess. (Washington, D.C.: GPO, 1950); Frank Porter Graham Papers, University of North Carolina at Chapel Hill Library.

ANALYZING THE EVIDENCE

➤ On what grounds do Fulton Lewis Jr. and HUAC assert that Frank Graham was a security risk? Do they charge that he was a Communist? Is there any evidence in these documents that he might have been a security risk?

➤ How does Graham defend himself? Are you persuaded by his defense?

➤ Do you see any similarity between McCarthy's famous speech at Wheeling, West Virginia, and the suspicions voiced against Dr. Graham by Fulton Lewis Jr. and HUAC a year earlier?

Eisenhower's gesture in this direction was his secretary of state, John Foster Dulles, a lawyer highly experienced in world affairs, but ill-suited by his self-righteous temperament for the craft of diplomacy. Dulles despised "atheistic Communism," and, rather than settling for the status quo, he argued for the "liberation" of the "captive countries" of eastern Europe. This was bombast. The power realities that had called forth containment still applied, as was evident in Eisenhower's first important act as president. Redeeming his campaign pledge to resolve the Korean war, Eisenhower went to Korea. More importantly he stepped up the negotiations that led to an agreement essentially fixing in place the military stalemate at the thirty-eighth parallel.

The Khrushchev Era. Stalin's death in March 1953 precipitated an intraparty struggle in the Soviet Union, which lasted until 1956, when Nikita S. Khrushchev emerged as Stalin's successor. He soon startled Communists around the world by denouncing Stalin and detailing his crimes and blunders. Khrushchev also surprised Westerners by calling for "peaceful coexistence." But any hopes of a thaw evaporated when Hungarians rose up in 1956 and demanded that the country leave the Warsaw Pact. Soviet tanks moved into Budapest and crushed the rebellion—an action the United States condemned but could not realistically resist. Some of the blood was on Dulles's hands because he had embolded the Hungarians with his rhetoric of "rolling back" the Iron Curtain—a pledge that the reality of nuclear weapons made impossible to fulfill.

With no end to the Cold War in sight, Eisenhower turned his attention to containing the cost of containment. Like Truman before him, he hoped to economize by relying on a nuclear arsenal as an alternative to expensive conventional forces. Nuclear weapons delivered "more bang for the buck," explained Defense Secretary Charles E. Wilson. Under the "New Look" defense policy, the Eisenhower administration stepped up production of the hydrogen bomb, approved extensive atmospheric testing, developed the long-range bombing capabilities of the Strategic Air Command, and installed the Distant Early Warning line of radar stations in Alaska and Canada. The Soviets, however, matched the United States weapon for weapon in an escalating arms race. By 1958 both nations had intercontinental ballistic missiles (ICBMs). When an American nuclear submarine launched an atomic-tipped Polaris missile in 1960, Soviet engineers raced to produce an equivalent weapon.

Eisenhower had second thoughts about a nuclear policy aptly named MAD (Mutually Assured Destruction)—based on the premise of annihilating the enemy even if one's own country was destroyed. Eisenhower tried to negotiate an arms-limitation agreement with the Soviet Union. Progress along those lines was cut short, however, when on May 5, 1960, the Soviets shot down an American U-2 spy plane over their territory. Eisenhower at first denied that the plane was engaged in espionage, but when the Soviet Union produced the captured pilot, Francis Gary Powers, Eisenhower admitted that he had authorized secret flights over the Soviet Union. In the midst of the dispute, a proposed summit meeting with Khrushchev was canceled, and Eisenhower's last chance to negotiate an arms agreement evaporated.

Containment in the Post-Colonial World

Containment policy had been devised in response to Soviet threats in Europe but, as intervention in Korea suggested, it was an infinitely expandable concept. The early Cold War era was a time when new nations were emerging across the **Third World**, inspired by powerful anticolonialist movements that went back before World War II. Between 1947 and 1962 the British, French, Dutch, and Belgian empires in the Middle East, Africa, and Asia all but disintegrated. Committed to national self-determination, FDR had favored these developments, often to the fury of his British and French allies. He expected democracies to emerge, new partners in an American-led, free-market world system. But as the Cold War intensified, that confidence began to wane. Both the Truman and Eisenhower administrations often failed to recognize that indigenous nationalist or socialist movements in emerging nations had their own goals and were not necessarily pawns of the Soviet Union.

Believing that nations had to choose sides, the United States tried to draw them into collective security agreements, with the NATO alliance in Europe as a model. Dulles orchestrated the creation of the Southeast Asia Treaty Organization (SEATO), which in 1954 linked America and its major European allies with Australia, Pakistan, Thailand, New Zealand, and the Philippines. An extensive system of defense alliances eventually tied the United States to more than forty other countries (Map 26.4). The United States also signed

Why a Cold War Space Race?

Satellite Space Race. The Michael Barson Collection / Past Perfect.

"Wonder Why We're Not Keeping Pace?" © 1957 by Herblock in *The Washington Post*.

At the center of the Cold War was science—big science, evidenced most dramatically by the continuous development of nuclear weapons and advances in rocket technology. In the 1950s, the physicists who created the first atomic (and then thermonuclear) weapons—Robert Oppenheimer, Edward Teller, and others—became household names and part of the collective face of America's scientific superiority. Then, in 1957, the United States was startled when the Soviets successfully launched *Sputnik,* the first man-made satellite to orbit the earth. Almost overnight, the United States embarked on a "space race" aimed at catching up with and surpassing the Soviet Union, at a cost of billions of dollars and with far-reaching consequences for American education, science, and space exploration. The two illustrations above say something about America's initial reaction to the news about *Sputnik.*

ANALYZING THE EVIDENCE

➤ Few scientific or technological achievements spark a card game, yet *Sputnik* did. Under the rules of the game, anyone dealt the *Sputnik* card lost two turns. What does that tell you?

➤ Herblock was perhaps the most influential and widely syndicated political cartoonist of the Cold War era. What does his cartoon suggest are the reasons the United States didn't beat the Soviets into space?

➤ The Cold War was far more than geopolitical conflict. It was also a competition between rival economic and cultural systems. How is that battle to demonstrate superiority revealed by the *Sputnik* episode? And by the "space race" that followed?

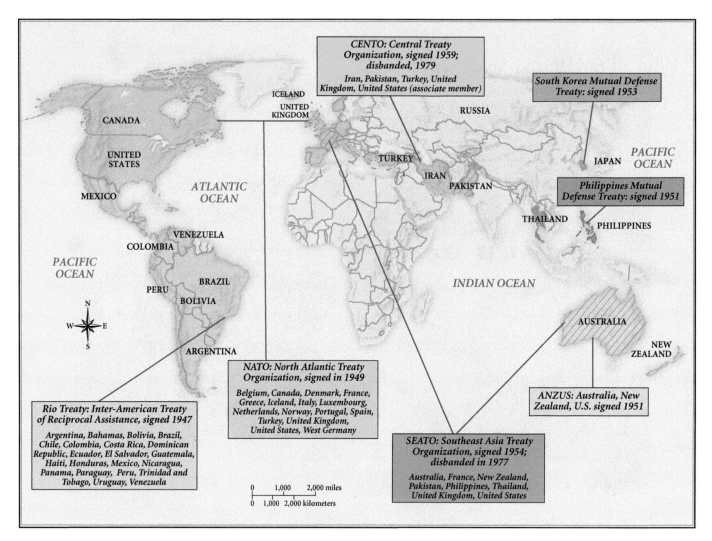

MAP 26.4   American Global Defense Treaties in the Cold War Era

The advent of the Cold War led to a major shift in American foreign policy — the signing of mutual defense treaties. Dating back to George Washington's call "to steer clear of permanent alliances with any portion of the foreign world," the United States had avoided treaty obligations that entailed the defense of other nations. As late as 1919, the U.S. Senate had rejected the principle of "collective security," the centerpiece of the League of Nations established by the Treaty of Versailles that ended World War I. But after World War II, in response to fears of Soviet expansion globally, the United States entered defense alliances with much of the non-Communist world, as this map vividly reveals.

bilateral defense treaties with South Korea and Taiwan, and sponsored a strategically valuable defensive alliance between Iran and Iraq on the southern flank of the Soviet Union.

The Eisenhower administration, less concerned about democracy than stability, tended to support governments, no matter how repressive, that were overtly anti-Communist. Some of America's staunchest allies — the Philippines, Korea, Iran, Cuba, and Nicaragua — were governed by

dictatorships or right-wing regimes that lacked broad-based support. Moreover, Dulles often resorted to covert operations against governments that, in his opinion, were too closely aligned with the Soviets.

For such tasks he used the Central Intelligence Agency (CIA) which had moved beyond its original mandate of intelligence-gathering into active, albeit covert, involvement in the internal affairs of foreign countries, even to the extent of overthrowing several governments. When Iran's nationalist premier, Muhammad Mossadegh, seized British oil properties in 1953, CIA agents helped depose him and installed the young Muhammad Reza Pahlavi as Shah of Iran. In 1954 the CIA engineered a coup in Guatemala against the popularly elected Jacobo Arbenz Guzman, who had expropriated land owned by the American-owned United Fruit Company and accepted arms from Czechoslovakia. Eisenhower specifically approved those CIA efforts. "Our traditional ideas of international sportsmanship," he confessed privately, "are scarcely applicable in the morass in which the world now [1955] flounders."

Vietnam. How Eisenhower's confession might entangle America was already unfolding on a distant stage, in a country of no strategic interest and utterly unknown to most Americans. This was Vietnam, part of French Indochina. When the Japanese occupiers surrendered in August 1945, the nationalist movement that had led the resistance, the Vietminh, seized control, with American encouragement. Their leader, Ho Chi Minh, admired the United States, and when he proclaimed an independent republic, he did so with words drawn from the American Declaration of Independence. But Ho was also a Communist, and as the Cold War took hold, being Communist outweighed America's commitment to self-determination. The next year, when France moved to restore its control over the country, Truman rejected Ho's plea for support in the Vietnamese struggle for independence and sided with France.

Eisenhower picked up where Truman left off. If the French failed, Eisenhower argued, the **domino theory**—a notion that would henceforth bedevil American strategic thinking—would one after the next lead to the collapse of all non-Communist governments in the region. Although the United States eventually provided most of the financing, the French still failed to defeat the tenacious Vietminh. After a fifty-six-day siege in early 1954, the French went down to stunning defeat at the huge fortress of Dienbienphu. The result was the 1954 Geneva Accords, which partitioned Vietnam temporarily at the seventeenth parallel (see Map 28.6, p. 877), committed France to withdraw from north of that line, and called for elections within two years that would lead to a unified Vietnam.

The United States rejected the Geneva Accords and immediately set about undermining them. With the help of the CIA, a pro-American government took power in South Vietnam in June 1954. Ngo Dinh Diem, an anti-Communist Catholic residing in the United States, returned as premier. The next year, in a rigged election, Diem became president of an independent South Vietnam. Facing certain defeat by the popular Ho Chi Minh, Diem called off the reunification elections that were scheduled for 1956. As the last French soldiers left in March 1956, the United States took over, with South Vietnam now the front line in the American battle to contain Communism in Southeast Asia. To prop him up, the Eisenhower administration sent Diem an average of $200 million a year in aid and stationed approximately 675 American military advisors in Saigon, the capital. Few Americans, including probably Eisenhower himself, had any inkling where this might lead.

The Middle East. If Vietnam was still of minor concern, the same could not be said for the Middle East, an area rich in oil and complications. The Zionist movement had long encouraged Jews to return to their ancient homeland of Israel (Palestine). After World War II, many survivors of the Nazi extermination camps resettled in Palestine, which

Future Israelis

In 1945 these survivors of the Buchenwald concentration camp, like many other Jewish survivors of Hitler's gas ovens, resettled in Palestine. International guilt over the Holocaust was one of the factors that led the United Nations in 1947 to the acceptance of a Jewish state and to the partition of Palestine making such a state possible. National Archives.

was still controlled by Britain under a World War I mandate (see Chapter 22). On November 29, 1947, the U.N. General Assembly voted to partition Palestine, between Jewish and Arab sectors. When the British mandate ended, Zionist leaders proclaimed the state of Israel. The Arab League nations invaded, but Israel survived. Many Palestinians fled or were driven from their homes during the fighting. The Arab defeat, which meant they could not return, left them permanently stranded in refugee camps. President Truman quickly recognized the new state, winning crucial support from Jewish voters in the 1948 election, but alienating the Arabs.

Long dominant in the Persian Gulf, Britain began a general withdrawal after giving up the mandate in Palestine. Two years after gaining independence from Britain, Egypt in 1954 came under the rule of Gamal Abdel Nasser, who pro-

claimed a form of pan-Arab socialism that aimed at leading the entire Middle East out of its dependent, colonial relationship with the West. When Nasser obtained promises of help from the Soviet Union in building the Aswan Dam on the Nile, Secretary of State Dulles countered with an offer of American assistance. Nasser refused to distance himself from the Soviets, however, and Dulles abruptly withdrew his offer in July 1956. A week later Nasser retaliated, nationalizing the Suez Canal, through which three-quarters of western Europe's oil was transported. After several months of fruitless negotiation, Britain and France, in alliance with Israel, attacked Egypt and retook the canal. The attack came just as Eisenhower was condemning the Soviet invasion of Hungary. The president demanded that France and Britain pull back. Egypt retook the Suez Canal and built the Aswan Dam with Soviet support.

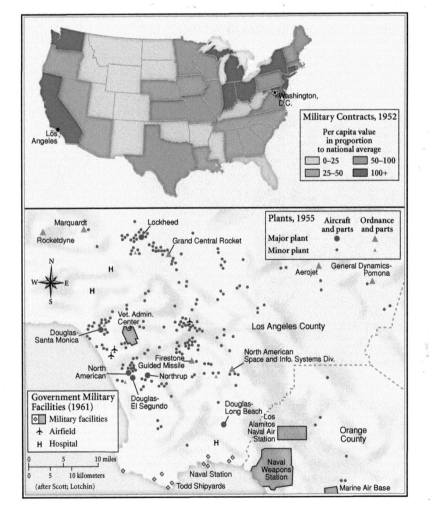

MAP 26.5 The Military-Industrial Complex

Defense spending gave a big boost to the Cold War economy, but, as the upper map suggests, the benefits were by no means equally distributed. The big winners were the Middle Atlantic states, the industrialized upper Midwest, Washington State (with its aircraft and nuclear plants), and California. The epicenter of California's military-industrial complex was Los Angeles, which, as is evident in the lower map, was studded with military facilities and major defense contractors like Douglas Aircraft, Lockheed, and General Dynamics. There was work a-plenty for engineers and rocket scientists.

The Suez Crisis, 1956

In this photograph, Egyptian President Gamal Abdel Nasser is greeted ecstatically by Cairo crowds after he nationalized the Suez Canal. Nasser's gamble paid off. Thanks to American intervention, military action by Britain, France, and Israel failed, and Nasser emerged the triumphant voice of Arab nationalism across the Middle East. The popular emotions he unleashed against the West survived his death in 1970 and are more potent today than ever, although now expressed more through Islamic fundamentalism than Nasser's brand of secular nationalism. Getty Images.

In early 1957, concerned that the USSR might step into the vacuum left by the British, the president announced the Eisenhower Doctrine, which stated that American forces would assist any nation in the region "requiring such aid, against overt armed aggression from any nation controlled by International Communism." Later that year, Eisenhower invoked the doctrine when he sent the U.S. Sixth Fleet to the Mediterranean Sea to aid King Hussein of Jordan against a Nasser-backed revolt. A year later he landed 14,000 troops to back up a pro-American government in Lebanon. The Eisenhower Doctrine was further proof of the global reach of containment, in this instance, accentuated by the strategic need to protect the West's access to steady supplies of oil.

Eisenhower's Farewell Address

In his final address to the nation, Eisenhower warned against the power of what he called the "military-industrial complex," which by then was employing 3.5 million Americans (Map 26.5). Its pervasive influence, he said, "is felt in every city, every statehouse, every office of the federal government." Even though his administration had fostered this growing defense establishment, Eisenhower was gravely concerned about its implications for a democratic people: "We must guard against the acquisition of unwarranted influence, whether sought or unsought, by the military-industrial complex," he warned. "We must never let the weight of this combination endanger our liberties or democratic processes." With those words Dwight Eisenhower showed how well he understood the impact of the Cold War on American life. Only by vigilance could the democratic values of a free people be preserved in an age of constant global struggle.

➤ Why do we say that Eisenhower was heir to FDR, not Herbert Hoover?

➤ Was Eisenhower an adherent to the concept of containment? How so?

➤ Why was America's deepening involvement in the Third World a phenomenon of the 1950s rather than the 1940s?

SUMMARY

We have seen how the Cold War began as a conflict between the United States and the Soviet Union over eastern Europe. Very early in the conflict the United States adopted a strategy of containment, and although initially intended only for Europe, the strategy quickly expanded to Asia when China was "lost" to Mao's Communists. The first effect of that expansion was the Korean War, after which, under Eisenhower, containment of Communism became America's guiding principle across the Third World. Cold War imperatives meant a major military buildup, a scary nuclear arms race, and unprecedented entanglements across the globe.

We have also seen how, on the domestic front, Truman started out with high hopes for an expanded New Deal, only to be stymied by the problems of reconversion, by resistance from Congress, and by competing spending demands of the Cold War. The greatest Cold War–inspired distraction, however, was a climate of fear over internal subversion by Communists that gave rise to McCarthyism. Truman's successor, Dwight Eisenhower, brought the Republicans back into power. Although personally conservative, Eisenhower actually proved a New Dealer in disguise.

He declined to cut back on social welfare programs and broke new ground in federal spending on highways, scientific research, and higher education. When he left office, it seemed that a "liberal consensus" prevailed, with old-fashioned, laissez-faire conservativism mostly marginalized.

Connections: Diplomacy and Politics

In the essay opening Part Six, we started with Walter Lippmann's boast at the close of World War II that "what Rome was to the ancient world . . . America is to be for the world of tomorrow." His confidence in America's future rested in part on his expectation that the Grand Alliance described in Chapter 25 would be durable. Had he gone further back to World War I (see Chapter 21), Lippmann might not have been so optimistic. Woodrow Wilson's hostile response to the Russian revolution had assumed that the two systems were irreconcilable, a belief that the Soviets fully shared. Once the Cold War began after 1945, it became the dominant event in American diplomatic history for the next half-century. In the case of the liberal consensus, its roots in the New Deal (Chapter 24) are entirely clear. Between 1945 and 1960, the liberal consensus held sway, even during Eisenhower's presidency, but after peaking in the mid-1960s with Johnson's Great Society (Chapter 28), it went into decline. The New Deal structure itself remained durable, despite the reaction against the War on Poverty, but the Democratic Party's grip on the country began to fail, and by the close of the Carter administration, conservatism and the Republican Party were clearly in the ascendancy (Chapter 29).

CHAPTER REVIEW QUESTIONS

➤ What factors gave rise to the Cold War between the United States and the Soviet Union?

➤ In what ways were President Truman's and Eisenhower's foreign policies similar? How did they differ?

➤ What was the domestic impact of the anti-Communist crusade of the late 1940s and 1950s?

TIMELINE

1945	Yalta and Potsdam conferences
	Harry S Truman succeeds Roosevelt
	End of World War II
	Senate approves U.S. participation in United Nations
1946	George Kennan outlines containment policy
	Baruch Plan for international control of atomic weapons fails
	War begins between French and Vietminh over control of Vietnam
1947	Taft-Hartley Act limits union power
	House Un-American Activities Committee (HUAC) investigates film industry
	Truman Doctrine promises aid to governments resisting Communism
	Marshall Plan aids economic recovery in Europe
1948	Communist coup in Czechoslovakia
	Truman signs executive order desegregating armed forces
	State of Israel created
	Stalin blockades West Berlin; Berlin airlift begins
1949	North Atlantic Treaty Organization (NATO) founded
	Soviet Union detonates atomic bomb
	Mao Zedong establishes People's Republic of China
1950–1953	Korean War
1950	Joseph McCarthy's "list" of Communists in government
	NSC-68 calls for permanent mobilization
1952	Dwight D. Eisenhower elected president
1953	Stalin dies
1954	Army-McCarthy hearings on army subversion
	French defeat at Dienbienphu in Vietnam
	Geneva Accords partition Vietnam at seventeenth parallel
1956	Crises in Hungary and at Suez Canal
	Interstate Highway Act
1957	Soviet Union launches *Sputnik*
1958	National Aeronautics and Space Administration (NASA) established
1960	U-2 incident leads to cancellation of U.S.-USSR summit meeting
1961	Eisenhower warns nation against military-industrial complex

FOR FURTHER EXPLORATION

James T. Patterson, *Grand Expectations: The United States, 1945–1974* (1996), offers a detailed, comprehensive account of this period. For a reconsideration of the Cold War from a post–Cold War perspective, see especially John Lewis Gaddis, *We Now Know: Rethinking Cold War History* (1997), and, for a more wide-ranging analysis, *The Cold War: A New History* (2005). On the Fair Deal, the best treatment is Alonso Hamby, *Beyond the New Deal: Harry S. Truman and American Liberalism* (1973). Jennifer Klein, *For All These Rights* (2003), is a probing analysis of why the United States failed to develop a national healthcare system. On McCarthyism, David Oshinsky, *A Conspiracy So Immense: The World of Joe McCarthy* (1983), is excellent. Key books containing documents and analysis of Soviet espionage are John E. Haynes and Harvey Klehr, *The Secret World of American Communism* (1995), and *Venona: Decoding Soviet Espionage in America* (1999). On the 1950s, see J. Ronald Oakley, *God's Country: America in the Fifties* (1986). David Halberstam's *The Fifties* (1993) offers a brief but searing account of CIA covert activities in Iran and Guatemala.

The Woodrow Wilson International Center for Scholars has established the Cold War International History Project at **www.wilsoncenter.org/index.cfm?topic_id=1409&fuseaction=topics.home**, an exceptionally rich Web site offering documents on the Cold War, including materials from former Communist-bloc countries. The Center for the Study of the Pacific Northwest's site, "The Cold War and Red Scare in Washington State," at **www.washington.edu/uwired/outreach/cspn/curcan/main.html**, provides detailed information on how the Great Fear operated in one state. Its bibliography includes books, documents, and videos. Project Whistlestop: Harry Truman at **www.trumanlibrary.org/whistlestop/student_guide.htm**, a program sponsored by the U.S. Department of Education, is a searchable collection of images and documents from the Harry S Truman Presidential Library. The site is organized into categories such as the origins of the Truman Doctrine, the Berlin airlift, the desegregation of the armed forces, and the 1948 presidential campaign. Users can also browse through the president's correspondence. "Korea + 50: No Longer Forgotten" is cosponsored by the Harry S Truman and Dwight D. Eisenhower Presidential Libraries, at **www.trumanlibrary.org/korea**. It offers official documents, oral histories, and photographs connected to the Korean War. It also features an audio recording of President Truman's recollections of his firing of General MacArthur in 1951.

TEST YOUR KNOWLEDGE

To assess your command of the material in this chapter, see the Online Study Guide at **bedfordstmartins.com/henretta**.

For Web sites, images, and documents related to topics and places in this chapter, visit **bedfordstmartins.com/makehistory**.

The Saturday Evening

POST

June 4, 1955 - 15¢

America's Mighty Mile:
THE SOO

LOOK, MOM—NO WHEELS!
The Vehicle That Floats on Land

Sargent

27 The Age of Affluence
1945–1960

I N 1959, VICE PRESIDENT RICHARD NIXON traveled to Moscow to open the American National Exhibit. It was the height of the Cold War. After sipping Pepsi-Cola, Nixon and Soviet Premier Nikita Khrushchev got into a heated debate about the relative merits of Soviet and American societies. Standing in the kitchen of a model American home, they talked dishwashers, toasters, and televisions, not rockets, submarines, and missiles. Images of the "kitchen debate" flashed across TV screens around the world.

What was so striking about the Moscow exhibition was the way its American planners enlisted affluence and mass consumption in service to Cold War politics. The suburban lifestyle trumpeted at the exhibition symbolized the superiority of capitalism over Communism.

During the postwar era, Americans did enjoy the highest standard of living in the world. But behind the affluence, everything was not as it seemed. The suburban calm masked contradictions in women's lives and cultural rebelliousness among young people. Suburban growth often came at the expense of urban life, sowing the seeds of inner-city decay and exacerbating racial tensions. Nor was prosperity ever as widespread as the Moscow exhibit implied. The suburban lifestyle was beyond the reach of the working poor, Spanish-speaking immigrants, and most African Americans. And in the South, a civil rights revolution was in the making.

Economic Powerhouse
Engines of Economic Growth
The Corporate Order
Labor-Management Accord

The Affluent Society
The Suburban Explosion
The Search for Security
Consumer Culture
The Baby Boom
Contradictions in Women's Lives
Youth Culture
Cultural Dissenters

The Other America
Immigrants and Migrants
The Urban Crisis
The Emerging Civil Rights Struggle

Summary
Connections: Economy

◀ **Life in the Suburbs**

In the 1950s the *Saturday Evening Post* celebrated the suburban ideal: family, leisure, and a nurturing wife and mother. © 1959 SEPS: Licensed by Curtis Publishing Company, Indianapolis, IN. All rights reserved. www.curtispublishing.com.

Economic Powerhouse

The United States enjoyed overwhelming political and economic advantages at the end of World War II. Unlike the Soviet Union, western Europe, and Japan, America emerged physically unscathed from the war and poised to take advantage of the postwar boom. Dominated by giant corporations, the American economy benefited from stable internal markets, heavy investment in research and development, and the rapid diffusion of new technology. For the first time, employers generally accepted collective bargaining, which for workers translated into rising wages, expanding benefits, and a growing rate of home ownership. At the heart of this postwar prosperity lay the involvement of the federal government. Federal outlays for defense and domestic programs gave a huge boost to the economy. Not least, the federal government recognized that prosperity rested on global foundations.

Engines of Economic Growth

By the end of 1945, war-induced prosperity launched the United States into an era of unprecedented economic growth. Pent-up demand after years of wartime mobilization made Americans eager to spend. Business applied scientific and technological innovations developed for military purposes, such as plastics and synthetic fibers, to the production of consumer goods. Over the next two decades, the gross domestic product (GDP) tripled, benefiting a wider segment of society than anyone would have dreamed possible in the dark days of the Depression.

The Bretton Woods System. American global supremacy rested in part on economic institutions created at a United Nations conference at Bretton Woods, New Hampshire, in July 1944. The International Bank for Reconstruction and Development (known commonly as the World Bank) provided private loans for the reconstruction of war-torn Europe as well as for the development of Third World countries. A second institution, the International Monetary Fund (IMF), was set up to stabilize the value of currencies and provide a predictable monetary environment for trade, with the U.S. dollar serving as the benchmark for other currencies. The United States dominated the World Bank and the IMF because it contributed the most capital and the strongest currency. In 1947, multinational trade negotiations resulted in the first General Agreement on Tariffs and Trade (GATT), which led to the establishment of an international body to oversee trade rules and practices.

The World Bank, the IMF, and GATT were the cornerstones of the so-called Bretton Woods system that guided the world economy after the war. These international organizations encouraged stable prices, the reduction of tariffs, flexible domestic markets, and international trade based on fixed exchange rates. The Bretton Woods system effectively served America's conception of the global economy, paralleling America's ambitious diplomatic aims in the Cold War.

The Kitchen Debate

At the Moscow Fair in 1959, the United States put on display the technological wonders of American home life. When Vice President Richard Nixon visited, he and Soviet Premier Nikita Khrushchev got into a heated debate over the relative merits of their rival systems, with the up-to-date American kitchen as a case in point. This photograph shows the debate in progress. Khrushchev is the bald man pointing his finger at Nixon. On the other side of Nixon stands Leonid Brezhnev, who would be Khrushchev's successor. Getty Images.

The Military-Industrial Complex. A second linchpin of postwar prosperity was defense spending. The military-industrial complex that President Eisenhower identified in his 1961 Farewell Address had its roots in the business-government partnerships of the world wars. But unlike after 1918, the massive commitment of government dollars for defense continued after 1945. Even though the country was technically at peace, the economy and the government operated practically on a war footing—in a state of permanent mobilization.

Based at the sprawling Pentagon in Arlington, Virginia, the Defense Department evolved into a massive bureaucracy. Defense-related industries entered into long-term relationships with the Pentagon in the name of national security. Some companies did so much business with the government that they became dependent on Defense Department orders. Over 60 percent of the income of Boeing, General Dynamics, and Raytheon eventually came from military contracts, while Lockheed received 81 percent and Republic Aviation 100 percent. All of them were giant enterprises, made even bigger by the Pentagon's inclination to favor the largest firms.

As permanent mobilization took hold, science, industry, and the federal government became increasingly intertwined. According to the National Science Foundation, federal money underwrote 90 percent of the cost of research on aviation and space, 65 percent of that on electricity and electronics, 42 percent of that on scientific instruments, and 24 percent of that on automobiles. With the government footing part of the bill, corporations transformed new ideas into useful products with amazing speed. After the Pentagon backed IBM's investment in integrated circuits in the 1960s, those new devices, which were crucial to the computer revolution, entered commercial production within three years.

The growth of this military-industrial establishment had a dramatic impact on national priorities. Between 1900 and 1930, excepting World War I, the country spent less than 1 percent of GDP on the military. By the early 1960s the figure had risen to nearly 10 percent. The defense buildup created jobs, and lots of them. Taking into account the indirect benefits (the additional jobs created to serve and support defense workers), perhaps one worker in seven nationally owed his or her job to the military-industrial complex. But increased military spending also limited the resources for domestic social needs. Critics of military spending calculated the trade-offs: The cost of a nuclear aircraft carrier and support ships equaled that of a subway system

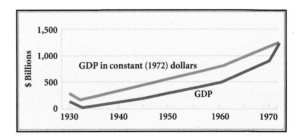

FIGURE 27.1 Gross Domestic Product, 1930–1972

After a sharp dip during the Great Depression, the GDP rose steadily in both real and constant dollars in the postwar period.

for Washington, D.C.; the money spent on one Huey helicopter could have built sixty-six units of low-income housing.

The Economic Record. America's annual GDP jumped from $213 billion in 1945 to more than $500 billion in 1960; by 1970, it exceeded $1 trillion (see Figure 27.1). To working Americans, this sustained economic growth meant a 25 percent rise in real income between 1946 and 1959. Postwar prosperity also featured low inflation. After the postwar reconversion period, inflation slowed to 2 to 3 percent annually during the 1950s, and it stayed low until the escalation of the Vietnam War in the mid-1960s. Low inflation meant stable and predictable prices. Feeling secure about the present and confident about the future, most Americans rightly felt that they were better off than they had ever been before. In 1940, 43 percent of American families owned their homes; by 1960, 62 percent did. Prosperity, as measured by the rate of income growth at different income levels, was quite equally distributed. Families in the 95th percentile did no better than lower-income families; the fastest rate of income growth, in fact, was at the 60th percentile.

Even so, the picture was not entirely rosy. The distribution of income remained stubbornly skewed, with the top 10 percent of Americans earning more than the bottom 50 percent. Moreover, the economy was plagued by periodic recessions, damaging especially to the most disadvantaged Americans. In *The Affluent Society* (1958) the economist John Kenneth Galbraith argued that the poor were only an "afterthought" in the minds of economists and politicians. Yet, as Galbraith noted, one in thirteen families at the time earned less than $1,000 a year.

The Corporate Order

For over half a century, American enterprise had favored the consolidation of economic power into big corporate firms. That tendency continued — indeed, it accelerated — as domestic and world markets increasingly overlapped after 1945. In 1970 the top four U.S. carmakers produced 91 percent of all motor vehicles sold in the country; the top four in tires produced 72 percent, in cigarettes 84 percent, and in detergents 70 percent. Despite laws restricting branch banking to a single state, in 1970 the four largest banks held 16 percent of the nation's banking assets; the top fifty banks held 48 percent.

The classic, vertically integrated corporation of the early twentieth century had produced a single line of products that served a national market (see Chapter 17). This strategy worked even better in the 1950s, when sophisticated media advertising enabled large corporations to break into hitherto resistant markets, for example, beer, where loyalty to local brews in their infinite variety was legendary. To erode that preference, Anheuser-Busch and other national producers sponsored televised sports, parlaying the aura of championship games into national acceptance of their standardized, "lighter" beers. "Bud, the King of Beers" — just as good for the little guy as for the big-league star. By 1970, big multiplant brewers controlled 70 percent of the beer market.

To this well-honed approach, national firms now added a new strategy of diversification. CBS, for example, hired the Hungarian inventor Peter Goldmark, who perfected color television during the 1940s, long-playing records in the 1950s, and a video recording system in the 1960s. As the head of CBS Laboratories, Goldmark patented more than a hundred new devices and created multiple new markets for his happy employer. Because big outfits like CBS had the deepest pockets, they were the firms best able to diversify through investment in industrial research.

More revolutionary was the sudden rise of the conglomerates, giant enterprises comprised of firms in unrelated industries. Conglomerate-building resulted in the nation's third great merger wave (the first two had taken place in the 1890s and the 1920s). Because of their diverse holdings, conglomerates shielded themselves from instability in any single market and seemed better able to compete globally. International Telephone and Telegraph transformed itself into a conglomerate by acquiring Continental Baking (famous for Wonder Bread), Sheraton Hotels, Avis Rent-a-Car, Levitt

and Sons home builders, and Hartford Fire Insurance. Ling-Temco-Vought, another conglomerate, produced steel, built ships, developed real estate, and brought cattle to market.

Expansion into foreign markets also spurred corporate growth. At a time when "made in Japan" still meant shoddy workmanship, U.S. products were considered the best in the world. American firms expanded into foreign markets when domestic demand became saturated or when recessions cut into sales. During the 1950s U.S. exports nearly doubled, giving the nation a trade surplus of close to $5 billion in 1960. By the 1970s, Gillette, IBM, Mobil, and Coca-Cola made more than half their profits from abroad.

In their effort to direct such giant enterprises, managers placed more emphasis on planning. Companies recruited top executives who had business-school training, the ability to manage information, and skills in corporate planning, marketing, and investment. A new generation of corporate chieftains emerged, operating in a complex environment that demanded long-range forecasting and close coordination with investment banks, law firms, the federal government, the World Bank, and the IMF.

The New Managerial Class. To man their bureaucracies, the postwar corporate giants required a huge supply of white-collar foot soldiers. They turned to the universities, which, fueled partly by the GI Bill, grew explosively after 1945. Better educated than their elders, the members of the new managerial class advanced more quickly, and at a younger age, into responsible jobs. As one participant-observer remarked: "If you had a college diploma, a dark suit, and anything between the ears, it was like an escalator; you just stood there and moved up." (He was talking about men; few women gained entrance to the managerial ranks.)

Corporations offered lifetime employment, but they also expected lifetime loyalty. Atlas Van Lines, in the business of moving them, estimated that corporate managers were transferred an average of fourteen times — once every two and a half years — during their careers. Perpetually mobile IBM managers joked that the company's initials stood for "I've Been Moved."

Climbing the corporate ladder rewarded men without hard edges — the "well adjusted." In *The Lonely Crowd* (1950) the sociologist David Reisman contrasted the independent businessmen and professionals of earlier years with the managerial class of the postwar world. He concluded that the new corporate men were "other-directed," more attuned

Organization Men (and a Few Women)

What happened when the 5:57 P.M. discharged commuters in Park Forest, Illinois, a suburb of Chicago? This was the subject of William H. Whyte's *The Organization Man* (1956). Were these hordes of commuters thinking about their stressful workdays at the office or the martinis waiting for them when they walked in the doors of their suburban homes? Photo by Dan Weiner, Courtesy Sarah Weiner.

to their associates than driven by their own goals. The sociologist William Whyte painted a somber picture of "organization men" who left the home "spiritually as well as physically to take the vows of organization life." A recurring theme of the 1950s, in fact, was that the conformity demanded of the man in the gray flannel suit (the title of Sloan Wilson's popular novel) was stifling creativity and blighting lives.

Labor-Management Accord

For blue-collar workers, collective bargaining became for the first time the normal means for determining how their labor would be rewarded. Anti-union employers had fought long and hard against collective bargaining, confining organized labor to a narrow band of craft trades and a few industries, primarily coal mining, railroading, and stove manufacture. The power balance shifted during the Great Depression (see Chapter 24), and by the time the dust settled after World War II, labor unions overwhelmingly represented America's industrial work force (Figure 27.2). The question then became: How would labor's power be used?

In late 1945, Walter Reuther of the United Auto Workers (UAW) challenged General Motors in a fundamental way. The youthful Reuther was thinking big, beyond a single company, or even a single industry. He aimed at nothing less than a reshaped, high-employment economy. To jumpstart it, he demanded a 30 percent wage hike with no price increase for GM cars, and when General Motors said no, it couldn't afford that, Reuther demanded that the company "open the books."

General Motors implacably resisted this "opening wedge" into the rights of management. The company took a 113-day strike, rebuffed the government's intervention, and soundly defeated the UAW. Having made its point, General Motors laid out the terms for a durable relationship. It would accept the UAW as its bargaining partner

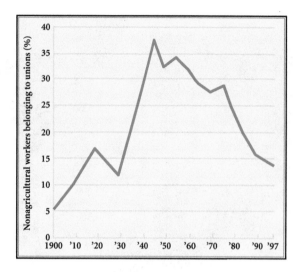

FIGURE 27.2   Labor Union Strength, 1900–1997

Labor unions reached their peak strength immediately after World War II, when they represented close to 40 percent of the nonfarm workforce. Although there was some decline after the mid 1950s, unions still represented nearly 30 percent in 1973. Thereafter, their decline was precipitous. SOURCE: AFL-CIO Information Bureau, Washington, D.C.

and guarantee GM workers an ever higher living standard. The price was that the UAW abandon its assault on the company's "right to manage." On signing the five-year GM contract of 1950 — the Treaty of Detroit, it was called — Reuther accepted the company's terms.

The Treaty of Detroit opened the way for a more broadly based "labor-management accord" — not industrial peace, because the country still experienced many strikes, but general acceptance of collective bargaining as the method for setting the terms and conditions of employment. For industrial workers, the result was rising real income, from $54.92 a week in 1949 to $71.81 (in 1947–1949 dollars) in 1959. The average worker with three dependents gained 18 percent in spendable real income in that period. In addition, collective bargaining delivered greater leisure (more paid holidays and lengthier vacations) and, in a startling departure, a social safety net.

In postwar Europe, America's allies were constructing welfare states. That was the preference of American unions as well. But having lost the bruising battle in Washington for national health care, the unions turned to the bargaining table. By the end of the 1950s, union contracts commonly provided defined-benefit pension plans (supplementing Social Security); company-paid health insurance; and, for two million workers, mainly in steel and auto, a guaranteed annual wage (via supplementary unemployment benefits). Collective bargaining had become, in effect, the American alternative to the European welfare state.

The sum of these union gains was a new sociological phenomenon, the "affluent" worker — as evidenced by relocation to the suburbs, by homeownership, by increased ownership of cars and other durable goods, and, an infallible sign of rising expectations, by installment buying. For union workers, the contract became, as Reuther boasted, the passport into the middle class. Generally overlooked, however, were the many unorganized workers with no such passport — those consigned to casual labor or low-wage jobs in the service sector. In retrospect, economists recognized that America had developed a two-tiered, inequitable labor system.

The labor-management accord that generated the good life for so many workers seemed in the 1950s absolutely secure. The union rivalries of the 1930s abated. In 1955 the industrial-union and craft-union wings joined together in the AFL-CIO, representing 90 percent of the nation's 17.5 million union members. At its head stood George Meany, a cigar-chomping former New York plumber who, in his blunt way, conveyed the reassuring message that organized labor had matured and was management's fit partner.

The labor-management accord, impressive though it was, never was as durable as it seemed. Vulnerabilities lurked, even in the accord's heyday. For one thing, the sheltered markets — the essential condition for passing on the costs of collective bargaining — were in fact quite fragile. In certain industries, the leading firms were already losing market share — for example, in meatpacking and steel — and nowhere, not even in auto, was their dominance truly secure. A second, more obvious vulnerability, was the non-union South, which, despite a strenuous postwar drive, the unions failed to organize. The South's success at attracting companies pointed to a third, most basic vulnerability, namely, the abiding anti-unionism of American employers. At heart, they regarded the labor-management accord as a negotiated truce, not a permanent peace. It was only a matter of time, and the onset of a more competitive environment, before the scattered anti-union forays of the 1950s turned into a full-scale counteroffensive.

The postwar labor-management accord, it turns out, was a transitory event, not a permanent condition of American economic life. And, in a larger sense, that was true of the postwar boom. It was a transitory event, not a permanent condition.

Lost in Levittown

This 1954 *New Yorker* cartoon humorously reflected what critics saw as the stifling uniformity of the new suburbs. Suburbanites didn't seem to mind. They understood that Levitt's houses were so cheap because he built them all alike. But, admittedly, Mrs. Barnes's confusion was a downside. The New Yorker Collection, 1954, Robert J. Day, from cartoonbank.com. All Rights Reserved.

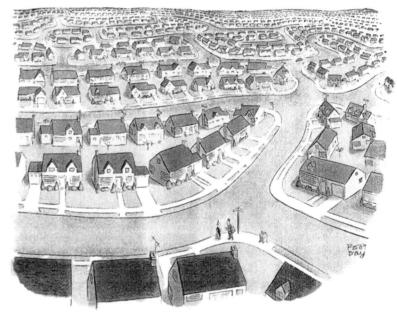

"I'm Mrs. Edward M. Barnes. Where do I live?"

➤ In what ways is the prosperity of the 1950s explained by the Cold War?

➤ Why is "the man in the gray flannel suit" the representative businessman of the 1950s?

➤ What do we mean by the "labor-management accord"?

The Affluent Society

Prosperity is more easily measured — how much an economy produces, how much people earn — than the good life that prosperity actually buys. For the 1950s, however, the contours of the American good life emerged with exceptional distinctness: a preference for suburban living, a high valuation on consumption, and a devotion to family and domesticity. In this section we ask, why those particular choices? And with what — not necessarily happy — consequences?

The Suburban Explosion

Suburban migration had been ongoing ever since the nineteenth century, but never on the explosive scale that the country experienced after World War II. Within a decade or so, developers filled up farmland on the outskirts of cities with tract housing and shopping malls. Entire counties once rural, like San Mateo, south of San Francisco, or Prince Georges, outside Washington, D.C., were built up. By 1960, more people lived in suburbs than in cities.

The Housing Boom. Home construction had virtually ended during the Great Depression, and returning veterans, dreaming of home and family, faced a critical housing shortage. After the war, construction surged to meet pent-up demand. A fourth of the country's entire housing stock in 1960 had not even existed a decade earlier.

An innovative Long Island building contractor, William J. Levitt, revolutionized the suburban housing market by applying mass-production techniques and turning out new homes at dizzying speed. Levitt's basic four-room house, complete with kitchen appliances, was priced at $7,990 in 1947. Levitt did not need to advertise; word of mouth brought buyers flocking to his developments in New York, Pennsylvania, and New Jersey (all called, naturally, Levittown). Dozens of other developers, including California's shipping magnate Henry J. Kaiser, were soon snapping up cheap farmland and building subdivisions around the country.

Even at $7,990, Levitt's homes were beyond the means of young families, or would have been, had the traditional home-financing standard — half down and ten years to pay off the balance — still prevailed. That's where the Federal Housing Administration (FHA) and the Veterans Administration (VA) came in. After the war, the FHA insured 30-year mortgages with as little as 5 percent down and interest at 2 or 3 percent. The VA was even more lenient, requiring only a token $1 down for qualified ex-GI's. FHA and VA mortgages best explain why, after hovering around 45 percent for the previous half-century, home ownership jumped to 60 percent by 1960.

What purchasers of Levitt's houses got, in addition to a good deal, were homogeneous communities. The developments contained few old people or unmarried adults. Even the trees were young. Owners agreed to cut their lawns once a week and not to hang out laundry on the weekends. Then there was the matter of race. Levitt's houses came with **restrictive covenants** prohibiting occupancy "by members of other than the Caucasian Race." (Covenants often applied to Jews and Catholics as well.)

Levitt, a marketing genius, knew his customers. The UAW learned the hard way. After the war, the CIO union launched an ambitious campaign for open-housing ordinances in the Detroit area. White auto workers rebelled, rebuking the union leadership by voting for racist politicans who promised to keep white neighborhoods white. A leading advocate of racial equality nationally, the UAW quietly shelved the fight at the local level. In *Shelley v. Kraemer* (1948) the Supreme Court outlawed restrictive covenants, but the practice persisted informally long afterward. Among America's bastions of racial segregation, the suburb was probably the last to fall.

The Sun Belt. Suburban living, although a nationwide phenomenon, was most at home in the Sun Belt, where taxes were low, the climate mild, and open space allowed for sprawling subdivisions (Map 27.1). Fueled by World War II, the South and

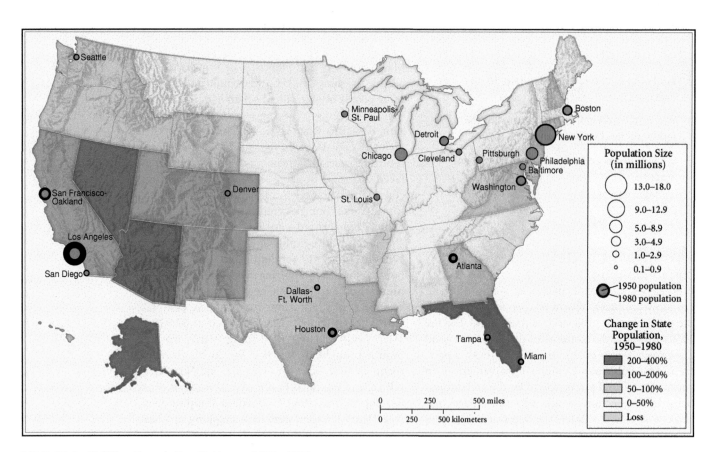

MAP 27.1 Shifting Population Patterns, 1950–1980

This map shows the two major, somewhat overlapping, patterns of population movement between 1950 and 1980. Most striking is the rapid growth of the Sun Belt states. All the states experiencing increases of over 100 percent in that period are in the Southwest, plus Florida. The second pattern involves the growth of metropolitan areas, defined as a central city or urban area and its suburbs. The central cities were themselves mostly not growing, however. The metropolitan growth shown in this map was accounted for by the expanding suburbs. And because Sun Belt growth was primarily suburban growth, that's where we see the most rapid metropolitan growth, with Los Angeles the clear winner.

West began to boom. Florida added 3.5 million people, many of them retired, between 1940 and 1970. Texas profited from an expanding petrochemical industry and profitable agriculture. Most dramatic was California's growth, spurred especially by lots of work in the state's defense-related aircraft and electronics industries. California's climate and job opportunites acted as magnets pulling people from all parts of the country. By 1970, California contained a tenth of the nation's population and surpassed New York as the most populous state.

Boosters heralded the booming development of the Sun Belt. But growth came at a price. In the arid Southwest, increasing demands for water and energy made for environmental and health problems. As cities competed for scarce water resources, they depleted underground acquifers and dammed scenic rivers. The proliferation of coal-burning power plants increased air pollution, and so did traffic. The West's nuclear industry, while good for the economy, also brought nuclear waste, uranium mines, and atomic test sites. And growth had a way of consuming the easy, uncongested living that attracted people to the Sun Belt in the first place. Still, for folks occupying those ranch-style houses, with their nice lawns, barbecues, and air-conditioning, suburban living seemed at its best in sunny California or Arizona.

Cars and Highways. Without automobiles, suburban growth on such a massive scale would have been impossible. Planners laid out subdivisions on the assumption that everybody would drive. And they did—to get to work, to take the children to Little League, to shop at the mall. With gas plentiful at 15 cents a gallon, no one cared about fuel efficiency, or seemed to mind the elaborate tail fins and chrome detail that weighed down their V-eights. In 1945 Americans owned twenty-five million cars; by 1965 the number had tripled to seventy-five million (see Voices from Abroad, "Hanoch Bartov: Everyone Has a Car," p. 840).

More cars required more highways, and the federal government obliged. In 1947 Congress authorized the construction of 37,000 miles of highways; major new legislation in 1956 increased this commitment by another 42,500 miles (Map 27.2). One of the largest civil-engineering projects in history, the new interstate system linked the entire country, with far-reaching effects on both the cities and the countryside. The interstate highways rerouted traffic away from small towns, bypassed well-traveled main roads like Route 1 on the East Coast and the cross-country Route 66, and cut wide swaths through old neighborhoods in the cities. Excellent mass transit systems, like those of Los Angeles and the San Francisco Bay Area, gave way to freeways. Federal highway funding specifically excluded mass transit, and the auto industry

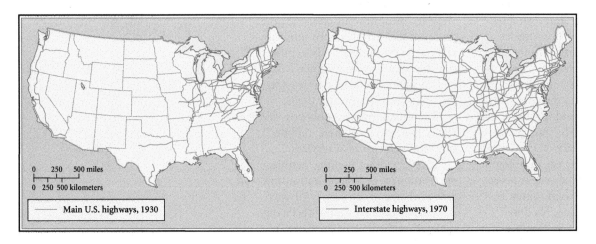

0   250   500 miles
0   250 500 kilometers
—— Main U.S. highways, 1930

0   250   500 miles
0   250 500 kilometers
—— Interstate highways, 1970

MAP 27.2   Connecting the Nation: The Interstate Highway System, 1930 and 1970

The 1956 Interstate and Defense Highways Act paved the way for an extensive network of federal highways throughout the nation. The act pleased American drivers and enhanced their love affair with the automobile, and also benefited the petroleum, construction, trucking, real estate, and tourist industries. The new highway system promoted the nation's economic integration, facilitated the growth of suburbs, and contributed to the erosion of America's distinct regional identities.

Hanoch Bartov

Everyone Has a Car

One of Israel's foremost writers and journalists, Hanoch Bartov spent two years in the United States working as a correspondent for the newspaper Lamerchav. *As a newcomer to Los Angeles in the early 1960s, he was both fascinated and appalled by Americans' love affair with the automobile.*

Our immediate decision to buy a car sprang from healthy instincts. Only later did I learn from bitter experience that in California, death was preferable to living without one. Neither the views from the plane nor the weird excursion that first evening hinted at what I would go through that first week.

Very simple — the nearest supermarket was about half a kilometer south of our apartment, the regional primary school two kilometers east, and my son's kindergarten even farther away. A trip to the post office — an undertaking, to the bank — an ordeal, to work — an impossibility.

Truth be told: the Los Angeles municipality . . . does have public transportation. Buses go once an hour along the city's boulevards and avenues, gathering all the wretched of the earth, the poor and the needy, the old ladies forbidden by their grandchildren to drive, and other eccentric types. But few people can depend on buses, even should they swear never to deviate from the fixed routes. . . . There are no tramways. No one thought of a subway. Railroads — not now and not in the future. Why? Because everyone has a car. A man invited me to his house, saying, "We are neighbors, within ten minutes of each other." After walking for an hour

and a half I realized what he meant — "ten minute drive within the speed limit." Simply put, he never thought I might interpret his remark to refer to the walking distance. The moment a baby sees the light of day in Los Angeles, a car is registered in his name in Detroit. . . .

At first perhaps people relished the freedom and independence a car provided. You get in, sit down, and grab the steering wheel, your mobility exceeding that of any other generation. No wonder people refuse to live downtown, where they can hear their neighbors, smell their cooking, and suffer frayed nerves as trains pass by bedroom windows. Instead, they get a piece of the desert, far from town, at half price, drag a water hose, grow grass, flowers, and trees, and build their dream house. . . .

The result? A widely scattered city, its houses far apart, its streets stretched in all directions. Olympic Boulevard from west to east, forty kilometers. Sepulveda Boulevard, from Long Beach in the south to the edge of the desert, forty kilometers. Altogether covering 1,200 square kilometers. As of now.

Why "as of now"? Because greater distances mean more commuting, and more commuting leads to more cars. More cars means problems that push people even farther away from the city, which chases after them.

The urban sprawl is only one side effect. Two, some say three, million cars require an array of services. . . .

. . . Why bother parking, getting out, getting in, getting up and sitting down, when you can simply "drive in"? Mailboxes have their slots facing the road, at the level of the driver's hand. That is how dirty laundry is deposited, electricity and water bills paid. That is how love is made, how children are taken to school. That is how the anniversary wreath is laid on

the graves of loved ones. There are drive-in movies. And, yes, we saw it with our own eyes: drive-in churches. Only in death is a man separated from his car and buried alone. . . .

SOURCE: Oscar and Lilian Handlin, eds., *From the Outer World* (Cambridge, MA: Harvard University Press, 1997), 293–296.

ANALYZING THE EVIDENCE

➤ From Bartov's observations, what are the pluses and minuses of America's car culture? In what ways was the automobile changing American society?

➤ Why did Bartov find owning a car was necessary, especially in southern California?

➤ Everyone, of course, didn't have a car. Who, according to Bartov, used public transportation?

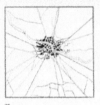

LIFE BELTS AROUND CITIES WOULD PROVIDE

A PLACE FOR BOMBED-OUT REFUGEES TO GO

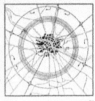

City Life Belts

What to do in case of nuclear attack? That was the problem Norbert Wiener, a renown cyberneticist at MIT, was thinking about when he and his colleagues came up with this design for an eight-lane "Life-Belt" around the country's major cities. Citizens who made it out would find safety at camp sites beyond the targeted areas. *Life* magazine, December 18, 1950.

was no friend either. General Motors made it a practice of buying up mass transit systems and scrapping them. By 1960 two-thirds of Americans drove to work each day. In Sun Belt cities like Los Angeles and Phoenix, the proportion came closer to 100 percent.

The postwar suburban explosion was distinctively American. In war-ravaged European cities, home construction was centered on high-density neighborhoods and along mass transit lines. Not until twenty years later did Europeans experiment with low-density suburban housing, and never with the disastrous effect, as in America, of gutting the central cities.

The Search for Security

There was a reason why Congress called the 1956 legislation creating America's modern freeway system

the National Interstate and *Defense* Highways Act. The four-lane freeways, used every day by commuters, might some day, in a nuclear war, evacuate them to safety. That captured as well as anything the underside of postwar life, when suburban living abided side by side with the shadow of annihilation.

The Cold War, reaching as it did across the globe, was omnipresent at home as well, permeating domestic politics, intruding on the debate over racial injustice, and creating an atmosphere that stifled dissent. For the first time, America had a peacetime draft. In every previous war, the country had quickly demobilized. But when World War II ended, the draft remained in place. Every neighborhood seemed to have a boy in the armed forces.

Most alarming was the nuclear standoff with the Soviet Union. Bomb shelters and civil defense drills

Duck and Cover

The nation's Civil Defense Agency's efforts to prepare Americans for a nuclear attack extended to children in schools, where repeated drills taught them to "duck and cover" when the alarm went off. Variations of this 1954 scene at Franklin Township School in Quakertown, New Jersey, were repeated all over the nation. Paul F. Kutta. Courtesy *Reminisce Magazine.*

provided a daily reminder of mushroom clouds. In the late 1950s a small but growing number of citizens raised questions about radioactive fallout from above-ground bomb tests. Federal investigators later documented illnesses, deaths, and birth defects among "downwinders"—people who lived near nuclear test sites. The most shocking revelations, however, came in 1993, when the Department of Energy released previously classified documents on human radiation experiments conducted in the late 1940s and 1950s under the auspices of the Atomic Energy Commission and other federal agencies. Many of the experiments were undertaken with little concern for or understanding of the adverse effects on the subjects.

By the late 1950s, public concern over nuclear testing had become a high-profile issue, and new antinuclear groups such as SANE (the National Committee for a Sane Nuclear Policy) and Physicians for Social Responsibility called for an international test ban.

Returning to the Church. In an age of anxiety, Americans yearned for a reaffirmation of faith. Church membership jumped from 49 percent of the population in 1940 and to 70 percent in 1960. People flocked especially into the evangelical Protestant denominations, who benefited from a remarkable new crop of preachers. Most notable was the young Reverend Billy Graham, who made brilliant use of television, radio, and advertising to spread the gospel. The religious reawakening meshed, in a time of Cold War, with Americans' view of themselves as a righteous people opposed

to "godless Communism." In 1954 the phrase "under God" was inserted into the Pledge of Allegiance, and after 1956 U.S. coins carried the words, "In God We Trust."

The resurgence of religion, despite its evangelical bent, had a distinctly moderate tone. An ecumenical movement bringing Catholics, Protestants, and Jews together flourished, and so did a concern for the here-and-now. In his popular television program, Catholic Bishop Fulton J. Sheen asked, "Is life worth living?" He and countless others answered that it was. None was more affirmative than Norman Vincent Peale, whose best-selling book *The Power of Positive Thinking* (1952) embodied the trend toward the therapeutic use of religion, an antidote to the stresses of modern life.

Consumer Culture

In some respects, postwar consumerism seemed like a return to the 1920s—an abundance of new gadgets and appliances, more leisure time, the craze for automobiles, and new types of mass media. Yet there was a significant difference. In the 1950s consumption became associated with citizenship. Buying things, once a sign of personal indulgence, now meant fully participating in American society and, moreover, fulfilling a social responsibility. By spending, Americans fueled a high-employment economy. What the suburban family consumed, asserted *Life* magazine in a photo essay featuring one such family, would help assure "full employment

Billy Graham, Evangelist

Billy Graham was the first great revival preacher of the postwar era, a worthy successor to Billy Sunday and Aimee Semple McPherson. In this photograph, the Reverend Graham is preaching to more than thirty thousand people jammed into Wall Street on July 10, 1957. In what he termed the "greatest service" of his New York Crusade, the evangelist gave a twenty-minute extemporaneous sermon from an improvised pulpit on the steps of the Federal Memorial Hall. In the foreground is the foot of the George Washington statue. At rear is the New York Stock Exchange.
© Bettmann/Corbis.

and improved living standards for the rest of the nation."

Advertising. As in the past, product makers sought to stimulate consumer demand through aggressive advertising. More money was spent in 1951 on advertising ($6.5 billion) than on primary and secondary education ($5 billion). The 1950s gave Americans the Marlboro Man; M&Ms that melt in your mouth, not in your hand; Wonder Bread to build strong bodies in twelve ways; and the "does she or doesn't she?" Clairol hair-coloring woman. Motivational research delved into the subconscious to suggest how the messages should be pitched. Like other features of the consumer culture, this one got its share of muckraking condemnation in Vance Packer's best-selling *The Hidden Persuaders* (1957).

Advertising heavily promoted the appliances that began to fill the suburban kitchen, many of them unavailable during the war, others new to the postwar market. In 1946 automatic washing machines replaced the old machines with hand-cranked wringers, and clothes dryers also came on the market. Commercial laundries across the country struggled to stay in business. Another new item was the home freezer, encouraging the dramatic growth of the frozen-food industry. Partly because of all the electrical appliances, consumer use of electricity doubled during the 1950s.

Television. TV's leap to cultural prominence was swift and overpowering. There were only 7,000 sets in American homes in 1947, yet a year later the CBS and NBC radio networks began offering regular programming, and by 1950 Americans owned 7.3 million TV sets. Ten years later, 87 percent of American homes had at least one television set.

Although licensed by the Federal Communications Commission (FCC), television stations, like radio, depended entirely on advertising for profits. Soon television supplanted radio as the chief diffuser of popular culture. Movies, too, lost the cultural dominance they had once enjoyed. Movie attendance shrank throughout the postwar period, and movie studios increasingly relied on overseas distribution to earn a profit.

What Americans saw on television, besides the omnipresent commercials, was an overwhelmingly white, Anglo-Saxon world of nuclear families, suburban homes, and middle-class life. A typical show was *Father Knows Best*, starring Robert Young and Jane Wyatt. Father left home each morning wearing a suit and carrying a briefcase. Mother was a full-time housewife, always tending to her three children, but, as a sterotypical female, prone to bad driving and tears. The children were sometimes rebellious, but family conflicts were invariably resolved. *The Honeymooners*, starring Jackie Gleason as a Brooklyn bus driver, and *Life of Reilly*, a situation comedy featuring a California aircraft worker, were rare in their treatment of working-class lives. Black characters such as Rochester in Jack Benny's comedy show appeared mainly as sidekicks and servants.

The types of television programs developed in the 1950s built on older entertainment genres but also pioneered new ones. Taking its cue from the movies, television offered some thirty westerns by 1959, including *Gunsmoke*, *Wagon Train*, and

Advertising in the TV Age

Aggressive advertising of new products, such as the color television, helped fuel the surge in consumer spending during the 1950s. Marketing experts emphasized the role of television in promoting family togetherness, while interior designers offered decorating tips that placed the television at the focal point of living rooms and the increasingly popular "family rooms." Here, the family watches a variety program starring singer Dinah Shore, who was the television spokeswoman for Chevrolet cars. Every American probably could hum the tune of the little song she sang in praise of the Chevy. Motorola.

Bonanza. Professional sports became big-time television—far exceeding the potential of radio. Programming geared to children, such as Walt Disney's *Mickey Mouse Club, Howdy Doody,* and *Captain Kangaroo,* created the first generation of children glued to the tube.

Although the new medium did offer some serious programming, notably live theater and documentaries, FCC Commissioner Newton Minow concluded in 1963 that television was "a vast wasteland." But it did what it intended, which was to sell products and fill America's leisure hours with reassuring entertainment.

The Baby Boom

A popular 1945 song was called "Gotta Make Up for Lost Time," and Americans did just that. Two things were noteworthy about the families they

formed after World War II. First, marriages were remarkably stable. Not until the mid-1960s did the divorce rate begin to rise sharply. Second, married couples were intent on having babies. Everyone expected to have two or more children—it was part of adulthood, almost a citizen's responsibility. After a century and a half of decline, the birthrate shot up: More babies were born between 1948 and 1953 than were born in the previous thirty years (Figure 27.3).

Among reasons for this baby boom, one was that everyone was having children at the same time. A second was a drop in the marriage age—down to twenty-two for men, twenty for women. Younger parents meant a bumper crop of children. Women who came of age in the 1930s averaged 2.4 children; their counterparts in the 1950s, 3.2 children. The baby boom peaked in 1957 and remained at a high level until the early 1960s. Thereafter, the

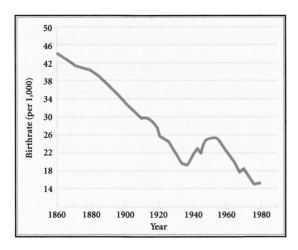

FIGURE 27.3 The American Birthrate, 1860–1980

When birthrates are viewed over more than a century, the postwar baby boom is clearly only a temporary reversal of the longterm downward trend in the American birthrate.

birthrate declined, returning to earlier long-term patterns.

"Scientific" Child Rearing. To keep all those baby-boom children healthy and happy, middle-class parents increasingly relied on the advice of experts. Dr. Benjamin Spock's best-selling *Baby and Child Care* sold a million copies a year after its publication in 1946. Spock urged mothers to abandon the rigid feeding and baby-care schedules of an earlier generation. New mothers found Spock's commonsense approach liberating, but it did not totally soothe their insecurities. If mothers were too protective, Spock and others argued, they might hamper their children's preparation for adult life. Mothers who wanted to work outside the home felt guilty because Spock recommended that they be constantly available for their children.

Less subject to fashion were the very real advances in diet, public health, and medical practice that made for healthier children. Serious illness turned routine after the introduction of such "miracle drugs" as penicillin (introduced in 1943), streptomycin (1945), and cortisone (1946). When Dr. Jonas Salk perfected a polio vaccine in 1954, he became a national hero. The free distribution of Salk's vaccine in the nation's schools, followed in 1961 by Dr. Albert Sabin's oral polio vaccine, demonstrated the potential of government-sponsored public health programs. The conquest of polio made the children of the 1950s the healthiest generation ever.

The baby boom had a vast impact on American society. All those babies fueled the economy as families bought food, diapers, toys, and clothing for their expanding broods. The nation's educational system also got a boost. The new middle class, America's first college-educated generation, placed a high value on education. Suburban parents approved 90 percent of proposed school bond issues during the 1950s. By 1970 school expenditures accounted for 7.2 percent of the gross national

Polio Pioneers

These Provo, Utah, children each received a "Polio Pioneer" souvenir button for participating in the trial of the Salk vaccine in 1954. Dr. Jonas Salk's announcement the next year that the vaccine was safe and effective made him a national hero. March of Dimes Birth Defect Foundation.

The Saturday Evening
POST
September 19, 1959 – 15¢

Does it Help
to Swap Visits
With the Russians?

A Woman's Dilemma in Postwar America

This 1959 cover of the *Saturday Evening Post* depicts the no-win situation facing women in the postwar era. But at least they could dream. Women consigned to low-paid, dead-end jobs in the service sector imagined suburban life with Mr. Wonderful helping do the dishes. In reality, Mr. Wonderful turned out to be that guy settled before the television set while Mrs. Homemaker scoured a dirty frying pan and the baby fussed. But of course Mrs. Homemaker's dream of a nice office job just was just as much an illusion. A no-win situation.

product, double the 1950 level. In the 1960s the baby-boom generation swelled college enrollments and, not coincidentally, the ranks of student protesters (see Chapter 28). The passage of time did not diminish the impact of the baby boom. When baby boomers competed for jobs during the 1970s, the labor market became tight. When career-oriented baby boomers belatedly began having children in the 1980s, the birthrate jumped. And in our own time, as baby boomers begin retiring, huge funding problems threaten to engulf Social Security and Medicare. Who would have thought that the intimate decisions of so many couples after World War II would be affecting American life well into the twenty-first century?

Contradictions in Women's Lives

"The suburban housewife was the dream image of the young American woman," the feminist Betty Friedan wrote of the 1950s. "She was healthy, beautiful, educated, concerned only about her husband, her children, and her home." Friedan gave up a psychology fellowship and a career as a journalist to marry, move to the suburbs, and raise three children. "Determined that I find the feminine fulfillment that eluded my mother . . . I lived the life of a suburban housewife that was everyone's dream at the time," she said.

The Feminine Mystique. The idea that a woman's place was in the home was, of course, not new. What Betty Friedan called the "feminine mystique" of the 1950s — that "the highest value and the only commitment for women is the fulfillment of their own femininity" — bore remarkable similarities to the nineteenth-century's cult of true womanhood.

The updated version drew on new elements of twentieth-century science and culture, even Freudian psychology. Psychologists equated motherhood with "normal" female identity and berated mothers who worked outside the home. Television and film depicted career women as social and sexual misfits, the heavies in movies like *Mildred Pierce*. The postwar consumer culture also emphasized women's domestic role as purchasing agents for home and family. "Love is said in many ways," ran an ad for toilet paper. Another asked, "Can a woman ever feel right cooking on a dirty range?"

Although the feminine mystique held cultural sway, it by no means was as all-encompassing as Friedan implied in her 1963 best-seller, *The Feminine Mystique*. Indeed, Friedan herself resisted the stereotype, doing freelance journalism while at home, and, as a result of that work, stumbling on the subject and writing the book that made her famous. Middle-class wives often found constructive outlets for their energy in the League of Women Voters, the PTA, and the Junior League. As in earlier periods, some women used the rhetoric of domesticity to justify political activism, which in this period involved community improvement, racial integration, and nuclear disarmament. As for working-class women, many of them doubtless would have loved to embrace domesticity, if only they could. The economic needs of their families demanded otherwise.

Women at Work. The feminine mystique notwithstanding, more than one-third of American women in the 1950s held jobs outside the home. As the service sector expanded, so did the demand for workers in jobs traditionally filled by women.

Occupational segmentation still haunted women. Until 1964 the classified sections of most newspapers separated employment ads into "Help Wanted Male" and "Help Wanted Female." More than 80 percent of all employed women did stereotypical "women's work" as salespersons, health-care technicians, waitresses, stewardesses, domestic servants, receptionists, telephone operators, and secretaries. In 1960 women represented only 3.5 percent of lawyers (many top law schools did not admit women at all) and 6.1 percent physicians, but 97 percent nurses, 85 percent librarians, and 57 percent social workers. Along with women's jobs went women's pay, which averaged 60 percent of men's pay in 1963.

What was new was the range of women at work. At the turn of the century, the typical female worker was young and unmarried. By midcentury she was in her forties, married, and with children in school. In 1940 only 15 percent of wives had worked. By 1960, 30 percent did, and by 1970 it was 40 percent.

Married women worked to supplement family income. Even in the prosperous 1950s, the wages of many men could not pay for what middle-class life demanded: cars, houses, vacations, and college educations for the children. Poorer households needed more than one wage earner just to get by.

How could American society so steadfastly uphold the domestic ideal when so many wives and mothers were out of the house and at work? In many ways the contradiction was hidden by the women themselves. Fearing public disapproval, women usually justified their work in family-oriented terms: "Of course I believe a woman's place is at home, but I took this job to save for college for our children." Moreover, when women took jobs outside the home, they still bore full responsibility for child care and household management. As one overburdened woman noted, she now had "two full-time jobs instead of just one — underpaid clerical worker and unpaid housekeeper."

Youth Culture

In 1956, only partly in jest, the CBS radio commentator Eric Sevareid questioned "whether the teenagers will take over the United States lock, stock, living room, and garage." Sevareid was grumbling about American youth culture, a phenomenon first noticed in the 1920s, that had its roots in lengthening years of education, the role of peer groups, and the consumer patterns of teenagers. Like so much else in the 1950s, the youth culture came down to having money.

Market research revealed a distinct teen market to be exploited. A 1951 *Newsweek* story noted with awe that the $3 weekly spending money of the average teenager was enough to buy 190 million candy bars, 130 million soft drinks, and 230 million sticks of gum. In 1956 advertisers projected an adolescent market of $9 billion for transistor radios (first introduced in 1952), 45-rpm records, clothing, and fads such as Silly Putty (1950) and Hula Hoops (1958). Increasingly, advertisers targeted the young, both to capture their spending money and to exploit their influence on family purchases. Note the changing slogans for Pepsi-Cola: "Twice as much for a nickel" (1935), "Be sociable — have a Pepsi" (1948), "Now it's Pepsi for those who think young" (1960), and finally "the Pepsi Generation" (1965).

Hollywood movies played a large role in fostering a teenage culture. At a time when Americans were being lured by television, young people made up the largest audience for motion pictures. Soon Hollywood studios catered to them with films like *The Wild One* (1951), starring Marlon Brando, and *Rebel without a Cause* (1955), starring James Dean. "What are you rebelling against?" a waitress asks Brando in *The Wild One*. "Whattaya got?" he replies.

What really defined this generation, however, was its music. Rejecting the romantic ballads of the 1940s, teenagers discovered rock 'n' roll, an amalgam of white country and western music and black-inspired rhythm and blues. The Cleveland disc jockey Alan Freed played a major role in introducing white America to the black-influenced sound by playing what were called "race" records. "If I could find a white man who had the Negro sound and the Negro feel I could make a billion dollars," said the owner of a record company. The performer fitting that bill was Elvis Presley, who rocketed into instant celebrity in 1956 with his hit records "Hound Dog" and "Heartbreak Hotel." Between 1953 and 1959 record sales increased from $213 million to $603 million, with rock 'n' roll as the driving force.

Many adults were not happy. They saw in rock 'n' roll music, teen movies, and magazines such as *Mad* (introduced in 1952) an invitation to race mixing, rebellion, and disorder. The media featured hundreds of stories on problem teens, and in 1955 a Senate subcommittee headed by Estes Kefauver conducted a high-profile investigation of juvenile delinquency and its origins in the popular media. Denunciations of the new youth culture, if anything, only increased its popularity.

Cultural Dissenters

Youth rebellion was only one aspect of a broader discontent with the conformist culture of the

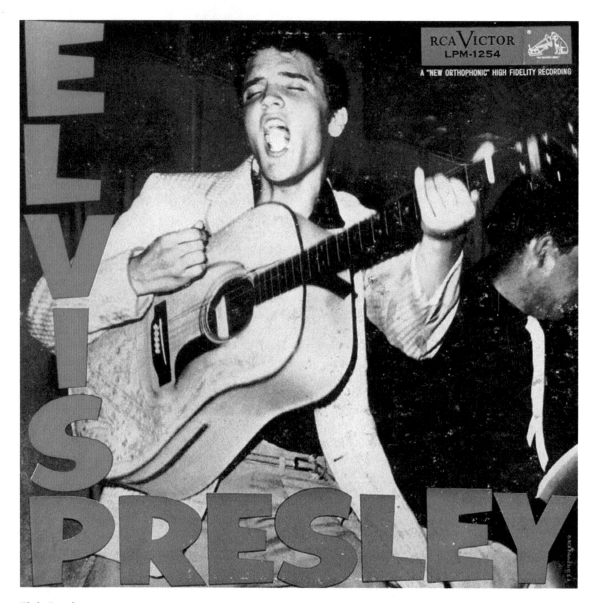

Elvis Presley

The young Elvis Presley, shown here on the cover of his first album in 1956, embodied cultural rebellion against the drabness of adult life in the 1950s. 1956 BGM Music.

1950s. Artists, jazz musicians, and writers expressed their alienation in a remarkable flowering of intensely personal, introspective art forms. In New York, Jackson Pollock and other painters developed an inventive style that became known as abstract expressionism. Swirling and splattering paint onto giant canvases, Pollock emphasized self-expression in the act of painting.

A similar trend characterized jazz, where black musicians developed a hard-driving improvisational style known as bebop. Whether the "hot" bebop of saxophonist Charlie Parker or the more subdued "cool" West Coast sound of the trumpeter Miles Davis, postwar jazz was cerebral, intimate, and individualistic. As such, it stood in stark contrast to the commercialized, dance-oriented "swing" bands of the 1930s and 1940s.

Black jazz musicians found eager fans not only in the African American community but among young white Beats, a group of writers and poets centered in New York and San Francisco who disdained middle-class conformity and suburban materialism. In his poem "Howl" (1956), which became a manifesto of the Beat generation, Allen Ginsberg lamented: "I saw the best minds of my generation destroyed by madness, starving hysterical naked, dragging themselves through the angry streets at dawn looking for an angry fix." In works such as Jack Kerouac's novel *On the Road* (1957), the Beats glorified spontaneity, sexual adventurism, drug

FIGURE 27.4 Legal Immigration to the United States by Region, 1931–1984

Historically, immigrants to the United States had come primarily from Europe. This figure shows the dramatic shift that began after 1960, as Latinos and Asians began to arrive in increasing numbers. Asians, who represented nearly 50 percent of all immigrants by the 1980s, especially benefited from the liberalization of U.S. immigration laws. SOURCE: Robert W. Gardner, Bryant Robie, and Peter C. Smith, "Asian Americans: Growth, Change, and Diversity," *Population Bulletin* 40, no. 4 (Washington, D.C.: Population Reference Bureau, 1985): 2.

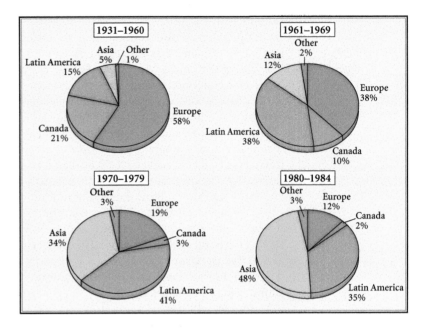

use, and spirituality. Like other members of the postwar generation, the Beats were apolitical; their rebellion was strictly cultural. In the 1960s, however, the Beats would inspire a new generation of young rebels angry at both the political and cultural status quo.

➤ In what ways does the growth of the Sun Belt reflect key themes of the suburban explosion?

➤ What was the relationship between consumer culture and the emphasis on family life in the postwar era?

➤ Is it correct to say that the 1950s was exclusively a time of cultural conformity?

The Other America

While middle-class whites flocked to the suburbs, an opposite stream of poor and working-class migrants, many of them southern blacks, moved into the cities. What these urban newcomers inherited was a declining economy and a decaying environment. To those enjoying prosperity, "the Other America"—as the social critic Michael Harrington called it in 1962—remained largely invisible. Only in the South, where African Americans organized to combat segregation, did the stain of social injustice catch the nation's attention.

Immigrants and Migrants

Ever since the passage of the National Origins Act of 1924 (see Chapter 23), U.S. immigration policy had aimed mainly at keeping foreigners out.

Anti-immigrant sentiment intensified during the Great Depression, hardly budging even to rescue Jews fleeing Nazi persecution. World War II caused the bar to be lowered slightly, enabling returning servicemen to bring home their war brides and, under the Displaced Persons Act (1948), permitting the entry of approximately 415,000 Europeans, among them former Nazis like Werner von Braun, the rocket scientist. The overt anti-Asian bias of America's immigration laws also became untenable. In a gesture to an important ally, the Chinese Exclusion Act was repealed in 1943. More far-reaching was the 1952 McCarran-Walter Act, which (in addition to barring Communists and other radicals) ended the exclusion under the 1924 act of Japanese, Koreans, and southeast Asians.

Although not many came until later, the immediate impact on Asian immigrant communities was considerable. On the eve of World War II, Chinatowns were populated primarily by men. Although largely married, their wives remained in China. The repeal of the Chinese Exclusion Act, and the granting of naturalization rights, encouraged those men to bring their wives to America. The result was a more normal, family-oriented community, a development also seen in the Filipino American and Japanese American communities. Approximately 135,000 men and 100,000 women of Chinese origin were living in the United States in 1960, mostly in New York State and California (Figure 27.4).

Latino Immigration. After the national-origins quota system went into effect in 1924, Mexico replaced eastern and southern Europe as the nation's labor reservoir. During World War II, the federal government introduced the *bracero* (temporary worker) program to ease wartime labor shortages (see Chapter 25), and then revived the program in 1951, during the Korean War. At its peak in 1959, Mexicans on temporary permits accounted for one-quarter of the nation's seasonal workers. The federal government's ability to control the flow, however, was strictly limited. Mexicans came illegally, and by the time the *bracero* program ended in 1964, many of that group — an estimated 350,000 — had managed to settle in the United States. When unemployment became a problem during the recession of 1953–1954, federal authorities responded by deporting many Mexicans in a program grimly named "Operation Wetback" (because Mexican migrants often waded across the Rio Grande River), but the Mexican population in the country continued to rise nonetheless.

Mostly they settled in to Los Angeles, Long Beach, El Paso, and other southwestern cities, following the crops during the harvest season or working in the expanding service sector. But many also went north, augmenting well-established Mexican American communites in Chicago, Detroit, Kansas City, and Denver. Although still important for American agriculture, more Mexican Americans by 1960 were employed as industrial and service workers.

Another major group of Spanish-speaking migrants came from Puerto Rico. American citizens since 1917, Puerto Ricans enjoyed an unrestricted right to move to the mainland. Migration increased dramatically after World War II, when mechanization of the island's sugarcane industry pushed many Puerto Ricans off the land. Airlines began to offer cheap direct flights between San Juan and New York City. With the fare at about $50, two weeks' wages, Puerto Ricans became America's first immigrants with the luxury of arriving by air.

Most Puerto Ricans went to New York, where they settled first in East ("Spanish") Harlem and then scattered in neighborhoods across the city's five boroughs. This massive migration, which increased the Puerto Rican population to 613,000 by 1960, transformed the ethnic composition of the city. More Puerto Ricans now lived in New York City than in San Juan. They faced conditions common to all recent immigrants: crowded and deteriorating housing, segregation, menial jobs, poor schools, and the problems of a bilingual existence.

Cuban refugees constituted the third largest group of Spanish-speaking immigrants. In the six years after Fidel Castro's seizure of power in 1959 (see Chapter 28), an estimated 180,000 people fled Cuba for the United States. The Cuban refugee community grew so quickly that it turned Miami into a cosmo-politan, bilingual city almost overnight. Unlike other migrants to urban America, Miami's Cubans quickly prospered, in large part because they had arrived with money and middle-class skills.

Indian Relocation. In western cities, an influx of Native Americans also contributed to the rise in the nonwhite urban population. In 1953, Congress passed a resolution authorizing a program to terminate the autonomous status of the Indian tribes and empty the reservations. The Bureau of Indian Affairs encouraged voluntary migration by subsidizing moving costs and establishing relocation centers in San Francisco, Denver, Chicago, and other cities. Despite the program's stated goal of assimilation, the 60,000 Native Americans who migrated to the cities mostly settled together in ghetto neighborhoods, with little prospect of adjusting successfully to an urban environment.

Black Migration. African Americans came in large number to cities from the rural South, continuing the "Great Migration" that had begun during World War I (see Chapter 22). Black migration was hastened by the transformation of southern agriculture. Synthetic fabrics cut into the demand for cotton, while mechanization cut into the demand for farm labor. The mechanical cotton picker, introduced in 1944, effectively destroyed the sharecropper system. Cotton acreage declined from 43 million acres in 1930 to less than 15 million in 1960, while the southern farm population fell from 16.2 million to 5.9 million. Although both whites and blacks left the land, the starkest decline was among blacks. By 1990 only 69,000 black farmers remained nationwide, a tiny fraction of the country's farmers.

Where did these displaced farmfolk go? White southerners from Appalachia moved north to "hillbilly" ghettos, such as Cincinnati's Over the Rhine neighborhood and Chicago's Uptown. As many as 3 million blacks headed to Chicago, New York, Washington, Detroit, Los Angeles, and other cities between 1940 and 1960. Certain sections of Chicago seemed like the Mississippi Delta transplanted, so pervasive were the migrants. By 1960 about half the nation's black population was living outside the South, compared with only 23 percent before World War II.

The Urban Crisis

Migration to American cities, whether from Europe or rural America, had always been attended by hardship — by poverty, slum housing, and cultural dislocation. So severe had these problems seemed

West Side Story

The influx of Puerto Rican immigrants after World War II inspired Leonard Bernstein's 1957 Broadway hit *West Side Story*. The plot recast Shakespeare's *Romeo and Juliet* in a Puerto Rican neighborhood on New York's West Side in the 1950s. Confrontations between members of youth gangs and adult figures of authority, as pictured here in a still from the movie version, were set to highly stylized song and dance routines. The Kobal Collection.

half a century earlier that they had helped spark the reform wave of the Progressive era (see Chapter 20). But hardship then had been temporary, a kind of waystation on the path to a better life. That had been true initially of the post-1941 migration, when blacks had found jobs in defense industry and, in the postwar boom, in Detroit auto plants and Chicago packing houses. Later migrants were not so lucky. By the 1950s, the economy was changing. The manufacturing sector was contracting, and technological advances — what people then called "automation" — hit unskilled and semiskilled jobs especially hard — "jobs in which Negroes are disproportionately concentrated," noted the civil rights activist Bayard

Rustin. Black migrants, Rustin warned, were becoming economically superfluous, and in that respect their situation was fundamentally different, far bleaker than anything faced by earlier immigrants.

A second difference involved race. Every immigrant wave — Irish, Italian, Slavic, Jewish — had been greeted by hostility, but none so virulent as that experienced by black migrants. In the 1950s, a more tolerant era, they were spared the race rioting that had afflicted their predecessors. But racism in its more covert forms held them back at every turn — by housing restrictions, by schools increasingly segregated, by an urban infrastructure underfunded and decaying because whites were fleeing to the suburbs.

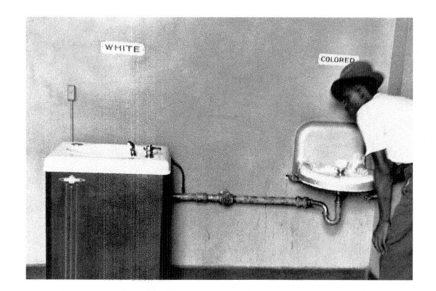

Racial Segregation, North Carolina, 1950

Until as recently as forty years ago, separate drinking fountains like the ones in this picture could be seen across the South. It was the resulting humiliation visited on blacks every day of their lives that explains why the Greensboro Four finally decided to sit down at that Woolworth's lunch counter in 1959 (see p. 855). Elliot Erwitt/Magnum Photos, Inc.

In the 1950s, the nation's twelve largest cities lost 3.6 million whites while gaining 4.5 million nonwhites.

Urban Renewal. As if joblessness and discrimination were not enough, black ghettoes were hit during the 1950s by a frenzy of urban renewal. Seeking to revitalize city centers, urban planners, politicians, and real-estate developers proposed razing blighted neighborhoods to make way for modern construction projects. Local residents were rarely consulted about whether they wanted their neighborhoods "renewed." In Boston, almost a third of the old city was demolished — including the historic West End, a long-established Italian neighborhood — to make way for a new highway, high-rise housing, and government and commercial buildings. In San Francisco some 4,000 residents of the Western Addition, a predominantly black neighborhood, lost out to an urban renewal program that built luxury housing, a shopping center, and an express boulevard. Between 1949 and 1967 urban renewal demolished almost 400,000 buildings and displaced 1.4 million people.

The urban experts knew what to do with these people. They would be relocated to federally funded housing projects, an outgrowth of New Deal housing policy, now much expanded and combined with generous funding for slum clearance. However well intentioned, these grim projects had a disastrous impact on black community life, destroying neighborhoods and relegating the inhabitants to social isolation. The notorious Robert Taylor Homes in Chicago, a huge complex of 28 sixteen-story buildings and 20,000 residents, almost all black, became a breeding ground for crime and hopelessness.

In 1962, the Swedish sociologist Gunnar Myrdal (author of *An American Dilemma,* a pioneering book about the country's race relations) wondered whether shrinking economic opportunity in the United States might not "trap an 'under-class' of unemployed and, gradually, unemployable and underemployed persons and families at the bottom of a society." Myrdal's term *underclass* — referring to a population permanently mired in poverty and dependency — would figure centrally in future American debates about social policy. In 1962, however, *underclass* was a newly coined word, describing a phenomenon not yet noticed but already well under way in the inner cities of 1950s America.

The Emerging Civil Rights Struggle

In the South, segregation prevailed. In most southern states, blacks could not eat in restaurants patronized by whites or use the same waiting rooms and toilets at bus stations. All forms of public transportation were rigidly segregated by custom or by law. Even drinking fountains were labeled "White" and "Colored."

Blacks understood that segregation would never be abolished without grassroots struggle. But that was not their only weapon. They also had the Bill of Rights and the great Reconstruction amendments to the Constitution. In this respect, fighting segregation was different from fighting poverty. Blacks had no constitutional right not to be poor, but they did have constitutional rights not to be discriminated against, if only these rights could be exercised. The Cold War, moreover, gave civil rights advocates added leverage because America's reputation in the world now counted to America's leaders. So the battle against racial injustice, as it took shape after World War II, proceeded on two tracks — on the ground, where blacks began to stand up for their rights, and in the courts and corridors of power, where words sometimes mattered more than action.

Civil Rights under Truman. During World War II, the National Association for the Advancement of Colored People (NAACP) redoubled its efforts to combat discrimination in housing, transportation, and other areas. Black demands for justice continued into the postwar years, spurred by symbolic victories, as when Jackie Robinson broke through the color line in major league baseball by joining the Brooklyn Dodgers in 1947. African American leaders also had hopes for President Truman. Although capable of racist language, Truman supported civil rights on moral grounds. He understood, moreover, the growing importance of the black vote in key northern states, a fact driven home by his surprise 1948 victory. Truman also worried about America's image abroad. It didn't help that the Soviet Union often compared the South's treatment of blacks with the Nazis' treatment of the Jews.

Lacking support in Congress, Truman turned to executive action. In 1946 he appointed a National Civil Rights Commission, whose 1947 report called for robust federal action on behalf of civil rights. In 1948, under pressure from A. Phillip Randolph's Committee Against Jim Crow in Military Service, Truman signed an executive order desegregating the armed forces. And then, with his hand strengthened by the victory for civil rights at the 1948 Democratic convention, Truman went on the offensive, pushing legislation on a variety of fronts, including voting rights and equal employment opportunity. Invariably, his efforts were defeated by filibustering southern Senators.

With Dwight Eisenhower as president, civil rights no longer had a champion in the White House. But in the meantime, NAACP lawyers Thurgood Marshall and William Hastie had been preparing the legal ground in a series of test cases challenging racial discrimination, and in 1954 they hit pay dirt.

Brown v. Board of Education. The case involved Linda Brown, a black pupil in Topeka, Kansas, who had been forced to attend a distant segregated school rather than the nearby white elementary school. The NAACP's chief counsel, Thurgood Marshall, argued that such segregation, mandated by the Topeka Board of Education, was unconstitutional because it denied Linda Brown the "equal protection of the laws" guaranteed by the Fourteenth Amendment. In a unanimous decision on May 17, 1954, the Supreme Court agreed, overturning the "separate but equal" doctrine of *Plessy v. Ferguson* (see Chapter 19). Speaking for the Court, the new Chief Justice Earl Warren wrote:

To separate Negro children . . . solely because of their race generates a feeling of inferiority as to their status in the community that may affect their hearts and minds in a way unlikely ever to be undone. . . . We conclude that in the field of public education the doctrine of "separate but equal" has no place. Separate educational facilities are inherently unequal.

In an implementing 1955 decision known as *Brown II,* the Court declared simply that integration should proceed "with all deliberate speed."

In the South, however, the call went out for "massive resistance." A Southern Manifesto signed in 1956 by 101 members of Congress denounced the *Brown* decision as "a clear abuse of judicial power" and encouraged their constituents to defy it. That year 500,000 southerners joined White Citizens' Councils dedicated to blocking school integration. Some whites revived the old tactics of violence and intimidation, swelling the ranks of the Ku Klux Klan to levels not seen since the 1920s.

President Eisenhower accepted the *Brown* decision as the law of the land, but he thought it was a mistake and was not happy about committing federal power to enforce it. A crisis in Little Rock, Arkansas, finally forced his hand. In September 1957 nine black students attempted to enroll at the all-white Central High School. Governor Orval Faubus called out the National Guard to bar them. Then the mob took over. Every day the nine students had to run a gauntlet of angry whites chanting "Go back to the jungle." As the vicious scenes played out on television night after night, Eisenhower acted. He sent 1,000 federal troops to Little Rock and nationalized the Arkansas National Guard, ordering them to protect the black students. Eisenhower thus became the first president since Reconstruction to use federal troops to enforce the rights of blacks (see Reading American Pictures, "The Cold War and the Civil Rights Movement," p. 854).

The *Brown* decision validated the NAACP's legal strategy, but white resistance also revealed that winning in court was not enough. Prompted by one small act of defiance, southern black leaders embraced nonviolent protest.

The Montgomery Bus Boycott. On December 1, 1955, Rosa Parks, a seamstress in Montgomery, Alabama, refused to give up her seat on a city bus to a white man. She was arrested and charged with violating a local segregation ordinance. Parks's act was not the spur-of-the-moment decision that it seemed. A woman of sterling reputation and a long-time NAACP member, she had been chosen to play that part. Rosa Parks fit the bill perfectly for the challenge the local NAACP intended against segregated buses.

The Cold War and the Civil Rights Movement

"Careful, the Walls Have Ears." *Oakland Tribune,* September 11, 1957.

"Right Into Their Hands." *Arkansas Democrat-Gazette,* September 11, 1957.

In 1957, in the far-off African nation of Mozambique, an official at the U.S. embassy worried that the school desegregation crisis in Little Rock, Arkansas, had "become a symbol of Negro-White relations in the United States." Similar worries about the impact of the Arkansas crisis on the Cold War struggle with the Soviet Union surfaced in many American newspapers and magazines, often in the form of political cartoons. The first cartoon above appeared in the *Oakland Tribune* on September 11, 1957, two weeks before President Eisenhower intervened by federalizing the Arkansas National Guard. The second cartoon appeared on the same day in the local newspaper, the *Arkansas Democrat-Gazette.*

ANALYZING THE EVIDENCE

➤ How has the artist's drawing for the *Arkansas Democrat-Gazette* depicted Little Rock segregationists? Are they the kind of people that the cartoonist thinks should be representing America before the world?

➤ Why do you suppose the *Oakland Tribune's* artist omitted African Americans and depicted the crisis as a battle between two groups of whites? Why is "The Whole Wide World" paying such close attention?

➤ Do both cartoons convey the same message, or do they suggest different perspectives on the issue?

➤ As historical evidence, how useful do you think these cartoons are at explaining why Americans began to take the civil rights struggle seriously in the 1950s?

The Greensboro Four

Pictured here are the four African American students who, entirely on their own, decided to demand service at the Woolworth's whites-only lunch counter in Greensboro, North Carolina, and started a sit-down protest movement across the South. Second from the left is Franklin McCain, whose interview appears in Comparing American Voices, "Challenging White Supremacy," on the following pages. © Bettmann/Corbis.

Once the die was cast, the black community turned for leadership to the Reverend Martin Luther King Jr., the recently appointed pastor of Montgomery's Dexter Street Baptist Church. The son of a prominent black minister in Atlanta, King embraced the teachings of Mahatma Gandhi, whose campaigns of passive resistance had led to India's independence from Britain in 1947. After Rosa Parks's arrest, King endorsed a plan by a local black women's organization to boycott Montgomery's bus system until it was integrated.

For the next 381 days Montgomery blacks formed car pools or walked to work. The bus company neared bankruptcy, and downtown stores complained about the loss of business. But only after the Supreme Court ruled in November 1956 that bus segregation was unconstitutional did the city of Montgomery finally comply. "My feets is tired, but my soul is rested," said one satisfied woman boycotter.

The Montgomery bus boycott catapulted King to national prominence. In 1957, along with the Reverend Ralph Abernathy, he founded the Southern Christian Leadership Conference (SCLC), based in Atlanta. The black church, long the center of African American social and cultural life, now lent its moral and organizational strength to the civil rights movement. Black churchwomen were a tower of strength, transferring the skills honed by years of church work to the fight for civil rights. Soon the SCLC joined the NAACP as one of the main advocacy groups for racial justice.

Greensboro. The battle for civil rights entered a new phase in Greensboro, North Carolina, on February 1, 1960, when four black college students

Challenging White Supremacy

No problem is more challenging to the historian than figuring out how long-oppressed, ordinary people finally rise up and demand justice. During the 1950s that liberating process was quietly under way among southern blacks, first bursting forth dramatically in the Montgomery bus boycott of 1955 and then, by the end of the decade, emerging across the South. Here we take the testimony of two individuals who stepped forward and took the lead in those struggles.

FRANKLIN McCAIN
Desegregating Lunch Counters

Franklin McCain was one of the four African American students at North Carolina A&T College in Greensboro, North Carolina, who sat down at the Woolworth's lunch counter on February 1, 1960, setting off by that simple act a wave of student sit-ins that rocked the South and helped initiate a national civil rights movement. In the following interview, McCain describes how he and his pals took that momentous step.

The planning process was on a Sunday night, I remember it quite well. I think it was Joseph who said, "It's time that we take some action now. We've been getting together, and we've been, up to this point, still like most people we've talked about for the past few weeks or so — that is, people who talk a lot but, in fact, make very little action." After selecting the technique, then we said, "Let's go down and just ask for service." It certainly wasn't titled a "sit-in" or "sit-down" at that time. "Let's just go down to Woolworth's tomorrow and ask for service, and the tactic is going to be simply this: we'll just stay there."

. . . Once getting there . . . we did make purchases of school supplies and took the patience and time to get receipts for our purchases, and Joseph and myself went over to the counter and asked to be served coffee and doughnuts. As anticipated, the reply was, "I'm sorry, we don't serve you here." And of course we said, "We just beg to disagree with you. We've in fact already been served." . . . The attendant or waitress was a little bit dumbfounded, just didn't know what to say under circumstances like that. . . .

At that point there was a policeman who had walked in off the street, who was pacing the aisle . . . behind us, where we were seated, with his club in his hand, just sort of knocking it in his hand, and just looking mean and red and a little bit upset and a little bit disgusted. And you had the feeling

that he didn't know what the hell to do. . . . Usually his defense is offense, and we've provoked him, yes, but we haven't provoked outwardly enough for him to resort to violence. And I think this is just killing him; you can see it all over him.

If it's possible to know what it means to have your soul cleansed — I felt pretty clean at that time. I probably felt better on that day than I've ever felt in my life. Seems like a lot of feelings of guilt or what-have-you suddenly left me, and I felt as though I had gained my manhood. . . . Not Franklin McCain only as an individual, but I felt as though the manhood of a number of other black persons had been restored and had gotten some respect from just that one day.

The movement started out as a movement of nonviolence and a Christian movement. . . . It was a movement that was seeking justice more than anything else and not a movement to start a war. . . . We knew that probably the most powerful and potent weapon that people have literally no defense for is love, kindness. That is, whip the enemy with something that he doesn't understand. . . . The individual who had probably the most influence on us was Gandhi . . . . Yes, Martin Luther King's name was well-known when the sit-in movement was in effect, but . . . no, he was not the individual we had upmost in mind when we started the sit-in movement.

SOURCE: Howell Raines, *My Soul Is Rested.* Copyright ©1977 by Howell Raines. Originally published by Penguin Putnam, 1977. Reprinted with permission of PFD, Inc.

JOHN McFERREN
Demanding the Right to Vote

In this interview, given about ten years after the events he describes, John McFerren tells of the battle he undertook in 1959 to gain the vote for the blacks of Fayette County, Tennessee. By the time of the interview, he had risen in life and become a grocery-store owner and property holder, thanks, he says, to the economic boycott imposed on him by angry whites. Unlike Greensboro, the struggle in Fayette County never made national headlines. It was just one of many local struggles that signaled the beginning of a new day in the South.

My name is John McFerren. I'm forty-six years old. I'm a Negro was born and raised in West Tennessee, the county of Fayette, District 1. My foreparents was brought here from North Carolina five years before the Civil War . . . because the rumor got out among the slaveholders that West Tennessee was still goin to be a slaveholdin state. And my people was brought over here and sold. And after the Civil War my people settled in West Tennessee. That's why Fayette and Haywood counties have a great number of Negroes.

Back in 1957 and '58 there was a Negro man accused of killin a deputy sheriff. This was Burton Dodson. He was brought back after he'd been gone twenty years. J. F. Estes was the lawyer defendin him. Myself and him both was in the army together. And the stimulation from the trial got me interested in the way justice was bein used. The only way to bring justice would be through the ballot box.

In 1959 we got out a charter called the Fayette County Civic and Welfare League. Fourteen of us started out in that charter. We tried to support a white liberal candidate that was named L. T. Redfearn in the sheriff election and the local Democrat party refused to let Negroes vote.

We brought a suit against the Democrat party and I went to Washington for a civil-rights hearing. Myself and Estes and Harpman Jameson made the trip. It took us twenty-two hours steady drivin. . . . I was lookin all up — lotsa big, tall buildins. I had never seen old, tall buildins like that before. After talkin to [John Doar] we come on back to the Justice Department building and we sat out in the hall while he had a meetin inside the attorney general's office. And when they come out they told us they was gonna indict the landowners who kept us from voting. . . .

Just after that, in 1960, in January, we organized a thousand Negroes to line up at the courthouse to register to vote. We started pourin in with big numbers — in this county it was 72 percent Negroes — when we started to register to vote to change the situation.

In the followin . . . October and November they started puttin our people offa the land. Once you registered you had to move. Once you registered they took your job. Then after they done that, in November, we had three hundred people forced to live in tents on Shepard Towles's land. And when we started puttin em in tents, then that's when the White Citizens Council and the Ku Klux Klan started shootin in the tents to run us out.

Tent City was parta an economic squeeze. The local merchants run me outa the stores and said I went to Washington and caused this mess to start. . . . They had a blacklist . . . And they had the list sent around to all merchants. Once you registered you couldn't buy for credit or cash. But the best thing in the world was when they run me outa them stores. It started me thinkin for myself. . . .

The southern white has a slogan: "Keep em niggers happy and keep em singin in the schools." And the biggest mistake of the past is that the Negro has not been teached economics and the value of a dollar. . . . Back at one time we had a teacher . . . from Mississippi — and he pulled up and left the county because he was teachin the Negroes to buy land, and own land, and work it for hisself, and the county Board of Education didn't want that taught in the county. And they told him, "Keep em niggers singin and keep em happy and don't teach em nothin."

. . . You cannot be free when you're beggin the man for bread. But when you've got the dollar in your pocket and then got the vote in your pocket, that's the only way to be free. . . . And I have been successful and made good progress because I could see the only way I could survive is to stay independent. . . . The Negro is no longer goin back. He's goin forward.

SOURCE: Stanley I. Kutler, ed., *Looking for America*, 2d ed., 2 vols. (New York: Norton, 1979), 2: 449–453.

ANALYZING THE EVIDENCE

➤ McCain took a stand on segregated lunch counters. McFerren took a stand on the right to vote. Why did they choose different targets? Does it matter that they did?

➤ McCain speaks of the sense of "manhood" he felt as he sat at that Woolworth counter. Would that feeling have been enough to satisfy McFerren?

➤ Almost certainly, McCain and McFerren never met. Suppose they had. What would they have had in common? Would what they had in common have been more important than what separated them?

➤ McCain speaks knowingly of the figures and ideas that influenced him. Why do you suppose McFerren is silent about such matters? If he had spoken up, do you suppose he would have — or should have — mentioned Booker T. Washington (see Chapter 20)?

took seats at the "whites-only" lunch counter at the local Woolworth's. They were determined to "sit in" until they were served (see Comparing American Voices, "Challenging White Supremacy," pp. 856–857). Although they were arrested, the sit-in tactic worked—the Woolworth lunch counter was desegregated—and sit-ins quickly spread to other southern cities. A few months later Ella Baker, an administrator with the SCLC, helped to organize the Student Non-Violent Coordinating Committee (SNCC, known as "Snick") to facilitate student sit-ins. By the end of the year, about 50,000 people had participated in sit-ins or other demonstrations, and 3,600 of them had been jailed. But in 126 cities across the South blacks were at last able to eat at Woolworth lunch counters.

The victories so far had been limited, but the groundwork had been laid for a civil rights offensive that would transform the nation's race relations.

➤ What were the most significant migration trends in this era?

➤ What were the key components of the urban crisis?

➤ What is the significance of the *Brown v. Board of Education of Topeka* decision?

SUMMARY

We have explored how, at the very time it became mired in the Cold War, the United States entered an unparalleled era of prosperity. Indeed, the Cold War was one of the engines of prosperity. The postwar economy was marked especially by the dominance of big corporations. Corporate dominance in turn helped make possible the labor-management accord that spread the benefits of prosperity to workers beyond the dreams of earlier generations.

After years of depression and war-induced insecurity, Americans turned inward toward religion, home, and family. Postwar couples married young, had several children, and—if they were white and middle class—raised their children in a climate of suburban comfort and consumerism. The pro-family orientation of the 1950s celebrated social conformity and traditional gender roles, even though millions of women entered the workforce in those years. Cultural conformity, however, provoked resistance, both by the burgeoning youth culture and by a remarkably inventive generation of painters, musicians, and writers.

Not everyone, moreover, shared the postwar prosperity. Postwar cities increasingly became places of last resort for the nation's poor. Black migrants, unlike earlier immigrants, encountered an urban economy that had little use for them. Without opportunity, and faced by pervasive racism, they were on their way to becoming, many of them, an American underclass. In the South, however, discrimination produced a civil rights uprising that white America could not ignore. Many of the smoldering contradictions of the postwar period—Cold War anxiety in the midst of suburban domesticity, tensions in women's lives, economic and racial inequality—helped spur the protest movements of the 1960s.

Connections: Economy

"In the 1950s," we noted in the essay opening Part Six, "no country was competitive with America's economy." The roots of that supremacy went back into the late nineteenth century when, as we discussed in Chapter 17, heavy industry, mass-production technology, and corporate business structure emerged. In the 1920s (Chapter 23) this industrial economy was refined and, after the hiatus of the Great Depression, became the basis for the post–World War II economic boom. In Chapter 29, we describe the first stages in the decline of this manufacturing economy during the 1970s. The postwar consumer culture had roots that went back into the 1920s (Chapter 23), while the accompanying suburbanization went back even earlier, into the nineteenth century (Chapter 18). Similarly, we can trace back to earlier discussions the migratory patterns (to Chapters 17 and 22) and the decay of the cities (to Chapter 18).

CHAPTER REVIEW QUESTIONS

➤ How do you acount for the economic prosperity of the postwar era?

➤ Why did the suburb achieve paramount significance for Americans in the 1950s?

➤ Who were the people who occupied "the Other America"? Why were they there rather than in mainstream America?

TIMELINE

1944	Bretton Woods economic conference World Bank and International Monetary Fund (IMF) founded
1946	First edition of Dr. Spock's *Baby and Child Care*
1947	First Levittown built Jackie Robinson joins the Brooklyn Dodgers
1948	Beginning of network television
1950	Treaty of Detroit initiates labor-management accord
1953	Operation Wetback
1954	*Brown v. Board of Education of Topeka*
1955	Montgomery bus boycott begins AFL and CIO merge
1956	National Interstate and Defense Highways Act Elvis Presley's breakthrough records
1957	Peak of postwar baby boom Eisenhower sends U.S. troops to enforce integration of Little Rock Central High School Southern Christian Leadership Conference (SCLC) founded
1960	Student sit-ins in Greensboro, North Carolina

FOR FURTHER EXPLORATION

Two engaging introductions to postwar society are Paul Boyer, *Promises to Keep* (1995), and David Halberstam, *The Fifties* (1993). John K. Galbraith, *The Affluent Society* (1958), is a lively and influential contemporary analysis of the postwar economy. Nelson Lichtenstein, *State of the Union: A Century of American Labor* (2002), offers a searching account of the labor-management accord. The best book on the consumer culture, wide-ranging in perspective, is Lizabeth Cohen, *A Consumers' Republic: The Politics of Mass Consumption in Postwar America* (2003). Elaine Tyler May, *Homeward Bound* (1988), is the classic introduction to postwar family life. For insightful essays on the impact of television, see Karal Ann Marling, *As Seen on TV* (1996). An excellent, award-winning memoir of the Beat generation is Joyce Johnson, *Minor Characters* (1983). For youth culture, see William Graebner, *Coming of Age in Buffalo* (1990), and, a classic of the period, Paul Goodman, *Growing Up Absurd* (1960). On the urban crisis, see especially Nicholas Lemann, *The Promised Land: The Great Migration and How It Changed America* (1991), and Thomas J. Sugrue, *The Origins of the Urban Crisis: Race and Inequality in Postwar Detroit* (1996). Taylor Branch's biography of Martin Luther King Jr., *Parting the Waters: America in the King Years, 1954–1963* (1988), while focusing on King's leadership, provides an engaging account of the early civil rights movement.

Literary Kicks: The Beat Generation, at **www.litkicks.com/ BeatPages/msg.jsp?what=BeatGen**, is an independent site created by New York writer Levi Asher devoted to the literature of the Beat generation. The site includes writings by Jack Kerouac, Allen Ginsberg, Neal Cassady, and others; material on Beats, music, religion, and film; an extensive bibliography; biographical information; and photographs.

The Arkansas *Democrat Gazette* has compiled materials from two Arkansas newspapers covering the Central High School crisis in Little Rock in 1957 at **www.ardemgaz.com/ prev/central**. Editorials and daily news coverage, including photographs, are featured, as well as later commentary by such diverse political figures as former president and Arkansas governor Bill Clinton and former Arkansas governor Orval Faubus.

TEST YOUR KNOWLEDGE

To assess your command of the material in this chapter, see the Online Study Guide at **bedfordstmartins.com/henretta**.

For Web sites, images, and documents related to topics and places in this chapter, visit **bedfordstmartins.com/makehistory**.

28 The Liberal Consensus: Flaming Out

1960–1968

ON INAUGURATION DAY, 1961, STANDING bare-headed in the wintry January brightness, the freshly sworn-in president issued a ringing declaration: "Let the word go forth from this time and place, to friend and foe alike, that the torch has passed to a new generation of Americans, born in this century, tempered by war, disciplined by a hard and bitter peace, proud of our ancient heritage." John F. Kennedy challenged Americans everywhere: "Ask not what your country can do for you, ask what you can do for your country." And, more than anyone might have expected, Americans responded. "There's a moral wave building among today's youth," said a civil rights volunteer in 1964, "and I intend to catch it." Kennedy's politics of expectation might have been initially mostly a matter of atmospherics, but over time it built into the greatest burst of liberal reform since the New Deal—landmark civil rights laws, Medicare, the War on Poverty, and much else. All this—the triumph of the liberal consensus—starts with the indelible image of the youthful Kennedy exhorting the country on that Inauguration Day, 1961.

Fast forward to 1968, to the Democratic National Convention in Chicago. Kennedy is dead, assassinated. His civil rights mentor, Martin Luther King Jr., is dead, assassinated. His younger brother and heir apparent, Bobby, is dead, assassinated. And his successor in the White

John F. Kennedy and the Politics of Expectation
The New Politics
The Kennedy Administration
The Civil Rights Movement Stirs
Kennedy, Cold Warrior
The Kennedy Assassination

Lyndon B. Johnson and the Great Society
The Momentum for Civil Rights
Enacting the Liberal Agenda

Into the Quagmire, 1963–1968
Escalation
Public Opinion on Vietnam
Student Activism

Coming Apart
The Counterculture
Beyond Civil Rights

1968: A Year of Shocks
The Politics of Vietnam
Backlash

Summary
Connections: Diplomacy and Politics

◄ **Peace Demonstrators**

Antiwar demonstrators wave a red flag bearing the peace sign near the Washington Monument where thousands gathered for a Moratorium Day rally in Washington, D.C., November 15, 1969. © Bettmann/Corbis.

House, Lyndon B. Johnson, is so discredited that he has withdrawn his name from nomination. On the streets the Chicago police teargassed and clubbed demonstrators, who screamed (as the TV cameras rolled), "The whole world is watching!" Some of them had once been the idealistic young people of Kennedy's exhortation. Now they detested everything that Kennedy's liberalism stood for. Inside the convention hall, the proceedings were chaotic, the atmosphere poisonous, the delegates bitterly divided over Vietnam. As expected, Johnson's vice president, Hubert Humphrey, easily won the nomination, but he hadn't been done any favors. He acknowledged going home feeling not triumphant, but "heartbroken, battered, and defeated." The Chicago convention had been "a disaster."

In this chapter we undertake to explain how Kennedy's stirring Inauguration metamorphosed into the searing Democratic National Convention of 1968. Between those two events, indelible in America's memory, the liberal consensus flamed out.

John F. Kennedy and the Politics of Expectation

Since the days of FDR and the New Deal, Americans had come increasingly to look to Washington and the president for answers to the nation's prob-

lems. Few presidents were happier to oblige than John Kennedy. He came to Washington primed for action, promising that his "New Frontier" would get America moving again. The British journalist Henry Fairley called this activist impulse "the politics of expectation." Soon enough, expectation came up against unyielding reality, but Kennedy's can-do style nevertheless left a lasting impression on American politics.

The New Politics

Charisma, style, and personality — these, more than platforms and issues — were hallmarks of a new brand of politics that we associate with John F. Kennedy. With the power of the media in mind, a younger generation of politicians saw in television a new way to reach directly to the voters. Candidates drifted away from traditional party organizations, with their ward bosses, state committees, and party machines that had once delivered the votes on election day. By using the media, campaigns could bypass the party structures and touch, if only with a 30-second commercial, the ordinary citizen.

The new politics was Kennedy's natural environment. A Harvard alumnus, World War II hero, senator from Massachusetts, he had inherited his love of politics from his grandfathers, both colorful Irish-Catholic politicians in Boston. Ambitious, hard-driving, and deeply aware of style, the forty-three-year-old Kennedy made full use of his many

The Kennedy Magnetism

John Kennedy, the Democratic candidate for president in 1960, used his youth and personality to attract voters. Here the Massachusetts senator draws an enthusiastic crowd on a campaign stop in Elgin, Illinois. AP Images.

advantages to become, as novelist Norman Mailer put it, "our leading man." His one disadvantage—that he was Catholic in a country that had never elected a Catholic president—he masterfully neutralized. His family's wealth and his energetic fund-raising financed an exceptionally expensive campaign. And thanks to media advisers and his youthful, attractive personality, he projected a superb television image.

His Republican opponent, Eisenhower's vice president Richard M. Nixon, was a more seasoned politician, but personally awkward and ill-endowed for combat in the new politics. The great innovation of the 1960 campaign was a series of four nationally televised debates. Nixon, less photogenic than Kennedy, looked sallow and unshaven under the intense studio lights. Polls showed that television did sway political perceptions: Voters who heard the first debate on the radio concluded that Nixon had won, but those viewing it on television favored Kennedy.

Despite the edge Kennedy enjoyed in the debates, he won only the narrowest of electoral victories, receiving 49.7 percent of the popular vote to Nixon's 49.5 percent. Kennedy attracted Catholics, black voters, and the labor vote; his vice presidential running mate, Lyndon Johnson from Texas, brought in southern Democrats. Yet only 120,000 votes separated the two candidates, and the shift of a few thousand votes in key states such as Illinois (where Chicago Mayor Richard Daley's machine miraculously generated the needed margin) would have reversed the outcome. Despite his razor-thin margin, Kennedy won 303 electoral votes, compared to Nixon's 219, revealing once again the distorting effect of the electoral college on the people's choice.

The Kennedy Administration

Unlike Eisenhower, Kennedy believed in a federal government that was visibly active and a presidency that set the tone for bold leadership. Kennedy's vigor attracted unusually able and ambitious people, including Robert McNamara, a renowned systems analyst and former head of Ford, at Defense, and C. Douglas Dillon, a highly admired Republican banker, as secretary of the Treasury. A host of trusted advisers and academics— "the best and the brightest," the journalist David Halberstam called them—flocked to Washington to join the New Frontier. Included on the team as attorney-general was Kennedy's kid brother, Robert, a trusted adviser who had made a name as a hard-hitting investigator of organized crime. Not everyone was enchanted.

Kennedy's people "might be every bit as intelligent as you say," House Speaker Sam Rayburn told his old friend Lyndon Johnson, "but I'd feel a whole lot better about them if just one of them had run for sheriff once." Sure enough, the new administration immediately got into hot water.

The Bay of Pigs. In January 1961 Soviet Premier Nikita Khrushchev announced that the USSR intended to support "wars of national liberation" wherever in the world they occurred. Kennedy took Khrushchev's words as a challenge, especially as they applied to Cuba, where in 1959 Fidel Castro had overthrown the dictator Fulgencio Batista and declared a revolution. Determined to keep Cuba out of the Soviet orbit, Kennedy took up plans by the Eisenhower administration to dispatch Cuban exiles from Nicaragua to foment an anti-Castro uprising. The invaders had been trained by the Central Intelligence Agency, but they were ill prepared for their task and betrayed by the CIA's inept planning. Upon landing at Cuba's Bay of Pigs on April 17, the force of 1,400 was apprehended and crushed by Castro's troops. The anticipated rebellion never happened. Kennedy had the good sense to reject CIA pleas for a U.S. air strike. And he was gracious in defeat. He went before the American people and took full responsibility for the fiasco.

Peace Corps, Foreign Aid, Astronauts. Kennedy redeemed himself with a series of bold initiatives. One was the Peace Corps, which embodied his call to public service in his inaugural address. Thousands of men and women agreed to devote two or more years to programs teaching English to Filipino schoolchildren or helping African villagers obtain adequate supplies of water. Exhibiting the idealism of the early 1960s, the Peace Corps was also a Cold War weapon intended to show developing countries of the so-called Third World that there was a better way than Communism (Map 28.1). Also embodying this aim were ambitious programs of economic assistance. The State Department's Agency for International Development coordinated foreign aid for the Third World, and its Food for Peace program distributed surplus agricultural products. In 1961 the president proposed a "ten-year plan for the Americas" called the Alliance for Progress, a $20 billion partnership between the United States and the republics of Latin America, to reverse the cycle of poverty and stimulate economic growth.

Kennedy was also keen on space exploration. Early in his administration, Kennedy proposed that the nation commit itself to landing a man on the

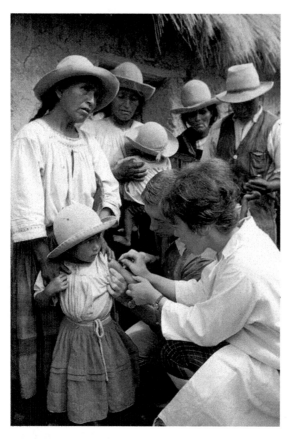

The Peace Corps

The Peace Corps, a New Frontier program initiated in 1961, attracted thousands of idealistic young Americans, including these volunteers who worked in a vaccination program in Bolivia. David S. Boyer/National Geographic Society Image Collection.

moon within the decade. Two weeks later, on May 5, 1961, Alan Shepard became the first American in space (beaten there by the Soviet cosmonaut Yuri Gagarin's 108-hour flight). The following year, John Glenn manned the first space mission to orbit the earth. Capitalizing on America's fascination with space flight, Kennedy persuaded Congress to greatly increase funding for the National Aeronautics and Space Administration (NASA), enabling the United States to pull ahead of the Soviet Union. (Kennedy's men on the moon arrived in 1969.)

Domestic Agenda. Kennedy's most striking domestic achievement—another of his bold moves—was the application of modern economic theory to government fiscal policy. New Dealers had lost faith in a balanced budget, turning instead to the Keynesian approach of deliberate deficit spending to stimulate economic growth. Now, in addition to deficit spending, Kennedy and his economic advisers proposed a reduction in income taxes. A tax

cut, they argued, would put money in the hands of consumers, thereby generating more demand, more jobs, and ultimately higher tax revenues. Congress balked at this unorthodox proposal, but it made its way through in 1964, marking a milestone in the use of tax cuts to encourage economic growth, an approach later embraced by Republican fiscal conservatives (see Chapter 30).

But Kennedy was less engaged by the more humdrum matters of social policy, notwithstanding that he had given lip service to an ambitious agenda during his presidential campaign. In part, he was stymied by the lack of a strong popular mandate in the election's outcome. He was also a cautious politician, unwilling to expend capital where the odds were against him. Kennedy managed to push through legislation raising the minimum wage and expanding Social Security, but on other emerging issues—federal aid to education, mass transportation, medical insurance for the elderly—he gave up in the face of conservative opposition in Congress.

The Civil Rights Movement Stirs

Kennedy was equally cautious about civil rights. Despite his campaign commitment, in his first two years he failed to deliver on a civil rights bill. The opposition in Congress, where segregationist southern Democrats dominated key committees, just seemed too formidable. But civil rights was not like other domestic issues. Its fate was going to be decided not in the halls of Congress, but on the streets of southern cities.

Freedom Riders. Emboldened by the success of SNCC's sit-in tactics at integrating lunch counters (see Chapter 27), the interracial Congress of Racial Equality (CORE) organized a series of "freedom rides" in 1961 on interstate bus lines throughout the South. The aim was to call attention to blatant violation of recent Supreme Court rulings against segregation in interstate commerce. The activists who signed on, mostly young, both black and white, knew they were taking their lives in their hands. In Anniston, Alabama, club-wielding Klansmen attacked one of the buses with stones and set it on fire. The freedom riders escaped only moments before the bus exploded. Other riders were brutally beaten in Montgomery and Birmingham. State authorities refused to intervene. "I cannot guarantee protection for this bunch of rabble rousers," declared Governor John Patterson. That left it up to Washington. Although Kennedy discouraged the freedom rides, films of beatings and burning buses

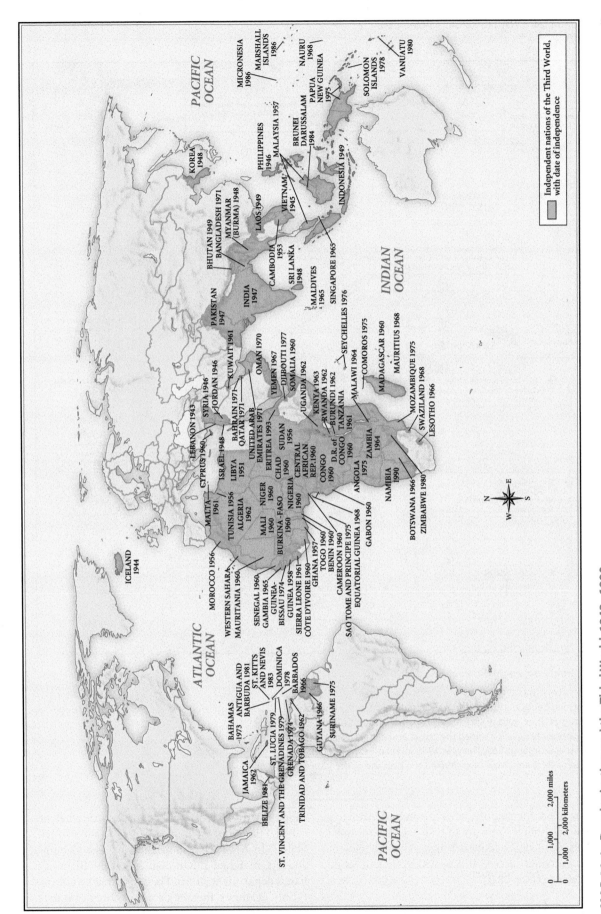

MAP 28.1 Decolonization and the Third World, 1943–1990

At the end of World War II, the colonial empires built up over the previous centuries by European countries were still formally intact. After 1945, movements for national self-determination swept across Africa, India, and Southeast Asia. This map shows the many nations carved out of that struggle, all of them parts of the "Third World," a Cold War term designating countries not formally aligned either with the Western or the Soviet blocs. Courted by both the United States and the Soviet Union, some Third World nations like Vietnam and Angola became key battlegrounds of the Cold War, often with disastrous results for the local populations.

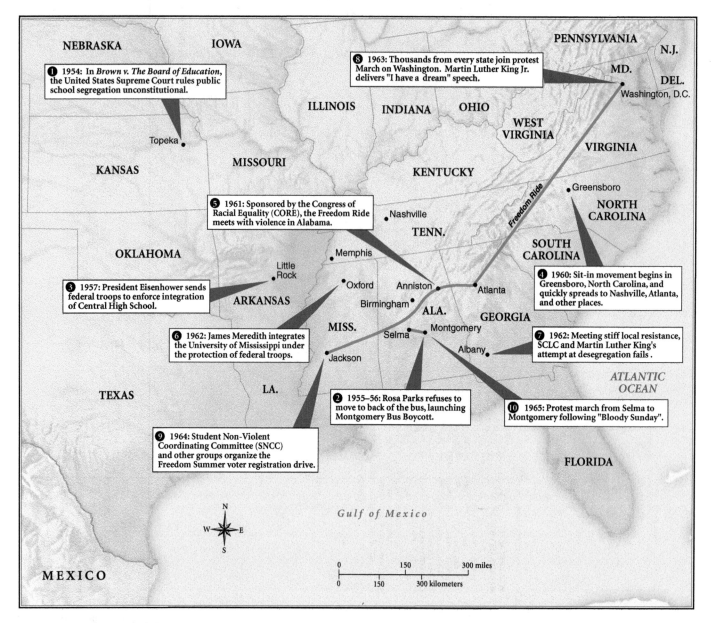

NEBRASKA   IOWA   PENNSYLVANIA   N.J.

❶ 1954: In *Brown v. The Board of Education*, the United States Supreme Court rules public school segregation unconstitutional.

ILLINOIS   INDIANA   OHIO   WEST VIRGINIA   MD.   DEL.

Washington, D.C.

❽ 1963: Thousands from every state join protest March on Washington. Martin Luther King Jr. delivers "I have a dream" speech.

Topeka

KANSAS   MISSOURI   KENTUCKY   VIRGINIA

❺ 1961: Sponsored by the Congress of Racial Equality (CORE), the Freedom Ride meets with violence in Alabama.

Nashville   Greensboro

NORTH CAROLINA

TENN.   SOUTH CAROLINA

OKLAHOMA   Memphis

Little Rock

❸ 1957: President Eisenhower sends federal troops to enforce integration of Central High School.

ARKANSAS   Oxford   Anniston   Atlanta

❹ 1960: Sit-in movement begins in Greensboro, North Carolina, and quickly spreads to Nashville, Atlanta, and other places.

Birmingham   ALA.   GEORGIA

❻ 1962: James Meredith integrates the University of Mississippi under the protection of federal troops.

MISS.   Montgomery   Selma

❼ 1962: Meeting stiff local resistance, SCLC and Martin Luther King's attempt at desegregation fails.

Jackson   Albany

ATLANTIC OCEAN

TEXAS   LA.

❷ 1955–56: Rosa Parks refuses to move to back of the bus, launching Montgomery Bus Boycott.

❿ 1965: Protest march from Selma to Montgomery following "Bloody Sunday".

❾ 1964: Student Non-Violent Coordinating Committee (SNCC) and other groups organize the Freedom Summer voter registration drive.

FLORIDA

MEXICO   *Gulf of Mexico*

0   150   300 miles
0   150   300 kilometers

MAP 28.2   The Civil Rights Struggle, 1954–1965

In the postwar battle for black civil rights, the first major victory was the NAACP litigation of *Brown v. Board of Education*, which declared public school segregation unconstitutional. As indicated on this map, the struggle then quickly spread, raising other issues and seeding new organizations. Other organizations quickly joined the battle and shifted the focus away from the courts to mass action and organization. The year 1965 marked the high point, when violence against the Selma, Alabama, marchers spurred the passage of the Voting Rights Act (see p. 872).

shown on the nightly news prompted Attorney General Robert Kennedy to dispatch federal marshals. Civil rights activists learned that nonviolent protest could succeed if it provoked violent white resistance (Map 28.2).

Birmingham. This lesson was confirmed in Birmingham, Alabama, when Martin Luther King Jr.

called for protests against conditions in what he called "the most segregated city in the United States." In April 1963 thousands of black demonstrators marched downtown to picket Birmingham's department stores. They were met by Eugene ("Bull") Connor, the city's commissioner of public safety, and his police, who used snarling dogs, electric cattle prods, and high-pressure fire hoses to

Racial Violence in Birmingham

When thousands of blacks marched through downtown Birmingham, Alabama, to protest racial segregation in April 1963, they were met with fire hoses and attack dogs unleashed by Police Chief "Bull" Connor. The violence, which was televised on the national evening news, shocked many Americans and helped build sympathy for the civil rights movement among northern whites. AP Images/Bill Hudson.

break up the crowds. Television cameras captured the scene for the evening news.

Outraged by the brutality, President Kennedy decided it was time to step in. On June 11, 1963, after Alabama Governor George Wallace barred two black students from the state university, Kennedy went on television and delivered a passionate speech denouncing racism and announcing a new civil rights bill. Black leaders hailed the speech as a "Second Emancipation Proclamation." That night Medgar Evers, president of the Mississippi chapter of the NAACP, was shot in the back and killed in his driveway in Jackson. The martyrdom of Evers became a spur to further action.

The March on Washington. To marshal support for Kennedy's bill, civil rights leaders adopted a tactic that A. Philip Randolph had first advanced in 1941 (see Chapter 25): a massive demonstration in

Washington. Although the planning was not primarily Martin Luther King's, he was truly the public face of the March on Washington on August 28, 1963. It was King's dramatic "I Have a Dream" speech, ending with the exclamation from an old Negro spiritual — "Free at last! Free at last! Thank God Almighty, we are free at last!" — that captured the nation's imagination. The sight of 250,000 blacks and whites marching solemnly together marked the high point of the civil rights movement and confirmed King's position, especially among white liberals, as the leading spokesperson for the black cause.

Although the March on Washington galvanized public opinion, it changed few congressional votes. Southern senators continued to block Kennedy's legislation by threatening a filibuster. In September a Baptist church in Birmingham was bombed and four black Sunday school students were killed,

The March on Washington

The Reverend Martin Luther King Jr. (1929–1968) was the most eloquent advocate of the civil rights movement. For many, his "I Have a Dream" speech of the 1963 March on Washington was the high point of the day, and, for some, of the entire civil rights struggle. The focus on the charismatic King, however, meant that the importance of other civil rights leaders was frequently overlooked.　Bob Adelman/Magnum Photos, Inc.

shocking the nation and bringing the civil rights demonstrations to a boiling point.

Kennedy, Cold Warrior

Foreign affairs gave greater scope for Kennedy's fertile mind. A resolute cold warrior, Kennedy took a hard line against Communism. In contrast to Eisenhower, whose cost-saving New Look program had built up the American nuclear arsenal at the expense of conventional weapons, Kennedy proposed a new policy of "flexible response," stating that the nation must be prepared "to deter all wars, general or limited, nuclear or conventional, large or small." Congress quickly granted Kennedy's military requests, and by 1963 the defense budget reached its highest level as a percentage of total federal expenditures in the Cold War era.

Already strained by the Bay of Pigs invasion, U.S.-Soviet relations deteriorated further in June 1961 when Soviet Premier Khrushchev deployed soldiers to isolate Communist-controlled East Berlin from the western sector controlled by West Germany. With congressional approval, Kennedy responded by adding 300,000 troops to the armed forces and promptly dispatching 40,000 of them to Europe. In mid-August, to stop the exodus of East Germans, the Soviets ordered construction of the Berlin Wall, and East German guards began policing the border. Until it was dismantled in 1989, the Berlin Wall remained the supreme symbol of the Cold War.

The climactic confrontation of the Cold War came in October 1962. In a somber televised address,

Kennedy revealed that reconnaissance planes had spotted Soviet-built bases for intermediate-range ballistic missiles in Cuba. Some of those weapons had already been installed, and more were on the way. Kennedy announced that the United States would impose a "quarantine on all offensive military equipment" intended for Cuba (Map 28.3). As the two superpowers went on full military alert, people around the world feared an imminent nuclear war. But as the world held its breath, the ships carrying Soviet-made missiles turned back. After a week of tense negotiations, both Kennedy and Khrushchev made concessions: Kennedy pledged not to invade Cuba, and Khrushchev promised to dismantle the missile bases.

The risk of nuclear war, greater during the Cuban missile crisis than at any other time in the postwar period, led to a slight thaw in U.S.-Soviet relations. As national security advisor McGeorge Bundy put it, both sides were chastened by "having come so close to the edge." Kennedy softened his Cold War rhetoric and Soviet leaders, similarly chastened, agreed to talk. In August 1963 the three principal nuclear powers—the United States, the Soviet Union, and Great Britain—announced a ban on the testing of nuclear weapons in the atmosphere, although underground testing was allowed to continue. The new emphasis on peaceful coexistence also led to the establishment of a Washington-Moscow telecommunications "hotline" in 1963 so that leaders could contact each other quickly in a crisis.

But no matter how much American leaders talked about opening channels of communication with Moscow, relations with the Soviet Union

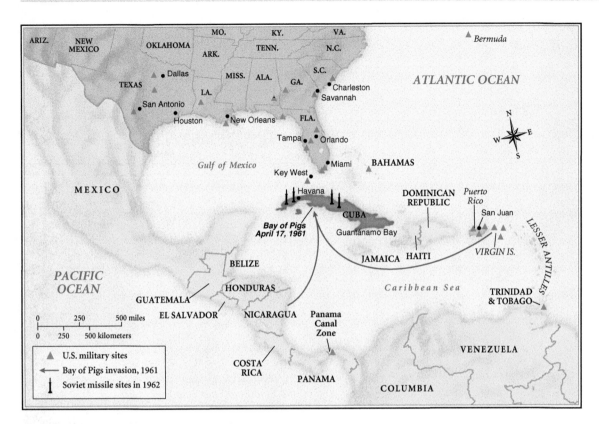

MAP 28.3   The United States and Cuba, 1961–1962

Fidel Castro's takeover in Cuba in 1959 brought Cold War tensions to the Caribbean. In 1961 the United States tried unsuccessfully to overthrow Castro's regime by supporting the Bay of Pigs invasion of Cuban exiles launched from Nicaragua and other points in the Caribbean. In 1962 a major confrontation with the Soviet Union occurred over Soviet construction of nuclear missile sites in Cuba. The Soviets removed the missiles after President Kennedy ordered a naval blockade of the island. Despite the fall of the Soviet Union in 1991 and the official end of the Cold War, the United States continues to view Cuba, still governed in 2006 by Fidel Castro, as an enemy nation.

remained tense, and containment remained the cornerstone of U.S. policy.

The Vietnam Puzzle. When Kennedy became president, he inherited Eisenhower's involvement in Vietnam. Kennedy saw Vietnam in very much the same Cold War terms. But what really grabbed him was the chance to test the counterinsurgency doctrine associated with his "flexible response" military strategy. The army was training U.S. Special Forces, called Green Berets for their distinctive headgear, to engage in unconventional, small-group warfare. Kennedy and his advisers wanted to try out the Green Berets in the Vietnamese jungles.

Despite American aid, the corrupt and repressive Diem regime installed by Eisenhower in 1954 was losing ground (see Chapter 26). By 1961 Diem's opponents, with backing from North Vietnam, had formed a revolutionary movement known as the National Liberation Front (NLF). The NLF's guerrilla forces—the Vietcong—found a receptive audience among peasants alienated by Diem's "strategic hamlet" program, which uprooted whole villages and moved them into barbed-wire compounds. Buddhists charged Diem, a Catholic, with religious persecution. Starting in May 1963, militant Buddhists staged dramatic demonstrations, including several self-immolations recorded by American television crews. Losing patience with Diem, Kennedy let it be known in Saigon that the United States would support a military coup. On November 1, 1963, Diem was overthrown and assassinated—an eventuality evidently not anticipated by Kennedy. At that point, there were about 16,000 American "advisers" (an elastic term that included helicopter crews and Special Forces) in Vietnam.

In a CBS interview, Kennedy had remarked that it was up to the South Vietnamese whether "their war"

The Berlin Wall

A West Berlin resident walks alongside a section of the Berlin Wall in 1962, a year after its construction. Note the two border guards on the East Berlin side, plus the numerous loud speakers, which East German Communists used to broadcast propaganda over the barricade that divided the city. © Bettmann/Corbis.

would be won or lost. Advisers close to the president later argued that, had he run strongly in the 1964 election, he would have felt emboldened to cut America's losses and leave. But that argument downplays the geopolitical issues at stake in Vietnam. The United States was now engaged in a global war against Communism. Giving up in Vietnam would be weakening America's "credibility" in that struggle. And, under the prevailing "domino theory," other pro-American states would topple after Vietnam's loss. Kennedy subscribed to these received Cold War tenets. Whether he might have surmounted them down the road is, like how Lincoln might have handled Reconstruction after the Civil War had he lived, an unanswerable historical question.

The Kennedy Assassination

On November 22, 1963, Kennedy went to Texas on a political trip. As he and his wife, Jacqueline, rode in an open car past the Texas School Book Depository in Dallas, he was shot through the head and neck by a sniper. Kennedy died within the hour. (The accused killer, Lee Harvey Oswald, a twenty-four-year-old loner, was himself killed while in custody a few days later.) Before Air Force One left Dallas to take the president's body back to Washington, a grim-faced Lyndon Johnson was sworn in as president. Kennedy's stunned widow, still wearing her bloodstained pink suit, looked on.

Kennedy's youthful image, the trauma of his assassination, and the nation's sense of loss contributed to a powerful Kennedy mystique. His canonization after death actually capped an extraordinarily successful effort at stage-managing the presidency. An admiring country saw in Jack and Jackie Kennedy an ideal American marriage (he was in fact an obsessive womanizer); in Kennedy the man the epitome of robust good health (although he was actually afflicted by Addison's disease and

Buddhist Protest, 1966

Buddhist nun Thich Nu Thanh Quang burns to death at the Dieu de Pagoda in Hue, South Vietnam, in a ritual act of suicide in protest against the Catholic Saigon regime on May 29, 1966. Its inability to win over the Buddhist population was a major source of weakness for the South Vietnamese government. AP Images.

kept going by potent medications); and in the Kennedy White House a glamorous world of high fashion and celebrity. No presidency ever matched the Kennedy aura of "Camelot"—after the mythical realm of King Arthur in the hit musical of that title—but every president after him embraced the idea, with greater or lesser success, that image mattered as much as reality—maybe more—in conducting a politically effective presidency. In Kennedy's case, the ultimate irony was that his image as martyred leader produced grander legislative results than anything he might have achieved as a live president in the White House.

➤ Why was Kennedy an effective politican?

➤ Why did civil rights become a big issue during the Kennedy years?

➤ What were the results of Kennedy's foreign policy?

Lyndon B. Johnson and the Great Society

Lyndon Johnson was a seasoned politician from Texas, a longtime Senate leader at his best negotiating in the back rooms of power. Compared to Kennedy, Johnson was a rough-edged character who had scrambled his way up, without too many scruples, to wealth and political eminence. But unlike other bootstrap successes, he never forgot his hill-country origins or lost his sympathy for the down-

trodden. Johnson was no match for the Kennedy style, but he capitalized on Kennedy's assassination, applying his astonishing energy and negotiating skills to bring to fruition many of Kennedy's stalled programs and more than a few of his own in an ambitious program he called the "Great Society."

The Momentum for Civil Rights

On assuming the presidency, Lyndon Johnson promptly pushed for civil rights legislation as a memorial to his slain predecessor. His motives were a combination of the political and the personal. As a politician, he wanted the Democratic Party to benefit from the national groundswell for civil rights, although he was too shrewd an operative not be aware of the price the party would pay in the South. It was more important to him, as a president from the South, to reach across regional lines and appeal to a broad national audience. Achieving historic civil rights legislation would, he hoped, place his mark on the presidency.

The Civil Rights Act of 1964. Overcoming a southern filibuster, Congress approved in June 1964 the most far-reaching civil rights legislation since Reconstruction. The keystone of the Civil Rights Act, Title VII, outlawed discrimination in employment on the basis of race, religion, national origin, or sex. Another section guaranteed equal access to public accommodations and schools. The law granted new enforcement powers to the U.S. attorney general and established the Equal Employment Opportunity Commission (EEOC) to implement

Freedom Summer, 1964

In the summer of 1964 — "Freedom Summer" — hundreds of civil rights volunteers converged on Mississippi and Alabama to conduct voter registration drives. In this photograph, college students in Oxford, Ohio, sing and hold hands before their departure for Mississippi. They knew that rough days were ahead of them. Shapiro/Black Star/Stockphoto.com.

the prohibition against job discrimination. It was a law with real teeth. But it left untouched obstacles to black voting rights.

Freedom Summer. So protesters went back into the streets. In 1964 black organizations and churches mounted a major civil rights campaign in Mississippi. Known as "Freedom Summer," the effort drew several thousand volunteers from across the country, including many idealistic white college students. Freedom Summer workers established freedom schools, which taught black children traditional subjects as well as their own history; conducted a major voter registration drive; and organized the Mississippi Freedom Democratic Party, a political alternative to the all-white Democratic organization in Mississippi. Some southerners reacted swiftly and violently. Fifteen civil rights workers were murdered; only about 1,200 black voters were registered that summer.

The need for federal action became even clearer in March 1965, when Martin Luther King Jr. and other black leaders called for a massive march from Selma, Alabama, to the state capitol in Montgomery to protest the murder of a voting-rights activist. As soon as the marchers left Selma, mounted state troopers attacked them with tear gas and clubs. The scene was shown on national television that night. Calling the episode "an American tragedy," President Johnson redoubled his efforts to persuade Congress to pass the pending voting-rights legislation.

The Voting Rights Act. The Voting Rights Act, which passed on August 6, 1965, outlawed the literacy tests and other measures most southern states used to prevent blacks from registering to vote and

authorized the attorney general to send federal examiners to register voters in any county where less than 50 percent of the voting-age population was registered. Together with the Twenty-fourth Amendment (1964), which outlawed the poll tax in federal elections, the Voting Rights Act enabled millions of blacks to register and vote for the first time since after Reconstruction.

In the South the results were stunning. In 1960 only 20 percent of blacks of voting age had been registered to vote; by 1964 the figure had risen to 39 percent, and by 1971 it was 62 percent (Map 28.4). As Hartman Turnbow, a Mississippi farmer who risked his life to register in 1964, later declared, "It won't never go back where it was."

Enacting the Liberal Agenda

Johnson's success in pushing through the Voting Rights Act had stemmed in part from the 1964 election, when he had faced the Republican Barry Goldwater of Arizona. An arch-conservative, Goldwater ran on a anti-Communist, anti-government platform, offering "a choice, not an echo." There would be no Republican "Dime Store New Deal" this time around. The voters didn't buy it. Johnson and his running mate Hubert H. Humphrey of Minnesota won in a landslide (Map 28.5). In the long run, Goldwater's candidacy marked the beginning of a grassroots conservative revolt that would eventually transform the Republican Party and American politics. In the short run, however, Johnson's sweeping victory enabled him to bring to fruition the legislative programs of the "Great Society."

Like most New Deal liberals, Johnson held an expansive view of the role of government. Now he

MAP 28.4 Black Voter Registration in the South, 1964 and 1975

After passage of the Voting Rights Act of 1965, black registration in the South increased dramatically. The bars on the map show the number of blacks registered in 1964, before the act was passed, and in 1975, after it had been in effect for ten years. States in the Deep South, such as Mississippi, Alabama, and Georgia, had the biggest increases.

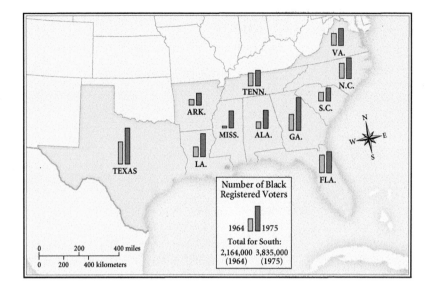

had a popular mandate and, equally important, the filibuster-proof majority he needed to push his programs forward (see Table 28.1).

One of Johnson's first successes was breaking the congressional deadlock on aid to education. Passed in April 1965, the Elementary and Secondary

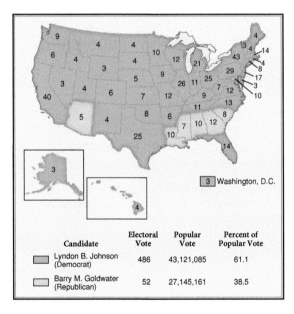

Candidate	Electoral Vote	Popular Vote	Percent of Popular Vote
Lyndon B. Johnson (Democrat)	486	43,121,085	61.1
Barry M. Goldwater (Republican)	52	27,145,161	38.5

MAP 28.5 Presidential Election of 1964

This map reveals how one-sided Lyndon Johnson's victory was over Barry Goldwater in 1964. Except for Arizona, his home state, Goldwater won only five states in the deep South — not of much immediate consolation to him, but a sure indicator that the South was cutting its historic ties to the Democratic Party. Moreover, although soundly rejected in 1964, Goldwater's Far Right critique of "big government" laid the foundation for a Republican resurgence in the 1980s.

Education Act authorized $1 billion in federal funds, sidestepping the religious issue by dispensing aid to public and parochial schools alike on the basis of the number of needy children in attendance. Six months later, Johnson signed the Higher Education Act, providing federal scholarships for college students.

The Eighty-ninth Congress also gave Johnson the votes he needed to achieve some form of national health insurance. Realizing the game was up, the American Medical Association fell back to a demand that services be provided through the existing private system of doctors and hospitals. On that basis, two new programs came forth: Medicare, a health plan for the elderly funded by a surcharge on Social Security payroll taxes, and Medicaid, a health plan for the poor paid for by general tax revenues and administered by the states.

Johnson's programs targeted not only the disadvantaged; the middle class benefited, too. Federal urban renewal and home mortgage assistance helped those who could afford to live in single-family homes or modern apartments. Medicare covered every elderly person eligible for Social Security, regardless of need. Much of the federal aid to education went to the children of the middle class.

And everyone benefited from the Great Society's environmental reforms. President Johnson pressed for expansion of the national park system, improvement of the nation's air and water, protection for endangered species and the wilderness, and stronger land-use planning. At the insistence of his wife, Lady Bird Johnson, he promoted the Highway Beautification Act of 1965. His approach marked a break with past conservation efforts, which had concentrated on husbanding the nation's natural

TABLE 28.1	Major Great Society Legislation

Civil Rights

1964	Twenty-fourth Amendment	Outlawed poll tax in federal elections
	Civil Rights Act	Banned discrimination in employment and public accommodations on the basis of race, religion, sex, or national origin
1965	Voting Rights Act	Outlawed literacy tests for voting; provided federal supervision of registration in historically low-registration areas

Social Welfare

1964	Economic Opportunity Act	Created Office of Economic Opportunity (OEO) to administer War on Poverty programs such as Head Start, Job Corps, and Volunteers in Service to America (VISTA)
1965	Medical Care Act	Provided medical care for the poor (Medicaid) and the elderly (Medicare)
1966	Minimum Wage Act	Raised hourly minimum wage from $1.25 to $1.40 and expanded coverage to new groups

Education

1965	Elementary and Secondary Education Act	Granted federal aid for education of poor children
	National Endowment for the Arts and Humanities	Provided federal funding and support for artists and scholars
	Higher Education Act	Provided federal scholarships for postsecondary education

Housing and Urban Development

1964	Urban Mass Transportation Act	Provided federal aid to urban mass transit
	Omnibus Housing Act	Provided federal funds for public housing and rent subsidies for low-income families
1965	Housing and Urban Development Act	Created Department of Housing and Urban Development (HUD)
1966	Metropolitan Area Redevelopment and Demonstration Cities Acts	Designated 150 "model cities" for combined programs of public housing, social services, and job training

Environment

1964	Wilderness Preservation Act	Designated 9.1 million acres of federal lands as "wilderness areas," barring future roads, buildings, or commercial use
1965	Air and Water Quality Acts	Set tougher air quality standards; required states to enforce water quality standards for interstate waters

Miscellaneous

1964	Tax Reduction Act	Reduced personal and corporate income tax rates
1965	Immigration Act	Abandoned national quotas of 1924 law, allowing more non-European immigration
	Appalachian Regional and Development Act	Provided federal funding for roads, health clinics, other public works projects in economically depressed regions

resources. Secretary of the Interior Stewart Udall emphasized quality of life, battling the problem "of vanishing beauty, of increasing ugliness, of shrinking open space, and of an overall environment that is diminished daily by pollution and noise and blight." In a similar vein, the National Endowment for the Arts and the Humanities was established in 1965 to support the work of artists, writers, and scholars.

In the prevailing reform climate, it even became possible to tackle the nation's discriminatory immigration policy, which since 1924 had used a national-origins quota system that favored northern Europeans. The Immigration Act of 1965 abandoned the quota system, replacing it with more equitable numerical limits on immigration from all nations. To promote family reunification, the law also

provided that close relatives of individuals already legally resident in the United States could be admitted outside the numerical limits, an exception that especially benefited Asian and Latin American immigrants. The ethnic diversity of our nation today—and of our campuses—goes back to that 1965 Immigration Act.

The War on Poverty. What drove Johnson hardest, however, was his determination to "end poverty in our time." The president called it a national disgrace that, in the midst of plenty, a fifth of all Americans—hidden from sight in Appalachia, in urban ghettos, in migrant labor camps, on Indian reservations—lived in poverty. Many had fallen through the cracks and were not served by New Deal welfare programs.

The "Johnson Treatment"

Lyndon B. Johnson, a shrewd and adroit politician, learned many of his legislative skills while serving as majority leader of the Senate from 1953 to 1960. Here he zeroed in on Senator Theodore Francis Green of Rhode Island. After assuming the presidency, Johnson remarked, "They say Jack Kennedy had style, but I'm the one who got the bills passed." George Tames, *The New York Times.*

So one tactic was shoring up those programs. The Great Society broadened Social Security to include waiters and waitresses, domestic servants, farmworkers, and hospital employees. Social welfare expenditures increased rapidly, especially for Aid to Families with Dependent Children (AFDC), as did public housing and rent subsidy programs. Food stamps, begun in 1964 mainly to stabilize farm prices, grew into a major source of assistance to low-income families.

The Office of Economic Opportunity (OEO), established by the Economic Opportunity Act of 1964, was the Great Society's showcase in the War on Poverty. Built around the twin principles of equal opportunity and community action, OEC advanced programs so numerous and diverse that they recalled the alphabet agencies of the New Deal. Head Start provided free nursery schools to prepare disadvantaged preschoolers for kindergarten. The Job Corps and Upward Bound provided young people with training and jobs. Volunteers in Service to America (VISTA), modeled on the Peace Corps, provided technical assistance to the urban and rural poor. An array of regional development programs aimed, like foreign aid, at spurring economic growth in impoverished areas. The Community Action Program encouraged its clients to demand "maximum feasible participation" in decisions that affected them. Community Action organizers worked closely with lawyers employed by the Legal Services Program to provide the poor with access to the legal system.

The Limits of the Great Society. By the end of 1965, the Johnson administration had compiled the most impressive legislative record since the New Deal and put issues of poverty, justice, and access at the center of national political life. Yet the Great Society never quite measured up to the extravagant promises made for it.

The proportion of Americans living below the poverty line dropped from 20 percent to 13 percent between 1963 and 1968 (Figure 28.1). African Americans did even better. In the 1960s the black poverty rate fell by half as millions of blacks moved into the middle class. Critics, however, credited the decade's booming economy more than government programs. Moreover, distribution of wealth remained highly skewed. In relative terms, the bottom 20 percent remained as far behind as ever.

An inherent problem was the limited funding, which was set at less than $2 billion annually. It also proved impossible to hold together the extraordinarily diverse political coalition first forged by Franklin Roosevelt in the 1930s — middle-class and poor; white and nonwhite; Protestant, Jewish, and Catholic; urban and rural — that Johnson rallied for the Great Society. Inevitably, the demands of certain groups — such as blacks' demands for civil rights and the urban poor's demands for increased political power — conflicted with the interests of other Democrats. In the end Johnson's coalition was not strong enough to withstand a growing challenge by conservatives who resisted expanded civil rights and social welfare benefits.

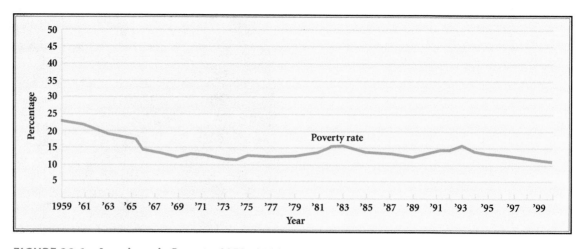

FIGURE 28.1 Americans in Poverty, 1959–2000

Between 1959 and 1973 the poverty rate among American families dropped by more than half — from 23 percent to 11 percent. There was, however, sharp disagreement about the reasons for that notable decline. Liberals credited the War on Poverty, while conservatives favored the high-performing economy, with the significant poverty dip of 1965–1966 caused by military spending, not Johnson's domestic programs.

Democrats were themselves plagued by disillusionment over the shortcomings of their reforms. In the early 1960s the lofty rhetoric of the New Frontier and the Great Society had raised people's expectations. But competition for federal largesse was keen, and the shortage of funds left many promises unfulfilled, especially after 1965 when the Vietnam War siphoned funding away from domestic programs. In 1966 the government spent $22 billion on the Vietnam War and only $1.2 billion on the War on Poverty. Ultimately, as Martin Luther King Jr. put it, the Great Society was "shot down on the battlefields of Vietnam."

➤ Why, after years of resistance, did Congress pass the great civil rights acts of 1964 and 1965?

➤ What were the key components of the Great Society?

➤ What factors limited the success of the War on Poverty?

Into the Quagmire, 1963–1968

Just as Kennedy inherited Vietnam from Eisenhower, so Lyndon Johnson inherited Vietnam from Kennedy. Only the inheritance was now more burdensome, for it became clear that only massive American intervention could prevent the collapse of South Vietnam (Map 28.6). Johnson was a subscriber, like Kennedy, to the Cold War tenets of global containment—that America's credibility was at stake in Vietnam and that the domino effect would have devastating consequences. But whereas, in Kennedy's case, second thoughts might have prevailed, that was an impossibility with Johnson. "I am not going to lose Vietnam," he vowed upon taking office. "I am not going to be the President who saw Southeast Asia go the way China went."

Escalation

Johnson was unwilling to level with the American people. For one thing, he doubted that they had the

MAP 28.6 The Vietnam War, 1968

The Vietnam War was a guerrilla war, fought in skirmishes rather than set-piece battles. Despite repeated airstrikes, the United States was never able to halt the flow of North Vietnamese troops and supplies down the Ho Chi Minh Trail, which wound through Laos and Cambodia. In January 1968 Vietcong forces launched the Tet offensive, a surprise attack on cities and provincial centers across South Vietnam. Although the attackers were pushed back with heavy losses, the Tet offensive revealed the futility of American efforts to suppress the Vietcong guerrillas and marked a turning point in the war.

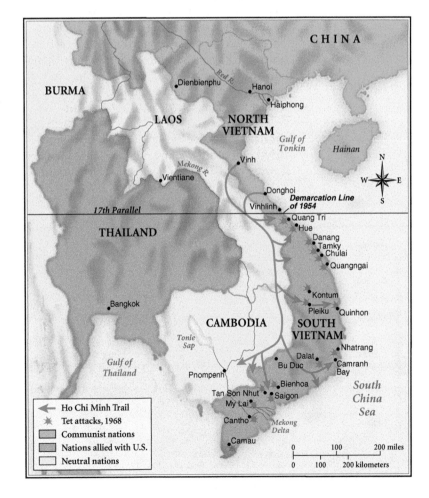

stomach for the course he was contemplating. And he did not want to endanger his grand domestic agenda. He felt he "had no choice but to keep my foreign policy in the wings" because "the day it exploded into a major debate on the war, that day would be the beginning of the end of the Great Society." So he ran in 1964 on the pledge that there be no escalation—no American boys fighting Vietnam's fight—although he intended to do exactly that. And while he wanted congressional approval, perhaps even a declaration of war, Johnson needed a good excuse, which he found even before the 1964 campaign was over.

The Gulf of Tonkin Resolution. During the summer, while American naval forces were conducting reconnaissance missions off the North Vietnamese coast, Johnson got reports that North Vietnamese torpedo boats had fired on the destroyer *Maddox* in international waters. In the first attack, on August 2, the damage inflicted was limited to a single bullet hole; a second, on August 4, later proved to be only misread radar sightings. It didn't matter. In a national emergency—real or imagined—the president's call to arms is hard to resist. In the entire Congress, House and Senate, only two lone Senators voted against Johnson's request for authorization to "take all necessary measures to repel any armed attack against the forces of the United States and to prevent further aggression." The Gulf of Tonkin resolution handed Johnson a mandate to conduct operations in Vietnam as he saw fit.

Americanizing the War. With the 1964 election safely behind him, Johnson began an American takeover of the war in Vietnam. The escalation, which was accomplished in the early months of 1965, took two forms: deployment of American ground troops and the intensification of bombing against North Vietnam.

On March 8, 1965, the first Marines waded ashore at Da Nang, ostensibly to protect the huge American air base there. Soon they were skirmishing with the enemy. Over the next three years, the number of American troops in Vietnam grew dramatically (Figure 28.2). By 1966 more than 380,000 American soldiers were stationed in Vietnam; by 1967, 485,000; and by 1968, 536,000. The escalating demands of General William Westmoreland, the commander of U.S. forces, confirmed a fear Kennedy had expressed before his death that requesting troops was like taking a drink: "The effect wears off and you have to take another."

In the meantime, in an operation called Rolling Thunder, Johnson unleashed a bombing campaign against North Vietnam. A special target was the Ho Chi Minh Trail, an elaborate network of trails, bridges, and shelters that stretched from North Vietnam through Cambodia and Laos into South Vietnam. By 1968 a million tons of bombs had fallen on North Vietnam, 800 tons a day for three-and-a-half years. Twice that tonnage was dropped on the jungles of South Vietnam as U.S. forces tried to flush out the Vietcong fighters.

To the surprise of American planners, the bombing had little effect on the Vietcong's ability to wage war. The flow of troops and supplies continued unabated as the North Vietnamese quickly rebuilt roads and bridges, moved munitions plants underground, and constructed a network of tunnels and shelters. Instead of destroying North Vietnamese morale, Operation Rolling

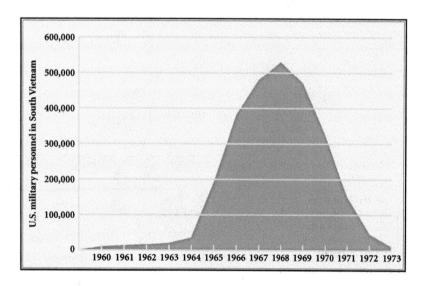

FIGURE 28.2 U.S. Troops in Vietnam, 1960–1973

This figure graphically tracks America's involvement in Vietnam. After Lyndon Johnson decided on escalation in 1964, troop levels jumped from 23,300 to a peak of 543,000 personnel in 1968. Under Richard Nixon's Vietnamization program, beginning in the summer of 1969, levels drastically declined; the last U.S. military forces left South Vietnam on March 29, 1973.

Thunder intensified their nationalism and hardened their will to fight.

The massive commitment of troops and air power devastated Vietnam's countryside. After one harsh but not unusual engagement, a commanding officer reported, using the logic of the time, "It became necessary to destroy the town in order to save it." Besides the bombing, a defoliation campaign began to deprive guerrillas of cover, destroying crops and undercutting the economic and cultural base of Vietnamese society. (In later years defoliants such as Agent Orange were found to have highly toxic effects on humans, including the G.I.s serving in Vietnam.) In Saigon and other South Vietnamese cities, the influx of American soldiers and dollars distorted local economies, fostered corruption and prostitution, and triggered uncontrollable inflation and black-market activity.

In Washington the debate intensified about why the increased American presence was failing to turn the tide of the war. Some advisors argued that military action could accomplish little without reform in Saigon. Other critics claimed that the United States never fully committed itself to a "total victory" (see Comparing American Voices, "The Toll of War," pp. 880–881). Military strategy was inextricably tied to political considerations. For domestic reasons policymakers often searched for an elusive "middle ground" between all-out invasion of North Vietnam (and the possibility of war with China) and the politically unacceptable alternative of disengagement. Hoping to win a war of attrition, the Johnson administration gambled that American superiority in personnel and weaponry would ultimately triumph.

Public Opinion on Vietnam

A big part of Johnson's gamble was that he could retain the support of the American people. He had reason for confidence on that score: A broad, steady consensus had formed in earlier years favorable to Washington's conduct of the Cold War. Both Democrats and Republicans approved Johnson's escalation in Vietnam, and so did public opinion polls in 1965 and 1966. But then public opinion began to shift.

In July 1967 a Gallup poll revealed that for the first time a majority of Americans disapproved of Johnson's Vietnam policy and believed the war had reached a stalemate. Every night Americans saw on television U.S. soldiers advancing steadily and heard about staggering Vietcong "body counts," but increasingly television screens showed the carnage of war and dead and wounded Americans. Journalists

began to warn that the Johnson administration suffered from a "credibility gap." The administration, they charged, was concealing discouraging information about the war's progress. In February 1966 television coverage of hearings by the Senate Foreign Relations Committee (chaired by J. William Fulbright, an outspoken critic of the war) raised further questions about the administration's policy.

The Rise of the Antiwar Movement. Out of these troubling developments an antiwar movement began to crystallize. Its core was, in addition to longstanding pacifist groups, a new generation of peace activists like SANE (the National Committee for a Sane Nuclear Policy) that in the 1950s had protested atmospheric nuclear testing. After the escalation in 1965, they were joined by student groups, clergy, civil rights advocates, even Dr. Spock. The antiwar coalitions were soon capable of mounting mass demonstrations in Washington, bringing out 20,000 to 30,000 people at a time. Although they were a diverse lot, participants in these rallies shared a common skepticism about U.S. policy in Vietnam. They charged variously that intervention was morally wrong and antithetical to American ideals; that an independent, anti-Communist South Vietnam was unattainable; and that no American objective justified the suffering inflicted on the Vietnamese people (see Voices from Abroad, "Che Guevara: Vietnam and the World Freedom Struggle," p. 883).

Economic developments put Johnson even more on the defensive. The Vietnam War cost the taxpayers $27 billion in 1967, and the deficit jumped from $9.8 billion to $23 billion. The cost of the war nudged the inflation rate upward. Only in the summer of 1967 did Johnson ask for a 10 percent surcharge on income taxes, an increase that Congress did not approve until 1968. By then the inflationary spiral that would plague the U.S. economy throughout the 1970s was well under way.

Student Activism

No group was more visible in these antiwar protests than college students. Many of them had been inspired by the black college students of Greensboro, North Carolina, who had sparked the wave of sit-ins that did so much to challenge segregation in the South (see Chapter 27). Galvanized by the struggle for racial justice, white students — many of whom had been raised in a privileged environment and inculcated with faith in American goodness — began to question U.S. foreign and domestic policy and middle-class conformity.

The Toll of War

The Vietnam War produced a rich and graphic literature: novels, journalists' reports, interviews, and personal letters. These brief selections suggest the war's profound impact on those Americans who experienced it firsthand.

DONALD L. WHITFIELD

Donald L. Whitfield was a draftee from Alabama, who was interviewed some years after the war.

I'm gonna be honest with you. I had heard some about Vietnam in 1968, but I was a poor fellow and I didn't keep up with it. I was working at a Standard Oil station making eight dollars a day. I pumped gas and tinkered a little with cars. I had a girl I saw every now and then, but I still spent most of my time with a car. When I got my letter from the draft lady, I appealed it on the reason it was just me and my sister at home. We were a poor family and they needed me at home, but it did no good.

My company did a lot of patrolling. We got the roughest damn deal. Shit, I thought I was going to get killed every night. I was terrified the whole time. We didn't have no trouble with the blacks. I saw movies that said we done the blacks wrong, but it wasn't like that where I was. Let's put it like this: they make pretty good soldiers, but they're not what we are. White Americans, can't nobody whip our ass. We're the baddest son of a bitches on the face of this earth. You can take a hundred Russians and twenty-five Americans, and we'll whip their ass. . . .

I fly the Rebel flag because this is the South, Bubba. The American flag represents the whole fifty states. That flag represents the southern part. I'm a Confederate, I'm a Southerner. . . .

I feel cheated about Vietnam, I sure do. Political restrictions — we won every goddamned battle we was in, but didn't win the whole goddamn little country. . . . Before I die, the Democratic-controlled Congress of this country — and I blame it on 'em — they gonna goddamn apologize to the Vietnam veterans.

SOURCE: James R. Wilson, *Landing Zones: Southern Veterans Remember Vietnam* (Durham, NC: Duke University Press, 1990), 203, 204, 207, 209, 210.

GEORGE OLSEN

George Olsen served in Vietnam from August 1969 to March 1970, when he was killed in action. He wrote this letter to his girlfriend.

31 Aug '69
Dear Red,
Last Monday I went on my first hunter-killer operation. . . .
The frightening thing about it all is that it is so very easy to kill in war. There's no remorse, no theatrical "washing of the hands" to get rid of nonexistent blood, not even any regrets. When it happens, you are more afraid than you've ever been in your life — my hands shook so much I had trouble reloading. . . . You're scared, really scared, and there's no thinking about it. You kill because that little SOB is doing his best to kill you and you desperately want to live, to go home, to get drunk or walk down the street on a date again. And suddenly the grenades aren't going off any more, the weapons stop and, unbelievably fast it seems, it's all over. . . .

I have truly come to envy the honest pacifist who honestly believes that no killing is permissible and can, with a clear conscience, stay home and not take part in these conflicts. I wish I could do the same, but I can't see letting another take my place and my risks over here. . . . The only reason pacifists such as the Amish can even live in an orderly society is because someone — be they police or soldiers — is taking risks to keep the wolves away. . . . I guess that's why I'm over here, why I fought so hard to come here, and why, even though I'm scared most of the time, I'm content to be here.

SOURCE: Bernard Edelman, ed., *Dear America: Letters Home from Vietnam* (New York: Pocket Books, 1985), 204–205.

ARTHUR E. WOODLEY JR.

Arthur E. Woodley Jr. was a Special Forces Ranger and gave this interview a decade after his return.

You had to fight to survive where I grew up. Lower east Baltimore. . . . It was a mixed-up neighborhood of Puerto Ricans, Indians, Italians, and blacks. Being that I'm light-skinned, curly hair, I wasn't readily accepted in the black community. I was more accepted by Puerto Ricans and some rednecks. They didn't ask what my race classification was. I went with them to white movies, white restaurants, and so forth. But after I got older, I came to the realization that I was what I am and came to deal with my black peers. . . .

I figured I was just what my country needed. A black patriot who could do any physical job they could come up with. Six feet, one hundred and ninety pounds, and healthy. . . .

I didn't ask no questions about the war. I thought communism was spreading, and as an American citizen, it was my part to do as much as I could to defeat the Communist from coming here. Whatever America states is correct was the tradition that I was brought up in. And I thought the only way I could possibly make it out of the ghetto was to be the best soldier I possibly could. . . .

Then came the second week of February of '69. . . . We recon this area, and we came across this fella, a white guy, who was staked to the ground. His arms and legs tied down to stakes. . . . He had numerous scars on his face where he might have been beaten and mutilated. And he had been peeled from his upper part of chest to down to his waist. Skinned. Like they slit your skin with a knife. And they take a pair of pliers or a instrument similar, and they just peel the skin off your body and expose it to the elements. . . .

And he start to cryin', beggin' to die.

He said, "I can't go back like this. I can't live like this. I'm dying. You can't leave me here like this dying." . . .

It took me somewhere close to 20 minutes to get my mind together. Not because I was squeamish about killing someone, because I had at that time numerous body counts. Killing someone wasn't the issue. It was killing another American citizen, another GI. . . . We buried him. We buried him. Very deep. Then I cried. . . .

When we first started going into the fields, I would not wear a finger, ear, or mutilate another person's body. Until I had the misfortune to come upon those American soldiers who were castrated. Then it got to be a game between the Communists and ourselves to see how many fingers and ears that we could capture from each other. After a kill we would cut his finger or ear off as a trophy, stuff our unit patch in his mouth, and let him die.

With 89 days left in country, I came out of the field. What I now felt was emptiness. . . . I started seeing the atrocities that we caused each other as human beings. I came to the realization that I was committing crimes against humanity and myself. That I really didn't believe in these things I was doin'. I changed.

SOURCE: Wallace Terry, *Bloods: An Oral History of the Vietnam War by Black Veterans* (New York: Ballantine, 1984), 243–263.

GAYLE SMITH

Gayle Smith was a nurse in a surgical unit in Vietnam in 1970–1971 and gave this interview a few years later.

I objected to the war and I got the idea into my head of going there to bring people back. I started thinking about it in 1966 and knew that I would eventually go when I felt I was prepared enough. . . .

Boy, I remember how they came in all torn up. It was incredible. The first time a medevac came in, I got right into it. I didn't have a lot of feeling at that time. It was later on that I began to have a lot of feeling about it, after I'd seen it over and over and over again. . . . I turned that pain into anger and hatred and placed it onto the Vietnamese. . . . I did not consider the Vietnamese to be people. They were human, but they weren't people. They weren't like us, so it was okay to kill them. It was okay to hate them. . . .

I would have dreams about putting a .45 to someone's head and see it blow away over and over again. And for a long time I swore that if the Vietnamese ever came to this country I'd kill them.

It was in a Vietnam veterans group that I realized that all my hatred for the Vietnamese and my wanting to kill them was really a reflection of all the pain that I had felt for seeing all those young men die and hurt. . . . I would stand there and look at them and think to myself, "You've just lost your leg for no reason at all." Or "You're going to die and it's for nothing." For nothing. I would never, never say that to them, but they knew it.

SOURCE: Albert Santoli, ed., *Everything We Had* (New York: Random House, 1981), 141–148.

ANALYZING THE EVIDENCE

➤ Why did these four young people end up in Vietnam?

➤ How would you describe their experiences there?

➤ How were they changed by the war? What do their reflections suggest about the war's impact on American society?

In June 1962 forty students from Big Ten and Ivy League universities met in Port Huron, Michigan, to found Students for a Democratic Society (SDS). Tom Hayden wrote a manifesto, the Port Huron Statement, which expressed their disillusionment with the consumer culture and the gulf between rich and poor. These students rejected Cold War foreign policy, including but not limited to the Vietnam conflict. The founders of SDS referred to their movement as the "New Left" to distinguish themselves from the "Old Left"— Communists and Socialists of the 1930s and 1940s. Consciously adopting the activist tactics pioneered by the civil rights movement, they turned to grassroots organizing in cities and on college campuses.

The Free Speech Movement. The first major student demonstrations erupted in the fall of 1964 at the University of California at Berkeley, after administrators banned political activity in Sproul Plaza, where student groups had traditionally distributed leaflets and recruited members. In protest, the major student organizations formed the Free Speech Movement (FSM) and organized a sit-in at the administration building. Some students had just returned from Freedom Summer in Mississippi, radicalized by their experience. Mario Savio spoke for many of them when he compared the conflict in Berkeley to the civil rights struggle in the South: "The same rights are at stake in both places—the right to participate as citizens in a democratic society and to struggle against the same enemy." Emboldened by the Berkeley movement, students across the nation were soon protesting

their universities' academic policies and then, more passionately, the Vietnam War.

The Draft. A spur to student protest was a change in the military's Selective Service system, which in January 1966 abolished automatic student deferments. To avoid the draft, young men enlisted in the National Guard, or declared themselves conscientious objectors, or became draft dodgers. Some left the country, most often for Canada or Sweden. In public demonstrations, opponents of the war burned their draft cards, picketed induction centers, and on a few occasions broke into Selective Service offices and destroyed records.

As antiwar and draft protests multiplied, students realized that their universities were deeply implicated in the war effort. In some cases as much as 60 percent of a university's research budget came from government contracts. Protesters blocked recruiters from the Dow Chemical Company, the producer of napalm and Agent Orange. Arguing that universities should not train students for war, they demanded that the Reserve Officer Training Corps (ROTC) be removed from college campuses.

After 1967, nationwide student strikes, mass demonstrations, and other organized protests became commonplace. In October 1967 more than 100,000 antiwar demonstrators marched on Washington, D.C., as part of "Stop the Draft Week." The event culminated in a "siege of the Pentagon," in which protesters clashed with police and federal marshals. Hundreds of people were arrested and several demonstrators beaten. Lyndon Johnson, who had once dismissed antiwar protesters as "nervous Nellies," rebellious children, or Communist dupes,

Free Speech at Berkeley, 1964

Students at the University of California's Berkeley campus protested the administration's decision to ban political activity in the school plaza. Free speech demonstrators, many of them active in the civil rights movement, relied on tactics and arguments that they learned during that struggle. University of California at Berkeley, Bancroft Library.

Che Guevara

Vietnam and the World Freedom Struggle

Che Guevara was a middle-class, medically trained Argentinian who enlisted in Castro's Cuban Revolution and became a world icon of guerrilla resistance. In 1965 he left Cuba in order to foment revolutionary struggle in Africa and Latin America. Two years later he was captured in Bolivia and executed. Between his departure from Cuba and his death in Bolivia in 1967, he made only one public statement, which he titled "Vietnam and the World Freedom Struggle."

This is the painful reality: Vietnam, a nation representing the aspirations and the hopes for victory of the entire world of the disinherited, is tragically alone. . . .

And — what grandeur has been shown by this people! What stoicism and valor in this people! And what a lesson for the world their struggle holds!

It will be a long time before we know if President Johnson ever seriously thought of initiating some of the popular reforms necessary to soften the sharpness of the class contradictions that are appearing with explosive force and more and more frequently.

What is certain is that the improvements announced under the pompous label of the Great Society have gone down the drain in Vietnam.

The greatest of the imperialist powers feels in its own heart the drain caused by a poor, backward country; and its fabulous economy feels the effect of the war. . . .

And for us, the exploited of the world, what should our role be in this? . . .

Our part, the responsibility of the exploited and backward areas of the world, is to eliminate the bases sustaining imperialism — our oppressed peoples, from whom capital, raw materials, technicians and cheap labor are extracted, and to whom new capital, means of domination, arms and all kinds of goods are exported, submerging us in absolute dependence.

The fundamental element of this strategic goal will be, then, the real liberation of the peoples, a liberation that will be obtained through armed struggle in the majority of cases, and which, in the Americas, will have almost unfailingly the property of becoming converted into a socialist revolution.

In focusing on the destruction of imperialism, it is necessary to identify its head, which is none other than the United States of North America. . . .

The adversary must not be underestimated; the North American soldier has technical ability and is backed by means of such magnitude as to make him formidable. He lacks the essential ideological motivation which his most hated rivals of today have to the highest degree — the Vietnamese soldiers. . . .

Over there, the imperialist troops encounter the discomforts of those accustomed to the standard of living which the North American nation boasts. They have to confront a hostile land, the insecurity of those who cannot move without feeling that they are walking on enemy territory; death for those who go outside of fortified redoubts; the permanent hostility of the entire population.

All this continues to provoke repercussions inside the United States; it is going to arouse a factor that was attenuated in the days of the full vigor of imperialism — the class struggle inside its own territory.

SOURCE: Ernesto C. Guevara, *Che Guevara Speaks* (New York: Pathfinder Press, 1967), 144–159.

ANALYZING THE EVIDENCE

➤ Guevara was a Latin American. He had never been to Southeast Asia. So why was he interested in Vietnam?

➤ How does Guevara define the struggle going on in Vietnam? How does he describe the two warring sides? Can you see, on the basis of that description, why Guevera was confident the United States couldn't win the Vietnam war?

➤ Why whould Guevara have bothered to speak about Johnson's Great Society program?

➤ Can you explain, based on this document, why Guevara was an inspirational figure to many student antiwar protesters?

now had to face the reality of large-scale public opposition to his policies.

> ➤ What difficulties did the United States face in fighting a war against North Vietnam and the Vietcong in South Vietnam?

> ➤ Why did President Johnson suffer a "credibility gap" over Vietnam?

> ➤ What was the student role in the antiwar movement? How can we explain students' willingness to protest the war?

Coming Apart

In the student protests, in the SDS, and in the Berkeley Free Speech Movement, more obviously was at stake than Vietnam. Indeed, antiwar protest merged into a variegated, broad-based attack on the status quo — "the Movement," to its participants — that not only challenged Cold War assumptions, but blasted America's liberal consensus.

The roots of this assault go back to the 1950s, back to when the Beats denigrated capitalism, teenagers defied their elders, and African American sit-ins protested racial injustice. By the mid-1960s this angry disaffection had broadened into a many-sided attack on mainstream America.

The Counterculture

While the New Left plotted against the political and economic "system," a growing number of young Americans embarked on a general revolution against authority and middle-class respectability. The "hippie" — attired in ragged blue jeans, tie-dyed T-shirts, beads, and army fatigues, with long, unkempt hair — symbolized the new counterculture.

Not surprisingly, given the importance of rock 'n' roll in the 1950s, popular music helped define the counterculture. Folk singer Pete Seeger set the tone for the era's political idealism with songs such as the antiwar ballad "Where Have All the Flowers Gone?" In 1963, the year of the Birmingham demonstrations and President Kennedy's assassination, Bob Dylan's "Blowin' in the Wind" reflected the impatience of people whose faith in America was wearing thin.

Other winds of change in popular music came from the Beatles, four working-class Brits who burst onto the American scene early in 1964. The Beatles' music, by turns lyrical and driving, was remarkably successful, spawning a commercial and cultural phenomenon called "Beatlemania." American youths' eager embrace of the Beatles deepened the generational divide between teenagers and their elders. The Beatles also helped to pave the way for the more rebellious, angrier music of other British groups, notably the Rolling Stones.

Drugs intertwined with music in the rituals of the youth culture. The recreational use of drugs — especially marijuana and the hallucinogenic popularly known as LSD or "acid" — was celebrated in popular music. San Francisco bands such as the Grateful Dead and Jefferson Airplane and musicians like guitarist Jimi Hendrix developed a musical style known as "acid rock," which was characterized by long, heavily amplified guitar solos accompanied by psychedelic lighting effects. In August 1969, 400,000 young people journeyed to Bethel, New York, to "get high" on music, drugs, and sex at the three-day Woodstock Music and Art Fair.

Jimi Hendrix at Woodstock

The three-day outdoor Woodstock concert in August 1969 was a defining moment in the rise of the counterculture. The event attracted 400,000 young people, who journeyed to Bethel, New York, for a weekend of music, drugs, and sex. Jimi Hendrix closed the show early Sunday morning with an electrifying version of "The Star-Spangled Banner." More overtly political than most counterculture music, Hendrix's rendition featured sound effects that seemed to evoke the violence of the Vietnam War. Michael Wadleigh, who directed the documentary *Woodstock*, called Hendrix's performance "his challenge to American foreign policy." Allan Koss/The Image Works.

For a brief time adherents of the counterculture believed a new age was dawning. They experimented in communal living and glorified uninhibited sexuality. In 1967 the "world's first Human Be-In" drew 20,000 people to Golden Gate Park in San Francisco. The Beat poet Allen Ginsberg "purified" the site with a Buddhist ritual, and the LSD advocate Timothy Leary, a former Harvard psychology teacher, urged the gathering to "turn on to the scene, tune in to what is happening, and drop out." That summer — dubbed the "Summer of Love" — San Francisco's Haight-Ashbury, New York's East Village, and Chicago's Uptown neighborhoods swelled with young dropouts, drifters, and teenage runaways dubbed "flower children." Their faith in instant love and peace quickly turned sour, however, as they suffered bad drug trips, sexually transmitted diseases, loneliness, and violence. Although many young people kept their distance, media cov-

erage made it seem as if all of American youth was rejecting the nation's social and cultural norms.

Beyond Civil Rights

Among young blacks, knocking the mainstream meant something else. It meant rejecting the established civil rights leadership, with its faith in the courts and legislative change. It meant an eye-for-an-eye, not Martin Luther King's nonviolence. It meant wondering why blacks wanted to be integrated with whites anyway. Above all, it expressed fury at the poverty of blacks and at white racism that was beyond the reach of civil rights laws.

Malcolm X. Black rage had expressed itself historically in demands for racial separation, espoused in the late nineteenth century by the Back-to-Africa movement and in the 1920s by Marcus Garvey (see

Malcolm X (1925–1965)

Malcolm X has an assistant hold up the picture of a fallen black as he addresses a Harlem rally on May 14, 1963, in support of civil rights demonstrations in Birmingham, Alabama. The photograph was not in fact related to the brutal police attack on Birmingham demonstrators, but it represented what Malcolm X considered to be the norm for how blacks were treated in America. From a Birmingham jail, Martin Luther King Jr. warned that if his appeal for racial justice went unheeded, African Americans would turn to "people who have lost faith in America … and who have concluded that the white man is an incurable 'devil.'" He had Malcolm X in mind. © Bettmann/Corbis.

Chapter 23). In the 1960s the leading exponent of black separatism was the Nation of Islam, which fused a rejection of Christianity with a strong dose of self-improvement. Black Muslims, as they were known, adhered to a strict code of personal behavior, with the men always recognizable by their dark suits and white shirts, the women by their long dresses and head coverings. Black Muslims preached an apocalyptic brand of Islam, anticipating the day when Allah would banish the white "devils" and give the black nation justice. Although its full converts numbered only about 10,000, the Nation of Islam had a wide popular following in urban ghettoes.

The most charismatic Black Muslim was Malcolm X (the X stood for his African family name lost under slavery). A spellbinding speaker, Malcolm X preached a philosophy of militant protest and separatism, though he advocated violence only for self-defense. Hostile to the traditional civil rights organizations, he caustically referred to the 1963 March on Washington as the "Farce on Washington." In 1964, after a power struggle with the founder, Elijah Muhammad, Malcolm X broke with the Nation of Islam. While remaining a black nationalist, his anti-white views moderated, and he began to talk in terms of class struggle uniting poor whites and blacks. But he got no further. On February 21, 1965, Malcolm X was assassinated while delivering a speech in Harlem. Three Black Muslims were later convicted of his murder.

Black Power. A more secular brand of black nationalism emerged in 1966 when young black SNCC and CORE activists, following the lead of Stokely Carmichael, began to call for black self-reliance and racial pride under the banner of "Black Power." Amid growing distrust of whites, SNCC declared itself a blacks-only organization and ejected its white members. In the same year Huey Newton and Bobby Seale, two college students in Oakland, California, founded the Black Panthers, a militant self-defense organization dedicated to protecting blacks from police violence. The Panthers' organization quickly spread to other cities, where members undertook a wide range of community organizing projects. Their rhetoric, however, declared their affinity for Third World revolutionary movements and armed struggle.

Among the most significant legacies of Black Power was the assertion of racial pride. Rejecting white society, blacks wore African clothing and hairstyles and awakened interest in black history, art, and literature. By the 1970s many colleges and universities were offering programs in black studies.

Urban Riots. The rage expressed by Black Power boiled over, in inchoate form, in a wave of riots that struck the nation's cities. The first "long hot summer" began in July 1964 in New York City, when police shot a black criminal suspect in Harlem. Angry youths looted and rioted there for a week. Over the next four years, the volatile issue of police brutality set off riots in dozens of cities. In August 1965 the arrest of a young black motorist in the Watts section of Los Angeles sparked six days of rioting that left thirty-four dead. The riots of 1967 were the most serious, engulfing twenty-two cities in July and August. The most devastating outbreaks occurred in Newark and Detroit. Forty-three people were killed in Detroit alone, nearly all of them black, and $50 million worth of property was destroyed.

The Assassination of Martin Luther King Jr. Stirred by this turmoil, and by disappointment with his civil rights achievements, Martin Luther King began to confront the deep-seated problems of poverty and racism facing American blacks. He spoke out eloquently against the Vietnam War and planned a poor people's campaign to fight economic injustice and inequality. In support of that cause, he went to Memphis, Tennessee, to support a strike by predominantly black sanitation workers, and there, on April 4, 1968, he was assassinated. King's death set off a further round of urban rioting, with major violence breaking out in many cities.

Although King died unfulfilled, he had set in motion permanent, indeed revolutionary, changes in American race relations. He had helped end Jim Crow segregation, won federal legislation ensuring black Americans' most basic civil rights, and broke the white monopoly on political power in the South. And not least, his example inspired other oppressed groups in America to enter the struggle for equal rights.

César Chavez and the Chicano Movement. For Mexican Americans, the counterpart to Martin Luther King was César Chavez, although, in Chavez's case, the conversion to economic struggle came much earlier. He and Dolores Huerta had begun in the Community Service Organization, a California group founded in the 1950s to promote Mexican political participation and civil rights. Leaving that organization in 1962, Chavez concentrated on the agricultural region of Delano, California, and with Huerta, organized the United Farm Workers (UFW), a union for migrant workers. While Huerta, a brilliant organizer, was crucial

César Chavez

Mexican American labor leader César Chavez, seen here addressing a rally in Guadalupe, California, won national attention in 1965 during a strike of migrant farmworkers, most of them Mexican Americans, against California grape growers. Drawing on tactics from the civil rights movement, Chavez called for nonviolent action and effectively mobilized nationwide support for a boycott of nonunion table grapes. FPG/Getty Images.

to the movement, it was Chavez, with his deep spirituality and commitment to nonviolent protest, who became the symbol for what was popularly called *La Causa*. A 1965 grape pickers' strike led the UFW to call a nationwide boycott of table grapes, bringing Chavez huge publicity and backing from the AFL-CIO. In a bid for attention to the struggle, Chavez staged a hunger strike in 1968, which ended dramatically after twenty-eight days with Senator Robert F. Kennedy at his side to break the fast. Victory came in 1970 when California grape growers signed contracts recognizing the UFW.

On a parallel track, Mexican Americans had since the 1930s (see Chapter 24) actively worked to surmount the poverty, uncertain legal status, and language barriers that made political mobilization difficult. That situation began to change when the Mexican American Political Association (MAPA)

mobilized support for John F. Kennedy. Over the next four years, MAPA and other organizations worked successfully to elect Mexican American candidates such as Edward Roybal of California and Henry González of Texas to Congress.

Younger Mexican Americans grew impatient with MAPA, however. The barrios of Los Angeles and other western cities produced the militant Brown Berets, modeled on the Black Panthers (who wore black berets). Rejecting the assimilationist approach of their elders, 1,500 Mexican American students met in Denver in 1969 to hammer out a new political and cultural agenda. They proclaimed a new term, *Chicano*, to replace Mexican American, and later organized a new political party, La Raza Unida (The United Race), to promote Chicano interests and candidates. In California and other southwestern states, students staged demonstrations

Wounded Knee Revisited

In 1973 members of the American Indian Movement staged a seventy-one-day protest at Wounded Knee, South Dakota, site of the 1890 massacre of two hundred Sioux by U.S. soldiers (see Chapter 16). The takeover was sparked by the murder of a local Sioux by a group of whites but quickly expanded to include demands for basic reforms in federal Indian policy and tribal governance. © Bettmann/Corbis.

to press for bilingual education, the hiring of more Chicano teachers, and the creation of Chicano studies programs. By the 1970s dozens of such programs were offered at universities throughout the region.

The Native American Movement. American Indians also found a model in black struggles for equality. Numbering nearly 800,000 in the 1960s, they were exceedingly diverse, divided by language, tribal history, region, and degree of integration into American life. As a group, they shared a staggering unemployment rate (ten times the national average), the worst housing, the highest disease rates, and the least access to education of any group in the United States.

Since World War II, the National Congress of American Indians had lobbied for reform. In the 1960s the prevailing spirit of protest swept through Indian communities. Young militants, like their counterparts in the black civil rights movement, challenged the accommodationist approach of their elders. Proposing a new name for themselves — Native Americans — they embraced the concept of "Red Power." Beginning in 1968 with the formation of the militant American Indian Movement (AIM), young Native Americans staged escalating protests, occupying the deserted federal penitentiary on Alcatraz Island in San Francisco Bay and sitting-in at the headquarters of the hated Federal Bureau of Indian Affairs in Washington, D.C. In February 1973, a siege at Wounded Knee, South Dakota, the site of the infamous 1890 massacre of the Sioux, ended in a gun battle with the FBI.

Although upsetting to many white onlookers, Native American protest did spur government action on tribal issues.

> What are the elements in the counterculture of the 1960s?

> How do you account for the Black Power movement?

> How do you explain the spillover of the black civil rights struggle into the Mexican American and Native American communities?

1968: A Year of Shocks

By 1968, a sense of crisis gripped the country. Riots in the cities, campus unrest, and a nose-thumbing counterculture seemed on the verge of tearing America apart. What crystallized the crisis was the fact that 1968 was an election year.

The Politics of Vietnam

President Johnson had gambled in 1965 on a quick victory, before the political cost of escalation at home came due. But there was no quick victory. North Vietnamese and Vietcong forces fought on, the South Vietnamese government enjoyed little popular support, and American casualties mounted. By early 1968, the death rate reached several hundred a week. Johnson and his generals kept insisting that there was "light at the end of the tunnel." Facts on the ground showed otherwise.

The Tet Offensive. On January 30, 1968, the Vietcong unleashed a massive, well-coordinated assault in South Vietnam. Timed to coincide with Tet, the lunar Vietnamese new year holiday, the offensive struck thirty-six of the forty-four provincial capitals and five of the six major cities, including Saigon, where Vietcong nearly overran the supposedly impregnable U.S. embassy. In strictly military terms, the Tet offensive was a failure, with very heavy Vietcong losses and the South Vietnamese government still intact. But psychologically, the effect was devastating. Television brought into American homes the shocking images — the American embassy under siege, with a pistol-wielding staff member peering warily from a window, the Saigon police chief placing a pistol to the head of a Vietcong suspect and, live on TV, executing him.

The Tet offensive made a mockery of official pronouncements that the United States was winning the war. Just before, a Gallup poll found that 56 percent of Americans considered themselves "hawks" (supporters of the war), while only 28 percent identified with the "doves" (war opponents). Three months later doves outnumbered hawks 42 to 41 percent. Without embracing the peace movement, many Americans simply concluded that the war was unwinnable (see Reading American Pictures, "War and Its Aftermath: Images of the Vietnam Conflict, 1968 and 1982," p. 890).

So did a growing faction within the Democratic Party. Even before Tet, Senator Eugene J. McCarthy of Minnesota had entered the Democratic primaries as an antiwar candidate. A core of student activists "went clean for Gene" by cutting their hair and putting away their jeans. President Johnson won the early New Hampshire primary, but McCarthy received a stunning 42.2 percent of the vote. To make matters worse for the president, McCarthy's showing propelled Senator Robert Kennedy, a far more formidable opponent, into the race.

Johnson realized that his political support was evaporating. At the end of an otherwise routine televised address on March 31, he stunned the nation by announcing that he would not seek reelection. He also called a partial halt to the bombing and vowed to devote his remaining months in office to the search for peace. On May 10, 1968, preliminary peace talks between the United States and North Vietnam opened in Paris.

Political Turmoil. Just four days after Johnson's withdrawal from the presidential race, Martin Luther King Jr. was assassinated in Memphis. The *(James Earl Ray)* ensuing riots in cities across the country left forty-three people dead. Soon afterward, students protesting Columbia University's plans for expanding into a neighboring ghetto occupied several campus buildings. The brutal response of the New York City police helped to radicalize even more students.

Then came the final tragedy of the year. On June 5, 1968, as he celebrated his victory in the California primary over Eugene McCarthy, Robert Kennedy was shot dead by a young Palestinian. *(Sirhan Sirhan)* Robert Kennedy's assassination was a calamity for the Democratic Party because only he had seemed able to surmount the party's Vietnam problem. In his brief but dramatic campaign, Kennedy had reached beyond the antiwar elements to traditional members of the New Deal coalition, including blue-collar workers, who were becoming susceptible to patriotic appeals from the right.

With Kennedy gone, the energy went out of the antiwar Democrats. McCarthy's campaign limped along, while Senator George S. McGovern of South Dakota entered the Democratic race in an effort to keep the Kennedy forces together. Meanwhile, Vice President Hubert H. Humphrey lined up pledges from traditional Democratic constituencies — unions, urban machines, and state political organizations. Democrats found themselves on the verge of nominating not an antiwar candidate but a public figure closely associated with Johnson's war policies.

The Siege of Chicago. At the August Democratic convention, the political divisions generated by the war consumed the party. Most of the drama occurred not in the convention hall but outside on the streets of Chicago. Thousands of protesters descended on the city. The most visible group, led by Jerry Rubin and Abbie Hoffman, a remarkable pair of troublemakers, claimed to represent the Youth International Party. To mock those inside the convention hall, these "Yippies" nominated a pig, Pigasus, for president. Their stunts, geared for maximum media exposure, diverted attention from the more serious, far more numerous activists who had come to Chicago to protest the war.

Richard J. Daley, the Democratic mayor, increasingly angry as protesters disrupted his convention, ordered the police to break up the demonstrations. Several nights of skirmishes between protesters and police culminated on the evening of the nominations. In what an official report later described as a "police riot," police officers attacked protesters with Mace, tear gas, and clubs. As the nominating speeches proceeded, television networks broadcast films of the riot, cementing a popular impression of the Democrats as the party of disorder. Inside the hall the Democrats dispiritedly nominated Hubert

War and Its Aftermath:
Images of the Vietnam Conflict, 1968 and 1982

America's Longest War. Copyright Tim Page.

The Vietnam Veterans Memorial. Peter Marlow / Magnum Photos, Inc.

The Vietnam War ended in 1975, but it remains a painful and contested event in the American memory. Images of both combat and remembrance continue to shape our understanding not only of the conflict itself, but also of the meaning of U.S. participation in wars abroad today. The first photograph shows the brutal aftermath of a combat operation by U.S. soldiers in Vietnam during the war. The second photo captures a group of U.S. veterans embracing in front of the Vietnam Veterans' Memorial in Washington, D.C. Dedicated in 1982, the monument, designed by architect Maya Ling, contains the names of over 58,000 U.S. servicemen and -women killed in the war.

ANALYZING THE EVIDENCE

➤ What does the first photo, "America's Longest War," reveal about how the war was fought and experienced by ordinary soldiers?

➤ Given the political climate of the late 1960s, what effect on their feelings about the war do you think this image of carnage and others like it had on those who viewed it?

➤ Why are the veterans embracing in front of the memorial? What is the significance of the clothing and items they are wearing?

➤ Traditionally, war memorials featured statues of combatants or generals in heroic poses; this one has only the names of those killed in combat. Yet the Vietnam monument is widely seen as being emotionally evocative. What does this suggest about the American view of the Vietnam War? See **www.nps.gov/vive** for more information about the memorial.

H. Humphrey, who chose Senator Edmund S. Muskie of Maine as his running mate. The delegates approved a middle-of-the-road platform that endorsed continued fighting in Vietnam while urging a diplomatic solution to the conflict.

Backlash

Political realignments are infrequent in American history. The last one had been 1932, when many Republicans, despairing over the Great Depression, had switched sides and voted for FDR. The year 1968 was another such pivotal moment. Consider a forty-seven-year-old machinist's wife from Dayton, Ohio, described by the social scientists Ben J. Wattenberg and Richard Scammon in their book, *The Real Majority* (1970):

> That lady in Dayton is afraid to walk the streets alone at night . . . she has a mixed view about blacks and civil rights because she lived in a neighborhood that became all black . . . her brother-in-law is a policeman [and] she is deeply distressed that her son is going to a community junior college where LSD was found on campus.

Growing up in the Great Depression, she was likely a great admirer of FDR, maybe with his picture on her living room wall. Such working-class people were the heart and soul of the New Deal democracy. But now, in the sour aftermath of the Chicago convention, their votes were up for grabs. And as always, politicians with their noses to the wind were eager to oblige.

Governor George C. Wallace of Alabama, a third-party candidate, skillfully exploited working-class anxieties over student protests and urban riots. He called for "law and order" in the streets and denounced welfare mothers who, thanks to Johnson's Great Society, were "breeding children as a cash crop." Wallace skewered "overeducated, ivory-towered folks with pointed heads looking down their noses at us." Although no longer overtly a racist, Wallace traded on his fame as the segregationist governor who had stood up to the federal government during the Selma crisis of 1965. His hope was that, by carrying the South, he could deny the major parties an electoral majority and force the 1968 election into the House of Representatives. That strategy failed, and Wallace's political star faded after a near-fatal shooting in 1972 left him paralyzed, but he had defined hot-button issues—liberal elitism, welfare queens, law and order—of immense utility to the next generation of mainstream conservatives.

The Republican candidate, Richard Nixon, offered a more sophisticated version of Wallace's populism. After losing the presidential campaign in 1960, and after losing again in the California gubernatorial race in 1962, Nixon had seemed finished, but he engineered an amazing political comeback and in 1968 won the Republican presidential nomination. As part of what his advisers called the "southern strategy," he chose Spiro Agnew, the conservative governor of Maryland, as his running mate. Nixon hoped to attract southern voters still smarting over Democratic civil rights legislation. Nationally, Nixon appealed to people who came to be known as the "silent majority." He pledged to represent the "quiet voice" of the "great majority of Americans, the forgotten Americans, the nonshouters, the nondemonstrators."

Despite the Democratic debacle in Chicago, the election actually proved to be close. In the last weeks of the campaign, Humphrey rallied by disassociating himself from Johnson's war policies. When on October 31 President Johnson announced a complete halt to the bombing of North Vietnam, Nixon countered by intimating that he had his own plan to end the war (in reality no such plan existed). On election day Nixon received 43.4 percent of the vote to Humphrey's 42.7 percent, defeating him by a scant 500,000 votes out of the 73 million that were cast (Map 28.7). Wallace finished with 13.5 percent of the popular vote.

The closeness of the outcome masked the fact that 1968 really was a pivotal election. Humphrey received almost 12 million fewer votes than had Johnson in 1964. The South, except for Texas, abandoned the Democratic Party, never to return. Nixon's "southern strategy" had worked. In the North, he and Wallace made significant inroads among traditionally Democratic voters. And while party divisions over Vietnam had been briefly patched up, the underlying ideological differences—signified by the rivalry of Hubert Humphrey and George McGovern—persisted, with corrosive effect on the party's effectiveness. New Deal Democrats would never again have the unity of purpose that had served them for thirty years. Assaulted from both left and right, the liberal consensus was coming apart.

➤ What were the critical events of 1968 that have led historians to describe it as a "watershed year"?

➤ Why did the Democrats lose their grip as the majority party in the late 1960s?

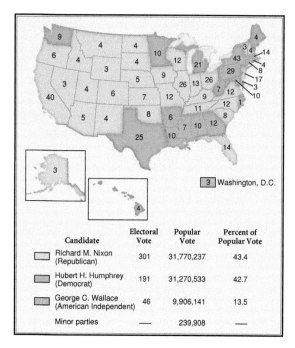

Candidate	Electoral Vote	Popular Vote	Percent of Popular Vote
Richard M. Nixon (Republican)	301	31,770,237	43.4
Hubert H. Humphrey (Democrat)	191	31,270,533	42.7
George C. Wallace (American Independent)	46	9,906,141	13.5
Minor parties	—	239,908	—

MAP 28.7 Presidential Election of 1968

With Lyndon B. Johnson's surprise withdrawal and the assassination of the party's most charismatic contender, Robert Kennedy, the Democrats faced the election of 1968 in disarray. Governor George Wallace of Alabama, who left the Democrats to run as a third-party candidate, campaigned on the backlash against the civil rights movement. As late as mid-September Wallace held the support of 21 percent of the voters. But in November he received only 13.5 percent of the vote, winning five southern states. Republican Richard M. Nixon, who like Wallace emphasized "law and order" in his campaign, defeated Hubert H. Humphrey with only 43.4 percent of the popular vote, but it was now clear, given that Wallace's southern support would otherwise have gone to Nixon, that the South had shifted decisively to the Republican side.

SUMMARY

In this chapter, we saw how the liberal consensus — agreement about a New Deal approach to the nation's social and economic ills — peaked in the mid-1960s and then, under the combined pressure of the Vietnam War and cultural conflict, flamed out. John F. Kennedy opened the politics of expectation in the 1960 campaign, although the domestic accomplishments of the New Frontier were limited. Following John Kennedy's assassination in 1963, Lyndon Johnson advanced the most ambitious liberal reform program since the New Deal, securing not only civil rights legislation, but an array of programs in education, medical care, transportation, and, above all, his War on Poverty. But the Great

Society fell short of its promise as Johnson escalated the American involvement in Vietnam.

The war bitterly divided Americans. Galvanized by the carnage of war and the draft, the antiwar movement spread rapidly among young people. The spirit of rebellion spilled beyond the antiwar movement. The New Left challenged the corporate dominance of society, while the more apolitical counterculture preached personal liberation through sex, drugs, music, and spirituality. Moving beyond civil rights, the Black Power movement encouraged racial pride and assertiveness, serving also as a model for Mexican Americans and Native Americans.

In 1968, the nation was rocked by the assassinations of Martin Luther King and Robert F. Kennedy and a wave of urban riots, fueling a growing popular desire for law and order. Adding to the national disquiet was a Democratic convention that summer, divided by the Vietnam war and under siege by rioting in the streets. A new wave of conservatism took hold of the country, contributing to the resurgence of the Republican Party under Richard Nixon.

Connections: Diplomacy and Politics

In the Part Six opening essay, we remark that "the interaction of domestic and global — the links between liberalism and the Cold War — was especially clear [in the 1960s] because it was Vietnam that, more than anything else, undermined the Great Society and the liberal consensus." In Chapter 26, we showed how that link between liberalism and the Cold War was forged during the Truman and Eisenhower administrations. Unlike in earlier periods, anti-Communism in its McCarthyite phase was not regarded as an attack on liberal reform. In the wake of Vietnam this changed, and prosecution of the Cold War increasingly became an attack on the liberal consensus, a development that, as we shall see in Chapter 30, culminated under the leadership of Ronald Reagan in the 1980s.

CHAPTER REVIEW QUESTIONS

➤ How do you explain the preeminence of civil rights in the politics of the 1960s?

➤ What are the differences between Kennedy's New Frontier and Johnson's Great Society?

➤ Why is the United States' involvement in the Vietnam War so often called a "quagmire"?

TIMELINE

1960	John F. Kennedy elected president
1961	Peace Corps established
	Bay of Pigs invasion
	Berlin Wall erected
1962	Cuban missile crisis
	Students for a Democratic Society (SDS) founded
	César Chavez and Dolores Huerta organize the United Farm Workers (UFW)
1963	Betty Friedan's *The Feminine Mystique*
	Civil rights protest in Birmingham, Alabama
	March on Washington
	Nuclear test-ban treaty
	John F. Kennedy assassinated; Lyndon B. Johnson assumes presidency
1964	Freedom Summer; Civil Rights Act
	Economic Opportunity Act inaugurates War on Poverty
	Free Speech Movement at Berkeley
	Gulf of Tonkin Resolution authorizes military action in Vietnam
1965	Immigration Act abolishes national quota system
	Voting Rights Act
	Medicare and Medicaid programs established
	Malcolm X assassinated
	Operation Rolling Thunder escalates bombing campaign
	First U.S. combat troops arrive in Vietnam
	Race riot in Watts district of Los Angeles
1966	Stokely Carmichael proclaims black power
1967	Hippie counterculture's "Summer of Love"
	100,000 march in antiwar protest in Washington, D.C.
1968	Tet offensive dashes American hopes of victory
	Martin Luther King Jr. and Robert F. Kennedy assassinated
	Riot at Democratic National Convention in Chicago
	Richard Nixon elected president
	American Indian Movement (AIM) organized

FOR FURTHER EXPLORATION

Good starting points for understanding Kennedy's presidency are W. J. Rorabaugh, *Kennedy and the Promise of the Sixties* (2002), and David Halberstam, *The Best and the Brightest* (1972). Arthur M. Schlesinger Jr., *A Thousand Days* (1965), offers a detailed insider's account. For Lyndon Johnson, see Robert Dallek, *Flawed Giant* (1998).

Henry Hampton and Steve Fayer's oral history, *Voices of Freedom* (1991), and Harvard Sitkoff, *The Struggle for Black Equality*, 2nd ed. (1993), offer engaging accounts of the civil rights movement. On Martin Luther King Jr., see Taylor Branch's three-part biography, *Parting the Waters: 1954–1963* (1988), *Pillar of Fire: 1963–1965* (1998), and *At Canaan's Edge: 1965–1968* (2005). On Vietnam, the basic history is George Herring, *America's Longest War: The United States and Vietnam* (1986). Vivid accounts of dissent in the 1960s are Todd Gitlin, *The Sixties: Years of Hope, Days of Rage* (1987), and Maurice Isserman and Michael Kazin, *America Divided: The Civil War of the 1960s* (1999).

The period is unusually rich in compelling primary accounts. *Takin' It to the Streets* (1995), edited by Alexander Bloom and Wini Breines, offers an impressive array of documents that encompass the war, counterculture, civil rights, feminism, gay liberation, and other issues. Henry Hampton and Steve Fayer's oral history, *Voices of Freedom* (1991), and *The Autobiography of Malcolm X* (1965), cowritten with Alex Haley, provide insight into black struggle. Memoirs of Vietnam are numerous. Secretary of Defense Robert McNamara offers an insider's view and belated apologia in his *In Retrospect* (1995). Ron Kovic's *Born on the Fourth of July* (1976) is one soldier's powerful account of the war experience and its aftermath.

The John F. Kennedy Library and Museum's site at **www.jfklibrary.org** provides a large collection of records from Kennedy's presidency, including transcripts and recordings of JFK's speeches, a database of his executive orders, and a number of other resources. Civil Rights in Mississippi Digital Archive, at **www.lib.usm.edu/~spcol/crda/oh/index.html**, offers 150 oral histories relating to the civil rights movement in Mississippi. Audio clips are also included, as are short biographies, photographs, newsletters, FBI documents, and arrest records. A useful Vietnam site that includes state papers and official correspondence from 1941 to the fall of Saigon in 1975 is at **www.mtholyoke.edu/acad/intrel/vietnam.htm**.

TEST YOUR KNOWLEDGE

To assess your command of the material in this chapter, see the Online Study Guide at **bedfordstmartins.com/henretta**.

For Web sites, images, and documents related to topics and places in this chapter, visit **bedfordstmartins.com/makehistory**.

The 1970s: Toward a Conservative America

"THE UNITED STATES STEEL CORPORATION announced yesterday that it was closing 14 plants and mills in 8 states. About 13,000 production and white-collar workers will lose their jobs." "Weyerhaeuser Co. may trim about 1,000 salaried employees from its 11,000 member workforce over the next year." "Philadelphia: Food Fair Inc. plans to close 89 supermarkets in New York and Connecticut." Imagine a citizen of the 1950s emerging from a time capsule into the 1970s. She is bewildered by these gloomy newspaper headlines. What happened to America's vaunted economic supremacy? Equally bewildering is the sight of the all-powerful United States withdrawing from Vietnam, defeated by a third-tier country this citizen has probably never heard of. And she is utterly stunned, as one whose notion of an American president is Dwight D. Eisenhower, to be told that the current president, charged with obstruction of justice, has resigned in disgrace and left the White House.

Yet it's not all bad news. Who would have imagined Americans, in a time of joblessness and runaway inflation, mounting robust consumer and environmental movements? Yet that's what happened in the 1970s. Or the struggle for civil rights, far from pausing after the strenuous 1960s, intensifying and, in the case of women's and gay rights, breaking

The Nixon Years
Nixon's Domestic Agenda
Détente
Nixon's War
The 1972 Election
Watergate

Battling for Civil Rights:
The Second Stage
The Revival of Feminism
Enforcing Civil Rights

Lean Years
Energy Crisis
Environmentalism
Economic Woes

Politics in the Wake of Watergate
Jimmy Carter: The Outsider as
*   President*
Carter and the World

Summary
Connections: Society

◀ **No Gas**

During the energy crisis of 1973, American motorists faced widespread gasoline shortages for the first time since World War II. Although gas was not rationed, gas stations were closed on Sundays, and some communities instituted further restrictions such as creating systems by which motorists with license plates ending in even numbers could purchase gas on certain days, with alternate days being reserved for odd numbers. Tom Ebenhoh/Black Star/Stockphoto.com.

new ground? Or a grassroots conservative movement, rising up in the millions in defense of traditional values?

If the historian is hard put making sense of the 1970s, it's because these crosscurrents suggest a country in the throes of change. But with Ronald Reagan's election in 1980, Americans better understood what was happening. They were leaving the liberal America behind and entering an age of political conservatism.

The Nixon Years

Richard Nixon was a master of the subtle art of politics. In the 1968 campaign his "southern strategy" and appeal to the "silent majority" had worked wonders at undermining the New Deal coalition. But Nixon was not, in fact, prepared to offer a genuine alternative. And insofar as he tried, he came up against a Democrat-controlled Congress — itself a stubborn legacy of the liberal age. Like Kennedy, moreover, Nixon much preferred foreign affairs. But here, too, while more adept a strategist, he was enmeshed by his inheritance of Vietnam. So we have to put Nixon down as a transitional figure — with one foot in the liberal past, the other in the conservative future — except in one respect. His departure was not transitional. He left with a big bang.

Nixon's Domestic Agenda

As a Republican candidate, it was incumbent on Nixon to run on an antigovernment platform. He called his approach the "New Federalism," vowing to "reverse the flow of power and resources from the states and communities to Washington and start power and resources flowing back . . . to the people." Nixon's particular take on this pledge was his revenue-sharing program, which distributed a portion of federal tax revenues to the states as block grants to be spent as state officials saw fit — an approach that became a fixture on the Republican agenda. Nixon also scaled back government programs that had grown dramatically during the Johnson administration. War on Poverty programs were reduced and the Office of Economic Opportunity entirely dismantled in 1971. Nixon also refused to spend billions of dollars appropriated by Congress for urban renewal, pollution control, and other environmental initiatives, and vetoed a 1971 bill to establish a comprehensive national child-care system on the grounds that such "communal approaches to child rearing" endangered the American family.

Yet Nixon could be imaginative, even daring, when it came to social welfare. He was much influenced by a key White House adviser, Daniel Moynihan, a Democrat and an independent-minded expert on urban affairs. In 1969 Nixon proposed a Family Assistance Plan, which would guarantee a family of four an income of $1,600 a year, plus $600 in food stamps. The appeal of this proposal lay in its simplicity: It would eliminate multiple layers of bureaucracy and pare down the nation's jerry-built welfare system. Attacked in the Senate both by conservatives and liberals, however, Nixon's plan failed. Welfare reform was postponed for another day. And so was national health insurance, another of Nixon's failed initiatives, in which he proposed a public/private system that would guarantee universal coverage.

No enemy of the major **entitlement programs**, Nixon approved generous advances in Medicare, Medicaid, and Social Security. And his administration expanded the regulatory apparatus of the modern state. New government agencies — the Environmental Protection Agency (EPA) in 1970, the Occupational Safety and Health Administration (OSHA), and the Consumer Products Safety Commission in 1972 — brought the federal government deep into areas hitherto only lightly regulated or not regulated at all.

Nixon's mixed record reflected the political crosscurrents of his time. His conservative base pushed in one direction; the Democratic Congress pushed in another. Consumer and environmental protections loomed large for the middle class. Social Security and Medicare mattered to working-class voters he was appealing to. But Nixon was himself not a laissez-faire conservative, and — what especially distinguished him — he had a zest for experimenting with the mechanics of government.

Détente

Richard Nixon regarded himself a "realist" in foreign affairs. That meant, above all, advancing the national interest. Everything else — commitments to allies, extending democracy abroad, championing human rights — came second, if that. Nixon's realism was fervently seconded by his national security adviser, Henry Kissinger, although Kissinger had arrived at Nixon's view by a more scholarly route. As a Harvard professor, he had closely studied the nineteenth-century diplomat Metternich, who at the Vienna Congress of 1815 crafted a balance-of-power system that stabilized Europe for an entire century.

Conducting foreign affairs Metternich's way, however, required a degree of secrecy that was antithetical to America's constitutional system. Nixon and Kissinger did the best they could. They bypassed Congress, cut out the State Department (including the secretary of state, William Rogers), and established "back channels" to agencies whose expertise they needed. It was a dangerous game, but for a time, a game they played successfully. Nixon and Kissinger were preparing to take advantage of international conditions ripe for change.

For one thing, all the major players faced significant internal unrest. It was not only the United States that was rocked by student protesters. Street rioting almost brought down the French government in May 1968. German universities were hotbeds of protest. On the Communist side, it had taken Russian tanks to put down a reformist challenge — the "Prague Spring" — in Czechoslovakia. But tanks only put down people; they couldn't put down dissident ideas, which seeped even into the Soviet Union. And in China, Mao Zedong's Cultural Revolution had gotten out of hand, with young Red Guards turning on the regime. A shared sense of internal fragility made all the major powers receptive to an easing of international tensions.

Ultimately of greater importance, however, was an upheaval in the original arrangement of the Cold War. The notion of a bipolar world no longer held. Once the Cold War stalemated around 1950, neither superpower found it possible to keep its side in line. In America's case, the most difficult partner was France, which under the imperious Charles de Gaulle, thumbed its nose at the United States and walked away from NATO. That, however, was nothing compared to Soviet relations with China, which by 1969 had deteriorated from eternal friendship into outright border warfare, with the possibility of a nuclear exchange not excluded.

Nixon saw his chance. In 1971 he sent Kissinger secretly to Beijing (Peking) to explore an accommodation. Mao was actually thinking along the same lines. So an arrangement was not difficult to arrive at. The United States would back away from the Chinese Nationalists on Taiwan, permit China's admission to the United Nations (with a permanent seat on the Security Council), and eventually grant recognition (in 1978). In February 1972, President Nixon arrived in Beijing in a blaze of publicity to ratify the deal. This was the man who had clawed his

Nixon in China

When President Nixon arrived in China in February 1972 to ratify détente with Mao Zedong, a required part of the visit was a tour of the Great Wall. In this photograph, Mao is on the president's left, Secretary of State William Rogers on his right. @ Bettmann/Corbis.

way into prominence by railing against the Democrats for "losing" China and hounding Alger Hiss into prison. Nixon's credentials as an anti-Communist were impeccable. That was why he felt free to come to Beijing, he remarked genially to Mao. "Those on the right can do what those on the left only talk about." Mao responded: "I like rightists."

Nixon then turned to the Soviet Union. He had already reached a secret understanding with Leonid Brezhnev, the Soviet premier, about Cuban issues left hanging after the missile crisis of 1962. In exchange for an American promise not to invade, the Soviets agreed to dismantle a submarine base and withhold offensive missiles from Castro. Three months after the Beijing summit, Nixon journeyed in another blaze of publicity to Moscow to sign the first Strategic Arms Limitations Treaty (SALT I) limiting the production and deployment of intercontinental ballistic missiles (ICBMs) and antiballistic missile systems (ABMs). SALT I, while technically modest, was intended only as a first step toward comprehensive arms limitation.

The summits in Beijing and Moscow inaugurated what came to be known as **détente** (in French: "relaxation of tensions"). Although the agreements themselves were quite limited, and rocky times lay ahead, the fact was the Cold War had reached a turning point. Nixon had parlayed a strategic advantage—the dangerous rift in the Communist world—into a new tripartite balance of power. The world had become a less dangerous place. And Nixon hoped for a dividend over Vietnam.

Nixon's War

Vietnam became an American project in the 1950s on the assumption that containing Communism was a global struggle, East against West, with Vietnam on the front line. The concept of a bipolar world, already outmoded in Lyndon Johnson's time, was utterly refuted by Richard Nixon's embrace of détente. Yet, when it came to Vietnam, Nixon picked up where Johnson had left off. Abandoning Vietnam, Nixon insisted, would damage America's "credibility" and make it seem "a pitiful, helpless giant." And, like Johnson, Nixon had himself to consider. He was not going to be the first American president to lose a war. Nixon wanted peace, but only "peace with honor."

The North Vietnamese were not about to oblige him. The only outcome acceptable to them was a unified Vietnam under their control. What remained negotiable were the details, the terms of surrender, and that, plus the wiliness of the North Vietnamese negotiators, enabled the Paris talks begun by Johnson to continue, intermittently. But on the essentials, North Vietnam was immovable. So Nixon fashioned a two-pronged response.

To damp down criticism at home, he began withdrawing American troops while delegating the ground fighting to the South Vietnamese. Under this new policy of "Vietnamization," American troop levels dropped from 543,000 in 1968, to 334,000 in 1971, to barely 24,000 by early 1973. American casualties, and the political liabilities they entailed, dropped correspondingly. But the killing in Vietnam continued. As the U.S. ambassador to Vietnam, Ellsworth Bunker, noted cynically, it was just a matter of changing "the color of the bodies."

The companion policy called for an intensified bombing campaign, concealed from the war-weary American public. To step up the pressure, Nixon in March 1969 ordered secret air attacks on neutral Cambodia, through whose territory the North Vietnamese had been moving supplies and reinforcements. The secret war on Cambodia culminated on April 30, 1970, in an "incursion" into Cambodia to destroy enemy havens there. In late 1971, as American troops withdrew from the region, Communist forces infiltrated back in and stepped up their attacks. The next spring North Vietnamese forces launched a major offensive against South Vietnam. In April, as the fighting intensified, Nixon ordered B-52 bombing raids against North Vietnam, and a month later he approved the mining of North Vietnamese ports, something Johnson had never dared do. Nixon had a freer hand because, in the "spirit" of détente, China no longer threatened to intervene. Nor was Brezhnev deterred from welcoming Nixon in May 1972 at the height of the B-52 bombing onslaught (causing some Soviet casualties). The North Vietnamese might have felt more isolated, but supplies from China and the USSR continued, and they fought on.

At home, Nixon's war exacted a huge toll. Far from abating, the antiwar movement intensified. On November 16, 1969, Mobilization Day brought a record half a million protesters to Washington. A secret war, moreover, could be kept secret only for so long. When news of the invasion of Cambodia came out, American campuses exploded in outrage and, for the first time, students died. On May 4, 1970, at Kent State University in Ohio, panicky National Guardsmen fired into an antiwar rally, killing four students and wounding eleven. At Jackson State College in Mississippi, Guardsmen stormed a dormitory, killing two black students. More than 450 colleges closed in protest; across the country the spring semester was essentially canceled.

Pro-War Rally

Under a sea of American flags, construction workers in New York City march in support of the Vietnam War. Tens of thousands of them wearing "hard hats" jammed Broadway for four blocks opposite City Hall, and the overflow crammed the side streets. Working-class patriotism became a main source of support for Nixon's war. Paul Fusco/Magnum Photos, Inc.

The Vietnam poison infected even the military. In November 1969, the story of the My Lai Massacre broke, revealing the slaughter of 350 Vietnamese villagers by U.S. troops in retaliation for earlier casualties they had taken. The young lieutenant in command, William Calley, was court-martialed, sentenced to life imprisonment, then released to his barracks at Nixon's order, and eventually paroled. As the war dragged on, morale sank. Troops refused to go into combat; thousands deserted or turned to drugs. Many sewed peace symbols on their uniforms. In the heat of battle, overbearing junior officers were sometimes "fragged" — killed or wounded by grenades of their own soldiers. At home, a group called Vietnam Veterans against the War turned in their combat medals at demonstrations outside the U.S. Capitol.

Despite everything, Nixon persevered, hunkering down in the White House, castigating student protesters as "bums," and rallying a potent backlash against them. "Hardhat" became a patriotic symbol after New York construction workers beat demonstrators at a peace rally in May 1970. Slowly, Vietnamization eroded the antiwar opposition. With the army's manpower needs reduced, the draft was cut back (and ended entirely in 1973), deflating the ardor of many antiwar students. And militant groups, like the SDS, splintered and became ineffective, while the SDS's violent offshoot, the Weathermen, were arrested or driven underground. In the end, Nixon outlasted his critics. What he couldn't outlast was North Vietnam.

With the 1972 election approaching, Nixon sent Henry Kissinger back to the Paris peace talks. In a key concession, Kissinger accepted the continued

The Fall of Saigon

After the 1973 U.S. withdrawal from Vietnam, the South Vietnamese government lasted another two years. In March 1975 the North Vietnamese forces launched a final offensive and by April they had surrounded the capital of Saigon. Here, panicked Vietnamese seek sanctuary at the U.S. embassy compound. Nik Wheeler/Sipa Press.

presence of North Vietnamese troops in South Vietnam. North Vietnam then agreed to an interim arrangement whereby the Saigon government would stay in power while a tripartite commission arranged elections and a final settlement. American prisoners of war would be returned, and the remaining U.S. troops withdrawn. With Kissinger's announcement that "peace is at hand," Nixon got the election lift he wanted, but the agreement was then sabotaged by General Nguyen Van Thieu, the South Vietnamese president. So Nixon, in one final spasm of blood-letting, unleashed the two-week "Christmas bombing," the most savage of the entire war. On January 27, 1973, the two sides signed the Paris Peace Accords, essentially restating the cease-fire agreement of the previous October. The United States might have achieved that agreement four years earlier had it been willing to accept North Vietnamese troops in the South.

Nixon hoped that, with massive U.S. aid, the Thieu regime might survive. But Congress was in revolt. It refused appropriations for bombing Cam-

bodia after August 15, 1973, and gradually cut back aid to South Vietnam. In March 1975 North Vietnamese forces launched a final offensive. On television, horrified American viewers watched as South Vietnamese officials and soldiers battled American embassy personnel to board the last helicopters out of Saigon. On April 29, 1975, Vietnam was reunited. Saigon was renamed Ho Chi Minh City, after the founding father of the Communist regime.

Did this sad outcome matter? Yes, certainly, for America's Vietnamese allies, who lost jobs and property, spent years in "re-education" camps, or fled the country. Yes, for next-door Cambodia, where the maniac Khmer Rouge took over, murdered 1.7 million people, and drove the country nearly back to the Stone Age. For the United States, yes, for the wasted lives (58,000 dead, 300,000 wounded), the $150 billion spent, the slow-to-heal internal wounds, the lost confidence in America's political leaders. But in geopolitical terms? Not really. Defeat in South Vietnam did not mean, as successive American administrations had feared, victory for the Communist side because there no longer was a Communist "side." The Hanoi regime called itself Communist, but never intended to be anybody's satellite, least of all China's, an ancient enemy. (Within a few years the two countries fell to fighting over disputed borders.) Today, after twenty years of embargo, America's relations with the People's Republic of Vietnam are normal, with diplomatic recognition granted in 1995. That event would hardly be worth mentioning but for the fact that it is a postscript to America's most disastrous military adventure of the twentieth century.

The 1972 Election

The Democrats had fallen into disarray after 1968. Swept up by reform enthusiasms, followers of George McGovern took over the party, adopting new rules intended to encourage grassroots participation and assure that women, blacks, and young people held delegate seats "in reasonable relation to their presence in the population." Benefiting from these guidelines, McGovern's army of antiwar activists blitzed the precinct-level caucuses, winning delegate commitments far beyond McGovern's actual party support. Fresh faces filled the 1972 convention—38 percent women, 15 percent black, 23 percent under thirty (compared to 2.6 percent in 1968)—bursting with enthusiasm, but mostly innocent of national politics. In the past, an alliance of urban machines, labor unions, and ethnic groups—the heart of the New Deal coalition—would almost certainly have rejected an upstart candidate like McGovern. But few of the party faithful qualified as delegates under the changed rules. The crowning insult came when the convention rejected the credentials of Chicago Mayor Richard Daley and his delegation, seating instead an Illinois delegation led by Jesse Jackson, a firebrand young black minister and former aide of Martin Luther King.

Capturing the party was one thing; winning a national election quite another. McGovern was, in fact, a weak campaigner. He started badly at the convention, which was in bedlam when he finally delivered his acceptance speech at 2:30 A.M. His running mate, Senator Thomas Eagleton of Missouri, turned out to have a history of mental illness and had to be replaced. And McGovern failed to mollify key party backers like the AFL-CIO, which, for the first time in memory, refused to endorse the Democratic ticket.

McGovern was no match for Nixon, who pulled out all the stops. Using the advantages of incumbency, he gave the economy a well-timed lift and

proclaimed (prematurely) a cease-fire in Vietnam. Nixon's appeal to the "silent majority"—people who "care about a strong United States, about patriotism, about moral and spiritual values"—was by now well-honed, with added wrinkles about "forced" busing and law and order.

Nixon won in a landslide, receiving nearly 61 percent of the popular vote and carrying every state except Massachusetts and the District of Columbia. The returns revealed how fractured traditional Democratic voting blocs had become. McGovern received only 38 percent of the big-city Catholic vote, and overall lost 42 percent of self-identified Democrats. The 1972 election marks a pivotal moment in the country's shift to the right. The full effect of that shift was delayed, however, by the president's soon-to-be-discovered self-inflicted wounds.

Watergate

On June 17, 1972, a funny thing happened at the Watergate complex in Washington, D.C. Early that morning, five men carrying wiretapping equipment were apprehended breaking into the Democratic National Committee's (DNC) headquarters. The arrest of two accomplices soon followed. Queried by the press, a White House spokesman dismissed the episode as "a third-rate burglary attempt." Wiretap equipment? At the DNC headquarters? Pressed further, Nixon himself denied any White House involvement in "this very bizarre incident."

In fact, the two kingpins, G. Gordon Liddy and E. Howard Hunt, were former FBI and CIA agents currently working for Nixon's Committee to Reelect the President (CREEP). Earlier they had been on the White House payroll, hired in 1971 after the publication by the *New York Times* of the Pentagon Papers, a classified history of American involvement in Vietnam up to 1967, before Nixon's time. Even so, Nixon was enraged at the leak by Daniel Ellsberg, one of Washington's "best and brightest" and a trusted Pentagon insider. In response, the president set up a clandestine squad, known as the "plumbers" because their job was to plug administration leaks and do other nasty jobs. Hunt and Liddy, two of the plumbers, burglarized Ellsberg's psychiatrist's office in an unsuccessful effort to discredit him. Now, as CREEP operatives, they were arranging illegal wiretaps at DNC headquarters, part of a campaign of "dirty tricks" against the Democrats.

The Watergate burglary was no isolated incident. It was part of a broad pattern of illegality and misuse of power by a White House obsessed with the antiwar movement and prepared to fight its critics by any means, fair or foul. That siege mentality best explains why Nixon took a fatal misstep. He could have dissociated himself from the break-in by dismissing his guilty aides, or even just by letting justice take its course. But it was election time, and Nixon hung tough. He arranged hush money for the burglars and instructed the CIA to stop an FBI investigation into the affair. This was obstruction of justice, a criminal offense.

The Wheels of Justice. Nixon kept the lid on until after the election, but then, as the wheels of justice turned, the lid came off. In January 1973, the Watergate burglars were found guilty. One of them, the security chief for CREEP, began to talk. In the meantime, two tenacious reporters at the *Washington Post*, Carl Bernstein and Bob Woodward, uncovered CREEP's illegal "slush fund" and its links to key White House aides. (Their informant, famously known as Deep Throat, was finally revealed in 2005 to be the second-in-command at the FBI, W. Mark Felt.) In May a Senate investigating committee began holding nationally televised hearings, at which Assistant Secretary of Commerce Jeb Magruder confessed his guilt and implicated former Attorney General John Mitchell, White House Counsel John Dean, and others. Dean, in turn, implicated Nixon. Just as startling, a former White House aide revealed that Nixon had installed a secret taping system in the Oval Office.

Citing executive privilege, Nixon refused to surrender his tapes. Under enormous pressure, he eventually released sanitized transcripts and some of the tapes, but with a highly suspicious eighteen-minute gap. Finally, on June 23, 1974, the Supreme Court ordered Nixon to release the unexpurgated tapes. Lawyers were astounded to find in them incontrovertible evidence that the president had ordered the cover-up six days after the break-in. By then, the House Judiciary Committee was already considering articles of impeachment. Certain that he would be convicted by the Senate, on August 9, 1974, Nixon became the first U.S. president to resign his office.

The next day Vice President Gerald Ford was sworn in as president. Ford, the Republican minority leader in the House of Representatives, had replaced Vice President Spiro Agnew, who had himself resigned in 1973 for accepting kickbacks while governor of Maryland. The transfer of power proceeded smoothly. A month later, however, Ford stunned the nation by granting Nixon a "full, free, and absolute" pardon "for all offenses he had committed or might have committed during his presidency." Ford took

that action, he said, to spare the country the agony of Nixon's criminal prosecution.

Aftermath. In Moscow, puzzled Kremlin leaders suspected a giant right-wing conspiracy against Nixon. They could not understand, recalled the Soviet ambassador to Washington at the time, "how a powerful president could be forced to resign . . . because of what they saw as a minor breach of conduct. Soviet history knew no parallel." That was one meaning of Watergate—that, in America, the rule of law prevailed (just barely; Nixon likely would have survived had he destroyed the tapes). A second meaning involved the constitutional separation of powers. As commander-in-chief, Nixon asserted unlimited authority, including wiretapping or worse, in the name of national security and, like the Kremlin leaders, he was perplexed at being brought down by a "pigmy-sized" incident like Watergate.

Congress pushed back, passing a raft of laws against the abuses of the Nixon administration—the War Powers Act (1973), reining in the president's ability to deploy U.S. forces without congressional approval; the Freedom of Information Act (1974), protecting privacy and access to federal records; the Fair Campaign Practices Act (1974), limiting and regulating contributions in presidential campaigns; and the Federal Intelligence Surveillance Act (1978), prohibiting domestic wiretapping without a warrant. Only in the short run, however, can it be said that these measures curbed America's tendency to embrace an imperial presidency.

➤ Why is the Nixon presidency considered a transitional one between the liberalism of the preceding decades and the conservatism that emerged in the 1980s?

➤ What do we mean when we say that Nixon was a "realist" in foreign affairs?

➤ Why did it take Nixon four years to reach a settlement with North Vietnam?

➤ How do you account for the Watergate scandal? What was its significance?

Battling for Civil Rights: The Second Stage

In the midst of Nixon's travail, the civil rights struggle continued, now entering a second, more complicated stage. In the first stage, the landmark achievements—*Brown v. Board of Education* (1954), the Civil Rights Act of 1964, and the Voting Rights Act of 1965—had been bitterly resisted, but once those battles ended, the moral atmosphere shifted. In principle, at any rate, Americans no longer defended segregation, or racial discrimination, or the denial of voting rights. But now the time came for enforcing those rights, sometimes, it turned out, at the expense of other Americans—and that meant strife. In the 1970s, moreover, the battle lines shifted from race to gender, as women, and then gays, mobilized and demanded equal rights. For many Americans, that was a great deal harder to handle because equality of the sexes hit closer to home than did racial equality. The effect was galvanizing. If the battle for equal rights had entered a second stage, so did the evolution of the conservative movement, increasingly driven as it now was by moral values and religious faith.

The Revival of Feminism

In the postwar years feminism was a languishing movement, with few advocates and no burning issues. That changed dramatically during the 1960s, initially sparked by the black civil rights movement, and then by the decade's broader social upheaval. But the revival of feminism also sprang from the deeply felt needs of many women at this juncture in their lives.

One spark was Betty Friedan's indictment of suburban domesticity, *The Feminine Mystique,* which appeared in 1963 (see Chapter 27). White, college-educated, middle-class women read Friedan's book and thought, "She's talking about me." *The Feminine Mystique,* after a slow start, became a runaway best seller. It gave women a vocabulary with which to express their dissatisfaction and made them believe that self-realization was attainable through jobs, education, and escape from mind-deadening domesticity.

Paradoxically, *The Feminine Mystique* was a bit out of date by the time it appeared. The domesticity it described was already crumbling. More and more women were working, including married women (40 percent by 1970) and mothers with preschool children (30 percent by 1970). After the postwar baby boom, women were again having fewer children, aided now by the birth control pill, first marketed in 1960, and the intrauterine device (IUD). At the same time the divorce rate, on the rise for the past century, speeded up as the states liberalized divorce laws. Educational levels were also rising; by 1970 women made up 42 percent of the college population. All these changes undermined

traditional gender roles and enabled women, as they read *The Feminine Mystique,* to embrace its liberating prescriptions.

Budding feminists also received positive signals from Washington. In 1961, Kennedy appointed a Presidential Commission on the Status of Women, which issued a 1963 report documenting employment and educational discrimination against women. The result was some minor legislation, but, more importantly, a rudimentary network of activist women in public life that had formed in the course of the commission's work. A bigger breakthrough resulted by sheer inadvertence. Hoping to derail the pending Civil Rights Act of 1964, a key conservative, Representative Howard Smith of Virginia, mischievously added "sex" to the categories protected against discrimination under Title VII. The act passed anyway, and, to everyone's surprise, women suddenly had a powerful tool for fighting sex discrimination—provided, of course, that the Equal Employment Opportunity Commission (EEOC) could be prodded into doing its job.

With that objective in mind, Friedan and others founded the National Organization for Women (NOW) in 1966. Modeled on the NAACP, NOW intended to be a civil rights organization for women, with the aim of bringing "women into full participation in . . . American society now, exercising all the privileges and responsibilities thereof in truly equal partnership with men"—a classic statement of feminism. Under Friedan, who served as NOW's first president, membership grew from 1,000 in 1967 to 15,000 in 1971, and NOW became, like the NAACP, a powerful voice for equal rights.

The 1960s spawned another branch of feminists, the women's liberationists, primarily younger, college-educated women who had earned their spurs in the civil rights, New Left, and the antiwar movements. To their chagrin, they discovered that the male leaders of these movements were no better than the frat boys they had known in college. Women who tried to raise feminist issues were shouted off the platform with jeers like "Move on, little girl, we have more important issues to talk about here than women's liberation."

Fed up with this treatment, women radicals broke away and began their own movement. Unlike NOW, women's liberation had little formal structure and was best described as an alliance of loose collectives that had formed in New York, San Francisco, and other big cities. "Women's lib," as it was dubbed by a skeptical media, went public in 1968 at the Miss America pageant. Most eye-catching was a "freedom trash can" into which women were invited to fling false eyelashes, hair curlers, brassieres, and girdles—all

Women's Liberation

Arguing that beauty contests were degrading to women, members of the National Women's Liberation Party staged a protest against the Miss America pageant held in Atlantic City, New Jersey, in September 1968. AP Images.

branded as symbols of female oppression. Women's liberation was a phenomenon of the 1960s, mirroring the identity politics of Black Power activists and the self-dramatization of the counterculture.

An activity more broadly experienced was "consciousness raising" — group sessions in which women shared their experiences. Swapping stories about being passed over for a promotion, needing a husband's signature on a credit card application, or enduring whistles and leers on the streets, participants began to realize that their individual problems were part of a wider pattern of oppression.

Feminism at High Tide. Before 1969 most women heard about NOW and other feminist organizations

by word of mouth. After that, the media brought women's issues to a wider audience. New terms such as *sexism* and *male chauvinism* became part of the national vocabulary. As converts flooded in, the two branches of the women's movement began to converge. Radical women realized that key feminist goals — child care, equal pay, and abortion rights — could best be achieved in the political arena. At the same time, more traditional activists developed a broader view of women's oppression. Although still largely white and middle class, feminists began to think of themselves as part of a broad and growing social crusade. Only later did the movement grapple with the fact that as much divided women — race, class, age, sexual preference — as united them.

U.S. Women's Lightweight Crew

Crew was one of those muscle sports from which college women had traditionally been excluded until Title IX came along and opened the sport to women. Some of the best of that first generation of college rowers ended up on the U.S. women's team competing in the Canadian Regatta in 1982, shown at left. The rower in the bow seat (far right) is the daughter of one of the co-authors of this text. Private collection.

Women's opportunities expanded dramatically in higher education. Formerly all-male bastions, such as Yale, Princeton, and the U.S. Military Academy, admitted women undergraduates for the first time. Hundreds of colleges started women's studies programs, and the proportion of women attending graduate and professional schools rose markedly. With the adoption of Title IX in 1972, Congress broadened the 1964 Civil Rights Act to include educational institutions, prohibiting colleges and universities that received federal funds from discriminating on the basis of sex. By requiring comparable funding for sports programs, Title IX made women's athletics a real presence on college campuses.

Women also became increasingly visible in public life. The National Women's Political Caucus, founded in 1971, actively promoted the election of women to public office. Bella Abzug, Elizabeth Holtzman, Shirley Chisholm, Patricia Schroeder, and Geraldine Ferraro served in Congress; Ella T. Grasso became Connecticut's governor in 1974, as did Dixie Lee Ray in Washington State in 1976. Women's political mobilization produced significant legislative and administrative gains. Congress authorized child-care tax deductions for working parents in 1972, and in 1974 passed the Equal Credit Opportunity Act, which enabled married women to get credit, including credit cards and mortgages, in their own names. In 1977, 20,000 women went to Houston for the first National Women's Conference. Their "National Plan of Action" represented a hard-won consensus on topics ranging from violence against women to homemakers' rights, the needs of older women, and, most controversially, abortion and other reproductive issues.

Phyllis Schlafly: The Equal Rights Amendment, Defeated. Buoyed by its successes, the women's movement renewed the fight for an Equal Rights Amendment (ERA) to the Constitution. First introduced in Congress in 1923, the ERA stated in its entirety, "Equality of rights under the law shall not be denied or abridged by the United States or any State on the basis of sex." In the early days, the ERA had split the women's movement, with social reformers fearing that the amendment would jeopardize protective legislation for women. That fear, while not wholly gone, no longer prevented feminists of all varieties from favoring the amendment. As much as anything, the ERA became a symbolic statement of women's equality. Congress enthusiastically adopted the amendment in 1972, and within two

years thirty-four states ratified it. But then progress abruptly halted (Map 29.1).

For this, credit goes chiefly to a remarkable woman, Phyllis Schlafly, a lawyer, outspoken anti-Communist, and long-time activist in conservative causes. Despite her own flourishing career, Schlafly advocated traditional roles for women. She liked to bait feminists by opening her speeches with "I'd like to thank my husband for letting me be here tonight." The ERA, she proclaimed, would create an unnatural "unisex society," with women drafted into the army and forced to use single-sex toilets and locker rooms. Her STOP ERA organization galvanized a "silent" population of conservative Americans. Grassroots networks mobilized, showing up at statehouses with home-baked bread and apple pies. As labels on baked goods at one anti-ERA rally expressed it, "My heart and hand went into this dough / For the sake of the family please vote no." It was a message that

Phyllis Schlafly

Phyllis Schlafly, leader of the Stop ERA movement, talks with reporters during a rally at the Illinois State Capitol on March 4, 1975, at a time when the state legislature was considering whether to ratify the Equal Rights Amendment. Schlafly described herself as a housewife and called her strenuous political career a "hobby."
© Bettmann/Corbis.

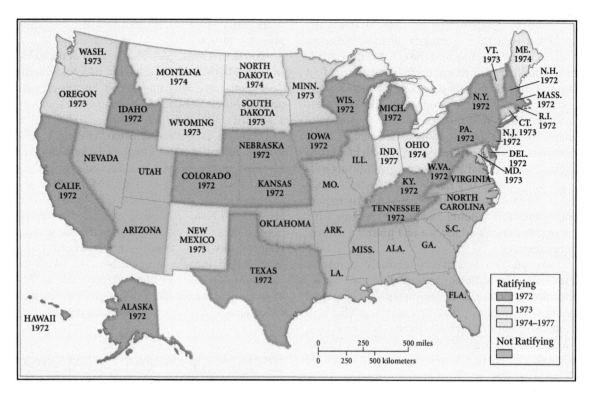

Map 29.1 States Ratifying the Equal Rights Amendment, 1972–1977

The ratifying process for the Equal Rights Amendment (ERA) went smoothly in 1972 and 1973 but then stalled. The turning point came in 1976, when ERA advocates lobbied extensively, particularly in Florida, North Carolina, and Illinois, but failed to sway the conservative legislatures in those states. After Indiana ratified in 1977, the amendment still lacked three votes toward the three-fourths majority needed for adoption. Efforts to revive the ERA in the 1980s were unsuccessful, and it became a dead issue.

resonated widely, especially among those troubled by the rapid pace of social change (see Comparing American Voices, "Debating the Equal Rights Amendment," pp. 908–909). The ERA never was ratified, despite a congressional extension of the deadline until June 30, 1982.

Gays and Lesbians. Parallel to, and inspired by, the feminist movement, homosexual men and women launched their own protest movement. The crystallizing event was the "Stonewall riot" of 1969 in New York City, when patrons of a gay bar fought back against police harassment. In the assertion of pride that followed, activists began to call themselves *gay* rather than homosexual; founded advocacy groups, newspapers, and political organizations; and offered emotional support to those who "came out" and publicly affirmed their homosexuality. In New York's Greenwich Village, San Francisco's Castro district, and other urban enclaves, vibrant gay communities emerged. In 1973 the National Gay Task Force launched a campaign to make gay men and lesbians a

protected group under laws covering employment and housing rights. These efforts succeeded mostly at the local level. During the 1970s Detroit, Boston, Los Angeles, Miami, San Francisco, and other cities passed laws barring discrimination on the basis of sexual preference.

Like the ERA, gay rights came under attack from conservatives. When the Miami city council passed a measure banning discrimination against gay men and lesbians in 1977, the singer Anita Bryant led a campaign to repeal the law by popular referendum. Later that year voters overturned the measure by a two-to-one majority, prompting similar antigay campaigns around the country. Once again, the country was witnessing the clash between equal rights for an oppressed minority and the moral values of a conservative majority.

Enforcing Civil Rights

The Equal Rights Amendment provoked a *political* struggle. Supporters and opponents mobilized and lobbied their legislators. The losing side, bitter though it might be, could not say its voice had been unheard. But to a large degree the civil rights struggle bypassed this democratic process. For one thing, under the American constitutional system fundamental rights trumped majority rule — which was, for example, the basis on which *Brown v. Board of Education* had struck down state-mandated segregated schooling. For another thing, and perhaps more important, *enforcing* civil rights was a judicial and/or executive function. Courts and federal agencies did the heavy lifting. And that — the unaccountability of the key actors — fed the outrage of many Americans already feeling adversely affected by the gains of protected minorities.

Affirmative Action. When Congress banned job discrimination in the Civil Rights Act (1964), all that it intended was that employers hire on a merit basis and without regard to race, religion, ethnicity, or sex. The wave of urban riots made the Johnson administration think again. The Kerner Commission (1968), after investigating the causes behind the rioting, strongly urged a massive federal effort at countering the white racism that held blacks back and deprived them of hope. One result was *affirmative action* — procedures designed to take into account the disadvantaged position of minorities after centuries of discrimination. First advanced by the Labor Department in 1968, affirmative action was refined by a series of court rulings that identified acceptable procedures, including hiring and enrollment goals, special recruitment and training programs, and *set-asides* (specially reserved slots).

Aided by affirmative action, African Americans enrolled in colleges and universities doubled between and 1970 and 1977, to 1.1 million, or 9.3 percent of total student population. Blacks moved into white-collar professions, found new opportunities in civil service, or got better access to union jobs. Latinos did as well, and white women far better.

Affirmative action, however, did not sit well with many whites, who felt the deck was being stacked against them. Complaints began to be heard about "reverse discrimination." Especially troubling were quotas because they were easily abused, tempting employers and college administrators to shoot for the numbers, without too much concern about whether the minorities hired or admitted really merited affirmative action.

In 1978 Allan Bakke, a white man, sued the University of California at Davis Medical School for rejecting him in favor of less qualified minority candidates. The Supreme Court rejected the medical school's quota system, which set aside 16 of 100 places for "disadvantaged" students. The Court ordered Bakke admitted, but indicated that a more flexible approach, in which racial factors could be considered along with other factors, would still pass muster. *Bakke v. University of California* thus upheld affirmative action, but by rejecting straightforward implementation, also called it into question. "Reverse discrimination" had become a rallying cry for conservatives.

Busing. The other main civil rights objective — desegregating the schools — produced far more fireworks. For fifteen years southern states, by a variety of stratagems, had fended off court directives that they move to integration "with all deliberate speed" (see Chapter 27). In 1968, hardly a third of all black children in the South attended schools with whites. At that point, the federal courts got serious and, in a series of stiff decisions, ordered an end to "dual school systems." Where this did not happen, the courts intervened directly. In 1971, in a landmark decision, the Supreme Court imposed a county-wide busing plan on Charlotte-Mecklenburg, North Carolina. In this case, integration went smoothly, and, in fact, the South as a whole essentially gave up the fight. By the mid-1970s, 86 percent of black children were attending school with whites.

But in the North, where segregated schooling was also a fact of life — arising, however, from residential patterns, not legally mandated separation — busing orders sparked intense and sometimes violent opposition. In South Boston, a strongly Irish-Catholic working-class neighborhood, mobs attacked African American students bused in from Roxbury. Armed police were required to keep South Boston High School open.

As a solution to segregation, busing came up against cherished attachments to neighborhood schooling. Busing also had the perverse effect of speeding up "white flight" to the suburbs. The result was egregiously evident in Detroit, where a black city was encircled by white suburbs. To integrate Detroit schools would have required merging city and suburban districts, which in fact was what a lower court ordered in 1971. But in *Milliken v. Bradley* (1974) the Supreme Court overruled the lower court. Thereafter, busing as a means of achieving racial balance fell out of favor. But in the meantime "forced busing," much touted by Nixon in the 1972 campaign, added to the grievances of conservatives, not least by reminding them of how much they hated what they perceived as the arrogance of unelected judges.

Debating the Equal Rights Amendment

Fifty years after it had first been introduced, Congress in 1972 finally approved the Equal Rights Amendment ("Equality of rights under the law shall not be denied or abridged by the United States or by any State on account of sex") and sent it off to the states for ratification. The amendment set off a furious debate, especially in the South and Midwest. Following are four of the voices in that debate.

J. MARSE GRANT

J. Marse Grant was the editor of the Biblical Recorder *and Chairman of the Baptist State Convention of North Carolina. He delivered these remarks to the Constitutional Amendments Committee of the state legislature.*

Recently I received a letter in which the writer told me to pick up my Bible. . . . He told me to read what God would have me do about ERA. I told him that this is exactly what I had done. And from my Bible I learned long ago that God loves all His children. That He gave them talents and abilities, and that in Him there is no male or female. . . .

The New Testament reveals countless ways in which women are an integral art of Jesus' ministry. He gave them new respect and dignity. He forsook the old traditions of his day — He talked to women in public — He visited in their homes — and it's little wonder, and not just accidentally, in my opinion, that women were the last ones at the cross. They were the first ones at the Resurrection, too. How anyone can distort the teachings of Christ and try to say that Christ was against equality and freedom for all people is hard for me to understand. . . .

It is unfortunate that I am here to apologize today that some here in the church oppose this amendment, but some in the church also opposed the Civil Rights Act in 1964. Some in the church defended slavery and quoted scripture to try to prove it. Some opposed the right of women to vote using many of the fallacious arguments that they are now using against ERA, but they were wrong. Dead wrong.

SOURCE: William A. Link, ed., *The South in the History of the Nation* (Boston: Bedford/St. Martin's, 1999), 293–294.

JERRY FALWELL

Jerry Falwell was a fundamentalist Baptist preacher in Virginia, a television evangelist, and the founder of the Moral Majority (see p. 929 for his photograph).

I believe that at the foundation of the women's liberation movement there is a minority core of women who were once bored with life, whose real problems are spiritual problems. Many women have never accepted their God-given roles. . . . God Almighty created men and women biologically different and with differing needs and roles. He made men and women to complement each other and to love each other. . . . Women who work should be respected and accorded dignity and equal rewards for equal work. But this is not what the present feminist movement and equal rights movement are all about.

The Equal Rights Amendment is a delusion. I believe that women deserve more than equal rights. And, in families and in nations where the Bible is believed, Christian women are honored above men. Only in places where the Bible is believed and practiced do women receive more than equal rights. Men and women have differing strengths. The Equal Rights Amendment can never do for women what needs to be done for them. Women need to know Jesus Christ as their Lord and Savior and be under His Lordship. They need a man who knows Jesus Christ as his Lord and Savior, and they need to be part of a home where their husband is a godly leader and where there is a Christian family. . . . ERA is not merely a political issue, but a moral issue as well. A definite violation of holy Scripture, ERA defies the mandate that "the husband is the head of the wife, even as Christ is the head of the church" (Ep. 5:23). In 1 Peter 3:7 we read that husbands are to give their wives honor as unto the weaker vessel, that they are both heirs together of the grace of life. Because a woman is weaker does mean that she is less important.

SOURCE: Jerry Falwell, *Listen America* (New York: Doubleday, 1980), 150–151.

SAM ERVIN JR.

Sam Ervin Jr. represented North Carolina in the U.S. Senate from 1954 to 1974 and was a key figure in the Watergate investigation. In 1971, he inserted these remarks into the Congressional Record.

Let us consider for a moment whether there be a rational basis for reasonable distinctions between men and women in any of the relationships or undertakings of life.

When He created them, God made physiological and functional differences between men and women. These differences confer upon men a greater capacity to perform arduous and hazardous physical tasks. Some wise people even profess the belief that there may be psychological differences between men and women. To justify their belief, they assert that women possess an intuitive power to distinguish between wisdom and folly, good and evil.

To say these things is not to imply that either sex is superior to the other. It is simply to state the all important truth that men and women complement each other in the relationships and undertakings on which the existence and development of the race depend. . . . The physiological and functional differences between men and women constitute the most important reality. Without them human life could not exist.

For this reason, any country which ignores these differences when it fashions its institutions and makes its laws is woefully lacking in rationality. . . .

The Congress and the legislatures of the various states have enacted certain laws based upon the conviction that the physiological and functional differences between men and women make it advisable to exempt or exclude women from certain arduous and hazardous activities in order to protect their health and safety. . . . Among federal laws of this nature are the Selective Service Act, which confines compulsory military service to men. . . . Among the state laws of this kind are laws which limit hours during which women can work, and bar them from engaging in occupations particularly arduous and hazardous such as mining.

If the Equal Rights Amendment should be interpreted by the Supreme Court to forbid any legal distinctions between men and women, all existing and future laws of this nature would be nullified.

SOURCE: *Congressional Record*, 15 February 1972 (Washington, D.C.: GPO, 1972).

ELIZABETH DUNCAN KOONTZ

Elizabeth Duncan Koontz was a distinguished educator, the first black woman to head the National Education Association and the U.S. Women's Bureau. At the time she made this statement at state legislative hearings on the ERA in 1977, she was assistant state superintendent for public instruction in North Carolina.

A short time ago I had the misfortune to break my foot. . . . The pain . . . did not hurt me as much as when I went into the emergency room and the young woman upon asking me my name, the nature of my ailment, then asked me for my husband's social security number and his hospitalization number. I asked her what did that have to do with my emergency. And she said, "We have to be sure of who is going to pay your bill." I said, "Suppose I'm not married, then." And she said, "Then give me your father's name."

I did not go through that twenty years ago when I was denied the use of that emergency room because of my color. I went through that because there is an underlying assumption that all women in our society are protected, dependent, cared for by somebody who's got a social security number and hospitalization insurance. Never once did she assume I might be a woman who might be caring for my husband, instead of him by me, because of some illness. She did not take into account the fact that one out of almost eight women heading families in poverty today [is] in the same condition as men in families and poverty. . . .

My greater concern is that so many women today . . . oppose the passage of the ERA very sincerely and . . . tell you without batting an eye, "I don't want to see women treated that way." And I speak up, "What way is that?" . . . Women themselves have been a bit misguided. We have mistaken present practice for law, and women have . . . assumed too many times that their present condition cannot change. The rate of divorce, the rate of desertion, the rate of separation, and the death rate of male supporters is enough for us to say: "Let us remove all legal barriers to women and girls making their choices—this state cannot afford it."

SOURCE: Lind & Wheeler, *op cit.*, 295–296.

ANALYZING THE EVIDENCE

> J. Marse Grant and Jerry Falwell were both southern Baptists. Both appealed to the Bible in discussing the ERA. Yet they came to opposite conclusions. How do you explain that?

> Senator Ervin characterizes his opposition to the ERA as being based on "rational" grounds. What does he mean by that? Would he agree with Falwell that the ERA was "not merely a political issue, but a moral issue as well"?

> Falwell speaks of women as "the weaker vessel." Why does Elizabeth Duncan Koontz disagree with that characterization? And what does her disagreement suggest to you about the social divisions underlying the debate over the ERA?

An Antibusing Confrontation in Boston

Tensions over court-ordered busing ran high in Boston in 1976. When a black lawyer tried to cross the city hall plaza during an antibusing demonstration, he became a victim of Boston's climate of racial hatred and violence. This Pulitzer Prize–winning photograph by Stanley Forman for the Boston *Herald American* shows a protester trying to impale the man with a flagpole.
Stanley Forman.

Judicial Activism. The decision that initiated the tumult over busing — *Brown v. Board of Education* (1954) — also triggered a larger judicial revolution. Traditionally, it was liberals, not conservatives, who favored *judicial restraint*, which roughly meant that courts defer to legislatures. After many years, the liberal espousal of judicial restraint finally triumphed in 1937, when the Supreme Court reversed itself and let stand key New Deal laws — to the shock and outrage of conservatives.

That history explains why many respected liberal jurists and legal scholars, while favoring racial equality, objected to the *Brown* decision. They felt it violated principles of judicial restraint they had spent lifetimes defending. What ultimately persuaded them was a shift in the big issues coming before the Court. When property rights had been at stake, conservatives favored activist courts willing to curb antibusiness legislatures. Now that personal rights came to the fore, it was liberals' turn to celebrate activist judges and, preeminently, the man whom President Eisenhower appointed chief justice of the Supreme Court in 1953, Earl Warren. A popular Republican governor of California, Warren surprised many, including Eisenhower, by his robust advocacy of civil rights and civil liberties issues. If conservatives found reason to bewail judicial activism, there was no one they blamed more than Chief Justice Warren.

Consider these landmark Warren Court decisions. On the treatment of criminals: that they had a constitutional right to counsel, including at initial interrogations (1963, 1964), and to be informed by arresting officers of their right to remain silent (1966). On indecency: that pornography was protected by freedom of the press unless shown to be "utterly without redeeming social importance" (1964). On prayers and Bible reading in the schools: that religious ritual of any kind violated the constitutional separation of church and state (1962, 1963). In *Griswold v. Connecticut* (1965), the Supreme Court struck down an 1879 state law prohibiting the purchase and use of contraceptive devices by couples as a violation of their constitutional right of privacy.

Griswold opened the way for *Roe v. Wade* (1973), which declared the anti-abortion laws of Texas and Georgia unconstitutional. Abortions performed during the first trimester were protected by the right of privacy (following *Griswold*). At the time, and afterward, some legal authorities questioned whether the Constitution recognized any such privacy right (which the Court extracted from the Third and Eighth Amendments). Moreover, individual states were already legalizing abortion. Nevertheless, the Supreme Court chose to move forward, translating a policy matter traditionally state-regulated into a national, constitutionally protected right. For the women's movement and liberals generally, *Roe v. Wade* was a great, if unanticipated, victory; for evangelical Christians, Catholics, and conservatives generally, it was a bitter pill. Other rights-creating issues — "coddling" criminals, prohibiting school prayer, protecting pornography — had a polarizing effect. But *Roe v. Wade* was in a class by itself. In 1976 opponents convinced Congress to deny Medicaid funds for abortions, an opening round in a protracted campaign against *Roe* that continues to this day.

➤ What were the sources of growth for the women's rights movement?

➤ Why did enforcing civil rights prove more controversial than passing civil rights legislation?

➤ Why did the conservative/liberal alignment on judicial restraint change after 1954?

Lean Years

On top of everything else, the economy went into a tailspin. Oil supplies suddenly fell short, disrupting industry and sending gas prices sky-high. At the same time the United States found itself challenged by foreign competitors making better and cheaper products. All the economic indicators — inflation, employment, productivity, growth — turned negative. In such times, quality-of-life concerns normally get short shrift. Not in the 1970s, when, alongside economic distress, environmental and consumer movements began to flourish.

Energy Crisis

Modern economies run on oil. And if the oil stops, woe follows. Something like that happened to the United States in the 1970s. Once the world's leading producer, the United States by the late 1960s was heavily dependent on imported oil, which mostly came from the Persian Gulf (Figure 29.1). American and European oil companies had discovered and developed the Middle Eastern fields, but control had been wrested away by the emerging Muslim states as they threw off the remnants of European colonialism. Foreign companies still extracted and marketed the oil — only they had the expertise at the time — but under profit-sharing agreements that recognized ownership by the Persian Gulf states. In 1960, they and other oil-rich developing countries formed the Organization of Petroleum

Exporting Countries (OPEC). OPEC was a cartel, and had it been a domestic enterprise, it would have been treated as an unlawful conspiracy in restraint of trade. But nothing prevented independent countries from conspiring in restraint of trade. During the 1960s, with the world awash in oil, the OPEC cartel was in fact ineffective.

That changed in 1973, when Egypt and Syria invaded Israel, initiating the Yom Kippur War. Israel prevailed, but only after being resupplied by an emergency American airlift. Already resentful of Western support for Israel (and encouraged by the Soviets), the Arab states declared an oil embargo against the United States, western Europe, and Japan. The effect was devastating, forcing Americans to spend long hours in line at the pumps and pushing gas prices up by 40 percent. Oil had become a political weapon. And the West's vulnerability stood revealed. In 1979, after a second shortage caused by the Iranian revolution, oil prices peaked at $34 a barrel, $31 dollars more than in 1973.

The United States scrambled to meet its energy needs. A national speed limit of 55 miles an hour was imposed to conserve fuel. Americans began to buy smaller, more fuel-efficient cars, only not from Detroit, which was tooled up to produce "gas guzzlers." Pretty soon VWs, Toyotas, and Datsuns (Nissans at a later date) dotted American highways, while sales of American cars slumped. The effect on the economy was considerable because one of every six jobs in the country was generated directly or indirectly by the auto industry. Even worse was the

FIGURE 29.1 U.S. Energy Consumption, 1900–2000

Coal was the nation's primary source of energy until the 1950s, when it was surpassed by oil and natural gas. The revival of coal consumption after 1960 stemmed from new open-pit mining in the West that provided cheaper fuel for power plants. The decline in oil consumption in 1980 reflects the nation's response to the oil crisis of the 1970s, including, most notably, fuel-efficient automobiles. Nuclear energy became an important new fuel source, but after 1990 its contribution leveled off as a result of the safety concerns triggered by the Three Mile Island incident (see pp. 913–914). SOURCE: *World Almanac 2002.*

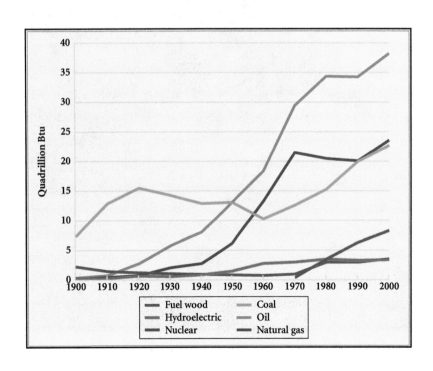

raging inflation set off by the oil shortage. Worst of all perhaps was the psychic shock to Americans at the discovery that their well-being was hostage to forces beyond their control.

Environmentalism

The energy crisis — and the realization it drove home that the earth's resources were not limitless — gave a huge boost to the environmental movement. In some ways, environmentalism was an offshoot of the 1960s counterculture. Activists talked about the "rights of nature," just as they had about the rights of women or blacks. Civil rights and antiwar activism readily translated into protest tactics against polluters and wilderness destroyers. More fundamentally, however, environmentalism was a feature of America's advanced consumer society. Now that they had the basic necessities, and then some, Americans wanted a quality of life defined by a healthy environment and by access to unspoiled nature.

The modern movement began in 1962 when Rachel Carson published *Silent Spring,* a stunning analysis of the impact of pesticides, most especially DDT, on the food chain. There followed a succession of galvanizing issues — concern over an environmentally destructive Alaskan oil pipeline, a proposed airport in the Florida Everglades, and a huge oil spill in January 1969 off the coast of Santa Barbara, California. Environmentalism became certifiably a mass movement on the first Earth Day, April 22, 1970, when 20 million citizens gathered in communities across the country to express their support for the endangered planet.

Earth Day, 1970

No single event better encapsulated the growing environmental awareness of Americans than the nationwide celebration of the first Earth Day on April 22, 1970. In this photograph, young people in Dallas have just hoisted their placard on a heap of garbage swept up from the city streets. TimeLife Pictures/Getty Images.

Nuclear Energy. The mother of environmental wars in the 1970s was the controversy over nuclear power. Electricity from the atom—what could be better? That was how Americans had greeted the arrival of power-generating nuclear technology in the 1950s. By 1974, utility companies were operating forty-two nuclear power plants, with a hundred more planned. Given the oil crisis, nuclear energy might have seemed a godsend. Besides, unlike coal- or oil-driven plants, nuclear operations produced no air pollutants. But environmentalists saw only the dangers. A meltdown would be catastrophic and so, in slow motion, might be the unsolved problem of radioactive wastes. These fears seemed to be confirmed in March 1979 when the reactor core at a nuclear plant at Three Mile Island near Harrisburg, Pennsylvania, came close to meltdown. A prompt shutdown saved the plant, but the near-catastrophe enabled environmentalists to win the battle over nuclear energy (see Reading American Pictures, "A Near Meltdown at Three Mile Island, 1979," p. 914). After Three Mile Island, the utility industry backed down and stopped building nuclear-powered plants.

The Consumer Movement. Environmentalism helped rekindle a consumer movement that had languished since the Progressive era (see Chapter 20). The key figure was Ralph Nader, a young Harvard-educated lawyer whose book, *Unsafe at Any Speed* (1965), attacked General Motors for putting flashy styling ahead of safety in the engineering of the rear-engine Chevrolet Corvair. Buoyed by his success, Nader in 1969 launched a Washington-based consumer protection organization that spawned a national network of activists fighting everything from consumer fraud to dangerous toys. Staffed largely by student volunteers known as "Nader's Raiders," the organization pioneered such legal tactics as the class-action suit, which enabled lawyers to represent an entire pool of grievants in a single litigation. In Nader's wake, dozens of other groups emerged in the 1970s and afterward to combat the tobacco industry, unethical insurance and credit practices, and a host of other consumer problems.

Environmental Legislation. Environmentalists proved remarkably adept at sparking governmental action. In 1969 Congress passed the National Environmental Policy Act, which required the developers to file environmental impact statements assessing the impact of their projects on particular ecosystems. The next year Nixon established the Environmental Protection Agency (EPA) and signed the Clean Air Act, which established standards for auto emissions that caused air pollution. Following the lead of several states, Congress banned the use of DDT in 1972, and in 1980 created the Superfund to finance the cleanup of toxic waste sites. The Endangered Species Act (1973) expanded the scope of the Endangered Animals Act of 1964, granting species such as snail darters and spotted owls protected status. On the consumer front, a big victory was the establishment of the federal Consumer Products Safety Commission in 1972.

These environmental successes were not, however, universally appreciated. Fuel-economy standards for cars was said to hinder the auto industry as it struggled to keep up with foreign competitors. Corporations resented environmental regulations, but so did many of their workers, who believed that tightened standards threatened their jobs. "IF YOU'RE HUNGRY AND OUT OF WORK, EAT AN ENVIRONMENTALIST" read one labor union's bumper sticker. In a time of rising unemployment, activists clashed head-on with proponents of economic growth and global competitiveness.

Economic Woes

While the energy crisis had dealt a hard blow, the economy was also beset by a host of longer-term problems. The high cost of the Vietnam War and the Great Society contributed to a growing federal deficit and spiraling inflation. In the industrial sector, the country faced growing competition from Germany and Japan. America's share of world trade dropped from 32 percent in 1955 to 18 percent in 1970, and was headed down. As a result, in 1971 the value of the dollar fell to its lowest level since World War II, and the United States posted its first trade deficit in almost a century.

In the 1970s, the country's economic performance turned dismal. Gross domestic product (GDP), which had been increasing at a sizzling 4.1 percent per year in the 1960s, dropped after 1970 to 2.9 percent. In a blow to national pride, nine western European countries surpassed the United States in per capita GDP by 1980. The economy was also characterized by stagnating wages, unemployment, and galloping inflation (Figure 29.2). The devastating combination of unemployment and inflation—*stagflation,* so-called—contradicted a basic principle taught by economists: Prices were not supposed to rise in a stagnant economy. In the 1970s, they did. For ordinary Americans, the reality of

A Near Meltdown at Three Mile Island, 1979

Goldsboro, PA. National Archives.

Crisis Management. Jimmy Carter Presidential Library.

Hardly had atomic bombs devastated Japan in 1945 than American leaders began touting the "peaceful" uses of atomic technology, especially the generation of electrical power by nuclear-powered steam turbines. By 1979, nuclear plants were producing 11 percent of the nation's electricity. At that point, dreams of a nuclear-powered America suddenly ended, punctured by a nearly catastrophic accident at the Three Mile Island plant near Harrisburg, Pennsylvania.

On March 28, 1979, the pumps for the Unit 2 reactor shut down, stopping the flow of cooling water and initiating a meltdown of the radioactive core. Had a full meltdown occurred, it would have breached the walls of the containment building and released huge amounts of radiation into the atmosphere. Fortunately, a full meltdown at Three Mile Island was averted. But for several days it was touch-and-go.

ANALYZING THE EVIDENCE

➤ When talk about nuclear energy began, not a lot was said about the fact that the huge plants would have to be placed in somebody's backyard. The first photo shows the neighborhood abutting the Three Mile Island facility. Look carefully at the houses. What sort of people might live there? Would you be happy to live there? What are the social implications of your answer?

➤ The second photograph shows President Carter and his wife Rosalynn inspecting the facility on April 1, 1979, just as the crisis was ending. Carter had been a nuclear engineer. Do you suppose he was there to offer his expertise? If not, what was he doing there?

Nervous Humor. © Batom. North American Syndicate.

➤ The cartoon is a commentary on Carter's visit. What does it portend about the future of nuclear energy in America? What details in the cartoon can you point to that support your answer?

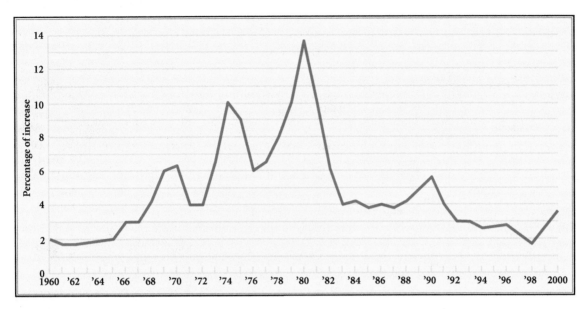

FIGURE 29.2 The Inflation Rate, 1960–2000

The impact of the oil crisis of 1973 on the inflation rate appears all too graphically in Figure 29.2. The dip in 1974 reflects the sharp recession that began that year, after which the inflation rate zoomed up to a staggering 14 percent in 1980. The return to normal levels after 1980 stemmed from very harsh measures by the Federal Reserve Board, which, while they succeeded, came at the cost of a painful slowdown in the economy. SOURCE: *Statistical Abstract of the United States, 2000.*

stagflation was a noticeable decline in the standard of living, as discretionary income per worker dropped 18 percent between 1973 and the early 1980s. Many families were kept afloat only by the second income brought in by working wives.

Deindustrialization. America's economic woes struck hardest in the industrial sector, which suddenly—shockingly—began to be dismantled. Worst hit was the steel industry, which for seventy-five years had been the economy's crown jewel. Its problems were, ironically, partly a product of good fortune. Only the American steel industry had been left unscathed by the devastation of World War II. In the postwar years, that gave U.S. producers an open, hugely profitable field, but it also saddled them with outdated plants and equipment.

When the German and Japanese industries rebuilt—with the aid of American funding and technology—they incorporated the latest and best of everything. Moreover, the American industry's natural advantages were eroding. With its abundant iron-ore reserves exhausted, the industry competed for raw materials on global markets like everyone else. Meanwhile, advances in international shipping deprived it of the comparative advantage of location. Distant from

markets and with no natural resources, Japan built a powerhouse of an industry. When Japanese steel flooded in during the 1970s, the American industry was simply overwhelmed. A massive dismantling began, including the entire Pittsburgh district. By the time the smoke cleared in the mid-1980s, the American industry was competitive again, but it was a shadow of its former self.

The steel industry was the prime example of what became known as *deindustrialization*. The country was in the throes of an economic transformation that left it largely stripped of its industrial base. A swath of the Northeast and Midwest, the country's manufacturing heartland, became the nation's "Rust Belt" (Map 29.2), strewn with abandoned plants and dying communities.

Many thousands of blue-collar workers lost well-paid union jobs. What they faced is revealed by the 4,100 steelworkers left jobless by the shutdown of the Campbell Works of the Youngstown Sheet & Tube Co. in 1977. Two years later, a third had retired early, at half pay. Ten percent had moved, mostly to the Sun Belt. Fifteen percent were still jobless, with unemployment benefits long gone. Forty percent had found local work, but mostly in low-paying, service-sector jobs. Most of these Ohio

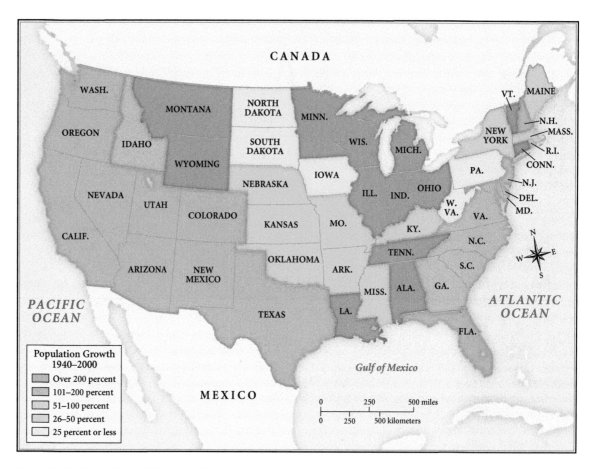

Map 29.2 From Rust Belt to Sun Belt, 1940–2000

One of the most significant developments of the post–World War II era was the growth of the Sun Belt. Sparked by federal spending for military bases, the defense industry, and the space program, states of the South and Southwest experienced an economic boom in the 1950s (see Map 27.1 on page 838). This growth was further enhanced in the 1970s, as the heavily industrialized regions of the Northeast and Midwest declined, and migrants from what was quickly dubbed the "Rust Belt" headed to the South and West in search of jobs.

steelworkers had fallen from their perch in the middle class.

Organized Labor in Decline. Deindustrialization dealt harshly with the labor movement. In the early 1970s, as inflation hit, the number of strikes surged; 2.4 million workers participated in work stoppages in 1970 alone. Challenged by foreign competition, industry became more resistant to union demands, and labor's bargaining power waned. In these hard years, the much-vaunted labor-management accord of the 1950s went bust. Instead of higher wages, unions now mainly fought to save jobs. In the 1970s union membership dropped sharply, with industrial unions — the Rust Belt unions — especially hard hit. By the end of the 1980s, only 16 percent of American workers were organized (See Figure 27.2, p. 836).

The impact on liberal politics was huge. With labor's decline, a main buttress of the New Deal coalition was coming undone.

Taxpayer Revolts. The economic crisis also hardened anti-tax sentiment, reversing a postwar spirit of generous public investment. The premier example was California, which after World War II created, among other achievements, an unrivaled system of higher education. With stagflation, real estate values rocketed upward, and so did property taxes. Especially hard hit were retirees and others on fixed incomes. Into this dire situation stepped Howard Jarvis, an anti-New Dealer cut to the same cloth as the ERA-hating Phyllis Schlafly and, like her, a genius at mobilizing a grassroots movement. Despite opposition by virtually the entire state establishment, Californians in 1978 voted overwhelmingly

Symbol of the Rust Belt

A padlock on the gate of Youngstown, Ohio's United States Steel mill symbolizes the creation of the Rust Belt in the 1970s. Economic hard times caused widespread plant closures in the industrial areas of the Midwest and Northeast and an exodus to the booming Sun Belt (see Map 29.2). © Bettmann/Corbis.

for Proposition 13, which rolled back property taxes, capped future increases, and harnessed all tax measures, state or local, to a two-thirds voting requirement. As a vehicle for hobbling public spending, Prop 13 was extraordinarily effective. Per capita funding of California public schools plunged from the top tier to the bottom (next to Mississippi). Prop. 13 also pulled off the neat trick of hugely benefiting, under the shelter of California's elderly, wealthy homeowners and businesses (commercial property got the same protection). More broadly, Prop. 13 inspired tax revolts across the country and gave conservatives an enduring issue: No New Taxes.

> ➤ Why did the United States enter an energy crisis in the 1970s?

> ➤ What were the major concerns of the environmentalist movement?

> ➤ What were the causes and effects of deindustrialization?

Politics in the Wake of Watergate

Nixon's resignation in 1974 left American politics in limbo. Popular disdain for politicians, already evident in declining voter turnout, deepened. "Don't vote. It only encourages them," read one bumper stick in 1976. Watergate damaged short-term Republican prospects, but also created an opening for the party's right wing. It was telling

that Gerald Ford, in advance of his 1976 reelection bid, dumped his vice president, Nelson Rockefeller, a liberal Republican, for a conservative running mate, Senator Robert Dole of Kansas. As for the Democrats, Watergate granted them a reprieve, a second chance at recapturing their eroding base. But that required leadership, not something the party's freewheeling rules for choosing a candidate could guarantee. Any governor with a nice head of hair, a winning manner, some money in the bank, and a semblance of organization had a shot at the party's nomination.

Jimmy Carter: The Outsider as President

"Jimmy Who?" was how journalists first responded when James E. Carter, governor of Georgia and self-styled peanut farmer, emerged from the pack and went on to win the Democratic nomination. Trading on Watergate, Carter pledged to restore morality to the White House. "I will never lie to you," he promised voters. Carter played up his credentials as a Washington outsider, although he made sure, in selecting Senator Walter F. Mondale of Minnesota, to have a running mate with ties to traditional Democratic voting blocs. Ford, still wounded by his pardon of Nixon and with little to boast about as a caretaker president, was a fairly easy mark. Carter won with 50 percent of the popular vote to Ford's 48 percent.

For a time, Carter got some mileage out of casting himself as an outsider, the common man who walked back to the White House after the Inauguration, delivered fireside chats in a cardigan sweater,

A Framework for Peace

After two weeks of intense personal diplomacy, President Jimmy Carter persuaded President Anwar el-Sadat of Egypt (left) and Prime Minister Menachem Begin of Israel (right) to sign a peace treaty in 1978. The signing of the Camp David Accords marked an important first step in constructing a framework for peace in the Middle East. This was Carter's greatest foreign-policy achievement. David Rubinger/TimeLife Pictures/Getty Images.

and carried his own bags. The fact that he was a born-again Christian also played well. But Carter's inexperience began to tell. His outsider strategy distanced him from established congressional leaders. Shying away from the Democratic establishment, Carter relied heavily on inexperienced advisers and friends from Georgia. And he himself, a prodigious worker, was an inveterate micromanager, exhausting himself over details best left to subordinates.

Economic Policy. On the domestic front, Carter's big challenge was managing the economy. The problems he faced defied easy solution. Most confounding was stagflation. If the government focused on the inflation side — forcing prices down by increasing taxes or raising interest rates — unemployment became worse. If the government tried to stimulate employment, inflation became worse. Seeking to cut through this conundrum, Nixon had imposed price and wage controls in 1971, a brave try, but one that created more problems than it solved.

Carter lacked Nixon's daring. At heart, in fact, he was an economic conservative. He toyed with the idea of an "industrial policy" to bail out the ailing manufacturing sector, but moved instead in a free-market direction by lifting the New Deal–era regulation of the airline, trucking, and railroad industries. **Deregulation** stimulated competition and cut prices, but also drove firms out of business and hurt unionized workers.

Taking office after a sharp mid-1970s downturn, Carter offered a stimulus package that was at cross-purposes with his Federal Reserve Board's program of attacking inflation by raising interest rates. Then turmoil in the Middle East in 1979 curtailed oil supplies, and gas prices jumped again. In a major TV address, Carter lectured Americans about the nation's "crisis of confidence" and "crisis of the spirit." He called energy conservation "the moral equivalent of war" — or, in the media's shorthand, "MEOW," aptly capturing the nation's assessment of Carter's homily. By then, his approval rating had fallen below 30 percent. And no wonder: an inflation rate over 11 percent, failing

Fei Xiaotong

America's Crisis of Faith

Fei Xiaotong, a Chinese anthropologist and sociologist, wrote influential books on the United States during World War II and the 1950s. Despite his criticism of U.S. foreign policy, his often sympathetic treatment of America contributed to twenty years of political ostracism in China. Regaining prominence in the late 1970s, he joined an official delegation to the United States in 1979. When he returned to China, Fei wrote a series of essays entitled "Glimpses of America." In this passage, he responds to President Jimmy Carter's assertion in his famous "malaise" speech of 1979 that Americans faced a spiritual crisis.

I read in the newspaper that the energy crisis in the United States is getting worse and worse. I hear that after spending several days of quiet thought in his mountain retreat, President Carter decided that America's real problem is not the energy crisis but a "crisis of faith." The way it is told is that vast numbers of people have lost their faith in the present government and in the political system, and do not believe that the people in the government working with current government methods can solve the present series of crises. Even more serious, he believes that the masses have come to have doubts about traditional American values, and if this continues, in his opinion, the future of America is terrible to imagine. He made a sad and worried speech. I have not had an opportunity to read the text of his speech, but if he

has truly realized that the present American social system has lost popular support, that should be considered a good thing because at least it shows that the old method of just treating the symptoms will no longer work.

In fact, loss of faith in the present social system on the part of the broad masses of the American people did not begin with the energy crisis. The spectacular advances in science and technology in America in the last decade or two and the unceasing rise in the forces of production are good. But the social system remains unchanged, and the relations of production are basically the same old capitalism. This contradiction between the forces of production and the relations of production has not lessened but become deeper. The ruling class, to be sure, still has the power to keep on finding ways of dealing with the endless series of crises, but the masses of people are coming increasingly to feel that they have fallen unwittingly into a situation where their fate is controlled by others, like a moth in a spiderweb, unable to struggle free. Not only the blacks of Harlem—who are clearly able to earn their own living but still have to rely on welfare to support themselves without dignity—but even well-off families in gardenlike suburban residences worry all day that some accident may suddenly rob them of everything. As the dependence of individuals on others grows heavier and heavier, each person feels in his heart that this society is no longer to be relied on. . . . No wonder people complain that civilization was created by humans, but humans have been enslaved by it. Such a feeling is natural in a society like America's. Carter is right to call this feeling of helplessness a "crisis of faith," for it is a doubting of the present culture.

Only he should realize that the present crisis has been long in the making and is already deep. . . .

These "Glimpses of America" essays may be brought to a close here, but to end with the crisis of faith does violence to my original intention. History is a stream that flows on and cannot be stopped. Words must be cut off, but history goes bubbling on. It is inconceivable that America will come to a standstill at any crisis point. I have full faith in the great American people and hope that they will continue to make even greater contributions to the progress of mankind. . . .

SOURCE: R. David Arkush and Leo O. Lee, trans. and eds., *Land Without Ghosts: Chinese Impressions of America from the Mid-Nineteenth Century to the Present* (Berkeley: University of California Press, 1989).

ANALYZING THE EVIDENCE

➤ Xiaotong is writing about America as someone schooled in Marxist (or Communist) analysis. Can you point to elements in his essay that indicate that perspective?

➤ Xiaotong agrees with Carter that America's problem is not the energy crisis, but a "crisis of faith." Does that mean he agrees with the president about the nature of the crisis?

➤ As a historical document, what value, if any, do you think a historian would find in Xiaotong's essay?

Afghanistan, 1980

Afghani fighters stand in triumph on a destroyed Soviet helicopter. The weapon that brought it down might well have been a shoulder-launched missile from the American-supplied arsenal, courtesy of the CIA. When the defeated Soviets left Afghanistan, the CIA congratulated itself on its smart moves, only to experience what experts call "blow back," as empowered mujahaddin such as those depicted here turned on the United States and made Afghanistan under the Taliban a haven for Al Qaeda. As for those shoulder-launched missiles, they have become a major headache for the West in the battle against Islamic terrorism. © Alain DeJean/Sygma/Corbis.

industries, long lines at the pumps. It seemed the worst of all possible economic worlds (see Voices from Abroad, "Fei Xiaotong: America's Crisis of Faith," p. 919).

Carter and the World

In foreign affairs, President Carter had a firmer sense of what he was about. He was the anti-Nixon, a world leader who rejected Kissinger's "realism" in favor of human rights and peacemaking. Carter established the Office of Human Rights in the State Department and withdrew economic and military aid from repressive regimes in Argentina, Uruguay, and Ethiopia, although he was unable to budge equally repressive U.S. allies like the Philippines, South Korea, and South Africa. In Latin America, Carter punctured an enduring symbol of Yankee imperialism by signing a treaty on September 7,

1977, turning control over the Panama Canal to Panama (effective December 31, 1999). Despite a conservative outcry, the Senate narrowly approved the treaty.

President Carter scored his greatest success by tackling the intractable Arab-Israeli conflict. In 1978 he invited Israel's prime minister Menachem Begin and Egyptian president Anwar el-Sadat to Camp David, the presidential retreat in Maryland. For two weeks, Carter kept the discussions going and finally, after promising additional economic aid, persuaded Sadat and Begin to adopt a "framework for peace," under which Egypt recognized Israel and received back the Sinai Peninsula, which Israel had occupied since 1967.

Though deploring "inordinate fear of Communism," Carter's efforts at improving relations with the Soviet Union foundered. He caused resentment by criticizing the Kremlin's record on

American Hostages in Iran

Images of blindfolded, handcuffed American hostages seized by Iranian militants at the American embassy in Tehran in November 1979 shocked the nation and created a foreign-policy crisis that eventually cost President Carter his chance for reelection. Alain Mingam/Gamma Press Images.

human rights. Negotiations for arms reductions went slowly, and when the SALT II agreement limiting bombers and missiles was finally signed in 1979, Senate hawks objected. Hopes for Senate ratification collapsed when the Soviet Union invaded Afghanistan that December. Treating the invasion as a major crisis, Carter placed an embargo on wheat shipments to the USSR, called for increased defense spending, and declared an American boycott of the 1980 summer Olympics in Moscow (in return the USSR boycotted the 1984 games in Los Angeles). In a fateful decision, Carter began providing covert assistance to anti-Soviet fighters in Afghanistan, some of whom metamorphosed into anti-American Islamic radicals in later years.

Carter's undoing, however, came in Iran. The Shah, Muhammad Reza Pahlavi, was an American client, installed by the CIA in 1953 (see Chapter 26) to prevent the nationalization of Iran's oil industry. Thereafter, the United States counted Iran as a faithful ally, a bulwark in the troubled Middle East, and a steady source of oil. Notwithstanding his fine words, Carter followed the same path as his Cold War predecessors, overlooking the crimes of Iran's CIA-trained secret police, SAVAK, the growing fragility of the Shah's regime, and mounting popular enmity toward the United States. Early in 1979, the Shah was driven into exile, overthrown by

an Iranian revolution that brought the Shiite cleric Ayatollah Ruhollah Khomeini to power.

In October 1979, the United States admitted the deposed Shah, who was suffering from cancer, for medical treatment. In response, Iranian students seized the U.S. embassy in Teheran, taking sixty-six Americans hostage. The captors demanded that the Shah be returned to Iran for trial, but the United States refused. Instead, President Carter suspended arms sales to Iran and froze Iranian assets in American banks.

For the next fourteen months, the hostage crisis paralyzed Jimmy Carter's presidency. Night after night, humiliating pictures of blindfolded hostages appeared on television newscasts. An attempt to mount a military rescue in April 1980 had to be aborted because of equipment failures in the desert. During the withdrawal, one of the helicopters collided with a transport plane, setting off ammunition explosions and causing multiple American casualties. After this fiasco, the torturous negotiations, simplified by the Shah's death, finally succeeded. As a parting shot, the Iranians waited until the day Carter left office to deliver the hostages.

Every war president in the twentieth century—Wilson, FDR, Truman, Johnson—had been a Democrat. So Carter performed a remarkable feat. Single-handedly, he marked the Democrats indelibly as the party of wimps. All the elements were now in place for the triumph of the conservatives. All they needed was a leader.

> ➤ Why did Jimmy Carter have so much trouble managing the economy?

> ➤ What distinguished Carter's conduct of foreign policy from Nixon's? Which foreign policy would you say was more successful? Nixon's or Carter's?

SUMMARY

As we have seen, the 1970s constitute a transitional period, with one foot in the liberal past, the other foot in the conservative future. This was evident in Richard Nixon's presidency, which tried to consolidate a new Republican majority, yet also accepted, and in some ways expanded, an activist state. In foreign policy, similarly, Nixon moved in two directions, capitalizing on Communist divisions to move toward détente, yet adhering to Cold War assumptions in Vietnam. The drift toward Republican supremacy was cut short by the Watergate scandal, which forced Nixon to resign in 1974.

For much of the 1970s, Americans struggled with economic problems, including inflation, energy shortages, stagnation of income, and deindustrialization. Despite diminishing expectations, Americans actively supported movements for environmental and consumer protection. The battle for civil rights entered a second stage, expanding to encompass women's and gay rights and, in the realm of racial justice, focusing more on problems of enforcement. One effect, however, was a new, more conservative social mood that began to challenge liberal values in politics and society more generally.

The presidencies of Gerald Ford and Jimmy Carter did little to restore Americans' faith in their political leaders. Carter failed to resolve the eco-nomic crisis besetting the nation, and his foreign policy, while high-minded, ran into comparable difficulties, topped off by the Iranian hostage crisis of 1979.

Connections: Society

In this chapter, we discussed the "second stage" of the civil rights revolution, which, like the first stage, prompted strong opposition. In the 1960s, however, the resistance was regional, limited to the South, whereas in the 1970s, the resistance became national and, as compared to the defense of racial segregation, touched concerns that many Americans considered legitimate and important. In the case of women's rights, we can trace back to the battle over woman suffrage (see Chapter 19) how strongly felt the belief had historically been about the proper role of women. In the case of enforcement of civil rights, the roots of resistance cannot be located in a single chapter, but are embedded in traditions of individual rights, going back to the Revolutionary era, that made Americans uncomfortable with arguments that favored affirmative action or court-mandated busing. Historically, the obligations of citizenship had not entailed parting with rights or privileges to advance the rights or privileges of others. As we will see in Chapter 30, the potency of these conservative views fueled a political revolution in the age of Ronald Reagan.

CHAPTER REVIEW QUESTIONS

> ➤ What impact did the Nixon administration have on American politics?

> ➤ Why are the 1970s considered an era of "declining expectations" for Americans?

> ➤ What were the major causes of the apparent weakening of the United States as a superpower during this period?

TIMELINE

1966	National Organization for Women (NOW) founded
1968	Richard Nixon elected president
1969	Stonewall riot leads to gay liberation movement
	Mobilization Day climaxes Vietnam war protests
1970	Earth Day first observed
	Environmental Protection Agency established
	Nixon orders invasion of Cambodia; renewed antiwar protests
	Killings at Kent State and Jackson State
1971	Pentagon Papers published
1972	Watergate break-in; Nixon reelected
	Nixon visits People's Republic of China
	SALT I Treaty with Soviet Union
1973	*Roe v. Wade* legalizes abortion
	Endangered Species Act
	Paris Peace Accords
	War Powers Act
	Arab oil embargo; gas shortages
1974	Nixon resigns over Watergate; Ford becomes president and pardons Nixon
	Busing controversy in Boston
1975	Fall of Saigon
1976	Jimmy Carter elected president
1978	Carter brokers Camp David accords between Egypt and Israel
	Proposition 13 reduces California taxes
	Bakke v. University of California limits affirmative action
1979	Three Mile Island nuclear accident
	Soviet Union invades Afghanistan
	Hostages seized at American embassy in Tehran, Iran
1980	"Superfund" created to clean up toxic land sites

FOR FURTHER EXPLORATION

Peter N. Carroll, *It Seemed Like Nothing Happened* (1982), provides a general overview of the period. Gary Wills, *Nixon Agonistes*, rev. ed. (1990), judges Nixon to be a product of his times. For Watergate, a starting point is the books by the *Washington Post* journalists who broke the scandal, Carl Bernstein and Bob Woodward: *All the President's Men* (1974) and *The Final Days* (1976). Stanley Kutler, *The Wars of Watergate* (1990), is the definitive history. Gary Sick, a Jimmy Carter White House advisor on Iran, offers an insider's account of the hostage crisis in *All Fall Down: America's Tragic Encounter with Iran* (1986). For documents on the Carter presidency and his "malaise" speech, see Daniel Horowitz, *Jimmy Carter and the Energy Crisis of the 1970s* (2005). Thomas Byrne Edsall with Mary D. Edsall, *Chain Reaction: The Impact of Race, Rights, and Taxes on American Politics* (1991), examines some of the divisive social issues of the 1970s. J. Anthony Lukas, *Common Ground* (1985), tells the story of the Boston busing crisis through the biographies of three families. Barbara Ehrenreich examines the backlash against feminism in *Hearts of Men* (1984).

For the Watergate scandal, see the National Archives and Record Administration's Watergate Trial Tapes and Transcripts at **nixon.archives.gov/index.php**, which provides transcripts of the infamous tapes as well as other useful links to archival holdings concerning Richard Nixon's presidency. Watergate, at **watergate.info**, is a textual, visual, and auditory survey of the scandal. Created by Australian political science professor Malcolm Farnsworth, the site's materials include a Nixon biography with speech excerpts, a Watergate chronology, an analysis of the significance of the "Deep Throat" informant, and an assessment of the Watergate legacy. Relevant links provide access to primary documents. The Oyez Project at Northwestern University, at **www.oyez.org/oyez/frontpage**, is an invaluable resource for over one thousand Supreme Court cases, with audio transcripts, voting records, and summaries. For this period, see, for example, its materials on *Roe v. Wade, Bakke v. University of California*, and *Griswold v. Connecticut*. Documents from the Women's Liberation Movement, culled from the Duke University Special Collections Library, emphasize the women's movement of the late 1960s and early 1970s. This searchable site, at **scriptorium.lib.duke.edu/wlm**, includes books, pamphlets, and other written materials on categories that include theoretical writings, reproductive health, women of color, and women's work and roles.

TEST YOUR KNOWLEDGE

To assess your command of the material in this chapter, see the Online Study Guide at **bedfordstmartins.com/henretta**.

For Web sites, images, and documents related to topics and places in this chapter, visit **bedfordstmartins.com/makehistory**.

PART SEVEN

Entering a New Era: Conservatism, Globalization, Terrorism

1980–2006

	DIPLOMACY	GOVERNMENT	ECONOMY	SOCIETY	TECHNOLOGY AND SCIENCE
	Beyond the Cold War	**Conservative Ascendancy**	**Uneven Affluence and Globalization**	**Demographic Change and Culture Wars**	**Media and the Information Revolution**
1980	▸ Reagan begins arms buildup ▸ Intermediate Nuclear Forces Treaty (1988) ▸ Berlin Wall falls (1989)	▸ New Right and evangelical Christians help to elect Ronald Reagan president ▸ Reagan cuts taxes and federal regulatory system	▸ Reaganomics; budget and trade deficits soar ▸ Labor union membership declines	▸ Rise of "Yuppies" ▸ Rise in Latino and Asian immigration ▸ Crime and drug crises in the cities ▸ AIDS epidemic	▸ Cable News Network (CNN) founded (1980) ▸ Television industry deregulation ▸ Compact discs and cell phones invented
1990	▸ Persian Gulf War (1990) ▸ USSR collapses; end of the Cold War ▸ U.S. peacekeeping forces in Bosnia	▸ Republican "Contract with America" (1994) ▸ Bill Clinton advances moderate Democratic policies; wins welfare reform ▸ Clinton impeached and acquitted (1998–1999)	▸ New technology prompts productivity rise ▸ Global competition cuts U.S. manufacturing; jobs outsourced overseas	▸ Los Angeles race riots (1992) ▸ "Culture Wars" over affirmative action, feminism, abortion, and gay rights	▸ Dramatic growth of the Internet and World Wide Web ▸ America Online rises and declines ▸ Biotech revolution
2000–	▸ Radical Muslim attacks on Twin Towers and the Pentagon (2001) ▸ U.S. and allies oust Taliban in Afghanistan ▸ United States invades Iraq (2003) ▸ North Korea tests a nuclear weapon (2006); stalemate with Iran over its nuclear program	▸ George W. Bush narrowly elected president (2000) ▸ Bush pushes Faith-Based Initiatives and No Child Left Behind ▸ USA PATRIOT Act passed (2002) ▸ *Hamdan v. Rumsfeld* (2006) overturns administration's policies on the treatment of detainees	▸ Bush tax cuts ▸ Huge trade deficits with China and Asia ▸ Rising budget deficits ▸ Illegal immigration boosts low-wage work ▸ Stock market and hedge fund boom ▸ Fall in value of dollar	▸ Many states ban gay marriages ▸ "Minutemen" patrol Mexican border; immigration changes proposed ▸ Baby boomers begin to retire; new federal drug benefits for elderly	▸ Broadband access grows ▸ "Blogging" increases ▸ "Creation Science" controversy ▸ Bush limits on stem-cell research challenged ▸ Global warming increases

In a 1972 interview, President Richard M. Nixon remarked, "History is never worth reading until it's fifty years old. It takes fifty years before you're able to come back and evaluate a man or a period of time." Nixon's comments remind us that writing recent history poses a particular challenge; not knowing the future course of events, we can't say for certain which present-day trends will prove to be the most important. Part Seven is therefore a work-in-progress; its perspective will change as events unfold. At this point, it focuses on five broad themes: the ascendancy in American politics of the New Right, the impact of economic globalization, social conflicts stemming from cultural diversity, the revolution in information technology, and the end of the Cold War and the rise of Muslim terrorism.

DIPLOMACY In a surprising development in the late 1980s, the Soviet Union and its satellite Communist regimes in Eastern European suddenly collapsed. The Soviet demise produced, in the words of President George H. W. Bush, a "new world order" and left the United States as the only military superpower. Accepting that role, the United States worked to counter civil wars, terrorist activities, and military aggression in many parts of the world and especially in the Middle East. In 1991, it fought the Persian Gulf War in response to Iraq's invasion of Kuwait and, in the late 1990s, led military action and peacekeeping efforts in Serbia and Bosnia. In 2001, in response to terrorist attacks on New York and Washington by the radical Islamic group Al Qaeda, President George W. Bush attacked Al Qaeda's bases in Afghanistan. He then ordered an invasion of Iraq in 2003 that quickly toppled the regime of dictator Saddam Hussein but triggered civil chaos and a violent insurgency that is still ongoing.

GOVERNMENT With Ronald Reagan's election in 1980, "New Right" conservatism began its ascendancy. The conservative agenda was to roll back the social welfare state created by liberal Democrats during the New Deal and the Great Society. Presidents Reagan, George H. W. Bush, and George W. Bush cut taxes, limited the regulatory activities of federal agencies, transferred some powers and resources to state governments, and appointed conservative-minded judges to the federal courts. The most important change in the federal welfare system, however, came during the Clinton administration in 1996, with new legislation designed to shift families from dependency on welfare payments to employment in the labor market. Evangelical Christians and conservative lawmakers brought abortion, gay rights, and other cultural issues into the political arena, setting off controversies that revealed sharp divisions among the American people.

ECONOMY The American economy grew substantially during the quarter century beginning in 1980, thanks to the increased productivity of workers and the controversial tax and spending policies of the federal government. Tax cuts spurred investment and government spending for military purposes boosted production; these policies also created huge budget deficits, a dramatic increase in the national debt, and a widening gap between rich and poor Americans. Equally significant, the end of Cold War allowed the spread of capitalist enterprise around the globe. As multinational corporations set up manufacturing facilities in China and other low-wage countries, they undercut industrial production and wage rates in the United States and helped to create a massive American trade deficit. Because of the trade and budget deficits, American prosperity rested on an increasingly shaky foundation.

SOCIETY The increasing heterogeneity of American society — in demographic composition and in cultural values — was yet another characteristic of life in the first decade of the twenty-first century. Increased immigration from Latin America and Asia added to cultural tensions and produced a new nativist movement. Continuing battles over affirmative action, abortion, sexual standards, homosexuality, feminism, and religion in public life took on an increasingly passionate character, inhibiting the quest for politically negotiated solutions.

TECHNOLOGY AND SCIENCE One effect of faith-based politics was a significant challenge to scientific evidence and research, most especially against the claims of evolution and the advent of stem-cell research. Even the dramatic changes in technology, which boosted economic productivity and provided easy access to information and entertainment, posed new challenges. Would cable technology, with its multitude of choices, further erode a common American culture? Would the World Wide Web facilitate the outsourcing of American middle-class jobs? Would computer technology allow corporations — and government agencies — to track the lives and limit the freedom of American citizens? Like any revolution, the innovations in computer technology had an increasingly significant impact on many spheres of American life.

A "new world order," a New Right ascendancy, a new global economy, massive new immigration, and a technological revolution: We live in a time of rapid political and social changes and continuing diplomatic and technological challenges that will test the resiliency of American society and the creativity of American leaders.

30 The Reagan Revolution and the End of the Cold War

1980–2001

O N NOVEMBER 9, 1989, MILLIONS of television viewers worldwide watched jubilant Germans knock down the Berlin Wall. The wall, which had divided the city since 1961, was a vivid symbol of Communist repression and the Cold War division of Europe. More than four hundred East Germans had lost their lives trying to escape to freedom on the other side. Now East and West Berliners, young and old, danced on the remains of the forbidding wall. Two years later, in 1991, the Soviet Union itself dissolved, ending the Cold War. A new world order was in the making.

The end of the Cold War was the result, in part, of a dramatic change in American political life. The election of President Ronald Reagan began a conservative political ascendancy that continues to the present. Supported by the Republican Party's New Right, Reagan declared political war against both the Soviet Union and the liberal ideology that had informed American public policy since the New Deal of Franklin D. Roosevelt (1933–1945). However, the Republicans' domestic agenda was complicated by a split between religious conservatives, who demanded strong government action to implement their faith-based agenda, and economic conservatives, who favored limited government and free markets. Moreover, the Democratic Party remained a potent — and flexible — political force. Acknowledging the rightward shift in the country's mood,

The Rise of Conservatism
Reagan and the Emergence of the New Right
The Election of 1980

The Reagan Presidency, 1981–1989
Reaganomics
Reagan's Second Term

Defeating Communism and Creating a New World Order
The End of the Cold War
The Presidency of George H. W. Bush
Reagan, Bush, and the Middle East, 1980–1991

The Clinton Presidency, 1993–2001
Clinton's Early Record
The Republican Resurgence
Clinton's Impeachment
Foreign Policy at the End of the Twentieth Century

Summary
Connections: Government and Politics

◄ **The Wall Comes Down**
As the Communist government of East Germany collapsed, West Berliners showed their contempt for the wall dividing the city by defacing it with graffiti. Then, in November 1989, East and West Berliners destroyed huge sections of the wall with sledgehammers, an act of psychic liberation that symbolized the end of the Cold War. Alexandria Avakian / Woodfin Camp & Associates.

Democrat Bill Clinton trod a centrist path that led him to the White House in 1992 and again in 1996. "The era of big government is over," Clinton declared. At home as well as abroad, a new order emerged during the last decades of the century.

The Rise of Conservatism

The Great Depression of the 1930s and World War II had discredited the traditional conservative program of limited government at home and an isolationist-oriented foreign policy. Although the conservatives' crusade against communism revived their political fortunes during the height of the Cold War in the 1950s, they failed to articulate an ideology and a set of policies that would command the support of a majority of American voters. Then, in the late 1970s, conservative Republicans took advantage of serious blunders by liberal Democrats and built a formidable political coalition.

Reagan and the Emergence of the New Right

The personal odyssey of Ronald Reagan embodies the story of "New Right" Republican conservatism. Before World War II, Reagan was a well-known movie actor — and a New Deal Democrat and admirer of Franklin Roosevelt. He turned away from the New Deal partly out of self-interest (he disliked paying high taxes) and partly out of principle. As head of the Screen Actors Guild from 1947 to 1952, he had to deal with communist union organizers — the left wing of the liberal New Deal. Dismayed by their hard-line tactics and goals, he became a militant anti-communist and a conservative. Giving up his fading movie career, Reagan became a well-known spokesperson for the General Electric Corporation. By the early 1960s, he had become a Republican and threw himself into California politics, speaking for conservative causes and candidates.

Ronald Reagan came to national prominence in 1964. Speaking to the Republican convention on national television, he delivered a powerful speech supporting the presidential nomination of archconservative Barry Goldwater (see Chapter 28). Just as the "Cross of Gold" speech elevated William Jennings Bryan to fame in 1896, so Reagan's address — titled "A Time for Choosing" and delivered again and again throughout the mid-1960s — secured his political future. With the financial backing of wealthy southern California business interests, he won the governorship of California in

1968 and again in 1972. His impassioned rhetoric supporting limited government, low taxation, and law and order won broad support among citizens of the most populous state and made him a force in national politics. Narrowly defeated in his bid for the Republican presidential nomination in 1976, Reagan counted on his growing popularity to make him the party's candidate in 1980.

Liberal Decline and Conservative Resurgence. In 1964, the conservative message preached by Ronald Reagan and Barry Goldwater appealed to few American voters. Then came the series of events that mobilized opposition to the Democratic Party and its liberal agenda: a stagnating economy, the failed war in Vietnam, African American riots, a judiciary that legalized abortion and enforced school busing, and an expanded federal regulatory state. By the mid-1970s, conservatism commanded greater popular support. In the South, long a Democratic stronghold, whites hostile to federal support of civil rights for African Americans voted Republican in increasing numbers. Simultaneously, middle-class suburbanites and migrants to the Sun Belt states endorsed the conservative agenda of combating crime, limiting social welfare spending, and increasing expenditures on military defense.

Strong "New Right" grassroots organizations spread the message. In 1964, 3.9 million volunteers had campaigned for Barry Goldwater, twice as many as worked for Lyndon B. Johnson; in the late 1970s, they swung their support to Ronald Reagan. Skilled conservative political operatives such as Richard Viguerie, a Louisiana-born Catholic and antiabortion activist, applied new computer technology to political campaigning. They used computerized mailing lists to solicit campaign funds, drum up support for conservative causes and candidates, and get out the vote on election day.

Other organizational support for the New Right came from think tanks funded by wealthy conservatives. The Heritage Foundation, American Enterprise Institute, and the Cato Institute issued policy proposals and persistently attacked both liberal social policy and the permissive culture they claimed it spawned. These organizations blended the traditional conservative themes of unrestrained individualism and a free-market economy with the hot-button "social issues" of affirmative action, the welfare state, and changing gender and sexual values. They also fostered the growth of a cadre of conservative intellectuals. For decades, William F. Buckley, the founder and editor of the *National*

Review, and Milton Friedman, the Nobel Prize–winning laissez-faire economist at the University of Chicago, were virtually the only prominent conservative intellectuals. Now they were joined on the public stage by the so-called neoconservatives—well-known intellectuals such as Jeane Kirkpatrick, Nathan Glazer, and Norman Podhoretz, editor of *Commentary* magazine. Many neoconservatives had once advocated radical and liberal causes; vehemently recanting their former views, they provided intellectual respectability to the Republican Right. As liberal New York Senator Daniel Moynihan remarked, suddenly "the GOP has become a party of ideas."

The Religious Right. The most striking new entry into the conservative coalition was the Religious Right. Drawing its membership from conservative Catholics and Protestant evangelicals, the Religious Right condemned growing public acceptance of divorce, abortion, premarital sex, and feminism. Charismatic television evangelists, such as Pat Robertson, the son of a U.S. senator, and Jerry Falwell, the founder of the Moral Majority, emerged as the champions of a faith-based political agenda. As these cultural and moral conservatives attacked Democratic liberals for supporting lenient punishments for criminals, permissive sexuality, and welfare payments to unmarried mothers with multiple children, economic conservatives called for cuts in taxes and government regulations. Ronald Reagan endorsed the programs of both groups and, with their support, captured the Republican nomination for president in 1980 (see Comparing American Voices, "Christianity and Public Life," pp. 930–931). To win the votes of more moderate Republicans, Reagan chose former CIA director George H. W. Bush as his running mate.

The Election of 1980

In the election of 1980, President Jimmy Carter's sinking popularity virtually doomed his campaign. When the Democrats renominated him over his liberal challenger, Edward (Ted) Kennedy of Massachusetts, Carter's approval rating was stunningly low—a mere 21 percent of Americans believed he was an effective president. The reasons were readily apparent. Economically, millions of citizens were feeling the pinch from stagnant wages, high inflation, crippling mortgage rates, and an unemployment rate of nearly 8 percent (see Chapter 29). Diplomatically, the nation blamed Carter for failing to respond strongly to Soviet expansion and to the Iranian hostage crisis.

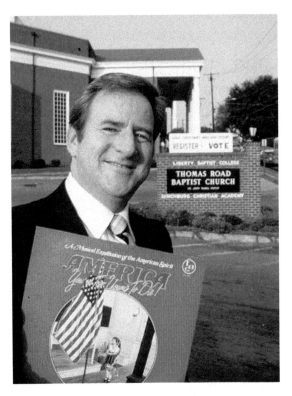

Jerry Falwell

The resurgence of evangelical religion in the 1970s was accompanied by a conservative movement in politics known as the New Right or the Christian Right. Founded in 1979 by televangelist Jerry Falwell, the Moral Majority was one of the earliest New Right groups, committed to promoting "family values" and (as the title to the record album suggests) patriotism in American society and politics. Wally McNamee/Corbis.

The incumbent president found himself constantly on the defensive, while Reagan remained upbeat and decisive. "This is the greatest country in the world," Reagan reassured the nation in his warm baritone voice, "we have the talent, we have the drive.... All we need is the leadership." To emphasize his intention to be a formidable international leader, Reagan hinted that he would take strong action to win the hostages' return. To signal a rejection of the Democrats' liberalism, the California governor declared his opposition to affirmative action and forced busing, and promised to get "the government off our backs." Most important, Reagan effectively appealed to the many Americans who felt financially insecure. In a televised debate between the candidates, Reagan emphasized the economic plight of working- and middle-class Americans in an era of "stagflation"—stagnant wages amidst rapidly rising prices. He posed the rhetorical question, "Are you better off today than you were four years ago?"

Christianity and Public Life

Modern social welfare liberalism embodies an ethic of moral pluralism and favors the separation of church and state. Conservative Christians challenge the legitimacy of pluralism and secularism and seek, through political agitation and legal action, to make religion an integral part of public life.

PRESIDENT RONALD REAGAN
"The Rule of Law under God"

Reagan's candidacy was strongly supported by Christian conservatives. He delivered these remarks to the National Association of American Evangelicals in 1983.

I want you to know that this administration is motivated by a political philosophy that sees the greatness of America in you, her people, and in your families, churches, neighborhoods, communities — the institutions that foster and nourish values like concern for others and respect for the rule of law under God.

Now, I don't have to tell you that this puts us in opposition to, or at least out of step with, a prevailing attitude of many who have turned to a modern-day secularism, discarding the tried and time-tested values upon which our very civilization is based. No matter how well intentioned, their value system is radically different from that of most Americans. And while they proclaim that they're freeing us from superstitions of the past, they've taken upon themselves the job of superintending us by government rule and regulation. Sometimes their voices are louder than ours, but they are not yet a majority. . . .

Freedom prospers when religion is vibrant and the rule of law under God is acknowledged. When our Founding Fathers passed the First Amendment, they sought to protect churches from government interference. They never intended to construct a wall of hostility between government and the concept of religious belief itself.

Last year, I sent the Congress a constitutional amendment to restore prayer to public schools. Already this session, there's growing bipartisan support for the amendment, and I am calling on the Congress to act speedily to pass it and to let our children pray. . . .

SOURCE: Ronald Reagan, *Speaking My Mind: Selected Speeches* (New York: Simon & Schuster, 1989), 169–180.

DONALD E. WILDMON
Network Television as a Moral Danger

Wildmon is a Christian minister and a grassroots religious activist. This selection comes from The Home Invaders *(1985).*

One night during the Christmas holidays of 1976, I decided to watch television with my family. . . . Not far into the program was a scene of adultery. I reacted to the situation in the manner as I had been taught. I asked one of the children to change channels. Getting involved in the second program, we were shocked with some crude profanity. . . .

As I sat in my den that night, I became angry. I had been disturbed by the deterioration of morals I had witnessed in the media and society during the previous twenty-five years. This was accompanied by a dramatic rise in crime, a proliferation of pornography, increasingly explicit sexual lyrics in music, increasing numbers of broken homes, a rise in drug and alcohol use among the youth, and various other negative factors. I had managed to avoid those unpleasant changes to a large degree by staying away, turning my head, justifying my actions with the reasons most commonly expressed: freedom of speech, pluralism, tolerance. . . .

Realizing that these changes were being brought into the sanctity of my home, I decided I could and would no longer remain silent. . . . Out of that decision came the National Federation for Decency (and out of the NFD came the Coalition for Better Television). . . . But the more I dealt with the problems, the more I realized that I was dealing only with symptoms not the disease. . . .

This great struggle is one of values, particularly which ones will be the standard for our society and a base for our system of justice in the years to come. For 200 years our country has based its morals, its sense of right and wrong, on the Christian view of man. The Ten Commandments and the Sermon on the Mount have been our solid foundation . . . the most perfect system ever devised in the history of mankind.

Television is the most pervasive and persuasive medium we have. At times it is larger than life. It is our only true national medium. Network television is the greatest educator we have. . . . It is teaching that adultery is an acceptable and approved lifestyle. . . . It is teaching that hardly anyone goes to church, that very few people in our society are Christian or live by Christian principles. How? By simply censoring Christian characters, Christian values, and Christian culture from the programs.

If within the next five years we fail to turn the tide of this humanist value system which seeks to replace our Christian heritage, then we have . . . lost the battle.

SOURCE: Donald E. Wildmon, *The Home Invaders* (Elgin, IL: Victor Books, 1985), 3–7.

A. BARTLETT GIAMATTI
The Moral Majority as a Threat to Liberty

A. Bartlett Giamatti was the president of Yale University (1978–1986) and subsequently president of the National (Baseball) League. He offered these remarks to the entering class of Yale undergraduates in 1981.

A self-proclaimed "Moral Majority," and its satellite or client groups, cunning in the use of a native blend of old intimidation and new technology, threaten the values [of pluralism and freedom]. . . .

From the maw of this "morality" come those who presume to know what justice for all is; come those who presume to know which books are fit to read, which television programs are fit to watch. . . . From the maw of this "morality" rise the tax-exempt Savonarolas who believe they, and they alone, possess the "truth." There is no debate, no discussion, no dissent. They know. . . . What nonsense. What dangerous, malicious nonsense. . . .

We should be concerned that so much of our political and religious leadership acts intimidated for the moment and will not say with clarity that this most recent denial of the legitimacy of differentness is a radical assault on the very pluralism of peoples, political beliefs, values, forms of merit and systems of religion our country was founded to welcome and foster.

Liberty protects the person from unwarranted government intrusions into a dwelling or other private places. In our tradition the State is not omnipresent in the home. And there are other spheres of our lives and existence, outside the home, where the State should not be a dominant presence. Freedom extends beyond spatial bounds. Liberty presumes an autonomy of self that includes freedom of thought, belief, expression, and certain intimate conduct.

SOURCE: Yale University Archives.

ANTHONY KENNEDY
The Constitution Protects Privacy

Kennedy, a Roman Catholic, was named to the Supreme Court by Ronald Reagan in 1988. In Lawrence v. Texas *(2003), he wrote the opinion for five of the six justices in the majority; Sandra Day O'Connor wrote a concurring opinion.*

The question before the Court is the validity of a Texas statute making it a crime for two persons of the same sex to engage in certain intimate sexual conduct.

In Houston, Texas, officers of the Harris County Police Department were dispatched to a private residence in response to a reported weapons disturbance. They entered an apartment where one of the petitioners, John Geddes Lawrence, resided. . . . The officers observed Lawrence and another man, Tyron Garner, engaging in a sexual act. The two petitioners were arrested, held in custody over night, and charged and convicted before a Justice of the Peace.

The complaints described their crime as "deviate sexual intercourse, namely anal sex, with a member of the same sex (man)." . . .

We conclude the case should be resolved by determining whether the petitioners were free as adults to engage in the private conduct in the exercise of their liberty under the Due Process Clause of the Fourteenth Amendment to the Constitution.

[The Texas statute in question seeks] to control a personal relationship that, whether or not entitled to formal recognition in the law, is within the liberty of persons to choose without being punished as criminals. . . . The liberty protected by the Constitution allows homosexual persons the right to make this choice. . . .

The present case does not involve minors. It does not involve persons who might be injured or coerced or who are situated in relationships where consent might not easily be refused. It does not involve public conduct or prostitution. It does not involve whether the government must give formal recognition to any relationship that homosexual persons seek to enter. The case does involve two adults who, with full and mutual consent from each other, engaged in sexual practices common to a homosexual lifestyle. The petitioners are entitled to respect for their private lives. The State cannot demean their existence or control their destiny by making their private sexual conduct a crime. Their right to liberty under the Due Process Clause gives them the full right to engage in their conduct without intervention of the government. "It is a promise of the Constitution that there is a realm of personal liberty which the government may not enter."

SOURCE: *Lawrence v. Texas*, 539 U.S. 558, 562–563, 567, 571, 579 (2003).

ANALYZING THE EVIDENCE

➤ What would Ronald Reagan think of the opinion written by Justice Kennedy, his appointee? Would Reagan agree with it, given his condemnation of those who are intent on "subordinating us to government rule and regulation"?

➤ According to Wildmon and Giamatti, what should be shown on television, and who should make those decisions?

➤ When should the government police private conduct? Consider the criteria outlined in the final paragraph of Justice Kennedy's opinion.

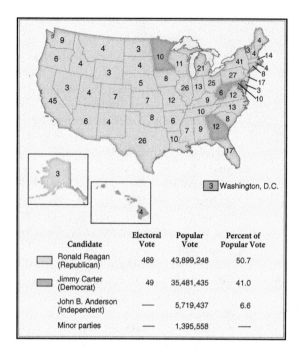

Candidate	Electoral Vote	Popular Vote	Percent of Popular Vote
Ronald Reagan (Republican)	489	43,899,248	50.7
Jimmy Carter (Democrat)	49	35,481,435	41.0
John B. Anderson (Independent)	—	5,719,437	6.6
Minor parties	—	1,395,558	—

MAP 30.1 Presidential Election of 1980

Ronald Reagan easily defeated Democratic incumbent Jimmy Carter, taking 51 percent of the popular vote to Carter's 41 percent and winning the electoral vote in all but six states and the District of Columbia. Reagan cut deeply into the traditional Democratic coalition by wooing many southern whites, urban ethnics, and blue-collar workers. More than five million Americans expressed their discontent with Carter's ineffectiveness and Reagan's conservatism by voting for Independent candidate John Anderson, a longtime Republican member of the House of Representatives.

In November, the voters gave a clear answer. They repudiated Carter, giving him only 41 percent of the vote. Independent candidate John Anderson garnered 7 percent, and Reagan won easily, with 51 percent of the popular vote nationwide and higher percentages in the South (Map 30.1). Equally important, the Republicans elected thirty-three new members of the House of Representatives and twelve new senators, which gave them control of the U.S. Senate for the first time since 1954.

Superior financial resources contributed to the Republican success: Two-thirds of all corporate donations to political action committees went to conservative Republican candidates. While the Demo-cratic Party saw its key constituency—organized labor—dwindle in size and influence, the GOP used its ample funds to reach voters through a sophisticated campaign of television and direct-mail advertisements. "Madison Avenue" advertising techniques—long used to sell commercial products—had begun to shape political campaigns in the 1960s. Now they became the primary means of trumpeting the virtues of a political candidate and attacking the credentials of his or her opponent.

Political Realignment. This aggressive campaigning continued the realignment of the American electorate that had begun during the 1970s. The core of the Republican Party remained the relatively affluent, white, Protestant voters who supported balanced budgets, opposed government activism, feared crime and communism, and believed in a strong national defense. But "Reagan Democrats" had now joined the Republican cause; prominent among these formerly Democratic voters were southern whites, who opposed civil rights legislation, and Catholic blue-collar workers, who were alarmed by antiwar protestors, feminist demands, and welfare expenditures. Reagan Republicanism also struck a responsive note among young voters, who increasingly identified themselves as "moderates" or "conservatives," and among the socially mobile residents of rapidly growing suburban communities in Texas, Arizona, and California.

The Religious Right was another significant contributor to the Republican victory. The Moral Majority claimed that it registered two million new voters for the 1980 election, and the Republican Party's platform reflected its influence. The platform called for a constitutional ban on abortion, voluntary prayer in public schools, and a mandatory death penalty for certain crimes. The Republicans also demanded an end to court-mandated busing and, for the first time in forty years, opposed the Equal Rights Amendment. Within the Republican Party, conservatism had triumphed.

Reagan's victory led some observers to predict a long-lasting alteration in American voting patterns. As *U.S. News & World Report* proclaimed, "A Massive Shift . . . Right." Other commentators offered more cautious assessments. They noted that Reagan won a bare majority of the votes cast and that turnout was unusually low because many working-class voters—disillusioned Democrats—stayed home. Rather than an endorsement of conservatism, one analyst called the election a "landslide vote of no confidence in an incompetent administration." Whatever the verdict, Ronald Reagan's victory raised the possibility of a dramatic shift in government policies and priorities. As he entered office, the new president claimed the American public had given him a mandate for sweeping change. His success—or failure—would determine the significance of the election and the New Right.

➤ What were the key groups of the new Republican coalition? Were their goals complementary? Contradictory?

➤ What factors led to Ronald Reagan's election in 1980?

The Reagan Presidency, 1981–1989

Ronald Reagan's personality was as important as his policies. Frayed by the cultural turmoil of the 1960s and the economic malaise of the 1970s, the majority of voters embraced the former movie actor's optimistic message of national pride and purpose. Even when major scandals threatened his administration, Reagan maintained his popularity, leading critics to dub him "the Teflon president" since nothing damaging seemed to stick. More sympathetic observers called him "the Great Communicator"; they praised his ability to address the anxieties of Americans and to win support for the Republicans' conservative economic and cultural agenda.

Reaganomics

First elected at age sixty-nine, Ronald Reagan was the oldest man ever to serve as president. His appearance and demeanor belied his age. Concerned since his acting days with his physical fitness, the president conveyed a sense of vigor and purpose (see Reading American Pictures, "Image Warfare: Fighting to Define the Reagan Presidency," p. 934). His folksy humor endeared him to millions, who overlooked his frequent misstatements and indifference to details of public policy. He kept his political message clear and simple. "Government is not the solution to our problem," Reagan declared. "Government is the problem."

In his first year of office, Reagan and his chief advisor, James A. Baker III, moved quickly to set new government priorities. To roll back the expanded liberal state, they launched a coordinated three-pronged assault on federal taxes, social welfare spending, and the regulatory bureaucracy. To win the Cold War, they advocated a vast increase in defense spending. And, to match the resurgent economies of Germany and Japan, whom the United States had defeated in World War II and then helped to rebuild, they set out to restore American leadership of the world's capitalist societies.

"Supply-Side" Theory. To achieve this goal, the new administration advanced a new set of economic and tax policies. Quickly dubbed "Reaganomics," these policies sought to boost the economy by increasing the supply of goods. The theory underlying "supply-side economics," as this approach was called, emphasized the need to increase investment in productive enterprises. According to George Gilder, a major supply-side theorist, the best way to bolster investment was to reduce the taxes paid by business corporations and wealthy Americans, who could then use these funds to expand production. Supply-siders maintained that the resulting economic expansion would increase government revenues and offset the loss of tax dollars stemming from the original tax cuts.

Taking advantage of Republican control of the Senate and his personal popularity following a failed assassination attempt, Reagan won congressional approval of the Economic Recovery Tax Act (ERTA). The act reduced income tax rates paid by most Americans by 23 percent over three years. For the wealthiest Americans — those with millions to invest — the highest marginal tax rate dropped from 70 to 50 percent. The act also slashed estate taxes, the levies on inheritances instituted around 1900 to prevent the transmission of huge fortunes from one generation to the next. Finally, the new legislation trimmed the taxes paid by business corporations by $150 billion over a period of five years. As a result of ERTA, by 1986 the annual revenue of the federal government had been cut by $200 billion.

Shifts in Spending. David Stockman, Reagan's budget director, hoped to match this sizable reduction in tax revenue with a comparable cutback in federal expenditures. To meet this ambitious goal, he proposed substantial cuts in Social Security and Medicare. But Congress — and the president — rejected such efforts because they were not willing to antagonize middle-class and elderly voters who viewed these government entitlements as sacrosanct. As neoconservative columnist George Will noted ironically, "Americans are conservative. What they want to conserve is the New Deal." This contradiction between Republican ideology and practical politics would frustrate the GOP into the twenty-first century.

In a futile attempt to balance the budget, Stockman advocated spending cuts on programs for food stamps, unemployment compensation, and welfare assistance such as Aid to Families with Dependent Children (AFDC). In the administration's view, these programs represented the worst features of Lyndon Johnson's Great Society — a huge

Image Warfare: Fighting to Define the Reagan Presidency

As might be expected, U.S. presidents and their staffs attempt to project a positive image of the chief executive and the administration's policies. But contradictions often arise between the image and values cultivated by a president and the actual policies pursued by the White House. The presidency of Ronald Reagan is a case in point. As the text points out, Reagan helped to stimulate a conservative movement in American politics and society during the 1980s. Images of Reagan quickly became vital for the White House to deliver its message of conservative reform to the American people. As the cartoon published by the *Arkansas Gazette* illustrates, powerful imagery could also be wielded by Reagan's political opponents.

ANALYZING THE EVIDENCE

➤ Examine the photo of Reagan at his ranch in California. This image was taken by a White House photographer. What message does the image convey about Reagan as a person? How does this message reinforce the policies created by Reagan that you read about in the text?

➤ What message does the cartoon convey about Reagan policies? How does this differ from the official White House message expressed in the photo of Reagan?

➤ Together, what do these two images tell us about the image and reality of the Reagan presidency? Do you think that cartoons or photographs are a more accurate source of information for understanding the historical meaning of a particular president and his administration? Why or why not?

President Reagan at His Ranch in Southern California. Ronald Reagan Presidential Library.

Presidential Landscaping. Courtesy *Arkansas Gazette*, 1984.

FIGURE 30.1 The Annual Federal Budget Deficit (or Surplus), 1940–2005

During World War II, the federal government incurred an enormous budget deficit. But between 1946 and 1965, it ran either an annual budget surplus or incurred a relatively small debt. As measured in 2005 dollars, the accumulated national debt increased by about $50 billion during that twenty-year period or about $2.5 billion a year. The annual deficits rose significantly during the Vietnam War and the stagflation of the 1970s, but they really exploded between 1982 and 1994, in the budgets devised by the Ronald Reagan and George H. W. Bush administrations, and again between 2002 and 2005, in those prepared by George W. Bush. The Republican presidents increased military spending while cutting taxes, an "enjoy-it-now" philosophy that transferred the cost to future generations of Americans.

SOURCE: National Priorities Project. See also *U.S. Budget for Fiscal Year 2007*, Historical Tables, Table 15.6.

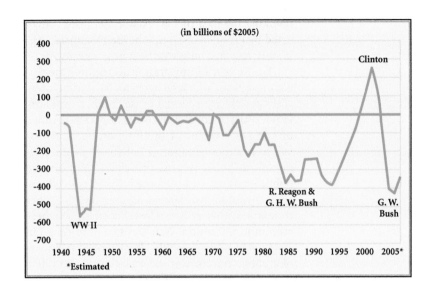

handout to economic drones at the expense of hardworking taxpayers. Congress approved some cutbacks but preserved most of these welfare programs because of their importance; in 1980, some 21 million people relied on the food stamp program. It likewise continued to lavish huge subsidies and tariff protection on wealthy farmers and business corporations — "welfare for the rich," as some critics put it. As the administration's spending cuts fell far short of its goal, the federal budget deficit increased dramatically.

Military spending accounted for the bulk of the growing federal deficit, and President Reagan was its strongest supporter. "Defense is not a budget item," he declared, "you spend what you need." To "make America number one again," Reagan and Defense Secretary Caspar Weinberger pushed through Congress a five-year, $1.2 trillion military spending program that accelerated an arms buildup begun in 1978 by President Carter after the emergence of a pro-Soviet government in Afghanistan. The administration revived the B-1 bomber, which Carter had canceled because of its great expense and limited usefulness, and continued development of the MX, a new missile system approved by Carter. Reagan's most ambitious and controversial weapons plan, proposed in 1983, was the Strategic Defense Initiative (SDI). Popularly known as "Star Wars" because of its science-fiction-like features, SDI would consist of a system of laser-equipped satellites that would detect and destroy incoming ballistic missiles carrying atomic weapons. Would it work? Most scientists were dubious; Secretary of State George Shultz thought

it was "lunacy," and even Weinberger, who liked every weapons system he saw, dismissed the idea. Nonetheless, Congress approved initial funding for the controversial — and enormously expensive — project. During Reagan's presidency military spending accounted for nearly one-fourth of all federal expenditures.

The combination of lower taxes and higher defense spending led to a skyrocketing national debt (Figure 30.1). By the time Reagan left office, the federal deficit had tripled — rising from $930 billion in 1981 to $2.8 trillion in 1989. Every American citizen — from small baby to senior citizen — now owed a hidden debt of $11,000.

Regulatory Cutbacks. Advocates of Reaganomics also asserted that excessive regulation by federal government agencies impeded economic growth. Some of these bureaucracies, such as the U.S. Department of Labor, had risen to prominence during the New Deal; others, such as the Environmental Protection Agency (EPA) and the Occupational Safety and Health Administration (OSHA), were created by Democratic Congresses during the Great Society and the Nixon administration (see Chapters 24, 28, and 29). Although these agencies provided many services to business corporations, they also increased their costs — by assisting labor unions to organize, ordering safety improvements in factories, and requiring expensive equipment to limit the release of toxic chemicals into the environment. To reduce the reach of federal regulatory agencies, the Reagan administration cut their budgets — by an average of 12 percent. And, invoking the idea of the "New Federalism" advocated by President Nixon, it began to transfer regulatory responsibilities to the state governments.

The Reagan administration also limited the regulatory efforts of federal agencies by staffing them with leaders who were hostile to their mission. James Watt, an outspoken conservative who headed up the Department of the Interior, explicitly attacked environmentalists as "a left-wing cult." Acting on his free-enterprise principles, Watt opened public lands for use by private businesses — oil and coal corporations, large-scale ranchers, timber companies. Already under heavy criticism for these economic give-aways, Watt was forced to resign in 1983 when he dismissively characterized members of a public commission as "a black, a woman, two Jews, and a cripple." Anne Gorsuch Buford, whom Reagan appointed to head the EPA, likewise resigned when she was implicated in a money scandal and was cited for contempt of Congress for refusing to provide documents regarding the Superfund program, which cleans up toxic waste sites.

The Sierra Club and other environmental groups roused enough public outrage about these appointees and their policies that the administration changed its position. During President Reagan's second term, he significantly increased the EPA's budget, created new wildlife preserves, and added acreage to the National Wilderness Preservation System and animals and plants to the endangered species lists.

Reaganomics Stalled. Ultimately, politics in a democracy is "the art of the possible," and savvy politicians know when to advance and when to retreat. Having attained two of his prime goals — a major tax cut and a dramatic increase in defense spending — Reagan did not carry through on his promises to scale back big government and the welfare state. When Reagan left office in 1989, federal spending stood at 22.1 percent of the gross domestic product (GDP) and federal taxes at 19 percent of GDP, both virtually the same as in 1981. In the meantime, the federal deficit had tripled in size, and the number of civilian government workers had increased from 2.9 to 3.1 million. This outcome — so different from the president's lofty rhetoric — elicited harsh criticism from conservative commentators. As one of them angrily charged, there was no "Reagan Revolution."

That verdict was too narrow. Despite its failed promises, the presidency of Ronald Reagan set the nation on a new political and ideological path. Social welfare liberalism, ascendant since 1933, was now thoroughly on the defensive. Moreover, the Reagan presidency restored popular belief that America — and individual Americans — could enjoy increasing prosperity.

Reagan's Second Term

As Ronald Reagan campaigned in 1984 for a second term in the White House, he claimed credit for a resurgent economy. On coming into office in 1981, he had supported the "tight" money policy implemented by the Federal Reserve Board headed by Paul Volker. By raising interest rates to the extraordinarily high level of 18 percent, Volker had quickly cut the high inflation rates of the Carter years. But this deflationary policy caused an economic recession that put some ten million Americans out of work. President Reagan's approval rating plummeted, and in the elections of 1982, Democrats picked up twenty-six seats in the House of Representatives and seven state governorships.

The economy — and the president's popularity — quickly revived. During the 1984 election campaign, Reagan hailed his tax cuts as the reason for the economic resurgence. His campaign theme, "It's Morning in America," suggested that a new day of prosperity and pride had dawned. The Democrats nominated former vice president Walter Mondale of Minnesota. With strong ties to labor unions, ethnic groups, and party leaders, Mondale epitomized the New Deal coalition that had dominated the Democratic Party since Franklin Roosevelt. To appeal to women voters, Mondale selected Representative Geraldine Ferraro of New York as his running mate — the first woman to run on the presidential ticket of a major political party. Neither Ferraro's presence nor Mondale's credentials made a difference. The incumbent president carried the entire nation except for Minnesota and the District of Columbia and won a landslide victory. Still, Democrats retained their majority in House and, in 1986, regained control of the Senate.

The Iran-Contra Affair. A major scandal marred Reagan's second term. Early in 1986 news leaked out that the administration had negotiated an "arms-for-hostages" deal with the revolutionary Islamic government of Iran. For years the president had denounced Iran as an "outlaw state" and a supporter of terrorism. Now he wanted its help. To win Iran's assistance in freeing some American hostages held by Hezbollah, a pro-Iranian Shiite terrorist group in Lebanon, the administration covertly sold arms to the "outlaw state." While this secret Iranian arms deal was diplomatically suspect and politically controversial, the use of resulting profits in

Nicaragua was patently illegal. In 1981, the Reagan administration had suspended aid to the Sandinista government of Nicaragua. It charged that the Sandinistas, a left-wing movement that had overthrown dictator Anastasio Somoza Debayle, were pursuing socialist policies detrimental to American interests, forming a military alliance with Fidel Castro in Cuba, and supporting a leftist rebellion in neighboring El Salvador (Map 30.2). To overthrow the Sandinista government, President Reagan ordered the Central Intelligence Agency (CIA) to aid an armed Nicaraguan opposition group called the Contras. Although Reagan praised the Contras as "freedom fighters," Congress worried that the pres-

ident and other executive branch agencies were assuming war-making powers that the Constitution reserved to the legislature. In 1984 it strengthened the Boland Amendment, thereby banning the CIA and other government officials from providing any military support to the Contras.

Oliver North, a lieutenant colonel in the U.S. Marines and an aide to the National Security Council, consciously defied that ban. With the tacit or explicit consent of high-ranking administration officials, including the president, he used the profits from the Iranian arms deal to assist the Contras. When asked if he knew of North's illegal actions, Reagan replied, "I don't remember." Still swayed by

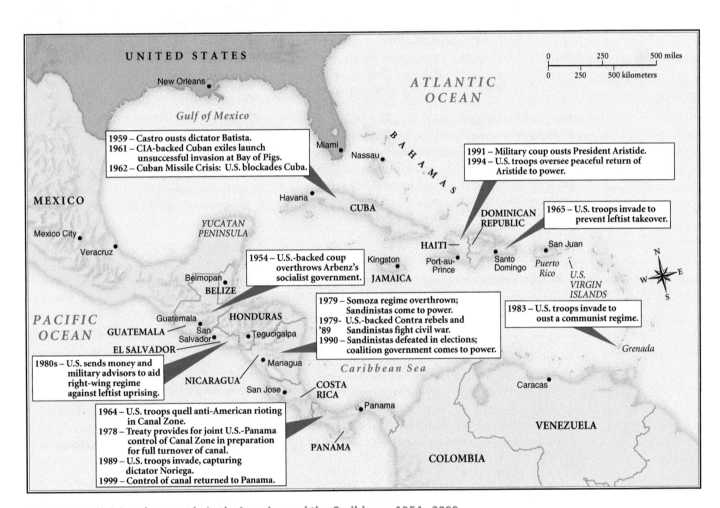

MAP 30.2   U.S. Involvement in Latin America and the Caribbean, 1954–2000

Ever since the Monroe Doctrine (1823), the United States has claimed a special interest in Latin America. During the Cold War, U.S. foreign policy throughout Latin America focused on containing instability and the appeal of communism in a region plagued by poverty and military dictatorships. Providing foreign aid was one approach to addressing social and economic needs, but the United States frequently intervened with military forces (or by supporting military coups) to remove unfriendly or socialist governments. The Reagan administration's support of the Contra rebels in Nicaragua, some of which was contrary to U.S. law, was one of those interventions.

Reagan's charm, the public accepted this convenient loss of memory. Nonetheless, the Iran-Contra affair resulted in the prosecution of Colonel North and several other officials and jeopardized the president's historical reputation. It was not only that administration officials (as Lawrence Walsh, the special prosecutor appointed to investigate the scandal, concluded) carried out "two programs contrary to congressional policy and contrary to national policy [and] . . . broke the law," but also that President Reagan—of all people—had bribed terrorists. Most Americans were shocked by Reagan's dealings with Iran and its terrorist allies.

The Reagan Legacy. Deeply stung by the Iran-Contra scandal, Reagan proposed no bold domestic policy initiatives in his last two years in office. He had entered office promising to limit the federal government and to give free-market forces freer rein. His success was only partial. Although he reordered the priorities of the federal government, he failed to reduce its size or scope. Social Security and other entitlement programs remained untouched, and the enormous military buildup outweighed cuts in other programs. Concerned to unite the country, Reagan did not actively advocate the agenda of the Religious Right. The president called for tax credits for private religious schools, restrictions on abortions, and a constitutional amendment to permit prayer in public schools, but refused to expend his political capital to secure these measures.

Perhaps Reagan's most significant institutional legacy was his judicial appointments. During his two terms, he appointed 368 federal court judges, many of them with conservative credentials, and three Supreme Court justices, Sandra Day O'Connor, Antonin Scalia, and Anthony Kennedy. O'Connor became the first woman to serve on the Supreme Court and wrote an important decision supporting a woman's right to an abortion. Both she and Kennedy won a reputation as judicial moderates, leaving Scalia as Reagan's only genuinely conservative appointee. But Reagan also elevated Justice William Rehnquist, a conservative Nixon appointee, to the position of chief justice. Under Rehnquist's conservative leadership (1986–2005), an often-divided court watered down, but did not usually overturn, the liberal rulings of the Warren Court (1954–1967) with respect to individual liberties, abortion rights, affirmative action, and the rights of criminal defendants.

Reagan failed to roll back the social welfare and regulatory state of the New Deal–Great Society era, but he did change the dynamic of American politics.

Another Barrier Falls

In 1981, Sandra Day O'Connor, shown here with Chief Justice Warren Burger, was appointed to the Supreme Court by President Ronald Reagan, the first woman to serve on that body. In 1993, she was joined by Ruth Bader Ginsburg, an appointee of President Bill Clinton. O'Connor emerged as a leader of the "moderate" bloc on the Court during the 1990s; she retired in 2006. Fred Ward/ Black Star/Stockphoto.com.

His antigovernment rhetoric won many adherents, as did his bold and fiscally dangerous tax cuts. As one historian has summed up Reagan's domestic legacy, "For the next twenty years at least, American policies would focus on retrenchment and cost-savings, budget cuts and tax cuts, deregulation and policy redefinitions."

> ➤ What were the key elements of Reagan's domestic policy?

> ➤ What limits did Reagan face in promoting conservative goals? What successes did he achieve?

Defeating Communism and Creating a New World Order

Ronald Reagan entered office determined to confront the Soviet Union diplomatically and militarily. Backed by Republican hard-liners, Reagan unleashed some of the harshest Cold War rhetoric since

Reagan and Gorbachev: Fellow Political Revolutionaries

Both Ronald Reagan and Mikhail Gorbachev changed the political outlook of their nations. As Reagan undermined social welfare liberalism in the United States, Gorbachev challenged the rigidity of the Communist Party and state socialism in the Soviet Union. Although they remained ideological adversaries, by the mid-1980s the two leaders had established a personal rapport, which helped to facilitate agreement on a series of arms reduction measures. © Bettmann/Corbis.

the 1950s, labeling the Soviet Union an "evil empire" and vowing to make certain it ended up "on the ash heap of history." By his second term Reagan had decided that this goal was best achieved by actively cooperating with Mikhail Gorbachev, its young and reform-minded leader. The collapse of the Soviet Union in 1991 ended the nearly fifty-year-long Cold War, but a new set of foreign challenges quickly appeared: the creation of a viable new world order (see Voices from Abroad, "Zhu Shida: China and the United States: A Unique Relationship," p. 940).

The End of the Cold War

The collapse of the Soviet Union and the end of the Cold War were the most dramatic developments in foreign affairs during the 1980s and early 1990s. The fall of the Soviet regime was the result of external pressure from the United States and the internal weaknesses of the Communist economy and soci-

ety. To defeat the Soviets, the administration pursued a two-pronged strategy. First, it abandoned the policy of "détente" and set about to rearm America. This buildup in American military strength, reasoned Secretary of Defense Caspar Weinberger, a determined hard-liner, would force the Soviets into an arms race that would strain their economy and undermine support for the Communist regime. Second, the president supported the policy of CIA Director William Casey to fund guerrillas who were trying to overthrow pro-Communist governments in Angola, Mozambique, Afghanistan, and Central America—and thereby roll back Soviet influence in the Third World.

The Weaknesses of the Soviet Union. These strategies succeeded because they exploited the internal weaknesses and policy mistakes of the Communist regime. Its system of state socialism and central economic planning had transformed Russia

Zhu Shida

China and the United States: A Unique Relationship

To understand the dynamics of American society and American foreign policy, the government-funded Chinese Academy of Social Sciences created an Institute of American Studies. Zhu Shida is a research associate at the Institute; in 2002, he published this piece on a semiofficial Chinese government Web site.

The relationship between China, one of the oldest civilizations with the biggest population, and the United States, one of the youngest civilizations with the strongest economy, is significant not only for the two peoples but also for the future of the whole world.

The factors influencing the Sino-US relationship include economic, strategic, diplomatic and cultural elements. Undoubtedly, among them the economic factor is the most important one. Economic interests are at the heart of China-US relations. In 2001, trade volume between the two nations hit US $8.4 billion, 8.1 percent higher than the previous year. Tempted by the colossal Chinese market, the US has become China's biggest investor with an investment of US $4.8 billion in 2001 and an accumulated investment of US $35.5 billion....

Strategically, China and the US have common interests. The White House needs China's assistance and influence to handle North Korea and non-proliferation issues. America also needs China's cooperation in fighting terrorism. On the Taiwan question that remains the most sensitive issue, China asks the United States to abide by the three joint communiqués and pursue the one-China policy....

To handle the Sino-US relationship appropriately, both sides should realize the necessity to further understanding and respect for each other's cultures, which, unfortunately, often has been neglected.

The origins of American culture lie in a combination of Puritanism, liberalism, individualism and republicanism. Reflected in politics, American culture takes the form of hegemonism with a strong religious flavor and labeled by its self-defined freedom, democracy and human rights standard.... Beginning with the original immigrating Puritans, Americans have regarded themselves as the chosen people, superior to any other peoples in the world. Meanwhile, in free and open America, there is no room for the strict consensus system characteristic of traditional societies. Therefore, without a unified attitude and consistent account in all fields of its political culture, discordant voices can be heard from time to time in American society, which is unimaginable and almost impossible in China.

The essence of Chinese culture is family affection and attachment. Any individual behavior damaging national dignity and group honor is not encouraged in Chinese society that thinks highly of collective benefits and reputation, which is beyond the understanding of American people.

In addition to the cultural differences between the two nations, we also need to realize the inherent discrepancies in American culture that influence American politics and foreign policies frequently. On the one hand, in terms of Puritanism, one of the origins of the American culture, since the earliest Puritans came to the New World due to the religious persecutions they suffered in England, the freedom and right for individuals to pursue welfare have occupied a special position in Puritanism. Naturally, Puritans harbor religious fer-

vor for human rights. On the other, the protracted existence of racial discrimination and segregation did not change until after the Civil Rights movement during the 1950s and 1960s. Even today, the deep-rooted barrier between whites and minorities is still hard to be removed completely in the United States. The cultural contradictions are the source of America's double standards on the human rights issue.

The aggressive American culture with a short history of a little more than 200 years is built on the basis of individualism and liberalism, while the introversive Chinese culture with a 5000 years' tradition lays stress on collectivism and cultural consensus at the expense of individual voices. Obviously, the essences of these two cultures are contradictory. This cultural contradiction is the main reason for the constant Sino-US clashes. Nevertheless, mutual complementarities in economy magnetize the two nations, forcing them to compromise for their cultural discrepancies.

SOURCE: China Internet Information Center, www.china.org.cn/english/2002/Mar/29138.htm.

ANALYZING THE EVIDENCE

➤ Ronald Reagan frequently evoked Puritan John Winthrop's image of America as a shining "city on a hill" and a beacon for mankind. How does Zhu Shida interpret the impact of Puritan ways of thinking on American foreign policy? Based on your reading in this textbook, how accurate is his understanding of American culture?

➤ Given the institutional status of the writer and the essay's place of publication, how should we interpret it?

➤ According to the author, what factors pull China and the United States together? Which ones push them apart?

Pope John Paul II in Poland, 1979

Polish-born Karol Joseph Wojtyla (1920–2005) was named a cardinal of the Roman Catholic Church in 1967 and was selected as pope in 1978. The following year he visited Poland, where he reiterated his opposition to Communist rule. His visit sparked the formation of the Solidarity workers' movement and, as its founder Lech Walesa put it, "started this chain of events that led to the end of communism." © Bettmann/Corbis.

from an agricultural to an industrial society. But it had done so very inefficiently; lacking the discipline and opportunities of a market economy, most enterprises hoarded raw materials, employed too many workers, and did not develop new products. Except in military weaponry and space technology, the Russian economy fell farther and farther behind those of capitalist societies in the post–World War II years, and most people in the Soviet bloc endured a low standard of living. Moreover, the Soviet invasion of Afghanistan, like the American war in Vietnam, turned out to be major blunder — an unwinnable war that cost vast amounts of money, destroyed military morale, and undermined popular support of the Communist government.

Mikhail Gorbachev, a younger Russian leader who became general secretary of the Communist Party in 1985, recognized the need for internal economic reform, technological progress, and an end to the Afghanistan war. His policies of *glasnost* (openness) and *perestroika* (economic restructuring) spurred widespread criticism of the rigid institutions and authoritarian controls of the Communist regime. To lessen tensions with the United States, Gorbachev met with Reagan in 1985, and the two leaders established a warm personal rapport. By 1987, they agreed to eliminate all intermediate-range nuclear missiles based in Europe. A year later, Gorbachev ordered Soviet troops out of Afghanistan, and Reagan replaced many of his hard-line advisors with policymakers who favored a renewal of détente.

The Collapse of Communism in Europe. As Gorbachev's reforms revealed the flaws of the Soviet system, the peoples of eastern and central Europe demanded the ouster of their Communist governments. In Poland, the Roman Catholic Church and its pope — Polish-born John Paul II — joined with Solidarity, the trade union movement led by Lech Walesa, to push for the overthrow of the pro-Soviet regime. In 1956, 1964, and 1968, Russian troops had quashed popular uprisings in Hungary, East Germany, and Czechoslovakia. Now they did not intervene, and a series of peaceful uprisings — "Velvet Revolutions" — created a new political order throughout the region. The destruction of the Berlin Wall in November 1989 symbolized the end of the Communist rule in central Europe. Two years later, the Soviet Union collapsed. Alarmed by Gorbachev's reforms, Soviet military leaders seized the premier in August 1991. But widespread popular opposition led by Boris Yeltsin, the president of the Russian Republic, thwarted their efforts to oust him from office. Their failure broke the dominance of the Communist Party. On December 25, 1991, the Union of Soviet Socialist Republics formally dissolved to make way for an eleven-member Commonwealth of Independent States (CIS). The Russian Republic assumed leadership of the CIS, but the USSR was no more (Map 30.3).

In 1956 Nikita Khrushchev had told the United States, "We will bury you," but now the tombstone read, "The Soviet Union, 1917–1991." For more than forty years the United States fought a bitter economic and ideological battle against its Communist foe, a struggle that had an enormous impact on American society. By linking the campaign for African American rights to the diplomatic competition with the Soviet Union in the Third World, liberal politicians advanced the cause of racial equality in the United States; conversely, by labeling social welfare legislation as "communistic," conservative politicians limited its extent, as did the staggering cost of Cold War. American taxpayers spent some *$4 trillion* on nuclear weapons and trillions more on conventional arms. The physical and psychological costs were equally high: radiation from atomic weapons tests, anti-Communist witchhunts, and — most pervasive of all — a constant fear of nuclear annihilation. "Nobody — no country, no party, no person — 'won' the cold war," concluded George Kennan, the architect in 1947 of the American policy of "containment," because both sides paid such a heavy price to wage the war and both benefited greatly from its end. Of course, many

MAP 30.3   The Collapse of the Soviet Union and the Creation of Independent States, 1989–1991

The collapse of Soviet Communism dramatically altered the political landscape of central Europe and central Asia. The Warsaw Pact, the USSR's answer to NATO, vanished. West and East Germany reunited, and the nations created by the Versailles Treaty of 1919 — Estonia, Latvia, Lithuania, Poland, Czechoslovakia, Hungary, and Yugoslavia — reasserted their independence or split into smaller ethnically defined nations. The Soviet republics bordering Russia, from Belarus in the west to Kyrgyzstan in the east, also became independent states, while remaining loosely bound with Russia in the Commonwealth of Independent States (CIS).

Americans had no qualms about proclaiming victory, and advocates of free-market capitalism, particularly conservative Republicans, celebrated the outcome. The collapse of Communism in Eastern Europe and the disintegration of the USSR itself, they argued, demonstrated that they had been right all along. Thus, Ronald Reagan's role in facilitating the end of the Cold War, for reasons both international and domestic, was his most important achievement.

The Presidency of George H. W. Bush

George H. W. Bush, Reagan's vice president and successor, was a man of intelligence, courage, and ambition. Born to wealth and high status, he served with great distinction as a naval aviator during World War II and then graduated Phi Beta Kappa from Yale University. Bush prospered as a Texas oil developer and Member of Congress, and then served, under Richard Nixon, as ambassador to the United Nations and head of the CIA. Although Bush lacked Reagan's extraordinary charisma and commanding presence, he had many other strengths that his predecessor lacked.

George Bush won the Republican nomination in 1988 and chose as the vice presidential candidate a young conservative Indiana senator, Dan Quayle. In the Democratic primaries, Governor Michael Dukakis of Massachusetts easily outpolled the charismatic civil rights leader Jesse Jackson, whose populist Rainbow Coalition brought together minority and liberal groups within the party. Dukakis chose Senator Lloyd Bentsen of Texas as his running mate.

The election campaign had a harsh tone as brief television "attack ads" took precedence over a thoughtful discussion of policy issues. The Republican's mantra was "Read My Lips: No New Taxes," a sound bite drawn from a Bush speech. The Bush campaign charged that Dukakis was "a card-carrying member" of the American Civil Liberties Union and was "soft on crime." Bush supporters repeatedly ran TV ads focused on Willie Horton, a convicted African American murderer who had raped a woman while on furlough from a prison in Dukakis's state of Massachusetts. Placed on the defensive by these attacks, Dukakis failed to unify the liberal and moderate factions within Democratic Party and to mount an effective campaign. Bush carried thirty-eight states, winning the popular vote by 53.4 percent to 45.6 percent, but Democrats retained control of the House of Representatives and the Senate.

Democratic Legislative Initiatives. Faced with a Democratic Congress and personally interested in foreign affairs, George H. W. Bush proposed few distinctive domestic initiatives. Rather, congressional Democrats took the lead. They enacted legislation allowing workers to take leave for family and medical emergencies, a measure that Bush vetoed. Then, over the president's opposition, they secured legislation enlarging the rights of workers who claimed discrimination because of their race or gender. With the president's support, congressional liberals also won approval of the Americans with Disabilities Act, a major piece of legislation that significantly enhanced the legal rights of physically disabled people in employment, public transportation, and housing.

Activist Republican Judges. As Democratic politicians seized the initiative in Congress, conservative Republican judges made their presence known in the courts. In *Webster v. Reproductive Health Services* (1989), the Supreme Court upheld the authority of state governments to limit the use of public funds and facilities for abortions. The following year, the justices approved a regulation that prevented federally funded health clinics from discussing abortion with their clients. Then, in the important case of *Planned Parenthood of Southeastern Pennsylvania v. Casey* (1992), the court upheld a Pennsylvania law requiring a twenty-four-hour waiting period prior to an abortion. Surveying these and other decisions, a reporter suggested that 1989 was "The Year the Court Turned Right," with a conservative majority ready and willing to limit or invalidate liberal legislation and legal precedents.

This observation was only partly correct. While the Court was no longer a bastion of liberal jurisprudence, it was not yet firmly conservative in character. Although the *Casey* decision, written by Reagan appointee Sandra Day O'Connor, upheld certain restrictions on abortions, it affirmed the "essential holding" in *Roe v. Wade* that women had a constitutional right to control their bodies. Justice David Souter, appointed to the Court by Bush in 1990, voted with O'Connor to uphold *Roe* and, like her, emerged as an ideologically "moderate" justice on a range of issues.

Bush's other appointment to the Court was Clarence Thomas, an African American conservative with little judicial experience or legal expertise. Thomas's nomination proved controversial; he was opposed by leading black organizations, such as the NAACP and the Urban League, and accused of sexual harassment by Anita Hill, a black law professor. Hill told the all-male Senate Judiciary Committee that Thomas had sexually harassed her when they were colleagues at a federal agency. Despite these charges, Republicans in the Senate won Thomas's

Anita Hill Challenges a Supreme Court Nominee

University of Oklahoma law professor Anita Hill accused Clarence Thomas, an African American nominated to the Supreme Court by President George H. W. Bush, of sexual harassment. Hill's charges sparked controversy during Thomas's confirmation hearings, but the Senate, voting largely on party lines, narrowly approved his appointment by a vote of 52 to 48. Subsequently, women's rights activists embarked on a campaign to elect more women to Congress. Brad Markel/Getty Images.

confirmation by a narrow margin. Once on the bench, Thomas took his cues from his conservative colleagues, Chief Justice William Rehnquist and Justice Antonin Scalia.

"Read My Lips." The controversy over Clarence Thomas hurt Bush at the polls. Politically minded women accused Republicans of ignoring sexual harassment — an issue of concern to many men and women — and vowed to mobilize voters. In the election of 1992, the number of women, mostly Democrats, elected to the Senate increased from three to seven, and in the House it increased from thirty to forty-eight.

Bush's main political problems stemmed from the huge budget deficit bequeathed to his administration by Ronald Reagan. In 1985 Congress had enacted the Gramm-Rudman Act, which mandated automatic cuts in government programs in 1991 if the budget remained wildly out of balance. That moment had now come. Unless Congress and the

president acted, there would be a shutdown of all nonessential government departments and the lay-off of thousands of employees. To resolve the crisis, Congress enacted legislation that cut spending and significantly increased taxes. Abandoning his pledge of "No New Taxes," Bush signed the legislation, earning the enmity of conservative Republicans and diminishing his chances for reelection in 1992.

Bush also struggled with an economic recession that began in 1990 and stretched into the middle of 1991. As unemployment mounted, the president could do little because the funding for many federal programs — including housing, public works, and social services — had been shifted to state and local governments during the Reagan administration. The states faced problems of their own because the economic slowdown sharply eroded their tax revenues. Indeed, to balance their budgets, as required by their constitutions, they laid off workers and cut social spending. The combination of the tax increase, which alienated Republican conservatives, and a tepid federal response to the recession, which turned independent voters against the administration, became crucial factors in denying George H. W. Bush reelection in 1992.

Reagan, Bush, and the Middle East, 1980–1991

The end of the Cold War left the United States as the only military superpower and raised the prospect of a "new world order" dominated by the United States and its European and Asian allies. But there were problems. American diplomats now confronted an array of regional, religious, and ethnic conflicts that defied easy solutions. Those in the Middle East — the oil-rich lands stretching between Afghanistan and Morocco — remained the most pressing and the most threatening to American interests.

Israel and the Palestinians. Like previous presidents, Ronald Reagan had little success in resolving the conflicts between the Jewish state of Israel and its Muslim Arab neighbors. In 1982 the Reagan administration initially supported Israel's invasion of Lebanon to attack forces of the Palestine Liberation Organization (PLO), which had taken over part of that country. As the violence escalated in 1984, the administration urged an Israeli withdrawal and dispatched an American military force as "peacekeepers," a decision it quickly regretted. Lebanese Muslim militants, angered by U.S. support for Israel, targeted American marines with a truck bomb, killing 241 soldiers; rather than confront the bombers, the administration withdrew American forces. Three years later, Palestinians in the Gaza

Men — and Women — at War

Women played visible roles in the Persian Gulf War, comprising approximately 10 percent of the American troops. In the last decades of the twentieth century, increasing numbers of women chose military careers and, although prohibited from most fighting roles, were increasingly assigned to combat zones. Luc Delahaye/ Sipa Press.

Strip and along the West Bank of the Jordan River — territories occupied by Israel since 1967 — mounted an *intifada,* a civilian uprising against Israeli authority. In response, American diplomats stepped up their efforts to persuade the PLO and Arab nations to accept the legitimacy of Israel and to convince the Israelis to allow the creation of a Palestinian state. Neither initiative met with much success.

Iran and Iraq. American policymakers faced a second set of problems in the oil-rich nations of Iran and Iraq. In September 1980 the revolutionary Islamic government of Iran, headed by Ayatollah Khomeini, found itself at war with Iraq, a secular state headed by the ruthless dictator Saddam Hussein and his Sunni Muslim followers. The war started over a series of boundary disputes, in particular, access to deep water ports in the Persian Gulf essential to shipping oil. Fighting quickly escalated into a war of attrition that claimed a million casualties. The Reagan administration ignored Hussein's brutal repression of his political opponents in Iraq and the murder (using poison gas) of tens of thousands of Iraqi Kurds and Shiite Muslims. Anxious to preserve a balance of power in the Middle East, the administration provided Hussein with military intelligence and other aid. Finally, in 1988, an armistice ended the inconclusive war, with both sides still claiming the territory that sparked the conflict.

The Gulf War, 1990–1991. Two years later, in August 1990, Saddam Hussein again went to war to expand Iraq's boundaries. His troops quickly conquered Kuwait, Iraq's small oil-rich neighbor and threatened Saudi Arabia, the site of one-fifth of the world's known oil reserves and an informal ally of the United States. In response, President George H. W. Bush quickly sponsored a series of resolutions in the United Nations Security Council condemning Iraq, calling for its withdrawal from Kuwait, and imposing an embargo and trade sanctions. When Hussein refused to withdraw, Bush successfully prodded the UN to authorize the use of force against "the butcher of Baghdad" if Iraq did not withdraw by January 15. Demonstrating great diplomatic finesse, the president organized a military coalition of thirty-four nations. The House of Representatives authorized American participation by a vote of 252 to 182; dividing mostly along party lines, the Senate voted for war by the close vote of 52 to 47.

The war for the "liberation of Kuwait" was quickly won by the coalition forces led by the United States. A month of American air strikes crushed the communication network of the Iraqi army, destroyed its air forces, and weakened the morale of its soldiers. A land offensive then quickly forced the withdrawal of Iraqi forces from Kuwait (see Map 32.2, p. 1001). To avoid a protracted war and retain French and Russian support for the UN coalition, President Bush did not try to occupy Iraq and remove Saddam Hussein from power. Instead, he won the passage of United Nations Resolution 687, which imposed economic sanctions against Iraq unless it allowed unfettered inspection of its weapons systems, destroyed all biological and chemical arms, and unconditionally pledged not to develop nuclear weapons.

The military victory, low incidence of American casualties, and quick withdrawal produced a euphoric reaction at home. "By God, we've kicked the Vietnam syndrome once and for all," Bush gloated, as his approval rating shot up precipitously. The president spoke too soon. Throughout the 1990s, Saddam Hussein would remain a problem for American policymakers. Indeed, his secretive policies were one factor that, in March 2003, caused Bush's son, President George W. Bush, to initiate another war in Iraq—one that was much more protracted, expensive, and bloody for Americans and Iraqis alike (see Chapter 32).

Thus, the end of the Cold War resulted not in an era of peace but rather two very hot wars in the Middle East. For half a century, the United States and the USSR had tried to divide the world into two rival commercial and ideological blocs— Communist and capitalist. The next half century promised a new set of struggles, one of them between a Western-led agenda of economic and cultural globalization and an anti-Western ideology of Muslim and Arab regionalism.

➤ What factors led to the end of the Cold War?

➤ How did the composition and decisions of the Supreme Court change during the Reagan-Bush administrations?

➤ Why did the United States intervene in the conflicts between Iraq and Iran and Iraq and Kuwait? What were American goals in each case?

The Clinton Presidency, 1993–2001

The election of 1992 brought a Democrat, Arkansas Governor Bill Clinton, to the White House. A profound admirer of John F. Kennedy, Clinton hoped to rekindle the idealistic vision of the slain president. Like Kennedy, Clinton was a political pragmatist; distancing himself from party liberals and special-interest groups, he styled himself as a "New Democrat" who would bring "Reagan Democrats" and middle-class voters back to the party.

Clinton's Early Record

Raised in Hope, Arkansas, by an alcoholic stepfather who abused his mother, Clinton left home to study at Georgetown University. He won a Rhodes scholarship to Oxford and earned a law degree at Yale, where he married a classmate, Hillary Rodham. Returning to Arkansas, he entered politics and won election to six 2-year terms as governor. In 1991 at age forty-five, he was energetic, ambitious, and a policy "wonk"—extraordinarily well informed about political issues.

The Election of 1992. Clinton became the Democratic candidate, but only after surviving charges that he dodged the draft to avoid service in Vietnam, smoked marijuana, and cheated repeatedly on his wife. Although all of those stories had an element of truth, Clinton adroitly talked his way into the presidential nomination—he had charisma and a way with words. For his running mate he chose Al Gore, a second-term senator from Tennessee. At age forty-four, Gore was about the same age as Clinton, making them the first baby-boom national ticket, as well as the first all-southern ticket.

President Bush easily won renomination over his lone opponent, the conservative columnist Pat Buchanan. But Bush allowed the Religious Right to dominate the Republican convention and write a conservative platform that alienated many political moderates. The Bush campaign also suffered from the independent candidacy of Texas billionaire H. Ross Perot, whose condemnation of the rising federal deficit and the influence of corporate lobbyists on Congress appealed to many middle-class voters.

The Democrats mounted an aggressive campaign that focused on Clinton's domestic agenda: He promised a tax cut for the middle classes, universal health insurance, and a reduction of the huge Republican budget deficit. Freed from the demands of the Cold War, Democrats hoped that an emphasis on domestic issues where they traditionally ran strong would sweep them to victory. They were right. On election day, Bush could not overcome voters' discontent over the weak economy and conservatives' disgust at his tax hikes. He received only 37 percent of the popular vote, as millions of Republicans cast their ballots for Ross Perot, who won more votes (19 percent) than any independent candidate since Theodore Roosevelt in 1912. With 44 percent of the vote, Clinton won the election handily (Map 30.4). Moreover, the Democratic Party retained control of both houses of Congress, ending twelve years of divided government. Still, even as

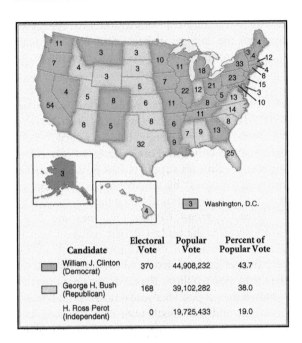

Candidate	Electoral Vote	Popular Vote	Percent of Popular Vote
William J. Clinton (Democrat)	370	44,908,232	43.7
George H. Bush (Republican)	168	39,102,282	38.0
H. Ross Perot (Independent)	0	19,725,433	19.0

MAP 30.4 Presidential Election of 1992

The first national election after the end of the Cold War focused on the economy, which had fallen into a recession in 1991. The first-ever all-southern Democratic ticket of Bill Clinton (Arkansas) and Al Gore (Tennessee) won support across the country but won the election with only 44 percent of the popular vote. The Republican candidate, Vice President George H. W. Bush, ran strongly in his home state of Texas and the South, an emerging Republican stronghold. Independent candidate H. Ross Perot, a wealthy technology entrepreneur, polled an impressive 19 percent of the popular vote by capitalizing on voter dissatisfaction with the huge federal deficits of the Reagan-Bush administrations.

the sun again shown on the Democrats, dark clouds appeared on the horizon. Bill Clinton entered the White House supported by a minority of voters and opposed by political enemies who considered him "a pot-smoking, philandering, draft-dodger" unqualified for the highest office in the land. He would need great political skills and more than a little good fortune to lead the country successfully, especially since he longed to go down in history as a great president.

The Failure of Health-Care Legislation. Clinton's ambition exceeded his abilities. The first year of his administration was riddled by mistakes — failed nominations of two attorney generals, embarrassing patronage revelations about the White House travel office, and an unsuccessful attempt to end a ban on homosexuals in the military. The president looked like a political amateur, out of his depth. He

compounded these minor errors by selecting health reform, an enduring liberal cause since the Truman administration but also an enormously complex issue, as the major objective of his first year in office.

Clinton's goal was to provide a system of health care that would cover all Americans. Though the United States spent a higher percentage of its GNP on medical care than any other nation, it was the only major industrialized country that did not provide government-guaranteed health insurance to all citizens. With medical costs and insurance premiums spiraling out of control, the president designated his wife, attorney Hillary Rodham Clinton, to head a task force to draft new legislation. This appointment was controversial because no First Lady had ever played a formal role in policymaking, but it also suited the times: In many American families, both husbands and wives held responsible positions in the workforce.

The recommendations of the task force were even more controversial. Recognizing the potency of Reagan's attack on "big government," the task force proposed a system of "managed competition": Market forces and private insurance companies, not government bureaucrats, would control health-care costs. The cost of the new system would fall heavily on employers, who had to pay 80 percent of their workers' health benefits, and many smaller businesses and insurance companies campaigned strongly against it. By September 1994, congressional Democratic leaders admitted that the Clintons' liberal health-care proposal was dead. Its failure left about forty million Americans, or 15 percent of the population, without health coverage.

Addressing other concerns of social welfare Democrats, Clinton appointed two pro-choice liberal jurists, Ruth Bader Ginsburg and Stephen Breyer, to the Supreme Court. He also placed women and racial minorities in cabinet positions. Janet Reno became attorney general, the first woman to head the Department of Justice; Donna E. Shalala headed the Department of Health and Human Services; and, in Clinton's second term, Madeleine Albright served as secretary of state. Clinton chose an African American, Ron Brown, as secretary of commerce, and two Latinos, Henry Cisneros and Frederico Peña, to head the Department of Housing and Urban Development (HUD) and the Department of Transportation, respectively.

The Clinton administration's policies toward social welfare, abortion, and crime likewise appealed to liberal Democrats. In 1993, Clinton signed the Family and Medical Leave Act, which had twice been

A Forceful and Controversial First Lady and Senator

Drawing inspiration from Eleanor Roosevelt, Hillary Rodham Clinton hoped the country was ready for a First Lady who actively shaped policy. It wasn't, or at least it wasn't ready for her health-care plan. Subsequently, Hillary Rodham Clinton assumed a less visible role in administration policymaking. In 2000, and again in 2006, she won election to the U.S. Senate from New York.
Robert Trippet / Sipa Press.

vetoed by President Bush, and the Clinic Entrance Act, which made it a federal crime to obstruct people entering hospitals or abortion clinics. Clinton's administration also won approval of two gun-control measures, on handguns and assault weapons, though neither had much affect on gun sales or the murder rate. To counter criticism from conservatives, Clinton "got tough on crime" and included funding in this legislation for 100,000 new police officers in local communities across the nation.

Clinton's Centrist Agenda. The president was more successful with the "centrist" New Democrat elements of his political agenda. Shortly before he left office, George H. W. Bush had signed the North American Free Trade Agreement (NAFTA), an arrangement among the United States, Canada, and Mexico to create a free-trade zone covering all of North America. The Clinton administration presided over Congress's consideration of the agreement, which was bitterly fought. Manufacturers looking for new markets or hoping to move their plants to Mexico, where workers' wages were much lower, strongly supported NAFTA. Labor

unions — a traditional Democratic constituency — opposed the agreement because it cut American jobs. Environmentalists likewise condemned the pact because antipollution laws were weak (and even more weakly enforced) south of the border. However, the Clinton administration was filled with advocates of free trade, including Treasury Secretary Lloyd Bentsen, Labor Secretary Robert Reich, and Economic Policy adviser Robert Rubin. With Clinton's support, they pushed NAFTA through Congress by assembling a coalition of free-trade Democrats and Republicans.

More important, Clinton took meaningful action to reduce the budget deficits of the Reagan-Bush presidencies. In 1993 Clinton secured a five-year budget package that would reduce the federal deficit by $500 billion. Republicans unanimously opposed the proposal because it raised taxes on corporations and individuals with high incomes, and liberal Democrats complained because it limited social spending. Clinton also paid a price because he had to abandon his campaign promise to lower taxes for the middle class. But shared sacrifice led to shared rewards. By 1998, Clinton's fiscal policies had balanced the federal budget and had begun to pay down the federal debt — at a rate of $156 billion a year between 1999 and 2001. As fiscal sanity returned to Washington, the economy boomed, thanks in part to the low interest rates stemming from deficit reduction. Ready access to cheap oil between 1986 and 2001 also fueled the growing economy. During Clinton's two terms in office, unemployment fell from 6 to 4 percent, the GNP increased at an annual rate of 3 percent (twice that of Japan), the stock market more than doubled in value, and home ownership rose to an all-time high.

The Republican Resurgence

The failure of health reform and the passage of NAFTA discouraged liberal Democrats even as Clinton's policies on homosexuals, guns, and abortion energized conservative Republicans in Congress and throughout the country. "Clinton-haters" — those who denied his fitness to be president — hammered away at his conduct as governor, and his participation in an allegedly fraudulent Arkansas real estate deal that became known as "Whitewater." Hoping to prove that the president and Hillary Clinton were free from any taint of fraud, the Clinton administration appointed an independent prosecutor to investigate the case.

In the meantime, the midterm election of 1994 became a referendum on Clinton and his presidency, and its results transformed the political

A Bipartisan Balanced Budget

Throughout his time in the White House, Bill Clinton worked to reduce federal deficits by increasing taxes and restraining spending. On August 5, 1997, a smiling President Clinton signed a balanced budget bill, surrounded by congressional leaders including Republican John Kasich of Ohio (front row, far right), Chair of the House Budget Committee, and Republican Newt Gingrich of Georgia (front row, second from right), the Speaker of the House. Also looking on with satisfaction was Vice President Al Gore, who already had hopes for the presidency in 2000. Ron Edmonds/AP Images.

landscape. In a well-organized and well-funded campaign strongly supported by the National Rifle Association and the Religious Right, Republicans gained 52 seats in the House of Representatives, giving them control for the first time in forty years; they also retook control of the Senate and captured eleven governorships.

The "Contract with America." Leading the Republican charge was Representative Newt Gingrich, an intellectually aggressive conservative from Georgia, who became the new Speaker of the House. During the campaign, Gingrich announced a Republican "Contract with America," a list of proposals that he vowed would be voted on in the first one hundred days of the new session. The contract included constitutional amendments to balance the budget and term limits for members of Congress. It also promised significant tax cuts, reductions in welfare and other entitlement programs, anticrime initiatives, and cutbacks in federal regulations. These initiatives, and Republican control of Congress after 1994, represented the completion of the conservative-backed Reagan Revolution of 1980. The president and the Democrats were now on the defensive. In his State of the Union message of 1996, Clinton suggested that "the era of big government is over." For the rest of his presidency, he eschewed expansive liberal social welfare policies and sought Republican support for a centrist, New Democrat program.

The Budget Struggle and Welfare Reform. Despite Clinton's acceptance of governmental restraint, the Republican-dominated Congress failed to make significant reductions in the size of the federal budget. Most big-budget items were politically or economically untouchable. The Treasury had to pay interest on the national debt; the military budget had to be met; the Social Security system had to be funded. When Republicans passed a government funding act in 1995 that included tax cuts to the wealthy and less money for Medicare, Clinton vetoed the legislation, thereby shutting down many government offices for three weeks. Depicted by Democrats and many independent observers as heartless opponents of aid for senior citizens, the Republicans admitted defeat and gave the president a bill he would sign.

Republicans had greater success in reforming the welfare system, a measure that saved relatively little money but carried a big ideological message. The program for Aid to Families with Dependent Children (AFDC) provided annual payments (including food stamps) to families earning less than $7,740, well below the established poverty line. Still, many taxpaying Americans believed, with some justification, that the AFDC program perpetuated poverty by encouraging women recipients to bear children and to remain on welfare rather than to seek productive employment. Various state legislatures — both Democrat- and Republican-run — had already imposed work requirements and denied benefits for additional children born to women who were already on AFDC. In August 1996, the federal government did the same. After vetoing two Republican-authored bills, President Clinton signed the Personal Responsibility and Work Opportunity Act. This historic overhaul of federal entitlements ended the guarantee of cash assistance by abolishing AFDC, required most adult recipients to find work within two years, and gave states wide discretion in running their welfare programs.

The 1996 Election. The Republican takeover of Congress had one unintended consequence: It united the usually fractious Democrats behind the president. Unopposed in the 1996 primaries, Clinton burnished his image as a moderate by endorsing welfare reform. He also benefited from the continuing strength of the economy. The Republicans settled on Senate Majority Leader Bob Dole of Kansas as their presidential candidate. A veteran of World War II, in which he lost the use of an arm, Dole was a safe but uninspiring candidate, lacking both personal charisma and innovative policies. He called for a 15 percent tax cut *and* a balanced budget, a fiscal combination that few Americans believed possible. On election day, Clinton took 49 percent of the popular vote to 41 percent for Dole. Ross Perot, who failed to build his independent movement of 1992 into a coherent political party, received 8 percent. By dint of great effort — dozens of risky vetoes, centrist initiatives, determined fundraising — Clinton had staged a heroic comeback from the electoral disaster of 1994. Still, Republicans remained in control of Congress and, angry at Clinton's reelection, returned to Washington eager to engage in partisan combat.

Clinton's Impeachment

Clinton's hopes for a distinguished place in history unraveled halfway through his second term when a sex scandal led to his impeachment. The impeachment charges stemmed from Clinton's sworn testimony in a lawsuit filed by Paula Jones, a former Arkansas state employee. In that testimony and later on national television, Clinton denied having sexually harassed Jones during his governorship. These denials may well have been truthful. But during the testimony Clinton also denied having a sexual affair with Monica Lewinsky, a former White House intern — a charge that was undoubtedly true. Kenneth Starr, a conservative Republican who had taken over as independent counsel in the Arkansas Whitewater land deal, now widened his probe to include the Jones affair. Starr's report of September 1998 concluded that Clinton had lied under oath regarding Lewinsky and obstructed justice, and that these actions were grounds for impeachment.

Viewed historically, Americans have usually defined "high crimes and misdemeanors" — the constitutional standard for impeachment — as involving a serious abuse of public trust that threatened the integrity of the republic. In 1998, many conservative Republicans favored a much lower standard because they had never accepted "Slick Willy" Clinton's legitimacy as president. In reply to the question, "Why do you hate Clinton so much?",

The Politics of Impeachment

As this cartoon shows, the Republicans caught President Clinton with his pants down. But they failed to persuade a majority of Americans that Clinton's sexual escapades with White House intern Monica Lewinsky (and his lies about it while under oath) were "high crimes and misdemeanors" that merited his removal from office. The episode is best seen as an expression of the harsh ideological politics of the 1990s and, in retrospect, as an unnecessary and dangerous diversion of the nation's energies away from the looming threat of terrorism.

Auth ©1998 *The Philadelphia Inquirer.* Reprinted with permission Universal Press Syndicate. All Rights Reserved.

one conservative declared, "I hate him because he's a womanizing, Elvis-loving, non-inhaling, truth-shading, war-protesting, draft-dodging, abortion-protecting, gay-promoting, gun-hating baby boomer. That's why." Seeing Clinton as an exemplar of the permissive social values of the 1960s, conservative Republicans vowed to use the sex scandal to oust him from office. On December 19 the House of Representatives narrowly approved two articles of impeachment against Clinton: one for perjury for lying to a grand jury about his liaison with Lewinsky, and a second for obstruction of justice by encouraging others to lie on his behalf. Most Americans did not applaud the House's action; according to a CBS news poll, 38 percent supported impeachment while 58 percent opposed it.

Lacking public support, Republicans in the Senate fell well short of the two-thirds majority they needed to remove the president. Like Andrew Johnson, the only other president to be tried by the Senate (see Chapter 15), Bill Clinton paid a high price for this victory. The president spent so much time in his defense that he was unable to fashion a coherent Democratic alternative to the Republicans' conservative domestic agenda and, equally important, to address important problems of foreign policy.

Foreign Policy at the End of the Twentieth Century

Unlike George H. W. Bush, Clinton claimed no expertise in international affairs and did not desire to develop one. "Foreign policy is not what I came here to do," he lamented as he faced a series of minor international crises. Neither of his main advisors, Secretary of State Warren Christopher and Secretary of Defense Les Aspin, had a strategic vision of America's role in the post–Cold War world. Consequently, Clinton pursued a cautious diplomatic policy. Unless important American interests were directly threatened, the president avoided a commitment of U.S. influence and troops.

"Peacekeeping" in Somalia and Haiti. Clinton's caution stemmed in part from a harrowing episode in the east African country of Somalia, where ethnic warfare had created political chaos and massive famine. President Bush had approved American participation in a UN peacekeeping force, and Clinton had added additional troops. When bloody fighting in October 1993 killed eighteen American soldiers and wounded eighty-four, Clinton gradually withdrew the troops. The United States had few economic and diplomatic interests in Somalia, and even a sizeable peacekeeping force would be unable to quell the factional violence and restore national unity. For similar reasons, Clinton refused in 1994 to dispatch American forces to the central African nation of Rwanda, where ethnic conflict had escalated to genocide—the killing by Hutu extremists of at least 800,000 people, mostly ethnic Tutsis.

The Caribbean was much closer to home, and Clinton consequently gave it closer attention. In 1991 a military coup in Haiti had deposed Jean-Bertrand Aristide, the democratically elected president. Then a candidate for president, Clinton had criticized President Bush's refusal to grant asylum to refugees from the oppressive new Haitian regime. Once in the White House, Clinton reversed his stance: To thwart a massive influx of impoverished Haitian "boat people" who would strain welfare services and increase racial tension, the new president called for Aristide's return to power. Threatening a U.S. invasion, Clinton forced Haiti's military rulers to step down. American troops maintained Aristide in power until March 1995, when the United Nations took over responsibility for keeping the peace.

Intervention in the Balkans. An even more intractable set of internal conflicts—based on ethnicity, religion, and nationality—led to the disintegration of the Communist nation of Yugoslavia in 1991. Initially, the Roman Catholic regions of Slovenia and Croatia declared independence from Yugoslavia, which was dominated by Russian Orthodox Serbians. In 1992, the heavily Muslim province of Bosnia and Herzegovina declared its independence, but its substantial Serbian population refused to live in a Muslim-run multiethnic state. Supported financially and militarily by Slobodan Milosevic, the uncompromisingly nationalistic leader of Yugoslavia, they formed their own breakaway state and, to make it an all-Serbian society, launched a ruthless campaign of "ethnic cleansing." They drove tens of thousands of Bosnian Muslims and Croats from their homes, executed tens of thousands of men, raped equal numbers of women, and forced the survivors into crowded refugee camps.

America's European allies, particularly Germany, had long-standing economic ties to the Balkans, and the United States had taken an active role in its affairs during the Cold War. However, both Clinton and NATO leaders feared that military action against the Serbs would result in a Vietnam-like quagmire. Finally, in November 1995, Clinton organized a NATO-led bombing campaign and peacekeeping effort, backed by twenty thousand American troops, that ended the Serbs' vicious expansionist drive. Four years later a new crisis emerged in Kosovo, another province of the Serbian-dominated Federal Republic of Yugoslavia. Most Kosovo residents were ethnic Albanian Muslims, whom the Russian Orthodox Serbs vowed to drive out of the region. Again led by the United States, NATO intervened with aircraft strikes and military forces to preserve Kosovo's autonomy (Map 30.5). While always acting prudently in defense of American interests, the Clinton administration had slowly developed a policy of active "engagement" in nations beset with internal conflict.

Islamic Radicalism. In the Middle East, Clinton was as unsuccessful as previous presidents in mediating the long-standing conflict between Jews and Arabs. In 1994 he arranged a meeting in Washington

MAP 30.5   Ethnic Conflict in the Balkans: The Breakup of Yugoslavia, 1991–1992

The collapse of the Soviet Union spurred the disintegration of the independent Communist state of Yugoslavia, a multiethnic and multireligious state held together after 1945 by the near-dictatorial authority of Josip Broz Tito (1892–1980). Fanned by ethnic and religious hatreds, Yugoslavia splintered into warring states. Slovenia and Macedonia won their independence in 1991, but Russian Orthodox Serbia, headed by president Slobodan Milosevic, tried to rule the rest of the Balkan peoples. Roman Catholic Croatia freed itself from Serb rule in 1995, and, after ruthless Serbian aggression against Muslims in Bosnia and later in Kosovo, the United States and NATO intervened militarily to create the separate states of Bosnia-Herzegovina (1995) and Montenegro (2006) and the autonomous Muslim province of Kosovo (1999).

between Israeli prime minister Yitzhak Rabin and Yasir Arafat, chairman of the Palestine Liberation Organization. Urged on by Clinton, they negotiated an agreement that allowed limited Palestinian self-rule in the Gaza Strip and Jericho. The hope that this breakthrough would lead to a general peace settlement was short lived. In 1995, a Jewish religious fanatic assassinated Rabin, and the new prime minister, Benjamin Netanyahu of the religious Likud Party, reverted to a hard-line policy against the Palestinians. Despite Clinton's continuing efforts, the "peace process" failed to produce substantial progress.

Terrorists Bomb USS *Cole*

On October 12, 2000, a radical Muslim group with ties to Al Qaeda detonated a powerful bomb near the USS *Cole,* which was refueling in the port of Aden in Yemen. The explosion killed seventeen American sailors and injured thirty-seven others. After repairs costing $250 million, the USS *Cole* returned to active duty in April 2002. © Bettmann/Corbis.

Indeed, the rise of radical Muslim organizations undermined the prospects of a Middle Eastern peace and challenged security and stability throughout the world. During the 1990s, radical Islamic movements staged armed insurgencies in parts of Russia and China and threatened existing governments in the Muslim states of Algeria, Egypt, Pakistan, and Indonesia. These terrorist groups likewise mounted a series of attacks against the United States, which they condemned as the main agent of economic globalization and cultural imperialism. In 1993 radical Muslim immigrants set off a bomb in the World Trade Center in New York City. Five years later, Muslim terrorists used truck bombs to blow up the American embassies in Kenya and Tanzania, and in 2000 they bombed an American warship, the USS *Cole*, in the port of Aden in Yemen. The Clinton administration knew these attacks were the work of Al Qaeda, a network of terrorists organized by the wealthy Saudi exile Osama bin Laden, but no one—in the State Department, CIA, or Pentagon—had yet figured out how to deal with these Islamic extremists (see Chapter 32).

As the Soviet Union collapsed in 1991, the director of the CIA had seen little cause to celebrate. "We have slain a large dragon," he admitted, "but we live now in a jungle filled with a bewildering variety of poisonous snakes. And in many ways, the dragon was easier to keep track of." As the century ended, his assessment rang true. The Balkan and African crises, the Middle Eastern morass, and radical Islamic terrorist groups served as potent reminders of a world in conflict and the limits of American power. If not quite as dangerous as the Cold War era, the "new world order" was no less problematic.

➤ In what ways did Clinton's administration suggest that he was a "New Democrat"?

➤ What was the goal of the Republicans' "Contract with America"?

➤ What foreign policy challenges did Clinton face, and how did he address them?

SUMMARY

As we have seen, the concluding decades of the twentieth century were a time of momentous change. In the international arena, the collapse of the Soviet Union and the end of the Cold War diminished the prospect of nuclear war. Nonetheless, regional and ethnic conflicts continued to pose a serious challenge to U.S. foreign policy. Militarily dominant, the United States found its economy challenged by strong competitors in Europe and Asia and its security endangered by ruthless terrorist groups.

The shifting economic fortunes of the nation affected domestic politics. The "stagflation" of the 1970s helped to ensure the electoral triumph of Ronald Reagan in 1980, and his administration's massive expenditures on defense boosted the domestic economy while creating an enormous federal deficit. Rather than getting "the government off our backs," Reagan simply used its power in different ways. "Reaganomics" shifted wealth into the hands of military planners and affluent Americans, mostly at the expense of the poor. Middle-class Americans — the majority of the population — generally prospered during the 1980s but divided ever more sharply over cultural issues. Influenced by the powerful lobby of the Religious Right, the Republican Party vigorously attacked the welfare state and the liberal cultural values that it represented.

These economic and cultural issues played out in the politics of the 1990s. The economic recession of 1991 assisted the election of Bill Clinton in 1992, as did his centrist, "New Democrat" policies that reflected the conservative movement's call for limited government. The Republican congressional landslide of 1994 limited Clinton's options, as did his sexual misconduct, which in 1998 led to his impeachment and loss of political effectiveness. As the century ended, American society was experiencing a massive technological revolution that promised to transform many aspects of life.

Connections: Government and Politics

Far into the future historians will debate Ronald Reagan's personal impact on the two great events presented in this chapter — the triumph of the conservative movement in America and the end of the Cold War. Still, there is no doubt, as we observed in the opening essay for Part Seven (p. 925), that President Ronald Reagan and his conservative successors were determined to carry out a governmental revolution:

The conservatives' agenda was to roll back the social welfare state created by liberal Democrats during the New Deal and the Great Society. Presidents Reagan, George H. W. Bush, and George W. Bush cut taxes, reduced spending on social welfare programs, and limited the regulatory activities of federal agencies.

In previous chapters, we have watched the slow construction of the governmental system that the conservatives attacked. Although prefigured in the regulatory legislation of the Progressive era (Chapter 20), it had its origins in the New Deal of Franklin Roosevelt. As we saw in Chapter 24, in response to the Great Depression the Roosevelt administration created a phalanx of federal agencies to oversee the American economy and, in the Social Security Act of 1935, laid the groundwork of a system to ensure the welfare of all Americans. But the powerful federal government of today is also the product of World War II and the Cold War. Those conflicts, as we saw in Chapters 25 and 26, brought a massive increase in government spending, taxes, and employees, as well as an influential "military-industrial complex" of private corporations. In fact, as our discussion of the decades since 1945 suggests, many private-interest groups have become reliant on favorable legislation or outright government subsidies. Because the modern state is so deeply implicated in the social and economic welfare of the American people as well as in their military defense, conservative politicians — as we explained in this chapter — have been unable to shrink substantially the size or scope of governmental activity.

CHAPTER REVIEW QUESTIONS

➤ How did the domestic policies of Presidents Reagan, Bush, and Clinton reflect the rise of conservatism in American politics?

➤ What comparisons can you make between the Iran-Contra scandal of Ronald Reagan's administration and the impeachment crisis of Bill Clinton's?

➤ What new challenges did the end of the Cold War bring to American foreign policy?

1970s	Rise of the New Right
1981	Ronald Reagan becomes president; Republicans win control of Senate
	Economic Recovery Tax Act (ERTA) cuts taxes
	Military expenditures increase sharply
	Reagan cuts budgets of regulatory agencies
	Sandra Day O'Connor appointed to the Supreme Court
1981–1989	National debt triples
	Emergence of New Right think tanks: Heritage Foundation, American Enterprise Institute, and the Cato Institute
	U.S. assists Iraq in war against Iran (1980–1988)
1983	Strategic Defense Initiative (Star Wars)
1985	Gramm-Rudman Budget Act
	Mikhail Gorbachev takes power in Soviet Union
1986	Iran-Contra scandal weakens Reagan presidency
	William Rehnquist named chief justice
1987	United States and USSR agree to limit missiles in Europe
1988	George H. W. Bush elected president
1989	Destruction of Berlin Wall; "Velvet Revolutions" in eastern Europe
	Webster v. Reproductive Health Services limits abortion services
1990–1991	Persian Gulf War
	Americans with Disabilities Act
1991	Dissolution of Soviet Union ends Cold War
	Clarence Thomas named to the Supreme Court
1992	Democratic moderate Bill Clinton elected president in three-way race
	Planned Parenthood of Southeastern Pennsylvania v. Casey upholds *Roe v. Wade*
1993	Congress passes Family and Medical Leave Act
	North American Free Trade Agreement (NAFTA)
1994	Clinton fails to win health insurance but reduces budget deficit and national debt
	Republicans gain control of Congress
1995	U.S. troops enforce peace in Bosnia
1996	Personal Responsibility and Work Opportunity Act reforms welfare system
1998–1999	Bill Clinton impeached and acquitted
	American intervention in Bosnia and Serbia
	Rise of radical Muslim movements and Al Qaeda terrorists

FOR FURTHER EXPLORATION

James T. Patterson, *Restless Giant: The United States from Watergate to Bush v. Gore* (2005), provides a solid analysis of the 1980s and 1990s. For evangelical politics, see Frances FitzGerald, *Cities on a Hill* (1986), which has a section on Jerry Falwell and the Moral Majority; William Martin, *With God on Our Side: The Rise of the Religious Right in America* (1996); and Lisa McGerr, *Suburban Warriors: The Origins of the New American Right* (2001). Two valuable overviews of the Reagan presidency are Lou Cannon, *President Reagan: The Role of a Lifetime* (2000), and Haynes Johnson, *Sleepwalking through History: America in the Reagan Years* (1992). John Greene, *The Presidency of George Bush* (2000), discusses the policies of the senior Bush.

On foreign policy, consult Richard A. Melanson, *American Foreign Policy since the Vietnam War* (2005), which covers the years from 1970 to 2000, and Raymond Garthoff, *The Great Transition: Russian-American Politics and the End of the Cold War* (1994). Two fine Web sites that document various Cold War incidents are The National Security Archive, at **www.gwu.edu/~nsarchiv**, and The Cold War International History Project, at **www.wilsoncenter.org/index.cfm?fuseaction= topics.home&topic_id=1409**. For the Gulf War, see Michael Gordon and Bernard Trainor, *The Generals' War: The Inside Story of the Conflict in the Gulf* (1995), and **www.pbs.org/ wgbh/pages/frontline/gulf**, a site with maps, documents, and interviews with decision makers and soldiers.

For the Clinton years, consult William Berman, *From the Center to the Edge: The Politics and Policies of the Clinton Presidency* (2001), and Joe Klein, *The Natural: The Misunderstood Presidency of Bill Clinton* (2002). Richard A. Posner, *An Affair of State: The Investigation, Impeachment, and Trial of President Clinton* (1999), probes the legal aspects of that affair. For online materials on Clinton's impeachment, consult Jurist, the Law Professors' Network, at **jurist.law.pitt.edu/impeach.htm**.

Other interesting political studies include Steven Gillon, *"That's Not What We Meant to Do": Reform and Its Unintended Consequences in Twentieth Century America* (2001); Fred Greenstein, *The Presidential Difference: Leadership Style from FDR to Clinton* (2000); and Ted Halstead and Michael Lind, *The Radical Center: The Future of American Politics* (2001). Information on all U.S. presidents is available at **www.ipl.org/div/potus**.

TEST YOUR KNOWLEDGE

To assess your command of the material in this chapter, see the Online Study Guide at **bedfordstmartins.com/henretta**.

For Web sites, images, and documents related to topics and places in this chapter, visit **bedfordstmartins.com/makehistory**.

A Dynamic Economy, A Divided People

1980–2000

A S 1999 CAME TO A CLOSE, a technological disaster threatened millions of computers around the world. For decades programmers had used a two-digit field to describe dates, recording 1950 as simply "50." What would happen when the clock flashed to "Y2K" — shorthand for the year 2000? Would millions of personal, corporate, and government computers clock it as 1900, magically shifting the world a century back in time? Or would the computers crash and wipe out the data of millions of users? As it turned out, the great "Y2K" fear proved unfounded, as thousands of software programmers managed to patch the world's computer systems and avoid a disaster.

The moment was nonetheless symbolic. As the world entered the third millennium of the Christian era, the fates of its many peoples were directly tied to one another electronically and in many other ways. In centuries past, periodic waves of epidemical diseases — the Black Death, cholera, and influenza — had joined the peoples of the world, and then only in death. Now millions of people across the globe were linked together on a daily basis — working in export-oriented factories, watching television programs created in distant nations, flying thousands of miles in jet planes to other continents, and — perhaps most amazing of all — having pictures of their towns and fields snapped by satellite cameras

America in the Global Economy and Society
The Economic Challenge
A Turn to Prosperity
Globalization

The New Technology
The Computer Revolution
Technology and the Control of Popular Culture

Culture Wars
An Increasingly Pluralistic Society
Conflicting Values: Women's and Gay Rights

Summary
Connections: Society and Technology

◀ **www.TimBerners-Lee**

Nothing represents the globalization of the world's economy and culture better than the World Wide Web, which allows instant access to Web sites around the globe. The technology behind the Web was invented between 1989 and 1991 by Tim Berners-Lee, an English computer scientist working at the time at CERN, the European Particle Physics Laboratory in Geneva, Switzerland. This photomosaic picture of Berners-Lee, who presently teaches at MIT, is composed of 2,304 Web sites. Tim Berners-Lee.

high in the stratosphere and beamed instantly around the world. The globe was growing smaller.

But not necessarily more harmonious. "Globalization"—the movement of goods, ideas, and organizations across political boundaries—created as many conflicts as it solved. Likewise, increased contact among Americans through modern means of communications made them more conscious of their differences—racial, ethnic, religious, ideological—and sharpened cultural conflict at home. In particular, New Right conservatives, who had come into their own in the Reagan-Bush years, squared off against social welfare liberals, who adhered to many of the social values that had flourished from the 1930s through the 1960s. The resulting "culture wars" strained social harmony as the twentieth century drew to a close.

America in the Global Economy and Society

When Bill Clinton ran for president in 1992, a large sign in his campaign "war room" underlined the main issue: "THE ECONOMY, STUPID." Throughout the last quarter of the century, bread-and-butter issues loomed large in the minds of many Americans. The abrupt rise in global oil prices in the 1970s had triggered a corrosive "stagflation" that had heaped hardship on the poor, shrunk middle-class expectations, and shaken the confidence of policymakers and business executives. It would take time, ingenuity, and a bit of luck to restore America's self-confidence.

The Economic Challenge

The 1980s began on a depressing economic note. Unemployment remained above 7 percent, and the cost of living continued to soar at a rate of 8 percent a year. When the Federal Reserve jacked up interest rates (to nearly 20 percent) to combat inflation (see Chapter 30), the nation experienced a sharp recession in 1981–1982, with nearly 10 percent of the workforce without jobs.

However, the economy quickly revived and turned the rest of the decade into one of relative prosperity. The wealthiest one-fifth of Americans, the primary beneficiaries of President Reagan's tax

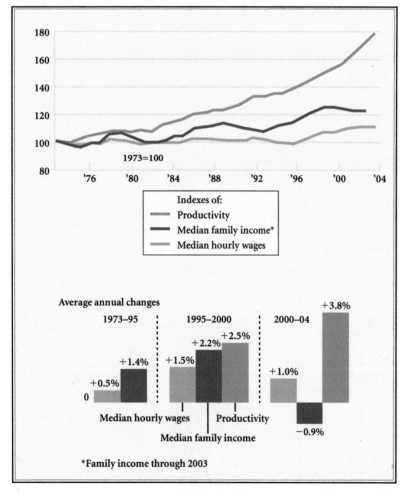

FIGURE 31.1 Productivity, Family Income, and Wages, 1970–2004

This chart tells a complex and not altogether happy story. The median hourly wages of American workers (adjusted for inflation) stagnated between 1970 and 1995. The rise in median family income reflected the increasing proportion of two-earner families, as more married women entered the workforce. The dramatic increases in productivity did not lead to higher wages for workers. Rather, businesses used those gains either to cut prices to compete in the global marketplace or to reward owners, shareholders, and, particularly, corporate executives.

Akio Morita and the Sony Corporation

In 1946 Akio Morita and Masaru Ibuka founded the Tokyo Telecommunications Engineering Corporation, which evolved into the Sony Corporation. Its first great sales success came in the mid-1950s with a pocket-sized transistor radio. Other innovative products followed in subsequent decades: in the 1960s, the popular Trinitron TV; in the 1970s, the Betamax video recorder and the Walkman radio; in the 1980s, the compact disc, the three-and-a-half inch diskette, and, shown here in a picture of Morita in 1985, the Handycam. In the 1990s, Sony devised the PlayStation, the memory stick, and many more electronic products. In 2005, Sony employed 150,000 workers and sold goods worth $18 billion in the United States and $67 billion worldwide. Photo by Bill Pierce/Time Life Pictures/Getty Images.

cuts and economic policies, did especially well. Many middle-class Americans also enjoyed a modest affluence, but the real wages of manufacturing and retail workers continued to stagnate (Figure 31.1). The poor — the thirty million citizens below the poverty line — struggled to survive.

Domestic Affluence and Foreign Debts. The fate of the poor was of little concern to the well-educated "baby boom" children who entered the labor force in the early 1980s. Many took high-paying jobs in the rapidly growing professional and technology sectors of the economy. These young urban professionals — the Yuppies, as they were called — set the tone for a strikingly materialistic culture. Yuppies (and Buppies, their black counterparts) dined at gourmet restaurants, enjoyed vacations at elaborate resorts, and lived in large suburban houses filled with expensive consumer goods. Their example shaped the outlook of the next generation. Surveys reported that 80 percent of college students in the 1980s placed a high value on individual economic success while only 40 percent gave importance to enlightened social values — an exact reversal of student attitudes during the 1960s. The majority of Americans who could not afford the new luxuries experienced them vicariously by watching *Lifestyles of the Rich and Famous,* a popular TV series that debuted in 1984. Every week, host Robin Leach took audiences into the mansions of people who enjoyed "champagne wishes and caviar dreams."

Tempering this enthusiasm, commentators warned of the nation's economic decline. Until the 1970s the United States had been the world's leading exporter of agricultural products, manufactured goods, and investment capital. Then, American exports began to fall, undercut in world markets by cheaper and often better designed products from Germany and Japan (see Chapter 29). By 1985, for the first time since 1915, the United States registered a negative balance of international payments. It now imported more goods than it exported, a trade deficit fueled by soaring imports of foreign oil, which increased between 1960 and 2000 from two to twelve million barrels per day. Moreover, America's earnings from foreign investments did not offset the imbalance in trade. The United States had become a debtor (rather than a creditor) nation; each year, it had to borrow money, in the form of credit or investment capital, to maintain the standard of living many Americans had come to expect.

Japan's Rise, America's Decline. The rapid ascent of the Japanese economy to the second largest in the world was a key factor in this historic reversal. Japan's Nikkei stock index tripled in value between 1965 and 1975, and then tripled again by 1985. Now more than a third of the American annual trade deficit of $138 billion was with Japan, whose corporations exported huge quantities of electronic goods (TVs, VCRs, microwave ovens) and other consumer products. Indeed, Japanese auto companies accounted for nearly a quarter of all cars bought in the United States. Using the profits of these sales, Japanese businesses bought up prime pieces of real estate, such as New York City's Rockefeller Center, and took over well-known American corporations. The purchase by Japan's Sony Corporation of two American icons, Columbia Pictures and CBS Records, frightened politicians and ordinary citizens. The post-1945 economic primacy of the United States was in rapid decline.

While Japan and Germany prospered, American businesses grappled with a worrisome decline in productivity. Between 1973 and 1992, the productivity of American workers grew at the meager rate of 1 percent a year, a far cry from the post–World War II rate of 3 percent annually. As a consequence, the wages of most employees stagnated and the number of high-paying, union-protected manufacturing jobs shrank. Unemployed industrial workers took whatever jobs they could find, usually minimum-wage positions as sales "associates" in fast-food franchises or in big-box stores, such as Wal-Mart or Home Depot. By 1985, more people in the United States worked for McDonald's slinging Big Macs than labored in the nation's steel industry, rolling out rails, girders, and sheet steel. Middle-class Americans—baby boomers included—also found themselves with less economic security. To remain competitive internationally, corporations reduced the number of middle-level managers and back-office accountants. Most laid-off middle managers eventually found new jobs, but many had to take sizeable cuts in pay.

As middle-class families struggled to make ends meet, poor Americans just held their own. The number remained stable, at about 31 million, and despite the Reagan-era budget cuts, Americans entitled to Medicare, food stamps, and Aid to Families

with Dependent Children received about the same level of benefits in 1990 than they had in 1980. Still, the number of homeless citizens doubled. A Community Services Society report movingly described how thousands of people found themselves without a place to live: "Something happens—a job is lost, unemployment benefits run out, creditors and banks move in to foreclose, eviction proceedings begin—and quite suddenly the respectable poor find themselves among the disreputable homeless."

The Impact on Family Life. Challenging economic times accelerated changes already underway in family life and gender roles. As early as the 1960s, married women entered the paid workforce in increasing numbers, both to exercise their talents and to bolster their families' income (Figure 31.2). As men's wages stagnated during the 1970s, women increasingly sought paid employment—even though their pay averaged only about 70 percent of that paid to men. By 1994, 58 percent of adult women were in the labor force, up from 38 percent in 1962. Many women, especially those with young children, did double duty; as one working mother remarked, "You're on duty at work. You come home, and you're on duty" again.

Some women entered male-dominated fields, such as medicine, law, skilled trades, law enforce-

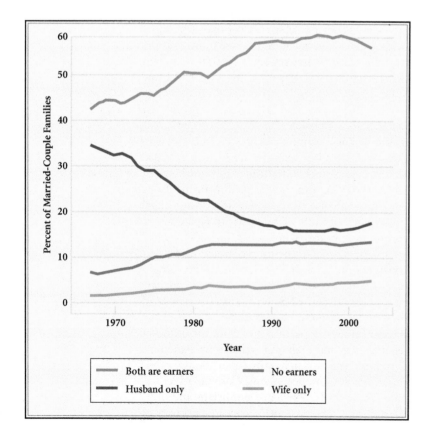

FIGURE 31.2 The Increase in Two-Worker Families

In 1968, about 43 percent of married couples sent both the husband and the wife into the workforce; thirty years later, 60 percent were two-earner families. The percentage of families in which the wife alone worked doubled (from 3 percent to 5 percent) during these years, while those with no earners (welfare recipients and, increasingly, retired couples) rose from 8 percent to 13 percent. Because these figures do not include unmarried persons and most illegal immigrants, they do not give a complete picture of the American workplace. But there is no doubt that women now play a major role in the workforce.

Barbie Goes to Work

Since 1959, the shapely Barbie doll has symbolized the "feminine mystique," the female as sexual object, and diffused this view of American womanhood around the nation and the globe. More than 500 million Barbies have been sold in 140 countries. But Barbie moves with the times. In 1985, she got her first computer, and in 1999, this doll and CD set transformed Barbie into a working woman, earning her own bread in the corporate workplace and, perhaps, with something intelligent to say! © Mattel.

ment, and the military, but the majority still labored in traditional fields, such as teaching, nursing, and sales work. In fact, one in five women held a clerical or secretarial job, the same proportion as in 1950. Still, as women flooded the labor force, cultural expectations and ideals began to change. Men learned to accept women as coworkers — and even as their bosses — and took responsibility for more household tasks. By the 1990s, only about 15 percent of U.S. households conformed to the model of the ideal American family depicted by the Hollywood script writers of the 1950s: employed father, homemaker wife, and young children.

The Turn to Prosperity

Between 1985 and 1990, American corporate executives and workers learned how to compete against their German and Japanese rivals. One key was technology and especially the use of information processing, which had been pioneered by Microsoft, Cisco, Sun, and other American companies. As corporations fitted out their plants and offices with computers, robots, and other "smart" machines, the productivity of the workforce rose. Bethlehem Steel, which invested $6 billion to modernize its operations during the late 1980s, soon doubled its productivity. Other firms retooled their corporate vision. Between 1980 and 1981, the Ford Motor Company lost $2.5 billion because of high expenses and stagnating sales. Responding to this desperate situation, Ford made fundamental reforms that improved the quality of its cars, enhanced the morale of assembly-line workers, and cut costs by adopting the Japanese system of rapid inventory resupply.

The stock market quickly reflected these initiatives, as ambitious and aggressive baby-boom brokers took control of Wall Street and government policy encouraged private investors. Prompted by the deregulation policies of the Carter administration, the Securities and Exchange Commission enacted new rules that made the financial industry more open and competitive (see Chapter 29). These measures encouraged the creation of discount brokerage firms, whose low fees prompted more small-scale investors to enter the stock market. Between 1980 and 2000, the percentage of American families owning some stock quadrupled from 13 to 51 percent. As the economic expansion gathered steam, stock prices spurted upward. In a six-month period in 1986, the value of stocks rose $400 billion. Even a major financial scandal in the savings and loan industry (which eventually cost taxpayers $132 billion) and a startling Wall Street crash in October 1987, in which stocks lost a fourth of their value, did not deter investors. Within two years, the market had regained its former level and continued to rise.

Goats and Heroes of the 1980s: Ivan Boesky, Lee Iacocca, and Donald Trump. The rise in stock values unleashed a wave of corporate mergers, as companies used stock to buy up competitors. As these deals multiplied, so too did the number of traders who profited illegally from insider knowledge. The most notorious of the white-collar criminals was Ivan Boesky, who acquired a fortune — and a reputation as an astute financier — as he arranged takeovers and buyouts. Invited to deliver the commencement address to graduates of the Business School at the University of California at Berkeley, Boesky said, "I think greed is healthy. You can be greedy and still feel good about yourself." At least until scandal strikes! Convicted of illegal trading, Boesky was sentenced to three-and-a-half years in prison (he served two years) and had to disgorge $50 million from his illicit profits and another $50 million in fines.

While sleazy financiers like Boesky gave corporate millionaires a bad name, successful business executives basked in the Reagan administration's adulation of wealth. When the president christened self-made entrepreneurs "the heroes for the eighties," he probably had Lee Iacocca in mind. The son of Italian immigrants, Iacocca personified the American Dream. Trained as an engineer, he rose through the ranks to become president of the Ford Motor Corporation; resigning from that position in 1978, he took over the ailing Chrysler auto company. Over the next decade, Iacocca turned Chrysler into a profitable company — securing a crucial $1.5 billion loan from the U.S. government and pushing the

An Automated Assembly Line

Most basic manufacturing is now done by machines, like these robotic welders on an automobile assembly line. The use of these machines increases productivity, in part by eliminating the jobs traditionally done by welders. But this advance in technology also creates new jobs in making and servicing the robots and other automated machines. © Bettmann/Corbis.

development of new cars. To encourage Americans to buy improved Chrysler models, Iacocca starred in TV advertisements and echoed Reagan's rhetoric: "Let's make American mean something again."

Simultaneously, real estate entrepreneur Donald Trump revived the morale of many aspiring residents of New York City, whose government had long teetered on the brink of bankruptcy. In 1983, the flamboyant Trump built the equally flamboyant Trump Towers. At the entrance of the $200 million apartment building stood two enormous bronze "T's," a display of self-promotion reinforced by the media. Calling him "The Donald," a nickname used by his first wife, TV reporters and magazines commented relentlessly on his marriages and divorces and the extravagant lifestyle that his $3 billion real estate empire made possible.

Trump personified the materialistic values of the Reagan era. Accustomed to the elegance and extravagance of Hollywood, Ronald and Nancy Reagan created an affluent atmosphere in the White House that contrasted sharply with the austerity of the 1970s and Jimmy and Rosalynn Carter's subdued lifestyle. At Carter's inauguration in 1977, the Carter family dressed simply, walked to the ceremony, and led an evening of restrained merrymaking; four years later, Reagan and his wealthy Republican supporters racked up inauguration expenses of $16 million. Critics lambasted the extravagance of Trump and the Reagans, but many Americans joined with them in celebrating the return of American prosperity and promise.

The Boom Years of the 1990s. The economic resurgence of the late 1980s did not restore America's once dominant position in the international economy. The nation's heavy industries — steel, autos, chemicals — continued to lose market share, both because of weak executive leadership and because of the relatively high wages paid to American workers. Nonetheless, during the 1990s the economy of the United States grew at the impressive average rate of 3 percent per year. Moreover, its main international competitors were now struggling. In Germany, France, and other European industrial nations, high taxes and high wages stifled economic growth, while in Japan spectacular busts in the speculative-driven real estate and stock markets in 1989 crippled the economy. Its banking system burdened by billions of yen in bad debts, Japan limped though the 1990s with a meager growth rate of 1.1 percent a year.

Meanwhile, boom times came to the United States. During Bill Clinton's two terms in the White House (1993–2001), the stock market value of American companies nearly tripled. This boom, which was fueled by the flow of funds into high-tech and e-commerce firms, enriched American citizens and their governments. Middle-income families who were covered by pension plans saw their retirement savings suddenly double and felt good about the future. Simultaneously, the taxes collected on stock sales and profits provided a windfall for the state and federal governments. By 2000, the Clinton administration had paid off half of the enormous national debt created during the Reagan and Bush presidencies and was sending balanced budgets to Congress. Indeed, on the basis of recent events, the Congressional Budget Office projected an astonishing surplus of $4.6 trillion in governmental revenue during the coming decade.

As was the case during the Reagan era, the prosperity of the Clinton years was not equally distributed. By 1998 the income of the wealthiest 13,000 families in the United States was greater than the poorest 20 *million* families. Moreover, the good times did not last. A spectacular "bust" hit the over-inflated stock market in late 2000; within two years

Donald Trump

Some people are larger than life, and Donald Trump is certainly one of them. The beneficiary of an inheritance of $200 million from his father, "The Donald" built a series of spectacular hotels and condominiums, first in New York City and later in Atlantic City and Palm Beach. Trump's grandiose vision — of himself and his projects — has often placed him in vulnerable personal and financial situations. But neither a bitter divorce nor brushes with bankruptcy have dented his ego and ambition. He is pictured here in 1989 in the atrium of the Trump Tower in New York City.
Photo by Ted Thai/Time Life Pictures/Getty Images.

stock values fell about 40 percent (Figure 31.3). Their savings suddenly worth less, older Americans delayed their retirements. Faced by falling tax revenues, state governments cut services to balance their budgets, and the federal government again spent billions more than it collected.

Globalization

As Americans sought economic security, they recognized that their success depended in part on developments in the world economy. In one sense, this situation was not new. Over the centuries, Americans had depended on foreign markets for their tobacco, cotton, wheat, and industrial goods, and they had long received manufactures and millions of immigrants from other countries. But the *intensity* of international exchange varied over time, and it was again on the upswing. The end of the Cold War had shattered the political barriers that had restrained international trade and impeded capitalist development of vast areas of the world. Moreover, new communication systems — satellites, fiber optic cables, global positioning networks — would shrink

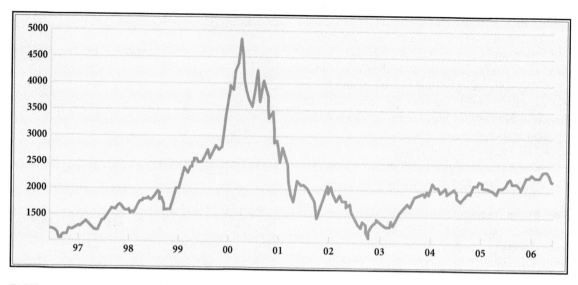

FIGURE 31.3 Boom and Bust in the Stock Market

In late 1999, the stock market took off. The rise of stocks listed on the NASDAQ (National Association of Security Dealers) Exchange was particularly rapid because of its heavy emphasis on technology companies. In little more than a year, the NASDAQ (pronounced *nass-dak*) index tripled in value. Its descent was equally quick. By mid-2002, the index was back where it started, and it continued to fall until early 2003. As in all booms and busts, fortunes were made — and lost — overnight.

the world to a degree unimaginable at the beginning of the twentieth century. The global economy was about to enter a new phase.

International Organizations. During the final decades of the Cold War, the leading capitalist industrial nations formed the Group of Seven (or G-7) to discuss — and manage — global economic policy. The G-7 nations — the United States, Britain, Germany, Italy, Japan, Canada, and France — largely controlled the activities of the major international financial organizations: the World Bank, the International Monetary Fund (IMF), and the General Agreement on Tariffs and Trade (GATT). During the 1990s these organizations became more inclusive. Russia joined the G-7, which became the Group of Eight (G-8), and in 1995 GATT evolved into the World Trade Organization (WTO), with nearly 150 member nations.

Working through the WTO, the promoters of freer global trade achieved many of their goals. They won reductions in tariff rates in many nations and removed many restrictions to the free international movement of capital investments (and profits). The WTO also negotiated agreements that facilitated international telecommunications, the settlement of contractual disputes, and (with less success) the protection of intellectual property rights. Many agreements benefited the wealthier nations; in return, the industrial nations agreed to

increase their imports of agricultural products, textiles, and raw materials from developing countries. Thanks to such measures, the value of American imports and exports rose from 17 percent of GNP in 1978 to 25 percent in 2000. By then, the worldwide volume of international exchange in goods and money had risen to about $1 trillion per day.

As globalization — the worldwide flow of capital, trade, and people — accelerated, so did the integration of regional economies. In 1991 the nations of western Europe created the European Union (EU) and began to move toward the creation of a single federal state (somewhat like the United States). Beginning as a free-trade zone, the EU subsequently promoted the free movement of its peoples among countries without passports and, in 2002, introduced a single currency, the euro (Map 31.1).

To offset the economic clout of the Euro-bloc, in 1993 the United States, Canada, and Mexico signed the North American Free Trade Agreement (NAFTA). This treaty, as ratified by the U.S. Congress, provides for the eventual creation of a free-trade zone covering all of North America; in 2005, some of its provisions were extended to the Caribbean and South America. In East Asia, the capitalist nations of Japan, South Korea, Taiwan, and Singapore consulted on matters of economic policy; as China gradually developed a quasi-capitalist economy, they included its Communist government in their deliberations.

MAP 31.1 Growth of the European Community, 1951–2005

The European Community (EU) began in the 1950s as a loose organization of western European nations. Over the course of the following decades, it created stronger common institutions, such as a European Parliament in Strasbourg, the EU Commission in Brussels, and a Court of Justice in Luxembourg. With the collapse of communism, the EU has expanded to include the nations of eastern and central Europe. It now includes twenty-five nations and 450 million people.

Multinational Corporations and American Labor.

The growing number of multinational business corporations testified to the extent of globalization. In 1970, there were 7,000 corporations with offices and factories in multiple countries; by 2000, the number had exploded to 63,000. Many of the most powerful multinationals are American based. Wal-Mart, the biggest retailer in the United States, is also the world's largest corporation, with 1,200 stores in other nations and $32 billion in foreign sales. The McDonald's restaurant chain is equally pervasive. In 1980, McDonald's had 1,000 outlets outside the United States; twenty years later, there were nearly 13,000 and "McWorld" had become a popular short-hand term for globalization. While retaining its emphasis on American-style fast food, the company adapted its menu to local markets. In Finland, customers purchased a McRye; in Chile, a McNifica; and in India, Veg McCurry Pan.

The intensification of globalization dealt another blow to the fragile position of organized labor in the United States. In the 1950s, 33 percent of nonfarm American workers belonged to unions; by 1980, the number had fallen to 20 percent, and President Reagan helped to push it still lower. Shortly after coming into office, he crushed a major union of public employees. When federal workers represented by PATCO (the Professional Air Traffic Controllers' Or-

ganization) went on strike for higher pay and benefits, the president declared the strike to be illegal, fired 11,000 controllers who did not return to work, and broke the union. Heartened by Reagan's firm stance, corporate managers resisted the demands of labor unions at Eastern Airlines and Caterpillar Tractors. A few unions — such as the West Coast Longshoremen's Union and the Teamsters' Union — won important strikes, but their successes did not reverse the long decline of organized labor. By 1998, union members represented only 13.9 percent of the labor force, and by 2004, only 12.5 percent.

Globalization was partly responsible for the recent declines. To take advantage of low-cost labor, many multinational corporations closed their factories in the United States and "outsourced" manufacturing jobs to plants in Mexico, eastern Europe, and especially Asia. The athletic sportswear firm Nike was a prime example. Ignoring ideological boundaries, the company established manufacturing plants for its shoes and apparel in Communist Vietnam and China as well as capitalist Indonesia. By the mid-1990s, Nike had 150 factories in Asia that employed more than 450,000 workers, most of whom received low wages and endured harsh working conditions. Highly skilled jobs were outsourced as well. American corporations — Chase Manhattan Bank, Dell Computer, General Electric, and many

"McWorld" and Globalization in Saudi Arabia
Many of the leading multinational corporations transforming the world's economy are purveyors of American-style consumer goods like Nike and Disney products. So successful was McDonald's in extending its international markets with 13,000 foreign outlets that many critics refer to the results of globalization in general as "McWorld." AP Images.

others—hired English-speaking Indians to staff consumer call centers; and many American firms hired electrical engineers and computer technicians in Bangalore and other Indian high-tech centers.

From the standpoint of corporate profits, outsourcing made sense. In 2005 an American graduate of the California Institute of Technology could expect a starting salary of $56,000, while a graduate of the Indian Institute of Technology commanded only one-third as much. Viewed from a national economic perspective, the outsourcing of skilled American jobs seemed more problematic. Unlike the "brain drain" that brought tens of thousands of foreign-born doctors, engineers, scientists, and technicians to the United States, where they enriched its society, outsourcing undermined the wages of American workers and threatened the long-term vitality of its economy.

Outsourcing had a cultural as well as an economic impact. One of Nike's advertising campaigns, focused on American basketball superstar Michael Jordan, sold millions of pairs of shoes and made Jordan an international celebrity. It also spread American entrepreneurial values as Nike's ads urged people around the world to "Just Do It." Some of them took up the challenge. Yao Ming, a 7′6″ basketball star in China, joined the Houston Rockets, one of a dozen or more players from European and Asian countries who now played in the National Basketball Association. In professional sports, as in other businesses, owners now drew their employees from around the world. In the pursuit of productivity and profit in the new global economy, the political boundaries of nation-states became increasingly irrelevant.

Disease and Death in an Interconnected World.
An exponential growth in the movement of people and ideas across borders was yet another marker of a shrinking world. On any given day in the late twentieth century, an estimated two million travelers and immigrants crossed an international border. Ideas moved even faster. Communications satellites transmitted phone conversations, television programs, and business data through the air, while fiber optic cables instantaneously connected e-mail users and World Wide Web servers in distant continents.

As the globe shrank in size, certain dangers increased in magnitude. In 1918 and 1919, soldiers from distant lands spread a killer flu virus from the battlefields of Europe to most of the world (see Chapter 22). That vicious pandemic killed fifty million people. An equally deadly disease, the human immunodeficiency virus (HIV), spread from Africa to the United States during the 1970s. In 1981 American physicians recognized HIV as a new disease, one that was killing hundreds of gay males, who had become its main carriers. Within two decades HIV, which causes AIDS (acquired immune deficiency syndrome), had spread worldwide, infected over fifty million people of both sexes, and killed more than twenty million.

Within the United States, AIDS took thousands of lives—more than died in the Korean and Vietnam wars combined. Then, between 1995 and 1999, American deaths from HIV dropped 30 percent. This decline—the result of new treatment strategies using a combination of drugs, or a "cocktail"—led to cautious optimism about controlling the disease, for which there is no cure. The high cost of

A Nike Factory in China

In 2005, Nike produced its shoes and sportswear at 124 plants in China; additional factories were located in other low-wage countries. Most of the Chinese plants are run by subcontractors, who house the workers — mostly women between the ages of sixteen to twenty-five — in crowded dormitories. The wages are low, about $3 a day, but more than the women could earn if they remained in their rural villages. AP Images.

these drugs limited their availability, particularly in poor nations. In sub-Saharan Africa, the HIV crisis has reached epidemic proportions, with 30 million infections. South and Southeast Asia, as well as countries of the former Soviet Union, also have millions of infected people — five million in India alone.

Other life-threatening diseases have the potential to spread around the world in days. In February 2003, a viral respiratory illness called SARS (severe acute respiratory syndrome) appeared in China. Within a few months, the disease spread to more than two dozen countries in North America, South America, Europe, and Asia. Despite elaborate public health measures, the virus infected over eight thousand people and killed almost eight hundred of them. And in 2006 a bird virus infected — and killed — a few dozen people and raised the prospect of a new pandemic, if the bird virus mutates to a form that easily spreads among humans.

The Endangered Environment. The expanding global economy also threatened the health of the world's peoples by polluting the environment. In some countries, the rapid rise in the number of mines, factories, and power plants destroyed irreplaceable natural resources or rendered them unusable. During the last three decades in Brazil, land-hungry peasants, lumber companies, and agribusinesses have cut down roughly a third of the region's ancient rain forests. In Taiwan and China, waste products from new industries and farms have polluted nearly every river — killing fish and rendering the water unsafe to drink.

The industrialized nations also threatened the environment. As millions of cars and thousands of

AIDS in Africa

AIDS (acquired immune deficiency syndrome) originated in Africa, where a chimpanzee virus jumped to humans in the 1960s, and it has taken its greatest toll on that continent. This man, from the Rakai province in southern Uganda, is dying — slowly wasting away — and is completely dependent for support on his twelve-year-old daughter. The Uganda government has implemented an AIDS-prevention program in Rakai and elsewhere and has reported a decline in the prevalence of HIV, the virus that causes AIDS. But it appears that the decline in the number of HIV-infected people is primarily the result of the deaths of many of them. In 2002 in Rakai, 200 people with long-standing HIV infections died, and 125 people became newly infected. Photo by Michael Jensen/www.world-photo.dk.

power plants in Europe and North America burned coal, oil, and other hydrocarbons, they raised the temperature of the atmosphere and the acidity of the oceans — a "greenhouse" effect with potentially momentous consequences. Similarly, the decades-long release into the atmosphere of chlorofluorocarbons (CFCs) — compounds used in industrial cleaning agents, refrigerators, and aerosol cans — significantly depleted the layer of ozone that protects humans from the sun's dangerous ultraviolet rays.

These dangers prompted thousands of Americans to join environmental-protection organizations, such as the Sierra Club and the Nature Conservatory. These groups, and officials of the Environmental Protection Agency, successfully curtailed some pollution. But they were unable to alter

government policy on major issues or to convince their fellow citizens of the wisdom of conservation. Ignoring warnings of tightening of oil supplies, the Reagan and Bush administrations refused to support legislation raising mileage requirements for car manufacturers. General Motors and Ford likewise rejected such warnings because they wanted to sell more high-profit gas-guzzling SUV's and small trucks. Nor would most American consumers voluntarily change their lifestyles to reduce energy consumption and cut pollution.

Still, the United States supported a few environmental initiatives. In 1987 the United States was one of thirty-four nations that signed the Montreal Protocol, which banned the production of ozone-damaging CFCs by 1999. The American government likewise joined sixty-three other countries in the Basel Convention of 1994, which ended the export of hazardous wastes to developing countries. Still, American businesses and their political allies resisted efforts to prevent global warming. Although President Clinton signed the Kyoto Treaty of 1998, which committed industrialized countries to reduce greenhouse-gas emissions, the U.S. Senate refused to ratify the agreement. In 2001, the administration of George W. Bush rejected the Kyoto accord, both because it did not apply to underdeveloped countries—which were some of the worst polluters—and because it would restrict or raise the cost of American economic production.

Globalization and Its Critics. President George W. Bush has celebrated globalization as "the triumph of human liberty stretching across national borders . . . [and holding] the promise of delivering billions of the world's citizens from disease and hunger and want." Critics are less optimistic. Some see globalization as a new form of imperialism, whereby the industrialized nations exploit the peoples and natural resources of the rest of the world. Giving political form to these criticisms, Lori Wallach founded Public Citizens' Global Watch, an organization whose goal was to promote "democracy by challenging corporate globalization." Condemning multinational corporations for their failure to protect workers or the environment, Global Watch spearheaded a massive protest at the World Trade Organization meeting in Seattle in 1999. Thousands of activists, including union organizers, environmentalists, and concerned students, disrupted the city and prevented the WTO from convening. As one protestor explained, people "can't go to the

WTO Demonstration, Seattle, 1999

In November 1999, an estimated 75,000 people from many states and foreign nations staged an effective protest at a World Trade Organization (WTO) meeting in Seattle. The goals of the protesters were diffuse; many feared that the trend toward a system of free (capitalist-run) trade would primarily benefit multinational corporations and would hurt both developing nations and the working classes in the industrialized world. Protests have continued at subsequent meetings of the WTO and the World Bank. Hector Mata/AFP/Getty Images.

polls and talk to these big conglomerates. So they had to take to the streets and talk to them." Similar protests against globalization have occurred at meetings of the World Bank, International Monetary Fund, and the G-8 nations.

Indeed, on the occasion of a G-8 meeting in Scotland in 2005, critics mounted a worldwide protest against the financial impact of globalization on poor countries. "Live-8" assembled an international cast of music stars who gave free concerts at ten venues — stretching from London to Tokyo and from Philadelphia to Johannesburg. Broadcast on television and the World Wide Web, the concerts reached a huge audience. Although the concerts helped to persuade the G-8 nations to forgive billions of dollars of debts owned by African nations, they did little to address the internal corruption that has gravely hindered those countries' development. Still, by using the communication infrastructure of the global world, critics had forced a discussion of its effects.

➤ What were the sources of the American economic recovery of the 1980s and 1990s? Who were its heroes, and what were its shortcomings?

➤ What factors promoted "globalization"?

➤ Outline the arguments for and against globalization. Who is making these arguments? Why?

The New Technology

The technological advances that enabled Live-8 had already changed the character of everyday life for millions of Americans. Computers, cell phones, the Internet, and other electronic-based devices altered work, leisure, and access to knowledge in stunning ways.

The Computer Revolution

Scientists devised the first computers — information-processing machines that stored and manipulated data — for military purposes during World War II. Subsequently, the federal government funded computer research as part of the drive for American military superiority during the Cold War. Using this research, private companies began to build large "main frame" computers. In 1952, CBS News used UNIVAC (Universal Automatic Computer), the first commercial computer system, to predict the outcome of the presidential election.

Innovation and Miniaturization. The first computers were cumbersome and finicky machines. They used heat-emitting vacuum tubes for computation power and punched cards for writing programs and analyzing data. UNIVAC and other main-frame computers occupied an entire air-conditioned room, and programming them took several days. In 1947, scientists at Bell Labs invented the transistor, a tiny silicon device that amplifies a signal or opens or closes a circuit many times each second. The transistor revolutionized the electronics industry and allowed technicians to build a second generation of computers — smaller, more powerful, and much cheaper to manufacture. Then in 1959, scientists invented the integrated circuit — a silicon microchip composed of large numbers of interconnected transistors — and ushered in the third computer generation.

Progress continued at an unrelenting pace, as computer wizards devised smaller and more sophisticated chips. A great breakthrough came in 1971 with the development of the microprocessor, which placed the entire central processing unit (CPU) of a computer on a single silicon chip about the size of the letter "O" on this page. By the mid-1970s, a few chips provided as much processing power as a World War II–era computer.

The day of the personal computer (PC) had arrived. In 1977, the Apple Corporation offered a personal computer for $1,195 (about $3,300 today), a price middle-class Americans could afford. When the Apple II became a runaway success, other companies scrambled to get into the market. International Business Machines (IBM) offered its first personal computer in 1981. In three decades, the computer had moved from a few military research centers, to thousands of corporate offices, and then to millions of people's homes. In the process, it created huge entrepreneurial opportunities and a host of overnight millionaires.

Bill Gates and Microsoft. Making computers user-friendly was the major challenge of the PC revolution. In the early 1970s, two former high-school classmates, Bill Gates, aged nineteen, and Paul Allen, twenty-one, set a goal of putting "a personal computer on every desk and in every home." They perceived that the key was "software," the programs that would tell the electronic components (the "hardware") what to do. In 1975 they founded the Microsoft Corporation, which soon dominated the software industry. The phenomenal success of Microsoft's MS-DOS and Windows operating systems stemmed primarily from the company's ability to anticipate industry trends, develop products

Triumph of the Geeks: Microsoft Employees, 1978

This group portrait shows eleven of Microsoft's thirteen employees as the company was about to relocate from Albuquerque, New Mexico, to Seattle, Washington. The oldest member was Paul Allen (front row, far right), age twenty-five; Bill Gates (front row, far left) was twenty-three. A quarter of a century later, Allen was worth $20 billion, Gates was worth nearly $100 billion, and Microsoft had more than fifty thousand employees. Courtesy, Bob Wallace.

quickly, and market them relentlessly. As a Microsoft veteran described the corporate strategy: "See where everybody's headed, then catch up and go past them." And pass them it did. By 2000, the company's products ran nine out of every ten personal computers in the United States and a majority of those around the world. Bill Gates became a billionaire, and Microsoft exploded into a huge company with 57,000 employees and annual revenue of $38 billion. Indeed, Microsoft's near-monopoly of basic computer operating systems prompted government regulators in the United States and the European Union to lodge antitrust suits against the company and force changes in its business practices.

The Impact of the Internet. During the 1990s, personal computers grew even more significant with the spread of the Internet and the World Wide Web. Like the computer itself, the Internet was the product of military-based research. During the 1970s, the Pentagon set up a system of hundreds of computers (or "servers") that were widely dispersed across the United States and connected to each other by copper wires (and now by fiber optic cables). Designed to preserve military communications in the event of a Soviet nuclear attack, the system was soon used by government scientists, academic specialists, and military contractors to exchange text-based e-mail messages via their computers.

The debut in 1991 of the graphics-based World Wide Web, a vast collection of interconnected documents, enhanced the popular appeal and commercial possibilities of the Internet. By 2006, nearly 70 percent of all Americans and slightly more than one billion people worldwide used the Internet to send messages or to view material on the Web. The Web al-

lowed companies, organizations, and individuals to create their own "home pages," incorporating visual, audio, and textual information. Businesses used the Internet to sell their products and services; the volume of e-commerce transactions grew steadily, to $114 billion in 2003 and $172 billion in 2005. During his unsuccessful bid for the 2004 Democratic presidential nomination, Governor Howard Dean of Vermont demonstrated the political potential of the Internet, by using it to raise money and mobilize grassroots support for his campaign. Other politicians and social activists have followed his lead, using the Internet and the Web in ever more creative ways.

Already thousands of businesses were using networked computers — creating the modern electronic office. Small companies kept their records and did all their correspondence and billing on a few desktop machines; large corporations set up linked computers that shared a common database. Some employees no longer came physically to the office; some days they worked as "telecommuters" with their home computers and fax machines connected to the office network by telephone lines, fiber optic cables, and wireless relay systems.

Computers and the Internet transformed leisure as well as work. Millions of Americans took advantage of e-mail to stay in close touch with family and friends. More anonymously, they joined online chat rooms, dating services, and interactive games. Those with broadband connections to the Internet watched "streaming videos" of news events and downloaded music videos and feature films. Interestingly — and importantly — millions of users tried to persuade others to see the world as they do. In 1997 a few people began personal online diaries called Web logs or "blogs"; by 2004, the number of bloggers had grown to eight million, and they offered their authors' perspectives on a wide range of issues: politics, diplomacy, and consumer affairs.

More profoundly, the Web empowered people by providing easy access to knowledge. For nearly two centuries, local public libraries had served that function; now, much of the content of a library was instantly available in a home or office. Using powerful "search engines" such as Google and Yahoo!, people easily located information—some wonderfully accurate and some distressingly problematic—on nearly every subject under the sun. Millions of Americans regularly read newspapers online and used the Web to acquire medical information about diet, drugs, and disease. Students and scholars mined the Web's digital archives and online journals; lawyers used Lexis-Nexis programs for immediate access to hundreds of cases on specific legal issues. Many things that libraries did well, the Web did wonderfully.

Small Electronics. Advances in electronic technology fostered the rapid creation of new leisure and business products. The 1980s saw the introduction of videocassette recorders (VCRs), compact disc (CD) players, cellular telephones, and inexpensive fax machines. Hand-held video camcorders joined film-based cameras as instruments for preserving family memories; parents video-taped their children's lives—sports achievements, graduations, and marriages—and played them on the home television screen. By 2000, cameras took digital pictures that could be stored and transmitted on computers, digital video discs (DVDs) became the newest technology for viewing movies, and TiVo (a direct video recording system) gave television viewers enormous flexibility in watching programs. At the same time, higher resolution television sets, flat plasma screens, and home theater setups became more affordable and widely disseminated.

Wireless telephones (or cell phones), which became available in the 1980s, presaged a communications revolution. By 2003, two-thirds of American adults carried these portable devices, and people under thirty used them in an increasing variety of ways—to take pictures, play games, connect to the Internet, and send text messages. Building on wireless technology for computers, prosperous families created a home network of telephones, computers, and media/entertainment systems. In 2001, Apple Computer revolutionized the pop music industry with the iPod, a hand-sized unit that stored up to 5,000 songs, and iTunes, a system for downloading music from the Web. By 2006, iPods could store and play video. This revolution in technology, like the cultural revolution of the 1960s, was increasingly the work of the young, who dragged their parents into the new information age.

Legal, Ethical, and Social Issues. Like all new technologies, the computers-Internet-electronics revolution raised a host of social issues and legal conflicts. Many disputes involved the "pirating" of intellectual property through the illegal reproduction of a computer program or a content file. Microsoft and other software companies devised a variety of technical and legal stratagems to protect their copyrighted products, which usually cost millions of dollars to develop. Similarly, the recording industry used lawsuits to shut down the NAPSTER program, which allowed music buffs to share songs through the Internet and burn their own CDs for virtually no cost. Yet intellectual piracy continues, both because of the refusal of governments in China and elsewhere to protect copyrights and because of the decentralized character of the new technology. Just as the Defense Department's system of hundreds of servers would "work around" a Soviet attack, so the existence of millions of personal computers (and skilled operators) has thwarted efforts to police their use.

Computers empowered scientists as well as citizens. Researchers in many scientific disciplines used powerful "supercomputers" to analyze complex natural and human phenomena ranging from economic forecasting to nuclear fusion to human genetics. In 1990, officials at the National Science Foundation allocated $350 million for the Human Genome Project. The Project's goal was to map the human genetic code and unravel the mysteries of DNA (deoxyribonucleic acid), the basic building block of all living things. In 1998, Celera Genomics, a private company backed by pharmaceutical corporations, launched a competing project in hopes of developing profitable drugs. Eventually the two groups pooled their efforts and, by 2003, had built a map of every human gene and posted it, free of charge, on the Web.

As scientists used computers and other technological innovations to probe the mysteries of life, they revived long-standing moral debates. Should employers or insurance companies be permitted to use genetic testing for purposes of hiring or health-care coverage? Should the stem cells from aborted (or in vitro produced) fetuses be used in the search for cures for Alzheimer's, AIDS, and other debilitating diseases (see Chapter 32)? As commentators debated these biomedical issues, other observers worried about the negative impact of the new computer-based technology. Would the use of automatic telephone menus, bank ATMs, and scanners in retail stores gradually create a machine-driven world in which people had little contact with each other? Would the use of the Web by children and

The Biotech Revolution

In 1953, scientists James Watson, Francis Crick, and Roslyn Franklin discovered the double helix structure of DNA (deoxyribonucleic acid), the molecule that carries the distinct genetic blueprint of specific living things. Once DNA's structure was understood, it became theoretically possible to isolate the genetic codes that control nearly every human characteristic — from height and hair color to inherited diseases and certain cancers. But the process would be enormously complicated, given that there are nearly three billion nucleic acid base pairs in just one set of human chromosomes. With the assistance of computer-linked, automated gene-sequencing machines (like these at the Whitehead Institute at MIT), scientists produced a genetic blueprint of the human species in 2003. The medical payoffs are still to come. © Sam Ogden, Photo Researchers.

youths expose them to sexual abuse? Could personal and financial privacy be preserved in a digital world in which businesses and governments could easily create an electronic "profile" of people's lives and hack into their computers?

Political questions were equally challenging. What were the implications of the Patriot Act of 2001 (see Chapter 32), which permits the federal government to monitor electronically citizens' telephone, e-mail, Web, and library usage? Is the loss of civil privacy and liberty an acceptable price to pay for increased security from terrorists? Such questions, debated throughout the twentieth century, acquired increased urgency in the electronic age.

Finally, would a "digital divide" accentuate existing class and racial divisions? Would affluent Americans who could afford computers and Internet access race ahead of poorer citizens? The evidence was contradictory. In 2005, fewer than half of the families with incomes of $30,000 or less had home access to the Internet. Yet most poorer children and adults had access to the new technology and the global communications network because the local, state, and federal governments have connected computers in schools and public libraries to the Internet and the Web.

Technology and the Control of Popular Culture

Americans have reveled in mass-consumer culture ever since the 1920s, when the spread of automobiles, electric appliances, movies, and radio enhanced the quality of everyday life and leisure. By exposing citizens to the same movies and radio programs, the new communication technologies also helped to forge a homogeneous national popular culture. During the 1950s, the spread of television — and its domination by three networks: ABC, CBS, and NBC — likewise encouraged the emergence of a uniform perspective among a majority of middle-class Americans.

Fragmentation in the Television Industry.
During the 1970s, new technological developments reshaped the television industry and the cultural landscape. The advent of cable and satellite broadcasting brought more specialized networks and programs into American living rooms. People now got news round-the-clock from Ted Turner's CNN (Cable News Network), watched myriad sports events on the ESPN channels, and tuned into the Fox network for innovative entertainment. By the 1990s, millions of viewers had access to scores, sometimes hundreds, of specialized channels. They could watch old or new

movies, golf tournaments, and cooking classes; view religious or African American or Hispanic programming; and buy goods on home-shopping channels. By 1998, such specialized programming had captured 53 percent of the prime-time TV audience.

One of the most successful niche channels was MTV (Music TV), which debuted in 1981. Initially, its main offerings were slickly made videos featuring popular vocalists, who sang and acted out the words of their songs. Essentially advertisements for CDs, these videos were extremely popular among teenagers, who often watched the channel for two hours a day. With its flashy colors, creative choreography, and rapid cuts, MTV popularized singers such as Michael Jackson and Madonna and pushed forward the creation of a culture based on visual and aural "stimulation."

As television became more competitive, network and cable programmers increasingly laced their shows with sexual stimulation. As a television executive explained, "In a cluttering environment where there are so many more media, you have to be more explicit and daring to stand out." In the 1980s network stations began to feature steamier plots on daytime and evening soaps, like *Dallas* and *Dynasty*, while in the 1990s cable shows, such as Home Box Office's (HBO) *Sex in the City*, aired partial nudity and explicit discussion of sexual relations. Talk-show hosts, ranging from the respectable Oprah Winfrey to the shocking Jerry Springer, recruited ordinary Americans to share the secrets of their personal lives — which often involved sexuality, drug abuse, and domestic violence. As the American pop-artist Andy Warhol had predicted, ordinary people eagerly embraced the opportunity to expose their lives and to be "world-famous for 15 minutes."

As TV became more "stimulating" and "reality" oriented, critics argued that it negatively shaped people's outlooks and actions. For evidence they cited violent television dramas, such as HBO's critically acclaimed series *The Sopranos*, which interweaved the personal lives of a Mafia family with the amoral and

Oprah Winfrey

Oprah Winfrey is an American success story. She was born in 1954 to unwed parents, lived first with her grandmother in rural Mississippi and then with her mother in Milwaukee and her father in Nashville. After graduating from Tennessee State University, she became a radio broadcaster and hit the big time in the mid-1980s, with a successful debut as a movie actress and as a national television daytime talk show host. Presently the *Oprah Winfrey Show* boasts a weekly audience of 21 million in 105 countries. Here she chats with author Toni Morrison, whose prize-winning novels Oprah has publicized on her Book Club. © Reuters / Corbis.

relentless violence of their business deals. Did the impact of the dozens of such violence-focused dramas, combined with the widespread availability of guns, increase the already high American murder rate? Did it play a role in a series of shootings by high school students, which culminated in 1991 with the murder of twelve students and one teacher at Columbine High School in Littleton, Colorado? Some lawmakers thought so. In a half-hearted effort to thwart youthful violence, Congress stipulated in the Telecommunication Reform Act of 1996 that manufacturers include a "V-chip" in new TV sets to allow parents to block specific programs.

Deregulation and Media Giants: Warner-AOL and Rupert Murdoch.

As the controversy over TV violence indicates, technology never operates in a social and political vacuum. The expansion of cable television and specialized programming stemmed in part from policies set by the Federal Communications Commission (FCC) during the Reagan administration. Mark Fowler, the FCC chair, shared the president's disdain for government regulation of business. "Television is just another appliance. . . . It's a toaster with pictures," Fowler suggested, as the FCC eliminated requirements that stations provide extensive news programming and allow full debate on controversial political issues. Freed from such "public service" responsibilities, TV newscasts increasingly shunned serious coverage of political and economic events and focused on lurid events, such as floods, fires, murders, and scandals connected to celebrities. The troubled marriage and divorce of Prince Charles of England and Lady Diana—and her subsequent death—saturated the airwaves, and the distinction between news and entertainment became blurred.

Fowler's FCC also minimized controls over children's programming. Soon cartoon programs such as *G.I. Joe* and *Care Bears* became extended advertisements for licensed replicas of their main characters. Even the characters of the Public Broadcasting Service's popular *Sesame Street* joined the parade of licensed replicas, as consumer culture extended into the lives of the youngest Americans. Responding to complaints from parents and children's advocates, Congress enacted the Children's Television Act of 1990, which reinstated some restrictions, but the commercialization of virtually every aspect of childhood proceeded nonetheless.

Whatever the programming, the television stations that carried them were increasingly owned by a handful of large companies. In 1985, Congress raised the number of television stations a company could own from seven to twelve. Subsequent regulations promoted even more concentration in media ownership; by 2003, one company owned eight radio stations and three television stations in a single city, in addition to a newspaper and a TV cable system. On the national level, there was a similar trend toward monopolization. In 1990 Warner Communications merged with Time/Life to create an enormous entertainment corporation that included the Warner Brothers film studio, HBO, TNT, Six Flags, the Atlanta Braves, Atlantic Records, and the magazines of Time, Inc. (*Time, Fortune, Sports Illustrated,* and *People*). In 1995, the company brought in $21 billion in revenues. Subsequently, Warner Communications merged with America Online (renamed simply "AOL" in 2006), the largest provider of Internet access. Although this merger turned out to be a poor business decision, it testified to the growing cultural influence of a few giant corporations.

Australian-born entrepreneur Rupert Murdoch stands as the exemplar of concentrated media ownership in the new global economy. As of 2004, Murdoch owned satellite TV companies in five countries and a worldwide total of 175 newspapers; in the United States, his holdings included Direct TV, the Fox TV Network, the Twentieth Century Fox Studio, the *New York Post,* and thirty-five television stations. A conservative ideologue as well as an entrepreneur, Murdoch has used his news empire to promote his political views. His career indicates not only the technological dimensions of globalization but also the influence of conservative individuals, institutions, and ideas at the beginning of the twenty-first century.

➤ What are the most important aspects of the computer revolution? What are the social consequences of this changing technology?

➤ How is the computer revolution related to globalization?

➤ How did the television industry change after 1980? Why does it matter?

Culture Wars

Times of economic affluence, like the 1950s, often encourage social harmony by damping down class conflict. Such was not the case in the 1980s and 1990s, a prosperous era that was marked by unrelenting warfare over cultural issues. Rooted in the social divisions of the 1960s, these "culture wars" generally pitted religious conservatives against secular liberals. Often instigated by politicians to advance their candidacies, they focused primarily on issues of racial and ethnic pluralism, on challenges to traditional "family values," and on the

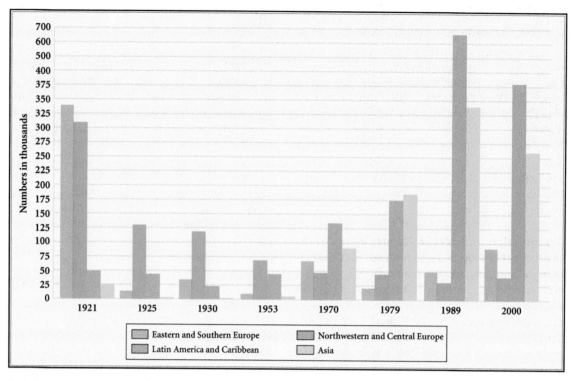

FIGURE 31.4 American Immigration, 1920–2000

Legislation inspired by nativism slowed the influx of immigrants after 1920, as did the dislocations brought on by economic depression and war in the 1930s and 1940s. Note the high rate of non-European immigration since the 1970s, the result of new eligibility rules in the Immigration Act of 1965 (see Chapters 27 and 28). The dramatic increase since 1980 in the number of migrants from Latin America and Asia reflects American economic prosperity, traditionally a magnet for migrants, and the rapid acceleration of illegal immigration.

rights of sexual minorities, especially gay men and women.

An Increasingly Pluralistic Society

In 1992, Republican presidential hopeful Patrick Buchanan warned Americans that their country was "undergoing the greatest invasion in its history, a migration of millions of illegal aliens a year from Mexico." A sharp-tongued cultural warrior, Buchanan exaggerated — but not by much. According to the Census Bureau, the population of the United States grew from 203 million people in 1970 to 280 million in 2000 (and topped 300 million in October 2006). Of that increase of 77 million, immigrants accounted for 28 million, with legal migrants numbering about 21 million and illegal entrants adding another 7 million (Figure 31.4). Relatively few migrants — legal or illegal — came from Europe (2 million), Africa (about 600,000), and Canada (250,000), the historical homelands of most American citizens. The overwhelming majority, some 25 million, came either from East Asia (9 million) or Latin America (16 million).

These immigrants and their children profoundly altered the demography of various states and the entire nation. By 2000, 27 percent of California's population was foreign-born; and Asians, Latinos, and native-born blacks constituted a majority of the residents. Nationally, there were now more Latinos (about 35 million) than African Americans (34 million), and Asians numbered over 12 million. Based on present rates of immigration and births, demographers predicted that by 2050 Americans of European descent would be a minority of the population. As Buchanan had pointed out, a "great invasion" was indeed changing the character — and the color — of American society. Small wonder that ethnic and racial diversity, long a source of conflict in American society, emerged as a prominent theme of the culture wars.

Latino and Asian Immigration. The massive inflow of *legal* immigrants was the unintended result of the Immigration Act of 1965, which allowed family members to join migrants already in the United States. Spanish-speaking Latinos took advantage of this provision; millions of Mexicans came to the United States, and hundreds of thousands arrived

MAP 31.2 Hispanic and Asian Populations, 2000

In 2000, people of Hispanic descent made up more than 11 percent of the American population, and now outnumber African Americans as the largest minority group. Asian Americans accounted for an additional 4 percent of the population. Demographers predict that by the year 2050 only about half of the U.S. population will be composed of non-Hispanic whites. Note the high percentage of Hispanics and Asians in California and certain other states.

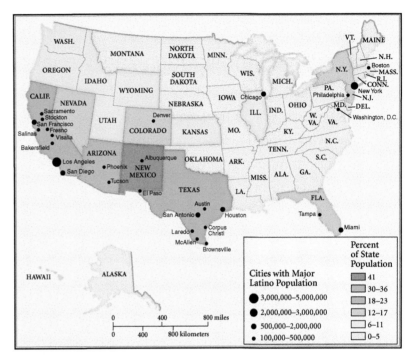

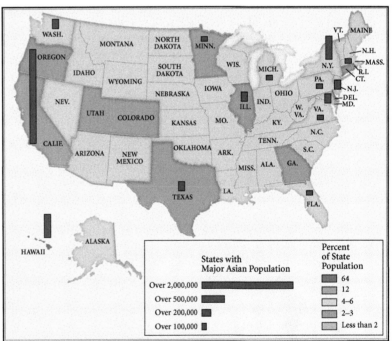

from El Salvador, Guatemala, and the Dominican Republic. Historically, most Latinos had lived in California, Texas, and New Mexico; now they settled in cities throughout the country—numbering 16 percent of the population in Florida and New York (see Map 31.2).

Most Latinos were poor men and women seeking a better life in the United States. They willingly worked for low wages—cleaning homes, tending lawns, servicing hotel rooms, painting houses,

working construction. Many labored "for cash, no questions asked"; as members of the "underground" economy, they did not pay income or Social Security taxes. Instead, many immigrants regularly sent funds to their families back home and urged them to migrate—legally or illegally. Their hopes lay in the future, especially in their American-born children, who could claim the rights of U.S. citizens (see Comparing American Voices, "Cheap Labor: Immigration and Globalization," pp. 978–979).

Cheap Labor: Immigration and Globalization

Immigrants populated the United States and they continue to remake it. But for whose benefit? Under what conditions? And at whose expense? Those are three of the questions raised by these testimonials from men and women employed in the labor-intensive industries of garment manufacturing and agricultural production.

GEORGE STITH AND JUANITA GARCIA
"Local farm workers could not get jobs at all"

George Stith and Juanita Garcia were farmworkers and union members. In 1952, they testified before a congressional committee considering whether to expand or restrict the Mexican "guest worker" (braceros) program.

STITH: Mr. Chairman and members of the committee, My name is George Stith. My address is Star Route Box 5, Gould, Ark. All my life I have worked on cotton plantations. When I was 4 years old my family moved to southern Illinois, near Cairo. We picked cotton in southeast Missouri, and west Tennessee nearly every year. We later moved across the river into Missouri and share-cropped. In 1930 we moved back to Arkansas. I don't know whether I am a migratory worker or not, but we certainly did a lot of migrating.

In 1936 when I was share cropping in Woodruff County, Ark. I joined the union which was then called the Southern Tenant Farmers Union. It is now the National Farm Labor Union, A. F. of L. I have been a member of the union ever since. . . .

For a long time I had heard about labor shortages in the West and how Mexican workers were being imported. I was sure that no people would be imported from Mexico to work on farms in Arkansas. There were too many people living in the little towns and cities who go out to chop and pick cotton. . . .

The importation of Mexican nationals into Arkansas did not begin until the fall of 1949. Cotton-picking wages in my section were good. We were getting $4 per 100 pounds for picking. As soon as the Mexicans were brought in the wages started falling. Wages were cut to $3.25 and $3 per 100 pounds. In many cases local farm workers could not get jobs at all. . . . The cotton plantation owners kept the Mexicans at work and would not employ Negro and white pickers. . . .

GARCIA: My name is Juanita Garcia. I live in Brawley, Calif. I work in the field and in the packing sheds. I lost my job in a packing shed about 2 weeks ago. I was fired because I belonged to the National Farm Labor Union. . . . My father, my brothers, and sisters also work on the farms. For poor people like us who are field laborers, making a living has always been hard. Why? Because the ranchers and companies have always taken over. . . .

In the Imperial Valley we have a hard time. It so happens that the local people who are American citizens cannot get work. . . . The wetbacks [illegal immigrants] and nationals from Mexico have the whole Imperial Valley. . . . The nationals and wetbacks take any wages the ranchers offer to pay them. The wages get worse every year. . . .

Last year they fired some people from the shed because they had nationals to take their jobs. There was a strike. . . . They took the nationals from the camps to break our strike. They had 5,000 scabs that were nationals. We told the Mexican consul about this. We told the Labor Department. They were supposed to take the nationals out of the strike. They never did take them away.

SOURCE: Migratory Labor, Hearings before Subcommittee on Labor and Labor-Management Relations, 82nd Congress, 2nd Session (Washington, D.C., Government Printing Office, 1952), 89–90, 93–94.

TRONG AND THANH NGUYEN
"We're political refugees. . . . We spend our money here."

Trong and Thanh Nguyen fled from Communist Vietnam in the mid-1970s.

TRONG: When my wife and I came to Chicago, our major concern was to feed our five small children. We had Vietnamese pride and did not want to take public aid. We wanted the American community and authorities to respect us.

Just trying to begin a new life here, we had so many difficulties. When I worked as a janitor at Water Tower Place, a co-worker told me, "Trong, do you know that America is overpopulated? We have more than two hundred million people. We don't need you. Go back where you belong." I was shocked to hear people trying to chase us out. . . .

THANH: When we first came to Chicago, I cried a lot. In the factory where I worked, there weren't many Americans. Most were Mexicans, some legal, but also many illegal aliens. . . . They cursed our people. Some Mexicans said, "You come here and take our jobs. Go back wherever you came from." . . . "You come here to make money, then go back home and live like kings." That was too much. I couldn't hold it in any more.

I told them in a very soft voice, "We are Vietnamese people. You don't have enough education to know where our country is. Vietnam is a small country, but we did not come to America to look for jobs. We're political refugees. We can't go back home." I didn't call them bad names or anything, but I said, "You are the ones who come here to make money to bring back to your country. We spend our money here." After that, they didn't bother us very much.

SOURCE: Paul S. Boyer, ed., *Enduring Voices*, 3rd ed. (Boston: Houghton Mifflin, 1996), 408–409.

PETRA MATA AND FEIYI CHEN

"Garment workers . . . made a decent living before free trade"

Petra Mata and Feiyi Chen are immigrants from low-wage countries who were "insourced"; on coming to the United States they worked as low-paid garment workers. Then, their jobs were "outsourced"—sent abroad to even lower-paid workers as a result of free trade and globalization.

MATA: My name is Petra Mata. I was born in Mexico. I have completed no more than the sixth grade in school. In 1969, my husband and I came to the U.S. believing we would find better opportunities for our children and ourselves. We first arrived without documents, then became legal, and finally became citizens. For years I moved from job to job until I was employed in 1976 by the most popular company in the market, Levi Strauss & Company. I earned $9.73 an hour and also had vacation and sick leave. Levi's provided me and my family with a stable situation, and in return I was a loyal employee and worked there for fourteen years.

On January 16, 1990, Levi's closed its plant in San Antonio, Texas, where I had been working, leaving 1,150 workers unemployed, a majority of whom were Mexican-American women. The company moved its factory to Costa Rica. . . .

As a result of being laid off, I personally lost my house, my method of transportation, and the tranquility of my home. My family and I had to face new problems. My husband was forced to look for a second job on top of the one he already had. He worked from seven in the morning to six at night. Our reality was very difficult. At that time, I had not the slightest idea what free trade was or meant. . . .

Our governments make agreements behind closed doors without participation from the working persons who are most affected by these decisions—decisions that to my knowledge only benefit large corporations and those in positions of power. . . .

CHEN: My name is Feiyi Chen. I immigrated to the United States in December 1998 from China. I began my working career as a seamstress in a garment factory because I did not speak English and the garment manufacturing industry was one of the few employment opportunities available to me. I typically worked ten hours a day, six days a week, at a backbreaking pace. Most garment bosses know that new immigrants have few choices when it comes to work and so they take advantage by paying workers less than the minimum wage with no overtime pay. . . . I learned from some of the older garment workers that garment workers in San Francisco actually made a decent living before free trade lured many of the better-paying garment factories over to other countries and forced the smaller and rule-abiding factories to shut down because they could not compete with the low cost of production from neighboring countries. . . .

Working as a seamstress and an assembly worker has always been hard, but with so many of the factories leaving the country in search of cheaper labor, life for immigrant workers like myself is getting worse. For example, many garment workers who were paid one dollar for sewing a piece of clothing are now only making fifty cents for the same amount of work. There are a lot of garment workers who still work ten hours a day but make less than thirty dollars a day.

SOURCE: Christine Ahn, *Shafted: Free Trade and America's Working Poor* (Oakland, CA: Food First Books, 2003), 32–38.

ANALYZING THE EVIDENCE

➤ Describe the experiences of the workers as related in their statements. What generalizations can you make about the impact of immigration on wages? On the relations among ethnic groups in the United States?

➤ How does "globalization," a major focus of this chapter, affect the lives of these workers? Provide some specific examples from the documents that show its impact.

➤ What role would these workers like the federal government to play? According to the discussion in this chapter, what is American policy with respect to globalization?

➤ Consider the questions raised in the introduction: Who benefits from immigration, legal or illegal? How does it affect working conditions? Is there a cost, and who pays it?

New Immigrants

In the 1980s, many Korean immigrants opened small grocery and fruit stores in urban neighborhoods. Their economic success was hard won — the result of disciplined saving and long hours of work — and often led to conflicts with poor blacks and Hispanics, who resented their rapid economic mobility. Kay Chernush.

Most Asian migrants came from China, the Philippines, South Korea, India, and Pakistan. In addition, 700,000 refugees migrated to the United States from Indochina (Vietnam, Laos, and Cambodia) after the Vietnam War. Some of these Asians were well educated or entrepreneurial; they adapted quickly and successfully to life in their new homeland. But a majority lacked professional or vocational skills and took low-paying jobs.

As in the past, the immigrants congregated in ethnic conclaves. In Los Angeles, Koreans created the thriving community of "Koreatown"; in Brooklyn, New York, Russian Jews settled in "Little Odessa"; Latino migrants took over entire sections of Chicago, the District of Columbia, Dallas, and Houston. As the number of immigrants grew, ethnic entrepreneurs catered to their tastes — establishing restaurants, food stores, clothing shops, and native-language newspapers — while mainstream department stores, car dealers, and politicians vied for their dollars and votes. Although many migrants worked and shopped outside their ethnic enclaves, they usually socialized, attended church, and married within the community.

Anti-immigrant Sentiment. While some native-born Americans celebrated this renewal of the nation's ethnic pluralism, many others worried about its massive size. Similar concerns had fueled nativist opposition to Irish Catholic immigrants in the 1840s and to Jews and Catholics from eastern

and southern Europe around 1900. As in the past, critics argued that immigrants assimilated slowly, depressed wages for all workers, and raised crime rates (see Voices from Abroad, "Janet Daley: A U.S. Epidemic," p. 981). They also sounded new and potent themes: that the rapidly rising population endangered the environment and burdened governments with millions of dollars in costs for schools, hospitals, police, and social services. Responding to such concerns, the Welfare Reform Act of 1996 curtailed the access of legal immigrants to food stamps and other welfare benefits.

The most far-reaching challenges to mass immigration emerged at the state level. In 1986, California voters overwhelmingly supported Proposition 63, which established English as the state's "official language," and seventeen other states followed suit. Eight years later, Californians approved Proposition 187, a ballot initiative forthrightly named "Save Our State," which barred illegal aliens from public schools, nonemergency care at public health clinics, and all other state social services. The initiative also required law enforcement officers, school administrators, and social workers to report suspected illegal immigrants to the Immigration and Naturalization Service. When a federal judge ruled that Proposition 187 was unconstitutional, supporters of the measure demanded that Congress take action to curtail legal migration and expel illegal entrants.

An unlikely coalition of politicians prevented the passage of such federal legislation. Heeding the pleas of business owners and large-scale farmers, who wanted a plentiful supply of low-wage workers, conservative Republicans refused to restrict immigration. Liberal Democrats also opposed such legislation because they supported ethnic pluralism and cultural diversity. Indeed, in 1986 Congress enacted (and President Reagan signed) a measure that granted amnesty to nearly two million illegal aliens and, in its lack of rigorous enforcement provisions, ensured that the flood of illegal migrants would continue, as indeed it has. By 2006, Congress was again debating this contentious issue.

African Americans. The dramatic increase in Asians and Latinos brought some benefits to African Americans. As immigrant workers took the lowest paid jobs in the construction, manufacturing, and hotel service industries, many blacks used their experience and facility in English to move into supervisory positions. Some of these African Americans joined the ranks of the middle classes and moved to better lives in the suburbs. Yet the poorer blacks who remained in the inner cities now paid more for housing because the demand from

Janet Daley

A U.S. Epidemic

Around 8:30 p.m. on April 19, 1989, marauding gangs of youths began to beat up joggers and bicyclists in New York City's Central Park. About the same time, Trisha Meilli, a twenty-nine-year-old American investment banker of Italian descent, was brutally raped, beaten, and left for dead in the park. In a coma for twelve days, Meilli did not remember any details of the attack. Five black and Latino young men from Harlem, arrested initially because of the gang attacks, confessed to the assault and served prison terms of seven to eleven years. In 2002, long after Daley's article appeared in an English newspaper, The Independent, *DNA tests pinned the attack on Matias Reyes, a convicted serial rapist and murderer. Reyes, who was born in Puerto Rico, told prison officials that he alone raped and beat the jogger.*

[London, August 29, 1990]
THE TRIAL in New York of the Central Park rapists has brought into focus two tacit assumptions that underpin conventional wisdom about America and the prognosis for our own [English] future.

The first is that everything wrong with American society is a result of its "system" (that is, its political and economic organisation). The second is that as our "system" becomes more like that of the United States (more free-market based), we shall inevitably suffer the same problems of a mindlessly violent underclass....

Both of these contentions seem to me wrong. To begin with, the notion that a country's social mores and attitudes are brought about entirely by the form of its government and economy is a bit of Marxist theoretical baggage that ought to be thrown out. ... It is an absurd idea that whatever is wrong with our social relations, or even our family lives, must be accounted for by the structure of our national institutions. Juvenile crime is a plague in communist China and alcoholism—a more traditional kind of drug abuse—is endemic in the Soviet Union.

Many of the worst instances of anarchic violence in America—such as the attack on the Central Park jogger—do not arise from the underclass in the proper economic sense at all. These boys were not notably poor, or from families without aspirations.

Those aspects of American life that are most repugnant—its lunatic viciousness and criminality—can be accounted for by purely historical circumstances which the political system could influence in only the most marginal way. The United States is an enormous continental landmass which was settled in an ad hoc, opportunist fashion by disparate groups of people with different motivations and lifestyles. This Babel-like chaos was governed in the most minimal way. ... Each immigrant group created its own cohesiveness. The Irish, the East Europeans, the Jews all had their communities which gave them some sense of security. And when the geographical communities began to disperse, there were still networks of tribal feeling and attachment.

Into this mix early this century came a great wave of Sicilians who brought with them their own family industry. The Mafia gained a hold in America at a time when law enforcement was nominal and social insecurity was universal. Having had its roots in the Little Italy of New York, it now runs the gambling, prostitution and drug empires of America. It has had deep connections with whole swathes of the transport industry through its connections with certain unions....

This pervasive influence of organised crime which arose through a historical coincidence—the arrival of a particular subculture in a loosely organised country which, for separate historical reasons, had committed itself constitutionally to the citizen's right to bear arms—is more central to the current problems of the US than its capitalist economy or its political ideology.

To describe Britain as inevitably on the same road is simple historical ignorance. For a stable and deeply conservative society to come to grips with immigrant groups may present us with a challenge, but it can never lead to the conditions with which America is faced, and which are the result of attempting to build a society from scratch out of a diverse and discordant collection of peoples.

The oppressive conformity and intolerance of American life arise from this compulsion to create a homogeneous culture out of ethnic chaos. A society without a central historical axis breeds chronic anxiety.

SOURCE: *The Independent* (London), August 29, 1990, p. 18.

ANALYZING THE EVIDENCE

➤ According to Daley, why is violence so widespread in the United States? How convincing is her analysis?

➤ Does Daley's argument provide insight into the rape of the Central Park jogger?

➤ What are we to make of Daley's conclusion, given the bombing of the London subway system in 2005 by four Muslim youth, three of whom were born in England of Pakistani descent?

immigrants drove up rents. Massive immigration also adversely affected many inner-city black children because overcrowded and underfunded schools diverted scarce resources to bilingual education for Spanish- and Chinese-speaking students.

Still, government policy continued to provide African Americans (and Latinos and white women) with preferential treatment in areas such as hiring for public sector jobs, "set-aside" programs for minority-owned businesses, and university admissions. Conservatives had long argued that such programs were deeply flawed because they amounted to intrusive governmental "social engineering," promoted "reverse discrimination" against white men, and resulted in the selection and promotion of less-qualified applicants. During the 1990s, conservatives — along with many Americans who believed in "equal opportunity" — demanded an end to such legal privileges.

Once again, California stood at the center of the debate. In 1995, under pressure from the Republican governor, Pete Wilson, the regents of the University of California voted to scrap its twenty-year-old policy of affirmative action. A year later, California voters approved Proposition 209, which banished affirmative action privileges in state employment and public education. When the number of Latino and African Americans admitted to the flagship Berkeley campus of the University of California plummeted, conservatives hailed the result as proving that the previous admissions policy had lowered intellectual standards. Avoiding a direct reply to that charge, liberals maintained that state universities should educate potential leaders of all ethnic and racial groups.

Affirmative action remained controversial. In 2001, the California Regents devised a new admissions plan to assist minority applicants; two years later the U.S. Supreme Court invalidated an affirmative action plan at the University of Michigan, but allowed racial-preference policies that promoted a "diverse" student body. In the face of growing public and judicial opposition, the future of such programs was uncertain.

Race and Crime: Rodney King and O. J. Simpson.

While affirmative action programs assisted some African Americans to rise into the middle classes, they did not address the social problems of poorer blacks. Millions of African Americans lived in households headed by wage-earning single mothers, who had neither the time nor the energy to supervise their children's lives. Many of their daughters bore babies at an early age, while their sons ran with street gangs and dealt in illegal drugs. To address drug use and the crimes that it generated, the Reagan administration urged young people to "Just Say No." This campaign had some success in cutting

drug use among middle-class black and white teenagers, but did not staunch the dangerous flow of crack cocaine into poor African American neighborhoods. "The police are losing the war against crack," *Newsweek* noted grimly in 1986, "and the war is turning the ghettos of major cities into something like a domestic Vietnam." Indeed, the murderous competition among black drug dealers took the lives of thousands of young African American men, and police efforts to stop drug use and trafficking brought the arrest and imprisonment of tens of thousands more.

In April 1992, this seething underworld of crime and urban impoverishment erupted in five days of race riots in Los Angeles. The worst civil disorder since the 1960s, the violence took sixty lives and caused $850 million in damage. The riot was set off by the acquittal (on all but one charge) of four white Los Angeles police officers accused of using excessive force in arresting a black motorist, Rodney King, who had led them on a wild car chase. A graphic amateur video showing the policemen kicking and clubbing King did not sway the predominantly white jury, even as it highlighted police brutality and the harassment of minorities.

The riot exposed the fragility of urban America and acute rifts between urban blacks and their immigrant neighbors. Many Los Angeles blacks resented recent immigrants from Korea, who had set up successful small retail businesses. When they

To Live and Die in L.A.

As rioters looted stores in South-Central Los Angeles and burned over one thousand buildings, the devastation recalled that caused by the African American riots in Watts in 1965. But Los Angeles was now a much more diverse community. More than 40 percent of those arrested in 1992 were Hispanic, and the rioters attacked Koreans and other Asians as well as whites. Silvie Kreiss/Liason.

tried to loot and burn these businesses during the riot, the Koreans fought them off with guns. Frustrated by high unemployment and crowded housing conditions, Latinos joined in the rioting and accounted for more than half of those arrested and a third of those killed. The riots represented both an expression of black rage at white injustice and the class-based looting of property by poor African Americans and immigrant Latinos.

In 1995, Los Angeles police worried about another black-led riot as the trial of O. J. Simpson neared its end. A renowned African American college and professional football player and a well-paid representative for Hertz Rental Cars, Simpson was accused of the brutal murder of his ex-wife, Nicole Brown Simpson, a white woman. The prosecution produced damning evidence of Simpson's guilt, but black defense attorney Johnnie Cochran argued that a police detective tampered with the evidence. More important, Cochran played the "race card," encouraging the predominately black jury to view Simpson as a victim of racial prejudice and to acquit him. Although a substantial majority of whites, in Los Angeles and the nation, believed that Simpson was guilty, they peacefully accepted the jury's verdict of "not guilty." In the 1990s, unlike the 1920s and 1940s, whites no longer resorted to racial riots to suppress or take revenge against blacks. Now it was African Americans who took to the streets.

Multiculturalism. For most of the twentieth century, supporters of civil rights for African Americans and other ethnic groups advocated their "integration" into the wider society and culture. Integration had been the dream of Martin Luther King Jr. and César Chavez (see Chapter 28). Beginning in the 1970s, some blacks (and Latinos) rejected integration in favor of "multiculturalism" and set out to win political support for the creation of racially and ethnically distinct institutions. Some liberals supported this multicultural agenda, but Arthur Schlesinger Jr. (a well-known historian and advisor to President Kennedy) and many others opposed such separatist schemes. Conservative commentators, such as George F. Will, William Bennett, and Patrick Buchanan, uniformly condemned multiculturalism as a threat to core American values. Fearing the "balkanization," or fragmentation, of American culture, they opposed classroom instruction of immigrant children in their native languages and revisions of university curricula that deemphasized the importance of European culture.

This warfare over culture issues extended into Congress. Believing that the programs aired on public television and the grants awarded by the National Endowments for the Arts and the Humanities promoted multiculturalism, conservative lawmakers tried to cut off their funding. When that effort failed, they drastically reduced the organizations' budgets. Conservatives also took aim at the antiracist and antisexist regulations and speech codes that had been adopted by many colleges. Demanding the protection of the First Amendment right of free speech, conservatives (along with liberals in the American Civil Liberties Union) opposed attempts to regulate "hate" speech.

Conflicting Values: Women's and Gay Rights

Conservatives were equally worried about the state of American families. They pointed to the 40 percent rate of divorce among whites and the 70 percent rate of out-of-wedlock pregnancies among blacks. The "abrasive experiments of two liberal decades," they charged, had eroded respect for marriage and family values. To members of the Religious Right, there were a wide range of culprits: legislators who enacted liberal divorce laws, funded child care, and allowed welfare payments to unmarried mothers, and judges who banished religious instruction from public schools. While their celebration of "traditional family values" evoked all these issues, religious conservatives were particularly intent on resisting the new freedoms and rights claimed by women and homosexuals.

Feminists, the Religious Right, and Abortion. In the 1980s, public opinion polls showed strong support for many feminist demands, including equal pay in the workplace, an equitable sharing of household and child-care responsibilities, and personal control of reproductive decisions. But in *Backlash: The Undeclared War on American Women* (1991), journalist Susan Faludi warned that conservative social groups had launched an all-out campaign against the feminist movement and its agenda of civic equality for women. To resist this conservative onslaught, the National Organization of Women (NOW) expanded its membership and agenda to include "Third Wave" feminists. These new feminists adopted a multicultural perspective and advanced the distinctive concerns of women of color, lesbians, and working women. Younger feminist women also felt more secure of their sexuality; many of them identified with the pop music star Madonna, whose outrageous sexualized style seemed to empower her rather than make her a sex object.

Abortion became a central issue in the cultural warfare between feminists and religious conservatives, and also a defining issue between Democrats and Republicans. Feminists viewed the issue from the perspective of the pregnant woman; they argued that the right to a legal, safe abortion was crucial to her control over her life. Conversely, religious conservatives maintained that legalized abortion improperly gave a higher value to the woman's individual rights than to her sacred vocation of motherhood. They also viewed abortion from the perspective of the unborn fetus—claiming that its rights trumped those of the living mother. Indeed, in cases of a difficult childbirth, some conservatives would sacrifice the life of the mother to save that of the fetus. To dramatize the larger issues at stake, the antiabortion movement christened itself as "pro-life," while proponents of abortion rights described themselves as "pro-choice." Both ideologies had roots in the American commitment to "life, liberty, and the pursuit of happiness." The question remained: Whose life? Whose liberty? Whose definition of happiness?

The hierarchy of the Catholic Church gave its answer to these questions in 1971, when it sponsored the formation of the National Right to Life Committee. Church leaders launched a sophisticated media campaign to build popular support for its antiabortion stance, distributing films of late-term fetuses in utero and photographs of tiny fetal hands. By the 1980s, fundamentalist Protestants assumed leadership of the antiabortion movement, which became increasingly confrontational and politically powerful.

Pressed by antiabortion interest groups, state legislatures passed laws that regulated the provision of abortion services. These laws required underage girls to obtain parental permission for abortions, denied public funding for abortions for poor women, and mandated waiting periods and elaborate counseling. These laws navigated between conflicting conservative beliefs. Religious conservatives demanded laws prohibiting abortions; "free enterprise" conservatives responded that abortion decisions were private matters and, like businesses, should be immune from government control. However, both groups of conservatives agreed that parents—and not the state— had the right to make important decisions for their minor children. As we saw in Chapter 30, in two decisions, *Webster v. Reproductive Health Services* (1989) and *Planned Parenthood of Southeastern Pennsylvania v. Casey* (1992), the Supreme Court accepted the constitutionality of many of these restrictions. But the federal courts continued to overturn state laws that prohibited late-term abortions when the life of the mother was in danger.

The debate over abortion stirred deep emotions (see Reading American Pictures, "The Abortion Debate Hits the Streets," p. 985). During the 1990s, evangelical Protestant activists mounted protests outside abortion clinics and harassed their staffs and clients. Pro-life extremists advocated killing the

doctors and nurses who performed abortions, and a few carried out their threats. In 1994, an antiabortion activist killed a worker at two Massachusetts abortion clinics and wounded five others; other religiously motivated extremists murdered doctors in Florida and New York. Cultural warfare had turned deadly—resorting to terror to achieve its ends.

The Controversy over Gay Rights. The issue of homosexuality stirred equally deep feelings on both sides. As more gay men and women "came out of the closet" in the years after Stonewall (see Chapter 29), they formed groups that demanded a variety of protections and privileges. Defining themselves as a "minority" group, gays sought legislation that protected them from discrimination in housing, education, public accommodations, and employment. Public opinion initially opposed such initiatives, but by the 1990s, many cities and states banned discrimination on the basis of sexual orientation.

This legislation did not end the conflict. Gay groups asserted that civic equality included extensive legal rights for same-sex couples, such as eligibility for workplace health-care coverage on the same basis as married heterosexuals. Indeed, many homosexuals wanted their partnerships recognized as legal marriages and treated identically to opposite-sex unions. Proposals for gay marriage roused widespread opposition because they confounded traditional practices and would have immense implications for the American family system.

The Religious Right had long condemned homosexuality as morally wrong and a major threat to the traditional family. Pat Robertson, North Carolina senator Jesse Helms, and other conservatives campaigned vigorously against antidiscrimination measures for gays. Their arguments that such laws amounted to undeserved "special rights" struck a responsive chord in Colorado. In 1992, Colorado voters amended the state constitution to bar local jurisdictions from passing ordinances protecting gays and lesbians, a measure subsequently overturned as unconstitutional by the Supreme Court. In 1998, Congress entered the fray by enacting the Defense of Marriage Act, which allowed states to refuse to recognize gay marriages or civil unions formed in other jurisdictions. However, in *Lawrence v. Texas* (2003), the Supreme Court ruled that states may not prohibit private homosexual activity between consenting adults (see Chapter 30, Comparing American Voices, pp. 930–931). As the new century began, the debate over legal rights for gays and lesbians rivaled in fervor and importance those over immigration restriction, abortion, and affirmative action. Increasingly, these cultural issues shaped the dynamics of American politics.

The Abortion Debate Hits the Streets

Divided Women, Divided Public: Protesting in Washington, D.C., 2004. Declan McCullagh.

Few issues in U.S. history divided late-twentieth-century Americans as profoundly as abortion. Since the Supreme Court's *Roe v. Wade* decision (1973), protests and counterprotests have grown. As the text suggests, the issue intrudes constantly into the social, cultural, and political history of recent decades (see Chapters 29, 30, and 32). Because the battle involves a seemingly irreconcilable difference between conflicting moral principles, finding common ground for compromise has been difficult. Antiabortion activists sometimes compare their fight with that of the abolitionists in the pre–Civil War era (who argued that slavery was immoral) and liken *Roe v. Wade* to *Dred Scott*—the 1857 Supreme Court decision that protected slave property. Those who support abortion often stake their ground on the rights of the individual—a

woman's right to control her life and her body—and invoke the Constitution's protection of individual freedom and privacy. The photograph above suggests the character of the resulting political confrontation. What do you see?

ANALYZING THE EVIDENCE

▶ Describe the people marching in the street. Who is protesting on the sidewalk? What does the composition of the two groups say about the abortion controversy?

▶ Next, look at how the police are positioned. From what you've read in the narrative, why might this sort of police deployment be necessary?

▶ Finally, look at the signs both groups are holding up. What messages do they convey? How do the slogans frame the debate? What principles do they invoke?

▶ Abortion was a significant political issue in the mid-nineteenth century, when many states first outlawed the practice, and again in the 1960s, when five states repealed antiabortion laws and eleven others reformed their restrictive legislation. Since the late 1970s, abortion has become an important issue in national politics and often divides Democrats and Republicans. From what you've read in the text and see in this picture, how can you explain the political importance of this issue?

➤ Who were the new immigrants? What were the sources of hostility to them?

➤ How do you account for the cultural conflict over issues relating to women and homosexuals? Who are the sides in conflict?

SUMMARY

As we have seen, a number of factors contributed to the revival of the American economy between 1980 and 2000. The defense buildup and the Reagan tax cuts poured billions of dollars into the economy, and American corporations invested heavily in research and new technologies. As the Japanese and German economies faltered, the United States reasserted its leading role in the global economy. The increase in the number of multinational firms, many of them U.S.-based, pushed forward the process of globalization. While nation-states remained immensely important, people, goods, and investment capital moved easily across political boundaries.

Technological innovations strengthened the American economy and transformed daily life. The computer revolution and the spread of the Internet changed the ways in which Americans shopped, worked, learned, and stayed in touch with family and friends. Technology likewise altered the character of television programming and viewing, as cable and satellite technology, along with government deregulation, provided Americans with a wider variety of entertainment choices.

As our account has suggested, globalization and technological change accentuated various cultural conflicts within the United States. Advances in biomedical science revived old moral debates, and globalization facilitated the immigration of millions of Asians and Latin Americans. The new immigrants increased the anxieties of many citizens about ethnic diversity and multiculturalism, while the poverty and crime that characterized the inner cities highlighted the nation's class and racial problems. Conservatives spoke out strongly, and with increasing effectiveness, against what they viewed as serious threats to "family values." Debates over women's rights, access to abortion, affirmative action, and the legal rights of homosexuals intensified. As the nation entered the twenty-first century, its people were sharply divided by cultural values as well as by economic class and racial identity.

Connections: Society and Technology

Cultural conflict has been a significant feature of recent American life. As we noted in the essay that opened Part Seven (p. 925):

> Increased immigration from Latin America and Asia added to cultural tensions and produced a new nativist movement. Continuing battles over affirmative action, abortion, sexual standards, homosexuality, feminism, and religion in public life took on an increasingly passionate character.

Neither set of issues was new. During the 1920s, as we explained in Chapter 23, powerful nativist sentiment forced the passage of a National Origins Act that severely restricted immigration from many countries. That decade also witnessed nationwide Prohibition, a failed attempt to impose a moral code by force of law. Both immigration and moral issues came to the fore again in the 1960s, but with a far different result. As we saw in Chapter 28, the Immigration Act of 1965 opened the way for a more diverse and more numerous flow of migrants, while the countercultural revolution challenged traditional social strictures and moral values and overthrew many of them. The battle was far from over, as we have discovered in Chapter 31. Beginning in the 1970s and gaining force in subsequent decades, moral and sexual conservatives launched a cultural offensive intended to encourage and, if possible, to legislate a return to the social arrangements and values that were dominant in the first half of the twentieth century.

That attempt at cultural control will take place in a world shaped by the technology of the computer chip and the Internet. In assessing possible outcomes, we might look back at earlier technological revolutions—the impact of electricity and the telephone in Chapter 18, of the radio and automobiles in Chapter 23, and of television in Chapter 27—all of which expanded the range of people's knowledge and choices. In such ways does technology influence, but not determine, cultural outcomes.

CHAPTER REVIEW QUESTIONS

➤ In what ways did the new technology affect the American economy? What was its relation to globalization?

➤ What was the outcome of the various cultural wars of the 1980s and 1990s?

TIMELINE

1980s	Rise of "Yuppies" (young urban professionals)
	Japan emerges as major economic power
	Women enter workforce in increasing numbers
	Lee Iacocca revives Chrysler Corporation
	Bill Gates builds Microsoft as computer use spreads
	Immigration of Latinos and Asians expands
	Conservatives challenge affirmative action programs
1981	Reagan crushes air traffic controllers' strike
	AIDS epidemic identified; begins worldwide spread
1985	United States becomes debtor nation
1987	Montreal environmental protocol cuts ozone loss
1989	Savings and loan scandals and crises
1990s	Stock market boom continues after 1987 crash
	Globalization intensifies; American jobs outsourced
	Wal-Mart emerges as major economic force
	Decline of labor unions continues
	Personal computer and small electronics revolution
	Spread of World Wide Web (WWW)
	Human Genome Project unravels structure of DNA
	Deregulation of television industry; concentration of media ownership
	Opposition to immigration and multiculturalism grows
1991	European Union formed
1992	Los Angeles race riots
1993	North American Free Trade Agreement (NAFTA)
1995	World Trade Organization (WTO) created
1998	Battles over abortion, gay rights intensify; Congress passes Defense of Marriage Act
1999	Protests against WTO policies begin
2001	George W. Bush administration rejects Kyoto environmental treaty

FOR FURTHER EXPLORATION

Alfred Eckes Jr. and Thomas Zeilin, *Globalization and the American Century* (2003), link American prosperity during the twentieth century to participation in the global economy. For insight into the dynamics and character of American social classes, see David Brooks, *Bobos in Paradise: The New Upper Class and How They Got There* (2000); Barbara Ehrenreich, *Fear of Falling: The Inner Life of the Middle Class* (1989); and Nelson Lichtenstein, *State of the Union: A Century of American Labor* (2002). In *More Equal Than Others* (2004), Godfrey Hodgson points to increasing social inequality as a central theme of the United States in the late twentieth century. Two other authors put greater emphasis on ideological demands for equality: John Skrentny, *The Minority Rights Revolution* (2002), and Samuel Walker, *The Rights Revolution: Rights and Community in Modem America* (1998). Two fine studies of family life are Stephanie Coontz, *The Way We Never Were: American Families and the Nostalgia Trap* (1992), and Arlie Hochschild, *The Second Shift: Working Parents and the Revolution at Home* (2002). See also Susan Faludi, *Backlash: The Undeclared War against American Women* (1991).

Provocative studies of technology include Howard Segal, *Future Imperfect: The Mixed Blessings of Technology in America* (1994), and Edward Tenner, *Why Things Bite Back: Technology and the Revenge of Unintended Consequences* (1996). Mary Ann Watson, *Defining Visions: Television and the American Experience Since 1945* (1998), surveys the changing character of the TV era, while Leonard Downie Jr. and Robert G. Kaiser, *The News about the News: American Journalism in Peril* (2002), point to its impact on the press. For a discussion of environmental issues, consult Adam Rose, *The Bulldozer in the Countryside: Suburban Sprawl and the Rise of American Environmentalism* (2001). The course of the AIDS epidemic can be followed in the *New York Times*—go to **www.nytimes.com/ref/health/25years-aids.html**.

On the culture wars, see Gertrude Himmelfarb, *One Nation, Two Cultures* (1999), and James Hunter, *Culture Wars: The Struggle to Define America* (1991). For race relations, consult Terry Anderson, *The Pursuit of Fairness: A History of Affirmative Action* (2004), and Jennifer Hochschild, *Facing Up to the American Dream: Race, Class, and the Soul of America* (1996). In *Debating Immigration, 1882–Present* (2001), Roger Daniels and Otis Graham offer a historical perspective on a contemporary issue. For discussions of recent arrivals, consult Nicolaus Mills, ed., *Arguing Immigration* (1994) and "The New Americans" at **www.pbs.org/independentlens/newamericans**.

TEST YOUR KNOWLEDGE

To assess your command of the material in this chapter, see the Online Study Guide at **bedfordstmartins.com/henretta**.

For Web sites, images, and documents related to topics and places in this chapter, visit **bedfordstmartins.com/makehistory**.

The Declaration of Independence

In Congress, July 4, 1776,
The Unanimous Declaration of the
Thirteen United States of America

When in the Course of human events, it becomes necessary for one people to dissolve the political bands which have connected them with another, and to assume among the Powers of the earth, the separate and equal station to which the Laws of Nature and of Nature's God entitle them, a decent respect to the opinions of mankind requires that they should declare the causes which impel them to the separation.

We hold these truths to be self-evident, that all men are created equal, that they are endowed by their Creator with certain unalienable rights, that among these are Life, Liberty, and the pursuit of Happiness. That to secure these rights, Governments are instituted among Men, deriving their just powers from the consent of the governed. That whenever any Form of Government becomes destructive of these ends, it is the Right of the People to alter or to abolish it, and to institute new Government, laying its foundation on such principles and organizing its powers in such form, as to them shall seem most likely to effect their Safety and Happiness. Prudence, indeed, will dictate that Governments long established should not be changed for light and transient causes; and accordingly all experience hath shown, that mankind are more disposed to suffer, while evils are sufferable, than to right themselves by abolishing the forms to which they are accustomed. But when a long train of abuses and usurpations, pursuing invariably the same Object evinces a design to reduce them under absolute Despotism, it is their right, it is their duty, to throw off such Government, and to provide new Guards for their future security. — Such has been the patient sufferance of these Colonies; and such is now the necessity which constrains them to alter their former Systems of Government. The history of the present King of Great Britain is a history of repeated injuries and usurpations, all having in direct object the establishment of an absolute Tyranny over these States. To prove this, let Facts be submitted to a candid world.

He has refused his Assent to Laws, the most wholesome and necessary for the public good.

He has forbidden his Governors to pass Laws of immediate and pressing importance, unless suspended in their operation till his Assent should be obtained; and, when so suspended, he has utterly neglected to attend to them.

He has refused to pass other Laws for the accommodation of large districts of people, unless those people would relinquish the right of Representation in the Legislature, a right inestimable to them and formidable to tyrants only.

He has called together legislative bodies at places unusual, uncomfortable, and distant from the depository of their public Records, for the sole purpose of fatiguing them into compliance with his measures.

He has dissolved Representative Houses repeatedly, for opposing with manly firmness his invasions on the rights of the people.

He has refused for a long time, after such dissolutions, to cause others to be elected; whereby the Legislative powers, incapable of Annihilation, have returned to the People at large for their exercise; the State remaining in the mean time exposed to all the dangers of invasion from without and convulsions within.

He has endeavoured to prevent the population of these States; for that purpose obstructing the Laws of Naturalization of Foreigners; refusing to pass others to encourage their migrations hither, and raising the conditions of new Appropriations of Lands.

He has obstructed the Administration of Justice, by refusing his Assent to Laws for establishing Judiciary powers.

He has made Judges dependent on his Will alone, for the tenure of their offices, and the amount and payment of their salaries.

He has erected a multitude of New Offices, and sent hither swarms of Officers to harass our People, and eat out their substance.

He has kept among us, in times of peace, Standing Armies without the Consent of our legislature.

He has combined with others to subject us to a jurisdiction foreign to our constitution, and unacknowledged by our laws; giving his Assent to their Acts of pretended Legislation:

For quartering large bodies of armed troops among us:

For protecting them, by a mock Trial, from Punishment for any Murders which they should commit on the Inhabitants of these States:

For cutting off our Trade with all parts of the world:

For imposing taxes on us without our Consent:

For depriving us, in many cases, of the benefits of Trial by jury:

For transporting us beyond Seas to be tried for pretended offences:

For abolishing the free System of English Laws in a neighbouring Province, establishing therein an Arbitrary government, and enlarging its Boundaries so as to render it at once an example and fit instrument for introducing the same absolute rule into these Colonies:

For taking away our Charters, abolishing our most valuable Laws, and altering fundamentally the Forms of our Governments:

For suspending our own Legislatures, and declaring themselves invested with Power to legislate for us in all cases whatsoever.

He has abdicated Government here, by declaring us out of his Protection and waging War against us.

He has plundered our seas, ravaged our Coasts, burnt our towns, and destroyed the lives of our people.

He is at this time transporting large armies of foreign mercenaries to compleat the works of death, desolation, and tyranny, already begun with circumstances of Cruelty & perfidy scarcely paralleled in the most barbarous ages, and totally unworthy the Head of a civilized nation.

He has constrained our fellow Citizens taken Captive on the high Seas to bear Arms against their Country, to become the executioners of their friends and Brethren, or to fall themselves by their Hands.

He has excited domestic insurrections amongst us, and has endeavoured to bring on the inhabitants of our frontiers, the merciless Indian Savages, whose known rule of warfare, is an undistinguished destruction of all ages, sexes, and conditions.

In every stage of these Oppressions We have Petitioned for Redress in the most humble terms: Our repeated Petitions have been answered only by repeated injury. A Prince, whose character is thus marked by every act which may define a Tyrant, is unfit to be the ruler of a free people.

Nor have We been wanting in attention to our British brethren. We have warned them from time to time of attempts by their legislature to extend an unwarrantable jurisdiction over us. We have reminded them of the circumstances of our emigration and settlement here. We have appealed to their native justice and magnanimity, and we have conjured them by the ties of our common kindred to disavow these usurpations, which would inevitably interrupt our connections and correspondence. They too have been deaf to the voice of justice and of consanguinity. We must, therefore, acquiesce in the necessity, which denounces our Separation, and hold them, as we hold the rest of mankind, Enemies in War, in Peace Friends.

We, therefore, the Representatives of the United States of America, in General Congress, Assembled, appealing to the Supreme Judge of the world for the rectitude of our intentions, do, in the Name, and by Authority of the good People of these Colonies, solemnly publish and declare, That these United Colonies are, and of Right ought to be FREE AND INDEPENDENT STATES; that they are Absolved from all Allegiance to the British Crown, and that all political connection between them and the State of Great Britain, is and ought to be totally dissolved; and that as Free and Independent States, they have full Power to levy War, conclude Peace, contract Alliances, establish Commerce, and to do all other Acts and Things which Independent States may of right do. And for the support of this Declaration, with a firm reliance on the Protection of Divine Providence, we mutually pledge to each other our Lives, our Fortunes, and our sacred Honor.

John Hancock

Button Gwinnett	**George Wythe**	**James Wilson**	**Josiah Bartlett**
Lyman Hall	**Richard Henry Lee**	**Geo. Ross**	**Wm. Whipple**
Geo. Walton	**Th. Jefferson**	**Caesar Rodney**	**Matthew Thornton**
Wm. Hooper	**Benja. Harrison**	**Geo. Read**	**Saml. Adams**
Joseph Hewes	**Thos. Nelson, Jr.**	**Thos. M'Kean**	**John Adams**
John Penn	**Francis Lightfoot Lee**	**Wm. Floyd**	**Robt. Treat Paine**
Edward Rutledge	**Carter Braxton**	**Phil. Livingston**	**Elbridge Gerry**
Thos. Heyward, Junr.	**Robt. Morris**	**Frans. Lewis**	**Step. Hopkins**
Thomas Lynch, Junr.	**Benjamin Rush**	**Lewis Morris**	**William Ellery**
Arthur Middleton	**Benja. Franklin**	**Richd. Stockton**	**Roger Sherman**
Samuel Chase	**John Morton**	**John Witherspoon**	**Sam'el Huntington**
Wm. Paca	**Geo. Clymer**	**Fras. Hopkinson**	**Wm. Williams**
Thos. Stone	**Jas. Smith**	**John Hart**	**Oliver Wolcott**
Charles Carroll of Carrollton	**Geo. Taylor**	**Abra. Clark**	

The Articles of Confederation and Perpetual Union

Agreed to in Congress, November 15, 1777;
Ratified March 1781

BETWEEN THE STATES OF NEW HAMPSHIRE, MASSACHUSETTS BAY, RHODE ISLAND AND PROVIDENCE PLANTATIONS, CONNECTICUT, NEW YORK, NEW JERSEY, PENNSYLVANIA, DELAWARE, MARYLAND, VIRGINIA, NORTH CAROLINA, SOUTH CAROLINA, GEORGIA.*

Article 1

The stile of this confederacy shall be "The United States of America."

Article 2

Each State retains its sovereignty, freedom and independence, and every power, jurisdiction, and right, which is not by this confederation expressly delegated to the United States, in Congress assembled.

Article 3

The said states hereby severally enter into a firm league of friendship with each other for their common defence, the security of their liberties and their mutual and general welfare; binding themselves to assist each other against all force offered to, or attacks made upon them, or any of them, on account of religion, sovereignty, trade, or any other pretence whatever.

Article 4

The better to secure and perpetuate mutual friendship and intercourse among the people of the different states in this union, the free inhabitants of each of these states, paupers, vagabonds, and fugitives from justice excepted, shall be entitled to all privileges and immunities of free citizens in the several states; and the people of each State shall have free ingress and regress to and from any other State, and shall enjoy therein all the privileges of trade and commerce, subject to the same duties, impositions, and restrictions, as the inhabitants thereof respectively; provided, that such restrictions shall not extend so far as to prevent the removal of property, imported into any State, to any other State of which the owner is an inhabitant; provided also, that no imposition, duties, or restriction, shall be laid by any State on the property of the United States, or either of them.

If any person guilty of, or charged with treason, felony, or other high misdemeanor in any State, shall flee from justice and be found in any of the United States, he shall, upon demand of the governor or executive power of the State from which he fled, be delivered up and removed to the State having jurisdiction of his offence.

Full faith and credit shall be given in each of these states to the records, acts, and judicial proceedings of the courts and magistrates of every other State.

Article 5

For the more convenient management of the general interests of the United States, delegates shall be annually appointed, in such manner as the legislature of each State shall direct, to meet in Congress, on the 1st Monday in November in every year, with a power reserved to each State to recall its delegates, or any of them, at any time within the year, and to send others in their stead for the remainder of the year.

No State shall be represented in Congress by less than two, nor by more than seven members; and no person shall be capable of being a delegate for more than three years in any term of six years; nor shall any person, being a delegate, be capable of holding any office under the United States, for which he, or any other for his benefit, receives any salary, fees, or emolument of any kind.

Each State shall maintain its own delegates in a meeting of the states, and while they act as members of the committee of the states.

In determining questions in the United States, in Congress assembled, each State shall have one vote.

Freedom of speech and debate in Congress shall not be impeached or questioned in any court or place out of Congress: and the members of Congress shall be protected in their

---

*This copy of the final draft of the Articles of Confederation is taken from the *Journals*, 9:907-25, November 15, 1777.

persons from arrests and imprisonments, during the time of their going to and from, and attendance on Congress, except for treason, felony, or breach of the peace.

Article 6

No State, without the consent of the United States, in Congress assembled, shall send any embassy to, or receive any embassy from, or enter into any conference, agreement, alliance, or treaty with any king, prince, or state; nor shall any person, holding any office of profit or trust under the United States, or any of them, accept of any present, emolument, office or title, of any kind whatever, from any king, prince, or foreign state; nor shall the United States, in Congress assembled, or any of them, grant any title of nobility.

No two or more states shall enter into any treaty, confederation, or alliance, whatever, between them, without the consent of the United States, in Congress assembled, specifying accurately the purposes for which the same is to be entered into, and how long it shall continue.

No state shall lay any imposts or duties which may interfere with any stipulations in treaties entered into by the United States, in Congress assembled, with any king, prince, or state, in pursuance of any treaties already proposed by Congress to the courts of France and Spain.

No vessels of war shall be kept up in time of peace by any State, except such number only as shall be deemed necessary by the United States, in Congress assembled, for the defence of such State or its trade; nor shall any body of forces be kept up by any State, in time of peace, except such number only as, in the judgment of the United States, in Congress assembled, shall be deemed requisite to garrison the forts necessary for the defence of such State; but every State shall always keep up a well regulated and disciplined militia, sufficiently armed and accoutred, and shall provide, and constantly have ready for use, in public stores, a due number of field pieces and tents, and a proper quantity of arms, ammunition and camp equipage.

No State shall engage in any war without the consent of the United States, in Congress assembled, unless such State be actually invaded by enemies, or shall have received certain advice of a resolution being formed by some nation of Indians to invade such State, and the danger is so imminent as not to admit of a delay till the United States, in Congress assembled, can be consulted; nor shall any State grant commissions to any ships or vessels of war, nor letters of marque or reprisal, except it be after a declaration of war by the United States, in Congress assembled, and then only against the kingdom or state, and the subjects thereof, against which war has been so declared, and under such regulations as shall be established by the United States, in Congress assembled, unless such State be infested by pirates, in which case vessels of war may be fitted out for that occasion, and kept so long as the danger shall continue, or until the United States, in Congress assembled, shall determine otherwise.

Article 7

When land forces are raised by any State for the common defence, all officers of or under the rank of colonel, shall be appointed by the legislature of each State respectively, by whom such forces shall be raised, or in such manner as such State shall direct; and all vacancies shall be filled up by the State which first made the appointment.

Article 8

All charges of war and all other expences, that shall be incurred for the common defence or general welfare, and allowed by the United States, in Congress assembled, shall be defrayed out of a common treasury, which shall be supplied by the several states, in proportion to the value of all land within each State, granted to or surveyed for any person, as such land and the buildings and improvements thereon shall be estimated according to such mode as the United States, in Congress assembled, shall, from time to time, direct and appoint.

The taxes for paying that proportion shall be laid and levied by the authority and direction of the legislatures of the several states, within the time agreed upon by the United States, in Congress assembled.

Article 9

The United States, in Congress assembled, shall have the sole and exclusive right and power of determining on peace and war, except in the cases mentioned in the 6th article; of sending and receiving ambassadors; entering into treaties and alliances, provided that no treaty of commerce shall be made, whereby the legislative power of the respective states shall be restrained from imposing such imposts and duties on foreigners as their own people are subjected to, or from prohibiting the exportation or importation of any species of goods or commodities whatsoever; of establishing rules for deciding, in all cases, what captures on land or water shall be legal, and in what manner prizes, taken by land or naval forces in the service of the United States, shall be divided or appropriated; of granting letters of marque and reprisal in times of peace; appointing courts for the trial of piracies and felonies committed on the high seas, and establishing courts for receiving and determining, finally, appeals in all cases of captures; provided, that no member of Congress shall be appointed a judge of any of the said courts.

The United States, in Congress assembled, shall also be the last resort on appeal in all disputes and differences now subsisting, or that hereafter may arise between two or more states concerning boundary, jurisdiction or any other cause whatever; which authority shall always be exercised in the manner following: whenever the legislative or executive authority, or lawful agent of any State, in controversy with another, shall present a petition to Congress, stating the matter in question, and praying for a hearing, notice thereof shall be given, by order of Congress, to the legislative or executive authority of the other State in controversy, and a day assigned for the appearance of the parties by their lawful agents, who shall then be directed to appoint, by joint consent, commissioners or judges to constitute a court for hearing and determining the matter in question; but, if they cannot agree, Congress shall name three persons out of each of the United States, and from the list of such persons each party shall alternately strike out one, the petitioners beginning, until the number shall be reduced to thirteen; and from that number not less than seven, nor more than nine names, as Congress shall direct, shall, in the presence of Congress, be drawn out by lot; and the persons whose names shall be so drawn, or any five of them, shall be commissioners or judges to hear and finally determine the controversy, so always as a major part of the judges who shall hear the cause shall agree in the determination; and if either party shall neglect to attend at the day appointed, without shewing reasons which Congress shall judge sufficient, or, being present, shall refuse to strike, the Congress shall proceed to nominate three persons out of each State, and the secretary of Congress shall strike in behalf of such party absent or refusing; and the judgment and sentence of the court to be appointed, in the manner before prescribed, shall be final and conclusive; and if any of the parties shall refuse to submit to the authority of such court, or to appear or defend their claim or cause, the court shall nevertheless proceed to pronounce sentence or judgment, which shall, in like manner, be final and decisive, the judgment or sentence and other proceedings begin, in either case, transmitted to Congress, and lodged among the acts of Congress for the security of the parties concerned: provided, that every commissioner, before he sits in judgment, shall take an oath, to be administered by one of the judges of the supreme or superior court of the State where the cause shall be tried, "well and truly to hear and determine the matter in question, according to the best of his judgment, without favour, affection, or hope of reward:" provided, also, that no State shall be deprived of territory for the benefit of the United States.

All controversies concerning the private right of soil, claimed under different grants of two or more states, whose jurisdictions, as they may respect such lands and the states which passed such grants, are adjusted, the said grants, or either of them, being at the same time claimed to have originated antecedent to such settlement of jurisdiction, shall, on the petition of either party to the Congress of the United States, be finally determined, as near as may be, in the same manner as is before prescribed for deciding disputes respecting territorial jurisdiction between different states.

The United States, in Congress assembled, shall also have the sole and exclusive right and power of regulating the alloy and value of coin struck by their own authority, or by that of the respective states; fixing the standard of weights and measures throughout the United States; regulating the trade and managing all affairs with the Indians not members of any of the states; provided that the legislative right of any State within its own limits be not infringed or violated; establishing and regulating post offices from one State to another throughout all the United States, and exacting such postage on the papers passing through the same as may be requisite to defray the expences of the said office; appointing all officers of the land forces in the service of the United States, excepting regimental officers; appointing all the officers of the naval forces, and commissioning all officers whatever in the service of the United States; making rules for the government and regulation of the said land and naval forces, and directing their operations.

The United States, in Congress assembled, shall have authority to appoint a committee to sit in the recess of Congress, to be denominated "a Committee of the States," and to consist of one delegate from each State, and to appoint such other committees and civil officers as may be necessary for managing the general affairs of the United States, under their direction; to appoint one of their number to preside; provided that no person be allowed to serve in the office of president more than one year in any term of three years; to ascertain the necessary sums of money to be raised for the service of the United States, and to appropriate and apply the same for defraying the public expences; to borrow money or emit bills on the credit of the United States, transmitting, every half year, to the respective states, an account of the sums of money so borrowed or emitted; to build and equip a navy; to agree upon the number of land forces, and to make requisitions from each State for its quota, in proportion to the number of white inhabitants in such State; which requisitions shall be binding; and thereupon, the legislature of each State shall appoint the regimental officers, raise the men, and cloathe, arm, and equip them in a soldier-like manner, at the expence of the United States; and the officers and men so cloathed, armed, and equipped, shall march to the place appointed and within the time agreed on by the United States, in Congress assembled; but if the United States, in Congress assembled, shall, on consideration of circumstances, judge proper that any State should not raise men, or should raise a smaller number than its quota, and that any other State should raise a greater number of men than the quota thereof, such extra number shall be raised, officered, cloathed, armed, and equipped in the same manner as the quota of such State, unless the legislature of such State shall judge that such extra number cannot be safely spared out of the same, in which case they shall raise, officer, cloathe, arm, and equip as many of such extra number as they judge can be safely spared. And the officers and men so cloathed, armed, and equipped, shall march to the place appointed and within the time agreed on by the United States, in Congress assembled.

The United States, in Congress assembled, shall never engage in a war, nor grant letters of marque and reprisal in time of peace, nor enter into any treaties or alliances, nor coin money, nor regulate the value thereof, nor ascertain the sums and expences necessary for the defence and welfare of the United States, or any of them: nor emit bills, nor borrow money on the credit of the United States, nor appropriate money, nor agree upon the number of vessels of war to be built or purchased, or the number of land or sea forces to be raised, nor appoint a commander in chief of the army or navy, unless nine states assent to the same; nor shall a question on any other point, except for adjourning from day to day, be determined, unless by the votes of a majority of the United States, in Congress assembled.

The Congress of the United States shall have power to adjourn to any time within the year, and to any place within the United States, so that no period of adjournment be for a longer duration than the space of six months, and shall publish the journal of their proceedings monthly, except such parts thereof, relating to treaties, alliances or military operations, as, in their judgment, require secrecy; and the yeas and nays of the delegates of each State on any question shall be entered on the journal, when it is desired by any delegate; and the delegates of a State, or any of them, at his, or their request, shall be furnished with a transcript of the said journal, except such parts as are above excepted, to lay before the legislatures of the several states.

Article 10

The committee of the states, or any nine of them, shall be authorized to execute, in the recess of Congress, such of the powers of Congress as the United States, in Congress assembled, by the consent of nine states, shall, from time to time, think expedient to vest them with; provided, that no power be delegated to the said committee, for the exercise of which, by the articles of confederation, the voice of nine states, in the Congress of the United States assembled, is requisite.

Article 11

Canada acceding to this confederation, and joining in the measures of the United States, shall be admitted into and entitled to all the advantages of this union; but no other colony shall be admitted into the same, unless such admission be agreed to by nine states.

The Constitution of the United States of America

Agreed to by Philadelphia Convention,
September 17, 1787
Implemented March 4, 1789

We the People of the United States, in Order to form a more perfect Union, establish Justice, insure domestic Tranquility, provide for the common defence, promote the general Welfare, and secure the Blessings of Liberty to ourselves and our Posterity, do ordain and establish this Constitution for the United States of America.

Article I

Section 1. All legislative Powers herein granted shall be vested in a Congress of the United States, which shall consist of a Senate and a House of Representatives.

Section 2. The House of Representatives shall be composed of Members chosen every second Year by the People of the several States, and the Electors in each State shall have the Qualifications requisite for Electors of the most numerous Branch of the State Legislature.

No Person shall be a Representative who shall not have attained to the Age of twenty-five Years, and been seven Years a Citizen of the United States, and who shall not, when elected, be an Inhabitant of that State in which he shall be chosen.

Representatives and direct Taxes shall be apportioned among the several States which may be included within this Union, according to their respective Numbers, *which shall be determined by adding to the whole Number of free Persons, including those bound to Service for a Term of Years, and excluding Indians not taxed, three fifths of all other Persons.** The actual Enumeration shall be made within three Years after the first Meeting of the Congress of the United States, and within every subsequent Term of ten Years, in such Manner as they shall by Law direct. The Number of Representatives shall not exceed one for every thirty Thousand, but each State shall have at Least one Representative; and *until such enumeration*

shall be made, the State of New Hampshire shall be entitled to chuse three, Massachusetts eight, Rhode Island and Providence Plantations one, Connecticut five, New York six, New Jersey four, Pennsylvania eight, Delaware one, Maryland six, Virginia ten, North Carolina five, South Carolina five, and Georgia three.

When vacancies happen in the Representation from any State, the Executive Authority thereof shall issue Writs of Election to fill such Vacancies.

The House of Representatives shall chuse their Speaker and other Officers; and shall have the sole Power of Impeachment.

Section 3. The Senate of the United States shall be composed of two Senators from each State, *chosen by the Legislature thereof,*† for six Years; and each Senator shall have one Vote.

Immediately after they shall be assembled in Consequence of the first Election, they shall be divided as equally as may be into three Classes. The Seats of the Senators of the first Class shall be vacated at the Expiration of the second Year, of the second Class at the Expiration of the fourth Year, and of the third Class at the Expiration of the sixth Year, so that one-third may be chosen every second Year; and if Vacancies happen by Resignation, or otherwise, during the Recess of the Legislature of any State, the Executive thereof may make temporary Appointments until the next Meeting of the Legislature, which shall then fill such Vacancies.‡

No person shall be a Senator who shall not have attained to the Age of thirty Years, and been nine Years a Citizen of the United States, and who shall not, when elected, be an Inhabitant of that State for which he shall be chosen.

The Vice President of the United States shall be President of the Senate, but shall have no Vote, unless they be equally divided.

The Senate shall chuse their other Officers, and also a President pro tempore, in the absence of the Vice President, or when he shall exercise the Office of President of the United States.

The Senate shall have the sole Power to try all Impeachments. When sitting for that Purpose, they shall be on Oath or Affirmation. When the President of the United States is tried, the Chief Justice shall preside: And no Person shall be convicted without the Concurrence of two-thirds of the Members present.

Note: The Constitution became effective March 4, 1789. Provisions in italics are no longer relevant or have been changed by constitutional amendment.
*Changed by Section 2 of the Fourteenth Amendment.

---

†Changed by Section 1 of the Seventeenth Amendment.
‡Changed by Section 2 of the Seventeenth Amendment.

Judgment in Cases of Impeachment shall not extend further than to removal from Office, and disqualification to hold and enjoy any Office of honor, Trust or Profit under the United States: but the Party convicted shall nevertheless be liable and subject to Indictment, Trial, Judgment and Punishment, according to Law.

Section 4. The Times, Places and Manner of holding Elections for Senators and Representatives, shall be prescribed in each State by the Legislature thereof; but the Congress may at any time by Law make or alter such Regulations, except as to the Places of Chusing Senators.

The Congress shall assemble at least once in every Year, and such Meeting *shall be on the first Monday in December, unless they shall by Law appoint a different Day.**

Section 5. Each House shall be the Judge of the Elections, Returns and Qualifications of its own Members, and a Majority of each shall constitute a Quorum to do Business; but a smaller number may adjourn from day to day, and may be authorized to compel the Attendance of absent Members, in such Manner, and under such Penalties, as each House may provide.

Each House may determine the Rules of its Proceedings, punish its Members for disorderly Behavior, and, with the Concurrence of two-thirds, expel a Member.

Each House shall keep a Journal of its Proceedings, and from time to time publish the same, excepting such Parts as may in their Judgment require Secrecy; and the Yeas and Nays of the Members of either House on any question shall, at the Desire of one-fifth of those Present, be entered on the Journal.

Neither House, during the Session of Congress, shall, without the Consent of the other, adjourn for more than three days, nor to any other Place than that in which the two Houses shall be sitting.

Section 6. The Senators and Representatives shall receive a Compensation for their Services, to be ascertained by Law, and paid out of the Treasury of the United States. They shall in all Cases, except Treason, Felony and Breach of the Peace, be privileged from Arrest during their Attendance at the Session of their respective Houses, and in going to and returning from the same; and for any Speech or Debate in either House, they shall not be questioned in any other Place.

No Senator or Representative shall, during the Time for which he was elected, be appointed to any civil Office under the Authority of the United States, which shall have been created, or the Emoluments whereof shall have been increased, during such time; and no Person holding any Office under the United States, shall be a Member of either House during his Continuance in Office.

*Changed by Section 2 of the Twentieth Amendment.

Section 7. All Bills for raising Revenue shall originate in the House of Representatives; but the Senate may propose or concur with Amendments as on other Bills.

Every Bill which shall have passed the House of Representatives and the Senate, shall, before it becomes a Law, be presented to the President of the United States; If he approve he shall sign it, but if not he shall return it, with his Objections to that House in which it shall have originated, who shall enter the Objections at large on their Journal, and proceed to reconsider it. If after such Reconsideration two-thirds of that House shall agree to pass the Bill, it shall be sent, together with the Objections, to the other House, by which it shall likewise be reconsidered, and if approved by two-thirds of that House, it shall become a Law. But in all such Cases the Votes of both Houses shall be determined by Yeas and Nays, and the Names of the Persons voting for and against the Bill shall be entered on the Journal of each House respectively. If any Bill shall not be returned by the President within ten Days (Sundays excepted) after it shall have been presented to him, the Same shall be a Law, in like Manner as if he had signed it, unless the Congress by their Adjournment prevent its Return, in which Case it shall not be a Law.

Every Order, Resolution, or Vote to which the Concurrence of the Senate and the House of Representatives may be necessary (except on a question of Adjournment) shall be presented to the President of the United States; and before the Same shall take Effect, shall be approved by him, or being disapproved by him, shall be repassed by two-thirds of the Senate and House of Representatives, according to the Rules and Limitations prescribed in the Case of a Bill.

Section 8. The Congress shall have Power To lay and collect Taxes, Duties, Imposts and Excises, to pay the Debts and provide for the common Defence and general Welfare of the United States; but all Duties, Imposts and Excises shall be uniform throughout the United States;

To borrow money on the credit of the United States;

To regulate Commerce with foreign Nations, and among the several States, and with the Indian Tribes;

To establish an uniform Rule of Naturalization, and uniform Laws on the subject of Bankruptcies throughout the United States;

To coin Money, regulate the Value thereof, and of foreign Coin, and fix the Standard of Weights and Measures;

To provide for the Punishment of counterfeiting the Securities and current Coin of the United States;

To establish Post Offices and post Roads;

To promote the Progress of Science and useful Arts, by securing for limited Times to Authors and Inventors the exclusive Right to their respective Writings and Discoveries;

To constitute Tribunals inferior to the supreme Court;

To define and punish Piracies and Felonies committed on the high Seas, and Offenses against the Law of Nations;

To declare War, grant Letters of Marque and Reprisal, and make Rules concerning Captures on Land and Water;

To raise and support Armies, but no Appropriation of Money to that Use shall be for a longer Term than two Years;

To provide and maintain a Navy;

To make Rules for the Government and Regulation of the land and naval Forces;

To provide for calling forth the Militia to execute the Laws of the Union, suppress Insurrections and repel Invasions;

To provide for organizing, arming, and disciplining the Militia, and for governing such Part of them as may be employed in the Service of the United States, reserving to the States respectively, the Appointment of the Officers, and the Authority of training the Militia according to the discipline prescribed by Congress;

To exercise exclusive Legislation in all Cases whatsoever, over such District (not exceeding ten Miles square) as may, by Cession of particular States, and the acceptance of Congress, become the Seat of Government of the United States, and to exercise like Authority over all Places purchased by the Consent of the Legislature of the State in which the Same shall be, for the Erection of Forts, Magazines, Arsenals, dock-Yards, and other needful Buildings;— And

To make all Laws which shall be necessary and proper for carrying into Execution the foregoing Powers, and all other Powers vested by this Constitution in the Government of the United States, or in any Department or Officer thereof.

Section 9. The Migration or Importation of such Persons as any of the States now existing shall think proper to admit, shall not be prohibited by the Congress prior to the Year one thousand eight hundred and eight but a tax or duty may be imposed on such Importation, not exceeding ten dollars for each Person.

The privilege of the Writ of Habeas Corpus shall not be suspended, unless when in Cases of Rebellion or Invasion the public Safety may require it.

No Bill of Attainder or ex post facto Law shall be passed.

*No capitation, or other direct, Tax shall be laid, unless in Proportion to the Census or Enumeration herein before directed to be taken.**

No Tax or Duty shall be laid on Articles exported from any State.

No Preference shall be given by any Regulation of Commerce or Revenue to the Ports of one State over those of another: nor shall Vessels bound to, or from, one State, be obliged to enter, clear, or pay Duties in another.

No Money shall be drawn from the Treasury, but in Consequence of Appropriations made by law; and a regular Statement and Account of the Receipts and Expenditures of all public Money shall be published from time to time.

No Title of Nobility shall be granted by the United States: And no Person holding any Office of Profit or Trust under them, shall, without the Consent of the Congress, accept of any present, Emolument, Office, or Title, of any kind whatever, from any King, Prince, or foreign State.

———————————
*Changed by the Sixteenth Amendment.

Section 10. No State shall enter into any Treaty, Alliance, or Confederation; grant Letters of Marque and Reprisal; coin Money; emit Bills of Credit; make any Thing but gold and silver Coin a Tender in Payment of Debts; pass any Bill of Attainder, ex post facto Law, or Law impairing the Obligation of Contracts, or grant any Title of Nobility.

No State shall, without the Consent of the Congress, lay any Imposts or Duties on Imports or Exports, except what may be absolutely necessary for executing its inspection Laws: and the net Produce of all Duties and Imposts, laid by any State on Imports or Exports, shall be for the Use of the Treasury of the United States; and all such Laws shall be subject to the Revision and Control of the Congress.

No State shall, without the Consent of the Congress, lay any duty of Tonnage, keep Troops, or Ships of War in time of Peace, enter into any Agreement or Compact with another State, or with a foreign Power, or engage in War, unless actually invaded, or in such imminent Danger as will not admit of delay.

Article II

Section 1. The executive Power shall be vested in a President of the United States of America. He shall hold his Office during the Term of four Years, and, together with the Vice President, chosen for the same Term, be elected, as follows:

Each State shall appoint, in such Manner as the Legislature thereof may direct, a Number of Electors, equal to the whole Number of Senators and Representatives to which the State may be entitled in the Congress; but no Senator or Representative, or Person holding an Office of Trust or Profit under the United States, shall be appointed an Elector.

The Electors shall meet in their respective States, and vote by Ballot for two Persons, of whom one at least shall not be an Inhabitant of the same State with themselves. And they shall make a List of all the Persons voted for, and of the Number of Votes for each; which List they shall sign and certify, and transmit sealed to the Seat of the Government of the United States, directed to the President of the Senate. The President of the Senate shall, in the Presence of the Senate and House of Representatives, open all the Certificates, and the Votes shall then be counted. The Person having the greatest Number of Votes shall be the President, if such Number be a Majority of the whole Number of Electors appointed; and if there be more than one who have such Majority, and have an equal Number of Votes, then the House of Representatives shall immediately chuse by Ballot one of them for President; and if no Person have a Majority, then from the five highest on the List the said House shall in like Manner chuse the President. But in chusing the President, the Votes shall be taken by States, the Representation from each State having one Vote; a quorum for this Purpose shall consist of a Member or Members from two thirds of the States, and a Majority of all the States shall be necessary to a Choice. In every Case, after the Choice of the President, the Person having the greatest Number of Votes of the

*Electors shall be the Vice President. But if there should remain two or more who have equal Votes, the Senate shall chuse from them by Ballot the Vice President.**

The Congress may determine the Time of chusing the Electors, and the Day on which they shall give their Votes; which Day shall be the same throughout the United States.

No Person except a natural born Citizen, or a Citizen of the United States, at the time of the Adoption of this Constitution, shall be eligible to the Office of President; neither shall any Person be eligible to that Office who shall not have attained to the Age of thirty five Years, and been fourteen Years a Resident within the United States.

In Case of the Removal of the President from Office, or of his Death, Resignation, or Inability to discharge the Powers and Duties of the said Office, the same shall devolve on the Vice President, *and the Congress may by Law provide for the Case of Removal, Death, Resignation, or Inability, both of the President and Vice President, declaring what Officer shall then act as President, and such Officer shall act accordingly, until the Disability be removed, or a President shall be elected.*†

The President shall, at stated Times, receive for his Services a Compensation, which shall neither be increased nor diminished during the Period for which he shall have been elected, and he shall not receive within that Period any other Emolument from the United States, or any of them.

Before he enter on the Execution of his Office, he shall take the following Oath or Affirmation:—"I do solemnly swear (or affirm) that I will faithfully execute the Office of President of the United States, and will to the best of my Ability, preserve, protect and defend the Constitution of the United States."

Section 2. The President shall be Commander in Chief of the Army and Navy of the United States, and of the Militia of the several States, when called into the actual Service of the United States; he may require the Opinion, in writing, of the principal Officer in each of the executive Departments, upon any Subject relating to the Duties of their respective Offices, and he shall have Power to Grant Reprieves and Pardons for Offences against the United States, except in Cases of Impeachment.

He shall have Power, by and with the Advice and Consent of the Senate, to make Treaties, provided two thirds of the Senators present concur; and he shall nominate, and by and with the Advice and Consent of the Senate, shall appoint Ambassadors, other public Ministers and Consuls, Judges of the supreme Court, and all other Officers of the United States, whose Appointments are not herein otherwise provided for, and which shall be established by Law: but the Congress may by Law vest the Appointment of such inferior Officers, as they think proper, in the President alone, in the Courts of Law, or in the Heads of Departments.

The President shall have Power to fill up all Vacancies that may happen during the Recess of the Senate, by granting Commissions which shall expire at the End of their next Session.

Section 3. He shall from time to time give to the Congress Information of the State of the Union, and recommend to their Consideration such Measures as he shall judge necessary and expedient; he may, on extraordinary Occasions, convene both Houses, or either of them, and in Case of Disagreement between them, with Respect to the Time of Adjournment, he may adjourn them to such Time as he shall think proper; he shall receive Ambassadors and other public Ministers; he shall take Care that the Laws be faithfully executed, and shall Commission all the Officers of the United States.

Section 4. The President, Vice President and all civil Officers of the United States, shall be removed from Office on Impeachment for, and Conviction of, Treason, Bribery, or other high Crimes and Misdemeanors.

Article III

Section 1. The judicial Power of the United States, shall be vested in one supreme Court, and in such inferior Courts as the Congress may from time to time ordain and establish. The Judges, both of the supreme and inferior Courts, shall hold their Offices during good Behaviour, and shall, at stated Times, receive for their Services a Compensation, which shall not be diminished during their Continuance in Office.

Section 2. The judicial Power shall extend to all Cases, in Law and Equity, arising under this Constitution, the Laws of the United States, and Treaties made, or which shall be made, under their Authority;—to all Cases affecting Ambassadors, other public Ministers and Consuls;—to all Cases of admiralty and maritime Jurisdiction;—to Controversies to which the United States shall be a Party;—to Controversies between two or more States;—*between a State and Citizens of another State;*‡—between Citizens of different States;—between Citizens of the same State claiming Lands under Grants of different States, and between a State, or the Citizens thereof, and foreign States, Citizens or Subjects.

In all Cases affecting Ambassadors, other public Ministers and Consuls, and those in which a State shall be Party, the supreme Court shall have original Jurisdiction. In all the other Cases before mentioned, the supreme Court shall have appellate Jurisdiction, both as to Law and Fact, with such Exceptions, and under such Regulations as the Congress shall make.

---

*Superseded by the Twelfth Amendment.
†Modified by the Twenty-fifth Amendment.

‡Restricted by the Eleventh Amendment.

The trial of all Crimes, except in Cases of Impeachment, shall be by Jury; and such Trial shall be held in the State where said Crimes shall have been committed; but when not committed within any State, the Trial shall be at such Place or Places as the Congress may by Law have directed.

Section 3. Treason against the United States, shall consist only in levying War against them, or in adhering to their Enemies, giving them Aid and Comfort. No Person shall be convicted of Treason unless on the Testimony of two Witnesses to the same overt Act, or on Confession in open Court.

The Congress shall have Power to declare the Punishment of Treason, but no Attainder of Treason shall work Corruption of Blood, or Forefeiture except during the Life of the Person attainted.

Article IV

Section 1. Full Faith and Credit shall be given in each State to the public Acts, Records, and judicial Proceedings of every other State. And the Congress may by general Laws prescribe the Manner in which such Acts, Records, and Proceedings shall be proved, and the Effect thereof.

Section 2. The Citizens of each State shall be entitled to all Privileges and Immunities of Citizens in the several States.

A Person charged in any State with Treason, Felony, or other Crime, who shall flee from Justice, and be found in another State, shall on demand of the executive Authority of the State from which he fled, be delivered up, to be removed to the State having Jurisdiction of the Crime.

No Person held to Service or Labour in one State, under the Laws thereof, escaping into another, shall, in Consequence of any Law or Regulation therein, be discharged from such Service or Labour, but shall be delivered up on Claim of the Party to whom such Service or Labour may be due. *

Section 3. New States may be admitted by the Congress into this Union; but no new State shall be formed or erected within the Jurisdiction of any other State; nor any State be formed by the Junction of two or more States, or parts of States, without the Consent of the Legislatures of the States concerned as well as of the Congress.

The Congress shall have Power to dispose of and make all needful Rules and Regulations respecting the Territory or other Property belonging to the United States; and nothing in this Constitution shall be so construed as to Prejudice any Claims of the United States, or of any particular State.

Section 4. The United States shall guarantee to every State in this Union a Republican Form of Government, and shall protect each of them against Invasion; and on Application of the Legislature, or of the Executive (when the Legislature cannot be convened) against domestic Violence.

Article V

The Congress, whenever two-thirds of both Houses shall deem it necessary, shall propose Amendments to this Constitution, or, on the Application of the Legislatures of two-thirds of the several States, shall call a Convention for proposing Amendments, which, in either Case, shall be valid to all Intents and Purposes, as Part of this Constitution, when ratified by the Legislatures of three-fourths of the several States, or by Conventions in three-fourths thereof, as the one or the other Mode of Ratification may be proposed by the Congress; Provided that no Amendment which may be made prior to the Year One thousand eight hundred and eight shall in any Manner affect the first and fourth Clauses in the Ninth Section of the first Article; and that no State, without its Consent, shall be deprived of its equal Suffrage in the Senate.

Article VI

All Debts contracted and Engagements entered into, before the Adoption of this Constitution, shall be as valid against the United States under this Constitution, as under the Confederation.

This Constitution, and the Laws of the United States which shall be made in Pursuance thereof; and all Treaties made, or which shall be made, under the Authority of the United States, shall be the supreme Law of the Land; and the Judges in every State shall be bound thereby, any Thing in the Constitution or Laws of any State to the Contrary notwithstanding.

The Senators and Representatives before mentioned, and the Members of the several State Legislatures, and all executive and judicial Officers, both of the United States and of the several States, shall be bound by Oath or Affirmation, to support this Constitution; but no religious Test shall ever be required as a Qualification to any Office or public Trust under the United States.

Article VII

The Ratification of the Conventions of nine States shall be sufficient for the Establishment of this Constitution between the States so ratifying the Same.

Done in Convention by the Unanimous Consent of the States present the Seventeenth Day of September in the Year of our Lord one thousand seven hundred and Eighty seven and of the Independence of the United States of America the Twelfth. In Witness whereof We have hereunto subscribed our Names.

---

*Superseded by the Thirteenth Amendment.

Go. Washington
President and deputy from Virginia

New Hampshire
John Langdon
Nicholas Gilman

Massachusetts
Nathaniel Gorham
Rufus King

Connecticut
Wm. Saml. Johnson
Roger Sherman

New York
Alexander Hamilton

New Jersey
Wil. Livingston
David Brearley
Wm. Paterson
Jona. Dayton

Pennsylvania
B. Franklin
Thomas Mifflin
Robt. Morris
Geo. Clymer
Thos. FitzSimons
Jared Ingersoll
James Wilson
Gouv. Morris

Delaware
Geo. Read
Gunning Bedford jun
John Dickinson
Richard Bassett
Jaco. Broom

Maryland
James McHenry
Dan. of St. Thos. Jenifer
Danl. Carroll

Virginia
John Blair
James Madison, Jr.

North Carolina
Wm. Blount
Richd. Dobbs Spaight
Hu Williamson

South Carolina
J. Rutledge
Charles Cotesworth Pinckney
Pierce Butler

Georgia
William Few
Abr. Baldwin

Amendments to the Constitution with Annotations (Including the Six Unratified Amendments)

In their effort to gain Antifederalists' support for the Constitution, Federalists frequently pointed to the inclusion of Article 5, which provides an orderly method of amending the Constitution. In contrast, the Articles of Confederation, which were universally recognized as seriously flawed, offered no means of amendment. For their part, Antifederalists argued that the amendment process was so "intricate" that one might as easily roll "sixes an hundred times in succession" as change the Constitution.

The system for amendment laid out in the Constitution requires that two-thirds of both houses of Congress agree to a proposed amendment, which must then be ratified by three-quarters of the legislatures of the states. Alternatively, an amendment may be proposed by a convention called by the legislatures of two-thirds of the states. Since 1789, members of Congress have proposed thousands of amendments. Besides the seventeen amendments added since 1791, only the six "unratified" ones included here were approved by two-thirds of both houses but not ratified by the states.

Among the many amendments that never made it out of Congress have been proposals to declare dueling, divorce, and interracial marriage unconstitutional as well as proposals to establish a national university, to acknowledge the sovereignty of Jesus Christ, and to prohibit any person from possessing wealth in excess of $10 million.*

Among the issues facing Americans today that might lead to constitutional amendment are efforts to balance the federal budget, to limit the number of terms elected officials may serve, to limit access to or prohibit abortion, to establish English as the official language of the United States, and to prohibit flag burning. None of these proposed amendments has yet garnered enough support in Congress to be sent to the states for ratification.

Although the first ten amendments to the Constitution are commonly known as the Bill of Rights, only Amendments 1 through 8 provide guarantees of individual rights. Amendments 9 and 10 deal with the structure of power within the constitutional system. The Bill of Rights was promised to appease Antifederalists who refused to ratify the Constitution without guarantees of individual liberties and limitations to federal power. After studying more than two hundred amendments recommended by the ratifying conventions of the states, Federalist James Madison presented a list of seventeen to Congress, which used Madison's list as the foundation for the twelve amendments that were sent to the states for ratification. Ten of the twelve were adopted in 1791. The first on the list of twelve, known as the Reapportionment Amendment, was never adopted (p. D-16). The second proposed amendment was adopted in 1992 as Amendment 27 (p. D-24).

Amendment I [1791]†

Congress shall make no law respecting an establishment of religion, or prohibiting the free exercise thereof; or abridging the freedom of speech, or of the press; or the right of the people peaceably to assemble, and to petition the Government for a redress of grievances.

. . .

The First Amendment is a potent symbol for many Americans. Most are well aware of their rights to free speech, freedom of the press, and freedom of religion and their rights to assemble and to petition, even if they cannot cite the exact words of this amendment.

The First Amendment guarantee of freedom of religion has two clauses: the "free exercise clause," which allows individuals to practice or not practice any religion, and the "establishment clause," which prevents the federal government from discriminating against or favoring any particular religion. This clause was designed to create what Thomas Jefferson referred to as "a wall of separation between church and state." In the 1960s the Supreme Court ruled that the First Amendment prohibits prayer and Bible reading in public schools.

Although the rights to free speech and freedom of the press are established in the First Amendment, it was not until the twentieth century that the Supreme Court began to explore the full meaning of these guarantees. In 1919 the Court ruled in Schenck v. United States that the government could suppress free expression only where it could cite a "clear and present danger." In a decision that continues to raise controversies, the Court ruled in 1990, in Texas v. Johnson, that flag burning is a form of symbolic speech protected by the First Amendment.

---

*Richard B. Bernstein, *Amending America* (New York: Times Books, 1993), 177–81.

†The dates in brackets indicate when the amendment was ratified.

Amendment II [1791]

A well regulated Militia, being necessary to the security of a free State, the right of the people to keep and bear Arms shall not be infringed.

. . .

Fear of a standing army under the control of a hostile government made the Second Amendment an important part of the Bill of Rights. Advocates of gun ownership claim that the amendment prevents the government from regulating firearms. Proponents of gun control argue that the amendment is designed only to protect the right of the states to maintain militia units.

In 1939 the Supreme Court ruled in United States v. Miller *that the Second Amendment did not protect the right of an individual to own a sawed-off shotgun, which it argued was not ordinary militia equipment. Since then, the Supreme Court has refused to hear Second Amendment cases, whereas lower courts have upheld firearm regulations. Several justices currently on the bench seem to favor a broader interpretation of the Second Amendment, which would affect gun-control legislation. The controversy over the impact of the Second Amendment on gun owners and gun-control legislation will certainly continue.*

Amendment III [1791]

No Soldier shall, in time of peace, be quartered in any house, without the consent of the Owner, nor in time of war, but in a manner to be prescribed by law.

. . .

The Third Amendment was extremely important to the framers of the Constitution, but today it is nearly forgotten. American colonists were especially outraged that they were forced to quarter British troops in the years before and during the American Revolution. The philosophy of the Third Amendment has been viewed by some justices and scholars as the foundation of the modern constitutional right to privacy.

Amendment IV [1791]

The right of the people to be secure in their persons, houses, papers, and effects, against unreasonable searches and seizures, shall not be violated, and no Warrants shall issue, but upon probable cause, supported by Oath or affirmation, and particularly describing the place to be searched, and the persons or things to be seized.

. . .

In the years before the Revolution, the houses, barns, stores, and warehouses of American colonists were ransacked by British authorities under "writs of assistance" or general warrants. The British, thus empowered, searched for seditious material or smuggled goods that could then be used as evidence against colonists who were charged with a crime only after the items were found.

The first part of the Fourth Amendment protects citizens from "unreasonable" searches and seizures. The Supreme Court has interpreted this protection as well as the words search *and* seizure *in different ways at different times. At one time, the Court did not recognize electronic eavesdropping as a form of search and seizure, although it does today. At times, an "unreasonable" search has been almost any search carried out without a warrant, but in the two decades before 1969 the Court sometimes sanctioned warrantless searches that it considered reasonable based on "the total atmosphere of the case."*

The second part of the Fourth Amendment defines the procedure for issuing a search warrant and states the requirement of "probable cause," which is generally viewed as evidence indicating that a suspect has committed an offense.

In Weeks v. U.S. *(1994) and* Mapp v. Ohio *(1962), the Court excluded evidence seized in violation of constitutional standards. The justification is that excluding such evidence deters violations of the amendment, but doing so may allow a guilty person to escape punishment.*

Amendment V [1791]

No person shall be held to answer for a capital or otherwise infamous crime, unless on a presentment or indictment of a Grand Jury, except in cases arising in the land or naval forces, or in the Militia, when in actual service in time of War or public danger; nor shall any person be subject for the same offence to be twice put in jeopardy of life or limb; nor shall be compelled in any criminal case to be a witness against himself, nor be deprived of life, liberty, or property, without due process of law; nor shall private property be taken for public use, without just compensation.

. . .

The Fifth Amendment protects people against government authority in the prosecution of criminal offenses. It prohibits the state, first, from charging a person with a serious crime without a grand-jury hearing to decide whether there is sufficient evidence to support the charge and, second, from charging a person with the same crime twice. The best-known aspect of the Fifth Amendment is that it prevents a person from being "compelled . . . to be a witness against himself." The last clause, the "takings clause," limits the power of the government to seize property.

Although invoking the Fifth Amendment is popularly viewed as a confession of guilt, a person may be innocent yet still fear prosecution. For example, during the cold war era of the late 1940s and 1950s, many people who had participated in legal activities that were associated with the Communist Party claimed the Fifth Amendment privilege rather than testify before the House Un-American Activities Committee because the mood of the times cast those activities in a negative light. Because "taking the Fifth" was viewed as an admission of guilt, those people often lost their jobs or became unemployable. Nonetheless, the right to protect oneself against self-incrimination plays an important role in guarding against the collective power of the state.

Amendment VI [1791]

In all criminal prosecutions, the accused shall enjoy the right to a speedy and public trial, by an impartial jury of the State and district wherein the crime shall have been committed, which district shall have been previously ascertained by law, and to be informed of the nature and cause of the accusation; to be confronted with the witnesses against him; to have compulsory process for obtaining witnesses in his favor, and to have the Assistance of Counsel for his defence.

• • •

The original Constitution put few limits on the government's power to investigate, prosecute, and punish crime. This process was of great concern to many Antifederalists, and of the twenty-eight rights specified in the first eight amendments, fifteen have to do with it. Seven rights are specified in the Sixth Amendment. These include the right to a speedy trial, a public trial, a jury trial, a notice of accusation, confrontation of opposing witnesses, testimony by favorable witnesses, and the assistance of counsel.

Amendment VII [1791]

In suits at common law, where the value in controversy shall exceed twenty dollars, the right of trial by jury shall be preserved, and no fact tried by a jury, shall be otherwise reexamined in any Court of the United States, than according to the Rules of the common law.

• • •

This amendment guarantees people the same right to a trial by jury as was guaranteed by English common law in 1791. Under common law, in civil trials (those involving money damages) the role of the judge was to settle questions of law and that of the jury was to settle questions of fact. The amendment does not specify the size of the jury or its role in a trial, however. The Supreme Court has generally held that those issues be determined by English common law of 1791, which stated that a jury consists of twelve people, that a trial must be conducted before a judge who instructs the jury on the law and advises it on facts, and that a verdict must be unanimous.

Amendment VIII [1791]

Excessive bail shall not be required, nor excessive fines imposed, nor cruel and unusual punishments inflicted.

• • •

The language used to guarantee the three rights in this amendment was inspired by the English Bill of Rights of 1689. The Supreme Court has not had a lot to say about "excessive fines." In recent years it has agreed that despite the provision against "excessive bail," persons who are believed to be dangerous to others can be held without bail even before they have been convicted.

Although opponents of the death penalty have not succeeded in using the Eighth Amendment to achieve the end of capital punishment, the clause regarding "cruel and unusual punishments" has been used to prohibit capital punishment in certain cases, such as minors and the mentally retarded.

Amendment IX [1791]

The enumeration in the Constitution, of certain rights, shall not be construed to deny or disparage others retained by the people.

• • •

Some Federalists feared that inclusion of the Bill of Rights in the Constitution would allow later generations of interpreters to claim that the people had surrendered all rights not specifically enumerated there. To guard against this, James Madison added language that became the Ninth Amendment. Interest in this heretofore largely ignored amendment revived in 1965 when it was used in a concurring opinion in Griswold v. Connecticut *(1965). While Justice William O. Douglas called on the Third Amendment to support the right to privacy in deciding that case, Justice Arthur Goldberg, in the concurring opinion, argued that the right to privacy regarding contraception was an unenumerated right that was protected by the Ninth Amendment.*

In 1980 the Court ruled that the right of the press to attend a public trial was protected by the Ninth Amendment. Although some scholars argue that modern judges cannot identify the unenumerated rights that the framers were trying to protect, others argue that the Ninth Amendment should be read as providing a constitutional "presumption of liberty" that allows people to act in any way that does not violate the rights of others.

Amendment X [1791]

The powers not delegated to the United States by the Constitution, nor prohibited by it to the States, are reserved to the States respectively, or to the people.

• • •

The Antifederalists were especially eager to see a "reserved powers clause" explicitly guaranteeing the states control over their internal affairs. Not surprisingly, the Tenth Amendment has been a frequent battleground in the struggle over states' rights and federal supremacy. Prior to the Civil War, the Jeffersonian Republican Party and Jacksonian Democrats invoked the Tenth

Amendment to prohibit the federal government from making decisions about whether people in individual states could own slaves. The Tenth Amendment was virtually suspended during Reconstruction following the Civil War. In 1883, however, the Supreme Court declared the Civil Rights Act of 1875 unconstitutional on the grounds that it violated the Tenth Amendment. Business interests also called on the amendment to block efforts at federal regulation.

The Court was inconsistent over the next several decades as it attempted to resolve the tension between the restrictions of the Tenth Amendment and the powers the Constitution granted to Congress to regulate interstate commerce and levy taxes. The Court upheld the Pure Food and Drug Act (1906), the Meat Inspection Acts (1906 and 1907), and the White Slave Traffic Act (1910), all of which affected the states, but it struck down an act prohibiting interstate shipment of goods produced through child labor. Between 1934 and 1935 a number of New Deal programs created by Franklin D. Roosevelt were declared unconstitutional on the grounds that they violated the Tenth Amendment. As Roosevelt appointees changed the composition of the Court, the Tenth Amendment was declared to have no substantive meaning. Generally, the amendment is held to protect the rights of states to regulate internal matters such as local government, education, commerce, labor, and business as well as matters involving families such as marriage, divorce, and inheritance within the state.

Unratified Amendment

Reapportionment Amendment (proposed by Congress September 25, 1789, along with the Bill of Rights)

After the first enumeration required by the first article of the Constitution, there shall be one Representative for every thirty thousand, until the number shall amount to one hundred, after which the proportion shall be so regulated by Congress, that there shall be not less than one hundred Representatives, nor less than one Representative for every forty thousand persons, until the number of Representatives shall amount to two hundred; after which the proportion shall be so regulated by Congress, that there shall not be less than two hundred Representatives, nor more than one Representative for every fifty thousand persons.

• • •

If the Reapportionment Amendment had passed and remained in effect, the House of Representatives today would have more than 7,000 members rather than 435 to reflect the current U.S. population.

Amendment XI [1798]

The Judicial power of the United States shall not be construed to extend to any suit in law or equity, commenced or prosecuted against one of the United States by Citizens of another State, or by Citizens or subjects of any foreign state.

• • •

In 1793 the Supreme Court ruled in favor of Alexander Chisholm, executor of the estate of a deceased South Carolina merchant. Chisholm was suing the state of Georgia because the merchant had never been paid for provisions he had supplied during the Revolution. Many regarded this Court decision as an error that violated the intent of the Constitution.

Antifederalists and many other Americans feared a powerful federal court system because they worried that it would become like the British courts of this period, which were accountable only to the monarch. Furthermore, Chisholm v. Georgia prompted a series of suits against state governments by creditors and suppliers who had made loans during the war.

In addition, state legislators and Congress feared that the shaky economies of the new states, as well as the country as a whole, would be destroyed, especially if Loyalists who had fled to other countries sought reimbursement for land and property that had been seized. The day after the Supreme Court announced its decision, a resolution proposing the Eleventh Amendment, which overturned the decision in Chisholm v. Georgia, *was introduced in the U.S. Senate.*

Amendment XII [1804]

The Electors shall meet in their respective States and vote by ballot for President and Vice-President, one of whom, at least, shall not be an inhabitant of the same State with themselves; they shall name in their ballots the person voted for as President, and in distinct ballots the person voted for as Vice-President, and they shall make distinct lists of all persons voted for as President, and of all persons voted for as Vice-President, and of the number of votes for each, which lists they shall sign and certify, and transmit sealed to the seat of government of the United States, directed to the President of the Senate;—the President of the Senate shall, in the presence of the Senate and House of Representatives, open all the certificates and the votes shall then be counted;—The person having the greatest number of votes for President, shall be the President, if such number be a majority of the whole number of Electors appointed; and if no person have such majority, then from the persons having the highest numbers not exceeding three on the list of those voted for as President, the House of Representatives shall choose immediately, by ballot, the President. But in choosing the President, the votes shall be taken by States, the representation from each State having one vote; a quorum for this purpose shall consist of a member or members from two-thirds of the States, and a majority of all the States shall be necessary to a choice. And if the House of Representatives shall not choose a President whenever the right of choice shall devolve upon them, before *the fourth day of March* next following, then the Vice-President shall act as

President, as in the case of the death or other constitutional disability of the President.*—The person having the greatest number of votes as Vice-President, shall be the Vice-President, if such number be a majority of the whole number of Electors appointed; and if no person have a majority, then from the two highest numbers on the list, the Senate shall choose the Vice-President; a quorum for the purpose shall consist of two-thirds of the whole number of Senators, and a majority of the whole number shall be necessary to a choice. But no person constitutionally ineligible to the office of President shall be eligible to that of Vice-President of the United States.

. . .

The framers of the Constitution disliked political parties and assumed that none would ever form. Under the original system, electors chosen by the states would each vote for two candidates. The candidate who won the most votes would become president, and the person who won the second-highest number of votes would become vice president. Rivalries between Federalists and Republicans led to the formation of political parties, however, even before George Washington had left office. In 1796 Federalist John Adams was chosen as president, and his great rival, Thomas Jefferson (whose party was called the Republican Party), became his vice president. In 1800 all the electors cast their two votes as one of two party blocs. Jefferson and his fellow Republican nominee, Aaron Burr, were tied with seventy-three votes each. The contest went to the House of Representatives, which finally elected Jefferson after thirty-six ballots. The Twelfth Amendment prevents these problems by requiring electors to vote separately for the president and vice president.

Unratified Amendment

Titles of Nobility Amendment (proposed by Congress May 1, 1810)

If any citizen of the United States shall accept, claim, receive or retain any title of nobility or honor or shall, without the consent of Congress, accept and retain any present, pension, office or emolument of any kind whatever, from any emperor, king, prince or foreign power, such person shall cease to be a citizen of the United States, and shall be incapable of holding any office of trust or profit under them, or either of them.

. . .

This amendment would have extended Article I, Section 9, Clause 8 of the Constitution, which prevents the awarding of titles by the United States and the acceptance of such awards from foreign powers without congressional consent. Historians speculate that general nervousness about the power of the Emperor Napoleon, who was at that time extending France's empire throughout Europe, may have prompted the proposal. Though it

fell one vote short of ratification, Congress and the American people thought the proposal had been ratified, and it was included in many nineteenth-century editions of the Constitution.

The Civil War and Reconstruction Amendments (Thirteenth, Fourteenth, and Fifteenth Amendments)

In the four months between the election of Abraham Lincoln and his inauguration, more than two hundred proposed constitutional amendments were presented to Congress as part of a desperate attempt to hold the rapidly dissolving Union together. Most of these were efforts to appease the southern states by protecting the right to own slaves or by disfranchising African Americans through constitutional amendment. None were able to win the votes required from Congress to send them to the states. Ultimately, the Corwin Amendment seemed to be the only hope for preserving the Union by amending the Constitution.

The northern victors in the Civil War tried to restructure the Constitution just as the war had restructured the nation. Yet they were often divided in their goals. Some wanted to end slavery; others hoped for social and economic equality regardless of race; others hoped that extending the power of the ballot box to former slaves would help create a new political order. The debates over the Thirteenth, Fourteenth, and Fifteenth Amendments were bitter. Few of those who fought for these changes were satisfied with the amendments themselves; fewer still were satisfied with their interpretation. Although the amendments put an end to the legal status of slavery, it was nearly a hundred years after the amendments' passage before most of the descendants of former slaves could begin to experience the economic, social, and political equality the amendments were intended to provide.

Unratified Amendment

Corwin Amendment (proposed by Congress March 2, 1861)

No amendment shall be made to the Constitution which will authorize or give to Congress the power to abolish or interfere, within any State, with the domestic institutions thereof, including that of persons held to labor or service by the laws of said State.

. . .

Following the election of Abraham Lincoln, Congress scrambled to try to prevent the secession of the slaveholding states. House member Thomas Corwin of Ohio proposed the "unamendable" amendment in the hope that by protecting slavery where it existed, Congress would keep the southern states in the Union. Lincoln indicated his support for the proposed amendment in his first inaugural address. Only Ohio and Maryland ratified the Corwin Amendment before the war caused it to be forgotten.

---

*Superseded by Section 3 of the Twentieth Amendment.

Amendment XIII [1865]

Section 1. Neither slavery nor involuntary servitude, except as a punishment for crime whereof the party shall have been duly convicted, shall exist within the United States, or any place subject to their jurisdiction.

Section 2. Congress shall have power to enforce this article by appropriate legislation.

• • •

Because the Emancipation Proclamation of 1863 abolished slavery only in the parts of the Confederacy still in rebellion, Republicans proposed a Thirteenth Amendment that would extend abolition to the entire South. In February 1865, when the proposal was approved by the House, the gallery of the House was newly opened to black Americans who had a chance at last to see their government at work. Passage of the proposal was greeted by wild cheers from the gallery as well as tears on the House floor, where congressional representatives openly embraced one another.

The problem of ratification remained, however. The Union position was that the Confederate states were part of the country of thirty-six states. Therefore, twenty-seven states were needed to ratify the amendment. When Kentucky and Delaware rejected it, backers realized that without approval from at least four former Confederate states, the amendment would fail. Lincoln's successor, President Andrew Johnson, made ratification of the Thirteenth Amendment a condition for southern states to rejoin the Union. Under those terms, all the former Confederate states except Mississippi accepted the Thirteenth Amendment, and by the end of 1865 the amendment had become part of the Constitution and slavery had been prohibited in the United States.

Amendment XIV [1868]

Section 1. All persons born or naturalized in the United States, and subject to the jurisdiction thereof, are citizens of the United States and of the State wherein they reside. No State shall make or enforce any law which shall abridge the privileges or immunities of citizens of the United States; nor shall any State deprive any person of life, liberty, or property, without due process of law; nor deny to any person within its jurisdiction the equal protection of the laws.

Section 2. Representatives shall be apportioned among the several States according to their respective numbers, counting the whole number of persons in each State, excluding Indians not taxed. But when the right to vote at any election for the choice of electors for President and Vice-President of the United States, Representatives in Congress, the Executive and Judicial officers of a State, or the members of the Legislature thereof, is denied to any of the male inhabitants of such State, being twenty-one years of age and citizens of the United States, or in any way abridged, except for participation in rebellion, or other crime, the basis of representation therein shall be reduced in the proportion which the number of such male citizens shall bear to the whole number of male citizens twenty-one years of age in such State.

Section 3. No person shall be a Senator or Representative in Congress, or Elector of President and Vice-President, or hold any office, civil or military, under the United States, or under any State, who, having previously taken an oath, as a member of Congress, or as an officer of the United States, or as a member of any State legislature, or as an executive or judicial officer of any State, to support the Constitution of the United States, shall have engaged in insurrection or rebellion against the same, or given aid or comfort to the enemies thereof. Congress may, by a vote of two-thirds of each house, remove such disability.

Section 4. The validity of the public debt of the United States, authorized by law, including debts incurred for payment of pensions and bounties for services in suppressing insurrection or rebellion, shall not be questioned. But neither the United States nor any State shall assume or pay any debt or obligation incurred in aid of insurrection or rebellion against the United States, or any claim for the loss or emancipation of any slave; but all such debts, obligations, and claims shall be held illegal and void.

Section 5. The Congress shall have power to enforce, by appropriate legislation, the provisions of this article.

• • •

Less than a year after Lincoln's assassination, Andrew Johnson was ready to bring the former Confederate states back into the Union and Confederate leaders back into Congress. Anxious Republicans drafted the Fourteenth Amendment to prevent that from happening. Moreover, most Southern states had enacted "Black Codes" that restricted the legal, political, and civil rights of former slaves. The most important provisions of this complex amendment made all native-born or naturalized persons American citizens and prohibited states from abridging the "privileges or immunities" of citizens; depriving them of "life, liberty, or property, without due process of law"; and denying them "equal protection of the laws." In essence, it made all former slaves citizens and protected the rights of all citizens against violation by their own state governments.

As occurred in the case of the Thirteenth Amendment, former Confederate states were forced to ratify the amendment as a condition of representation in the House and the Senate. The intentions of the Fourteenth Amendment, and how those intentions should be enforced, have been the most debated point of constitutional history. The terms due process and equal protection have been especially troublesome. Was the amendment designed to outlaw racial segregation? Or was the goal simply to prevent the leaders of the rebellious South from gaining political power?

The framers of the Fourteenth Amendment hoped Section 2 would produce black voters who would increase the power of the Republican Party. The federal government, however, never used its power to punish states for denying blacks their right to vote. Although the Fourteenth Amendment had an immediate impact in giving black Americans citizenship, it did nothing to protect blacks from the vengeance of whites once Reconstruction ended. In the late nineteenth and early twentieth centuries, Section 1 of the Fourteenth Amendment was often used to protect business interests and strike down laws protecting workers on the grounds that the rights of "persons," that is, corporations, were protected by "due process." More recently, the Fourteenth Amendment has been used to justify school desegregation and affirmative action programs, as well as to dismantle such programs.

Amendment XV [1870]

Section 1. The right of citizens of the United States to vote shall not be denied or abridged by the United States or by any State on account of race, color, or previous condition of servitude—

Section 2. The Congress shall have power to enforce this article by appropriate legislation.

• • •

The Fifteenth Amendment was the last major piece of Reconstruction legislation. Although earlier Reconstruction acts had already required black suffrage in the South, the Fifteenth Amendment extended black voting rights to the entire nation. Some Republicans felt morally obligated to do away with the double standard between the North and South because many northern states had stubbornly refused to enfranchise blacks. Others believed that the freedman's ballot required the extra protection of a constitutional amendment to shield it from white counterattack in the South. But partisan advantage also played an important role in the amendment's passage because Republicans hoped that by giving the ballot to blacks, they could lessen their party's political vulnerability.

Many women's rights advocates had fought for the amendment. They had felt betrayed by the inclusion of the word male *in Section 2 of the Fourteenth Amendment and were further angered when the proposed Fifteenth Amendment failed to prohibit denial of the right to vote on the grounds of sex as well as "race, color, or previous condition of servitude." In this amendment, for the first time, the federal government exerted its power to regulate the franchise, or vote. It was also the first time the Constitution placed limits on the power of the states to regulate access to the franchise. Although ratified in 1870, the amendment was not enforced until the twentieth century.*

The Progressive Amendments (Sixteenth– Nineteenth Amendments)

No amendments were added to the Constitution between the Civil War and the Progressive Era. America was changing, however, in fundamental ways. The rapid industrialization of the United States after the Civil War led to many social and economic problems. Hundreds of amendments were proposed, but none received enough support in Congress to be sent to the states. Some scholars believe that regional differences and rivalries were so strong during this period that it was almost impossible to gain a consensus on a constitutional amendment. During the Progressive Era, however, the Constitution was amended four times in seven years.

Amendment XVI [1913]

The Congress shall have power to lay and collect taxes on incomes, from whatever source derived, without apportionment among the several States, and without regard to any census or enumeration.

• • •

Until passage of the Sixteenth Amendment, most of the money used to run the federal government came from customs duties and taxes on specific items, such as liquor. During the Civil War the federal government taxed incomes as an emergency measure. Pressure to enact an income tax came from those who were concerned about the growing gap between rich and poor in the United States. The Populist Party began campaigning for a graduated income tax in 1892, and support continued to grow. By 1909 thirty-three proposed income tax amendments had been presented in Congress, but lobbying by corporate and other special interests had defeated them all. In June 1909 the growing pressure for an income tax, which had been endorsed by presidents Roosevelt and Taft, finally pushed an amendment through the Senate. The required thirty-six states had ratified the amendment by February 1913.

Amendment XVII [1913]

Section 1. The Senate of the United States shall be composed of two Senators from each State, elected by the people thereof, for six years; and each Senator shall have one vote. The electors in each State shall have the qualifications requisite for electors of [voters for] the most numerous branch of the State legislatures.

Section 2. When vacancies happen in the representation of any State in the Senate, the executive authority of such State shall issue writs of election to fill such vacancies: Provided, that the Legislature of any State may empower the executive thereof to make temporary appointments until the people fill the vacancies by election as the Legislature may direct.

Section 3. This amendment shall not be so construed as to affect the election or term of any Senator chosen before it becomes valid as part of the Constitution.

. . .

The framers of the Constitution saw the members of the House as the representatives of the people and the members of the Senate as the representatives of the states. Originally, senators were to be chosen by the state legislators. According to reform advocates, however, the growth of private industry and transportation conglomerates during the late nineteenth century had created a network of corruption in which wealth and power were exchanged for influence and votes in the Senate. Senator Nelson Aldrich, who represented Rhode Island in this period, for example, was known as "the senator from Standard Oil" because of his open support of special business interests.

Efforts to amend the Constitution to allow direct election of senators had begun in 1826, but because any proposal had to be approved by the Senate, reform seemed impossible. Progressives tried to gain influence in the Senate by instituting party caucuses and primary elections, which gave citizens the chance to express their choice of a senator who could then be officially elected by the state legislature. By 1910 fourteen of the country's thirty senators received popular votes through a state primary before the state legislature made its selection. Despairing of getting a proposal through the Senate, supporters of a direct-election amendment had begun in 1893 to seek a convention of representatives from two-thirds of the states to propose an amendment that could then be ratified. By 1905 thirty-one of forty-five states had endorsed such an amendment. Finally, in 1911, despite extraordinary opposition, a proposed amendment passed the Senate; by 1913 it had been ratified.

Amendment XVIII [1919; repealed 1933 by Amendment XXI]

Section 1. After one year from the ratification of this article the manufacture, sale, or transportation of intoxicating liquors within, the importation thereof into, or the exportation thereof from the United States and all territory subject to the jurisdiction thereof, for beverage purposes, is hereby prohibited.

Section 2. The Congress and the several States shall have concurrent power to enforce this article by appropriate legislation.

Section 3. This article shall be inoperative unless it shall have been ratified as an amendment to the Constitution by the legislatures of the several States, as provided by the Constitution, within seven years from the date of the submission thereof to the States by the Congress.

. . .

The Prohibition Party, formed in 1869, began calling for a constitutional amendment to outlaw alcoholic beverages in 1872. A prohibition amendment was first proposed in the Senate in 1876

and was revived eighteen times before 1913. Between 1913 and 1919 another thirty-nine attempts were made to prohibit liquor in the United States through a constitutional amendment. Prohibition became a key element of the Progressive agenda as reformers linked alcohol and drunkenness to numerous social problems, including the corruption of immigrant voters. Whereas opponents of such an amendment argued that it was undemocratic, supporters claimed that their efforts had widespread public support. The admission of twelve "dry" western states to the Union in the early twentieth century and the spirit of sacrifice during World War I laid the groundwork for passage and ratification of the Eighteenth Amendment in 1919. Opponents added a time limit to the amendment in the hope that they could thereby block ratification, but this effort failed. (See also Amendment XXI.)

Amendment XIX [1920]

Section 1. The right of citizens of the United States to vote shall not be denied or abridged by the United States or by any State on account of sex.

Section 2. Congress shall have the power to enforce this article by appropriate legislation.

. . .

Advocates of women's rights tried and failed to link woman suffrage to the Fourteenth and Fifteenth Amendments. Nonetheless, the effort for woman suffrage continued. Between 1878 and 1912 at least one and sometimes as many as four proposed amendments were introduced in Congress each year to grant women the right to vote. Although over time women won very limited voting rights in some states, at both the state and federal levels opposition to an amendment for woman suffrage remained very strong. President Woodrow Wilson and other officials felt that the federal government should not interfere with the power of the states in this matter. And many people were concerned that giving women the vote would result in their abandoning traditional gender roles. In 1919, following a protracted and often bitter campaign of protest in which women went on hunger strikes and chained themselves to fences, an amendment was introduced with the backing of President Wilson. It narrowly passed the Senate (after efforts to limit the suffrage to white women failed) and was adopted in 1920 after Tennessee became the thirty-sixth state to ratify it.

Unratified Amendment

Child Labor Amendment
(proposed by Congress June 2, 1924)

Section 1. The Congress shall have power to limit, regulate, and prohibit the labor of persons under eighteen years of age.

Section 2. The power of the several States is unimpaired by this article except that the operation of State laws shall be suspended to the extent necessary to give effect to legislation enacted by Congress.

. . .

Throughout the late nineteenth and early twentieth centuries, alarm over the condition of child workers grew. Opponents of child labor argued that children worked in dangerous and unhealthy conditions, that they took jobs from adult workers, that they depressed wages in certain industries, and that states that allowed child labor had an economic advantage over those that did not. Defenders of child labor claimed that children provided needed income in many families, that working at a young age helped to develop character, and that the effort to prohibit the practice constituted an invasion of family privacy.

In 1916 Congress passed a law that made it illegal to sell through interstate commerce goods made by children. The Supreme Court, however, ruled that the law violated the limits on the power of Congress to regulate interstate commerce. Congress then tried to penalize industries that used child labor by taxing such goods. This measure was also thrown out by the courts. In response, reformers set out to amend the Constitution. The proposed amendment was ratified by twenty-eight states, but by 1925 thirteen states had rejected it. Passage of the Fair Labor Standards Act in 1938, which was upheld by the Supreme Court in 1941, made the amendment irrelevant.

Amendment XX [1933]

Section 1. The terms of the President and Vice-President shall end at noon on the 20th day of January, and the terms of Senators and Representatives at noon on the 3rd day of January, of the years in which such terms would have ended if this article had not been ratified; and the terms of their successors shall then begin.

Section 2. The Congress shall assemble at least once in every year, and such meeting shall begin at noon on the 3rd day of January, unless they shall by law appoint a different day.

Section 3. If, at the time fixed for the beginning of the term of the President, the President-elect shall have died, the Vice-President-elect shall become President. If a President shall not have been chosen before the time fixed for the beginning of his term, or if the President-elect shall have failed to qualify, then the Vice-President-elect shall act as President until a President shall have qualified; and the Congress may by law provide for the case wherein neither a President-elect nor a Vice-President-elect shall have qualified, declaring who shall then act as President, or the manner in which one who is to act shall be selected, and such person shall act accordingly until a President or Vice-President shall have qualified.

Section 4. The Congress may by law provide for the case of the death of any of the persons from whom the House of Representatives may choose a President whenever the right of choice shall have devolved upon them, and for the case of the death of any of the persons from whom the Senate may choose a Vice-President whenever the right of choice shall have devolved upon them.

Section 5. Sections 1 and 2 shall take effect on the 15th day of October following the ratification of this article.

Section 6. This article shall be inoperative unless it shall have been ratified as an amendment to the Constitution by the Legislatures of three-fourths of the several States within seven years from the date of its submission.

. . .

Until 1933, presidents took office on March 4. Because elections are held in early November and electoral votes are counted in mid-December, this meant that more than three months passed between the time a new president was elected and when he took office. Moving the inauguration to January shortened the transition period and allowed Congress to begin its term closer to the time of the president's inauguration. Although this seems like a minor change, an amendment was required because the Constitution specifies terms of office. This amendment also deals with questions of succession in the event that a president- or vice-president-elect dies before assuming office. Section 3 also clarifies a method for resolving a deadlock in the electoral college.

Amendment XXI [1933]

Section 1. The eighteenth article of amendment to the Constitution of the United States is hereby repealed.

Section 2. The transportation or importation into any State, Territory, or Possession of the United States for delivery or use therein of intoxicating liquors, in violation of the laws thereof, is hereby prohibited.

Section 3. This article shall be inoperative unless it shall have been ratified as an amendment to the Constitution by conventions in the several States, as provided in the Constitution, within seven years from the date of the submission thereof to the States by the Congress.

. . .

Widespread violation of the Volstead Act, the law enacted to enforce prohibition, made the United States a nation of lawbreakers. Prohibition caused more problems than it solved by encouraging crime, bribery, and corruption. Further, a coalition of liquor and beer manufacturers, personal liberty advocates, and constitutional scholars joined forces to challenge the amendment. By 1929 thirty proposed repeal amendments had been introduced in Congress, and the Democratic Party made repeal part of its platform in the 1932 presidential campaign. The Twenty-first Amendment was proposed in February 1933 and ratified less than a year later. The failure of the effort to enforce prohibition through a constitutional amendment has often been cited by opponents of subsequent efforts to shape public virtue and private morality.

Amendment XXII [1951]

Section 1. No person shall be elected to the office of the President more than twice, and no person who has held the office of President, or acted as President, for more than two years of a term to which some other person was elected President shall be elected to the office of President more than once. But this article shall not apply to any person holding the office of President when this Article was proposed by the Congress, and shall not prevent any person who may be holding the office of President, or acting as President, during the term within which this Article becomes operative from holding the office of President or acting as President during the remainder of such term.

Section 2. This article shall be inoperative unless it shall have been ratified as an amendment to the Constitution by the legislatures of three-fourths of the several States within seven years from the date of its submission to the States by the Congress.

• • •

George Washington's refusal to seek a third term of office set a precedent that stood until 1912, when former president Theodore Roosevelt sought, without success, another term as an independent candidate. Democrat Franklin Roosevelt was the only president to seek and win a fourth term, though he did so amid great controversy. Roosevelt died in April 1945, a few months after the beginning of his fourth term. In 1946 Republicans won control of the House and the Senate, and early in 1947 a proposal for an amendment to limit future presidents to two four-year terms was offered to the states for ratification. Democratic critics of the Twenty-second Amendment charged that it was a partisan posthumous jab at Roosevelt.

Since the Twenty-second Amendment was adopted, two of the three presidents who might have been able to seek a third term, had it not existed, were Republicans Dwight Eisenhower and Ronald Reagan. Since 1826, Congress has entertained 160 proposed amendments to limit the president to one six-year term. Such amendments have been backed by fifteen presidents, including Gerald Ford and Jimmy Carter.

Amendment XXIII [1961]

Section 1. The District constituting the seat of Government of the United States shall appoint in such manner as the Congress may direct: A number of electors of President and Vice-President equal to the whole number of Senators and Representatives in Congress to which the District would be entitled if it were a State, but in no event more than the least populous State; they shall be in addition to those appointed by the States, but they shall be considered for the purposes of the election of President and Vice-President, to be electors appointed by a State; and they shall meet in the District and perform such duties as provided by the twelfth article of amendment.

Section 2. The Congress shall have the power to enforce this article by appropriate legislation.

• • •

When Washington, D.C., was established as a federal district, no one expected that a significant number of people would make it their permanent and primary residence. A proposal to allow citizens of the district to vote in presidential elections was approved by Congress in June 1960 and was ratified on March 29, 1961.

Amendment XXIV [1964]

Section 1. The right of citizens of the United States to vote in any primary or other election for President or Vice-President, for electors for President or Vice-President, or for Senator or Representative in Congress, shall not be denied or abridged by the United States or any State by reason of failure to pay any poll tax or other tax.

Section 2. The Congress shall have the power to enforce this article by appropriate legislation.

• • •

In the colonial and Revolutionary eras, financial independence was seen as necessary to political independence, and the poll tax was used as a requirement for voting. By the twentieth century, however, the poll tax was used mostly to bar poor people, especially southern blacks, from voting. Although conservatives complained that the amendment interfered with states' rights, liberals thought that the amendment did not go far enough because it barred the poll tax only in national elections and not in state or local elections. The amendment was ratified in 1964, however, and two years later the Supreme Court ruled that poll taxes in state and local elections also violated the equal protection clause of the Fourteenth Amendment.

Amendment XXV [1967]

Section 1. In case of the removal of the President from office or of his death or resignation, the Vice-President shall become President.

Section 2. Whenever there is a vacancy in the office of the Vice-President, the President shall nominate a Vice-President who shall take office upon confirmation by a majority vote of both Houses of Congress.

Section 3. Whenever the President transmits to the President pro tempore of the Senate and the Speaker of the House of Representatives his written declaration that he is unable to discharge the powers and duties of his office, and until he transmits to them a written declaration to the contrary, such powers and duties shall be discharged by the Vice-President as Acting President.

Section 4. Whenever the Vice-President and a majority of either the principal officers of the executive departments or of such other body as Congress may by law provide, transmit to the President pro tempore of the Senate and the Speaker of the House of Representatives their written declaration that the President is unable to discharge the powers and duties of his office, the Vice-President shall immediately assume the powers and duties of the office as Acting President.

Thereafter, when the President transmits to the President pro tempore of the Senate and the Speaker of the House of Representatives his written declaration that no inability exists, he shall resume the powers and duties of his office unless the Vice-President and a majority of either the principal officers of the executive department[s] or of such other body as Congress may by law provide, transmit within four days to the President pro tempore of the Senate and the Speaker of the House of Representatives their written declaration that the President is unable to discharge the powers and duties of his office. Thereupon Congress shall decide the issue, assembling within forty-eight hours for that purpose if not in session. If the Congress, within twenty-one days after receipt of the latter written declaration, or, if Congress is not in session, within twenty-one days after Congress is required to assemble, determines by two-thirds vote of both Houses that the President is unable to discharge the powers and duties of his office, the Vice-President shall continue to discharge the same as Acting President; otherwise, the President shall resume the powers and duties of his office.

. . .

The framers of the Constitution established the office of vice president because someone was needed to preside over the Senate. The first president to die in office was William Henry Harrison, in 1841. Vice President John Tyler had himself sworn in as president, setting a precedent that was followed when seven later presidents died in office. The assassination of President James A. Garfield in 1881 posed a new problem, however. After he was shot, the president was incapacitated for two months before he died; he was unable to lead the country, and his vice president, Chester A. Arthur, was unable to assume leadership. Efforts to

resolve questions of succession in the event of a presidential disability thus began with the death of Garfield.

In 1963 the assassination of President John F. Kennedy galvanized Congress to action. Vice President Lyndon Johnson was a chain-smoker with a history of heart trouble. According to the 1947 Presidential Succession Act, the two men who stood in line to succeed him were the seventy-two-year-old Speaker of the House and the eighty-six-year-old president of the Senate. There were serious concerns that any of these men might become incapacitated while serving as chief executive. The first time the Twenty-fifth Amendment was used, however, was not in the case of presidential death or illness, but during the Watergate crisis. When Vice President Spiro T. Agnew was forced to resign following allegations of bribery and tax violations, President Richard M. Nixon appointed House Minority Leader Gerald R. Ford vice president. Ford became president following Nixon's resignation eight months later and named Nelson A. Rockefeller as his vice president. Thus, for more than two years, the two highest offices in the country were held by people who had not been elected to them.

Amendment XXVI [1971]

Section 1. The right of citizens of the United States, who are eighteen years of age or older, to vote shall not be denied or abridged by the United States or by any State on account of age.

Section 2. The Congress shall have power to enforce this article by appropriate legislation.

. . .

Efforts to lower the voting age from twenty-one to eighteen began during World War II. Recognizing that those who were old enough to fight a war should have some say in the government policies that involved them in the war, Presidents Eisenhower, Johnson, and Nixon endorsed the idea. In 1970 the combined pressure of the antiwar movement and the demographic pressure of the baby-boom generation led to a Voting Rights Act lowering the voting age in federal, state, and local elections.

In Oregon v. Mitchell (1970), the state of Oregon challenged the right of Congress to determine the age at which people could vote in state or local elections. The Supreme Court agreed with Oregon. Because the Voting Rights Act was ruled unconstitutional, the Constitution had to be amended to allow passage of a law that would lower the voting age. The amendment was ratified in a little more than three months, making it the most rapidly ratified amendment in U.S. history.

Unratified Amendment

Equal Rights Amendment (proposed by Congress March 22, 1972; seven-year deadline for ratification extended to June 30, 1982)

Section 1. Equality of rights under the law shall not be denied or abridged by the United States or by any State on account of sex.

Section 2. The Congress shall have the power to enforce, by appropriate legislation, the provisions of this article.

Section 3. This amendment shall take effect two years after the date of ratification.

• • •

In 1923, soon after women had won the right to vote, Alice Paul, a leading activist in the woman suffrage movement, proposed an amendment requiring equal treatment of men and women. Opponents of the proposal argued that such an amendment would invalidate laws that protected women and would make women subject to the military draft. After the 1964 Civil Rights Act was adopted, protective workplace legislation was partially removed.

The renewal of the women's movement, as a by-product of the civil rights and antiwar movements, led to a revival of the Equal Rights Amendment (ERA) in Congress. Disagreements over language held up congressional passage of the proposed amendment, but on March 22, 1972, the Senate approved the ERA by a vote of 84 to 8, and it was sent to the states. Six states ratified the amendment within two days, and by the middle of 1973 the amendment seemed well on its way to adoption, with thirty of the needed thirty-eight states having ratified it. In the mid-1970s, however, a powerful "Stop ERA" campaign developed. The campaign portrayed the ERA as a threat to "family values" and traditional relationships between men and women. Although thirty-five states ratified the ERA, five of those state legislatures voted to rescind ratification, and the amendment was never adopted.

Unratified Amendment

D.C. Statehood Amendment
(proposed by Congress August 22, 1978)

Section 1. For purposes of representation in the Congress, election of the President and Vice President, and article V of this Constitution, the District constituting the seat of government of the United States shall be treated as though it were a State.

Section 2. The exercise of the rights and powers conferred under this article shall be by the people of the District constituting the seat of government, and as shall be provided by Congress.

Section 3. The twenty-third article of amendment to the Constitution of the United States is hereby repealed.

Section 4. This article shall be inoperative, unless it shall have been ratified as an amendment to the Constitution by the legislatures of three-fourths of the several states within seven years from the date of its submission.

• • •

The 1961 ratification of the Twenty-third Amendment, giving residents of the District of Columbia the right to vote for a president and vice president, inspired an effort to give residents of the district full voting rights. In 1966 President Lyndon Johnson appointed a mayor and city council; in 1971 D.C. residents were allowed to name a nonvoting delegate to the House; and in 1981 residents were allowed to elect the mayor and city council. Congress retained the right to overrule laws that might affect commuters, the height of District buildings, and selection of judges and prosecutors. The district's nonvoting delegate to Congress, Walter Fauntroy, lobbied fiercely for a congressional amendment granting statehood to the district. In 1978 a proposed amendment was approved and sent to the states. A number of states quickly ratified the amendment, but, like the ERA, the D.C. Statehood Amendment ran into trouble. Opponents argued that Section 2 created a separate category of "nominal" statehood. They argued that the federal district should be eliminated and that the territory should be reabsorbed into the state of Maryland. Most scholars believe that the fears of Republicans that the predominantly black population of the city would consistently elect Democratic senators constituted a major factor leading to the defeat of the amendment.

Amendment XXVII [1992]

No law varying the compensation for the services of the Senators and Representatives, shall take effect, until an election of Representatives shall have intervened.

• • •

Whereas the Twenty-sixth Amendment was the most rapidly ratified amendment in U.S. history, the Twenty-seventh Amendment had the longest journey to ratification. First proposed by James Madison in 1789 as part of the package that included the Bill of Rights, this amendment had been ratified by only six states by 1791. In 1873, however, it was ratified by Ohio to protest a massive retroactive salary increase by the federal government. Unlike later proposed amendments, this one came with no time limit on ratification. In the early 1980s Gregory D. Watson, a University of Texas economics major, discovered the "lost" amendment and began a single-handed campaign to get state legislators to introduce it for ratification. In 1983 it was accepted by Maine. In 1984 it passed the Colorado legislature. Ratifications trickled in slowly until May 1992, when Michigan and New Jersey became the thirty-eighth and thirty-ninth states, respectively, to ratify. This amendment prevents members of Congress from raising their own salaries without giving voters a chance to vote them out of office before they can benefit from the raises.

The American Nation

Admission of States into the Union

State	Date of Admission	State	Date of Admission	State	Date of Admission
1. Delaware	December 7, 1787	18. Louisiana	April 30, 1812	35. West Virginia	June 20, 1863
2. Pennsylvania	December 12, 1787	19. Indiana	December 11, 1816	36. Nevada	October 31, 1864
3. New Jersey	December 18, 1787	20. Mississippi	December 10, 1817	37. Nebraska	March 1, 1867
4. Georgia	January 2, 1788	21. Illinois	December 3, 1818	38. Colorado	August 1, 1876
5. Connecticut	January 9, 1788	22. Alabama	December 14, 1819	39. North Dakota	November 2, 1889
6. Massachusetts	February 6, 1788	23. Maine	March 15, 1820	40. South Dakota	November 2, 1889
7. Maryland	April 28, 1788	24. Missouri	August 10, 1821	41. Montana	November 8, 1889
8. South Carolina	May 23, 1788	25. Arkansas	June 15, 1836	42. Washington	November 11, 1889
9. New Hampshire	June 21, 1788	26. Michigan	January 26, 1837	43. Idaho	July 3, 1890
10. Virginia	June 25, 1788	27. Florida	March 3, 1845	44. Wyoming	July 10, 1890
11. New York	July 26, 1788	28. Texas	December 29, 1845	45. Utah	January 4, 1896
12. North Carolina	November 21, 1789	29. Iowa	December 28, 1846	46. Oklahoma	November 16, 1907
13. Rhode Island	May 29, 1790	30. Wisconsin	May 29, 1848	47. New Mexico	January 6, 1912
14. Vermont	March 4, 1791	31. California	September 9, 1850	48. Arizona	February 14, 1912
15. Kentucky	June 1, 1792	32. Minnesota	May 11, 1858	49. Alaska	January 3, 1959
16. Tennessee	June 1, 1796	33. Oregon	February 14, 1859	50. Hawaii	August 21, 1959
17. Ohio	March 1, 1803	34. Kansas	January 29, 1861		

Territorial Expansion

Territory	Date Acquired	Square Miles	How Acquired
Original states and territories	1783	888,685	Treaty of Paris
Louisiana Purchase	1803	827,192	Purchased from France
Florida	1819	72,003	Adams-Onís Treaty
Texas	1845	390,143	Annexation of independent country
Oregon	1846	285,580	Oregon Boundary Treaty
Mexican cession	1848	529,017	Treaty of Guadalupe Hidalgo
Gadsden Purchase	1853	29,640	Purchased from Mexico
Midway Islands	1867	2	Annexation of uninhabited islands
Alaska	1867	589,757	Purchased from Russia
Hawaii	1898	6,450	Annexation of independent country
Wake Island	1898	3	Annexation of uninhabited island
Puerto Rico	1899	3,435	Treaty of Paris
Guam	1899	212	Treaty of Paris
The Philippines	1899–1946	115,600	Treaty of Paris; granted independence
American Samoa	1900	76	Treaty with Germany and Great Britain
Panama Canal Zone	1904–1978	553	Hay–Bunau-Varilla Treaty
U.S. Virgin Islands	1917	133	Purchased from Denmark
Trust Territory of the Pacific Islands*	1947	717	United Nations Trusteeship

*A number of these islands have been granted independence: Federated States of Micronesia, 1990; Marshall Islands, 1991; Palau, 1994.

Presidential Elections

Year	Candidates	Parties	Percentage of Popular Vote	Electoral Vote	Percentage of Voter Participation
1789	**George Washington**	No party designations	*	69	
	John Adams[†]			34	
	Other candidates			35	
1792	**George Washington**	No party designations		132	
	John Adams			77	
	George Clinton			50	
	Other candidates			5	
1796	**John Adams**	Federalist		71	
	Thomas Jefferson	Democratic-Republican		68	
	Thomas Pinckney	Federalist		59	
	Aaron Burr	Democratic-Republican		30	
	Other candidates			48	
1800	**Thomas Jefferson**	Democratic-Republican		73	
	Aaron Burr	Democratic-Republican		73	
	John Adams	Federalist		65	
	Charles C. Pinckney	Federalist		64	
	John Jay	Federalist		1	
1804	**Thomas Jefferson**	Democratic-Republican		162	
	Charles C. Pinckney	Federalist		14	
1808	**James Madison**	Democratic-Republican		122	
	Charles C. Pinckney	Federalist		47	
	George Clinton	Democratic-Republican		6	
1812	**James Madison**	Democratic-Republican		128	
	De Witt Clinton	Federalist		89	
1816	**James Monroe**	Democratic-Republican		183	
	Rufus King	Federalist		34	
1820	**James Monroe**	Democratic-Republican		231	
	John Quincy Adams	Independent Republican		1	
1824	**John Quincy Adams**	Democratic-Republican	30.5	84	26.9
	Andrew Jackson	Democratic-Republican	43.1	99	
	Henry Clay	Democratic-Republican	13.2	37	
	William H. Crawford	Democratic-Republican	13.1	41	
1828	**Andrew Jackson**	Democratic	56.0	178	57.6
	John Quincy Adams	National Republican	44.0	83	
1832	**Andrew Jackson**	Democratic	54.5	219	55.4
	Henry Clay	National Republican	37.5	49	
	William Wirt	Anti-Masonic	8.0	7	
	John Floyd	Democratic	‡	11	
1836	**Martin Van Buren**	Democratic	50.9	170	57.8
	William H. Harrison	Whig		73	
	Hugh L. White	Whig		26	
	Daniel Webster	Whig	49.1	14	
	W. P. Mangum	Whig		11	
1840	**William H. Harrison**	Whig	53.1	234	80.2
	Martin Van Buren	Democratic	46.9	60	
1844	**James K. Polk**	Democratic	49.6	170	78.9
	Henry Clay	Whig	48.1	105	
	James G. Birney	Liberty	2.3		

Year	Candidates	Parties	Percentage of Popular Vote	Electoral Vote	Percentage of Voter Participation
1848	**Zachary Taylor**	Whig	47.4	163	72.7
	Lewis Cass	Democratic	42.5	127	
	Martin Van Buren	Free Soil	10.1		
1852	**Franklin Pierce**	Democratic	50.9	254	69.6
	Winfield Scott	Whig	44.1	42	
	John P. Hale	Free Soil	5.0		
1856	**James Buchanan**	Democratic	45.3	174	78.9
	John C. Frémont	Republican	33.1	114	
	Millard Fillmore	American	21.6	8	
1860	**Abraham Lincoln**	Republican	39.8	180	81.2
	Stephen A. Douglas	Democratic	29.5	12	
	John C. Breckinridge	Democratic	18.1	72	
	John Bell	Constitutional Union	12.6	39	
1864	**Abraham Lincoln**	Republican	55.0	212	73.8
	George B. McClellan	Democratic	45.0	21	
1868	**Ulysses S. Grant**	Republican	52.7	214	78.1
	Horatio Seymour	Democratic	47.3	80	
1872	**Ulysses S. Grant**	Republican	55.6	286	71.3
	Horace Greeley	Democratic	43.9		
1876	**Rutherford B. Hayes**	Republican	48.0	185	81.8
	Samuel J. Tilden	Democratic	51.0	184	
1880	**James A. Garfield**	Republican	48.5	214	79.4
	Winfield S. Hancock	Democratic	48.1	155	
	James B. Weaver	Greenback-Labor	3.4		
1884	**Grover Cleveland**	Democratic	48.5	219	77.5
	James G. Blaine	Republican	48.2	182	
1888	**Benjamin Harrison**	Republican	47.9	233	79.3
	Grover Cleveland	Democratic	48.6	168	
1892	**Grover Cleveland**	Democratic	46.1	277	74.7
	Benjamin Harrison	Republican	43.0	145	
	James B. Weaver	People's	8.5	22	
1896	**William McKinley**	Republican	51.1	271	79.3
	William J. Bryan	Democratic	47.7	176	
1900	**William McKinley**	Republican	51.7	292	73.2
	William J. Bryan	Democratic; Populist	45.5	155	
1904	**Theodore Roosevelt**	Republican	57.4	336	65.2
	Alton B. Parker	Democratic	37.6	140	
	Eugene V. Debs	Socialist	3.0		
1908	**William H. Taft**	Republican	51.6	321	65.4
	William J. Bryan	Democratic	43.1	162	
	Eugene V. Debs	Socialist	2.8		
1912	**Woodrow Wilson**	Democratic	41.9	435	58.8
	Theodore Roosevelt	Progressive	27.4	88	
	William H. Taft	Republican	23.2	8	
	Eugene V. Debs	Socialist	6.0		
1916	**Woodrow Wilson**	Democratic	49.4	277	61.6
	Charles E. Hughes	Republican	46.2	254	
	A. L. Benson	Socialist	3.2		

Year	Candidates	Parties	Percentage of Popular Vote	Electoral Vote	Percentage of Voter Participation
1920	**Warren G. Harding**	Republican	60.4	404	49.2
	James M. Cox	Democratic	34.2	127	
	Eugene V. Debs	Socialist	3.4		
1924	**Calvin Coolidge**	Republican	54.0	382	48.9
	John W. Davis	Democratic	28.8	136	
	Robert M. La Follette	Progressive	16.6	13	
1928	**Herbert C. Hoover**	Republican	58.2	444	56.9
	Alfred E. Smith	Democratic	40.9	87	
1932	**Franklin D. Roosevelt**	Democratic	57.4	472	56.9
	Herbert C. Hoover	Republican	39.7	59	
1936	**Franklin D. Roosevelt**	Democratic	60.8	523	61.0
	Alfred M. Landon	Republican	36.5	8	
1940	**Franklin D. Roosevelt**	Democratic	54.8	449	62.5
	Wendell L. Willkie	Republican	44.8	82	
1944	**Franklin D. Roosevelt**	Democratic	53.5	432	55.9
	Thomas E. Dewey	Republican	46.0	99	
1948	**Harry S Truman**	Democratic	49.6	303	53.0
	Thomas E. Dewey	Republican	45.1	189	
1952	**Dwight D. Eisenhower**	Republican	55.1	442	63.3
	Adlai E. Stevenson	Democratic	44.4	89	
1956	**Dwight D. Eisenhower**	Republican	57.6	457	60.6
	Adlai E. Stevenson	Democratic	42.1	73	
1960	**John F. Kennedy**	Democratic	49.7	303	64.0
	Richard M. Nixon	Republican	49.5	219	
1964	**Lyndon B. Johnson**	Democratic	61.1	486	61.7
	Barry M. Goldwater	Republican	38.5	52	
1968	**Richard M. Nixon**	Republican	43.4	301	60.6
	Hubert H. Humphrey	Democratic	42.7	191	
	George C. Wallace	American Independent	13.5	46	
1972	**Richard M. Nixon**	Republican	60.7	520	55.5
	George S. McGovern	Democratic	37.5	17	
1976	**Jimmy Carter**	Democratic	50.1	297	54.3
	Gerald R. Ford	Republican	48.0	240	
1980	**Ronald W. Reagan**	Republican	50.7	489	53.0
	Jimmy Carter	Democratic	41.0	49	
	John B. Anderson	Independent	6.6	0	
1984	**Ronald W. Reagan**	Republican	58.4	525	52.9
	Walter F. Mondale	Democratic	41.6	13	
1988	**George H. W. Bush**	Republican	53.4	426	50.3
	Michael Dukakis	Democratic	45.6	111**	
1992	**Bill Clinton**	Democratic	43.7	370	55.1
	George H. W. Bush	Republican	38.0	168	
	H. Ross Perot	Independent	19.0	0	
1996	**Bill Clinton**	Democratic	49	379	49.0
	Robert J. Dole	Republican	41	159	
	H. Ross Perot	Reform	8	0	
2000	**George W. Bush**	Republican	47.8	271	51.3
	Albert Gore	Democratic	48.4	267	
	Ralph Nader	Green	0.4	0	
2004	**George W. Bush**	Republican	50.7	286	60.3
	John Kerry	Democratic	48.3	252	
	Ralph Nader	Independent	.38	0	

*Prior to 1824, most presidential electors were chosen by state legislators rather than by popular vote.
†Before the Twelfth Amendment was passed in 1804, the Electoral College voted for two presidential candidates; the runner-up became vice president.
‡Percentages below 2.5 have been omitted. Hence the percentage of popular vote might not total 100 percent.
**One Dukakis elector cast a vote for Lloyd Bentsen.

Supreme Court Justices

Name	Terms of Service	Appointed by	Name	Terms of Service	Appointed by
John Jay, * N.Y.	1789–1795	Washington	Samuel Blatchford, N.Y.	1882–1893	Arthur
James Wilson, Pa.	1789–1798	Washington	Lucius Q. C. Lamar, Miss.	1888–1893	Cleveland
John Rutledge, S.C.	1790–1791	Washington	**Melville W. Fuller**, Ill.	1888–1910	Cleveland
William Cushing, Mass.	1790–1810	Washington	David J. Brewer, Kan.	1890–1910	B. Harrison
John Blair, Va.	1790–1796	Washington	Henry B. Brown, Mich.	1891–1906	B. Harrison
James Iredell, N.C.	1790–1799	Washington	George Shiras Jr., Pa.	1892–1903	B. Harrison
Thomas Johnson, Md.	1792–1793	Washington	Howell E. Jackson, Tenn.	1893–1895	B. Harrison
William Paterson, N.J.	1793–1806	Washington	Edward D. White, La.	1894–1910	Cleveland
John Rutledge, S.C.	1795	Washington	Rufus W. Peckham, N.Y.	1896–1909	Cleveland
Samuel Chase, Md.	1796–1811	Washington	Joseph McKenna, Cal.	1898–1925	McKinley
Oliver Ellsworth, Conn.	1796–1800	Washington	Oliver W. Holmes, Mass.	1902–1932	T. Roosevelt
Bushrod Washington, Va.	1799–1829	J. Adams	William R. Day, Ohio	1903–1922	T. Roosevelt
Alfred Moore, N.C.	1800–1804	J. Adams	William H. Moody, Mass.	1906–1910	T. Roosevelt
John Marshall, Va.	1801–1835	J. Adams	Horace H. Lurton, Tenn.	1910–1914	Taft
William Johnson, S.C.	1804–1834	Jefferson	Charles E. Hughes, N.Y.	1910–1916	Taft
Brockholst Livingston, N.Y.	1807–1823	Jefferson	**Edward D. White**, La.	1910–1921	Taft
Thomas Todd, Ky.	1807–1826	Jefferson	Willis Van Devanter, Wy.	1911–1937	Taft
Gabriel Duvall, Md.	1811–1835	Madison	Joseph R. Lamar, Ga.	1911–1916	Taft
Joseph Story, Mass.	1812–1845	Madison	Mahlon Pitney, N.J.	1912–1922	Taft
Smith Thompson, N.Y.	1823–1843	Monroe	James C. McReynolds, Tenn.	1914–1941	Wilson
Robert Trimble, Ky.	1826–1828	J. Q. Adams	Louis D. Brandeis, Mass.	1916–1939	Wilson
John McLean, Ohio	1830–1861	Jackson	John H. Clarke, Ohio	1916–1922	Wilson
Henry Baldwin, Pa.	1830–1844	Jackson	**William H. Taft**, Conn.	1921–1930	Harding
James M. Wayne, Ga.	1835–1867	Jackson	George Sutherland, Utah	1922–1938	Harding
Roger B. Taney, Md.	1836–1864	Jackson	Pierce Butler, Minn.	1923–1939	Harding
Philip P. Barbour, Va.	1836–1841	Jackson	Edward T. Sanford, Tenn.	1923–1930	Harding
John Cartron, Tenn.	1837–1865	Van Buren	Harlan F. Stone, N.Y.	1925–1941	Coolidge
John McKinley, Ala.	1838–1852	Van Buren	**Charles E. Hughes**, N.Y.	1930–1941	Hoover
Peter V. Daniel, Va.	1842–1860	Van Buren	Owen J. Roberts, Pa.	1930–1945	Hoover
Samuel Nelson, N.Y.	1845–1872	Tyler	Benjamin N. Cardozo, N.Y.	1932–1938	Hoover
Levi Woodbury, N.H.	1845–1851	Polk	Hugo L. Black, Ala.	1937–1971	F. Roosevelt
Robert C. Grier, Pa.	1846–1870	Polk	Stanley F. Reed, Ky.	1938–1957	F. Roosevelt
Benjamin R. Curtis, Mass.	1851–1857	Fillmore	Felix Frankfurter, Mass.	1939–1962	F. Roosevelt
John A. Campbell, Ala.	1853–1861	Pierce	William O. Douglas, Conn.	1939–1975	F. Roosevelt
Nathan Clifford, Me.	1858–1881	Buchanan	Frank Murphy, Mich.	1940–1949	F. Roosevelt
Noah H. Swayne, Ohio	1862–1881	Lincoln	**Harlan F. Stone**, N.Y.	1941–1946	F. Roosevelt
Samuel F. Miller, Iowa	1862–1890	Lincoln	James R. Byrnes, S.C.	1941–1942	F. Roosevelt
David Davis, Ill.	1862–1877	Lincoln	Robert H. Jackson, N.Y.	1941–1954	F. Roosevelt
Stephen J. Field, Cal.	1863–1897	Lincoln	Wiley B. Rutledge, Iowa	1943–1949	F. Roosevelt
Salmon P. Chase, Ohio	1864–1873	Lincoln	Harold H. Burton, Ohio	1945–1958	Truman
William Strong, Pa.	1870–1880	Grant	**Frederick M. Vinson**, Ky.	1946–1953	Truman
Joseph P. Bradley, N.J.	1870–1892	Grant	Tom C. Clark, Texas	1949–1967	Truman
Ward Hunt, N.Y.	1873–1882	Grant	Sherman Minton, Ind.	1949–1956	Truman
Morrison R. Waite, Ohio	1874–1888	Grant	**Earl Warren**, Cal.	1953–1969	Eisenhower
John M. Harlan, Ky.	1877–1911	Hayes	John Marshall Harlan, N.Y.	1955–1971	Eisenhower
William B. Woods, Ga.	1881–1887	Hayes	William J. Brennan Jr., N.J.	1956–1990	Eisenhower
Stanley Matthews, Ohio	1881–1889	Garfield	Charles E. Whittaker, Mo.	1957–1962	Eisenhower
Horace Gray, Mass.	1882–1902	Arthur	Potter Stewart, Ohio	1958–1981	Eisenhower

Name	Terms of Service	Appointed by	Name	Terms of Service	Appointed by
Bryon R. White, Colo.	1962–1993	Kennedy	Antonin Scalia, Va.	1986–	Reagan
Arthur J. Goldberg, Ill.	1962–1965	Kennedy	Anthony M. Kennedy, Cal.	1988–	Reagan
Abe Fortas, Tenn.	1965–1969	Johnson	David H. Souter, N.H.	1990–	Bush, G.H.W.
Thurgood Marshall, Md.	1967–1991	Johnson	Clarence Thomas, Ga.	1991–	Bush, G.H.W.
Warren E. Burger, Minn.	1969–1986	Nixon	Ruth Bader Ginsburg, N.Y.	1993–	Clinton
Harry A. Blackmun, Minn.	1970–1994	Nixon	Stephen G. Breyer, Mass.	1994–	Clinton
Lewis F. Powell Jr., Va.	1971–1987	Nixon	**John G. Roberts, Jr.**, Md.	2005–	Bush, G.W.
William H. Rehnquist, Ill.	1971–1986	Nixon	Samuel A. Alito Jr., N.J.	2006–	Bush, G.W.
John Paul Stevens, Ill.	1975–	Ford			
Sandra Day O'Connor, Ariz.	1981–2006	Reagan			
William H. Rehnquist, Va.	1986–2005	Reagan			

*Chief Justices are printed in bold type.

The American People: a Demographic Survey

A Demographic Profile of the American People

Year	Life Expectancy from Birth		Average Age at First Marriage		Number of Children Under 5 (per 1,000 Women Aged 22–24)	Percentage of Persons in Paid Employment		Percentage of Paid Workers Who Are Women
	White	Black	Men	Women		Men	Women	
1820					1,295		6.2	7.3
1830					1,145		6.4	7.4
1840					1,085		8.4	9.6
1850					923		10.1	10.8
1860					929		9.7	10.2
1870					839		13.7	14.8
1880					822		14.7	15.2
1890			26.1	22.0	716	84.3	18.2	17.0
1900	47.6	33.0	25.9	21.9	688	85.7	20.0	18.1
1910	50.3	35.6	25.1	21.6	643	85.1	24.8	20.0
1920	54.9	45.3	24.6	21.2	604	84.6	22.7	20.4
1930	61.4	48.1	24.3	21.3	511	82.1	23.6	21.9
1940	64.2	53.1	24.3	21.5	429	79.1	25.8	24.6
1950	69.1	60.8	22.8	20.3	589	81.6	29.9	27.8
1960	70.6	63.6	22.8	20.3	737	80.4	35.7	32.3
1970	71.7	65.3	22.5	20.6	530	79.7	41.4	38.0
1980	74.4	68.1	24.7	22.0	440	77.4	51.5	42.6
1990	76.1	69.1	26.1	23.9	377	76.4	57.4	45.2
2000	77.6	71.7	26.7	25.1	365	74.8	58.9	46.3
2004	78.2	73.4	27.4	25.8		73.3	59.2	46.5

SOURCE: U.S. Bureau of the Census, *Historical Statistics of the United States, Colonial Times to 1970 (1975); Statistical Abstract of the United States, 2001; Statistical Abstract of the United States, 2006.*

American Population

Year	Population	Percentage Increase	Year	Population	Percentage Increase
1610	350	—	1820	9,638,453	33.1
1620	2,300	557.1	1830	12,866,020	33.5
1630	4,600	100.0	1840	17,069,453	32.7
1640	26,600	478.3	1850	23,191,876	35.9
1650	50,400	90.8	1860	31,443,321	35.6
1660	75,100	49.0	1870	39,818,449	26.6
1670	111,900	49.0	1880	50,155,783	26.0
1680	151,500	35.4	1890	62,947,714	25.5
1690	210,400	38.9	1900	75,994,575	20.7
1700	250,900	19.2	1910	91,972,266	21.0
1710	331,700	32.2	1920	105,710,620	14.9
1720	466,200	40.5	1930	122,775,046	16.1
1730	629,400	35.0	1940	131,669,275	7.2
1740	905,600	43.9	1950	150,697,361	14.5
1750	1,170,800	29.3	1960	179,323,175	19.0
1760	1,593,600	36.1	1970	203,235,298	13.3
1770	2,148,100	34.8	1980	226,545,805	11.5
1780	2,780,400	29.4	1990	248,709,873	9.8
1790	3,929,214	41.3	2000	281,421,906	13.2
1800	5,308,483	35.1	2005	296,410,404	5.0
1810	7,239,881	36.4			

Note: These figures largely ignore the Native American population. Census takers never made any effort to count the Native American population that lived outside their reserved political areas and compiled only casual and incomplete enumerations of those living within their jurisdictions until 1890. In that year the federal government attempted a full count of the Indian population: The Census found 125,719 Indians in 1890, compared with only 12,543 in 1870 and 33,985 in 1880.

SOURCES: U.S. Bureau of the Census, *Historical Statistics of the United States, Colonial Times to 1970* (1975); *Statistical Abstract of the United States, 2001*; U.S. Bureau of the Census, Population Finder, http://factfinder.census.gov.

White/Nonwhite Population

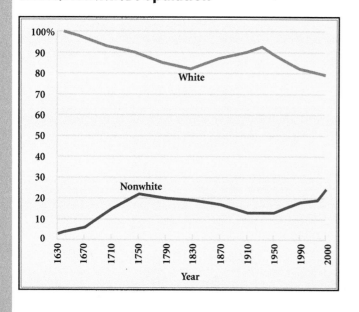

Urban/Rural Population

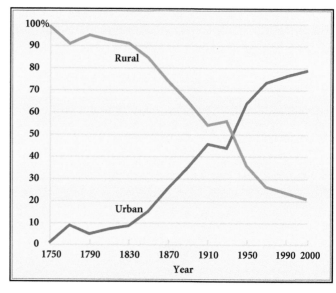

The Ten Largest Cities by Population, 1700–2000

		City	Population				City	Population
1700	1.	Boston	6,700		1930	1.	New York	6,930,446
	2.	New York	4,937*			2.	Chicago	3,376,438
	3.	Philadelphia	4,400†			3.	Philadelphia	1,950,961
1790	1.	Philadelphia	42,520			4.	Detroit	1,568,662
	2.	New York	33,131			5.	Los Angeles	1,238,048
	3.	Boston	18,038			6.	Cleveland	900,429
	4.	Charleston, S.C.	16,359			7.	St. Louis	821,960
	5.	Baltimore	13,503			8.	Baltimore	804,874
	6.	Salem, Mass.	7,921			9.	Boston	781,188
	7.	Newport, R.I.	6,716			10.	Pittsburgh	669,817
	8.	Providence, R.I.	6,380		1950	1.	New York	7,891,957
	9.	Marblehead, Mass.	5,661			2.	Chicago	3,620,962
	10.	Portsmouth, N.H.	4,720			3.	Philadelphia	2,071,605
1830	1.	New York	197,112			4.	Los Angeles	1,970,358
	2.	Philadelphia	161,410			5.	Detroit	1,849,568
	3.	Baltimore	80,620			6.	Baltimore	949,708
	4.	Boston	61,392			7.	Cleveland	914,808
	5.	Charleston, S.C.	30,289			8.	St. Louis	856,796
	6.	New Orleans	29,737			9.	Washington, D.C.	802,178
	7.	Cincinnati	24,831			10.	Boston	801,444
	8.	Albany, N.Y.	24,209		1970	1.	New York	7,895,563
	9.	Brooklyn, N.Y.	20,535			2.	Chicago	3,369,357
	10.	Washington, D.C.	18,826			3.	Los Angeles	2,811,801
1850	1.	New York	515,547			4.	Philadelphia	1,949,996
	2.	Philadelphia	340,045			5.	Detroit	1,514,063
	3.	Baltimore	169,054			6.	Houston	1,233,535
	4.	Boston	136,881			7.	Baltimore	905,787
	5.	New Orleans	116,375			8.	Dallas	844,401
	6.	Cincinnati	115,435			9.	Washington, D.C.	756,668
	7.	Brooklyn, N.Y.	96,838			10.	Cleveland	750,879
	8.	St. Louis	77,860		1990	1.	New York	7,322,564
	9.	Albany, N.Y.	50,763			2.	Los Angeles	3,485,398
	10.	Pittsburgh	46,601			3.	Chicago	2,783,726
1870	1.	New York	942,292			4.	Houston	1,630,553
	2.	Philadelphia	674,022			5.	Philadelphia	1,585,577
	3.	Brooklyn, N.Y.	419,921‡			6.	San Diego	1,110,549
	4.	St. Louis	310,864			7.	Detroit	1,027,974
	5.	Chicago	298,977			8.	Dallas	1,006,877
	6.	Baltimore	267,354			9.	Phoenix	983,403
	7.	Boston	250,526			10.	San Antonio	935,933
	8.	Cincinnati	216,239		2000	1.	New York	8,008,278
	9.	New Orleans	191,418			2.	Los Angeles	3,694,820
	10.	San Francisco	149,473			3.	Chicago	2,896,016
1910	1.	New York	4,766,883			4.	Houston	1,953,631
	2.	Chicago	2,185,283			5.	Philadelphia	1,517,550
	3.	Philadelphia	1,549,008			6.	Phoenix	1,321,045
	4.	St. Louis	687,029			7.	San Diego	1,223,400
	5.	Boston	670,585			8.	Dallas	1,188,580
	6.	Cleveland	560,663			9.	San Antonio	1,144,646
	7.	Baltimore	558,485			10.	Detroit	951,270
	8.	Pittsburgh	533,905					
	9.	Detroit	465,766					
	10.	Buffalo	423,715					

*Figure from a census taken in 1698.
†Philadelphia figures include suburbs.
‡Annexed to New York in 1898.
SOURCE: U.S. Census data.

Immigration by Decade

Year	Number	Percentage of Total Population	Year	Number	Percentage of Total Population
1821–1830	151,824	1.6	1921–1930	4,107,209	3.9
1831–1840	599,125	4.6	1931–1940	528,431	0.4
1841–1850	1,713,251	10.0	1941–1950	1,035,039	0.7
1851–1860	2,598,214	11.2	1951–1960	2,515,479	1.6
1861–1870	2,314,824	7.4	1961–1970	3,321,677	1.8
1871–1880	2,812,191	7.1	1971–1980	4,493,000	2.2
1881–1890	5,246,613	10.5	1981–1990	7,338,000	3.0
1891–1900	3,687,546	5.8	1991–2000	9,095,083	3.7
1901–1910	8,795,386	11.6	**Total**	**32,433,918**	
1911–1920	5,735,811	6.2			
Total	**33,654,785**		1821–2000		
			GRAND TOTAL	**66,088,703**	

SOURCES: U.S. Bureau of the Census, *Historical Statistics of the United States, Colonial Times to 1970* (1975), part 1, 105–106; *Statistical Abstract of the United States, 2001.*

Regional Origins

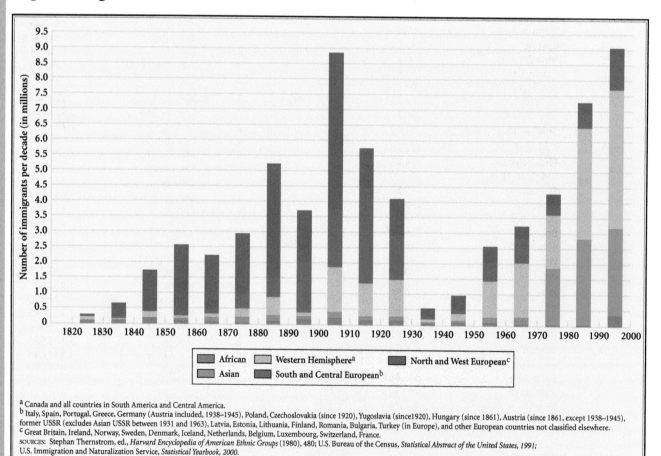

a Canada and all countries in South America and Central America.
b Italy, Spain, Portugal, Greece, Germany (Austria included, 1938–1945), Poland, Czechoslovakia (since 1920), Yugoslavia (since1920), Hungary (since 1861), Austria (since 1861, except 1938–1945), former USSR (excludes Asian USSR between 1931 and 1963), Latvia, Estonia, Lithuania, Finland, Romania, Bulgaria, Turkey (in Europe), and other European countries not classified elsewhere.
c Great Britain, Ireland, Norway, Sweden, Denmark, Iceland, Netherlands, Belgium, Luxembourg, Switzerland, France.
SOURCES: Stephan Thernstrom, ed., *Harvard Encyclopedia of American Ethnic Groups* (1980), 480; U.S. Bureau of the Census, *Statistical Abstract of the United States, 1991;* U.S. Immigration and Naturalization Service, *Statistical Yearbook, 2000.*

The Labor Force (Thousands of Workers)

Year	Agriculture	Mining	Manufacturing	Construction	Trade	Other	Total
1810	1,950	11	75	—	—	294	2,330
1840	3,570	32	500	290	350	918	5,660
1850	4,520	102	1,200	410	530	1,488	8,250
1860	5,880	176	1,530	520	890	2,114	11,110
1870	6,790	180	2,470	780	1,310	1,400	12,930
1880	8,920	280	3,290	900	1,930	2,070	17,390
1890	9,960	440	4,390	1,510	2,960	4,060	23,320
1900	11,680	637	5,895	1,665	3,970	5,223	29,070
1910	11,770	1,068	8,332	1,949	5,320	9,041	37,480
1920	10,790	1,180	11,190	1,233	5,845	11,372	41,610
1930	10,560	1,009	9,884	1,988	8,122	17,267	48,830
1940	9,575	925	11,309	1,876	9,328	23,277	56,290
1950	7,870	901	15,648	3,029	12,152	25,870	65,470
1960	5,970	709	17,145	3,640	14,051	32,545	74,060
1970	3,463	516	20,746	4,818	15,008	34,127	78,678
1980	3,364	979	21,942	6,215	20,191	46,612	99,303
1990	3,223	724	21,346	7,764	24,622	60,849	118,793
2000	2,464	475	19,644	9,931	15,763	88,260	136,891

SOURCES: U.S. Bureau of the Census, *Historical Statistics of the United States, Colonial Times to 1970* (1975), 139; *Statistical Abstract of the United States, 1998,* table 675; *Statistical Abstract of the United States, 2006.*

Changing Labor Patterns

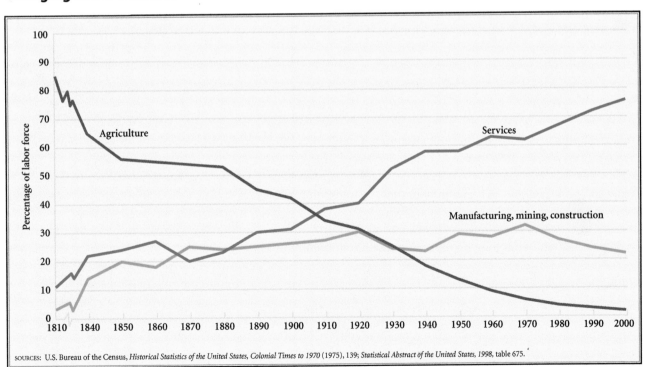

SOURCES: U.S. Bureau of the Census, *Historical Statistics of the United States, Colonial Times to 1970* (1975), 139; *Statistical Abstract of the United States, 1998,* table 675.

Birth Rate, 1820–2000

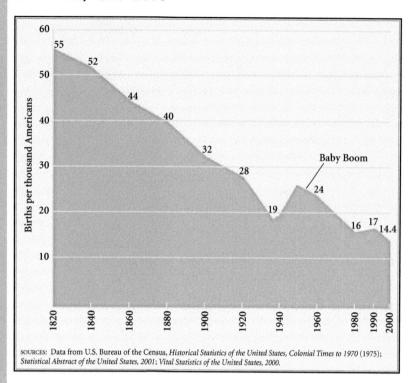

SOURCES: Data from U.S. Bureau of the Census, *Historical Statistics of the United States, Colonial Times to 1970* (1975); *Statistical Abstract of the United States, 2001*; *Vital Statistics of the United States, 2000*.

Death Rate, 1900–2000

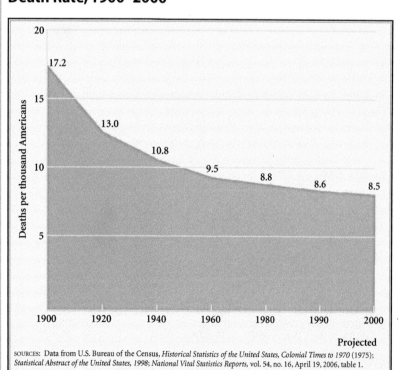

SOURCES: Data from U.S. Bureau of the Census, *Historical Statistics of the United States, Colonial Times to 1970* (1975); *Statistical Abstract of the United States, 1998*; *National Vital Statistics Reports*, vol. 54, no. 16, April 19, 2006, table 1.

Life Expectancy (at birth), 1900–2000

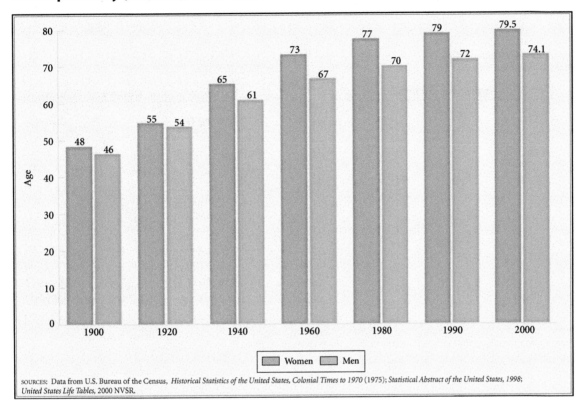

SOURCES: Data from U.S. Bureau of the Census, *Historical Statistics of the United States, Colonial Times to 1970* (1975); *Statistical Abstract of the United States, 1998*; *United States Life Tables*, 2000 NVSR.

The Aging of the U.S. Population, 1850–2000

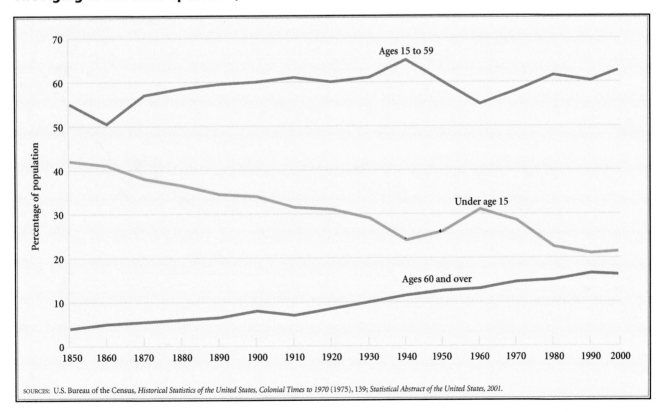

SOURCES: U.S. Bureau of the Census, *Historical Statistics of the United States, Colonial Times to 1970* (1975), 139; *Statistical Abstract of the United States, 2001.*

The American Government and Economy

The Growth of the Federal Government

Year	Employees (millions)		Receipts and Outlays ($ millions)	
	Civilian	Military	Receipts	Outlays
1900	0.23	0.12	567	521
1910	0.38	0.13	676	694
1920	0.65	0.34	6,649	6,358
1930	0.61	0.25	4,058	3,320
1940	1.04	0.45	6,900	9,600
1950	1.96	1.46	40,900	43,100
1960	2.38	2.47	92,500	92,200
1970	3.00	3.06	193,700	196,600
1980	2.99	2.05	517,112	590,920
1990	3.13	2.07	1,031,321	1,252,705
2000	2.88	1.38	2,025,200	1,788,800

SOURCES: *Statistical Profile of the United States, 1900–1980; Statistical Abstract of the United States, 2001.*

Gross Domestic Product, 1840–2000

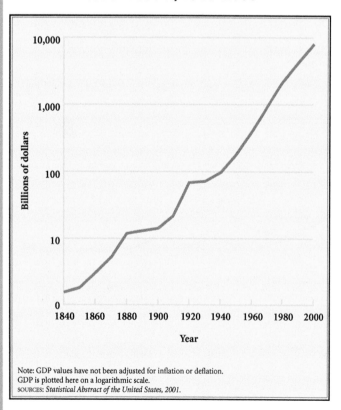

Note: GDP values have not been adjusted for inflation or deflation.
GDP is plotted here on a logarithmic scale.
SOURCES: *Statistical Abstract of the United States, 2001.*

GDP per Capita, 1840–2000

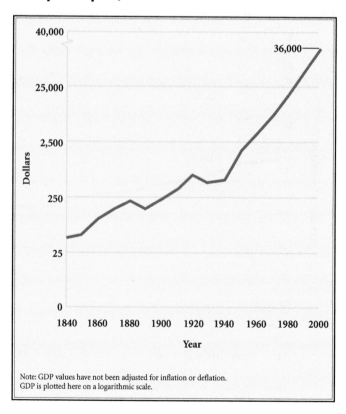

Note: GDP values have not been adjusted for inflation or deflation.
GDP is plotted here on a logarithmic scale.

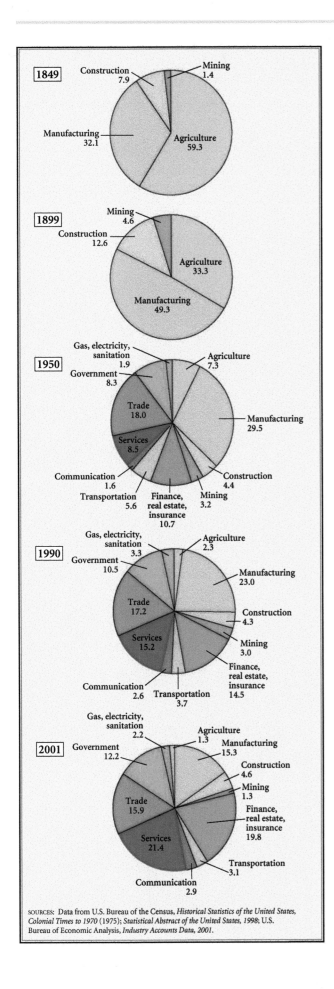

SOURCES: Data from U.S. Bureau of the Census, *Historical Statistics of the United States, Colonial Times to 1970* (1975); *Statistical Abstract of the United States, 1998*; U.S. Bureau of Economic Analysis, *Industry Accounts Data, 2001*.

Consumer Price Index

$100 in the year		
$100 in the year	1790 is equivalent to	$2,204 in 2005
	1800	1,605
	1810	1,640
	1820	1,720
	1830	2,185
	1840	2,330
	1850	2,580
Civil War Inflation	1860	2,425
	1870	1,540
	1880	1,970
$100 in the year	1890 is equivalent to	2,210 in 2005
	1900	2,400
World War I Inflation	1910	2,120
	1920	975
	1930	1,170
Post World War II	1940	1,400
Inflation	1950	810
	1960	660
	1970	500
	1980	240
$100 in the year	1990 is equivalent to	150 in 2005
	2000	115

This index provides a very rough guide to the purchasing power of $100 in various periods of American history. For example, in the early 1830s, day laborers earned about $1 a day or about $300 a year. This sum is the equivalent of about $6,555 a year in 2005 (3 × $2,185 = $6,555) or sixty percent of the gross income of a worker earing the federal government-designated minimum wage of $5.15 per hour.
SOURCE: Lawrece H. Officer and Samuel H. Williamson, "Purchasing Power of Money...1774–2005," MeasuringWorth.com, August 2006. www.measuringworth.com/calculculators/ppowerus/

◀ **Main Sectors of the U.S. Economy: 1849, 1899, 1950, 1990, and 2001**

anarchism The advocacy of a stateless society achieved by revolutionary means. Feared for their views, anarchists became the scapegoats for the 1886 Haymarket Square bombing. (p. 543)

Anglo-Saxonism A theory widely held in the late nineteenth century that the English-speaking peoples were racially superior and, for that reason, justified in colonizing and dominating the peoples of less-developed areas of the world. Combined with Social Darwinism, Anglo-Saxonism fueled American expansionism in the late nineteenth century. (p. 647)

armistice A temporary cession of military hostilities. World War I ended when the armistice of November 1918 simply continued because both sides had lost their will to fight further. (p. 679)

Black Codes Laws passed by southern states after the Civil War denying ex-slaves the civil rights enjoyed by whites and intended to force blacks back to the plantations. (p. 459)

blacklist Procedure used by employers throughout the nineteenth century to label and identify workers affiliated with unions. In the 1950s, blacklists were utilized to exclude alleged Communists from jobs in government service, the motion picture business, and many industries and unions.(p. 322)

business cycle The periodic rise and decline of business activity characteristic of capitalist-run, market economies. A quest for profit stimulates a level of production that exceeds demand and prompts a decline in output. In the United States, major periods of expansion (1802–1818, 1824–1836, 1846–1856, 1865–1873, 1896–1914, and 1922–1928) were followed by either relatively short financial panics (1819–1822 and 1857–1860) or extended depressions (1837–1843, 1873–1896, and 1929–1939). Since 1945, government intervention (through tax cuts, increased spending, interest rate hikes, etc.) has moderated the swings of the business cycle. (p. 239)

capitalism A system of economic production based on the private ownership of property and the contractual exchange for profit of goods, labor, and money (capital). Although some elements of capitalism existed in the United States before 1820, a full-scale capitalist economy—and society—emerged only with the Market Revolution (1820–1850) and reached its pinnacle during the final decades fo the century. *See* Market Revolution. (p. 520)

carpetbaggers A derisive name given by Southerners to Northerners who moved to the South during Reconstruction. Former Confederates despised these Northerners as transient exploiters. Carpetbaggers actually were a varied group, including Union veterans who had served in the South, reformers eager to help the ex-slaves, and others looking for business opportunities. (p. 470)

classical liberalism The political ideology, dominant in England and the United States during the nineteenth century, that celebrated individual liberty, private property, a competitive merket economy, free trade, and limited government. In the late twentieth-century United States, many economic conservatives embrace, the principles of classical liberalism (and oppose, the principles of social welfare liberalism). (p. 738)

closed shop Workplace in which a job seeker had to be a union member to gain employment. In the nineteenth century, the closed shop was favored by craft unions as a method of keeping out incompetent and lower-wage workers and of strengthening the unions' bargaining position with employers. (p. 540)

collective bargaining A process of negotiation between labor unions and employers, particularly favored by the American Federation of Labor (AFL). Led by Samuel Gompers, the AFL accepted the new industrial order, but fought for a bigger share of the profits for the workers. (p. 540)

common law Centuries-old body of English law based on custom and judicial interpretation, not legislation, and evolving case by case on the basis of precedent. The common law was transmitted to America along with English settlement and became the foundation of American law at the state and local levels. In the United States, even more than in Britain, the common law gave the courts supremacy over the legislatures in many areas of law. (p. 622)

conservationist Advocacy for the protection of the natural environment for sustained use. As applied by Theodore Roosevelt at the start of the twentieth century, conservation accepted development of public lands, provided this was in the public interest and not wastefully destructive. In contrast, preservationists valued wilderness in its natural state and were more broadly opposed to development. (p. 629)

cultural pluralism A term coined in 1924 that posits that diversity, especially religious and ethnic diversity, can be a source of strength in a democratic nation and that cultural differences should be respected and valued. (p. 755)

deficit spending High government spending in excess of tax revenues based on the ideas of British economist John Maynard Keynes, who proposed in the 1930s that governments should be prepared to go into debt to stimulate a stagnant economy. (p. 748)

deflation The sustained decline of prices, generally accompanying an economic depression, but in the United States after the Civil War, the result of rapidly rising productivity, market competition, and a tight money supply. (p. 604)

deregulation Process of removing or limiting federal regulatory mechanisms, justified on the basis of promoting competition and streamlining government bureaucracy. President Carter began deregulation in the 1970s, starting with the airline, banking, and communications industries. The process continued under subsequent administrations. (p. 918)

détente From the French word for "a relaxation of tension," this term was used to signify the new foreign policy of President Nixon, which sought a reduction of tension and hostility between the United States and the Soviet Union and China in the early 1970s. (p. 898)

direct primary The selection of party candidates by a popular vote rather than by the party convention, this progressive reform was especially pressed by Robert La Follette, who viewed it as an instrument for breaking the grip of machines on the political parties. In the South, where it was limited to whites, the primary was a means of disfranchising blacks. (p. 624)

dollar diplomacy Policy adopted by President Taft emphasizing the connection between America's economic and political interests overseas. The benefits would flow in both directions. Business would gain from diplomatic efforts in its behalf, while the strengthened American economic presence overseas would give added leverage to American diplomacy. (p. 664)

domino theory An American Cold War concept associated with the containment policy that posited that in areas of East-West conflict, the loss of one country to communism would lead to the toppling of other non-communist regimes. The term was first used by President Eisenhower, who warned of "falling dominos" in Southeast Asia if Vietnam became Communist. (p. 825)

entitlement programs Government programs that provide financial benefits to which recipients are entitled by law. Examples include Social Security, Medicare, unemployment compensation, and agricultural price supports. (p. 896)

ethnocultural Refers to the distinctive social characteristics of immigrants and religious groups, especially in determining their party loyalties and stance on political issues touching personal behavior and public morality. (p. 590)

feminism, feminist Doctrine advanced in the early twentieth century by women activists that women should be equal to men in all areas of life. Earlier women activists and suffragists had accepted the notion of separate spheres for men and women, but feminists sought to overcome all barriers to equality and full personal development. (p. 617)

fiscal policy The range of decisions involving the finances of the federal government. These decisions include how much to tax, how much to spend, and what level of resulting deficit or surplus is acceptable. Such decisions—fiscal policy—have a big effect on a nation's allocation of economic resources, the distribution of income, and the level of economic activity. (p. 864)

Fourteen Points President Wilson proposed these principles as a basis for peace negotiations at Versailles in 1919. Included in the points were open diplomacy, freedom of the seas, free trade, territorial integrity, arms reduction, national self-determination, and establishment of the League of Nations. (p. 694)

fundamentalism, fundamentalist Any religious movement that adopts a "pure" and rigid belief system. In the United States, it usually refers to evangelical Protestants who interpret the Bible literally. In the 1920s, fundamentalists opposed modernist Protestants, who tried to reconcile Christianity with Darwin's theory of evolution by natural selection and other scientific discoveries. Fundamentalists' promotion of anti-evolution laws for public schools led to the famous Scopes trial of 1925; in recent decades, fundamentalists have strongly supported legislation to prohibit abortions and gay marriages. (p. 721)

gang-labor system A system of work discipline used on southern cotton plantations in the mid-nineteenth century. White overseers or black drivers constantly supervised gangs of enslaved laborers to enforce work norms and secure greater productivity. (p. 464)

general strike A strike that draws in all the workers in a society, with the intention of shutting down the entire system. Radical groups like the Industrial Workers of the World (IWW), in the early twentieth century, saw the general strike as the means for initiating a social revolution. (p. 546)

gerrymander The political strategy (named after the early nineteenth-century politician Elbridge Gerry) of changing the boundaries of voting districts to give the dominant party an advantage. (p. 596)

ghetto Term describing an urban neighborhood composed of the poor, and occasionally used to describe any tight-knit community containing a single ethnic or class group. Ghettos came into being in the nineteenth century, in tandem with the enormous influx of immigrants to American cities. (p. 566)

Great American Desert The name given to the drought-stricken Great Plains by Euro-Americans in the early nineteenth century. Believing the region was unfit for cultivation or agriculture, Congress designated the Great Plains as permanent Indian country in 1834. (p. 488)

greenbacks Paper money issued by the U.S. Treasury during the Civil War to finance the war effort. Greenbacks had the status of legal tender in all public and private transactions. Because they were issued in large amounts and were not backed by gold or silver, the value of a greenback dollar fell during the war to 40 cents (but much less than the notes issued during the Revolutionary War, which became virtually worthless) and recovered only as the Union government won the war and proceeded to reduce its war-related debt. (p. 604)

habeas corpus Latin for "bring forth the body," a legal writ forcing government authorities ot justify their arrest and detention of an individual, Rooted in English common law, habeas corpus was given the status of a formal privilege in the U.S. Constitution (Article 1, Section 9), which also allows its suspension in cases of invasion or in-surrection, During the Civil War, Lincoln suspended habeas corpus to stop protests against the draft and other anti-Union activities. The USA PATRIOT Act (2001) likewise suspends this privilege in cases of suspected terrorism, but the constitutional legitimacy of this and other provisions of the act have yet to be decided by the courts. (p. 1012)

home rule A rallying cry used by southern Democrats painting Reconstruction governments as illegitimate—imposed on the South—and themselves as the only party capable of restoring the South to "home rule." By 1876, northern Republicans were inclined to accept this claim. (p. 480)

ideology A systematic philosophy or political theory that purports to explain the character of the social world or to prescribe a set of values or beliefs. (p. 587)

impeachment First step in the constitutional process for removing the president from office, in which charges of wrongdoing (articles of impeachment) are passed by the House of Representatives. A trial is then conducted by the Senate to determine whether the impeached president is guilty of the charges. (p. 468)

indenture, indentured servants A seventeenth-century labor contract that required service for a period of time in return for passage to North America. Indentures were typically for a term of four or five years, provided room and board in exchange for labor, and granted free status at the end of the contract period. (p. 511)

industrial union A group of workers in a single industry (for example, automobile, railroad, or mining) organized into a single association, regardless of skill, rather than into separate craft-based associations. The American Railway Union, formed in the 1880s, was one of the first industrial unions in the nation. (p. 544)

isolationism, isolationist A foreign-policy stance supporting the withdrawal of the United States from involvement with other nations, especially an avoidance of entangling diplomatic relations. The common view of post–World War I U.S. foreign policy is that it was isolationist, but in fact the United States played an active role in world affairs, particularly in trade and finance. (p. 712)

Jim Crow A term first heard in antebellum minstrel shows to designate black behavior and used in the age of segregation to designate facilities restricted to blacks, such as Jim Crow railway cars. (p. 598)

jingoism This term came to refer to the super-patriotism that took hold in the mid-1890s during the American dispute with Spain over Cuba. Jingoes were enthusiastic about a military solution as a way of showing the nation's mettle and, when diplomacy failed, they got their wish with the Spanish-American War of 1898. (p. 648)

Keynesian economics The theory, developed by British economist John Maynard Keynes in the 1930s, that purposeful government intention into the economy (through lowering or raising taxes, interest rates, and government spending) can affect the level of overall economic activity and thereby prevent severe depressions and runaway inflation. (p. 748)

laissez-faire The doctrine, based on economic theory, that government should not interfere in business or the economy. Laissez-faire ideas guided American government policy in the late nineteenth century and conservative politics in the twentieth. Business interests that supported laissez-faire in the late nineteenth century accepted government interference when it took the form of tariffs or subsidies that worked to their benefit. Broader uses of the term refer to the simple philosophy of abstaining from all government interference. (p. 587)

liberal, liberalism The ideology of individual rights and private property outlined by John Locke (circa 1690) and embodied in many American constitutions, bills of rights, and institutions of government. *See also* classical liberalism *and* social welfare liberalism. (p. 479)

liberal consensus Refers to widespread agreement among Americans in the decades after World War II that the pro-government policies of the New Deal were desirable and should be continued. In politics, the liberal consensus was reflected in the relatively small differences on economic and social policies between Republicans and Democrats until the advent of Ronald Reagan. (p. 819)

lien (crop lien) A legal device enabling a creditor to take possession of the property of a borrower, including the right to have it sold in payment of the debt. Furnishing merchants took such liens on cotton crops as collateral for supplies advanced to sharecroppers during the growing season. This system trapped farmers in a cycle of debt and made them vulnerable to exploitation by the furnishing merchant. (p. 474)

literacy test The requirement that an ability to read be demonstrated as a qualification for the right to vote. It was a device easily used by registrars to prevent blacks from voting, whether they could read or not, and was widely adopted across the South beginning with Mississippi in 1890. (p. 594)

machine tools Cutting, boring, and drilling machines used to produce standardized metal parts that were assembled into products like sewing machines. The development of machine tools by American inventors in the early nineteenth century facilitated the rapid spread of the Industrial Revolution. (p. 528)

mass production A system of factory production that often combines sophisticated machinery, a disciplined labor force, and assembly lines to turn out vast quantities of identical goods at low cost. In the nineteenth century, the textile and meatpacking industries pioneered mass production, which eventually became the standard mode for making consumer goods from cigarettes to automobiles, to telephones, radios, televisions, and computers. (p. 538)

military-industrial complex A term first used by President Eisenhower in his farewell address in 1961, it refers to the interlinkage of the military and the defense industry that emerged with the arms buildup of the Cold War. Eisenhower particularly warned against the "unwarranted influence" that the military-industrial complex might exert on public policy. (p. 827)

muckrakers Journalists in the early twentieth century whose stock-in-trade was exposure of the corruption of big business and government. Theodore Roosevelt gave them the name as a term of reproach. The term comes from a character in *Pilgrim's Progress*, a religious allegory by John Bunyan. (p. 614)

national debt The financial obligations of the U.S. government for money borrowed from its citizens and foreign investors. Alexander Hamilton wanted wealthy American to invest in the national debt so that they would support the new national government. In recent decades, that same thinking has led the United States to encourage individuals and institutions in crucial foreign nations—Saudi Arabia and Japan, for example—to invest billions of dollars in the American national debt. (p. 774)

national self-determination This concept holds that nations have the right to be sovereign states with political and economic autonomy. A central component of Woodrow Wilson's Fourteen Points for a World War I peace treaty, this concept challenged the existing colonial empires. The right of national self-determination continues to be invoked by nationalist, usually ethnic, groups, such as the Basques in Spain, the Kurds in Turkey and Iraq, and the Palestinians in Israel. (p. 695)

nationalize, nationalization Government seizure and ownership of a business or natural resource. In the 1890s the Populist Party demanded nationalization of American railroads; in the 1950s the seizure by Cuba of American-owned sugar plantations and gambling casinos sparked a long-lasting diplomatic conflict. (p. 712)

nativist, nativism Antiforeign sentiment in the United States that fueled drives against the immigration of Irish and Germans in the 1840s and 1850s, the Chinese and Japanese in the 1880s and 1890s, migrants from eastern and southern Europe in the 1910s and 1920s, and Mexicans in the 1990s and 2000s. Nativism prompted the Chinese Exclusion Act of 1882, the Immigration Restriction Act of 1924, and the interment of Japanese Americans during World War II. (p. 718)

oligopoly In economics, the situation in which a given industry (steel making, automobile manufacturing) is dominated by a small number of large-scale companies. (p. 709)

patronage The power of elected officials to grant government jobs. Beginning in the early nineteenth century, politicians systematically used—and abused—patronage to create and maintain strong party loyalties. After 1870, political reformers gradually introduced merit-based civil service systems in the federal and state governments. (p. 584)

peonage (debt peonage) As cotton prices declined during the 1870s, many sharecroppers fell into permanent debt. Merchants often conspired with landowners to make the debt a pretext for forced labor, or peonage. (p. 474)

pocket veto Presidential way to kill a piece of legislation without issuing a formal veto. When congressional Republicans passed the Wade-Davis Bill in 1864, a harsher alternative to President Lincoln's restoration plan, Lincoln used this method to kill it by simply not signing the bill and letting it expire after Congress adjourned. (p. 458)

political machines Nineteenth-century term for highly organized groups operating within and intending to control political parties. Machines were regarded as antidemocratic by political reformers and were the target especially of Progressive era leaders such as Robert La Follette. The direct primary was the factored antimachine instrument because it made the selection of party candidates the product of a popular ballot rather than conventions that were susceptible to machine control. (p. 569)

poll taxes A tax paid for the privilege of voting, used in the South beginning during Reconstruction to disfranchise freedmen. Nationally, the northern states used poll taxes to keep immigrants and others deemed unworthy from the polls. (p. 469)

pragmatism Philosophical doctrine developed primarily by William James that denied the existence of absolute truths and argued that ideas should be judged by their practical consequences. Problem solving, not ultimate ends, was the proper concern of philosophy, in James's view. Pragmatism provided a key intellectual foundation for progressivism. (p. 613)

preservationist, preservation Early-twentieth-century activists, like John Muir, who fought to protect the natural environment from commercial exploitation, particularly in the American West. (p. 629)

Prohibition Law dictated by the Eighteenth Amendment of the Constitution that banned the manufacture and sale of alcoholic beverages. Prohibition took effect in January of 1920, but public resistance was intense. "Speakeasies" (illegal saloons) sprang up around the country and bootleggers (illegal providers) supplied alcoholic beverages smuggled from Canada and Mexico. Organized crime invested heavily in bootlegging and gang-war slayings generated much publicity. Public pressure led to the repeal of prohibition by the Twenty-First Amendment in 1933. (p. 688)

pump priming Term first used during the Great Depression of the 1930s to describe the practice of increased government spending in the hope that it would generate additional economic activity throughout the system. It is the beginning of a process that is supposed to lead to significant economic recovery. (p. 730)

residual powers The constitutional principle that powers not explicitly granted to the federal government belong to the states. (p. 588)

restrictive covenants Limiting clauses in real estate transactions intended to prevent the sale or rental of properties to classes of the population considered "undesirable," such as African Americans, Jews, or Asians. Such clauses were declared unenforcable by the Supreme Court decision in *Shelley v. Kraemer* (1948), but continued to be instituted informally in spite of the ruling. (p. 838)

rural ideal Concept advanced by the landscape architect Andrew Jackson Downing urging the benefits of rural life, it was especially influential among middle-class Americans making their livings in cities but attracted to the suburbs. (p. 557)

scalawags Southern whites who joined the Republicans during Reconstruction and were ridiculed by ex-Confederates as worthless traitors. They included ex-Whigs and yeomen farmers who had not supported the Confederacy and who believed that an alliance with the Republicans was the best way to attract northern capital and rebuild the South. (p. 470)

scientific management A system of organizing work, developed by Frederick W. Taylor in the late nineteenth century, designed to get the maximum output from the individual worker and reduce the cost of production, using methods such as the time-and-motion study to determine how factory work should be organized. The system was never applied in its totality in any industry, but it contributed to the rise of the "efficiency expert" and the field of industrial psychology. (p. 538)

secondary boycott (secondary labor boycott) Technique used by unions in labor disputes to exert pressure on an employer involved in the dispute by targeting other parties not involved but having a relationship to the employer, for example, as a supplier or as a customer. A secondary labor boycott was used in the Great Pullman Boycott of 1894 and failed when the government intervened. (p.544)

secret ballot Before 1890, most Americans voted in "public." That is, voters either announced their vote to a clerk or handed in a ballot that had been printed by—and so was recognizable as the work of—a political party. Voting in "private" or in "secret" was first used on a wide scale in Australia. When the practice was adopted in the United States, it was known as the Australian ballot. (p. 594)

self-made man The nineteenth-century ideal that celebrated men who rose to wealth or social prominence from humble origins through self-discipline, hard work, and temperate habits. (p. 289)

separation of powers The constitutional arrangement that gives the three governmental branches—executive, legislative, and judicial—independent standing, thereby diffusing the federal government's overall power and reducing the chances that it might turn tyrannical and threaten the liberties of the people. (p. 458)

severalty Individual ownership of land. The term applied to the Dawes Severalty Act of 1890, which undertook to end tribal ownership and grant Indians deeds to individual holdings, i.e., severalty. (p. 503)

sharecropping The labor system by which freedmen agreed to exchange a portion of their harvested crops with the landowner for use of the land, a house, and tools. A compromise between freedmen and white landowners, this system developed in the cash-strapped South because the freedmen wanted to work their own land but lacked the money to buy it, while white landowners needed agricultural laborers but did not have money to pay wages. (p. 473)

Social Darwinism The application of Charles Darwin's biological theory of evolution by natural selection to the development of society, this late-nineteenth-century principle encouraged the notion that societies progress as a result of competition and the "survival of the fittest." Intervention by the state in this process was counterproductive because it impeded healthy progress. Social Darwinists justified the increasing inequality of late-nineteenth-century, industrial American society as natural. (p. 588)

"social welfare" liberalism   The liberal ideology implemented in the United States during the New Deal of the 1930s and the Great Society of the 1960s. It uses the financial and bureaucratic resources of the state and federal governments to provide economic and social security to individual citizens, interest groups, and corporate enterprises. Social welfare programs include old age pensions, unemployment compensation, subsidies to farmers, mortgage guarantees, and tax breaks for corporations. (p. 738)

spoils system   The widespread award of public jobs to political supporters following an electoral victory. Underlying this practice was the view that in a democracy rotation in office was preferable to a permanent class of officeholders. In 1829 Andrew Jackson began this practice on the national level, and it became a central, and corrupting, feature of American political life. (p. 584)

states' rights   An interpretation of the Constitution that exalts the sovereignty of the states and circumscribes the authority of the national government. Expressed first by Antifederalists in the debate over the Constitution, and then in the Virginia and Kentucky resolutions of 1798, the ideology of states' rights became especially important in the South. It informed white southerners' resistance to the high tariffs of the 1820s and 1830s, to legislation to limit the spread of slavery, and to attempts by the national government in the mid-twentieth century to end Jim Crow practices. (p. 585)

subtreasury system   A scheme deriving from the Texas Exchange, a cooperative in the 1880s, through which cotton farmers received cheap loans and marketed their crops. When the Texas Exchange failed in 1891, Populists proposed that the federal government take over these functions on a national basis through a "subtreasury," which would have the added benefit of increasing the stock of money in the country and thus push up prices. (p. 602)

suburbanization   The movement of the upper and middle classes beyond city limits to less crowded areas with larger homes that are connected to city centers by streetcar or subway lines. By 1910, 25 percent of the population lived in these new communities. The 1990 census revealed that the majority of Americans lived in the suburbs. (p. 560)

suffrage   The right to vote. In the early national period suffrage was limited by property restrictions. Gradually state constitutions gave the vote to all white men over the age of twenty-one. Over the course of American history, suffrage has expanded as barriers of race, gender, and age have fallen. In the late nineteenth and early twentieth centuries, women activists on behalf of the vote were known as "suffragists." (p. 466)

syndicalism   A revolutionary movement that, like socialism, believed in the Marxist principle of class struggle and advocated the organization of society on the basis of industrial unionism. This approach was advocated by the Industrial Workers of the World (IWW) at the start of the twentieth century. (p. 546)

tariff   A tax on imports, which has two purposes: raising revenue for the government and protecting domestic products from foreign competition. A hot political issue throughout much of American history, in the late nineteenth century the tariff became particularly controversial as protection-minded Republicans and pro-free-trade Democrats made the tariff the centerpiece of their political campaigns. (p. 585)

temperance, temperance movement   A long-term series of activities by reform organizations to encourage individuals and governments to limit the consumption of alcoholic beverages. Leading temperance groups include the American Temperance Society of the 1830s, the Washingtonian Association of the 1840s, the Women's Christian Temperance Union of the late nineteenth century, and Alcoholics Anonymous, which was founded in the 1930s. (p. 692)

Third World   This term came into use in the post-World War II era to describe developing or ex-colonial nations that were not aligned with either the Western capitalist countries led by the United States or the socialist states of eastern Europe led by the Soviet Union. It referred to developing countries in Asia, Africa, Latin America, and the Middle East. (p. 822)

trusts   A term originally applied to a specific form of business organization enabling participating firms to assign the operation of their properties to a board of trustees, but by the early twentieth century, the term applied more generally to corporate mergers and business combinations that exerted monopoly power over an industry. It was in this latter sense that progressives referred to firms like United States Steel and Standard Oil as trusts. (p. 627)

union shop   The requirement that, after gaining employment, a worker must join a union, as distinct from the closed shop, which requires union membership *before* gaining employment. (p. 814)

vaudeville   A professional stage show composed of singing, dancing, and comedy routines that changed live entertainment from its seedier predecessors like minstrel shows to family entertainment for the urban masses. Vaudeville became popular in the 1880s and 1890s, the years just before the introduction of movies. (p. 574)

voluntarism   The view that citizens should themselves improve their lives, rather than rely on the efforts of state. Especially favored by Samuel Gompers, voluntarism was a key idea within the labor movement, but one gradually abandoned in the course of the twentieth century. (p. 622)

war of attrition   A military strategy of small-scale attacks used, usually by the weaker side, to sap the resources and morale of the stronger side. Examples include the attacks carried out by Patriot militias in the South during the War of Independence, and the guerrilla tactics of the Vietcong and North Vietnamese during the Vietnam War. (p. 679)

welfare capitalism   A system of labor relations that stresses management's responsibility for employees' well-being. Originating in the 1920s, welfare capitalism offered such benefits as stock plans, health care, and old-age pensions and was designed to maintain a stable workforce and undercut the growth of trade unions. (p. 710)

welfare state   A nation that provides for the basic needs of its citizens, including such provisions as old-age pensions, unemployment compensation, child-care facilities, education, and other social programs. Major European countries began to provide such programs around 1900; the New Deal of the 1930s brought them to the United States. In the early twenty-first century, aging populations and the emergence of a global economy (the transfer of jobs to low-wage countries) threatens the economic foundation of the European and American welfare systems. (p. 615)

white-collar   Middle-class professionals who are salaried workers as opposed to business owners or wage laborers; they first appeared in large numbers during the industrial expansion in the late nineteenth century. Their ranks were composed of lawyers, engineers, and chemists, as well as salesmen, accountants, and advertising managers. (p. 529)

yellow-dog contract   An agreement by a worker, as a condition of employment, not to join a union. Employers in the late nineteenth century used this along with the blacklist and violent strikebreaking to fight unionization of their workforces. (p. 543)

yellow journalism   Term that refers to newspapers that specialize in sensationalistic reporting. The name came from the ink used in Hearst's *New York Journal* to print the first comic strip to appear in color in 1895 and is generally associated with the inflammatory reporting leading up to the Spanish-American War of 1898. (p. 577)

Chapter 25

Comparing American Voices: Evelyn Gotzion. From *Women Remember the War 1941–1945*, by Michael E. Stevens and Ellen D. Goldlust, editors. Copyright © 1993 by Michael E. Stevens and Ellen D. Goldlust. Reprinted with the permission of the Wisconsin Historical Society.

Comparing American Voices: Fanny Christina Hill. Excerpted from interview on pp. 37–42 in *Rosie the Riveter Revisited* by Sherna Berger Gluck. Copyright © 1987 by Sherna B. Gluck. Reprinted with permission of the author.

Comparing American Voices: Peggy Terry. Excerpt from *The Good War* by Studs Terkel. Copyright 1984 by Studs Terkel. Reprinted by permission of Donadio & Olson, Inc.

Voices from Abroad: Monica Itoi Sone. "Japanese Relocation." From *Nisei Daughter* by Monica Sone. Copyright © 1953 by Monica Sone. Copyright © renewed 1981 by Monica Sone. By permission of Little, Brown, and Company, Inc.

Chapter 26

Voices from Abroad: Jean Monnet: Truman's Generous Proposal. Excerpt from *Memoirs* by Jean Monnet, translated by Richard Mayne. Translation copyright © 1978 by Doubleday, a division of Bantam, Doubleday Dell, a division of Random House, Inc.

Comparing American Voices: Fulton Lewis, Jr's Radio Address, January 13, 1949. Manuscript Sept CB# 3926 Frank Porter Graham Papers #1819. Manuscript CB #3926 Wilson Library. Southern Historical Collection, University of North Carolina at Chapel Hill. Reprinted with permission.

Comparing American Voices: Frank Porter Graham's Telegram to Fulton Lewis Jr, January 13, 1949. Frank Porter Graham Papers #1819. Manuscript #3926 Wilson Library. Southern Historical Collection, Southern Historical Collection, Wilson Library, University of North Carolina at Chapel Hill. Reprinted with permission.

Comparing American Voices: House Un-American Activities Committee Report on Frank Graham. Frank Porter Graham Papers #1819. Manuscript Sept CB#3926 Wilson Library, University at Chapel Hill. Reprinted with permission.

Chapter 27

Voices from Abroad: Hanoch Bartov. "Everyone Has a Car." From *Arbaah Isrealim Vekhol America (Four Israelis and the Whole of America)* by Hanoch Bartov. Copyright © Hanoch Bartov, Acum House, Israel. Reprinted by permission of the author and Acum House.

Comparing American Voices: Franklin McCain. "Desegrating Lunch Counters." From *My Soul Is Rested: Movement Days in the Deep South Remembered*, by Howell Raines. Copyright © 1977 by Howell Raines. Originally published by Penguin Putnam, 1977. Reprinted with permission of PFD, Inc.

Comparing American Voices: John McFerren: "Demanding the Right to Vote." From *Looking for America*, Second Edition, Volume 1 by Stanley I. Kutler, editor. Copyright © 1979, 1976 by Stanley I. Kutler. Used by permission of W.W. Norton & Company, Inc.

Chapter 28

Comparing America Voices: James R. Wilson. Excerpts from *Landing Zones: Southern Veterans Remember Vietnam* by James R. Wilson. Copyright © 1990 Duke University Press. All rights reserved. Used by permission of the publisher.

Comparing American Voices: Arthur E. Woodley. Excerpt from *Bloods: An Oral History of the Vietnam War by Black Veterans* by Wallace Terry. Copyright © 1984 by Wallace Terry. Used by permission of Random House, Inc.

Comparing American Voices: Gayle Smith. Excerpt from *Everything We Had* by Albert Santoli. Copyright © 1981 by Albert Santoli and Vietnam Veterans of America. Used by permission of Random House.

Voices from Abroad: Che Guevara: "Vietnam and the World Freedom Struggle." From "Message to the Tricontinental" from *Che Guevara Speaks* by Ernesto Che Guevara. Copyright © 1967, 2000 by Pathfinder Press. Reprinted by permission.

Voices from Abroad: Fei Xiaotong. America's Crisis of Faith. From *Land Without Ghosts* by David Arkrush. Copyright © 1989 by the University of California Press Books. Reprinted by the permission of the California University of PressBooks in the format Textbook via Copyright Clearance Center.

Chapter 30

Comparing American Voices: Ronald Reagan. "The Rule of Law Under God." From *Speaking My Mind* by Ronald Reagan. Copyright © 1989 by Ronald Reagan. Reprinted with the permission of Simon & Schuster Adult Publishing Group.

Comparing American Voices: Donald E. Wildmon. "Network Television as a Moral Danger." Excerpt from *The Home Invaders* by Donald E. Wildmon. Copyright © 1985 by Donald E. Wildmon. Reprinted with permission.

Voices from Abroad.: Zhu Shida. "Chaina and the United States: A Unique Relationship." From the China Internet Information Center. Reprinted with permission. www.china.org.en/english/2002/mar/29138.

Chapter 31

Comparing American Voices: Trong and Thanh Nguyen. "We're Political Refugees. . . . We Spend Our Money Here." Excerpt from *Enduring Voices*, volume II. Copyright © 1966 by D.C. Heath and Company. Used with permission of Houghton Mifflin.

Comparing American Voices: Petra Mata and Feiyi Chen: "Garmet Workers made a decent living before free trade." From *Shafted: Free Trade and America's Working Poor* edited by Christine Ahn. Copyright © 2003 Food First/Institute for Food and Development Policy. Oakland, CA. Reprinted with permission.

Voices from Abroad : Janet Daley. A US Epidemic. From *The Independent*, August 29, 1990. Copyright 1990. Reprinted with permission of Independent Newspapers, A Division of Independent News & Media Ltd. Theindependentsyndication@independent.co.uk.

Chapter 32

Voices From Abroad.: Abu Musab al-Zarqawi. "A Strategy for the Iraq Insurgency." Reprinted by permission of Juan R.I. Cole. Jrcole@mich.edu.

Comparing American Voices: "The Promised Land." Reprinted with permission of Michael Chorost.

A note about the index: Names of individuals appear in boldface; biographical dates are included for major historical figures. Letters in parentheses following pages refer to: *(f)* figures, including charts and graphs; *(i)* illustrations, including photographs and artifacts; *(m)* maps; and *(t)* tables.

AAA. *See* Agricultural Adjustment Act; American Automobile Association
Abbott, Grace, 746
Abbott, Jacob, 564
Abernathy, Ralph, 855
Abilene, Kansas, 492
abolitionism, Douglass and, 624
abortion, 564, 924, 947–948, 955, 987
    opposition to, 910
    Roe v. Wade and, 910, 943, 985(*i*), 1008
    Supreme Court on, 985, 1008
Abramoff, Jack, 1006
abstract expressionism, 848
"The Absurd Attempt to Make the World Over" (Sumner), 588
Abu Ghraib prison, 1002, 1002(*i*), 1017
Abzug, Bella, 904
accommodationism, 624
Acheson, Dean, 807, 812
ADA. *See* Americans with Disabilities Act
Adams, Brooks, 647
Adams, Charles Francis, 654
Adams, Charles Francis, Jr., 592
Adams, Samuel Hopkins, 631
Adamson eight-hour law for railroad workers, 637
Addams, Jane, 612–615, 615(*i*), 654
Adelphia Communications, 995
adolescence, 564, 580. *See also* juvenile delinquency; youth
advertising
    automobile and, 714
    brand names and, 527, 527(*i*)
    consumer culture and, 670, 713–714, 734
    corporate growth and, 834
    of Kansas, 495(*i*)
    mass marketing and, 527, 527(*i*)
    New Deal and, 742
    in 1920s, 713–714
    political campaigns and, 932
    postwar, 843
    presidential campaign of 2004 and, 1005
    radio and, 717, 737(*i*)
    by railroads, 495, 513

religion and, 842
television and, 844(*i*)
of Wild West Show, 494(*i*)
youth culture and, 847
AFDC. *See* Aid to Families with Dependent Children
affirmative action, 907, 924, 928, 982, 987, 993
affluent society (1950s), 831–859
The Affluent Society (Galbraith), 833
Afghanistan, 939, 990, 998, 1000(*i*)
    Al Qaeda in, 925
    insurgencies in, 1002
    Soviet invasion of, 920(*i*), 921, 941
    Taliban in, 924
    U.S. aid to, 921
    U.S. attack on, 999, 1001(*m*), 1017
    U.S. invasion of Iraq and, 1001
AFL. *See* American Federation of Labor
AFL-CIO, 836, 838, 887, 901. *See also* American Federation of Labor; Congress of Industrial Organizations
Africa
    African American migration to, 726
    AIDS in, 967
    debts of, 970
    foreign trade and, 728
    North, 788(*m*), 789
    post-WWI colonialism in, 696–697
    WWI and, 674
African Americans. *See also* civil rights movement; desegregation; free blacks; racism; segregation; slavery; slaves
    affirmative action and, 907
    in Armed Forces, 681–683
    Back-to-Africa movement, 599
    Black Power and, 886, 892, 904
    as buffalo soldiers, 502
    Bush (George W.) and, 992–993
    in cattle industry, 493(*i*)
    changing demographics and, 976, 977(*m*), 980, 982
    churches of, 472
    civil rights movement and, 853–858, 879, 885–888, 892
    as cowboys, 492–493, 493(*i*)
    Democratic Party and, 754, 763
    Dred Scott and, 985(*i*)
    education of, 472(*i*)
    election of 1936 and, 747
    election of 1972 and, 901
    equality of, 597–599

as Exodusters, 496, 496(*i*), 517
Fifteenth Amendment and, 595–596, 598, 598(*i*)
Fourteenth Amendment and, 588, 595–596, 598
German propaganda toward, 682
Great Migration of, 685–687, 690(*m*), 703
Great Society and, 876
Harlem Renaissance and, 723(*i*), 723–726
Hurricane Katrina and, 1007(*i*)
immigrant workers and, 980, 982
in industrial jobs, 699
jazz and, 716(*i*), 716–717, 848
JFK and, 863
Korean immigrants and, 980(*i*)
labor unions and, 542–543, 750
LBJ and, 871
leadership of, 470–471
legal system and, 753, 753(*i*)
lynchings of, 599, 599(*i*), 698
militancy of, 734, 885–886, 892
in military, 652, 652(*i*), 681–683
music of, 848
Muslim, 886
New Deal and, 742
in New South, 529–530, 595–599, 608
1920s and, 708
nominating process and, 624
northward migration of, 567, 625, 685–687, 690(*m*), 703
as percent of population, 567
post-WWI, 698(*i*), 698–699
racial equality and, 946
Republican Party and, 470–471, 585
resettlement in Africa of, 599
rights of. *See* civil rights
riots by, 982(*i*), 982–983
rock 'n' roll and, 847–848
in Spanish-American War, 652, 652(*i*)
on television, 843
urban, 567–568, 572(*i*), 815
urban migration of, 742, 753, 850–851
urban rioting of, 886, 892. *See also* race riots
Vietnam War (1961-1975) and, 882
violence against, 476–478, 867
voting by, 465(*i*), 470
voting rights and, 586, 597(*m*), 597–599, 598(*i*), 608
War on Poverty and, 876
welfare system and, 747
white supremacy movement and, 597–599, 608

African Americans (*continued*)
  women, 708, 750
  working women among, 533
  WWI and, 676
  WWII and, 777, 780–781, 784
African Methodist Episcopal Church
    (AME), 472
Afrika Korps, 789
Agency for International Development, 863
Agent Orange, 879, 882
Agnew, Spiro, 891, 902
Agricultural Adjustment Act (AAA), 739–742,
    745, 747(*t*), 765
agriculture. *See also* corn; cotton; farmers;
    grain; sugar; tobacco; wheat; yeoman
    farmers
  in California, 511–514
  capital for, 498
  drought and, 757
  dry-farming, 497
  Granger movement and, 498, 602
  on Great Plains, 488(*m*), 488–489, 495–498
  immigrants and, 978–979
  irrigation for, 497, 515
  labor shortage in, 787
  migrant labor and, 511–512
  New Deal and, 742, 755–756
  in 1920s, 706, 710, 727
  orchards and, 512–513
  prices for, 602, 607
  in the South, 529, 529(*m*), 530, 530(*i*),
    685, 850
  subtreasury system and, 602
  technology for, 497
  in Texas, 587
  TVA and, 759–760
  WWII and, 774
Aguinaldo, Emilio, 653, 653(*i*), 654
Ahmadinejad, Mahmoud, 1014
AIDS (acquired immune deficiency
    syndrome), 924, 966–967, 968(*i*), 987
Aid to Dependent Children (ADC), 747, 876
Aid to Families with Dependent Children
    (AFDC), 747, 876, 933, 950, 960
Air and Water Quality Acts (1965), 874(*t*)
airline industry, 850. *See also* commercial
    aviation
air traffic controller strike, 965, 987
Alabama
  black registered voters in, 470
  coal mining in, 521
  iron industry in, 530
Alabama (Confederate warship), 642
Alaska, 643, 912
  Arctic National Wildlife Refuge in,
    994, 994(*m*)
Albright, Madeline, 947
alcohol
  blue laws and, 590, 592
  prohibition, 691–692

prohibition of, 590, 592, 594–595, 595(*i*).
    See also Prohibition
  taxes on, 585
Aldrich, Nelson W., 632
Alger, Horatio, 587, 587(*i*)
Algeria, radical Islamic movements in, 953
Aliquippa, Pennsylvania, 552
Alito, Samuel A., Jr., 1008, 1009(*i*), 1017
Allawi, Ayad, 1006
Allen, Paul, 970, 971(*i*)
Allen, Thomas, 471
Alliance for Progress, 863
Allied Powers (WWII), 674–675, 675(*i*),
    678–680, 683, 695, 697, 771, 787–791,
    796–797
  wartime debts and, 711
Al Qaeda, 925, 953, 989–990, 998–999,
    1000(*i*), 1001(*m*), 1002, 1014
  in Iraq, 1003
America First Committee, 771
American Automobile Association
    (AAA), 714
American Civil Liberties Union (ACLU),
    Scopes trial and, 721, 724
The American Commonwealth (Bryce),
    583, 628
American Communist Party, 816–817
An American Dilemma (Myrdal), 852
American Enterprise Institute, 928, 955
American Expeditionary Force (AEF),
    678–679, 681, 683
American Federation of Labor (AFL),
    542–543, 548, 622, 685, 749–750,
    836, 901
American Federation of Teachers, 724–725
American fever, 496
American Indian Movement (AIM), 888
American Indians, National Council of, 888
Americanization campaign, 693–694
American Legion, 683
American Medical Association (AMA),
    815, 873
American Peace Society, 666
American Plan, meaning of, 711
American Protective League, 693
American Railway Union (ARU), 544
The Americans at Home (Macrae), 460
Americans with Disabilities Act (ADA;
    1990–1991), 955
An American Tragedy (Dreiser), 723
American Union against Militarism, 676
The American Woman's Home (Beecher), 561
American Woman Suffrage Association, 469
America Online, 924
Ames, Adelbert, 478
amnesty
  for Confederates, 458
  for illegal aliens, 980
  for Southerners, 459
Amos 'n' Andy (radio program), 717

amusement parks, 574(*i*), 575
anarchism, 543
Ancona, Victor, 776
Anderson, John, 932
Anderson, Jourdon, 462–463
Angel's Camp, California, 513
Angelus Temple, 721(*i*)
Anglo-Saxonism, 647
Angola, West Africa, 939
Anheuser-Busch, 834
Anschutz, Thomas P., 537(*i*)
antelope, 489
Anthony, Susan B. (1820–1906), 469, 594
antiballistic missile systems (ABMs), 898
anticipatory self-defense, 999
Anti-Comintern Pact, 769, 797
anticommunism, 815–819, 828. *See also*
    McCarthy, Joseph R.
Antigua, 474
Anti-Imperialist Leagues, 654
Anti-Saloon League, 622
anti-Semitism, 838
  Holocaust and, 790
  racism and, 780
antitrust laws, 635–636, 707
  Microsoft Corporation, 971
  Sherman Antitrust Act (1890), 629, 632,
    635–636
  wartime suspension of, 684
antiwar movement (Vietnam War), 879–884,
    892, 901
  backlash against, 891, 899
  Chicago Democratic convention (1968),
    889, 891
  decline of, 899
  draft and, 882–883, 892
  hardhat protest and, 899, 899(*i*)
  Kent State and, 898
  student protests and, 882–884, 892
ANZUS (Australia, New Zealand, United
    States; 1951), 824(*m*)
AP. *See* Associated Press
A&P, 527, 713
Apache Indians, 498–499, 499(*m*)
Appalachia, 729(*m*), 874(*t*), 875
  migration from, 850
  War on Poverty and, 875
Appalachian Regional Development Act
    (1965), 874(*t*)
Appalachian Trail, 760
appeasement (WWII), 770
Apple Corporation, 970, 972
appliances, household, 843
Appomattox Court House, Virginia, 466
Arab League, 826
Arabs. *See also* Middle East; Muslims
  Islamic fundamentalism and, 944–945
  U.S. invasion of Iraq and, 1001
Arafat, Yasir, 952
Arapaho Indians, 498, 499(*m*)

arbitration, WWI and, 675
Arctic National Wildlife Refuge, 994(*m*)
Argentina, 728, 920
Arikara Indians, 489, 499(*m*)
Aristide, Jean-Bertrand, 951–952
Arizona
    Hispanic settlement in, 508
    Japanese internment in, 785, 785(*i*)
    Mexican Americans in, 685
    mining in, 510(*i*)
Arkansas, Japanese internment in, 785, 785(*i*)
Arkansas Democrat-Gazette, 854, 854(*i*)
Armistice (1918), 679, 685, 703
Armour & Co., 525
arms control, 939. *See also* weapons of
        mass destruction
    Carter and, 921
    nuclear test ban treaty (1963), 868
    SALT I, 898
    SALT II, 921
    Washington Naval Arms Conference
        (1921), 713
arms race, 803. *See also* atomic bomb;
        nuclear weapons
    nuclear, 802–803, 841–842, 898
    nuclear proliferation and, 841–842
Armstrong, Louis, 717
Army, U.S., 641, 701
    conscription for, 678–679
    in Germany, 767(*i*)
    Indian wars and, 499(*m*), 502–504
    in Philippines, 654
    in Pullman boycott, 545(*i*)
    racial segregation in, 681–683
    racial violence in, 681
    Special Forces of, 869
Army Corps of Engineers, U.S., 661
art
    cultural dissent and, 848
    New Deal and, 737(*i*), 760–762
    in 1920s, 710(*i*)
Arthur, Chester A. (1829–1886), as
        president (1881–1885), 583, 642
Arthur Andersen, 995
artisans. *See also* mechanics
    in industrial age, 520, 531, 537(*i*)
    Reconstruction and, 470
    trade unionism and, 540–541
art museums, 578
Ashcroft, John D., 1009
Asia. *See also* particular countries
    European empires in, 642, 645–646,
        663, 663(*m*)
    foreign powers in (1898–1910), 663(*m*)
    immigrants from, 849(*f*), 976(*f*)
    Nike in, 965
Asian Americans, 643(*i*)
    discrimination against, 838, 849
    New Deal and, 756–757
    population increase of, 977(*m*)

Asian immigrants
    in California, 784
    race riots by, 982(*i*)
Aspin, Les, 951
assembly lines, 539(*i*), 714. *See also* mass
       production
    for automobiles, 962(*i*)
Associated Press (AP), 717
associated state, 706–707
Aswan Dam, 826
Atkinson, Edward, 587
Atkins v. Children's Hospital, 711
Atlanta, Georgia, Ku Klux Klan in, 708(*m*)
Atlanta Journal (newspaper), 686
Atlantic Charter (1941), 771, 772(*m*),
    787, 797
Atlantic City, New Jersey, real estate in, 963(*i*)
Atlantic Monthly, 579
Atlas Van Lines, 834
atomic bomb, 796, 802, 808–810, 812, 816.
       See also nuclear power; nuclear weapons
    use of, 670, 767, 793(*m*), 794, 795(*i*), 797
Atomic Energy Commission (AEC), 842
Auschwitz concentration camp, 790
Australia, 643
    Chinese immigration to, 511
    gold rush in, 505
    secret ballot from, 594
    WWII and, 791
Austria, 696, 770
Austria-Hungary, 674
automobile
    culture of, 706, 709, 714, 836, 839–841
    foreign, 911
    fuel-efficient, 911(*f*)
    Great Depression and, 727
    interstate highways and, 839(*m*)
    1950s culture and, 840
    rural life and, 714
    suburbs and, 839–841
automobile industry
    assembly lines in, 962(*i*)
    consolidation in, 834
    energy crisis and, 911
    environmentalism and, 913
    international economy and, 963
    labor unions and, 749
    market share of U.S., 834, 836
    mass production in, 538, 539(*i*), 548
    mass transit systems and, 841
    in 1920s, 735
    quality in, 961
Axis, Rome-Berlin (WWII), 769, 787, 797
axis of evil (Iran, Iraq, and North Korea),
    999, 1017
Ayres, Thomas A., 487(*i*)

Baathist regime, 1002
Babbitt (Lewis), 723
Babcock, Orville, 479

Baby and Child Care (Spock), 845
baby-boom generation, 844–849, 924, 946,
    959, 996
*Backlash: The Undeclared War on American
    Women* (Faludi), 983
Back-to-Africa movement, 599
Baghdad, Iraq
    looting in, 1001–1002
    Persian Gulf War and, 999
    slums of, 1015(*i*)
    U.S. invasion of Iraq and, 1001
Bainbridge, Joseph, 752(*i*)
Baker, Ella, 858
Baker, Ray Stannard, 693
Bakke, Allan, 907
Bakke v. University of California (1978), 907
balance of power, 659, 663, 896, 898
Bali, Islamic terrorist bombing in, 1014
balkanization, 983
Balkans, 666, 674, 698, 952
Ballinger, Richard A., 633
Baltic provinces, 679, 696–697
Baltimore, Maryland, population of, 552(*t*)
bananas, 712(*i*)
bandits, 510
Banking Act (1863), 604
Banking Act (1935), 744, 747(*t*)
bankruptcy
    of Enron, 995
    of farmers, 730
    holding company pyramid and, 706
    of Northern Pacific Railroad, 479
    of railroads, 549, 727
bankruptcy laws, 995
banks
    consolidation of, 834
    corporate coordination with, 834
    economic expansion and (1920s), 709–711
    failure of, 479
    failures of, 727–728, 739, 739(*t*)
    gold standard and, 604–607, 606(*i*)
    Great Depression and, 733
    National Banking Acts and, 604
    New Deal and, 744
    postwar, 832
    reform of, 635
Baptists
    African American, 567–568
    National Convention of, 472
    prohibition and, 692
Barbados (West Indies), 474
barbed wire, 497
Barnum, P. T., 578
Barrow Plantation, 473(*m*)
Barry, Leonora M., 542
Bartov, Hanoch, 840
Baruch, Bernard, 684, 684(*i*), 739, 742, 803
Baruch Plan, 803
baseball, 576–577, 577(*i*)

Basel Convention (1994), 969
Bataan death march, 791
Batista, Fulgencio, 863
Bayard, Thomas F., 642
Bayer, 694
Bay of Pigs invasion (1961), 863, 869(m)
Beall, Lester, 737(i)
the Beatles, 884
Beats, 848–849, 884
beauty pageants, 903–904, 904(i)
bebop, 848
Beecher, Catharine, 561
Beecher, Henry Ward, 573, 579
beer, 834
    German immigrants and, 688(i)
    Prohibition and, 722(i)
    prohibition and, 692
Begin, Menachem, 918(i), 920
Belgium, 674, 770, 790
Bell, Alexander Graham, 555
Belleau Wood, Battle of, 679(m)
Bellow, Saul, 762
Below, Ernst, 593
benevolent hegemony, 998
Bennett, James Gordon, 577
Bennett, William, 983
Bentsen, Lloyd, 948
Berger, Victor, 619, 694
Berkman, Alexander, 700
Berle, Adolph A., Jr., 739
Berlin, Germany, 790, 805(i), 806, 808
    division of, 792, 806, 808
    JFK and, 868
Berlin Airlift, 808, 808(i)
Berlin Conference (1884), 645
Berlin Wall, 868, 870(i)
    fall of, 924, 927, 942, 955
Berners-Lee, Tim, 957(i)
Bernstein, Carl, 902
Bernstein, Leonard, 851(i)
Bessemer, Henry, 520
Bessemer furnace, 520–521, 521(i)
Betamax video recorder, 959(i)
Bethlehem Steel, 521(i), 961
Bethune, Mary McLeod, 754(i), 754–755
Bethune-Cookman College, 754, 754(i)
Beveridge, Alfred J., 648
Bevin, Ernest, 807
Bible, evolution and, 721–722
Bidault, Georges, 807
Big Foot, Chief of Sioux, 504
Big Four, 696
Big Three, 787–788
Billy the Kid (Copland), 760
bin Laden, Osama, 953, 989–990, 999, 1014
bintel brief, 570
biotechnology, 924, 973(i)
bipolar world system, 897–898
Bird, Caroline, 728
bird flu, 967

Birmingham, Alabama, 866–867, 867(i)
birth control, 910
    declining birth rate and, 903
    rhythm method of, 564
Birth of a Nation (film), 721
birth rate. *See also* population
    declining, 903
    increasing, 524
    in 1950s, 844, 845(f)
Black, Hugo, 748
black churches, 472, 568. *See also particular denominations* under African Americans
    in New York, 567–568
Black Codes, 459, 471, 481
Black Elk, Sioux holy man, 504(i)
Blackfeet Indians, 489, 499(m)
Blackfoot Indians, 755(i)
Black Hills, South Dakota, 502, 505
blacklist, 816, 828
black market, during WWII, 783
Black Muslims, 886
Black Panthers, 886–887
Black Star Line steamship company, 726
"Black Thursday" (Oct. 24, 1929), 727
"Black Tuesday" (Oct. 29, 1929), 727
Blaine, James G., 586, 586(m), 592, 643
Bland-Allison Act (1878), 604
blitzkrieg, 767, 770
blogging, 924
blogs, meaning of, 971–972
bloody shirt, the, 585–586
blue laws, 590, 592
Blue Ridge Parkway, 760
Boesky, Ivan, 962
Boland Amendment, 937
Bolivia, 643
Bolshevik Revolution (1917), 679, 700
Bolshevism, 674, 679, 700, 703. *See also* communism
Bonanza (television show), 844
Bonaparte, Charles J., 618
Bonn, Germany, 998
Bonnin, Gertrude Simmons (Zitkala-ša), 501
Bonsack, James A., 530
Bonus Army (1932), 731, 735
boodle, 572
boomer movement, 503
Booth, John Wilkes, 457–458
Borah, William E., 697
Bosnia, 674, 924–925, 952, 952(m), 955
Boston, Massachusetts
    art museum in, 578
    elite in, 558–559
    immigrants in, 566
    population of, 552(t)
    school busing in, 907, 910(i)
    suburbs of, 560
    urban renewal in, 852
Boston Guardian, 625

Bourke-White, Margaret, 762, 762(i)
Bourne, Rudolph, 692
Bow, Clara, 715(i), 715–716
Bowery, New York, 576
Bowman Dairy Company, 780(i)
Boxer rebellion (China; 1900), 663, 663(m)
Boyce, Ed, 546
boycotts
    by Atlanta African Americans, 599
    of California grapes, 887
    civil rights movement and, 879
    Pullman, 544, 545(i), 605, 611
    secondary, 544, 813–814
braceros program, 850, 978
Bradford, Perry, 716(i)
Bradley, Joseph P., 481
Brandeis, Louis D., 613, 615, 617, 635
Brando, Marlon, 847
Brauckmiller, John R., 783(i)
Brazil, 967
    foreign trade and, 728
    land distribution in, 474
breadlines, 731(i), 732
breaker boys, 536(i)
Brest-Litovsk, Treaty of, 679
Bretton Woods system, 832
breweries
    prohibition and, 692
    Volstead Act and, 722(i)
Breyer, Stephen G., 947, 991, 1009(i)
Brezhnev, Leonid, 832(i), 898, 1002
Briand, Aristide, 713
Britain. *See* Great Britain
British Caribbean, land distribution in, 474
British Columbia, gold in, 505
British Guiana, 474
broadband connections, 924, 971
brokerage firms, 962
Brooklyn, New York, 552(t)
Brooks, Phillips, 573
Brotherhood of Sleeping Car Porters, 780
Brown, Ron, 947
Brown Berets, 887
Brownlow, William G., 477
Brown v. Board of Education (1954), 853, 903, 907, 910
Bruce, Blanche K., 471
Bruce, William, 718
Brush, Charles F., 554, 555(i)
Brussels, 965(m)
Bryan, William Jennings, 605–607, 606(i), 607(m), 632, 654, 666–667, 722, 726, 928
Bryant, Anita, 906
Bryce, James, 583–584, 587, 592
    on America, 628
    on diplomacy, 644
Buchanan, Patrick, 946, 976, 983, 991
Buchenwald concentration camp, 790
Buckley, William F., 928

buffalo, 489, 492, 492(*i*)
Buffalo Bill, the King of the Border Men (Buntling), 494
buffalo soldiers, 502
Buford (vessel), 700
Buford, Anne Gorsuch, 936
Bulgaria, WWI and, 674
Bulge, Battle of, 790
Bulkley, William Lewis, 625
Bull Moose Party, 633
Bundy, McGeorge, 868
Bunker, Ellsworth, 898
Buntline, Ned, 494
Bunyan, John, 614
Burger, Warren, 910, 938(*i*)
Burgess, John W., 624
Burkitt, Frank, 597
Burma, 791
Burroughs, Edgar Rice, 563
Bush, George H. W. (1924-), 924–925, 929, 947(*i*), 955
    automobile mileage requirements and, 968
    Persian Gulf War and, 999
    as president (1989-1993), 943–946, 993(*i*)
    signing of NAFTA and, 948
Bush, George W. (1946-), 925, 946
    Air National Guard and, 1005
    approval ratings of, 1002, 1004, 1006
    dressed up as fighter pilot, 1001
    election of 2000 and, 990–991, 991(*i*), 1002, 1004–1005
    election of 2004 and, 1002, 1004–1005, 1017
    Enron and, 995
    favoritism to business by, 994–995
    globalization and, 969
    homeland security and, 995, 1004(*i*)
    Kyoto Treaty and, 969, 987, 998
    as president (2001-), 990–1017
    rollback of federal government and, 954, 996
    scandals during administration of, 995
    second term of, 1005–1016
    September 11 attacks and, 998
    State of the Union address of 2002, 999, 1009(*i*)
    stem cell research veto by, 1007–1008, 1010, 1017
    unilateralism of, 1012
Bush doctrine, 999
Bushnell, Horace, 579
Bush v. Gore (2000), 991
business. *See also* corporations
    Bush (George W.) and, 994–995
    Cheney and, 994
    consolidation of, 709–710
    energy industry and, 995(*i*)
    failures in, 728(*f*)
    government cooperation with, 706–713
    mobilization for war and, 774–777

modern management and, 537, 548
    New Deal and, 742, 763
    in 1920s, 709–711
    productivity decline in, 959–960
    U.S. interventions and, 937(*m*)
business cycles, 710, 727
busing, school, 907, 910(*i*)
butterfly ballots, 991
Byrnes, James F., 748

Cable New Network (CNN), 924
cable television, 973–975
Cahan, Abraham, 573
California
    affirmative action in, 907, 982
    agriculture in, 511–512
    Catholic missions in, 513
    Chinese immigrants in, 511
    climate of, 505, 513
    culture of, 512–513, 515
    Enron scam and, 995
    European immigrants in, 510
    gold rush (1849–1857) in, 517
    Hispanic settlement, 509
    immigration to, 976
    internal migration to, 491, 755–756, 783, 838(*m*), 839
    Japanese internment in, 785, 785(*i*)
    Latino immigrants in, 850
    Mexican Americans in, 685
    as mining frontier, 505–508, 506(*m*), 508(*i*), 515
    movie industry in, 714
    national parks in, 514
    Native Americans in, 509
    prohibition and, 691
    Proposition 13 in, 916–917
    racial antagonism in, 784
    racism in, 511–512
    Reagan and, 928
    settlement of, 489
    stem-cell research in, 1008
California, University of, Free Speech Movement and, 882, 882(*i*)
Californios, 509
Calley, William, 899
Cambodia
    Khmer Rouge in, 900
    Vietnam War and, 877(*m*), 878, 899–900
Camp David accords (1978), 918(*i*), 920
Canada, 642, 968, 987
    medication prices in, 993
    NAFTA and, 948, 964
    settlement of boundaries with, 659
    Sioux Indians in, 502
    U.S. invasion of Iraq and, 1001
    war on terrorism and, 1000(*i*)
Canby, Henry Seidel, 561
cancer, genetic codes and, 973(*i*)
Cannon, "Uncle Joe", 633

capital goods, 520
capitalism, 999(*i*)
    automobiles and, 713–714
    business cycles in, 710, 727
    corporate, 709–711, 832
    election of 1932 and, 733(*m*)
    free-market, 943
    industrialization and, 519–549
    New Deal and, 739
    in 1950s, 831
    postwar liberalism and, 832
    pyramid of holding companies and, 706
    robber barons and, 522–523
    Social Darwinism and, 588
    vs. communism, 831
    welfare, 710–711, 781, 796
    WWI and, 684
    WWII and, 787
Capra, Frank, 782
Caribbean Islands (West Indies)
    Asian migration to, 511
    expansionist foreign policy and, 655(*m*), 668
    military interventions in, 711
    U.S. as power in, 649
    U.S. intervention in, 937(*m*), 951–952
Caribbean Sea, 646–647, 655(*m*), 668
    "policing" of, 661–662, 662(*m*)
Carmichael, Stokely, 886
Carnegie, Andrew, 519(*i*), 520–521, 522(*i*), 526, 543, 549, 578–579, 587, 654, 676
Carolinas. *See* North Carolina; South Carolina
carpetbaggers, 470, 478
Carranza, Venustiano, 664–666
Carroll, James, 892
Carson, Rachel, 912
Carter, Jimmy (James E.; 1924-), 922, 963
    Camp David accords and, 918(*i*), 920
    defeat of, 929, 932, 932(*m*)
    defense spending of, 935
    as president (1977-1981), 917–922
cartoons, political, 523(*i*), 546(*i*), 584(*i*)
Cartwright, Alexander, 576
Casablanca (film), 782
Cascades mountains, 505
Casey, William, 939
caste labor system, 512
Castro, Fidel, 850, 863, 869(*m*), 898, 937
Caterpillar Tractors, 965
Catholicism
    Americanism and, 572–573
    election of 1928 and, 726
    ethnic identity and, 573
    of Mexican Americans, 685
    presidential elections and, 863, 901
    rhetoric against, 586
Catholics
    abortion and, 984
    California missions and, 513
    Democratic party and, 590, 590(*f*), 592
    immigration restriction and, 718

Catholics (continued)
  Irish, 573
  JFK and, 863
  Ku Klux Klan and, 719(i), 721
  in 1920s, 718, 726
  in 1950s, 842
  opposition to, 980
  in Poland, 941
  Religious Right and, 928
  in the Southwest, 509
Cato Institute, 928, 955, 1012
Catt, Carrie Chapman, 617, 688, 709(i)
cattle industry, 525, 525(m). See also meat
    packing industry; ranching
  African Americans in, 493, 493(i)
  on Great Plains, 492–493
  Hispanics in, 493, 493(i), 509
  and Long Drive, 493, 517
CBS Laboratories, 834
CBS News, 970
CBS Records, 959
"The Celebrated Jumping Frog of Calaveras
    County" (Twain), 513
Celera Genomics, 972
cellular telephones, 924, 972
CENTO. See Central Treaty Organization
Central America
  immigrants from, 976–977
  U.S. intervention in, 939
Central Asia, 942(m)
Central Europe, immigration from, 976(f)
Central Intelligence Agency (CIA)
  Afghanistan and, 921
  covert operations of, 824–825, 937
  creation of, 809
  Cuba and, 863
  Iran and, 921
  Nixon's dirty tricks and, 901–902
Central Pacific Railroad, 507
  building of, 492, 517
  Chinese labor for, 511, 512(i)
Central Park rapists, 981
Central Powers, 674–675, 675(i), 676,
    679–680, 697
Central Treaty Organization (CENTO),
    824(m)
centrist agenda, 948, 950
A Century of Dishonor (Jackson), 500, 503
CERN, 957(i)
Cervera, Pascual, 650, 652
CFC. See chlorofluorocarbons
Chamberlain, Neville, 770
Chambers, Whittaker, 816
Chaplin, Charlie, 713, 715
charitable activities
  Great Depression and, 729, 729(m), 733
  New Deal and, 742
Charles, Prince of England, 975
Chase, Salmon P., 468
Chase Manhattan Bank, 965

Chateau-Thierry, Battle of, 679, 679(m)
Chatel-Chehery, Battle of, 680
Chautauqua, New York, 578
Chavez, César, 756, 886–887, 887(i), 983
Chavez, Hugo, 1013
checks and balances, 468
Cheever, John, 762
chemical industry, 963
Chen, Feiyi, 979
Cheney, Richard, 991, 996, 1012
Chernobyl meltdown, 914
Cherokee Indians, 499, 499(m), 759(i)
Cherry family, 569(i)
Cheyenne, Wyoming, 492
Cheyenne Indians, 489, 498, 499(m), 502
Chiang Kai-shek (Jiang Jieshi), 810
Chicago, Burlington, and Quincy Railroad, 522
Chicago, Illinois, 551–553
  African Americans in, 567, 687
  art museum in, 578
  Berlin and, 558
  as center of meat industry, 498, 525, 525(m)
  expansion in, 554(m)
  fire of 1871, 556
  Haymarket bombing in, 549
  immigrants in, 566
  jazz and, 716
  Ku Klux Klan in, 708(m)
  mass transit in, 553(i)
  migration to, 718, 850
  population of, 552(t)
  race riots in, 698(i), 698–699, 703
  Robert Taylor Homes, 852
  Scopes trial and, 722
  skyline of, 554
  transportation and, 498
Chicago, University of, 793
Chicago Columbian Exposition (1893), 557
Chicago Commission on Race Relations, 686
Chicago Defender (newspaper), 686
Chicago Democratic Convention (1968),
    889, 891
Chicago Rapid Transit Company, 706
Chicago school of architecture, 553
Chicago Urban League, 686
Chicanos. See Mexican Americans
Chickasaw Indians, 499, 499(m)
Child, Lydia Maria, 469
child care programs, 896, 905
child labor, 536, 536(i)
  New Deal and, 742, 748
children
  attitudes toward, 564, 566
  inner-city, 982
  labor of, 536, 536(i)
  of Native Americans, 503
  in 1950s culture, 844–846
  Sheppard-Towner Act and, 709
  television regulation and, 975
Children's Television Act (1990), 975

Chile, 643, 965
China. See also People's Republic of
    China; Taiwan
  Boxer rebellion in, 663, 663(m)
  capitalism and, 1012
  civil war in, 810
  copyright issues and, 972
  Cultural Revolution in, 897
  European spheres of influence in, 645,
    651, 662–664, 663(m), 668
  foreign trade and, 728
  immigrants from, 756–757
  Japanese invasion of, 768, 797
  lobby for, 810
  multinational corporations and, 925
  Nationalist, 664, 810, 812, 897–898
  Nike and, 967(i)
  Nixon in, 897(i), 897–898
  pollution in, 967
  radical Islamic movements in, 953
  trade with, 645, 662–664
  U.S. relations with, 940
  WWI and, 674
  WWII and, 787, 792(m)
Chinatown, 511, 743(t)
Chinese Exclusion Act (1882), 511, 517, 849
Chinese immigrants, 510–512, 517, 849
  discrimination against, 505, 511, 517
  immigration restriction and, 511, 718, 849
  in the West, 510–512, 512(i), 515, 517
Chinn, Mae, 743(t)
chips. See silicone microchips
Chisholm, Shirley, 905
Chloe and Sam (Hovenden), 457(i)
chlorofluorocarbons (CFC), 968
Choctaw Indians, 499, 499(m)
Chorost, Michael, 1011
Christianity. See also evangelism; revivalism;
    particular denominations
  African-American, 568
  muscular, 574
  public life and, 930
  Reconstruction and, 478
  revivalism and, 574
  Social Gospel and, 612
Christopher, Warren, 951
Chrysler, 962
church and state, separation of, 573, 930, 992
Churchill, Winston
  Atlantic Charter and, 772(m), 787
  on division of Germany, 808
  at Potsdam Conference, 803
  United Nations and, 793
  wartime planning and, 771, 789
  at Yalta Conference, 791–792, 794(i), 802
Church of Jesus Christ of Latter-day Saints.
    See Mormons
Cincinnati, Ohio, 558–559
  migration to, 850
  population of, 552(t)

CIO. *See* Congress of Industrial
    Organizations
CIS. *See* Commonwealth of Independent
    States
Cisco, 961
Cisneros, Henry, 947
cities. *See also* urbanization
    African American migration to, 742,
        753, 850
    American *vs.* European, 553
    amusements in, 574–578
    in art and literature, 579
    crime increases in, 924
    decaying inner, 849–852
    drug crises in, 924
    election of 1928 and, 727(*i*)
    election of 1932 and, 733
    flapper in, 716
    gay communities in, 906
    growth of, 551–552, 552(*m*), 580, 838(*m*)
    high culture in, 578–580
    immigrants in, 551, 551(*i*), 566
    industrialization and, 487
    Korean immigrants in, 980, 980(*i*)
    Ku Klux Klan in, 708(*m*)
    life belts around, 841(*i*)
    life in, 566–580
    lighting of, 554–555
    mass media and, 718
    move to suburbs from, 831, 837–838
    population growth and, 551, 552(*t*), 735,
        849–850
    private/public, 555–558
    Protestantism in, 573–574
    race riots in, 698(*i*), 698–699, 703, 886,
        892, 982–983
    riots in, 797, 886
    skyscrapers in, 553–554
    sprawl of, 840
    Summer of Love (1967) in, 885
    in Sun Belt, 839
    ten largest U.S., 552(*t*)
    transportation in, 553, 553(*i*), 580
    urban development and, 873, 874(*t*)
    urban renewal and, 852, 896
City Beautiful movement, 556
Civil Defense Agency, 842(*i*)
Civilian Conservation Corps (CCC), 739,
    747(*t*), 752–754, 765
civil liberty, 817(*i*)
civil rights
    Bush (George W.) and, 993
    conservative opposition to, 875
    Eisenhower and, 853
    federal government and, 831
    Fifteenth Amendment and, 468(*t*), 469,
        477, 595–596, 598, 598(*i*), 624
    of former slaves, 459, 474
    Fourteenth Amendment and, 465–466,
        468(*t*), 477, 588, 595–596, 598

for homosexuals, 903, 906
integration and, 983
JFK and, 861, 864
LBJ and, 871–872
legislation on, 874(*t*)
for Mexican Americans, 886–888, 892
for Native Americans, 888, 892
in 1970s, 922
Nixon and, 896
nonviolent protest and, 853, 855
Truman and, 853
for women, 903–906
WWII and, 780(*i*), 784–787
Civil Rights Act (1866), 459, 465, 468(*t*),
    478, 483
Civil Rights Act (1964), 871–872, 874(*t*), 903
    Title IX and, 905
    women and, 903, 905
Civil Rights Bill (1870), 478
Civil Rights Commission, National, 853
civil rights movement, 852(*i*), 852–858,
    855(*i*), 855(*m*), 879, 885–888
    African Americans and, 853–858, 879,
        885–886, 892
    anticommunism and, 816
    Cold War and, 814–815, 852–858
    conflicts within, 858
    federal government and, 828, 864, 866
    feminism and, 903–906
    gay rights and, 906
    Harlem Renaissance and, 726
    in 1970s, 902–910
    sit-ins and, 855–858
    television and, 867, 872
    violence against, 858
    WWII and, 781
Civil Service Commission, 584
civil service reform, 479, 584–585, 624
civil unions, 984
civil war
    in Iraq, 1006, 1016
    in Russia, 679
Civil War (1861–1865)
    financing of, 604
    party loyalty and, 590
    Reconstruction and, 474
    roles of France and Britain in, 642
    warships of, 642
Civil Works Administration (CWA), 743–744,
    747(*t*)
    Native Americans and, 754
    women and, 743, 752
Clark, Champ, 634(*i*)
class. *See* social structure
class-action suits, 913
class distinctions
    Hurricane Katrina and, 1007(*i*)
    World War I and, 674
Clayton Antitrust Act (1914), 635–637
Clean Air Act (1970), 913, 994

Clemenceau, Georges, 695(*i*), 696
Clemens, Samuel. *See* Twain, Mark
Cleveland, Grover (1837–1908), 629
    election of 1884 and, 586, 592
    election of 1888 and, 582(*i*)
    as passive president (1885-1889), 584(*i*)
    as president (1885–1889; 1893–1897),
        584(*i*), 584–587, 589(*i*), 592, 602, 605,
        643, 648–649
    Pullman boycott and, 544, 549, 605
    as reformer, 586
Cleveland, Ohio
    African Americans in, 567
    oil refining in, 526
Clinic Entrance Act (1993), 948
Clinton, Bill (William Jefferson; 1946-)
    balanced budget and, 948, 949(*i*), 996
    big government and, 928, 950
    economy and, 958, 963
    first term of, 955
    impeachment of, 924, 950–951, 951(*i*),
        954–955
    Kyoto Treaty and, 969
    nuclear power and, 1013
    as president (1993–2001), 946–953
Clinton, Hillary Rodham, 946–948, 948(*i*)
clothing industry. *See* textile industry
Coalition Provisional Authority, 1002
coal mining, 521–522, 531, 536, 546, 622
    breaker boys and, 536, 536(*i*)
    decline of (1920s), 710, 727
    increase in, 911(*f*)
    in New South, 529(*m*)
    strikes and, 637
    strikes in, 813
coal shortages, 684
Coca-Cola, 834
Cochran, Johnnie, 983
Cody, William F. (Buffalo Bill), 493–494,
    494(*i*)
Cohan, George M., 678
Colbert, Claudette, 782
Cold War, 801–829, 897–898
    affluent society and, 831
    arms race in, 868
    beginning of, 807
    Berlin Wall and, 868, 870(*i*)
    civil rights movement and, 814–815,
        852–858
    Cuba in, 863, 869(*m*)
    détente and, 897
    domino effect and, 877
    end of, 925, 927, 939, 954–955, 1012
    in Europe, 805–806, 806(*m*)
    impact of, 841–842
    Iran and, 921
    mainframe computers and, 970
    in Middle East, 825–827
    nuclear test ban treaties and, 868
    Peace Corps and, 863

Cold War (*continued*)
staggering cost of, 942
Third World and, 865(*m*)
Vietnam War and, 877–884
WWII and, 768, 775, 796
Yalta and, 794(*i*)
Cole, U.S.S., attack on, 953, 953(*i*), 989, 1001(*m*)
collective bargaining, 540, 749
collective security, 771, 802, 822, 824
Collier, John, 754, 755(*i*)
Collier's magazine, 613, 631
Colombia, 659
colonialism, 822
colonization
end of, 865(*m*)
by Spain, 505
Colorado
Chinese in, 511
gay rights legislation in, 984
Japanese internment in, 785, 785(*i*)
migration to, 510
mining in, 505, 511, 607
Colorado Coal Company v. United Mine Workers, 711
Colorado plateau, 505
Colored Farmers' Alliance, 596–597
Colored Women, National Association of (NACW), 754
Colored Women's Clubs, National Association of, 625
Colored Women's League of Washington, D.C., 626(*i*)
Columbia Broadcasting Service (CBS), 717
Columbia Pictures, 959
Columbia plateau, 505
Columbia University, 889
Columbine High School, 975
Comanche Indians, 489, 499(*m*)
Comintern, 700, 769, 797
commercial aviation, WWI and, 681
Commission on Industrial Relations, 637
Committee Against Jim Crow in Military Service, 853
Committee on Public Information, 693, 703
Committee to Defend America by Aiding the Allies, 771
Committee to Re-Elect the President (CREEP), 901
common law, 622
Commonwealth Edison Company, 706
Commonwealth of Independent States (CIS), 942, 942(*m*)
communication systems, globalization and, 963–964, 966
communism
Carter and, 921
in China, 964
Chinese, 877, 897–898
Cold War and, 831, 832(*i*), 877–879, 892, 897–898

collapse of, 938–943, 941(*i*), 942(*m*)
conservatives and, 928
containment of, 804, 809–810
European economy and, 805–806
Federal Theatre Project and, 762
in Germany, 769
godless, 842
Great Fear of, 815–818
Greece and, 804–805
international, 822
Iran and, 921
JFK and, 863, 870
in Latin America, 937(*m*)
Nixon and, 897–898
Peace Corps and, 863
Soviet, 815–816, 898, 939
U.S. interventions and, 937(*m*)
Vietnam War and, 892, 901
vs. capitalism, 831
in Yugoslavia, 952
Communist Labor Party, 700
Communist Party, 770
election of 1932 and, 733, 733(*m*)
in Great Depression, 731, 735
popular protests and, 751(*m*)
in Russia, 679, 697, 700
in Soviet Union, 941–942
U.S., 700
Community Action Program, 876
compact discs (CD), 924, 959(*i*), 972, 974
compassionate conservatism, 990, 992
Compromise of 1877, 481, 483
computers
millennium fears and, 957
revolution, 987
computer technology, 970–972
Comstock, Anthony, 564
Comstock Lode (1859), 506
concentration camps, 791(*i*)
Coney Island, 575
Confederate States of America. *See also* Civil War; secession
radical Reconstruction of, 467(*m*)
conglomerates, rise of, 834
Congregationalism, politics of, 590(*f*)
Congress, U.S. *See also* House of Representatives, U.S.; Senate, U.S.
civil rights movement and, 867
declaration of war and, 678, 697, 771, 773
Democratic control of, 814, 896, 901, 946–947
drug benefit bill in, 993–994
FDR and, 748, 759
Federal Theatre Project and, 762
Great Depression and, 730
Gulf of Tonkin Resolution (1964), 878
illegal aliens and, 980
immigration restriction and, 718–719
Japanese internments and, 787

labor unions and, 780
Latin American countries and, 769
Medicare cuts and, 933
military veterans and, 781
Native Americans and, 850
New Deal and, 739, 742, 744, 748
Republicans in, 932, 949–950
Roosevelt recession and, 749
scheduled meeting of, 458–459
Schiavo case and, 1007
Supreme Court and, 708
television regulation and, 975
welfare programs and, 935
women in, 709, 944(*i*)
Congress of Industrial Organizations (CIO), 670, 749–750, 750(*i*), 756, 765, 836, 838, 887, 901
Congress of Racial Equality (CORE), 781, 864, 886
Conkling, Roscoe, 478, 585, 587
Connor, Eugene ("Bull"), 866, 867(*i*)
conscientious objectors, 678
consciousness raising, 904
conscription, 678–679, 770–771, 797. *See also* draft, military
conservation, 968–969. *See also* environment; pollution
Carter on, 918, 920
LBJ and, 873, 875
New Deal and, 759–760
Roosevelt (Theodore) and, 629, 631
conservationists, 629
conservatism, 934, 983, 986, 990, 992
creationism and, 1008
election of 1980 and, 932(*m*)
gay rights and, 906
Great Society and, 875
in 1970s, 895–896, 901, 907, 910, 922
political cartoons about, 997(*i*)
resurgence of, 891–892
rise of, 928–932
small government and, 997
stem-cell research and, 1008
vs. feminism, 905–906
Constitution, U.S.
acquired territories and, 654
amendments to, 684. *See also particular amendments*
electoral college and, 481
Japanese internments and, 787
New Deal and, 748
secession and, 458, 467
constitutions, state, 471, 511
construction industry, 520, 728(*f*)
consumerism
installment buying and, 836
interstate highways and, 839
in 1950s, 831, 840
women and, 847
consumer price index (CPI), 728

Consumer Products Safety Commission, 896, 913
consumers
  protection of, 631–632
  rights of, 913
Consumers' League, National, 615
consumer spending
  economic development and, 844
  postwar, 836
  television and, 844(i)
containment policy, 804, 822–827, 942
  in Asia, 810–814, 822, 825
  Eisenhower Doctrine and, 827
  LBJ and, 877
  meaning of, 804
  militarization of (NSC=68), 809–810
  Third World and, 822, 824–825
  in Truman administration, 822, 828
Contras, 937, 937(m)
Conwell, Russell H., 561, 587
Cooke, Jay, 479, 492
Coolidge, Calvin (1882–1933), 699
  ethics of, 707(i)
  as president (1923-1929), 707–708, 710, 718, 735
  as vice-presidential candidate, 706
Cooperstown, New York, 576
Copland, Aaron, 760
copper mines, 506
copyright issues, 972
Coral Sea, Battle of, 791, 792(m), 797
CORE. See Congress of Racial Equality
Corinne, Utah, 507
corn. See also grain
  price supports for, 710
corporate capitalism, 684
corporate executives, salaries of, 958(f)
corporate welfare programs, 775
corporations. See also business
  capitalism and, 709–711, 728
  computer networks and, 971
  conglomerates, 834
  consolidation of, 613, 709–710, 834
  consumer rights movement and, 913
  foreign competition and, 915–916
  foreign purchases of, 959
  information processing in, 961
  managerial class in, 834–835
  multinational, 925
  multinationalization of, 965–966, 966(i), 969
  outsourcing and, 965–966, 987
  political action committees and, 932
  power of, 613, 635–637
  radio and, 717
  rise of, 522
  scandals in, 995
  tariff protection for, 935
  taxation of, 684
  vertically integrated, 834

Corrigan, Michael A., 573
corruption
  in Harding administration, 707
  in Nixon administration, 901–902
  political, 471, 479, 613
cotton
  former slaves and, 464(i)
  prices for, 602
  price supports for, 710
  production of, 474
  sharecropping and, 473–474, 476
  in the South, 529(m), 530, 530(i)
  strikes and, 755(i), 756
  in Texas, 530(i), 598, 602
Coughlin, Charles, 744–745, 748, 751(m), 765
Council for Mutual Economic Assistance (COMECON), 808
counterculture
  drugs and, 884–885
  of 1950s, 847–849
  of 1960s, 879, 882, 884–885
  1970s activism and, 912
counterinsurgency, 863
courtship, parental control and, 576
court system. See also judiciary; Supreme Court
  conservative federal judges and, 925
covert interventions, meaning of, 824
cowboys, 492–493, 493(i)
Cowley, Malcolm, 760
Cox, James M., 706
Coxey, Jacob S., 605
craftsmen. See artisans
Crane, Stephen, 497, 579
Crazy Horse, 502
creationism, 924, 1008
credit. See also debt
  consumer, 836, 913
  Great Depression and, 728
Creek Indians, 499, 499(m)
Creel, George, 693
creeping socialism, 739
Crick, Francis, 973(i)
The Crisis, 625, 723(i)
Croatia, 952
Croats, 952(m)
Crocker, Charles, 511
cronyism, 479
crop-lien laws, 474, 476
crops. See agriculture
"Cross of Gold" speech, 928
Crow Indians, 489, 499(m)
Cruikshank, United States v., 478
Cuba
  Bay of Pigs in, 863, 868, 869(m)
  expansionism and, 642
  independence of, 652
  JFK and, 863, 870
  land distribution in, 474
  military alliance with, 937

Nixon and, 898
  refugees from, 850
  sensationalist journalism and, 648, 649(i), 649–650
  Spanish "reconcentration" camps in, 648–649, 651
  U.S. relations with, 661–662, 662(m), 769
  vs. Spain, 647–655
Cuban missile crisis (1962), 863, 868, 869(m)
Cullen, Countee, 723
cultural assimilation, Native Americans and, 850
cultural pluralism, 755
cultural values
  automobile and, 706
  conflict and, 718
culture. See also multiculturalism; popular culture
  automobile, 836, 839–841
  of California, 512–513, 515
  in cities, 578–579
  conflict, 958
  of corruption, 1006
  dissent and, 847–849
  fragmentation of, 983
  modern American (1920s), 733–734
  national, 706, 713–718
  of Native Americans, 513
  of 1950s, 847–849
  popular, 782
  technology and, 973–975
culture wars, 726, 924–925, 975–985
Cummins, Albert B., 624
currency. See also specie
  euro, 1013
  free silver and, 604, 606(i)
  renminbi, 1013
  U.S. as dominant, 832
Currie, Laughlin, 815
Cushman, Candi, 1010
Custer, George Armstrong, 502
Czechoslovakia, 696, 802, 805, 825, 942, 942(m)
  German invasion of, 770
  Prague Spring in, 897
Czolgosz, Leon F., 627

Dachau concentration camp, 790
Daily Worker (newspaper), 770
Dakota territory
  homesteaders in, 497
  Indian reservations in, 498–504, 499(m), 502(m)
  Scandinavian migration to, 496
Daley, Janet, 981
Daley, Richard J., 863, 889, 901
Dallas (TV program), 974
Damrosch, Leopold, 578
Dario, Ruben, 660
Darrow, Clarence, 722

Darwin, Charles, 588, 647, 721–722
Darwinism, 1008
Davis, David, 481
Davis, John W., 708
Davis, Miles, 848
Dawes, Charles G., 711
Dawes Plan (1924), 670, 711, 735
Dawes Severalty Act (1887), 503, 517, 754, 755(i)
Day, William R., 652–653
day care, corporations and, 775
"Day Under Communism" (Mosinee, Wisconsin), 801
D-Day (June 6, 1944), 789, 790(i), 797
DDT, 912–913
Dean, Howard, 971, 1004–1005
Dean, John, 902
death squads, 1016
Debayle, Anastasio Somoza, 937
Debs, Eugene, 544–545, 546(i), 548–549, 619, 635(m), 676, 694, 703
debt
    Asian migrants and, 511
    consumer, 710, 727–728
    farmers and, 474
    foreign, 711, 728, 959
    national, 774, 935, 948, 950, 955, 996. See also deficit spending
    of states, 471
    tax cuts and, 996
    of U.S., 963, 987
    during WWI, 683–684
decolonization, 865(m), 911
defense industry, women in, 777
Defense of Marriage Act (1998), 984, 987
defense spending, 774(f), 812, 813(f)
    economy and, 916(m)
    Eisenhower and, 863
    JFK and, 863
    postwar development and, 839
    Reagan and, 935–936, 954
    WWII, 774–775
deficit spending, 748, 913. See also debt
    economy and, 911, 925, 936
    in New Deal, 864
    by Nixon, 911
    Reaganomics and, 935, 935(f), 954
deflation, 604, 936
de Gaulle, Charles, 897
deindustrialization, 915–916, 917(i)
"De Kid Wot Works at Night" (Hard), 613
de Kooning, Willem, 760
DeLay, Tom, 991–993, 1006
De Leon, Daniel, 545
De Lesseps, Ferdinand, 642–643
Dellaire, Ohio, 752(i)
Dell Computer, 965
Del Monte, 750
de Lome, Dupuy, 649

democracy
    direct, 624
    Great Depression and, 732
    in Iraq, 999, 1015(i)
    militant Muslims and, 1015–1016
    New Deal and, 744
Democracy in America (Tocqueville), 583
Democratic National Committee, Women's Bureau of, 677(i), 751, 763
Democratic Party. See also elections; presidential elections
    African Americans and, 754, 763
    Catholics and, 590, 590(f), 592
    Chicago convention of (1968), 889, 891
    coalition of, 763, 863, 875, 917, 932(m), 948
    in Congress, 902
    control of Congress by, 814, 896, 902
    in 1870s, 479
    election of 1912 and, 635, 635(m)
    election of 1924 and, 707
    election of 1928 and, 726, 727(i)
    election of 1932 and, 733
    election of 1936 and, 747–748
    election of 1964 and, 873(m)
    election of 1972 and, 901
    election of 1980 and, 932, 932(m)
    election of 1982 and, 936
    election of 1992 and, 946
    election of 2004 and, 1004–1005
    FDR and, 748–749
    free trade and, 585
    Ku Klux Klan and, 476–477
    labor and, 622, 637, 750
    LBJ and, 871
    liberalism and, 892, 928
    "Lost Cause" and, 596
    Mexican Americans and, 756
    National Committee of, 677(i), 751, 763, 901
    New Deal and, 748, 889
    in New South, 596–599
    Nixon's dirty tricks and, 901
    organized labor and, 813
    progressive politics and, 612, 633
    Reagan and, 925, 928, 932
    Redeemers, 476, 478, 482
    in the South, 745(i)
    Southern, 814, 864
    split in (1948), 814
    states' rights and, 585
    urban liberalism and, 622
    women in, 751, 763
    during WWI, 684
    in WWII, 781
demographics
    African Americans and, 977(m), 980–981
    immigration and, 976–980
Dempsey, Jack, 718
Denmark, 770

depressions. See also Great Depression; Panics; recessions
    of 1873, 479
    of 1890s, 611, 629
deregulation, 918, 986
    of television industry, 924, 975, 987
desegregation, 871–872, 886, 907, 910(i)
detainees
    Abu Ghraib prison, 1002, 1002(i)
    at Guantanamo, 1012, 1017
    Muslim immigrants as, 1009
détente, 896–898, 939, 941
Detroit, Michigan
    busing in, 907
    Ku Klux Klan in, 708(m)
    riots in, 797, 886
Dewey, George, 650–651, 651(m), 655
Dewey, John, 692–693
Dewey, Thomas E., 781, 814
DeWitt, John, 785
Dewson, Molly, 751
Diana, 975
Díaz, Porfirio, 664–665
Dickinson, G. Lowes, 579
Diem, Ngo Dinh, 825, 869
Dies, Martin, 816
digital cameras, 972
Dillon, C. Douglas, 863
diplomacy
    Carter and, 920–922
    Clinton and, 951
    dollar, 664
    economic, 645–646
    isolationism and, 670
    in Latin America, 642–643
    military power as, 1012
    Senate and, 642
    U.S. expansion and, 642–644
discount brokerage firms, 962
discrimination. See also racism
    affirmative action and, 907
    against African Americans, 505, 530, 595–599, 752–754, 775
    against Chinese, 505, 511
    in employment, 768
    against gays, 984
    against Hispanics, 505, 510
    against Mexican Americans, 756
    in military, 775
    reverse, 907, 982
    against women, 902–906
    against women in military, 945(i)
    against women in workforce, 777
disease. See also influenza; smallpox
    epidemic, 681(i)
    globalization and, 966–967
    influenza, 682(i)
    malaria, 661, 661(i)
    Native Americans and, 489
diskettes, 959(i)

Displaced Persons Act, 849
Distant Early Warning line, 822
diversity. *See also* ethnic diversity
    Armed Forces and, 681–683
    cultural, 925
divorce, 905
Dixiecrats. *See* States' Rights Party
DNA (deoxyribonucleic acid), 972, 973(*i*)
Doar, John, 857
documentary impulse, 762
Dodge City, Kansas, 492
Dodson, Burton, 857
the dole, 742. *See also* welfare
Dole, Robert J. (Bob), 917, 950
dollar-a-year men, meaning of, 774
dollar diplomacy, 664
domestic servants
    African Americans as, 753
    Social Security and, 746, 763
    women as, 533
    WWII and, 777
Dominican Republic, 662, 712, 735
domino theory, 825, 870, 877
Dorr, Retha Childe, 594
Dos Passos, John, 723, 762
Doubleday, Abner, 576
Double V campaign, 780
doughboys, 678
Douglas, William O., 748
Douglass, Frederick (1818–1895), 469, 624
    home of, 626(*i*)
Dover, Pennsylvania, 1008
Dow Chemical Company, 882
Downing, Andrew Jackson, 560
draft, military, 678
    first in U.S., 770
    peacetime, 841
    Vietnam War and, 882, 892, 899
    WWII and, 775
Drake, Edwin L., 526
Dred Scott decision (*Dred Scott v. Sandford*; 1857), 985(*i*)
Dreiser, Theodore, 551, 559, 723
drought
    conservation and, 757
    federal building projects and, 756(*m*)
    on Great Plains, 488, 497, 517
    migration and, 757, 757(*i*)
    in Texas, 587
Droughty Kansas (Worrall), 495(*i*)
drug abuse, 982
drug benefits, for baby-boom generation, 924
drug use, 576
dry-farming methods, 497
Du Bois, W.E.B., 625, 625(*i*), 723, 723(*i*)
Dukakis, Michael, 992
Duke, James B., 530
Dulles, John Foster, 822, 824, 826
Dust Bowl (Oklahoma, Texas, New Mexico, Colorado, Arkansas, Kansas)

conservation and, 670, 757
    federal building projects in, 756(*m*)
Dutch Republic. *See* Netherlands
DVD (digital video discs), 972
Dylan, Bob, 884
Dynasty (TV program), 974

Earth Day, 912, 912(*i*)
the East, Native American rights and, 503
Eastern Airlines, 681, 965
Eastern Europe, 803, 822, 828, 965(*m*)
    end of Cold War and, 941–943, 942(*m*)
    immigration from, 976(*f*)
Eastern Front (WWI), 674, 679
East Germany. *See* German Democratic Republic
East St. Louis, Illinois, 698, 703
eavesdropping program, 1009, 1017
Economic Bill of Rights, 813
economic development. *See also* agriculture; industrialization; manufacturing; mining; ranching
    capital goods and, 520
    consumer spending and, 844
    fear of communism and, 801
    government spending and, 815
    industrial capitalism and, 519–549
    military-industrial complex in, 802
    in Sun Belt, 838–839
    tax cuts and, 864
    Whig program for, 585
Economic Growth and Tax Relief Act (2001), 995
Economic Opportunity, Office of (OEO), 876, 896
Economic Opportunity Act (1964), 874(*t*)
Economic Recovery Tax Act (ERTA; 1981), 933, 955
economic rights of women, 533–536
economic theory
    Keynesian, 748
    supply-side, 933
    tax cuts and, 864
economic transformations, Atlantic Charter and, 771, 787
economy. *See also* business; capitalism; depressions; inflation; market economy; Panics; recessions; trade, foreign
    agricultural, 473–474, 529, 529(*m*), 530, 530(*i*)
    balanced budget and, 864, 948, 949(*i*)
    budget deficits and, 925, 934(*i*), 935(*f*), 936, 944, 946, 947(*m*), 996
    business cycles in, 710, 727
    of China, 1013
    concentration of, 627, 629
    of diminished expectations, 911
    downsizing and, 895
    election of 1972 and, 902
    expansionism and, 643–646

federal role in, 469, 739, 742, 762
    Ford and, 917
    free-market, 928, 938
    Great Deflation and, 520
    Great Depression and, 670–671
    industrial, 613
    international, 711, 911, 916
    laissez-faire, 587, 603–604, 608, 613
    mass-consumption, 706
    Nixon and, 896
    postwar, 832–837
    productivity in, 960, 960(*f*)
    prohibition and, 692
    Reagan and, 954
    reconversion of, after Korean War, 813–815
    in the Southwest, 510
    in Soviet Union, 941
    tax cuts and, 996
    U.S. dominance of international, 911
    West German, 807–808
    women's rights and, 905
    WWI and, 683–685
    WWII and, 768, 774
Edison, Thomas A., 553, 555, 705
education
    about sexually transmitted diseases, 691
    affirmative action in, 907, 993
    of African Americans, 472(*i*)
    bilingual, 982
    child-care, 615, 615(*i*)
    in cities, 982
    federal aid to, 815, 831
    Freedmen's School, 472(*i*)
    GI Bill and, 781, 796–797, 834
    high school graduates, 565(*t*)
    JFK and, 864
    LBJ and, 873
    legislation on, 874(*t*)
    managerial class and, 834–835
    of Native American children, 503
    in 1950s, 845–846
    parochial, 592
    prayer in public schools and, 910
    public, 471–472
    school segregation and, 595–596, 886
    women and, 564, 903, 905
Educational Amendments Act (1972), 905
Egypt, 826–827
    Bush (George W.) and, 1016
    Camp David accords and, 918(*i*), 920
    invasion of Israel by, 911
    radical Islamic movements in, 953
Eighteenth Amendment (Prohibition; 1920), 693(*m*), 703, 722(*i*), 722–723, 735
Eighth Amendment, 910
eight-hour day, 479. *See also* work day
Einstein, Albert, 793
Eisenhower, Dwight D. (1890–1969), 895
    civil rights and, 853
    communism and, 822, 824

Eisenhower, Dwight D. (*continued*)
covert intervention and, 824
Cuba and, 863
defense spending and, 827–828, 863, 868
domino theory and, 825
Korea and, 822
McCarthy and, 819
on military-industrial complex,
827–828, 833
New Look in foreign policy of, 822, 868
as president (1953–1961), 818–819, 822,
824, 828
Suez crisis and, 826–827
U-2 spy plane and, 822
Vietnam and, 825, 869
in WWII, 789, 808
Eisenhower Doctrine, 827
elections. *See also* presidential elections
of 1866, 465
of 1868, 468–469
of 1872, 479
of 1876, 480–481
of 1896, 611
of 1916, 677–678
of 1940, 771
of 1942, 781
of 1944, 781
of 1982, 936
of 1992, 946–947, 947(*i*)
of 1994, 948–949
of 2006, 1006
voter turnout for, 590(*i*), 708
electoral college, 479, 481
election of 1940 and, 771
election of 1928 and, 726, 727(*i*)
election of 1932 and, 733(*m*)
election of 2000 and, 990
election of 2004 and, 1005
Wilson and, 678
electricity, 522
electric utility companies, 706, 708
electrification, 747(*t*)
rural, 737(*i*)
TVA and, 739, 759, 760(*m*)
electronic products
imports of, 959
inventions of, 959(*i*), 970, 972
Elementary and Secondary Education Act
(1965), 873–874
elevators, 553
Eliot, T. S., 723, 735
elite. *See also* middle class; social structure
national, 559
urban, 558–559, 580
Elk Hills, California, 707
Elkins Act (1903), 629
Ellington, Edward "Duke", 717
Ellison, Ralph, 762
Ellsberg, Daniel, 901
Ellsworth, Kansas, 492

el-Mokri, El-Hadj, 667(*i*)
El Paso, Texas, 508, 850
El Salvador, 937
embedded reporters, 1001
Emergency Banking Act (1933), 739, 747(*t*), 765
Emerson, Ralph Waldo (1803–1882), on
children, 564
employment. *See also* unemployment
equal opportunity in, 852
gay rights and, 906
Endangered Animals Act (1964), 913
Endangered Species Act (1973), 913
End Poverty in California (EPIC), 751(*m*)
energy. *See also* oil industry
alternative sources of, 913
coal as, 727
consumption of, 911(*f*)
electrical, 522, 747(*t*), 759
for manufacturing, 521–522
nuclear, 839, 911(*f*), 913
in Sun Belt, 838–839
energy crisis (1973–1974), 894(*i*),
911–913, 917
enforcement laws, 477
England. *See* Great Britain
English Channel, 789
English language, 980
Enron Corporation, 995, 995(*i*), 1017
entitlement programs, 896
entrepreneurs
corporate economy and, 706
gold rush and, 506
sports complexes and, 718
WWII and, 775
environment, 514, 839. *See also* national parks
effects of mining on, 508(*i*)
globalization and, 967–969
of Great Plains, 488, 488(*m*), 497
immigrants and, 980
LBJ and, 873, 875
legislation on, 873, 874(*t*), 913
NAFTA and, 948
Nixon and, 896
Tennessee Valley Authority and, 760(*m*)
urban, 556–558, 580
environmentalism, 514–515, 936
in 1970s, 896, 912–913, 922
Sierra Club and, 514
Environmental Policy Act, National
(1969), 913
Environmental Protection Agency (EPA),
896, 913, 935–936, 968, 994
EPA. *See* Environmental Protection Agency
epidemics. *See also* disease
influenza, 680(*i*)
Native Americans and, 489
Equal Credit Opportunity Act (1974), 905
Equal Employment Opportunity Commission
(EEOC), 903
equality

of African Americans, 597–599
before the law, 465
equal opportunity, 852, 982
Equal Rights Amendment (ERA), 905(*i*),
905–906, 906(*m*), 908–909
election of 1980 and, 932
opposition to, 908–909
Equal Rights Association, 469
Erdman Mediation Act (1898), 611
Erickson, Norman, 710(*i*)
Erie Railroad, 523, 523(*i*), 527
ERTA. *See* Economic Recovery Tax Act
Ervin, Sam, Jr., 908–909
Espionage Act (1917), 694, 703
Estonia, 696
Ethiopia, 769, 797, 920
ethnic cleansing, 790–791, 945, 952
ethnic conflict, 983. *See also* race riots
in the Balkans, 952, 952(*m*)
in Somalia, 951
ethnic diversity
in 19th-century America, 530–531, 590(*f*)
politics and, 589–592, 590(*f*),
606–607
ethnicity, 566, 568, 573. *See also* race
Prohibition and, 722
ethnic minorities
employment for, 674
prohibition and, 692
ethnocultural conflict, 590, 592
EU. *See* European Union
Europe. *See also* migration
Chinese spheres of influence and, 645,
651, 662–664, 663(*m*), 668
economic recovery of, 965(*i*)
growth of industrial regions in, 553
immigration from, 510, 849(*f*), 976(*f*)
jazz and, 717
mass transit in, 558
19th century alliances in, 666
oil embargo *vs.*, 911
radio in, 717
urban development in, 553
vs. postwar U.S., 832
welfare system in, 746
WWI and, 674–675, 694–698, 696(*m*)
WWII in, 788(*m*)
European Recovery Program. *See* Marshall
Plan
European Union (EU), 964, 965(*i*), 987,
1012–1013
evangelism, 573, 721, 721(*i*). *See also*
Protestantism; revivalism
abortion and, 984
Bush (George W.) and, 992
election of 2004 and, 1005
in 1950s, 842
in 1970s, 908–909
in 1980s, 924–925
Religious Right and, 928

Evans, Walker, 762
Evers, Medgar, 867
"evil empire," 939
evolution, 587–588, 721–722, 1008
Executive Order 8802 (minority employment rights), 781
Executive Order 9066 (Japanese internment), 784–785, 797
Exodusters, 496, 496(i), 517
expansionism, 655, 655(m)
    economy of, 644–646
    as foreign policy, 642–644
    ideology of, 647
    Manifest Destiny and, 647–648
    opposition to, 654
    roots of, 641–644
Ex Parte Endo (1944), 787
exports, 644–645. See also trade
    decline of, 959
    Great Depression and, 728
    during WWI, 684

factory system. See also industrialization; manufacturing; mills
    assembly line and, 539(i)
    industrialization and, 487
Fairbanks, Douglas, 715
Fair Campaign Practices Act (1974), 902
Fair Deal, 815, 819, 828
Fair Employment Practices Commission (FEPC), 781, 797
Fair Labor Standards Act (FLSA; 1938), 747(t), 748, 765
Fairley, Henry, 862
faith-based initiatives, 924–925, 929
faith-based politics, 992, 1008
Fall, Albert, 707
Faludi, Susan, 983
Falwell, Jerry, 908, 929, 929(i)
families, 561–566. See also birth control; children; women
    desertion of, 570
    feminism and, 905
    gay rights and, 984
    of immigrants, 976
    immigration and, 570–571
    income of, 958(f), 960(f)
    in 1950s, 844–846
    sharecropping and, 474
    television and, 844(i)
    wages and, 960–961
    wartime assistance for, 691
    women in workforce and, 777
    working-class, 529, 532–536
Family and Medical Leave Act (1993), 947, 955
Family Assistance Plan (Nixon), 896
family values, 908–909, 929(i), 975–976, 983, 986
    gay rights and, 984
A Farewell to Arms (Hemingway), 723, 735

Farmer, James, 781
farmers. See also agriculture; tenant farmers; yeoman farmers
    African American, 754
    drought and, 757
    economic problems of, 728
    election of 1936 and, 747
    as homesteaders, 495–498
    in Kansas, 495(i)
    Native Americans as, 503–504
    New Deal and, 742, 754, 762
    1920s and, 710, 727, 734
    Populism and, 602–604
    protests by, 751(m)
    rural electrification and, 737(i), 759
    socialism and, 545
    Social Security and, 746, 763
    subsidies for, 935
    War on Poverty and, 876
    during WWI, 684–685
Farmers' Alliance of the Northwest, 602
Farm Holiday Association, 730, 735, 751(m)
farming. See agriculture; farmers
Farm Loan Act (1916), 742
Farm Security Administration (FSA), 747(t), 762
Farnham, Dwight Thompson, 687
the Far West, 487, 505–515
fascism, 768–769, 782, 784, 796–797. See also Nazi (National Socialist) Party
Father Knows Best (TV program), 843
Faubus, Orval, 853
Fauset, Jessie, 723
fax (facsimile) machines, 972
FBI. See Federal Bureau of Investigation
FCC. See Federal Communications Commission
fedayeen, 1001
Federal Art Project (WPA), 760
Federal Bureau of Indian Affairs, 888
Federal Bureau of Investigation (FBI), 700, 901–902
Federal Communications Commission (FCC), 843–844, 975
Federal Deposit Insurance Corporation (FDIC), 739
Federal Emergency Relief Administration (FERA), 729(m), 742, 747(t), 754
Federal Farm Loan Act (1916), 637
federal government, 673
    activism of, 861, 875
    as broker state, 763
    bureaucracy of, 637, 637(f), 749, 762, 774, 896, 917
    Carter and, 917
    civil rights movement and, 828, 864, 867
    economy and, 815
    environmental legislation and, 913
    expansion of, 749, 768, 781, 876

highways and, 839, 841
housing and, 837–838
LBJ and, 872–873, 875–876
mining interests and, 546
New Deal and, 739–749, 762
in 1970s, 922
Nixon and, 896
photography and, 762
public cynicism and, 896, 918
railroads and, 522, 544, 588
Reagan and, 924, 936, 996
Republican Party and, 896
shrinking of, 936, 954, 996
states and, 896
wartime propaganda of, 685, 693
welfare capitalism and, 710–711
WWII and, 781
Federal Housing Administration (FHA), 837–838
Federal Intelligence Surveillance Act (1978), 902
Federal Music Project, 760
Federal Reserve Act (1913), 635
Federal Reserve system, 918
    inflation and, 936, 959
    New Deal and, 744, 763
    1970s recessions and, 915(f)
    Roosevelt recession and, 748
    tariff reform and, 635
Federal Theatre Project (FTP), 762, 765
Federal Trade Commission (FTC), 636, 707
Federal Writers' Project (FWP), 760–762
Fei Xiaotong, 919
fellow travelers, 770, 816
Felt, W. Mark, 902
The Feminine Mystique (Friedan), 846, 903
feminism, 904(i), 924
    in 1970s, 903–906, 922
    opposition to, 905–906, 908–909, 983
    revival of, 903–906
    rise of, 617–618, 638
    third-wave, 983
Fermi, Enrico, 793
Ferraro, Geraldine, 905, 936
Field, Stephen J., 588–589
Fifteenth Amendment, 468(t), 469, 477, 483, 595–596, 598, 598(i)
    African Americans and, 624
    enforcement laws, 477–478
fifties. See affluent society (1950s)
Filipinos, wartime treatment of, 654. See also Philippines
films. See movies
"final solution," 791(i)
Finland, 696, 802, 965
fireside chats, 738–740, 765
First Amendment, 816, 910, 983
First World War. See World War I
Fiske, John, 647
Fitzgerald, F. Scott, 723, 735
Flanagan, Hallie, 762

flappers, 715–716
Fleetwood, Sara Iredell, 626(*i*)
Fleming, Alexander, 692(*i*)
flexible response policy, 868–869
"flexible specialization," 528
Florida
  abortion clinic murders in, 984
  black registered voters in, 470
  election fiasco in, 990–991
  election of 2000 in, 991(*i*)
  migration to, 838(*m*), 839
  Reconstruction in, 467(*m*), 469–470
  Republican government in, 478, 480–481
  Schiavo case in, 1007
Foch, Ferdinand, 679
Foley, Mark, 1006
folk songs, 760
Food Administration (WWI), 684
Food and Drug Administration (FDA), 632
food conservation, 673, 673(*i*), 683(*i*)
Food for Peace program, 863
food rationing, 673(*i*)
food stamps, 876, 935, 950, 960
Foote, Edward Bliss, 564
Forbes, John Murray, 523
Ford, Gerald R. (1913–2006), 902, 922
  as president (1974–1977), 917
Ford, Henry, 538, 676, 685, 706, 710
Ford Model T, consumer culture and,
  713–714
Ford Motor Company, 644, 731,
  961–962, 968
Fordney-McCumber Tariff (1922), 711
Ford's Theatre, 457
Foreign Affairs, 803–804
foreign aid, 863, 937(*m*)
foreign policy. *See also* international relations
  acquisition of territories and, 654–655
  anti-imperialism in, 654
  in Asia, 662–664
  bipartisan, 814
  Bush (George H. W.), 944–946
  Bush (George W.), 996, 1012, 1015
  in Caribbean, 655(*m*), 668
  Carter, 920–922
  Clinton, 951–953
  Cold War and, 812, 892
  Eisenhower, 822, 824
  expansionist, 642–644, 655(*m*), 668
  Ford, 917
  globalization and, 646, 655
  imperial experiment in, 652–655
  JFK, 863, 871
  lack of purpose in, 642–644, 668
  "large," 646, 649
  neoconservatives and, 998
  in 1920s, 712–713
  Nixon, 896–898
  nonalignment, 642
  Reagan, 927, 936–943

trade and, 645–646, 662
  Venezuela and, 647
  Wilson's philosophy of reform and, 664, 693
Forman, Stanley, 910(*i*)
Forrest, Nathan Bedford, 476(*i*), 476–477
Fort Buford, Montana, 502
Fort Hall, 491
Fortounescere, Vito, 568
Fort Peck Dam, 762(*i*)
Fort Pillow, Tennessee, massacre at, 476
Fort Worth, Texas, 525, 525(*m*)
"forty-niners," 513. *See also* gold rush
Foster, William Z., 733
The Four Hundred, 559
four-minute men, 693
Four-Power Conference (1947), 807
Four Square Gospel Church, 721(*i*)
Fourteenth Amendment (1868), 465–467,
  468(*t*), 477–478, 483, 588, 595–596,
  598, 853
  abortion rights and, 910
  enforcement laws, 477–478
Fowler, Mark, 975
France, 770. *See also* Paris, Treaty of;
  Versailles, Treaty of
  appeasement and, 770
  Germany and, 769–770
  Great Depression and, 728
  in Indochina, 825
  jazz and, 717
  liberation of, 789(*i*)
  NATO and, 897
  Suez Canal and, 826
  U.S. invasion of Iraq and, 1001
  Washington Naval Arms Conference
    and, 713
  WWI and, 674, 679–680, 696–697
  WWII role of, 787, 789
Franco, Francisco, 768, 770
Franco-Prussian War (1870), 666
Frankfurter, Felix, 613, 700, 739, 748
Franklin, Roslyn, 973(*i*)
Franz Ferdinand, Archduke of Austria,
  assassination of (1914), 674
Frazer-Lemke debt relief act, 744
free blacks
  black churches and, 472
  economic independence and, 461
  education of, 472(*i*)
  labor of, 464(*i*), 474
  Reconstruction and, 459, 461–464, 470–471
  sharecropping and, 473–476
  terrorism against, 476–478
  voting rights for, 469
  wage labor and, 461, 464, 473, 479
  women, 474
Freed, Alan, 847
Freedman's Savings and Trust Company, 479
Freedmen's Bureau, 459, 461, 464, 471,
  473, 483

Freedom of Information Act, 902
freedom of speech, 694, 882, 882(*i*)
Freedom Riders, 864, 866
Freedom Summer (1964), 872, 872(*i*), 882
free-market capitalism, 943
free-market economy, 928, 938
free silver, 611, 633
free speech, Scopes trial and, 721–722, 735
Free Speech Movement (FSM), 882, 882(*i*)
Frick, Henry Clay, 543–544, 579
Friedan, Betty, 846, 903
Friedman, Milton, 929
Friends. *See* Quakers
Frist, Bill, 1007
frontier
  concept of, 647–648
  end of, 515, 517
  mythic, 487(*i*), 493–494
Fuel Administration, 684
Fujita, Jun, 698(*i*)
Fulbright, J. William, 879
fundamentalism
  abortion and, 984
  Scopes trial and, 721–722
  Taliban and, 998
F.W. Woolworth Company, 527

G-7 nations, 964
G-8 nations, 964, 970
Gagarin, Yuri, 864
Galbraith, John Kenneth, 833
Gandhi, Mahatma, 792, 855
gang-labor system, 464, 464(*i*), 474
gangs
  African Americans in, 982
  zoot suits and, 784, 784(*i*)
Garcia, Juanita, 978
Garfield, James A. (1831–1881),
  584–585
Garland, Hamlin, 496, 566
garment industry, 537, 545, 978–979
Garson, Greer, 782
Garvey, Marcus, 726, 885–886
Gary, Elbert H., 629, 699
Gary, Indiana, 710(*i*)
gasoline prices, 1013
Gates, Bill, 970–971, 971(*i*), 987
Gatling machine guns, 502
GATT. *See* General Agreement on Tariffs
  and Trade
gay rights, 903, 924
  conflicting values and, 984
  marriage and, 1005–1006
  in military, 947
  in 1970s, 922
  opposition to, 975, 987
Gay Task Force, National, 906
Gaza Strip, 944–945, 952, 1001(*m*)
GDP. *See* gross domestic product
Gellhorn, Martha, 762

gender roles, 928–929. *See also* men; women
  conservative view of, 908–909
  farming and, 496
  feminism and, 905–906
  of free blacks, 461, 464
  homesteaders and, 496
  in 1950s, 846–847
  sex-typing and, 532–533
  on television, 843
  wives and, 561–562
General Agreement on Tariffs and Trade
  (GATT), 832, 964
General Assembly (UN), 793, 826
General Electric (GE), 711, 713, 965
General Motors (GM), 711, 835–836, 841, 968
  sit-down strike and, 749, 765
general strike, 546
genetic codes, 973(i)
genetic testing, 972
Geneva Accords (1954), 825
*Gentle Measures in the Management and
  Training of the Young* (Abbott), 564
Gentlemen's Agreement (1907), 664
George, David Lloyd, 695(i), 696–697
George, Henry, 511
Georgia
  Barrow Plantation in, 473(m)
  Democratic Party in, 477
  sharecroppers in, 473(m), 475(i)
German Democratic Republic (East
  Germany), 808, 942
German immigrants, 496, 530–531,
  675–676, 688(i), 693–694
  nativism and, 718
  political activism of, 543, 545, 590(f), 591
  prohibition and, 692
  unionism of, 540
Germany. *See also* Berlin; Berlin Wall;
  German Democratic Republic
  anti-Semitism in, 769
  automobile industry in, 911
  Balkans and, 952
  defeat of, 806
  division of, 792
  domination by, 787
  fascism in, 768–770
  Great Depression and, 728
  imports from, 959–960
  invasion of Poland by, 767, 797
  Japan and, 771
  Nazi, 768(i)
  propaganda and, 682, 693–694, 700
  reunification of, 942(m)
  Soviet Union and, 787, 789(i)
  surrender of, 790, 797
  U-boats and, 677–678
  U.S. invasion of Iraq and, 1001
  war reparations of, 696–697, 711, 735,
  768–769
  welfare system in, 746

in WWI, 674–675, 677–679
  in WWII, 767(i), 788–789(i), 789, 791
  zones of occupation in, 806
Germany, Federal Republic of (West
  Germany), 808
Geronimo, Chief, 502
gerrymandering, 991–992, 1006
ghettoes, 566–567, 572, 572(i). *See also* cities
  urban renewal and, 852
ghost dance, 504
ghost towns, 506
Giamatti, A. Bartlett, 931
GI Bill of Rights (Servicemen's Readjustment
  Act; 1944), 781, 796–797, 834–835
Gibson, Charles Dana, 564, 566
Gibson girl, 564, 566
Gilbert Islands, 792(m)
Gilded Age (late 19th century), 579, 613, 627,
  642–644
The Gilded Age (Warner), 579
Gilder, George, 933
Gillette, 834
Gilman, Charlotte Perkins, 617
Gingrich, Newt, 949, 949(i), 991
Ginsberg, Allen, 848, 885
Ginsburg, Ruth Bader, 938(i), 947
glasnost, meaning of, 941
Glass-Steagall Banking Act (1932),
  739, 747(t)
Glazer, Nathan, 929
Glenn, John, 864
Global Crossing, 995
globalization, 925, 958, 963–970, 986. *See
  also* economy: international
  China and, 1013
  computers and, 973
  corporations and, 834
  endangered environment and, 967–969
  foreign policy and, 646, 655
  outsourcing and, 965–966, 987
  terrorism and, 954
Godkin, Edwin L., 558–559
Goethals, George W., 661(i)
gold, monetary system and, 604–607, 606(i)
Goldberg, Rube, 800(i)
Goldman, Emma, 700
Goldmark, Pauline, 681
Goldmark, Peter, 834
gold mining, 505(m), 505–506, 508(i), 607
  in California, 505, 515
  Chinese in, 510–511
gold rush (1849–1857), 505–506, 510, 517
gold standard, 604–607, 606(i), 728
Goldwater, Barry, 819, 872, 873(m), 928
Goldwyn, Samuel, 716
Gompers, Samuel, 542, 542(i), 622, 654, 685
Gonzales, Alberto, 1009
González, Henry, 887
Good Housekeeping (magazine), 561, 717
Good Neighbor Policy, 670, 769

Gorbachev, Mikhail, 939, 939(i), 941–942, 955
Gore, Albert (Al), Jr., 946, 947(i), 949(i),
  990–991, 991(i)
Gorgas, William C., 661(i)
Gorson, Aaron Henry, 519(i)
Gotzion, Evelyn, 778
Gould, Jay, 523, 542
government
  in America, 924, 954
  federal, 673
  limited, 479, 683, 685, 928, 936, 938, 954
  New Deal and, 737–738, 742, 745, 749
  partnership with business and, 706–713
  radio licenses and, 717
  women in, 750–752, 763
graft, in ward politics, 572
Graham, Billy, 842, 843(i), 992
Graham, Frank P., 820–821
grain. *See also* corn; rice; wheat
  prohibition and, 692
  during WWI, 684
Gramm-Rudman Act (1985), 944, 955
Grand Alliance, 801, 803
grandfather clauses, 597
Granger movement, 498, 517, 602
Grant, J. Marse, 908
Grant, Ulysses S. (1822–1885), 480(i)
  1868 election and, 468–469, 483
  1872 election and, 479, 483
  Ku Klux Klan Act of 1871 and, 478
  as president (1869–1877), 478–479,
  592, 642
  Reconstruction and, 467, 478, 481–482
  scandals during administration of, 479
The Grapes of Wrath (Steinbeck), 757,
  757(i), 762
grasslands, 488(m), 488–489, 497
Grasso, Ella T., 905
Grateful Dead, 884
Graves, Leslie, 794
Great American Desert, 488, 488(m), 489,
  495. *See also* Great Plains
Great Atlantic and Pacific Tea Company
  (A&P), 527, 713
Great Basin, 505
Great Britain, 647
  alliances of, 666
  appeasement and, 770
  Germany and, 769
  Great Depression and, 728
  invasion of Iraq and, 1001
  naval blockade by, 676
  neutrality of, 770–771
  nuclear test ban treaties and, 868
  Palestine and, 826
  steel production and, 487
  Suez Canal and, 826
  U.S. relations with, 659, 668, 771
  Washington Naval Arms Conference
  and, 713

Great Britain (*continued*)
  welfare system in, 746
  WWI and, 674–675, 696–697
  WWII role of, 787
Great Deflation (19th century), 520
Great Depression, 622–623, 670–671, 719,
  727–733, 729(*f*)
  beginning of, 706, 727–728
  causes of, 710
  conservatives and, 928, 954
  Hoover and, 726
  human face of, 759(*i*), 762
  labor unions in, 835
  popular protests in, 751(*m*)
  Prohibition and, 723
  WWII and, 768, 777, 781
Greater East Asia Co-Prosperity Sphere,
  771–772
The Great Gatsby (Fitzgerald), 723, 735
Great Lakes, iron ore in, 521
Great Migration, 685–687, 690(*m*), 703, 753
  WWII and, 784
Great Moments in History (radio program),
  713
Great Northern Railroad, 522–523
Great Plains
  climate of, 488(*m*), 488–489, 495, 497, 517
  ecosystem of, 488(*m*), 488–489
  as Great American Desert, 488(*m*), 495
  homesteaders on, 495–498, 496(*i*), 497,
    505, 515
  as Indian country, 489
  marketing of, 491–492, 495(*i*)5463(*i*)
  railroads and, 491(*m*), 491–492
  ranching on, 492–493
  settlement of, 488–504, 515
  sod houses on, 496(*i*), 497
Great Salt Lake, 497, 505
Great Smoky Mountain National Park, 760
Great Society, 871–877, 884, 892, 925,
  933, 935
  declining economy and, 911–912
  funding for, 876–877
  legislation of, 874(*t*)
Great Strike of 1877, 519–520
Great War. *See* World War I
Greece, 803, 805, 807
Greeley, Horace, 479, 488, 491
Green, Theodore Francis, 875(*i*)
greenbacks, 604. *See also* currency
Green Berets, 869
Greeneville, Tennessee, 458
greenhouse effect, 968–969
Green Party, 990
Greensboro Four, 852(*i*), 855(*i*)
Gresham, Walter Q., 646
Griffith, Beatrice, 756
Griffith, E. H., 692(*i*)
Grimes County, Texas, 598–599
Griswold v. Connecticut (1965), 910

gross domestic product (GDP), 644
  during 1920s, 710, 727
  postwar, 832, 833(*f*), 913
  under Reagan, 936
gross national product (GNP)
  under Clinton, 948
  decline of, 911
  defense spending and, 774, 774(*f*)
  globalization and, 964
  health care and, 947
  postwar, 833, 833(*f*)
  Roosevelt recession and, 748
  during WWI, 683
Group of Eight nations, 964, 970
Group of Seven nations, 964
Guadalcanal Diary (film), 782
Guam, 651–652, 655, 655(*m*), 791
Guantanamo Bay, Cuba, 653, 655(*m*), 661,
  662(*m*), 1012, 1017
Guatemala, 643, 825
guest worker program, 978
Guevara, Che (Ernesto C.), 883
Guggenheim, Harry, 705(*i*)
Guiteau, Charles, 584
Gulf of Tonkin Resolution (1964), 878
gun control, 948–949
guns
  Rifle Clubs, 478
  during WWI, 674–675, 683
Gunsmoke, 843
Guthrie, Oklahoma, 503
Guy, Seymour J., 560(*i*)
Guzman, Jacobo Arbenz, 825
Gypsies, Holocaust and, 790

Hague Peace Conference (1899), 666
Haiti, 642, 662, 951–952
  land distribution in, 474
  U.S. military intervention in, 712
Halberstam, David, 863
Hall, G. Stanley, 563
Halliburton, 994
Hamas, 1015–1017
Hamdan v. Rumsfield (2006), 924,
  1012, 1017
Hamilton, Mary Agnes, 732
Hancock, Winfield, 586(*m*)
Handlin, Oscar, 593
Handycam, 959(*i*)
Hanna, Mark, 606, 611
Hard, William, 614
Harding, Warren G. (1865–1923)
  corruption and, 707(*i*)
  death of, 707, 735
  as president (1921–1923), 706, 735
hardware, meaning of, 970
Harlan County, Kentucky, 735
Harlem, New York City, 567, 753–754, 765
Harlem Renaissance, 723(*i*), 723–726
Harman, Jane, 1012

Harper, Frances, 469
Harper's Weekly (journal), 465(*i*), 537(*i*), 634(*i*)
Harriman, Averell, 803, 807
Harrington, Michael, 849
Harrison, Benjamin (1833–1901)
  election of 1892 and, 584, 584(*i*),
    607(*m*)
  as president (1889-1893), 589, 589(*i*),
    602, 646
  on protective tariffs, 585
Harrison, William Henry (1773–1841), 584(*i*)
Harte, Bret, 513
Harvey, George, 634(*i*)
Hastie, William, 853
hat-in-the-ring squadron, 681(*i*)
hatters, 536, 540
Hawaii. *See also* Pearl Harbor, attack on
  annexation of, 651, 655, 655(*m*)
  Chinese immigration to, 511
  Japanese internment and, 785, 787
  strategic importance of, 646, 655(*m*)
  sugarcane in, 643, 643(*i*)
Hawley-Smoot Tariff (1930), 711, 728, 735
Hay, John, 663
Hayden, Tom, 882
Hayes, Rutherford B. (1822–1893)
  election of 1876 and, 584
  nomination of, 480
  as president (1877–1881), 481, 483
  Strike of 1877 and, 519–520
Haymarket affair, 543, 549
Hay-Pauncefote Agreement (1901), 659
Haywood, "Big Bill", 546
A Hazard of New Fortunes (Howells), 579
Head Start, 876
Health, Education, and Welfare, Department
  of (HEW), 819
health care
  attempts to reform, 947–948, 948(*i*)
  baby boom improvements in, 845
  biotechnology and, 972
  Bush (George W.) and, 993–994
  federal government and, 836
  gay rights and, 984
  illegal aliens and, 980
  JFK and, 861
  in shipbuilding industry, 774
  socialized, 815
health insurance, 622
  JFK and, 864
  labor unions and, 836
  national, 746, 815, 947–948, 955
  Social Security and, 746, 763
  welfare capitalism and, 709, 711
health savings accounts, 994
Hearst, William Randolph, 577–578, 578(*i*),
  648–649, 732
hegemony, meaning of, 996
Helms, Jesse, 984
Hemingway, Ernest, 723, 735

Hendrix, Jimi, 884, 884(*i*)
Henry Street Settlement, 612
Hepburn Railway Act (1906), 629
Hereford cattle, 493
Heritage Foundation, 928, 955
Her Wedding Night (film), 715(*i*)
Herzegovina, 674, 952
Hess, Jean, 660
Hetch Hetchy Valley, 515
HEW. *See* Health, Education, and Welfare, Department of
Heyward, Edward Barnell, 462
Hezbollah, *versus* Israel, 1015–1017
Hickok, Lorena, 762
Hicks, Clarence J., 623
The Hidden Persuaders (Packer), 843
high crimes and misdemeanors, 466, 951
Higher Education Act (1965), 873–874, 874(*t*)
high school shootings, 975
Highway Act, National Interstate and Defense (1956), 839(*m*), 841
Highway Beautification Act (1965), 873
highways
    automobile and, 714
    Interstate, 819, 839(*m*)
    move to suburbs and, 839, 841
    1950s culture and, 839, 841
    postwar growth of, 819, 839(*m*)
Hill, Anita, 943, 944(*i*)
Hill, Fanny Christina (Tina), 778
Hill, James J., 522–523
Hine, Lewis, 622(*i*)
hippies, 884. *See also* counterculture
Hirabashi, Gordon, 787
Hirabayashi v. United States (1943), 787
Hiroshima, 767, 793(*m*), 794, 795(*i*), 797, 809
Hispanics. *See also* Latinos
    in cattle industry, 493, 493(*i*)
    as cowboys, 492–493, 493(*i*)
    culture of, 512
    in the Far West, 508–510
    Korean immigrants and, 980, 980(*i*)
    migratory work and, 510
    population increase of, 977(*m*)
    race riots by, 982(*i*)
    as shepherds, 493
    in the Southwest, 505, 508–510
    welfare system and, 747
Hiss, Alger, 815–816, 818, 898
"The History of the Standard Oil Company" (Tarbell), 614(*i*)
Hitler, Adolph, 748, 768, 768(*i*), 769–771, 790, 797
    Holocaust and, 790, 791(*i*), 825(*i*)
HIV infection. *See also* AIDS
    AIDS and, 968(*i*)
    globalization and, 966–967
Hoar, George F., 654
Höbner, Joseph Alexander von, 507

Ho Chi Minh, 697, 825
Hoffman, Abbie, 889
Hohenberg, Duchess of, 674
Holland. *See* Netherlands
Hollywood, California, 714, 715(*i*), 742. *See also* Los Angeles, California; movies
Hollywood films, venereal diseases, 692(*i*)
Hollywood Ten, 816
Holmes, Oliver Wendell, Jr., 613, 694
Holocaust, 768, 790–791, 791(*i*), 825(*i*)
    homosexuals and, 790
Holtzman, Elizabeth, 905
Home Depot, 960
home front, during WWI, 683–694, 702
Home Insurance Building, 554
Homeland Security, Department of, 995, 1004(*i*)
homelessness (1990s), 960
Home Owners Loan Corporation, 739
home pages, meaning of, 971
home rule, 480
Homestead Act (1862), 495, 503, 517
homesteaders, 495–498, 496(*i*)–497(*i*), 505, 515
Homestead steel strike (1892), 487, 543–544
homosexuals, 983, 986. *See also* gay rights; lesbians
    civil rights for, 903, 906
    gay liberation movement and, 906
    Holocaust and, 790
    in military, 775
    in New York City, 576
The Honeymooners (TV program), 843
Hong Kong, 791, 792(*m*)
Hoover, Herbert (1874–1964), 684
    at Department of Commerce, 706–707, 733
    election of 1928 and, 726, 735
    election of 1932 and, 733(*m*)
    Great Depression and, 728–730, 738
    illegal immigrants and, 756
    New Deal and, 742, 744
    as president (1929–1933), 728–730, 734
Hoover, J. Edgar, 700
Hoovervilles, 730, 730(*i*)
Hopkins, Harry, 742–743
Horton, Willie, 992
House, Edward, 677
House Committee on Un-American Activities (HUAC), 816–818, 820–821
House of Representatives, U.S. *See also* Congress, U.S.; Senate, U.S.
    Clinton impeachment and, 951
    Democratic control of, 936, 1006
    Gulf War and, 945
    Republican gains in, 932, 949
    woman suffrage and, 691
    women in, 944(*i*)

housing
    in cities, 851–852
    discrimination in, 838, 852
    gay rights and, 906
    LBJ and, 873
    legislation on, 747(*t*), 815, 819, 874(*t*)
    postwar boom in, 837–838
    public, 876
    suburban, 560–561
    tenements, 556–557, 556(*f*), 569, 572(*i*)
    wartime migration and, 784
Housing and Urban Development, Department of (HUD), 947
Houston, Texas, 530(*i*), 681
Houston Astros, 995(*i*)
Hovenden, Thomas, 457(*i*)
Howard, Oliver O., 461
Howe, Frederic, 605
Howe, Julia Ward, 469
Howe, Marie Jenny, 617
Howells, William Dean, 579
"Howl" (Ginsberg), 848
HUAC. *See* House Committee on Un-American Activities
HUD. *See* Housing and Urban Development, Department of
Huerta, Victoriano, 664–665
Hughes, Charles Evans, 677, 706, 713
Hughes, Langston, 723
Hughes, Robert P., 657
Hull, Cordell, 769
Hull House, 612, 615, 615(*i*)
Human Genome Project, 987
human resources, WWII and, 775–777
human rights
    Carter and, 920, 922
    in China, 1013
Human Rights, Office of, 920
Humphrey, Hubert H., 814, 863
    election of 1968 and, 889, 891, 892(*m*)
Hundred Days (New Deal), 739–744
Hungarian immigrants, 531–532
Hungary, 674, 696, 803, 822, 826, 942
hunger marches, 735
hunger strikes, 690
Hunt, E. Howard, 901
Hurricane Katrina (2005), 1006, 1007(*i*), 1017
Hurston, Zora Neale, 723, 762
Hussein, King of Jordan, 827
Hussein, Saddam, 925, 945–946, 999–1001, 1004, 1016(*m*)
Huston, John, 762
Hutu extremists, 951
hydrogen bomb, 809, 822. *See also* nuclear weapons

Iacocca, Lee, 962, 987
IAEA. *See* International Atomic Energy Agency
IBM. *See* International Business Machines
Ibuka, Masaru, 959(*i*)

Ickes, Harold, 739, 743, 754, 759
Idaho
    Chinese in, 511
    Japanese internment in, 785, 785(i)
    mining in, 511, 546
idealism, 863
    progressive, 613
identity, in California, 512
identity politics, 904
ideology, 587
IED. See improvised explosive devices
illegal immigrants, 976, 980
    Bush (George W.) and, 993, 1006
Illinois
    prohibition and, 691
    wheat in, 498
illness. See disease
IMF. See International Monetary Fund
immigrants, 638. See also Chinese
        immigrants; German immigrants;
        immigration; Irish immigrants; migration
    Americanization of, 681, 693–694
    Asian, 849(f), 875, 924, 976–980
    Catholic, 573
    as cheap labor, 530–531, 548
    in cities, 551, 551(i), 566–568, 570–572
    Democratic Party and, 590–592, 590(f), 707
    deportation of, 850
    discrimination against, 734–735, 875
    disease and, 966
    Eastern European, 875
    European, 531, 531(f), 549, 567(m), 849(f)
    Filipino, 849
    German, 530–531, 540, 543, 545, 675–676,
        688(i), 693–694
    hostility to, 987
    Hungarian, 531–532
    Irish, 530–531, 537, 675, 692
    Italian, 530–531, 566, 567(i)
    Japanese, 718, 849
    Jewish, 716
    Korean, 849, 980
    Latino, 849–850, 924, 976–980
    legal, 849(f)
    Mexican, 924, 976
    newspapers and, 566
    in New York City, 552
    Norwegian, 496
    politics and, 735
    Puerto Rican, 850
    Scandinavian, 530–531
    South American, 850, 875
    Southeast Asian, 849
    Swedish, 496
    U.S. fear of anarchy and, 700–701
immigration
    of Asians, 987
    of Latinos, 987
    legislation on, 874(t), 875
    in 1920s, 718

    in 1950s, 847, 849–850
    restrictions on, 622, 718–721
    trends in, 976(f)
Immigration Act (1965), 875, 976, 986
Immigration and Naturalization Service
        (INS), 980
immigration laws, 719, 849(f)
    LBJ and, 875
    in 1950s, 849–850
Immigration Restriction League, 622
impeachment
    of Adelbert Ames, 478
    Clinton, 950–951, 951(i), 954
    Johnson, 467–468, 483, 951
    Nixon, 902
imperialism, U.S., 641–642, 652–655, 658(i)
    globalization and, 969
    opposition to, 654, 656–657, 660, 668
Imperial Presidency, 774
imports. See trade, foreign
improvised explosive devices (IED), 1002
inclusiveness, politics of, 992–993
income. See also wages
    of families, 958(f), 960(f)
    of farmers, 727
    of immigrants, 977–979
    of Native Americans, 754
    unequal distribution of, 713, 727
income taxes, 684–685
indentured servants
    Asians as, 511
    in Caribbean, 474
    laws against, 511
India, 1013
    McDonald's in, 965
    nuclear power and, 1013
    outsourcing and, 965–966
    WWII and, 791
Indiana
    Ku Klux Klan in, 721
Indian Affairs, Bureau of, 850
Indian Affairs, Office of, 499, 502–503
Indian Education (Morgan), 500
Indian Reorganization Act (1934), 754, 765
Indian reservations. See Native Americans:
        reservation system and
Indian Rights Association, 503
Indian Territory
    of Oklahoma, 503
individualism, 628, 928
    election of 1928 and, 726
    Great Depression and, 732
    ideology of, 587–588
    Lindbergh and, 705
individual rights, New Deal and, 737–738
Indochina, 771–772, 822. See also Cambodia;
        Vietnam
Indonesia, 1013
    foreign trade and, 728
    radical Islamic movements in, 953

industrialization. See also factory system;
        manufacturing; mills
    accumulation of wealth and, 587–589
    capitalism and, 519–549
    environmental pollution and, 519(i)
    immigrant labor and, 530–531, 548
    integrated systems within, 521, 525(m),
        526, 528
    large-scale enterprise and, 524–528
    in late 19th century, 487, 519(i), 519–538
    middle class and, 560–561
    mining and, 506
    in New South, 529(m), 529–530
    railroads and, 519–520, 522–524, 524(m)
    reversal of, 915–916
    robber barons and, 522–523
    skills for, 531
    urbanization and, 551–552, 580, 638
Industrial Revolution, in Great Britain, 520
industrial unionism, 544, 749. See also labor
        unions
Industrial Workers of the World (IWW;
        Wobblies), 546–547, 549, 637, 694, 700
industry
    automobiles and, 714
    decline of, 915–916
    development of, 628, 837
    employment in, 835–836
    foreign policy and, 827
    growth of, 642, 668
    interstate highways and, 839(m)
    managerial revolution and, 709
    new techniques in, 709
    postwar, 835–837
    during WWI, 683–685
infant mortality, 709
inflation
    after WWI, 699
    Carter and, 918, 920
    energy crisis and, 911–912
    interest rates and, 958
    in 1920s, 710
    in 1970s, 913, 915, 915(f), 922
    postwar, 833
    Roosevelt recession and, 748
    Vietnam War and, 879
    WWII and, 780
The Influence of Seapower upon History
        (Mahan), 646
influenza
    1918–1919 epidemic of, 680(i)
    wartime propaganda and, 693–694
information age, 972
information technology, 925
In His Steps (Sheldon), 574
In Our Time (Hemingway), 723
In Re Jacobs (1885), 588
insider knowledge, 962
installment plans, 713. See also credit
Insull, Samuel, 705–706

insurgencies
in Iraq, 1002–1003, 1006, 1016
in Vietnam, 1002
intellectual property rights, 964, 972
"intelligent design," 1008
Inter-American Treaty of Reciprocal Assistance (Rio Treaty; 1947), 824(m)
intercontinental ballistic missiles (ICBMs), 868, 898
Intermediate Nuclear Forces Treaty (1988), 924
Internal Revenue Service (IRS), 762. See also taxation
International Atomic Energy Agency (IAEA), 1013–1014
International Bank for Reconstruction and Development (World Bank), 832
International Business Machines (IBM), 834, 970
International Criminal Court, 998
International Harvester, 710
internationalism, 832. See also globalization; isolationism
International Monetary Fund (IMF), 832, 834, 964, 970
international relations
Cold War, 822, 824(m), 824–827
overseas bases and, 646, 668
U.S. dominance in, 659–662
before WWI, 674
International Telephone and Telegraph Corporation, 834
International Typographical Union (1852), 541
Internet, 924, 971–973
Interstate Commerce Commission (ICC), 629
Interstate Highway Act (1956), 819, 839, 839(m), 841
interventionism, 769–770
intifada, meaning of, 945
iPod, 972
Iran, 803, 825
dictatorship in, 824
nuclear power and, 1013–1014
oil production in, 911, 921
revolution in, 911, 921, 945
Shah of, 921
uranium enrichment by, 1017
Iran-Contra affair, 936–938, 937(m), 955
Iranian hostage crisis, 921, 921(i), 922, 929, 1001(m)
Iraq, 696(m)
creation of, 1016(i)
dead soldiers in, 990
insurgencies in, 1002–1003, 1006
invasion of Kuwait by, 925, 945
oil production in, 911
Persian Gulf War and (1990–1991), 945–946, 1001(m)

al-Sadr in, 1015(i)
U.S. invasion of, 924–925, 999–1002, 1016–1017
Ireland, famine in, 530
Ireland, John, 572
Irish Home Rule, 675
Irish immigrants, 675
Democratic Party and, 590, 590(f)
machine politics and, 572
nativism and, 718
19th-century, 530–531, 537
opposition to, 980
prohibition and, 692
iron industry, 537, 537(i), 540
coal in, 552
in Great Britain, 487
mining in, 529(m)
pig iron in, 520
steel and, 520
wrought iron in, 520
"Ironworkers-Noontime" (painting), 537(i)
irreconcilables, 697
irrigation
Mormons and, 497
water resources and, 515
Islam. See also Muslims; Shiite Muslims; Sunni Muslims
African American, 886
fundamentalist, 921, 1001(m)
militant terrorists, 1014–1016
radicalism, 952–953
Islamic extremism, 1014–1016
isolationism, 642, 644, 666, 670, 697
opposition to, 769–770
retreat from, 770–771
WWI and, 712
WWII and, 790
Israel, 999(i), 1014
Camp David accords and, 918(i), 920
in international politics, 911
oil embargo and, 911
Palestinians and, 825–826, 944–945, 1001(m)
versus Hezbollah, 1017
Italy, 674, 696
fascism in, 768–770, 797
immigration from, 530–531, 566, 567(i)
invasion of Ethiopia by, 769, 797
Japan and, 771
Washington Naval Arms Conference and, 713
WWII and, 788(m), 789
Iwo Jima, 791, 793(m), 797
IWW. See Industrial Workers of the World

Jackson, Helen Hunt, 500, 503, 513, 517
Jackson, Jesse, 901, 991(i)
Jackson, William Henry, 553(i)
Jackson State College, killing at, 898
James, Henry, 579

James, William, 613, 654
Japan, 645–646
automobile industry in, 911
defeat of, 813
domination by, 787
economic growth and, 963
as economic power, 959–960, 987
fascism in, 768–769
Germany and, 767(i)
immigrants from, 512, 756
imports from, 959–960
Indochina (Vietnam) and, 771–772
invasion of China by, 768–769, 771, 797
invasion of Manchuria by, 768
oil embargo vs., 911
Pearl Harbor and, 772–773, 773(i), 796–797
quality of products from, 834
surrender of, 794, 797
U.S. relations with, 663–664, 668
war with Russia (1905) and, 675
Washington Naval Arms Conference and, 713
WWI and, 674, 697
WWII and, 782, 791
Japanese Americans
internment of, 670, 784–787, 785(i)
Nisei (second-generation), 785, 787
Jarvis, Howard, 916
jazz, 716(i), 716–717, 848
Jazz Age (1920s), 718, 726
The Jazz Singer (film), 716
Jefferson Airplane, 884
Jenney, William Le Baron, 554
Jericho, Israel, 952
Jewish Daily Forward, 566, 570–571
Jews
Arabs and, 952
discrimination against, 838
election of 1936 and, 747
Holocaust and, 790–791
immigration restrictions and, 718
Ku Klux Klan and, 721
movie studios and, 716
Nazi view of, 769
in 1950s, 842
in Soviet Union, 920–921
Yiddish theater and, 566
Jiang Jieshi (Chiang Kai-shek), 810
jihad, meaning of, 989
jihadi bomber, meaning of, 1002
Jim Crow laws, 597–599, 624, 721, 886
jingoism, 648–650
Job Corps, 876
Joffre, Joseph, 678
John Paul II, Pope (1920–2005), 941, 941(i)
Johnson, Andrew (1808–1875), 458(i)
impeachment of, 467–468, 483, 951
as president (1865–1869), 458–466, 483

Johnson, Andrew (*continued*)
Reconstruction plan of, 458(*i*), 458–459, 461, 473, 481, 483
veto of civil rights bill by, 464
veto of Reconstruction Act by, 467
Johnson, Hiram W., 618, 697
Johnson, Lady Bird, 873
Johnson, Lyndon B. (1908–1973), 744, 862, 928, 996, 1002
affirmative action and, 907
civil rights movement and, 872
credibility gap of, 879
Great Society of, 871–877, 884, 892
as president (1963–1969), 871–877
Vietnam policy of, 877–878, 878(*f*), 884, 891–892
Jolson, Al, 716
Jones, Bobby, 718
Jones, Paula, 952
Jones Act (1916; 1917), 654
Jones and Laughlin steel works (Pittsburgh), 531
Jordan, 827, 1003
Joseph, Chief of Nez Percé, 502
journalism. *See also* mass media
national culture and, 717–718
reform, 613–614
sensationalist, 648–649, 649(*i*)
women in, 752
yellow, 577–578
Journal of Negro History, 686
judicial restraint, 910
judiciary. *See also* common law; court system; law; Supreme Court
Ku Klux Klan and, 478
on rights of private property, 588
supremacy of in late 19th century, 588–589
Julian, George, 466
The Jungle (Sinclair), 632
the Junta (Cuban exiles), 648
juvenile delinquency
music and, 847
WWII and, 784

Kaiser, Henry J., 774–775, 775(*i*), 783(*i*), 837
Kaiser Corporation, 784
Kaiser Permanente Medical Care Program, 775
kamikaze missions, 791
Kansas
advertising, 495(*i*)
African American exodus to, 496, 496(*i*)
Apache Indians in, 502
creationism and, 1008
farmers in, 495(*i*), 498
Long Drive and, 492
prohibition and, 693(*m*)
Kansas City, Missouri, 492, 557–558
jazz and, 716
stockyard centers in, 525, 525(*m*)
Kansas Pacific Railroad, 492(*i*)

Kashmir, 1013
Kasich, John, 949(*i*)
Kazakhstan, 1013
Kearney, Denis, 511
Keaton, Buster, 715
Keegan, John, 767
Kefauver, Estes, 847
Kelley, Florence, 615
Kelley, Oliver H., 498
Kellogg, Frank, 713
Kellogg-Briand Peace Pact (1928), 713, 735
Kennan, George F., 803–804, 804(*i*), 807
containment theory of, 804, 942
Kennedy, Anthony, 931, 938
Kennedy, Edward (Ted), 929
Kennedy, Jacqueline, 870
Kennedy, John Fitzgerald (1917–1963), 862(*i*)
assassination of, 870–871, 884, 892
civil rights and, 867
domestic policies of, 864
foreign policy of, 863
Mexican Americans and, 887
as president (1961–1963), 861–871
Vietnam policy and, 877–878, 892
Kennedy, Robert F., 863, 887
assassination of, 861, 889, 892, 892(*m*)
civil rights and, 866
Kent State University, killings at, 898
Kentucky, strikes in, 735
Kenya, 953, 989
Kerner Commission (1968), 907
Kerouac, Jack, 848
Kerry, John, 1004(*i*), 1004–1005
Keun, Odette, 758
Keynes, John Maynard, 748, 815
Khan, A.Q., 1013
Khomeini, Ayatollah Ruhollah, 921, 945
Khrushchev, Nikita S., 822, 832(*i*), 863, 868, 942
Kim Il Sung, 810
King, Constance, 743(*t*)
King, Martin Luther, Jr. (1929–1968), 855–856, 866–867, 868(*i*), 872, 876, 983
assassination of, 861, 886, 889, 892
Jesse Jackson and, 901
King, Rodney, 982
Kingfish. *See* **Long, Huey**
King's Canyon National Park, 514
King's College. *See* Columbia University
Kiowa Indians, 489, 499(*m*)
Kirkpatrick, Jeane, 929
Kissinger, Henry, 896–897, 899–900
"kitchen debate" (Nixon-Khrushchev), 831, 832(*i*)
Knickerbocker Trust Company, 635
Knights of Labor, 540, 541(*i*), 542–543, 548–549, 595
Knox, Frank, 771
Kodak, 644
Koehler, Karl, 776

Koontz, Elizabeth Duncan, 909
Korea, 772. *See also* North Korea; South Korea
dictatorship in, 824
immigrants from, 849, 980, 980(*i*)
Japanese and Chinese claims to, 646, 664
thirty-eighth parallel in, 811(*m*), 812–813
Koreans, race riots by, 982(*i*), 983
Korean War (1950–1953), 810–812, 811(*m*), 812(*i*)
beginning of, 810, 815
defense spending and, 774(*f*)
end of, 812
impact of, 812, 818
public support in U.S. for, 811, 819
Korematsu v. United States (1944), 787
Kosovo, 952(*m*)
K Street Project, 991, 1006
Kuhn, Loeb & Co., 524
Ku Klux Klan, 476(*i*)–477(*i*), 477–478, 483, 598(*i*), 670, 853, 857
civil rights movement and, 872
Democratic Party and, 477, 707
leader of, 476–477
revival of, 708(*m*), 734–735
women in, 719(*i*)
Ku Klux Klan Act (1871), 468(*t*), 477–478
Kurds, 945, 1016(*i*)
Kuwait
Iraq's invasion of, 925, 945, 1000
oil production in, 911
Persian Gulf War and, 1001(*m*)
Kyoto Treaty (1997), 969, 987, 998

labor. *See also* indentured servants; labor unions; slavery
Adamson eight-hour law for, 637
antiunion movement and, 699
autonomous, 536–538
capital and, 519–549
free black, 461, 464, 464(*i*)
gang, 464, 464(*i*), 474
shortage of, 777
Southern, 529–530
systematic control of, 537–538
wage, 464(*i*), 473, 479
work day and, 685
work week and, 677(*i*), 710, 718
yellow-dog contracts and, 543
Labor, U.S. Department of, 935
laborers
factory, 622
Jewish garment, 537, 545
migrant, 719, 849–850, 886–887
railroad, 637
labor force
aristocracy of, 537
changes in, 528–536, 528(*f*)
children in, 536, 536(*i*)
for manufacturing, 528–538
for mining, 536(*i*)

sex-typing and, 532–533
white-collar workers in, 529
women in, 531, 533–537, 545
Labor Relations Act. *See* Wagner Act
labor unions, 538–548, 622. *See also* strikes
African Americans and, 542–543, 750
Amalgamated Association of Iron and Steel Workers, 543
anti-unionism and, 636–637
Brotherhood of Locomotive Firemen, 544
Bush (George W.) damage to, 995
communism and, 816
decline of, 924, 987
Democratic Party and, 901
election of 1936 and, 747
emergence of, 540, 542–543, 670
immigration and, 718
industrial unions and, 544
Mexican Americans and, 886–887
in mining industry, 506
NAFTA and, 948, 966
need for, 538, 540
New Deal and, 742, 749–750, 756
organized shops and, 814
Populist Party and, 603
postwar strikes and, 813
post-WWI antiunion movement and, 685, 699, 699(i)
pure-and-simple unionism, 542–543
reform and, 540–542, 613
Seattle strike and, 699, 699(i)
seniority systems in, 749
steel industry and, 749–750, 750(i)
strength of, 835–836, 836(f)
in Sun Belt, 916
trade unionism and, 540–542
wages and, 780
welfare capitalism and, 711
women in, 541–544
working hours and, 543, 637
WWII and, 777, 780
Ladies' Home Journal (magazine), 561, 717
La Follette, Robert M., 613, 623–624, 627, 638, 676, 697, 708
laissez-faire principle, 896
Lakin, Kansas, 497(i)
Lakota. *See* Sioux Indians
land
livestock and, 509–510
Native Americans and, 755(i)
ownership of, 472–476, 478
sharecroppers and, 742
land grants
for railroads, 491, 495, 522
from Spain, 509–510
in Virginia, 489
Lange, Dorothea, 757, 757(i), 759(i), 762
languages
in California, 980
Catholic immigrants and, 573

English, 980
German, 676, 693
immigrants and, 983
Latino immigrants and, 976
of Native Americans, 755
Yiddish, 570, 572, 574
Laos, Vietnam War and, 877(m), 878, 900
Laredo, Texas, 720(i)
Latin America
immigration from, 719, 976, 976(f)
interventionism and, 769
military interventions in, 711
U.S. involvement in, 937(m)
Latinos. *See also* Hispanics
affirmative action and, 907
Bush (George W.) and, 993
employment discrimination and, 781
migration to cities of, 850
race riots and, 983
on television, 843
youth gangs of, 784, 784(i)
Latter-day Saints, Church of Jesus Christ of. *See* Mormons
Latvia, 696
law, 876. *See also* common law; court system; immigration laws; judiciary; Supreme Court
antitrust, 629, 635–636, 684
blue, 590, 592
child labor, 615, 633, 637
eight-hour, 637
equality before, 465
experience and, 613
Jim Crow, 597–599, 721, 886
minimum wage, 615, 617–618, 633, 815, 819
right-to-work, 814
on women's civil rights, 903, 905
The Law of Civilization and Decay (B. Adams), 647
Lawrence, William, 587
Lawrence v. Texas (2003), 931, 984
lawyers, 605
Leach, Robin, 959
lead mines, 506
League of Nations, 695, 696(m), 697, 702
U.S. and, 703, 706
WWII and, 768–769, 792
League of United Latin American Citizens (LULAC), 781
League of Women Voters, 708, 709(i)
Leary, Timothy, 885
Lease, Mary Elizabeth, 603, 603(i)
Lebanon, 696(m), 827, 944, 1016
Legal Services Program, 876
Leibowitz, Samuel, 753(i)
leisure
automobile and, 714
consumerism and, 714
labor unions and, 836
in 1920s, 714, 718

Lemke, William, 748
Lend-Lease Act (1941), 771, 772(m), 797
Lenin, Vladimir Ilych, 679
Leningrad, Soviet Union, 787, 788(m)
lesbians, 906
Leslie's Illustrated Weekly Newspaper, 673(i)
Le Temps (newspaper), 655, 659
Levitt, Arthur, 837(i), 837–838
Levittown, Long Island, 837(i), 837–838
Lewinsky, Monica, 950–951, 951(i)
Lewis, John L., 749, 780, 813
Lewis, Sinclair, 723
Lexis-Nexis programs, 972
Leyte Gulf, Battle of, 791
liability, limited, 522
Libby, 750
liberal consensus, 819
liberalism, 892
Fair Deal, 815
New Deal and, 737–738, 758, 762
postwar coalition of, 819
role of the state and, 815
urban, 618–626, 638
Liberal Republican Party, 479
Liberty League, 744
liberty of contract, 613
Liberty ships, 775, 775(i)
libraries
establishment of, 578–579
Internet and, 972
Liddy, G. Gordon, 901
liens, sharecropping and, 474, 476
Life (magazine), 658(i), 762, 762(i), 783(i), 790, 842
life belts, around cities, 841(i)
Life of Reilly (TV program), 843
Lifestyles of the Rich and Famous (TV program), 959
lightning war. *See* blitzkrieg
Likud Party (Israel), 952
Liliuokalani, Queen of Hawaii (r. 1891–1893), 643
limited liability, 522
Lincoln, Abraham (1809–1865), 754. *See also* Civil War
assassination of, 458, 483
paper money and, 604
Reconstruction and, 458, 870
second inaugural address of, 457
speeches of, 457
tariffs under, 585
Ten Percent Plan, 458, 483
Lincoln Brigade, American, 770
Lindbergh, Charles (1902–1974), 705, 705(i), 735, 771
Ling, Maya, 890
Ling-Temco-Vought, 834
Lippmann, Walter, 637, 828
literacy, voting rights and, 872
literacy tests, 593, 597

literature
  cultural dissent and, 848
  genteel tradition in, 579
Lithuania, 696
Little Big Horn, Battle of (1876), 502, 517
Little Richard, 716(i)
Little Rock, Arkansas, 853–854
Littleton, Colorado, 975
Litvinoff, Maxim, 803
Live-8 concert (2005), 970
living standards
  decline of, 911–912
  foreign trade and, 959
  Great Society and, 875
  postwar, 831, 836–837
Lloyd, Henry Demarest, 603–604
loans, to Allies, 676
Lochner v. New York (1905), 616(t)
Lodge, Henry Cabot, 646, 650–651,
  653, 697
London, England, Islamic terrorist bombing
  in, 1014
London Times (newspaper), 659
The Lonely Crowd (Reisman), 834–835
Long, Huey, 745(i), 746, 751(m), 765
  assassination of, 748, 765
  New Deal and, 744–745
Long, John, 650–651
Long, Stephen H., 489
Long Drive, 493, 517
Long Island, New York, Levittown in, 837(i),
  837–838
Long Telegram, 803–804
Look (magazine), 762
looting, in Iraq, 1001–1002
Los Alamos, New Mexico, 794
Los Angeles, California
  automobile in, 840
  beer breweries in, 688(i)
  growth of, 838(m)
  jazz and, 716
  Ku Klux Klan in, 708(m)
  Latino immigrants in, 850
  migration to, 718
  population in, 509(m)
  riots in, 886, 982(i), 982–983, 987
  wartime migration to, 783
  youth gangs in, 784, 784(i)
Los Angeles *Times* explosion, 636
Louisiana
  Huey Long in, 745
  Reconstruction in, 467(m), 469, 480, 482
  Republican government in, 478, 480–482
  sugar plantations of, 472
Lowell, Josephine Shaw, 614–615
Lowell, Lawrence, 701(i)
Loyalists, Spanish, 770
loyalty oaths, 816
"The Luck of Roaring Camp" (Harte), 513
Lusitania (ship), 677, 703

Luxembourg, 770, 965(m)
Luzon (Philippines), 653
Lybia, 1013
lynching
  laws against, 708
  New Deal and, 752–753
  in New South, 599
Lynd, Helen Merrell, 714
Lynd, Robert, 714

McAdoo, William, 684, 708
McAllister, Ward, 559
MacArthur, Arthur, 656–657
MacArthur, Douglas (1897–1978), 731, 791,
  810–812
McCain, Franklin, 856
McCallum, Daniel C., 527
McCarran-Walter Act (1952), 849
McCarthy, Eugene, 889
McCarthy, Joseph R., 817(i), 817–821
McCarthyism, 817–818, 820–821
McClure's magazine, 613–614
McColl, Ada, 497(i)
McCormick reaper works, 543
McCue, Martin, 622
McDonald's, 960, 965, 966(i)
McDowell, Mary, 612
McFerren, John, 856–857
McGovern, George, 889, 892(m), 901
McGuire, Thomas B., 540
machine guns, 502, 674–675
machinery, as capital goods, 520
machine tools, 528
machinists, 531, 536, 538
McKay, Claude, 723
McKee, Ray, 692(i)
McKinley, William (1843–1901), 611, 627,
  629, 632(i), 652
  election of 1896 and, 605(i), 606–607,
    607(i), 607(m)
  as president (1897-1901), 648–650, 654, 668
  tariffs under, 585, 602, 605, 643
McKinley Tariff (1890), 585, 602, 605, 643
McNamara, John J., 636
McNamara, Robert, 863, 902
McNary-Haugen bills (1927; 1928), 710
McNeill, 750
McPherson, Aimee Semple, 721, 721(i)
McPherson, Harold, 721(i)
Macrae, David, 460
MAD (Mutually Assured Destruction
  policy), 822
Madero, Francisco, 664
Madonna, 983
Madrid, Spain, Islamic terrorist bombing
  in, 1014
magazines, 613–614, 631, 658(i), 673(i), 735,
  762, 762(i)
  in the 1920s, 713–714, 717
Maggie: Girl of the Streets (Crane), 579

Magruder, Jeb Stuart, 902
Mahan, Alfred T., 646, 646(i), 653, 668
Maier and Zoblein Brewery, 688(i)
mail bombs, 700
Maine
  election of 1936 and, 748
  prohibition and, 693(m)
Maine (battleship), 649(i), 649–650
maize. *See* corn
"Making Steel and Killing Men" (Hard), 613
Malaya, 791
Malcolm X, 885(i), 885–886
management techniques, 709
  modern, 537, 548
  scientific, 538, 548–549
managerial revolution, 527–528
Manchuria, 768, 793(i)
Mandan Indians, 489, 499(m)
Manhattan, Kansas, 495(i)
Manhattan Island. *See* New York City
Manhattan Project, 793–794, 803, 816
Manifest Destiny, 647–648, 668
manufacturing. *See also* factory system;
  industrialization; mills
  during 1920s, 710, 727
  distribution for, 525
  energy for, 521–522
  labor force for, 528–538
  mass production and, 538, 548
Manzanar (Japanese internment camp),
  785(i)
Mao Zedong (Mao Tse-tung), 810, 897(i),
  897–898
March on Washington (1941), 780–781
March on Washington (1963), 867–868
Marianas Islands, 651
market economy, 941
  big business and, 627–629
  laissez-faire, 613
  mass marketing and, 526–527, 548
market forces, 709
marriage. *See also* women
  divorce and, 903
  farming's dual economy and, 496
  gay rights and, 924, 984, 1005–1006
  in late 20th century, 903
  in 1950s, 844
  slaves and, 461
  two-worker families and, 960(f)
  women's rights and, 564, 905
Marshall, George C., 805, 807
Marshall, Thomas R., 634(i)
Marshall, Thurgood, 853
Marshall Islands, 792(m)
Marshall Plan, 805–806
Martí, José, 575, 648
Martin, Joseph J., 811
Marx, Karl, 545
Marxism, 545
masculinity, cult of, 562–563, 563(i)

Massachusetts
  election of 1928 and, 726, 727(i)
  prohibition and, 691
mass marketing
  advertising and, 527, 527(i)
  market economy and, 526–527, 548
mass media. See also magazines; movies;
    newspapers; radio; television
  abortion and, 984
  Iranian hostage crisis and, 921, 929
  in 1990s, 973–975
  Vietnam War and, 877, 889, 900
  vs. feminism, 904
mass production
  of automobiles, 538, 539(i), 548,
    714
  in housing, 837–839
  industrial expansion and, 710
  in manufacturing, 538, 548
  1920s and, 714
mass transit, interstate highways and,
    839, 841
master race, 769
Mata, Petra, 979
Maxim, Hiram, 674
Maximilian, Ferdinand, Archduke of
    Mexico (r. 1864–1867), 642
Meany, George, 836
Meat Inspection Acts, 632
meatpacking industry, 526, 549
  centers of, 525, 525(m)
  postwar market share of, 836
mechanics. See also artisans
  trade union for, 540
Medicaid, 873–874, 876, 896, 910
Medical Care Act (1965), 874(t)
Medicare, 873–874, 876, 960, 996
  Bush (George W.) and, 1006
  drug benefit of, 993–994, 1017
  Nixon and, 896
  Reagan and, 933
medicine. See health care
medicine men, 489
Meilli, Trisha, 981
Mein Kampf (Hitler), 769
Melbourne, Australia, gold rush in, 505
Mellon, Andrew W., 706
memory sticks, 959(i)
Memphis, Tennessee, 465
men
  in breadlines, 731(i)
  Homestead Act and, 496
  voter turnout and, 708
merchant marine, 646
Mesabi Range, 521
Mesoamerica. See Central America
mestizos, 509
Methodism
  fundamentalism and, 721
  politics of, 590, 590(f), 592

Methodists
  African American, 567
  Prohibition and, 692
Metro-Goldwyn-Mayer, 716
Metternich, Klemens, 896
Meuse-Argonne campaign, 679, 679(m),
    680, 703
Mexican American Political Association
    (MAPA), 887
Mexican Americans. See also Hispanics
  Bush (George W.) and, 992–993
  in cities, 850
  civil rights for, 886–888, 892
  discrimination against, 505
  Great Depression and, 719
  labor activism of, 755(i)
  as migrant workers, 719
  in military, 775
  as miners, 510(i)
  movement into industrial jobs, 685, 699
  New Deal and, 755–756
  women, 750
  WWII and, 775, 781, 797
Mexican immigrants, 688(i)
Mexican Revolution (1911–1917), 664–666,
    668, 678, 712, 719
Mexico, 643
  foreign trade and, 728
  immigrants from, 512, 755–756, 976
  Loyalists and, 770
  migration and, 505, 510
  Minutemen border patrols, 924
  NAFTA and, 948, 964
  U.S. invasion of Iraq and, 1001
  U.S. involvement in, 664–666, 712
  WWI and, 678
Miami, Florida, Cuban refugees in, 850
Microsoft Corporation, 961, 970–971,
    971(i), 972, 987
middle class, 580
  in 1980s, 959
  African American, 875
  consumerism of, 713–714, 734
  education legislation and, 873
  election of 1936 and, 747
  European, 561
  free labor and, 479
  Great Society and, 875
  jazz and, 716
  JFK and, 863
  Medicare cuts and, 933
  movie industry and, 715
  in 1920s, 705, 713–714, 726
  in 1980s, 954
  in 1990s, 946, 948, 958, 960
  pension plans and, 963
  postwar, 831
  progressivism and, 612
  Protestant, 707
  suburban, 559–561

  on television, 843
  women of, 847
Middle East. See also particular countries
  Al Qaeda in, 1002, 1014
  Carter and, 920–921
  Cold War in, 826–827
  oil production in, 911, 921
  post-WWI colonialism in, 696(m), 697
  U.S. involvement in, 925, 944–946,
    952–953, 1001(m)
  in WWI, 674
middle management, 528
Midway, Battle of, 791, 792(m), 797
the Midwest
  election of 1928 and, 727(i)
  Ku Klux Klan in, 708(m), 721
Miers, Harriet, 1008
migrant workers, 512, 718, 755–756
migration. See also immigrants
  African American, 567, 685–687, 690(m),
    703, 742, 753, 850
  Asian, 510–512, 517
  to California, 491, 784, 838(m), 839
  difficulties of, 496
  of farmers, 742
  to Florida, 838(m), 839
  internal, 850
  from Mexico, 505
  postwar, 837–841
  to and from the South, 530
  to Sun Belt, 838(m), 838–839
  urban, 850. See also urbanization
  to the West, 496, 510, 838–839, 850,
    915, 916(m)
  WWII and, 783–784
militarism, Europe and, 713
military. See also Army, U.S.; defense spend-
    ing; draft, military; missiles; Navy, U.S.;
    weapons of mass destruction
  African Americans in, 652(i), 780(i)
  after WWII, 768
  budget for, 935, 950, 955
  diplomacy and, 1012
  economic growth and, 833, 916(m)
  gays in, 947
  growth of, 642, 668
  homosexuality and, 775
  JFK and, 868
  racism in, 775
  U.S. interventions and, 937(m)
  women and, 945(i)
military-industrial complex, 802, 826(m),
    827–828, 833, 954
military technology, during WWI,
    674–675
millennium fears, 957
Miller, Arthur, 762
Miller, J. Howard, 777(i)
Milliken v. Bradley (1974), 907
mills, 552. See also factory system

mills (*continued*)
  steel, 519(*i*), 520–522, 521(*i*)
  textile, 529(*m*), 529–530
Milosevic, Slobodan, 952, 952(*m*)
miltary tribunals, Guantanamo and, 1012, 1017
minimum wage
  JFK and, 864
  laws on, 615, 617–618, 633, 815, 819
  New Deal and, 742
  Supreme Court on, 748
  vs. unemployment, 960
  for women, 633, 750
  women and, 711
Minimum Wage Act (1966), 874(*t*)
mining
  in Arizona, 510(*i*)
  Chinese labor for, 510–511
  coal, 521–522, 531, 536
  copper, 506
  environmental pollution of, 508(*i*)
  in the Far West, 505–506
  free silver and, 604
  gold, 505(*m*), 505–506, 508(*i*), 607. *See also* gold rush
  labor force for, 531, 536(*i*)
  migrant labor and, 510, 531
  silver, 505(*m*), 605
  strikes against, 603
  strikes in, 546, 547(*i*)
  technology for, 508(*i*)
  zinc, 506
mining camps, 513
Minneapolis, Minnesota, 555(*i*)
Minneconjou Indians, 504
Minnesota, 496, 498
minorities. *See also particular groups*
  consumer culture and, 734
  1950s culture and, 847
  rights of, 906–907
  women, 750, 763
Minow, Newton, 844
Minutemen border patrols, 924
Miss America pageant, 903, 904(*i*)
missiles
  intercontinental ballistic (ICBMs), 822
  Polaris, 822
  "Star Wars" and, 955
"Mission Accomplished" banner, 1001
Mississippi, 478
  black registered voters in, 470
  Ku Klux Klan in, 478
Mississippi Freedom Democratic Party, 872
Missouri, stem-cell research in, 1008
Missouri Pacific Railroad, 492, 523
Missouri River, 762(*i*)
Mitchell, John, 902
Miyatake, Toyo, 785(*i*)
Mobil, 834

mobs. *See also* race riots; riots
  in San Francisco, 511
A Modern Instance (Howells), 579
modernism, Protestant, 721
Moley, Raymond, 739
Molotov, Vyacheslav, 803, 807
Mondale, Walter F., 917, 936
monkey trial. *See* Scopes ("monkey") trial
Monnet, Jean, 807
monopolies, 526
  computer operating systems, 971
  mining and, 506
  on nuclear weapons, 803
  railroads and, 498
  Standard Oil Company, 614, 614(*i*)
  television regulation and, 975
Monroe Doctrine (1823), 647, 937(*m*)
  Roosevelt Corollary to, 662
Montana
  gold in, 505
  mining in, 511
  Sioux Indians in, 502
Montgomery, Alabama, 853, 855
Montgomery Ward, 498, 527
Montreal environmental protocol, 987
Montreal protocol (1987), 968
Moody, Dwight L., 574
Moore, John Bassett, 655
Moral Majority, 908, 929, 929(*i*)
moral reform, after WWI, 691–692
Morgan, J. P., 578, 605, 627(*i*)
Morgan, Thomas J., 499–500
J.P. Morgan & Co., 524
Morgenthau, Henry, Jr., 739
Morita, Akio, 959(*i*)
Mormons, 505, 507
  as farmers, 497
  prohibition and, 692
Moroccan crisis, 666
Morrison, Tony, 974(*i*)
Morton, Ferdinand "Jelly Roll", 717
Morton, Oliver, 466
Moscow, 787
Mosinee, Wisconsin, mock Communist takeover, 801
Mossadegh, Muhammad, 825
motels, forerunners to, 714
Moussoaui, Zacarias, 998
movies, 574
  mass culture and, 670, 714–716
  "talkies," 715(*i*), 716, 735
  youth culture and, 847
movie theaters, 782
Moynihan, Daniel Patrick, 896, 929
Mozambique, 854, 939
Mrs. Miniver (film), 782
muckrakers, 613–614, 622
Mugwumps, 592, 594, 654
Muhammad, Elijah, 886
Muir, John, 514(*i*), 514–515, 629

Mulberry Street, New York City, 551(*i*)
Muller v. Oregon (1908), 615, 616(*t*), 617
multiculturalism, 983, 987. *See also* ethnic diversity
multi-polar world, 1012–1014
Munich Conference (1938), 770, 797
Murdoch, Rupert, 975
Murrow, Edward R., 782
museums, in cities, 578
music
  African American, 847–848
  the Beatles, 884
  bebop, 848
  of counterculture, 884, 892
  cultural dissent and, 848
  folk, 884
  jazz, 716(*i*), 716–717
  New Deal and, 760
  rhythm and blues, 847
  rock 'n' roll, 884
  of youth culture, 847–848
Muskie, Edmund S., 891
Muslims, 952, 952(*m*). *See also* Arabs; Islam
  African American, 886
  in Europe, 1017
  fundamentalist, 921, 1001(*m*)
  hatred of America by, 999(*i*)
  humiliating treatment of, 1002, 1002(*i*)
  militant, 1014–1016
  racial profiling and, 1009
  radical, 924, 944–945, 952–953, 953(*i*), 955
Muslim terrorism, rise of, 925, 953
Mussolini, Benito, 742, 748, 768, 789
My Lai massacre, 899
Myrdal, Gunnar, 852

NAACP. *See* National Association for the Advancement of Colored People
Nader, Ralph, 913, 990
NAFTA. *See* North American Free Trade Agreement
Nagasaki, 767, 793(*m*), 794, 797, 809
Nanking, sack of (1937), 771
NAPSTER, 972
NASA. *See* National Aeronautics and Space Administration
NASDAQ Exchange, 964(*i*)
Nasser, Gamal Abdel, 826–827, 827(*i*)
Nast, Thomas, 477(*i*)
National Advisory Commission (Kerner Commission; 1968), 907
National Aeronautics and Space Administration (NASA), 819, 864
National American Woman Suffrage Association, 709(*i*)
National Association for the Advancement of Colored People (NAACP), 638, 723(*i*), 853, 903
  Communists and, 816

formation of (1909), 625
  segregation and, 853, 855
  on segregation in military, 775
  in WWII, 781
National Basketball Association, 966
National Broadcasting Company (NBC), 717
National Consumer's League, 681
National Defense Advisory Commission, 685, 771
National Endowment for the Arts (NEA), 874(t), 875
National Endowment for the Arts and the Humanities, 983
National Endowment for the Humanities (NEH), 874(t), 875
National Environmental Policy Act (1969), 913
National Gay Task Force, 906
National Grange of the Patrons of Husbandry, 498, 517
National Guard, 882
National Housing Acts
  of 1937, 747(t), 748
  of 1949, 815
National Industrial Recovery Act (NIRA; 1933), 742, 745, 747(t), 749, 765
nationalism, 911
  Arab, 826–827
  jingoistic, 648–650
  New, 633, 638
nationalization, Mexican government and, 711
National Labor Relations Board (NLRB), 747(t), 750
National Labor Union, 479
national liberation, wars of, 863
National Liberation Front (NLF), 869
National Organization for Women (NOW), 903, 905, 983
National Origins Act (1924), 670, 719, 721, 849, 986
national parks, 514–515, 631(m), 760, 873
National Recovery Administration (NRA), 742, 743(i), 744, 753
National Review (periodical), 928–929
National Rifle Association, 949
National Science Foundation, 833, 972
National Security Act (1947), 809
National Security Agency, eavesdropping program of, 1009, 1017
National Security Council (NSC), 809
National Union for Social Justice, 744
National Union Party, 465
national unity, WWI and, 692–694
National Urban League, 625, 638, 816
National War Labor Board (NWLB), 685, 780
National Wilderness Preservation System, 936
National Woman's Party (NWP), 617, 690, 691(i)
National Woman Suffrage Association, 469, 470(i)

National Women's Conference (1977), 905
National Women's Liberation Party, 904(i)
National Women's Political Caucus, 905
National Women's Trade Union League, 615
National Youth Administration (NYA), 755
Nation of Islam, 886
Native Americans, 647. See also individual peoples/tribes
  in Armed Forces, 681–683
  assimilation of, 755
  civil rights of, 888, 892
  culture of, 513
  education of, 500–501, 503, 503(i), 888
  on Great Plains, 488(m), 489, 498, 515
  migration to cities of, 850
  in military, 775
  mission life and, 513
  mythic West and, 494
  New Deal and, 755, 755(i)
  religions of, 489
  reservation system and, 498–504, 499(m), 502(m), 517, 850
  termination policy and, 888
  unemployment among, 888
  War on Poverty and, 875
  wars with, 487, 499(m)
Native Son (Wright), 762
nativism, 718–721
NATO. See North Atlantic Treaty Organization
natural resources. See environment
natural selection, 588
Nature Conservancy, 968
Navajo Indians, 499, 499(m), 509
naval blockades, during WWI, 676
naval power. See Navy, U.S.
Naval War College, 642
Navy, U.S., 641–642, 678–679
  battleships and, 640(i), 668
  building of, 647, 659
  power of, 646–647, 659, 664, 668
  strategy of, 652–653
NAWSA. See Woman Suffrage Association, National American
Nazi movement, in America, 721
Nazi (National Socialist) Party, 768(i), 769, 796
Nebraska, 497–498
Neel, Alice, 760
Negro Labor Relations League, 780(i)
Negro National League, 718
Negro Women, National Council of (NCNW), 754
Negro World, 726
Nelson, Donald, 774
neoconservatives, 929, 933, 996, 998–999, 1004
nesters, 493
Netanyahu, Benjamin, 952
Netherlands, German invasion of, 770
neutrality, 670, 675–678

Neutrality Acts, 797
  of 1935, 769
  of 1937, 770
Nevada, 505, 513
Nevelson, Louise, 760
Newark, New Jersey, rioting in, 886
Newbold, Gregory, 1006
New Deal (1933–1939), 548, 673, 691, 726, 729(m), 730, 765, 813, 819, 927
  African Americans and, 752–754
  anticommunism and, 816
  banks and, 739
  capitalism and, 739
  coalition of, 875
  Cold War and, 802
  conservation and, 757, 759–760
  conservatism vs., 896
  deficit spending and, 864
  election of 1932 and, 733
  first (1933-1935), 738, 747(t)
  first Hundred Days of, 739–744
  Great Society and, 872, 875
  legacies of, 814
  legislation of, 739, 747(t)
  Native Americans and, 755
  postwar programs and, 832
  Republican Party and, 814
  rollback of, 819, 828
  second (1935–1938), 746–749
  Supreme Court on, 748, 750
  vs. Truman's Fair Deal, 815
  women and, 750, 763
  WWII and, 771, 774, 781
New Democrats, 946, 950, 954
New England, textile industry in, 529
New Federalism, 896
New Freedom, 634, 637–638
New Frontier, 862–864, 892
New Guinea, 791, 792(m)
New Jersey, rioting in, 886
Newlands Reclamation Act, 631
New Left, 882, 892, 903. See also Students for a Democratic Society (SDS)
New Look, 868
New Mexico
  Hispanic culture in, 508–509
  Mexican Americans in, 685
  mining in, 510(i)
  Native Americans in, 509
New Nationalism, 633–635, 638
New Orleans, Louisiana
  Hurricane Katrina and, 1006, 1007(i)
  population of, 552(t)
  railroad connections to, 492
New Right, 924–925, 927–928, 929(i), 954, 958
New Spain, 505, 508
newspapers, 655, 659. See also journalism
  African American, 686
  baseball and, 577

newspapers (*continued*)
circulation of, 577(*t*)
globalization and, 975
immigrants and, 566
mass culture and, 717
New York, 576–577, 648–649
propaganda and, 693
Red Scare and, 700
in San Francisco, 513
Treaty of Versailles and, 697
yellow journalism in, 577
newsreels, 762, 782
Newsweek, 847
Newton, Huey, 886
new world order, 944, 953
New York
abortion clinic murders in, 984
progressive reform in, 709
prohibition and, 691
New York Central Railroad, 522–523
New York City, 551(*i*), 552. *See also* Wall Street
African American migration to, 723
art museum in, 578
the Bowery in, 576, 576(*i*)
as financial capital, 709
gay rights movement in, 906
Great Depression in, 730(*i*), 732
Henry Street Settlement, 612
high society in, 559
homosexuals in, 576
housing in, 753
immigrants in, 552, 566, 568(*i*)
jazz and, 716
Lower East Side in, 568(*m*)
Metropolitan Opera in, 560(*i*)
migration to, 718
population of, 552(*t*)
Prohibition in, 722
prostitution in, 576
real estate in, 962, 963(*i*)
skyscrapers in, 554
subway in, 553
tenements in, 556–557, 569, 572(*i*)
V-J Day and, 767
New York Herald (newspaper), 576–577
New York Journal (newspaper), 648–649
New York Sun (newspaper), 577
New York Times (newspaper), 902, 1009, 1017
New York Tribune, 471, 479
New York World, 577, 648
Nez Percé Indians, 499(*m*), 502
Nguyen, Thanh, 978
Nguyen, Trong, 978
Niagara Movement, 625
Nicaragua, 662, 824
Contras in, 936–937, 937(*m*)
U.S. intervention in, 712
Nicholas II, Tsar, 679
nickelodeons, 574, 714
Nightlight Christian Adoptions, 1008

Nike, 965–966, 966(*i*)–967(*i*)
Nikkei stock index, 959
Nimitz, Chester W., 791
Nineteenth Amendment, 670, 691, 709(*i*)
NIRA. *See* National Industrial Recovery Act
Nisei (second-generation Japanese
Americans), 785, 787
Nisei Daughter (Sone), 786
Nixon, Richard M. (1913–1994), 831, 832(*i*),
896–902, 897(*i*), 922, 925, 935, 943
Alger Hiss and, 898
antiwar movement and, 898–899, 902
as Eisenhower's running mate, 818,
818(*i*)
election of 1968 and, 891, 892(*m*)
election of 1972 and, 901
environment and, 913
pardon of, 917
as president (1969–1974), 896–902
recognition of China, 897–898
on television, 863
Vietnamization and, 878(*f*), 898, 900
Vietnam War and, 892
Watergate and, 895, 901–902
noble experiment. *See* Prohibition
No Child Left Behind, 924
No Child Left Behind Act (2002), 993,
993(*i*), 1017
Nonaggression Pact, Nazi-Soviet (1939),
770–771, 797
nonviolent civil disobedience, 690
Normandy, France, D-Day (June 6, 1944) in,
789, 790(*i*), 797
Norris, George, 676
the North
African American migration to, 567,
685–687, 690(*m*), 703
election of 1928 and, 727(*i*)
racist propaganda in, 478
Reconstruction and, 476
North, Oliver, 937–938
North Africa, WWII in, 788(*m*), 789
North American Free Trade Agreement
(NAFTA), 948, 955, 964, 987
North Atlantic Treaty Organization (NATO),
806(*m*), 822, 824(*m*)
creation of (1949), 808
France's departure from, 897
Kosovo and, 952, 952(*m*)
peacekeeping forces of, 952
North Carolina
Democratic Party in, 477
election of 1928 and, 726
freedmen in, 461
North Dakota
farmers in, 498
homesteaders in, 497
prohibition and, 693(*m*)
Scandinavian migration to, 496
Northern Pacific Railroad, 479, 492

North Korea, 810–812, 822, 1013–1014,
1014(*i*), 1017
nuclear weapons and, 924
Norton, Charles Eliot, 654
Norway
German invasion of, 770, 788(*i*)
homesteaders from, 496
Norwood (Beecher), 579
NRA. *See* National Recovery Administration
NSC-68 (report of National Security Council),
809–810
Nuclear Non-Proliferation Treaty (1968), 1013
nuclear power, 839, 911(*f*)
Chernobyl and, 914
environmentalism and, 913
Three Mile Island and, 913–914
nuclear weapons, 800(*i*), 808–810, 822, 868.
See also atomic bomb
city life belts and, 841(*i*)
Cold War and, 942
Great Fear and, 816
interstate highways and, 841
in Iraq, 1000
Iraq and, 946
in North Korea, 1013–1014
North Korea and, 1014(*i*), 1017
radioactive fallout from, 842
testing of, 809(*i*), 842
U.S. monopoly of, 803
Nuremberg, Nazi Party in, 768(*i*)
nurses, in military, 777
NWLB. *See* National War Labor Board
NWP. *See* National Woman's Party
Nye, Gerald P., 769–770

Oakland Tribune (newspaper), 854, 854(*i*)
Oakley, Annie, 494
Occupational Safety and Health
Administration (OSHA), 896, 935
occupation army, U.S. troops as, 1002
O'Connor, Sandra Day, 931, 938, 938(*i*),
943, 955, 1008
Office of Economic Opportunity (OEO), 876
Office of Price Administration (OPA), 813
Ohio
electoral college and, 481
same-sex marriage and, 1005
unemployment in, 733
oil industry
energy consumption and, 911(*f*)
energy crisis and, 894(*i*), 911
environmentalism and, 913
gasoline prices and, 1013
in Middle East, 1001(*m*), 1013
in Pennsylvania, 526
in Persian Gulf, 911, 1000
pipeline and, 994(*m*)
prices of, 918
refineries in, 526
in Sun Belt, 915

Okies, 757. *See also* Dust Bowl
Okinawa, 791, 793(*m*), 797
Oklahoma
   Indian reservations in, 498–504, 499(*m*)
   Ku Klux Klan in, 721
   white settlement, 503–504, 517
Old Age Revolving Pension Plan, 765
oligopoly, 526, 709
Olmsted, Frederick Law, 557–558
Olney, Richard, 544, 611, 647
Olsen, George, 880
Olsen, Tillie, 762
Olympics, boycotts of, 921
Omaha, Nebraska, 492, 525, 525(*m*)
Omnibus Housing Act, 874(*t*)
On the Origin of Species (Darwin), 588
On the Road (Kerouac), 848
OPA. *See* Price Administration, Office of
OPEC. *See* Organization of Petroleum
   Exporting Countries
open-door policy, 663, 771
Operation Rolling Thunder, 878–879
Operation Wetback, 850
Oppenheimer, J. Robert, 794, 816, 823
oral histories, 760–762
Oregon, 505
   economy of, 506
   Ku Klux Klan in, 721
   migration to, 783(*i*)
   Native American march to, 502
   settlement of, 489, 505–506
Oregon Trail, 491
The Organization Man (Whyte), 835(*i*)
Organization of Petroleum Exporting
   Countries (OPEC), 911
organized crime, 723, 781
Orlando, Vittorio, 696
Orpen, William, 695(*i*)
Oswald, Lee Harvey, 870
Ottoman Empire, 666, 674, 696(*m*)
"The Outcasts of Poker Flat" (Harte), 513
outsourcing, 965–966, 987
overland freight lines, 491
"Over There" (Cohen), 678
Ovington, Mary White, 625
Owen, Reba, 610(*i*)
Owens Valley, California, 515
ownership society, 994, 1017
Oxford, Ohio, 872(*i*)
ozone, 987

pachuco (youth) gangs, 784
Pacific Crest Trail, 760
Pacific Mail Steamship Company, 511
Pacific region
   strategic importance of, 655(*m*)
   U.S. in, 643–644, 651–655, 661–662,
      663(*m*)
   WWII in, 791
Pacific slope, 506, 508, 509(*m*)

pacifism, Vietnam War and, 879
Packer, Vance, 843
Pago Pago (Samoa), 643
Pahlavi, Muhammad Reza, shah of Iran,
   825, 921
Paiute Indians, 499(*m*)
Pakistan, 999, 999(*i*)
   Afghanistan and, 921
   nuclear power and, 1013
   radical Islamic movements in, 953
   Taliban in, 1000(*i*)
Palestine, 696(*m*), 825–826, 1015, 1017
Palestine Liberation Organization (PLO),
   944–945, 952
Palestinian-Israeli conflict, 944–945,
   1001(*m*)
Palm Beach, Florida, 963(*i*), 991(*i*)
Palmer, A. Mitchell, 700
Palmer raids (1919–1920), 699(*i*), 700,
   703, 706
Panama (Isthmus of Darien), 642–643
Panama Canal, 626, 655(*m*), 659, 661, 668
   Colombia and, 659
   design of, 662(*m*)
   malaria at, 661, 661(*i*)
   U.S. return of, 920
Pan-American Union, 643
Panics. *See also* depressions
   of 1873, 479, 483, 492, 519, 549
   of 1893, 523, 544, 549, 602, 604, 646
Pankhurst, Christabel, 690
paper money. *See* currency
paper sons, 511
Paramount, 716
Paris, France, 679
Paris, Treaty of (1899), 654
Paris Peace Accords (1973), 900
Parker, Alton B., 629
Parker, Charlie, 848
Parks, Rosa, 853, 855
The Passion of Saco and Vanzetti (Shahn),
   701(*i*)
PATRIOT Act (2001), 787, 973
PATRIOT Act (2002), 924, 999, 1009, 1017
patriotism
   defense industries and, 777
   election of 2004 and, 1005
   ground zero and, 998
   labor unions and, 780
   New Right and, 929(*i*)
   Southern, 476
   taxation and, 774
   during WWI, 673–674
patronage
   after WWI, 699
   politics and, 584–585
   Republican Party and, 592
Patrons of Husbandry. *See* Granger
   movement
Patterson, Haywood, 753(*i*)

Patterson, John, 864
Patterson, Thomas, 656–657
Patton, George S., 789
Paul, Alice, 616–617, 688, 690, 691(*i*)
Pawnee Indians, 489, 499(*m*)
Payne-Aldrich Tariff Act (1909), 633
payroll deductions, 774
PC. *See* personal computers
Peace Corps, 863, 864(*i*)
peaceful coexistence, meaning of, 822
peacekeepers
   Reagan and, 944–945
   in Somalia, 951–952
peace movement, 666. *See also* antiwar
   movement
peace process, Clinton and, 952
peace ship, 676
Peale, Norman Vincent, 842
Pearce, Charles H., 472
Pearl Harbor, attack on (December 7, 1941),
   643, 771–773, 773(*i*), 791, 796–797, 998
peasants, in New Mexico, 509–510
Peña, Frederico, 947
Pendergast, Thomas, 781
Pendleton Act (1883), 584
penicillin, 692(*i*), 845
Pennsylvania
   abortion and, 943
   coal mining in, 521, 536
   creationism in, 1008
   hijacked airplane crash in, 998
   oil industry in, 526
   railroads in, 519, 521
   steel production in, 519(*i*), 521, 531–532
Pennsylvania Railroad, 519, 521
penny arcades, 574
pension plans, 836
pensions, 710–711, 744, 746–747, 762, 765
Pentagon, 833
   attack on, 998
   radical Muslim attack on, 924
   U.S. attack on Iraq and, 1001
Pentagon Papers, 902
peonage, meaning of, 474
People's (Populist) Party, 602–604
People's Republic of China, 810–811
   U.S. recognition of, 897–898
perestroika, meaning of, 941
Perkins, Frances, 619, 739, 746, 751–752
Perot, H. Ross, 946, 947(*i*), 950
Pershing, John J., 665(*i*), 666, 678–679
Persia. *See* Iran
Persian Gulf, 911, 1001(*m*)
Persian Gulf War (1990–1991), 924–925,
   945, 955, 999, 1001(*m*)
   women in, 945(*i*)
personal computers (PC), 970–972
Personal Responsibility and Work Opportu-
   nity Act (1996), 950, 955
Peru, 643

petrochemical industry, 839
petroleum industry. *See* oil industry
Philadelphia, Pennsylvania, 551, 552(*t*)
    department stores in, 549
    industrial development in, 553
    population of, 552(*t*)
philanthropy, 578–579
Philippines, 651–655. *See also* Filipinos
    acquisition from Spain of, 653–654, 668
    dictatorship in, 824
    human rights in, 920
    immigrants from, 756–757, 849
    Senate hearings on, 656–657
    Spanish-American War in, 651, 651(*m*),
        652–655
    vs. United States, 654–655
    in WWII, 791, 792(*m*)–793(*m*)
Phillips, David Graham, 614
phonograph, 717
photography, 762
photojournalism, 762
Physicians for Social Responsibility, 842
Pickford, Mary, 715
Pietism, 590
pig iron, 520
Pike, James M., 478
Pike's Peak, Colorado, 505
Pilgrim's Progress (Bunyan), 614
Pinchot, Gifford, 631
Pinckney, Thomas, 461
Pine Bluff, Arkansas, 464
Pinkerton Detective Agency, 543
pirates, 972, 1013
Pittsburgh, Pennsylvania, 556
    Catholic church in, 573(*i*)
    radio station in, 717
    railroad strike and, 519
    steel production in, 519(*i*), 521, 531–532
*Plain Home Talk on Love, Marriage, and
    Parentage* (Foote), 564
Plame, Valerie, 1004
*Planned Parenthood of Southeastern
    Pennsylvania v. Casey* (1992), 943, 955,
        984, 1008
plantations. *See also* the South
    impact of sharecropping on, 473(*m*), 476
    Reconstruction and, 478
Platt, Orville, 644
Platt Amendment, 661, 769
PlayStation, 959(*i*)
Pledge of Allegiance, 842
Plessy v. Ferguson (1896), 598, 853
PLO. *See* Palestine Liberation Organization
plumbers, Watergate, 901
Plunkitt, George Washington, 569
pluralism. *See also* ethnic diversity
    cultural, 619, 622, 930, 975–976
    ethnic, 975, 980, 983
pocket veto, 458
Podhoretz, Norman, 929

los pogres, 510
Poland, 679, 696, 790, 802
    German invasion of, 767, 770, 797
    Holocaust in, 790
    papal visit to, 941(*i*)
    Yalta and, 791–792, 794(*i*), 802–803, 815
police action, meaning of, 810, 811(*m*)
police brutality, 982
polio vaccine, 845
The Polish Peasant in Europe and America
        (Thomas; Znaniecki), 570
Political Action Committees (PAC), 750
political campaigns
    fundraising for, 902
    presidential, 818(*i*), 818–819, 971
    television and, 862–863
political cartoons
    about conservatism, 997(*i*)
    Grant and, 480(*i*)
    impeachment, 951(*i*)
    Muslim riots and, 1015, 1017
    racial equality and, 477(*i*)
political machines, 568–569, 572
political parties. *See also* elections; *particular
        parties*
    loyalty to, 590
    political machines and, 592, 608, 623
    priorities of, 585–586
politics
    African Americans in, 567
    computer revolution and, 973
    conservatism and, 929(*i*)
    corruption in, 471, 479, 611, 613
    culture wars and, 984
    direct primary in, 624
    energy crisis and, 911
    of expectation, 862–871
    faith-based, 992
    free labor and, 479
    government-business cooperation in,
        706–713
    of inclusiveness, 992–993
    initiative and recall in, 624
    international, 911
    international trade and, 963
    Ku Klux Klan and, 721
    labor unions in, 750
    of late nineteenth century, 582–609
    machine, 592, 608, 611, 613, 618–619, 638
    new, 862–863
    patronage and, 584–585
    post-Watergate, 917–922
    power, 624
    race and, 595–599
    reform in, 608, 623–624
    of resentment, 917
    television regulation and, 975
    ward, 568–569
    women in, 905–906
    in WWII, 768, 781

Pollock, Jackson, 760, 848
poll taxes, 598(*i*), 872
pollution, 967–969. *See also* environmentalism
    highways and, 839
    industrial, 519(*i*)
    from mining, 508(*i*)
    in Sun Belt, 839
    TVA and, 760(*m*)
Pony Express, 491
popular culture. *See also* advertising; mass
        media; movies; television
    in 1990s, 973–975
    WWII and, 782
Popular Front, 770
population
    of African Americans in armed forces, 681
    of African Americans in industrial
        heartland, 685
    in California, 756
    changes in, 977(*m*)
    of Chinese immigrants, 510–511
    in cities, 551, 552(*t*)
    in the Far West, 505–506
    growth in, 976
    of Hiroshima, 795(*i*)
    immigration and, 524
    in Iraq, 1016(*i*)
    life expectancy and, 846
    in Los Angeles, 688(*i*)
    migratory labor force, 757
    of Native Americans in armed forces,
        681
    of radio owners, 717, 717(*i*)
    shifting patterns in, 838(*m*)
    shift to cities, 718, 735
    in the West, 509(*m*)
Populism, 602–604, 607(*m*)
    African Americans and, 600–601
    of American West, 602(*m*), 607
    among farmers, 602–603, 603(*i*)
    Father Coughlin and, 744
    one party rule and, 596–597, 602, 608
    women's rights and, 603, 603(*i*)
Populist Party, 603–604
pornography, 910
Portland, Oregon, 506
posters, 673, 693
    of steel mills, 710(*i*)
    during WWII, 777(*i*)
Potsdam Conference, 803
Pound, Roscoe, 613
poverty, 876(*f*)
    in 1980s, 959
    Asian migration and, 511
    in California, 751(*m*)
    election of 1928 and, 726
    Hoover on, 726
    LBJ's war on, 875–876
    New Deal and, 744, 747, 754
    in 1950s, 849–850

in 1990s, 950, 960
of women, 950
Powderly, Terence V., 540, 541(*i*), 541–542
Powder River, 517
Powell, Colin, 992, 992(*i*), 1000
The Power of Positive Thinking (Peale), 842
Powers, Francis Gary, 822
POWs. *See* prisoners of war
pragmatism, 613
Prague Spring, 897
prairies, 488, 488(*m*)
Presbyterians, Republican Party and, 590, 592
preservationists, 629
Presidential Commission on the Status of
 Women (1963), 903
presidential elections
 Arthur, Chester A. (1880), 586(*m*), 642
 Bush, George H.W. (1988), 935(*i*)
 Bush, George W. (2000), 947(*m*),
  954–955, 990–991, 991(*i*), 1017
 Bush, George W. (2004), 1002, 1004–1005
 Cleveland, Grover (1884), 585–586,
  586(*m*), 592, 643
 Cleveland, Grover (1888), 586(*m*)
 Cleveland, Grover (1892), 584, 584(*i*), 585,
  607(*m*)
 Clinton, William Jefferson (1992),
  946–947, 947(*m*), 954–955
 Clinton, William Jefferson (1996), 950
 computer systems and, 970
 Coolidge, Calvin (1924), 707–708
 Eisenhower, Dwight D. (1952), 818(*i*),
  818–819, 822
 Garfield, James A. (1880), 586
 Grant, Ulysses S. (1868), 468–469
 Grant, Ulysses S. (1872), 479, 592
 Harding, Warren G. (1920), 706, 735
 Harrison, Benjamin (1888), 582(*i*), 585,
  586(*m*), 589(*i*), 602, 647
 Hayes, Rutherford B. (1876), 481, 584
 Hoover, Herbert (1928), 726, 727(*m*)
 Johnson, Lyndon B. (1964), 872, 873(*m*),
  878
 Kennedy, John F. (1960), 862–863
 McKinley, William (1896), 606–607,
  607(*i*), 607(*m*), 632(*i*), 649
 McKinley, William (1900), 654
 Nixon, Richard M. (1968), 891, 892(*m*),
  896
 Nixon, Richard M. (1972), 899–900, 901
 Reagan, Ronald (1980), 925, 932(*m*), 955
 Roosevelt, Franklin D. (1932), 731–733,
  733(*m*)
 Roosevelt, Franklin D. (1936), 745,
  747–748
 Roosevelt, Franklin D. (1940), 771
 Roosevelt, Franklin D. (1944), 781
 Roosevelt, Theodore (1904), 632, 632(*i*)
 Taft, William Howard (1908), 664
 Truman, Harry (1948), 814, 814(*m*)

 Watson, Tom (1904), 600–601
 Wilson, Woodrow (1912), 635(*m*), 664
presidential powers, terrorism and, 1009, 1012
Presley, Elvis, 847, 848(*i*)
preventive war policy, 999–1000
Price Administration, Office of (OPA), 782
prices. *See also* consumer price index
 agricultural, 602
 controls on, 707, 709–710, 896, 911
 of oil, 918
 WWII and, 782
Princip, Gavrilo, 674
prisoner abuse, 1002
prisoners of war (POWs)
 Bataan death march and, 791
 Japanese internment and, 785(*i*)
 in Vietnam War, 879
Progressive Era (1890–1914), 579, 610–639,
 815
 academic expertise in, 613
 consumer rights and, 913
 end of, 706, 726
 New Deal and, 737, 762
 shift from Republican dominance in, 622
Progressive Party, 632
 new, 633, 814, 816
progressivism
 definition of, 612
 fracturing of Republican, 632–633
 national politics and, 634–638
 of 1970s, 913
 Prohibition and, 691–692
 reform and, 692–693, 695
 science and, 613
 white supremacy and, 625
 women and, 612, 692
 in WWI, 678, 683–684
Prohibition, 594–595, 622, 670, 718,
 722–723, 986
 Al Smith on, 726
 Democratic Party and, 707
 Eighteenth Amendment on, 692, 693(*m*),
  703, 722–723, 735
 organized crime and, 781
 progressive reform and, 691–692
 repeal of (1933), 723, 739, 765
 rural areas *vs.* cities in, 691–692, 693(*m*)
 WWI impetus for, 691–692, 701
Prohibitionist Party, 595, 606
"The Promise of the New Deal" (Shahn),
 761(*i*)
Promontory Point, Utah, 492
propaganda
 German, 682
 in the North, 478
 Reagan presidency, 937
 wartime, 685, 693, 695
 during WWII, 776
property. *See* land
prospectors, 505–506

prostitution, 506
 after WWI, 691
 Asian migration and, 511
 in cities, 576
 in New York City, 576
 shelters for, 573
The Prostrate South (Pike), 478
protectionism, 585. *See also* tariffs: protective
Protestantism. *See also* evangelism; *individual
 denominations*
 abortion and, 984
 accumulation of wealth and, 587
 in cities, 573–574
 immigration restriction and, 718
 Ku Klux Klan and, 719
 middle class and, 707
 in 1950s, 842
 Prohibition and, 692
 Religious Right and, 928
 Republican Party, 590, 590(*f*), 592
 social reform and, 619, 622
 temperance and, 594–595
 work ethic and, 706
psychology, advertising and, 713
public assistance. *See* welfare
Public Citizens' Global Watch, 969
public health system, 682(*i*)
Public Lands Commission, 631
public opinion, on civil rights, 867
public works
 Great Depression and, 729
 in New Deal, 743–744, 747(*t*)
 War on Poverty and, 876
Public Works Administration (PWA), 743,
 747(*t*)
Puck, 480(*i*)
Pueblo Indians, 499(*m*), 509
Puerto Rico
 annexation of, 652, 655, 655(*m*)
 immigrants from, 850, 851(*i*)
Puget Sound, 689(*i*)
Pulaski, Tennessee, 477
Pulitzer, Joseph, 577–578, 648
Pullman, George M., 544
Pullman boycott (1894), 544, 545(*i*), 605,
 611–612
pump priming, meaning of, 730
pure-and-simple unionism, 542–543
Pure Food and Drug Act, 632
Putin, Vladimir, 1013

Quaker Oats Company, 527(*i*)
Quakers (Society of Friends), women
 and, 690
Quang, Thich Nu Thanh, 871(*i*)
Quinn, Anthony, 782

Rabin, Yitzhak, 952
race. *See also* ethnicity; *particular groups*
 Democratic coalition and, 763

race (*continued*)
    equal rights and, 946
    feminism and, 904
    in Haiti, 952
    lynchings and, 698
race riots
    African Americans and, 886, 892
    in Chicago, 698–699, 703
    in Harlem, 753–754, 765
    in Harlem (1935), 726, 734
    in Los Angeles, 924, 982(i), 982–983, 987
    police brutality and, 982
    post-WWI, 698–699
    Springfield (1908), 625
    WWII and, 797
racial profiling, 1009
racism. *See also* lynching; segregation
    anti-Asian, 663–664
    anti-Semitism and, 780
    in Armed Forces, 681–683
    in California, 511–512
    in cities, 567, 572, 851–852
    immigration restriction and, 664, 718
    Jim Crow laws and, 597–599, 886
    Ku Klux Klan and, 707
    in literature, 762
    in military, 775
    in New South, 595–599, 599(i)
    in 1920s, 707
    opposition to, 885–888, 892
    Philippine annexation and, 654
    post-WWI, 688, 698(i), 698–699
    race riots and, 982–983
    reform and, 624–626
    in the South, 595–596, 608, 886
    in Spanish-American War, 652, 652(i)
    in suburbs, 838
    in WWI, 674
radar, 822
radiation poisoning, in Hiroshima, 795(i)
radical Islamic terrorist groups, 953
radicalism, 544–548, 604
    fear of, 699–700
    in the West, 546, 547(i), 602(m), 607
Radical Republicans, 459, 466, 470–471, 481
radio
    clear-channel stations, 717(i)
    Father Coughlin on, 744
    FDR and, 738–739
    first commercial broadcast, 717, 735
    in Great Depression, 717(m)
    JFK-Nixon debates on, 863
    music and, 847
    national culture and, 713–714, 717–718
    religion and, 842
    rural electrification and, 737(i)
radioactive fallout, 842
Railroad Retirement Act, 744
railroads, 522–524, 529(m), 548. *See also
    individual railroads*

Adamson eight-hour law and, 637
advertising by, 495
Baltimore and Ohio Railroad, 519, 549
bankruptcy of, 602
Brotherhood of Locomotive Firemen, 544
Chinese labor and, 511
Chinese workers and, 511
completion of transcontinental (1869),
    491–492
development of California and, 511
elevated, 553, 553(i)
expansion of, 552
federal government and, 522, 544, 588
freight rates for, 498, 513, 523
government support for, 522, 544,
    585, 588
Great Depression and, 727
in Great Plains, 491(m), 491–493, 498
industrialization and, 519–520, 522–524,
    524(m)
investment in, 522
labor unions and, 544, 611
land grants for, 491, 522
managerial revolution and, 527–528
mining and, 506
nationalization of, 708
Native Americans and, 498
Pullman boycott (1894) of, 544, 545(i),
    605, 611
regulation of, 584–585, 629
segregation laws and, 596, 598–599, 599(i)
strikes against, 519, 544, 545(i), 549,
    603, 813
technology for, 523
transcontinental, 491(m), 491–492,
    512(i), 517
Wall Street and, 524
western expansion and, 522–523, 524(m)
Western Trunk lines, 491(m)
Railroad War Board, 684
Ramona (Jackson), 513, 517
ranching
    barbed wire and, 497
    on Great Plains, 493, 515
    in Texas, 492
Randolph, A. Philip, 676, 780, 853, 867
Rankin, Jeannette, 678, 773
rape, of slaves, 461
rationing, WWII, 670, 782–783, 797
Rauschenbush, Walter, 612
Ray, Dixie Lee, 904
Rayburn, Sam, 863
La Raza Unida (The United Race), 887
Readers Digest (magazine), 713
Reagan, Nancy, 934(i), 963
Reagan, Ronald (1911–2004), 934(i), 939(i),
    947, 995
    air traffic controllers and, 965, 987
    automobile mileage regulations and, 968
    Christianity and, 930

conservatism and, 896
extravagance of, 963
Iran-Contra Affair and, 937(m)
Just Say No campaign of, 982
as president (1981-1989), 924–925,
    927–973
rollback of federal power and, 954, 997,
    997(i)
scandals in administration of, 936
Star Wars of, 935, 955
Reagan Democrats, 932
Reaganomics, 924, 933
    budget deficits and, 935(f), 936,
    947(m), 954
Reagan Revolution, 936
real estate boom, in California, 513
realism, legal, 613
The Real Majority (Wattenberg,
    Scammon), 891
recessions. *See also* depressions
    of FDR, 748–749
    migrant workers and, 850
    of 1920-1921, 710, 735
    of 1975-1976, 918, 920
    of 1990s, 944
    of Reagan (1981-1982), 937, 954, 958
    vs. Great Depression, 727
Reconstruction (1865–1877), 457–483, 624
    end of, 481
    end of (1877), 596, 608
    Fourteenth Amendment and, 588
    Presidential, 458–466, 481
    Radical, 466–476, 467(m)
    Republicans and, 457, 585
    undoing of, 476–481
Reconstruction Act (1867), 466,
    468(t), 483
Reconstruction Finance Corporation (RFC),
    730, 735
Red Baron, 681
Red Cloud, Chief of the Sioux, 498
Redeemers, 476, 478, 482, 596, 599
Redfearn, L. T., 857
Red River Valley, North Dakota, 497
Red River Valley, Texas, 502
Red Scare, 670, 700, 703, 721. *See also*
    anti-communism
Red Shirts, 478
reform, 611, 613, 638. *See also* social reform
    labor, 618–619
    moral, 592, 608, 691–692
    municipal, 624
    party, 624
    progressive, 708–709
    racism and, 624–626
    Republican Party and, 632–633
    tariff, 635
Reform Party, 991
refugees
    Cuban, 850

Holocaust and, 790–791
in 1950s, 849
regionalism, 839(*m*)
regulation. *See also* deregulation
   public, 613
   of railroads, 584–585, 629
Rehnquist, William, 938, 944, 955, 1008, 1017
Reich, Robert, 948
Reisman, David, 834–835
relief. *See* welfare
religion. *See also* evangelism; revivalism;
      particular denominations
   African-American, 567
   conservative social values and, 927, 975, 992
   cultural conflict and, 718
   extremism in, 1014–1016
   Native American, 489
   in 1920s, 718
   in 1950s, 842
   parochial schools and, 592
   prayer in public schools and, 910, 938
   prohibition and, 692
   same-sex marriage and, 1005
   separation of church and state, 573,
      930, 992
   social meaning and, 574
religious factions. *See* Native Americans
Religious Right
   Bush (George W.) and, 992
   cultural values and, 927, 938, 949, 954
   election of 1980 and, 929
   election of 1992 and, 946
   family values and, 983
"Remember the Maine," 649(*i*)
rent riots, 731
Reorganized Church of Jesus Christ of
   Latter-day Saints. *See* Mormons
republicanism
   modern, 818–819
Republican Party, 677, 699
   affluence and, 932
   African Americans and, 754
   anti-communism and, 816
   on big government, 873(*m*)
   candidates of, 990
   in Congress, 933
   conservatism of, 891, 892(*m*)
   "Contract with America" and, 924, 949–950
   domestic policies of, 896
   election of 1924 and, 708
   election of 1928 and, 726, 727(*i*)
   election of 1932 and, 731–733
   election of 1936 and, 747–748
   election of 2004 and, 1005
   free silver and, 611
   Halfbreeds in, 585
   JFK and, 868
   Ku Klux Klan and, 477–478
   law and order campaign of, 891–892,
      892(*m*)

liberal, 479
   as majority party, 466, 469, 707, 733,
      932(*m*), 955, 991–992
   modern, 818–819
   Mugwumps and, 590, 592
   New Deal and, 744, 814
   in 1920s, 706
   organized labor and, 813–814
   pietism and, 590
   presidency and, 706
   progressive politics and, 612
   protectionism and, 585
   Protestants and, 590, 590(*f*), 592
   Reconstruction and, 457, 466, 478, 481
   reform and, 632–633
   Schiavo case and, 1007
   in Senate, 933
   silent majority and, 891
   small government and, 997
   in the South, 469–472, 481, 896
   Stalwarts in, 585
   stem-cell research and, 1008
   Theodore Roosevelt and, 627, 635
   veterans' benefits and, 585
   white supremacy and, 624
   women's rights groups and, 469
   in WWII, 781
Republic Steel Corporation, 750
reservations
   of Dakota territory, 498–504, 499(*m*),
      502(*m*), 504, 517, 850
   of Oklahoma territory, 499(*m*), 504, 517
Reserve Officer Training Corps (ROTC), 882
Resettlement Administration, 754
restrictive covenants, 838
Reuther, Walter, 835–836
Revels, Hiram, 471(*i*)
Revenue Acts
   of 1916, 703
   of 1935, 747(*t*)
   tax cuts and, 729
revenue-sharing program, 896
reverse discrimination, 907, 982
revisionist historians, 802
revivalism, 574, 721. *See also* evangelism
Reyes, Matias, 981
Reyneau, Betsy Graves, 754(*i*)
Rhee, Syngman, 810
Rhineland, 769, 797
Rhode Island
   election of 1928 and, 726
   election of 1928 and, 727(*i*)
   prohibition and, 691
Rice, Condoleeza, 992, 992(*i*)
rice, price supports for, 710
Richmond, California, 784
Richmond, Virginia, trolley cars in, 553
Richtofen, Manfred von (Red Baron), 681
Rickenbacker, Eddie, 680–681, 681(*i*)
Rifle Clubs, 478

Riis, Jacob, 557(*i*)
Rio Grande Valley, Hispanic settlement in,
   508, 510
Rio Treaty (Inter-American Treaty of Reciprocal Assistance; 1947), 824(*m*)
riots. *See also* mobs
   anti-U.S., 643
   armory construction and, 520
   in China, 897
   in Detroit, 797, 886
   in Europe, 897
   in Harlem, 726, 734
   in Los Angeles, 784, 784(*i*), 797, 886,
      982(*i*), 982–983, 987
   in Memphis, 465
   by Muslims, 1017
   in Newark, 886
   rent, 731
   in San Francisco, 517
   school busing and, 907, 910(*i*)
   urban, 886, 892
The Rise of David Levinsky (Cahan), 573
The Rise of Silas Lapham (Howells), 579
Roaring Twenties, 718, 722
Roberts, John, 1008, 1009(*i*), 1017
Robertson, Pat, 929, 984
Robert Taylor Homes, 852
Robinson, Jackie, 853
Rockefeller, John D., 526, 547, 614(*i*)
Rockefeller, Nelson, 917
Rockefeller Center, 959
rock 'n' roll, 847, 884
Rockwell, Norman, 777, 777(*i*)
Rocky Mountains, 488, 505
Rodeo (Copland), 760
Roe v. Wade (1973), 910, 943, 955, 1008
Rogers, William, 896, 897(*i*)
Rolling Stones, 884
Roman Catholic church. *See* Catholicism
Roman Catholics. *See* Catholics
Romania, 803
Rommel, Erwin, 789
Roosevelt, Eleanor, 733, 740, 751–752, 752(*i*)
   African Americans and, 754
   civil rights and, 780
   Stevenson and, 819
Roosevelt, Franklin Delano (1882–1945),
   670, 684, 738(*i*). *See also* New Deal
   Alger Hiss and, 815
   Atlantic Charter and, 772(*m*), 787
   conservation and, 759
   death of, 793, 797, 803
   declaration of war and, 787
   election of 1932 and, 733, 735
   Four Freedoms of, 797, 771
   Great Depression and, 729(*m*), 891
   Imperial Presidency and, 774
   isolationism and, 769
   labor unions and, 780
   New Deal of, 813, 862, 927–928

Roosevelt, Franklin Delano (*continued*)
on Pearl Harbor, 773, 796
popularity of, 738
as president (1933–1945), 734, 737–763, 765, 770–794
second term of, 815
on self-determination, 822
Soviet Union and, 802
Stalin and, 802
Supreme Court and, 748
third term of, 771
trade with Japan and, 771–772
United Nations and, 793
as vice-presidential candidate, 706
wartime planning and, 771
WWII and, 774, 780, 794, 796
at Yalta, 791–792, 794(*i*)
Roosevelt, Theodore (1858–1919), 563, 594, 614(*i*), 627–632, 636, 675, 677, 733
as assistant secretary of the navy, 646, 650
attack on legal system, 633
balance of power philosophy of, 659
conservation and, 629, 631
Japanese immigration and, 718
Moroccan intervention by, 666–667, 667(*i*)
popular vote of, 943
as president (1901-1909), 659, 663–664
presidential powers and, 739
as rancher, 493
as "Rough Rider," 650, 652
Spanish-American War and, 647, 650, 652
Square Deal of, 632, 632(*i*), 638
Taft and, 632
trust-busting and, 629, 632
Wall Street Giants and, 630(*i*)
Roosevelt Corollary (to Monroe Doctrine), 662
Root, Elihu, 661, 666
Root-Takahira Agreement (1908), 664
Rosie the Riveter, 777, 777(*i*)
Ross, Edward A., 622
Rough Riders, 650, 652
Rove, Karl, 990–992, 1005–1006
Rowe, Guy, 804(*i*)
Roybal, Edward, 887
rubber scarcity, 782
Rubin, Robert, 948
Ruef, Abe, 618
Rumsfeld, Donald, 924, 996, 999, 1001–1002, 1006, 1012, 1017
Rural Electrification Administration, 759, 765
rural ideal, 557
rural life
automobile and, 714
electrification and, 759
Prohibition and, 691–692, 693(*m*)
urbanization and, 718
Russia. *See also* Soviet Union
Bush (George W.) and, 1013
claims on China of, 646

Communist Party in, 679, 695–697
1917 revolution in, 679, 700
radical Islamic movements in, 953
war with Japan (1905) and, 675
in WWI, 674, 703
during WWII, 770, 789(*i*)
Russo-Japanese War (1904–1905), 663, 663(*m*)
Rust Belt, 915–916, 916(*m*)
Rustin, Bayard, 851
Ruth, Babe, 718
Rwanda, 951

Sabin, Albert, 845
Sacco, Nicola, 700–701, 701(*i*), 703
Sacco-Vanzetti case, 700–701, 703
Sackville-West, Lionel, 641
Sacramento, California, 492, 509(*m*)
al-Sadat, Anwar, 918(*i*), 920
al-Sadr, Moqtada, 1002, 1015(*i*)
safe for democracy, 678, 691
Safeway, 713
Saigon, Vietnam, 825, 869, 879, 889, 900, 900(*i*)
St. Louis, Missouri
Bush in, 993(*i*)
population of, 552(*t*)
St. Louis Post-Dispatch, 577
St. Mihiel, 679
St. Paul, Minnesota, 492
Salk, Jonas, 845
saloons, 595, 595(*i*)
SALT I (Strategic Arms Limitations Treaty), 898
SALT II (Strategic Arms Limitation Treaty), 921
Salvation Army, 573
Samoa, 643, 655
San Diego, California, 509(*m*), 513, 783
Sandinistas, 937
SANE (National Committee for a Sane Nuclear Policy), 842, 879
San Francisco, California
Anglo migration to, 509
anti-Chinese riots in, 517
Chinatown in, 511
Chinese businesses in, 756
earthquake (1906) in, 556
Eastern connections of, 508
as economic hub of the West, 508
elite in, 559
gay rights movement in, 906
gold rush and, 559
growth of, 505, 509, 509(*m*), 515
NRA codes and, 743(*i*)
population of, 552(*t*)
United Nations and, 793
urban renewal in, 852
wartime migration to, 783
San Francisco Chronicle (newspaper), 783
San Francisco Examiner (newspaper), 577

sanitary zone, 697
San Juan Hill, Battle of (1898), 627, 652, 652(*i*)
Santa Fe, New Mexico, 505, 508, 513
Santa Fe Railroad, 492, 513
Santanella, Zeno, 738(*i*)
Santiago (Cuba), 652
Santiago de Cuba, Battle of (1898), 640(*i*)
Santo Domingo, 642
Sarajevo, Serbia, 674
SARS. *See* severe acute respiratory syndrome
satellite television, 973–974
Saturday Evening Post (magazine), 717, 777, 846(*i*)
Saudi Arabia, 911, 921, 945, 966(*i*)
Savage, Augusta, 723
Saving Private Ryan (film), 790(*i*)
savings and loan scandals, 962, 987
Savio, Mario, 882
scalawags, 470
Scalia, Antonin, 938, 944
Scammon, Richard, 891
Schechter v. United States, 744, 765
Schenck, Charles T., 694
Schenck v. United States (1919), 694, 703
Schiavo, Terri, 1007
Schlafly, Phyllis, 905(*i*), 905–906, 916
Schlesinger, Arthur, Jr., 983
Schneiderman, Rose, 615–616, 620–621
Schroeder, Patricia, 905
Schurz, Carl, 592, 654
science, 924–925
art and, 579
management and, 538, 548, 613, 710
progressivism and, 613
SCLC. *See* Southern Christian Leadership Conference
Scopes, John T., 721–722
Scopes ("monkey") trial (1925), 724–725, 735
Scotland, Live-8 concert in, 970
Scott, Emmett J., 686
Scottsboro, Alabama, 753, 753(*i*)
Screen Actors Guild, 928
Scudder, Vida, 562
Seale, Bobby, 886
Seamen's Act (1916), 637
Sears, Roebuck, 527
SEATO. *See* Southeast Asia Treaty Organization
Seattle, Washington, 506, 509(*m*), 689(*i*)
Microsoft in, 971(*i*)
strike in, 699, 699(*i*)
WTO meeting in, 969(*i*)
SEC. *See* Securities and Exchange Commission
secession
champions of, 476
Constitution and, 458, 467
Second World War. *See* World War II
secret ballot, 594

secularism, 930
Securities and Exchange Commission (SEC), 744, 747(t), 765, 962
Security Council (UN), 792, 803, 810, 897, 1000–1001, 1014
Sedalia, Missouri, 492
Sedition Act (1918), 694
Seeger, Charles, 760
Seeger, Pete, 884
Seeger, Ruth Crawford, 760
segregation, 852(i), 907. *See also* busing, school; desegregation
  anti-Asian sentiment and, 664
  in Armed Forces, 681–683
  Jim Crow and, 598–599, 886
  laws supporting, 596, 598, 608
  in military, 775
  opposition to, 853–859
  school, 851, 907, 910(i)
  of transportation, 867
Selassie, Haile, 769
Selective Service, 882
Selective Service Act (1917), 678, 703
self-determination, national, 802, 825
  Atlantic Charter and, 771, 787
  movements for, 865(m)
  Yalta and, 792
self-determination principle, 695, 696(m), 696–697, 699
self-made man ideal, 731
Selle River (France), 678
Selma, Alabama, 872
Seminole Indians, 499, 499(m)
Semple, Robert, 721(i)
Senate, U.S. *See also* Congress, U.S.; House of Representatives, U.S.
  Clinton impeachment and, 951
  conduct of diplomacy and, 642
  Democratic Party control of, 936, 1006
  Gulf War and, 945
  hearings on the Philippines, 656–657
  Kyoto Treaty and, 969
  Republican control of, 932(m), 949
  Treaty of Versailles and, 697, 701
  Watergate Committee of, 902
  woman suffrage and, 691
  women in, 944(i)
Seneca Falls convention (1848), 691
Seoul, South Korea, 811
separation of church and state, 573, 930, 992
separation of powers, 458, 902. *See also* checks and balances
September 11, 2001, terrorist attacks, 924–925, 989(i), 998(i), 998–999, 1001(m), 1017
Sequoia National Park, 514
Serbia, 674, 925, 952, 952(m), 955
Servicemen's Readjustment Act (GI Bill; 1944), 781, 796–797
Sesame Street (TV program), 975

set-asides, 907
settlement houses, 610(i), 612, 614–615, 615(i), 625, 690
Sevareid, Eric, 847
severe acute respiratory syndrome (SARS), 967
Seward, William H., 642
Sex in the City (TV program), 974
sexual harassment, 777, 944, 944(i)
sexuality
  automobile and, 714
  changing views of, 563–564, 580
  disease and, 691
  jazz and, 716
  music and, 847
  rock 'n' roll and, 847
  women's rights and, 906
sexual values, 928–929
Seymour, Horatio, 468
Shahn, Ben, 701(i), 750(i), 761(i), 762
Shakespeare, William, 579
Shalala, Donna E., 947
sharecropping, 473–476, 475(i), 742. *See also* agriculture; tenant farmers
Share Our Wealth Society, 745, 745(i), 751(m), 765
Sheen, Bishop Fulton, 842
sheep raising, 493, 497, 509
Sheldon, Charles M., 574
Shelley v. Kraemer (1948), 838
shell shock, 646(i)
Shelterbelts, 760
Shenandoah National Park, 760
Shepard, Alan, 864
Shepard, William G., 620
Sheppard-Towner Act (1921), 709, 709(i), 735
Sheridan, Philip H., 492, 642
Sherman, William Tecumseh (1820–1891), 481
  land for liberated slaves and, 461
Sherman Antitrust Act (1890), 629, 632–633, 636
Sherman Silver Purchase Act (1890), 604–605
Shiite Muslims, 945, 999, 1002–1003, 1006, 1016, 1016(m)
Shiloh, Battle of, 476
shipbuilding industry
  Kaiser and, 774–775, 775(i), 783(i)
  wartime migration and, 783(i)
"shock and awe," 1001
Shore, Dinah, 844(i)
Shores, Jerry, 497(i)
Shultz, George, 935
Sicily, WWII in, 788(m), 789
sickness. *See* disease
Sierra Club, 514, 936, 968
Sierra Nevada mountains, 492, 505, 511, 514

"The Significance of the Frontier in American History" (Turner), 648
silent majority, 896
Silent Sentinels, 690
Silent Spring (Carson), 912
silicone microchips, 970
Simpson, Nicole Brown, 983
Simpson, O. J., 982–983
Sinai Peninsula, 920
Since You Went Away (film), 782
Sinclair, Upton, 632, 751(m)
Singer Sewing Machine Company, 527, 644, 644(i)
Sino-Japanese War (1894–1895), 646, 663–664
Sioux Indians, 498–499, 499(m), 502, 502(m), 504, 517
  AIM and, 888, 888(i)
  Battle of Little Big Horn and, 502, 517
  religion of, 489
  wars with, 494
  Wounded Knee massacre and, 487, 499(m), 504, 504(i), 517
Sister Carrie (Dreiser), 551
sit-ins, civil rights movement and, 781, 855–858
Sitting Bull, Chief of Sioux, 494, 502
Six Companies, 511
Sixteenth Amendment, 684
skyscrapers, 553–554
slackers, 678
slavery. *See also* cotton; plantations; the South
  anti-slavery movement and. *See* abolitionism
  white south and, 596
slaves
  former, 459, 464(i)
  labor gang system and, 464, 464(i), 474
Slavs, Holocaust and, 790
Sloan, John, 619(i)
Slovenia, 952
smallpox, 489
Smith, Adam, 709
Smith, Alfred E. (Al), 619, 708–709, 726, 727(i)
Smith, Bessie, 717
Smith, Gayle, 881
Smith, Howard, 903
Smith, Mamie, 716(i)
Smith-Connally Labor Act (1943), 780
smuggling, 722–723
SNCC. *See* Student Non-Violent Coordinating Committee
soap operas, radio and, 737(i)
Social Darwinism, 587–588, 613, 647, 668
Social Gospel, 612
social identity, in California, 512
social insurance, 622–623. *See also* health insurance; welfare
socialism, 544–547

socialism (continued)
  among farmers, 545
  "creeping," 815
  New Deal and, 739, 744
  pan-Arab, 826
  in Soviet Union, 939, 941
  women activists and, 545
Socialist Labor Party (1877), 545
Socialist Party, 619, 635(m), 676, 694, 700, 733, 733(m)
Socialist Party of America (1901), 545
social order, in Texas, 509
social reform
  blue laws and, 590, 592
  election of 1964 and, 873(m)
  in 1970s, 896, 907, 910, 922
  opposition to, 918
  radical Republicans and, 471
  sexually transmitted diseases and, 691
  urban liberalism and, 709
  women's rights and, 545
  WWI and, 674, 683, 700, 781, 783–784
Social Security Act (1935), 744, 746–747, 747(t), 762–763, 765
  Supreme Court on, 748
Social Security system, 709(i)
  Bush (George W.) and, 994, 996
  in Clinton administration, 950
  expansion of, 876
  increase in, 819
  JFK and, 864
  Nixon and, 896
  Reagan and, 933, 938, 954
  in Truman administration, 815
social structure, 558–559. See also elite; middle class; working class
  city amusements and, 574, 576
  Great Depression and, 727
  New Deal and, 749–763
  race riots and, 982–983
  revolt and, 611
  social order and, 580
  in the South, 596–599, 608
  welfare legislation and, 709, 709(i)
  welfare liberalism and, 738, 749, 762–763
social values
  during 1980s, 959
  computer revolution and, 972
society
  in 1980s, 924–925, 928
  in 1990s, 924
  in 2000s, 924
  communism and, 942
  global economy and, 958–970
  permissive values of, 951
  preservationism and, 515
Society of Friends. See Quakers
socioeconomic status. See social structure
sod houses, 496(i), 497, 497(i)

software, meaning of, 970
Soil Conservation Service, 759
Solidarity (Poland), 941, 941(i)
Solomon Islands, 791, 792(m)
Somalia, 951
Sone, Monica, 786
Sonntag, W. Louis Jr., 576(i)
Sony Corporation, 959, 959(i)
The Sopranos (TV program), 974
The Souls of Black Folk (Du Bois), 625
soup kitchens, 573
Souter, David, 943
the South. See also Civil War; cotton; plantations; slavery
  African American migration from, 685–687, 690(m), 703
  agricultural economy of, 529, 529(m), 530, 530(i)
  civil rights movement and, 866–867
  class distinctions in, 596–598, 608
  cotton and, 529(m), 530(i)
  Democratic Party in, 754, 814, 864, 928
  economic growth in, 915–916, 916(m)
  extractive natural-resources industries in, 530
  five military districts in, 466
  Great Depression and, 729(m)
  home rule for, 480
  Jim Crow laws in, 597–599, 886
  labor unions in, 916
  legal system in, 753(i)
  low wages in, 529–530, 596
  migration to and from, 530, 742, 836, 838–839, 850, 916, 916(m)
  New Deal and, 748
  New South (1900) and, 529(m), 529–530, 597(m)
  Nixon and, 896
  Populism in, 596–597, 602–604
  racism in, 595–599, 608, 886
  Radical Republicans in, 466
  Reconstruction and, 457–458, 469
  Republican rule in, 469–472
  segregation in, 595–596, 607
  sharecropping in, 474
  tenant farmers of, 596
  textile industry in, 529(m), 529–530
  voter registration in, 873(m)
South Africa, human rights in, 920
South America, 642–643
  foreign aid in, 863
  foreign investment in, 712(i)
  immigrants from, 840(f)
  U.S. intervention in, 642–643, 645, 937(m)
  U.S. relations with, 920
South Carolina
  black registered voters in, 470
  freedmen in, 461, 478
  Ku Klux Klan in, 478

  land redistribution plan, 472
  Reconstruction in, 467(m), 471, 480, 482
  Republican government in, 478, 480–482
South Dakota, 496–498, 502, 504
Southeast Asia Treaty Organization (SEATO), 822, 824(m)
Southern Christian Leadership Conference (SCLC), 855
Southern Homestead Act (1866), 472
Southern Manifesto, 853
Southern Negro League, 718
Southern Pacific Railroad, 492, 513
Southern Tenant Farmers Union (STFU), 742, 751(m), 765
South Improvement Company, 526
South Korea, 810–812, 822, 920
South Vietnam. See Vietnam War
the Southwest
  economic growth of, 915, 916(m)
  Hispanic settlement in, 505, 508–509
  Ku Klux Klan in, 719
Soviet Union, 700. See also Russia
  in Afghanistan, 921
  arms race with, 898
  Carter and, 920–921
  Chernobyl meltdown, 914
  Cold War and, 796
  collapse of (1991), 924, 927, 939, 941–942, 942(m), 952(m), 954–955
  communism in, 770, 815–816, 939
  Cuba and, 863
  détente with, 896–898
  Germany and, 769, 771, 797
  Greece and, 802, 805
  human rights in, 920–921
  intraparty struggle in, 822
  Jews in, 920–921
  JFK and, 863
  Marshall Plan and, 806
  Nasser and, 826
  Nixon and, 897
  nuclear test ban treaties and, 868
  Prague Spring and, 897
  space program of, 819
  U.S. relations with, 802–804, 810, 828, 896–898
  vs. postwar U.S., 832, 833(i)
  war in Pacific and, 793(m)
  in WWII, 768, 787, 788(m)
space program, 823, 864
  economic growth and, 916(m)
  JFK and, 863–864
  Soviet, 819, 823, 823(i)
Spain. See also New Spain; Spanish-American War
  acquisition of territories from, 651–652
  Cuba and, 648–650
  fascism in, 768, 770
  in North America, 505
  South American empire of, 648

Spanish-American War (1898), 627, 641, 648–655, 649(i), 655(m), 659, 668
  Hearst newspapers and, 648–649
Spanish civil war (1936–1939), 770
Sparkman, John A., 819
speakeasies, 722
Special Forces, Army, 869
specie, 604
speed limit, national, 782
Spencer, Herbert, 588
spheres of influence
  in China, 646, 651, 662–664, 663(m), 668
  meaning of, 802
Spielberg, Steven, 790(i)
Spirit of St. Louis (airplane), 705, 705(i)
Spock, Benjamin, 845
spoils system, 584–585
sports
  baseball, 576–577, 577(i)
  national culture and, 718
  Title IX and, 904(i), 905
Sprague, Frank J., 553
Springer, Jerry, 974
Springfield, Massachusetts, 685
Springfield race riot (1908), 625
Sputnik (Soviet satellite), 819, 823, 823(i)
Square Deal, 632, 632(i), 638
St. Lawrence Seaway, 819
stagflation, 913, 915, 929, 954, 958
Stalin, Joseph, 770, 794
  deal of with Hitler, 816
  death of, 822
  Kim Il Sung and, 810
  nuclear weapons and, 809
  in Poland, 802–803
  United Nations and, 793
  on U.S. aggression, 804
  wartime planning and, 771, 787–788
  at Yalta, 791–792, 794(i)
  Yalta Conference and, 802–803
Stalingrad, Battle of, 788, 788(m)
standardized products, market for, 524, 527
Standard Oil case (1911), 633
Standard Oil Company, 526, 547, 644, 711–712
  monopoly of, 614, 614(i)
Stanton, Edwin M., 467
Stanton, Elizabeth Cady, 469
Starr, Ellen Gates, 612
Starr, Kenneth, 950
"Star Wars" (Strategic Defense Initiative; SDI), 935, 955
state building, 683, 685
State Department, U.S., 642
state governments
  abortion and, 943
  Great Depression and, 729(m)
  health care and, 709
  Ku Klux Klan in, 719
  Prohibition and, 723
  shift of costs to, 925

  shift of powers to, 896
  shift of responsibilities to, 936
  Social Security and, 763
  welfare programs and, 949
  women's rights and, 752
state parks, 760
states
  abortion and, 984
  block grants to, 896
  constitutional amendments and, 468(t)
  constitutions of, 471, 511
  education and, 993
  price regulations by, 498
  prohibition and, 691–692, 693(m)
  stem-cell research in, 1008
  taxation and, 944
states' rights
  Fourteenth Amendment and, 588
  interstate commerce and, 588
States' Rights Party (Dixiecrats), 814
Statue of Liberty, 989(i)
"stay the course" policy, 1002, 1005–1006
steam power, manufacturing and, 521–522
steel industry, 963
  Bessemer furnace and, 520–521, 521(i)
  British, 487
  Homestead strike and, 487, 543–544
  iron industry and, 520
  labor unions and, 749–750
  in late 19th century, 519(i), 520–522, 521(i), 531–532, 543–544
  mills for, 519(i), 520–522, 521(i)
  in Pennsylvania, 519(i), 521, 531–532
  puddlers and, 520, 536
  rolling mills and, 521
  technology in, 520–522, 521(i)
Steel Workers Organizing Committee (SWOC), 750, 750(i)
Steffens, Lincoln, 614, 636
Steichen, Edward, 627(i)
Steinbeck, John, 757, 757(i), 762
stem-cell research, 924, 1007–1008, 1010–1011, 1017
Stephens, Alexander H., 459
Stephenson, David, 721
Steuer, Max D., 621
Stevens, Thaddeus, 466
Stevenson, Adlai E., 819
Steward, Ira, 479
Stimson, Henry, 771
Stith, George, 978
Stockman, David, 933
stock market. *See also* Wall Street
  boom of, 963, 964(i), 987
  capitalism and, 709, 711
  crash (1929), 706, 711, 727–728, 735
  crash (1987), 962
  government regulation of, 744
  growth in, 948
  technological advances and, 962

Stone, Harlan Fiske, 706
Stone, Lucy, 469, 594
Stonewall rebellion (1969), 906, 984
Strategic Air Command (SAC), 822
Strategic Arms Limitation Treaties (SALT I & II), 898, 921
Strategic Defense Initiative (SDI; "Star Wars"), 935, 955
Straton, John Roach, 724
streptomycin, 845
strikes, 542(i)
  agricultural, 730–731
  air traffic controllers, 965, 987
  Boston police (1919), 699
  in California, 750, 755(i), 756
  deindustrialization and, 915
  of 1877, 519
  general, 546
  in Great Depression, 735
  Great Strike of 1877, 519–520
  Haymarket affair, 543
  Homestead (1892), 487, 543–544, 549
  Memphis sanitation workers, 886
  middle class and, 750
  mining industry, 546, 547(i), 603, 633, 637, 731, 735
  in 1902, 633
  in 1919, 699(i), 699–700, 703
  Pullman boycott, 544, 545(i), 604
  railroad, 519, 544, 545(i), 603, 813
  sit-down, 749–750, 765
  in steel industry, 543–544, 749
  strikebreakers and, 731
  by suffrage movement, 703
  in textile industry, 637
  violence and, 543–544, 545(i), 547(i)
  welfare capitalism and, 711
  women and, 541
  WWII and, 780, 813, 836
Strong, Josiah, 552
Stryker, Roy, 762
Student Non-Violent Coordinating Committee (SNCC), 858, 886
Students for a Democratic Society (SDS), 882, 899. *See also* New Left
submarines
  nuclear, 822
  in WWI, 677–678
  in WWII, 771, 772(m)
suburbs, 830(i), 831, 837–842
  automobile and, 837, 839–841
  busing and, 907
  commuters from, 835(i)
  decay of inner cities and, 851–852
  growth of, 559–561, 837–841
  in 1950s, 849
  racism in, 838
  white flight to, 907
Sudetenland, German invasion of, 770
Suez Canal, Egypt, 642, 826, 827(i)

suffrage
  for African Americans, 466–467
  after Reconstruction, 470(i), 474
  universal, 479
  for women, 469, 470(i)
suffrage movement, 608, 618(m), 688–691,
      691(i), 702, 709(i). See also voting rights
  activists in, 594–595, 617, 617(i), 638
  American politics and, 617–618, 638
  Mugwumps and, 592, 594
  organizations in, 469, 594, 617, 703
  revival of, 615–617
sugar
  Asian laborers and, 643(i)
  plantations and, 643, 643(i), 648
  Puerto Rican immigrants and, 849
  U.S. foreign investment in, 711
sugarcane farming, 643(i)
suicide bombings, 1014
Sullivan, Louis, 554
Sumner, Charles, 466, 469, 478
Sumner, William Graham, 588
Sun, 961
The Sun Also Rises (Hemingway), 723
Sun Belt, 838–839, 915, 916(m)
Sun Dance, 489
Sunday, Billy, 574, 721
Sunni Muslims, 945, 1002–1003, 1006,
      1015(i), 1016, 1016(m)
supercomputers, 972
Superfund program, 913, 936
Supreme Court. See also individual decisions
  in 2006, 1009(i)
  on abortion, 984–985
  abortion rights and, 910. See also
      Roe v. Wade
  on affirmative action, 907
  affirmative action and, 982
  antitrust laws and, 707
  Bush (George W.) and, 1008
  Congress and, 708
  constitutionality of Civil Rights Bill
      (1870) and, 478
  decisions of, 616(t)
  election of 2000 and, 991
  FDR and, 748, 765
  gay rights and, 984
  on housing discrimination, 838
  on Japanese internment, 787, 797
  judicial restraint and, 910
  Ku Klux Klan and, 478
  New Deal and, 744
  on New York subway, 556
  on prayer in public schools, 910
  school busing and, 907
  strikes and, 750
  war prisoners and, 1012
  welfare capitalism and, 711
Sutter's Mill, discovery of gold (1848) at, 506
Swan Island, Oregon, 783(i)

swastika, 768(i)
Sweden, 496
Swift, Gustavus F., 524–527, 547, 549
Swift Boat controversy, 1005
symphony orchestras, 578
syndicalism, 546
synthetic rubber, 782
Syria, 696(m)
  invasion of Israel by, 911
Szilard, Leo, 793

Taft, William Howard (1857–1930), 624,
      632–633, 636
  as Philippines governor-general, 654
  as president (1909–1913), 664, 666, 707
  Roosevelt and, 632–633
Taft-Hartley Act, 813–814, 816
Taiwan, 812, 897, 967
Taliban, 921, 924, 998–999, 1000(i),
      1001(m), 1017
Tammany Hall, 569, 572, 619, 726
Tanzania, 953, 989
Taos, New Mexico, 513
Tarbell, Ida, 614, 614(i), 693
Tardieu, Andre, 667
tariffs
  McKinley and, 602, 605, 611, 643
  protective, 585, 602, 605, 632–633
Tarzan of the Apes (Burroughs), 563
taxation
  on agricultural commodities, 742
  under Bush (George W.), 944,
      995–996, 996(i)
  in Cold War, 810
  decay of inner cities and, 851–852
  estates, 933
  excess-profits, 684
  excise levies and, 585
  federal surplus and, 585
  for highway construction, 714
  income, 933
  on income, 588, 684, 774
  legislation on, 874(t)
  poll tax, 598(i), 872
  property, 471
  radical Republicans and, 471
  Reaganomics and, 933, 936, 954
  reductions in, 728, 864, 916–917, 924–925,
      936, 949, 954–955, 986, 995–996, 996(i)
  for Social Security, 746, 763
  taxpayers' revolts against, 916–917
  WWII and, 768
Tax Reduction Act (1964), 864
Taylor, Frederick W., 538, 548–549,
      613, 710
Teapot Dome scandal (1924), 707, 735
technology. See also machinery
  in agriculture, 497, 511
  alternative, 913
  capitalism and, 918

computer, 928, 957, 970–972
economic growth and, 986, 961–962
  in mining, 508(i)
  popular culture and, 973–975
  postwar development and, 839
  in railroad system, 523
  in steel production, 520–522, 521(i)
  U.S. Army and, 502
  WWII and, 767
teenagers. See adolescence; youth
Tehran, Iran, 788
Tejanos, 510
Telecommunications Reform Act
      (1996), 975
telecommuters, 971
telegrams, reports of death by, 782
telegraph, 491, 642
telephone
  cellular, 924, 972
  company, 533(i), 834
television
  civil rights movement and, 867, 872
  color, 834
  documentaries on, 844
  JFK-Nixon debates on, 863
  JFK's election and, 862–863
  1950s culture and, 843–844
  proliferation of channels, 973–974
  religion and, 842
  sitcoms on, 843
  as "vast wasteland," 844
  V-chips in, 975
Teller, Henry M., 650
temperance movement, Prohibition and,
      594–595, 595(i), 691–692
tenant farmers. See also sharecropping
  Populist party and, 596
Tenderloin, New York City, 576
Tenement House Law (1901; New York),
      556–557
tenements, 556–557
  dumbbell, 556(f)
  in New York City, 569, 572(i)
Tennessee
  Ku Klux Klan in, 477
  public education in, 471
  Reconstruction and, 465, 476–477
  Scopes trial in, 721–722, 724–725
  Thirteenth Amendment and, 459
Tennessee Coal and Iron Company, 633
Tennessee Valley Authority (TVA), 670, 739,
      747(t), 758–760, 760(m), 765
  Supreme Court on, 748
Ten Percent Plan, 458, 483
Tenure of Office Act (1867), 467–468,
      468(t), 483
Terkel, Studs, 768
terrorism, 955
  abortion clinic murders and, 984
  against blacks, 478

fears about, 973, 1004(*i*)
in Middle East, 1001(*m*)
Muslims and, 953
in 1980s, 954–955
1993 World Trade Center bombing, 998
presidential powers and, 1009, 1012
Red Scare and, 700
September 11, 2001, 989(*i*), 989–990,
  998(*i*), 998–999, 1001(*m*), 1017
U.S.S. *Cole* attack, 953, 953(*i*), 989, 1001(*m*)
Terry, Peggy, 779
Tet offensive, 877(*m*), 889
Texas
  cattle ranching in, 492, 509–510, 517
  cotton in, 496, 530(*i*), 598
  election of 1928 and, 726
  farming in, 509
  gay rights and, 984
  gerrymandering, 991–992, 1006
  Hispanics in, 493, 508–510
  Latino immigrants in, 850
  Mexican Americans in, 685
  migration to, 839
  segregation in, 781
Texas Rangers, 990
textile industry
  decline of, 710
  Jewish garment workers in, 537, 545
  in the South, 529(*m*), 529–530
  strikes in, 637
  women in, 533
Thailand, 992(*i*)
Thayer, Webster, 700, 701(*i*)
theater
  in New Deal, 762
  vaudeville, 574
  Yiddish, 566
Their Eyes Were Watching God (Hurston), 762
Thieu, Nguyen Van, 900
think tanks, New Right and, 928, 955
Third Amendment, 910
Third International, 700
Third World
  Cold War and, 822, 828
  meaning of, 865(*m*)
Thirteenth Amendment, 458–459, 468(*t*)
Thirty Seconds over Tokyo (film), 782
Thomas, Clarence, 943–944, 944(*i*),
  955, 1009(*i*)
Thomas, Norman, 733
Thomas, Theodore, 578
Thomas, William I., 570
Thompson, Florence, 759(*i*)
Thompson, LaMarcus, 574(*i*)
Thoughts for the Young Men of America
  (Alger), 587
Three Mile Island, Pennsylvania, 911(*f*),
  913–914
The Three Soldiers (Dos Passos), 723
Thurman, A.G., 582(*i*)

Thurmond, J. Strom, 814
tides of commerce, 626
Tilden, Samuel J., 480
Tilden Park, 760
Tillman, Ben, 598
Time (magazine), 705, 735, 770
time-and-motion study, 538
Time/Life, 975
time zones, 549
The Titan (Dreiser), 559
Title IX, Educational Amendments Act (1972),
  904(*i*), 905
Titusville, Pennsylvania, 526
TiVo system, 972
tobacco, 834
  duties on, 585
  price supports for, 710
  Southern production of, 529(*m*)
Tocqueville, Alexis de, 583
Tojo, Hideki, 768, 772
Tokyo Telecommunications Engineering
  Corporation, 959(*i*)
Toomer, Jean, 723
torture, Abu Ghraib prison, 1002, 1002(*i*),
  1017
Towles, Shepard, 857
Townsend, Francis, 744–746, 748, 751(*m*)
Townsend Clubs, 744, 765
Tracy, Benjamin F., 647
Tracy, Spencer, 782
trade. *See also* exports; *particular
  commodities*
  European domination of, 674
  free, 771, 787, 802
  with Japan, 772
  multi-polar world and, 1013
  restraint of, 635–636
  of Sioux Indians, 489
  during WWI, 676, 683
trade, foreign, 664, 959
  automobile and, 911
  balance of, 644–645, 645(*f*), 832, 911.
    See also trade deficits
  corporations and, 834
  Great Depression and, 728
  postwar, 832
  recessions and, 832
  restrictions on, 728
  surpluses in, 832
trade associations, 742
trade deficits, 911, 918, 924–925, 959
  under Bush (George W.), 996
  Reaganomics and, 924, 936, 947(*m*)
trade unionism, 479, 540–542, 622. *See also*
  labor unions
Trans-Alaska Pipeline, 994(*m*)
transistor, invention of, 970
transistor radio, 959(*i*)
Trans-Missouri case (1897), 629
Transportation, Department of, 947

transportation system. *See also* airline
  industry; highways; railroads
  cattle drives and, 493
  freight lines and, 491
  JFK and, 864
  legislation on, 874(*t*)
  public, 840
  segregation of, 867
  water, 521–522
  during WWI, 684
Treasury bonds, 774
treaties. *See also* arms control; *particular
  treaties by name*
  with Great Plains Indians, 498–499, 502
  mutual defense, 824(*m*)
  nuclear test ban, 868
Treitschke, Heinrich von, 558
trench warfare, 646(*i*)
Triangle Shirtwaist factory fire, 618–619,
  619(*i*), 620–621
Trinitron TV, 959(*i*)
Tri-Partite Pact (Germany, Japan, Italy;
  1940), 797
Triple Alliance, 666, 674
Triple Entente, 666, 674
Triumphant Democracy (Carnegie), 587
Trotter, William Monroe, 625
True Story (magazine), 713
Truman, Harry S (1884–1972), 781, 797,
  818–819
  atom bomb and, 793–795
  civil rights and, 815, 853
  Cold War and, 892
  communism and, 810, 825, 828
  death of Roosevelt and, 803
  desegregation of armed forces, 853
  election of 1948 and, 814, 814(*i*)
  Fair Deal of, 815, 819, 828
  George Kennan and, 803–804
  Korean War and, 810–812
  loyalty program of, 816
  Marshall Plan and, 805–807
  McCarthy and, 817–818
Truman, Harry S
  postwar price controls and, 813
  at Potsdam, 803
  as president (1945–1953), 803–819
  railroad strike and, 813
  recognition of Israel, 826
  Soviet Union and, 803
Truman Doctrine (1947), 804
Trumbull, Lyman, 459, 464
Trump, Donald, 962–963, 963(*i*)
trust-busting, 629. *See also* antitrust laws
trusts, 627, 629
Truth, Sojourner, 469
Tucson, Arizona, 509
Tugwell, Rexford, 739
turbine, 522
Turkey, 674, 803, 805, 1001

Turnbow, Hartman, 872
Turner, Frederick Jackson, 648
Turner, Henry M., 461
Tutsi, genocide of, 951
Twain, Mark (Samuel Clemens), 513, 555, 566, 579, 592, 594
Tweed, William Marcy "Boss", 572
"Tweed Days in St. Louis" (Steffens), 614
Twentieth Amendment (1933), 733
Twenty-first Amendment (1933), 692, 723, 765
Twenty-fourth Amendment (1964), 872, 874(t)
Twin Towers, radical Muslim attack on, 924
Tydings-McDuffie Act (1934), 757
Tyler, James G., 640(i)
Typographical Union (1852), 541

Udall, Stewart, 875
Uganda, 968(i)
Ukraine, 679, 788
Underwood Tariff Act (1913), 635
unemployment
    compensation for, 622, 746, 762, 819
    decay of inner cities and, 851–852
    decline of, 948
    declining economy and, 911
    environmentalism and, 913
    in Germany, 769
    Great Depression and, 729, 729(f), 731
    in late 19th century, 602
    migrant workers and, 849
    Native American, 888
    New Deal and, 742–744, 746–747
    in 1920s, 710, 728
    postwar, 835
    race riots and, 983
    rise in, 929, 944, 959–960
    Roosevelt recession and, 748, 765
    in Rust Belt, 916
    workers' compensation and, 622
    WWII and, 777
unemployment compensation, spending cuts for, 933
Union. *See* Civil War
Union Army, African Americans in, 471(i)
Union Pacific Railroad, 492, 507, 517, 523
Union Party, 748
unions. *See* labor unions
United Artists, 716
United Automobile Workers (UAW), 749, 835–836, 838
United Cannery, Agricultural, Packing, and Allied Workers, 750
United Farm Workers (UFW), 756, 886–887
United Fruit Company, 711, 712(i)
United Mine Workers (UMW), 749, 780
United Nations (UN), 794(i), 802–803
    Bush (George W.) and, 998
    China and, 810–811, 897

founding of, 670, 792–793, 797
General Assembly of, 793, 826
Gulf War and, 945–946
Haiti and, 952
Korean War and, 810–812
peacekeeping forces of, 810–811
Persian Gulf War and, 1001(m)
Security Council, 792, 803, 810, 897, 1000–1001, 1014
weapons inspectors from, 1000
United States Border Patrol, 720(i)
United States Steel Corporation, 629, 633, 707, 710(i), 749–750, 895
United States v. Cruikshank, 478
UNIVAC computer, 970
Universal Negro Improvement Association (UNIA), 726
Unsafe at Any Speed (Nader), 913
Upward Bound, 876
urbanization, 551–581. *See also* cities
    industrialization and, 552, 580, 638
Urban Mass Transportation Act, 874(t)
U'Ren, Harold, 624
Uruguay, 920
U.S. News & World Report (magazine), 932
USA trilogy (Dos Passos), 762
USS *Abraham Lincoln*, 1001
USS *Arizona*, 773(i)
Utah, 505
    Japanese internment in, 785, 785(i)
Ute Indians, 499, 499(m)

Valparaiso (Chile), anti-U.S. riot in, 643
Vanderbilt, Cornelius, 522–523, 560(i), 579
Vanderbilt, George W., 579
Vanderbilt, William H., 560(i)
Van Kleek, Mary, 681
Vanzetti, Bartolomeo, 700–701, 701(i), 703
vaudeville, 574
Vaya, Count Vay de, 531–532
VCR (videocassette recorders), 972
Velvet Revolutions, 942, 955
venereal diseases, 692(i)
Venezuela, 642, 647, 1013
Verdun, 675, 679
Vermont, election of 1936 and, 748
Versailles, Treaty of (1919), 684(i), 694–698, 695(i), 703, 824(m)
    Hitler and, 768(i), 769
    Senate refusal to ratify, 670, 697, 702
    states created by, 942(m)
    WWII and, 768–769
vertical integration, 525(m), 526, 528, 834
veterans, benefits for, 622–623, 819
Veterans Administration, 837–838
victory gardens, 782
video recording, invention of, 834
Vienna Congress (1815), 896
Vietcong, 869, 878–879, 889

Vietnam
    communism in, 825
    insurgencies in, 1002
Vietnam Veterans Memorial, 890, 890(i)
Vietnam War (1961–1975), 877–884. *See also* antiwar movement
    aftermath of, 890
    Agent Orange and, 879, 882
    bombing campaigns in, 878–879, 889, 898, 900
    Buddhist opposition to, 869, 871(i)
    Cambodian attacks and, 898–900
    credibility gap in, 879
    defense spending and, 774(f)
    détente and, 898
    economy and, 833, 879
    Eisenhower administration and, 877, 892
    election of 1968 and, 888, 892(m)
    election of 1972 and, 899–900
    fall of Saigon and, 900, 900(i)
    firsthand accounts of, 880–881
    Great Society and, 877
    guerrilla tactics in, 877(m), 879
    Gulf of Tonkin resolution and, 878
    Johnson administration and, 877–884, 878(f), 882, 884, 892
    Kennedy administration and, 877, 892
    legacy of, 890
    mass media and, 879, 889, 900
    My Lai massacre and, 899
    Nixon administration and, 878(f), 892, 898–901
    Operation Rolling Thunder and, 878–879
    opposition to, 879–884, 898. *See also* antiwar movement
    Paris peace talks and, 898–900
    Persian Gulf War and, 946
    poverty and, 876, 876(f)
    prisoners of war in, 879
    Tet offensive and, 877(i)
    troops in, 878(i), 878–879, 878(f)
    Vietnamization policy in, 878(i), 898–899
vigilantes, Ku Klux Klan as, 708(m)
Viguerie, Richard, 928
Villa, Pancho, 665(i), 665–666, 678
Virginia
    election of 1928 and, 726
    freed blacks in, 470
    Reconstruction in, 467(m), 469
Virginia City, Nevada, 506
The Virginian (Wister), 563
Volker, Paul, 936
Volstead Act (1919), 722(i)
voluntarism
    Hoover and, 728
    trade unions and, 622
    in WWI, 683–684
voluntary sacrifice, 673(i), 684
Volunteers in Service to America (VISTA), 876

voting rights, 461, 465(i). *See also* Fifteenth Amendment
  African Americans and, 466–467, 476, 595–599, 597(m), 598(i), 872
  civil rights movement and, 872
  federal protection of, 853
  literacy tests and, 593, 597, 598(i), 599
  poll tax and, 598(i)
  in the South, 873(m)
  universal suffrage, 479
  women, 691(i)
  for women, 469. *See also* suffrage movement
Voting Rights Act (1965), 872, 873(m), 874(t), 903

Wabash Railroad, 523
WACs (Women's Army Corps), 777
Wade, Benjamin F., 468
Wade-Davis Bill (1864), 458, 483
Wadleigh, Michael, 884(i)
wage differentials, 750, 752
wages. *See also* minimum wage
  controls on, 717
  gender gap in, 533–536, 983
  immigrants and, 977–979
  labor for, 461, 464, 464(i), 473, 479
  multinational corporations and, 925
  productivity and, 958(f), 960, 960(f)
  in the South, 529–530, 596
  welfare capitalism and, 710–711
wageworkers, Hispanics as, 510
Wagner, Robert F., 619, 709
Wagner Act (Labor Relations Act; 1935), 747(t), 748–750, 765, 813 0–814
Wagon Train (TV show), 843
wagon trains, 489, 491, 505
Wake Island, 791
Wake Island (film), 782
Walesa, Lech, 941, 941(i)
Walkman radio, 959(i)
Wallace, George C., 867, 891–892, 892(m)
Wallace, Henry A., 739, 771, 781, 814
Wallace, Henry C., 706
Wallach, Lori, 969
Wall Street, New York City, 524, 605, 709, 744. *See also* stock market
Wal-Mart, 960, 965, 987
Wanamaker, John, 527, 549
War Brides Act (1945), 849
ward politics, 568–569
War Finance Corporation, 730
Warhol, Andy, 974
War Industries Board, 742
War Information, Office of (OWI), 782
Warm Springs, Georgia, 793
Warner, Charles Dudley, 579
Warner Brothers, 716
Warner Communications, 975
War on Poverty, 875–876, 892, 896

War on Terror, 990, 998–1002, 1006
War Powers Act (1941), 774
War Powers Act (1973), 902
War Production Board (WPB), 774
War Refugee Board, 791
War Relocation Authority, 785
Warren, Earl, 853, 910, 938
War Revenue Bills (1917), 684
War Risk Insurance Act (1917), 691, 703
Warsaw Pact, 806(m), 808, 822
Wartime Industries Board, 684(i), 684–685, 703
war to end all wars, 694
Washington, Booker T., 624–625
Washington, George (1732–1799), on foreign alliances, 824(m)
Washington Naval Arms Conference (1921), 670, 713, 735
Washington Post (newspaper), Watergate and, 902
Washington state, 505
WASPs (Women Airforce Service Pilots), 777
The Waste Land (Eliot), 723, 735
Watch on the Rhine (film), 782
Watergate scandal, 895, 901–902, 922, 1012
water power, manufacturing and, 521–522
water resources
  agriculture and, 497, 515
  preservation of, 874(t)
  in Sun Belt, 839
  transportation and, 521–522
Watson, James, 973(i)
Watson, Tom, 596–598, 600–601
Watt, James, 936
Wattenberg, Ben J., 891
WAVES (Women Accepted for Volunteer Emergency Service), 777
Wayne, John, 782
wealth. *See also* economy
  creed of individualism and, 587
  distribution of, 875, 963
  increase of, 627, 629
  per capita income and, 520, 782
  Reagan administration and, 962
  taxation and, 670, 995–996
  tax cuts and, 925, 935, 958–959
  unequal distribution of, 727, 745, 745(i)
  during WWI, 684
weapons of mass destruction (WMD), 1000, 1001(m), 1002. *See also* atomic bomb; nuclear weapons
The Weary Blues (Hughes), 723
Weathermen, 899
Weaver, James B., 602, 602(m), 607(m)
Web. *See* World Wide Web
Web logs. *See* blogs
Webster v. Reproductive Health Service (1989), 943, 955, 984
Weinberger, Caspar, 935, 939
Welch, Joseph, 817(i)

welfare, 691, 748, 756–757, 928
  during 1990s, 960
  collective bargaining as, 836
  conservativism and, 875, 916, 942
  cuts for, 933, 936, 939(i)
  in Europe, 747
  federal involvement with, 819, 896
  Great Depression and, 729(m), 733
  legislation on, 874(t)
  maternalist, 615
  New Deal and, 742–744, 747, 762–763
  Nixon and, 896
  reform of, 896, 924–925, 947, 950, 955, 958
  resentment of, 916
  Truman and, 815
  War on Poverty and, 876
  women and, 638
  WWII and, 781
welfare capitalism, 670, 710–711, 781, 796
Welfare Reform Act (1996), 980
Welles, Orson, 762
Wells, David A., 524
Wells, Ida B., 599, 599(i)
the West. *See also* migration
  closing of frontier in, 647
  economic growth of, 916, 916(m)
  election of 1928 and, 727(i)
  Kaiser and, 774–775
  Ku Klux Klan in, 708(m), 721
  migration to, 755–759, 757(i), 838–839, 850, 915, 916(m)
  pension plans in, 744
  settlement of, 487–517
  transmountain, 487(i), 487–517. *See also* California; Pacific slope
West Bank, 945, 1001(m)
Western Federation of Miners (WFM), 546
Western Front (WWI), 674–675, 675(m), 679, 679(m)
Western Trail (periodical), 495
Western Union, 523
West Germany. *See* Germany, Federal Republic of
West Indies. *See also* Caribbean Islands
  exports to, 987
Westinghouse, George, 523
West Side Story, 851(i)
westward expansion. *See* migration
Weyl, Walter, 613
Weyler, Valeriano, 648–649
Wharton, Edith, 559
wheat
  in California, 511, 513
  on Great Plains, 497–498
  prices of, 602, 710
  during WWI, 684
Whiskey Ring, 479, 483
White, Harry Dexter, 815
White, Walter, 755

White, William Allen, 589, 771
White Citizens' Councils, 853
White Man's Union, 599
white supremacy, 464, 481, 597–599, 608, 624–626. *See also* Ku Klux Klan; racism
Whitewater investigation, 948, 950
Whitfield, Donald L., 880
Whitlock, Brand, 590, 619
wholesale prices, 520(*f*)
Whyte, William, 835, 835(*i*)
"Why We Fight" documentaries, 782
Wickersham, George, 633
Wiener, Norbert, 841(*i*)
Wilderness Preservation Act (1964), 874(*t*)
Wildmon, Donald E., 930
The Wild One, 847
Wild West Show, 494, 494(*i*)
Wilhelm II, Emperor of Germany (r. 1888–1918), 666
Will, George F., 933, 983
Willamette Valley, Oregon, 491, 505–506
Willard, Frances, 594–595
Williams, Charles, 682
Williams v. Mississippi (1898), 598
Willkie, Wendell, 771
Wilson, Charles E., 822
Wilson, Edith Bolling Galt, 697
Wilson, Joseph C., 1004
Wilson, Pete, 982
Wilson, Sloan, 835
Wilson, Woodrow (1856–1924), 624, 635, 706, 802, 1015
   on congressional government, 585
   as Democratic Party nominee, 634(*i*), 634–635
   "Fourteen Points" of, 670, 694–696, 703, 771
   isolationism and, 770
   neutrality in WWI and, 674–675, 677
   the New Freedom and, 633–638
   as president (1913–1921), 664–666, 668, 673, 677(*i*), 677–678, 683, 684(*i*), 684–685, 691, 693, 695(*i*), 697, 700, 702–703
   presidential powers and, 739
   social program of, 636–637
   suffragists and, 617(*i*)
   trusts and, 635–636
Wilson-Gorman Tariff (1894), 605
Winfrey, Oprah, 974, 974(*i*)
The Winning of the West (T. Roosevelt), 647
Wisconsin, wheat in, 498
Wise, Stephen S., 620
Wissler, Clark, 489
Wister, Owen, 563
WMD. *See* weapons of mass destruction
Wobbelin concentration camp, 791(*i*)
Wobblies. *See* Industrial Workers of the World
Wojtyla, Karol Joseph (1920–2005), 941(*i*)

Wolfowitz, Paul, 996, 999
Woman's Christian Temperance Union (WCTU), 594–595, 595(*i*)
Woman Suffrage Association, National American (NAWSA), 594, 617, 688–691
women. *See also* children; marriage
   advertising to, 843
   African American, 474
   Asian migration and, 511
   birth rates and, 903
   in breadlines, 731(*i*)
   in cabinet positions, 947
   changing roles of, 905
   in China, 967(*i*)
   in Congress, 678
   consumer culture and, 714
   discrimination against, 903–906
   divorce and, 903
   as domestic servants, 533
   education of, 564
   employment of, 674, 685, 688, 689(*i*)
   feminist movement and, 903–906
   free black, 464, 474
   in Hispanic culture, 510
   Homestead Act and, 496
   jazz and, 716, 716(*i*)
   Ku Klux Klan and, 719(*i*), 721
   in labor force, 531, 533(*i*), 533–537, 545
   labor unions and, 541–544, 750
   legal status of married, 564
   middle-class, 714
   in military, 777, 945(*i*)
   minimum wage for, 617–618, 633, 750, 752
   New Deal and, 763
   in 1920s, 708–709, 709(*i*), 711, 714
   in 1950s, 846(*i*), 846–847
   opportunities for, 852
   in politics, 708–709
   popular protests and, 751(*m*)
   Progressivism and, 612, 614–618
   Radical Reconstruction program and, 469, 471
   rural electrification and, 759
   sexual harassment of, 944
   as sexual objects, 961(*i*)
   sharecropping and, 474
   social reform and, 545
   Social Security Act and, 763
   in textile industry, 533
   voter turnout and, 708
   wage gap and, 533–536
   War on Poverty and, 876
   in wartime jobs, 685, 688, 689(*i*)
   welfare and, 638
   westward migration and, 496–497
   in workforce, 778–779, 835(*i*), 846(*i*), 846–847, 905, 958(*f*), 960–961, 960(*f*), 987
   WWI and, 684–685, 688–692
   WWII and, 777–779, 797

Women's Christian Temperance Union (WCTU), 594–595, 595(*i*)
Women's Division of Democratic National Committee, 677(*i*), 751, 763
Women's Joint Congressional Committee, 708
Women's Land Army, 689(*i*)
Women's Peace Party, 676
women's rights, 603. *See also* feminism; suffrage movement
   conflicting values and, 983–984
   economic, 533–536
   equal, 721
   feminist movement and, 903–906
   in labor force, 545
   media and, 905
   movement for, 541–542, 594–595, 603, 603(*i*)
   radical Republicans and, 471
   sex-typing and, 532–533
   Title IX and, 905
   Title VII and, 903, 905
   voting, 469, 470(*i*), 594–595, 691(*i*)
   women's liberation and, 903, 904(*i*), 905
Woodley, Arthur E., Jr., 880–881
Woodstock, rock concert at, 884, 884(*i*)
Woodward, Bob, 902
Woolworth Building, 554
Woolworths, 713
work day, length, 479, 685
workers. *See* labor; labor force
workers' compensation programs, 709
working class. *See also* laborers
   conservatism of, 916
   feminism and, 904
   movie industry and, 715
   in 1950s, 849
   Nixon and, 896, 899
   prohibition and, 692
   school busing and, 907
   strikes and, 699
   on television, 843
   Vietnam War and, 899
   women, 846–847
   during WWI, 688
Working Men's Party, 511
Works Progress Administration (WPA), 747, 747(*t*), 752, 762(*i*), 765
   African Americans and, 754
   Federal One of, 760
   Roosevelt recession and, 748
World Bank (International Bank for Reconstruction and Development), 832, 834, 964, 970
WorldCom, 995
World's Work (periodical), 698
World Trade Center, 989, 989(*i*), 998, 998(*i*). *See also* September 11, 2001 terrorist attacks
   1993 bombing of, 953, 998

World Trade Organization (WTO), 964, 969(i), 969–970, 987

World War I (WWI; 1914–1918), 674–694, 703, 824(m)
  domestic efforts during, 673(i)
  Eastern Front, 674, 679
  liberty bonds of, 673, 683(i), 684
  Lusitania and, 677, 703
  progressive reforms and, 691–692
  Prohibition and, 703
  propaganda in, 682, 685, 693
  Red Scare after, 815–818
  reparations for, 735
  social reform and, 781
  trench warfare in, 646(i)
  U-boats in, 677–678
  U.S. involvement in, 703
  Western Front, 674–675, 675(m), 679, 679(m)
  women and, 685, 688–692, 689(i)
  WWII and, 768

World War II (WWII; 1939–1945), 767–797
  budget deficits in, 935(f)
  casualties in, 767, 789–791
  causes of, 713
  decolonization and, 865(m)
  defense spending and, 774(f)
  in Europe (1941–1943), 788(m), 788–789(m)
  government spending and, 749
  in North Atlantic, 772(m)
  in Pacific, 792–793(m)

  reparations and, 806
  second front in, 787
  women during, 777, 777(i), 778–779
  WWI and, 768

World Wide Web, 924, 957(i), 966, 970–972, 987. *See also* Internet

Worrall, Henry, 495(i)

Wounded Knee, South Dakota
  massacre at, 487, 499(m), 504, 504(i), 517
  occupation of (1973), 888, 888(i)

Wovoka, Indian holy man, 503–504

Wright, Richard, 762

WTO. *See* World Trade Organization

WWI. *See* World War I

WWII. *See* World War II

Wyoming, 505, 785, 785(i)

Yalta meeting (1945), 791–792, 794(i), 797, 802–803, 815

Yalu River, 811

Yao Ming, 966

Yellow Bird, Sioux medicine man, 504, 504(i)

yellow-dog contracts, 543

yellow journalism, 577–578

The Yellow Kid (comic strip), 578

Yeltsin, Boris, 942

Yemen, 953(i), 989

yeoman farmers, 470

yippies, 889

YMCA. *See* Young Men's Christian Association

Yom Kippur War (1973), 911

York, Alvin, 680

Yosemite National Park, 515

Yosemite Valley, 487(i), 514, 517

Young Men's Christian Association (YMCA), 573, 593, 691

Young Women's Christian Association (YWCA), 573, 691

youth, 564, 580, 876. *See also* National Youth Administration
  WWII and, 784

youth culture, 564. *See also* counterculture
  music of, 847–848
  in 1950s, 847

Ypres, 675

Y2K fears, 957

Yugoslavia, 697, 942(m), 952, 952(m)

Yuppies, 924, 959, 987

YWCA. *See* Young Women's Christian Association

al-Zarqawi, Abu Musab, 1003

Zhu Shida, 940

Zimmerman, Arthur, 678

zinc mines, 506

Zionism, 825–826

Zitkala-Ša (Gertrude Simmons Bonnin), 501

Znaniecki, Florian, 570

Zola, Emile, 660

zoot suits, 784(i)

CANADA

MINNESOTA
Duluth

Lake Superior

MICHIGAN

WISCONSIN
Milwaukee
Madison

St. Paul
Minneapolis
x Falls

Wisconsin R.

Lake Michigan

Lansing

Lake Huron

MAINE
Augusta

Burlington
Montpelier
VT. N.H.
Concord
Manchester
Portland

Albany
MASS.
Hartford
Providence
Boston

St. Lawrence R.

Lake Ontario
Buffalo
NEW YORK

RHODE ISLAND
CONNECTICUT

IOWA
Des
Moines
Omaha
ncoln

Mississippi R.

Chicago
Gary

Detroit
Toledo
Lake Erie
Cleveland
Wheeling
OHIO
Columbus
Cincinnati
Ohio R.

Wabash R.

Illinois R.

INDIANA
Indianapolis

ILLINOIS
Springfield

Hudson R.
Newark
New York
Trenton
NEW JERSEY
Philadelphia
Harrisburg
PENNSYLVANIA
Pittsburgh
Allegheny R.
Baltimore
Dover
DELAWARE
MD.
Washington, D.C.
Annapolis

Potomac R.

Topeka
Kansas
City
Jefferson
City
MISSOURI

Missouri R.

St. Louis
Louisville
Frankfort
KENTUCKY
Cumberland R.

WEST
VIRGINIA
Charleston
VIRGINIA
Richmond
Norfolk
Roanoke R.

APPALACHIAN MOUNTAINS

ATLANTIC
OCEAN

Tulsa
oma
ARKANSAS
Little
Rock

Arkansas R.

adian R.

Memphis
Knoxville
Nashville
TENNESSEE

Tennessee R.

NORTH CAROLINA
Charlotte
Raleigh
Cape Fear R.

Mississippi R.

Birmingham
Atlanta
GEORGIA

SOUTH CAROLINA
Columbia
Charleston
Santee R.

Worth
Dallas
LOUISIANA

MISSISSIPPI
Jackson

ALABAMA
Montgomery

Alabama R.

Altamaha R.

Savannah

Chattahoochee R.

Sabine R.
Red R.
Trinity R.

Mobile
Baton Rouge
New Orleans
Houston

Tallahassee
Jacksonville

FLORIDA

Gulf of Mexico

Tampa

Miami

BAHAMAS

CUBA

ATLANTIC
OCEAN
San Juan
PUERTO RICO
Ponce
67 W   66 W
18 N
Caribbean Sea

0   25   50 miles
0   25   50 kilometers

Elevation

Feet		Meters
9,843		3,000
6,562		2,000
3,281		1,000
1,640		500
656		200
0		0
Below sea level		Below sea level

0   200   400 miles
0   200   400 kilometers

95 W   90 W   85 W   80 W   75 W

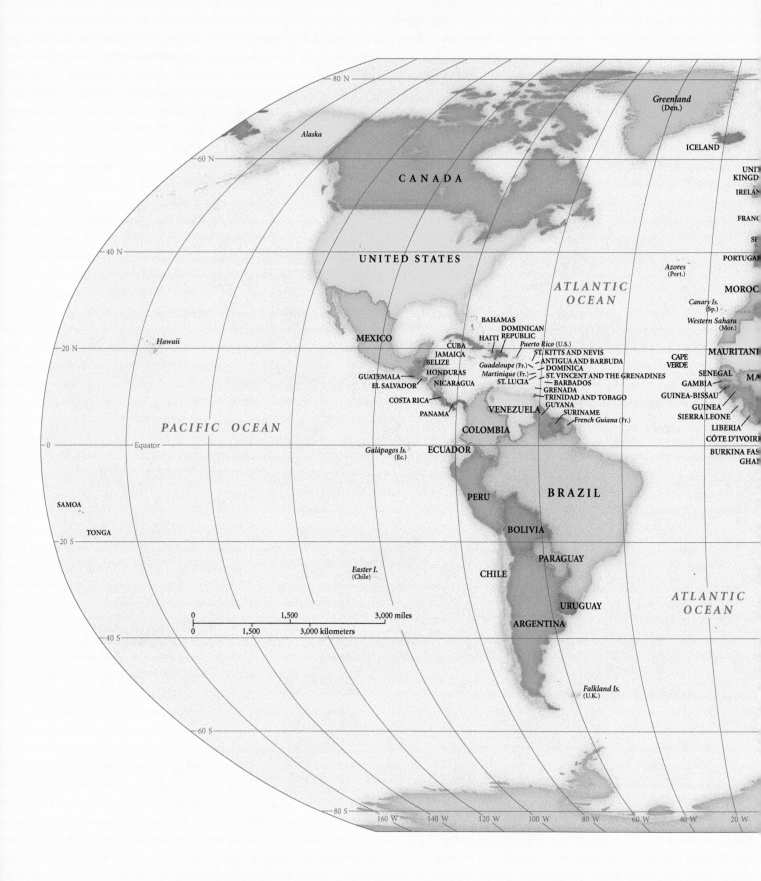

80 N

Greenland
(Den.)

Alaska

ICELAND

60 N

CANADA

UNIT
KINGD

IRELAN

40 N

FRANC

UNITED STATES

S

ATLANTIC
OCEAN

PORTUGA

Azores
(Port.)

MOROC

Canary Is.
(Sp.)

20 N

Hawaii

MEXICO

BAHAMAS

DOMINICAN
REPUBLIC

HAITI

Western Sahara
(Mor.)

CUBA

JAMAICA

Puerto Rico (U.S.)

ST. KITTS AND NEVIS

MAURITANI

CAPE
VERDE

BELIZE

ANTIGUA AND BARBUDA

SENEGAL

GUATEMALA

HONDURAS

Guadeloupe (Fr.)

DOMINICA

MA

GAMBIA

EL SALVADOR

Martinique (Fr.)

ST. VINCENT AND THE GRENADINES

GUINEA-BISSAU

NICARAGUA

ST. LUCIA

BARBADOS

GUINEA

COSTA RICA

GRENADA

SIERRA LEONE

PANAMA

TRINIDAD AND TOBAGO

LIBERIA

VENEZUELA

GUYANA

CÔTE D'IVOIR

SURINAME

French Guiana (Fr.)

BURKINA FAS

COLOMBIA

GHA

PACIFIC OCEAN

0

Galápagos Is.
(Ec.)

ECUADOR

Equator

PERU

BRAZIL

SAMOA

BOLIVIA

20 S

TONGA

PARAGUAY

Easter I.
(Chile)

CHILE

ATLANTIC
OCEAN

URUGUAY

0   1,500   3,000 miles

ARGENTINA

0   1,500   3,000 kilometers

40 S

Falkland Is.
(U.K.)

60 S

80 S

160 W   140 W   120 W   100 W   80 W   60 W   40 W   20 W

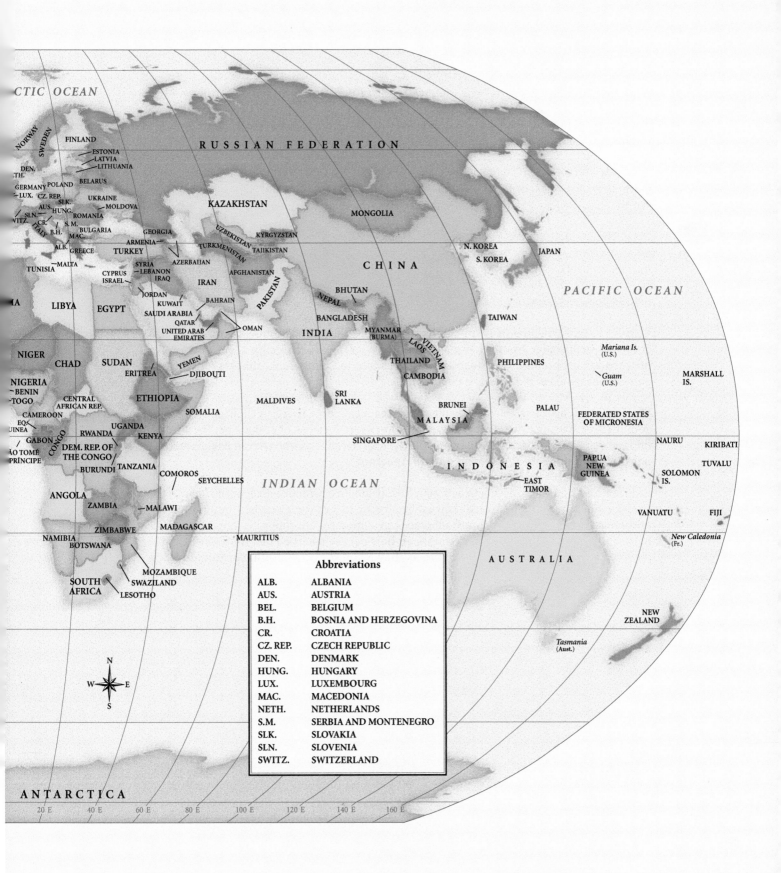

CTIC OCEAN

NORWAY
SWEDEN
FINLAND
ESTONIA
LATVIA
LITHUANIA
DEN.
TH.
GERMANY POLAND
LUX. CZ. REP.
BELARUS
AUS. HUNG.
SLN.
SWITZ.
CR.
ITALY B.H.
S.M.
MAC.
ALB.
GREECE
TUNISIA
MALTA
UKRAINE
MOLDOVA
ROMANIA
BULGARIA
GEORGIA
ARMENIA
TURKEY
SYRIA
LEBANON
CYPRUS
ISRAEL
IRAQ
AZERBAIJAN

RUSSIAN FEDERATION

KAZAKHSTAN

UZBEKISTAN
KYRGYZSTAN
TURKMENISTAN
TAJIKISTAN

MONGOLIA

N. KOREA
S. KOREA

JAPAN

CHINA

TAIWAN

PACIFIC OCEAN

A

LIBYA

EGYPT

NIGER

CHAD

SUDAN

NIGERIA
BENIN
TOGO
CAMEROON
EQ.
UINEA
GABON
ÃO TOMÉ
PRÍNCIPE

CENTRAL
AFRICAN REP.

RWANDA
CONGO
DEM. REP. OF
THE CONGO
BURUNDI

UGANDA
KENYA

ETHIOPIA

ERITREA

YEMEN
DJIBOUTI

SOMALIA

TANZANIA

COMOROS

SEYCHELLES

INDIAN OCEAN

JORDAN
KUWAIT
SAUDI ARABIA
QATAR
UNITED ARAB
EMIRATES

IRAN

BAHRAIN

OMAN

AFGHANISTAN

PAKISTAN

INDIA

NEPAL

BHUTAN

BANGLADESH

MYANMAR
(BURMA)

THAILAND

CAMBODIA

MALDIVES

SRI
LANKA

VIETNAM
LAOS

PHILIPPINES

Mariana Is.
(U.S.)

Guam
(U.S.)

MARSHALL
IS.

BRUNEI

PALAU

FEDERATED STATES
OF MICRONESIA

MALAYSIA

SINGAPORE

INDONESIA

EAST
TIMOR

PAPUA
NEW
GUINEA

NAURU

SOLOMON
IS.

KIRIBATI

TUVALU

VANUATU

FIJI

ANGOLA

ZAMBIA
MALAWI

NAMIBIA
BOTSWANA

ZIMBABWE
MADAGASCAR

MAURITIUS

New Caledonia
(Fr.)

AUSTRALIA

SOUTH
AFRICA

MOZAMBIQUE
SWAZILAND
LESOTHO

NEW
ZEALAND

Tasmania
(Aust.)

N
W E
S

ANTARCTICA

20 E   40 E   60 E   80 E   100 E   120 E   140 E   160 E

Abbreviations	
ALB.	ALBANIA
AUS.	AUSTRIA
BEL.	BELGIUM
B.H.	BOSNIA AND HERZEGOVINA
CR.	CROATIA
CZ. REP.	CZECH REPUBLIC
DEN.	DENMARK
HUNG.	HUNGARY
LUX.	LUXEMBOURG
MAC.	MACEDONIA
NETH.	NETHERLANDS
S.M.	SERBIA AND MONTENEGRO
SLK.	SLOVAKIA
SLN.	SLOVENIA
SWITZ.	SWITZERLAND

Understanding History through Maps

Working with maps deepens your understanding of the basic issues of geography and how they relate to historical studies. Understanding these five themes — location, place, region, movement, and interaction — will enrich your readings of maps and the historical situation they depict.

Location "When?" and "where?" are the first questions asked by historians and cartographers. Every event happens somewhere and at some point in time, and maps are the best devices to show a particular location at a particular time.

Place Human activity creates places. Locations exist on their own without the presence of people, but they become places when people use the spots in some way. As human enterprise thickens and generation after generation use a place, it accumulates artifacts, develops layers of remains, and generates a variety of associations held in a society's history and memory.

Region A region highlights common elements, tying certain places together as a group distinguishable from other places. Perceiving regional ties helps the reader of historical maps because they suggest the forces binding individual interests together and encouraging people to act in common.

Movement All historical change involves movement. People move in their daily activities, in seasonal patterns, and in migration to new places of residence. To understand a map fully, the reader must always envision it as one part of a sequence, not unlike a "still" excerpted from a motion picture.

Interaction The interaction between people and the environment goes both ways. On the one hand, people change their environment to suit their needs. Human ingenuity has found ways to put almost all places to some use. On the other hand, climate and topography present constraints on how people use the land and force people to change their behavior and culture as they adapt to their natural surroundings.